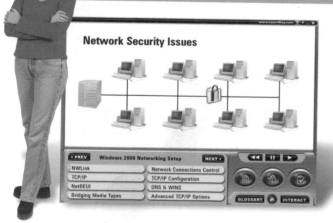

CompTIA A+® Certification
Study Guide, Sixth Edition

CompTIA A+® Certification
Study Guide, Sixth Edition

Jane Holcombe
Charles Holcombe

New York   Chicago   San Francisco   Lisbon   London   Madrid
Mexico City   Milan   New Delhi   San Juan   Seoul   Singapore   Sydney   Toronto

The McGraw·Hill Companies

Cataloging-in-Publication Data is on file with the Library of Congress

CompTIA A+® Certification Study Guide, Sixth Edition

4567890 DOC DOC 019

ISBN-13: Book p/n 978-0-07-148765-8 and CD p/n 978-0-07-148766-5
of set 978-0-07-148764-1
ISBN-10: Book p/n 0-07-148765-4 and CD p/n 0-07-148766-2
of set 0-07-148764-6

Sponsoring Editor Timothy Green	**Technical Editor** Eric Ecklund	**Composition** International Typesetting and Composition
Editorial Supervisor Janet Walden	**Copy Editor** Bob Campbell	**Illustration** International Typesetting and Composition
Project Manager Samik Roy Chowdhury (International Typesetting and Composition)	**Proofreader** Paul Tyler	**Art Director, Cover** Jeff Weeks
	Indexer Karin Arrigoni	
Acquisitions Coordinator Jennifer Housh	**Production Supervisor** James Kussow	**Cover Design** Pattie Lee

CompTIA Authorized Quality Curriculum

The logo of the CompTIA Authorized Quality Curriculum (CAQC) program and the status of this or other training material as "Authorized" under the CompTIA Authorized Quality Curriculum program signifies that, in CompTIA's opinion, such training material covers the content of CompTIA's related certification exam.

The contents of this training material were created for the CompTIA A+ exams covering CompTIA certification objectives that were current as of November 2006. CompTIA has not reviewed or approved the accuracy of the contents of this training material and specifically disclaims any warranties of merchantability or fitness for a particular purpose. CompTIA makes no guarantee concerning the success of persons using any such "Authorized" or other training material in order to prepare for any CompTIA certification exam.

How to Become CompTIA Certified

This training material can help you prepare for and pass a related CompTIA certification exam or exams. In order to achieve CompTIA certification, you must register for and pass a CompTIA certification exam or exams.

In order to become CompTIA certified, you must:

1. Select a certification exam provider. For more information please visit http://www.comptia.org/certification/general_information/exam_locations.aspx
2. Register for and schedule a time to take the CompTIA certification exam(s) at a convenient location.
3. Read and sign the Candidate Agreement, which will be presented at the time of the exam(s). The text of the Candidate Agreement can be found at http://www.comptia.org/certification/general_information/candidate_agreement.aspx
4. Take and pass the CompTIA certification exam(s).

For more information about CompTIA's certifications, such as its industry acceptance, benefits, or program news, please visit www.comptia.org/certification.

CompTIA is a not-for-profit information technology (IT) trade association. CompTIA's certifications are designed by subject matter experts from across the IT industry.

Each CompTIA certification is vendor-neutral, covers multiple technologies, and requires demonstration of skills and knowledge widely sought after by the IT industry.

To contact CompTIA with any questions or comments, please call (1) (630) 678-8300 or e-mail questions@comptia.org.

Jane Holcombe (CompTIA A+, CompTIA Network +, MCSE, and CTT+) was a pioneer in the field of PC support training. In 1983, she installed a LAN for her employer, a financial planning company. Since 1984, she has been an independent trainer, consultant, and course content author, creating and presenting courses on PC operating systems taught nationwide through the late 1980s and early 1990s. She also co-authored a set of networking courses for the consulting staff of a large network vendor. In the early 1990s she worked with both Novell and Microsoft server operating systems, finally focusing on the Microsoft operating systems and achieving early MCSE certification, recertifying for new versions of Windows. Since 2001 she has been the lead author, in collaboration with her husband, of numerous books and book chapters.

Charles Holcombe was a programmer of early computers in both the nuclear and aerospace fields. In his 15 years at Control Data Corporation, he was successively a programmer, technical sales analyst, salesman, and sales manager in the field marketing organization. At corporate headquarters he ran the Executive Seminar program, served as corporate liaison to the worldwide university community, and was market development manager for Plato, Control Data's computer-based education system.

For the past 28 years, he has been an independent trainer and consultant. He has authored and delivered training courses in many disciplines. He is a skilled writer and editor of books and online publications, and he collaborates with his wife, Jane, on many writing projects.

Together, Chuck and Jane Holcombe are a writing team who have authored the *MCSE Guide to Designing a Microsoft Windows 2000 Network Infrastructure* (Course Technology) and both the *A+ Certification Press Lab Manual* and the *MCSE Certification Press Windows 2000 Professional Lab Manual* (McGraw-Hill/Osborne). They authored *Survey of Operating Systems*, the first book in the Michael Meyer's Computer Skills series, and contributed chapters to *The Michael Meyers' Guide to Managing and Troubleshooting PCs*, *The Michael Meyer's All-in-One A+ Certification Exam Guide, Fifth Edition*, and *Windows 2000 Administration* (McGraw-Hill/Osborne). They also wrote several chapters for the Peter Norton *Introduction to Operating Systems, Sixth Edition* (McGraw-Hill). Their last book before tackling the one you are holding was a greatly expanded *Survey of Operating Systems, Second Edition* (McGraw-Hill/Higher Education).

About the Technical Editor

Eric Ecklund is an instructor in both Management and Computer Technology at Cambria-Rowe Business College, where he teaches courses ranging from Small Business Management and Marketing to Network Administration and Operating Systems. He is the author of *Introduction to Windows Server 2003* (McGraw-Hill, 2004) and *Windows XP: A Professional Approach* (Glencoe/McGraw-Hill, 2002). Eric has also contributed to, edited, and reviewed numerous other computer texts published by various divisions of McGraw-Hill.

Eric earned a B.S. degree and Pennsylvania teaching certificate from the University of Pittsburgh and an M.B.A degree from Seton Hill College. He lives in Johnstown, Pennsylvania, with his wife Charlotte and their daughters Lauren and Anna.

About LearnKey

LearnKey provides self-paced learning content and multimedia delivery solutions to enhance personal skills and business productivity. LearnKey claims the largest library of rich streaming-media training content that engages learners in dynamic media-rich instruction complete with video clips, audio, full motion graphics, and animated illustrations. LearnKey can be found on the Web at **www.LearnKey.com**.

CONTENTS AT A GLANCE

ix

CONTENTS

Part II
Laptops and Portable Devices

5   Using and Supporting Laptops and Portable Devices   223

Part III
Operating Systems

Part V
Networks

Part VI
Security

15 Computer Security Fundamentals 735

Part VIII
Communication and Professionalism

ACKNOWLEDGMENTS

We thank the many dedicated people at McGraw-Hill/Osborne who have been so helpful to us, demonstrating that writing a book is truly a team effort. A special thank you goes to Timothy Green, senior acquisitions editor, who convinced us to take on the enormous task of creating this updated and greatly expanded sixth edition of the best-selling *A+ Certification Study Guide*. He has consistently been creative, responsive, energetic, and dedicated to making this the best book of its kind available. Jenni Housh, acquisitions coordinator, has been a rock of support and responsiveness through some trying times. Both of them have smoothed the way for us and deserve great credit for the success of this book.

We also want to thank Eric Ecklund of Cambria-Rowe College, Johnstown, Pennsylvania, who has been our technical editor for several books, and who made many contributions to this one. As an instructor who uses our books in his classes, his insights are invaluable.

Many other people at McGraw-Hill have contributed to the creation of this book. Although we can't list all of their names, they know who they are, and we want them to know that we truly appreciate their outstanding efforts.

This book's primary objective is to help you prepare for and pass the required CompTIA A+ exams so that you can begin to reap the career benefits of certification. We believe that the only way to do this is to help you increase your knowledge and build your skills. After completing this book, you should feel confident that you have thoroughly reviewed all of the objectives that CompTIA has established for the exams.

In This Book

We have organized this book around the objectives of four CompTIA A+ 2006 exams: CompTIA A+ Essentials (referred to in this book as Exam 601), CompTIA A+ 220-602 (referred to here as Exam 602), CompTIA 220-603 (referred to here as Exam 603), and CompTIA 220-604 (referred to here as Exam 604). These objectives divide into domains, some of which appear in multiple exams. For example, the three domains titled Personal Computer Components, Printers and Scanners, and Security are included in all four exams. Two of the exams, 601 and 602, include the same eight domains, while Exam 603 covers six domains, and Exam 604 covers five domains. Therefore, there is some overlap in the coverage of domains between the exams, but in some cases, the scope and depth of knowledge differs. For instance, in the Essentials (601) exam objectives under domain 1.0, Personal Computer Components, subobjective 1.1 is "Identify the fundamental principles of using personal computers." Under 1.1 is a long list of components that an A+ candidate must be able to identify. This objective does not exist in the other exams. The Exam Readiness Charts at the end of this Introduction list the domains and each objective, along with the page number where you can find the discussion for each objective in the book.

In Every Chapter

We've created a set of chapter components that call your attention to important items, reinforce important points, and provide helpful exam-taking hints. Take a look at what you'll find in every chapter:

- Every chapter begins with the **Certification Objectives**—what you need to know in order to pass the section on the exam dealing with the chapter topic.

The Certification Objective headings identify the objectives within the chapter, so you'll always know an objective when you see it!

- **Exam Watch** notes call attention to information about, and potential pitfalls in, the exam. These helpful hints reinforce your learning and exam preparation.

- **Certification Exercises** are interspersed throughout the chapters. These are step-by-step exercises that mirror vendor-recommended labs. They help you master skills that are likely to be an area of focus on the exam. Don't just read through the exercises; they are hands-on practice that you should be comfortable completing. Learning by doing is an effective way to increase your competency with a product.

- **On the Job** notes describe the issues that come up most often in real-world settings. They provide a valuable perspective on certification- and product-related topics. They often go beyond certification objectives to point out common mistakes and address questions that have arisen from on-the-job discussions and experience.

- **Scenario & Solution** sections lay out problems and solutions in a quick-read format.

SCENARIO & SOLUTION

What are the most common bus architectures in use today?	PCI and PCIe
What drive interface standard is replacing PATA for hard drives?	SATA

- The **Certification Summary** is a succinct review of the chapter and a re-statement of salient points regarding the exam.

- The **Two-Minute Drill** at the end of every chapter is a checklist of the main points of the chapter. You can use it for last-minute review.

- The **Self Test** offers questions similar to those found on the certification exams. You can find the answers to these questions, as well as explanations of the answers, at the end of each chapter. By taking the Self Test after completing each chapter, you'll reinforce what you've learned from that chapter, while becoming familiar with the structure of the exam questions.

- The **Lab Question** at the end of the Self-Test section offers a unique and challenging question or project that requires the reader to demonstrate knowledge of the content or do some independent research related to the content. These questions or projects are more complex and more comprehensive than the other questions, as they test your ability to take knowledge you have gained from reading the chapter and to apply it to complicated, real-world situations. We intend these questions to be more difficult than what you will find on the exam. If you can answer these questions or complete the project, you have proven that you know the subject!

Some Pointers

Once you've finished reading this book, set aside some time to do a thorough review. You might want to return to the book several times and make use of all the methods it offers for reviewing the material:

1. *Re-read all the Two-Minute Drills*, or have someone quiz you. You also can use the drills as a way to do a quick cram before the exam.
2. *Review all the Scenario & Solutions* for quick problem solving.
3. *Retake the Self Tests.* Taking the tests right after you've read the chapter is a good idea, because it helps reinforce what you've just learned. However, it's an even better idea to go back later and do all the questions in the book in one sitting. Pretend you're taking the exam.
4. *Complete the exercises.* Did you do the exercises when you read through each chapter? If not, do them! These exercises cover exam topics, and there's no better way to get to know this material than by practicing.

ⓦatch **You should mark your answers to questions on a separate piece of paper when you go through this book for the first time so that you may go back and retake the Self Tests as you review for the exam.**

CompTIA A+ Certification

We designed this book to help you pass the CompTIA A+ certification exams. At the time we wrote this book, CompTIA had posted the objectives for the exams on its Web site, **www.comptia.org**. We wrote this book to give you a complete and incisive review of all the important topics the exams target. The information contained here will provide you with the required foundation of knowledge that will not only allow you to succeed in passing the CompTIA A+ certification exams, but will also make you a better CompTIA A+ Certified Technician.

Since the inception of the CompTIA A+ exams, CompTIA periodically revises them to bring them up to date in the rapidly changing world of computers. We have extensively revised and expanded this sixth edition of the *A+ Certification Study Guide* with much new material, to match the 2006 revisions to the CompTIA A+ examinations.

How to Take an A+ Certification Exam

This section discusses the importance of your CompTIA A+ certification and prepares you for taking the actual examinations. It gives you a few pointers on methods of preparing for the exam, including how to study and register, what to expect, and what to do on exam day.

Importance of CompTIA A+ Certification

The Computing Technology Industry Association (CompTIA) created the A+ certification to provide technicians with an industry-recognized and valued credential. Due to its acceptance as an industry-wide credential, it offers technicians an edge in a highly competitive computer job market. Additionally, it lets others know your achievement level and that you have the ability to do the job right. Prospective employers may use the CompTIA A+ certification as a condition of employment or as a means to a bonus or job promotion.

Earning CompTIA A+ certification means that you have the knowledge and the technical skills necessary to be a successful entry-level IT professional in today's environment. The recently revised exam objectives test your knowledge and skills in all the areas that today's computing environment requires. More than 5000 CompTIA A+ certified professionals and employers participated in validating the revised exam's objectives. Although the tests cover a broad range of computer software and hardware, they are not vendor specific.

With the 2006 exams, CompTIA introduced an entirely new structure to the exams. You will still need two exams to achieve your CompTIA A+ Certification. However, where previously the two exams were easily divided into a hardware exam and a software exam, the new exams are organized very differently, and each tests knowledge in a variety of areas. The first exam is the **CompTIA A+ Essentials (220-601) Exam**, which every candidate must pass. This exam measures the competencies required for an entry-level IT professional in a wide range of responsibilities.

Beyond the Essentials Exam, you can select your second exam from among three exam choices—each of which carefully targets specific job titles. For instance, the

CompTIA 220-602 Exam tests competencies required for such job titles as IT technician, enterprise technician, IT administrator, field service technician, and PC technician. The **CompTIA 220-603 Exam** targets the following job titles: remote support technician, help desk technician, call center technician, specialist, and representative. Finally, the **CompTIA 220-604 Exam** tests skills expected for such job titles as depot technician and bench technician.

CompTIA recognizes that soft skills are an important part of most jobs, so the exams for job titles that require interaction with customers include a domain called Communication and Professionalism, which deals with human interaction. This is the first time these skills are being measured in the CompTIA A+ exams.

Computerized Testing

As with Microsoft, Novell, Lotus, and various other company tests, the most practical way to administer tests on a global level is through Prometric or VUE testing centers, which provide proctored testing services for Microsoft, Oracle, Novell, Lotus, and CompTIA. In addition to administering the tests, Prometric and VUE also score the exam and provide statistical feedback on each section of the exam to the companies and organizations that use their services.

Typically, CompTIA develops several hundred questions for a new exam. Subject matter experts review the questions for technical accuracy and then present them in the form of a beta test. The beta test consists of many more questions than the actual test and helps provide statistical feedback to CompTIA to check the performance of each question.

Given the outcomes of the beta examination, CompTIA test designers discard questions according to how well or badly the examinees performed on them. If most of the test-takers answer a question correctly, they discard it as too being easy. Likewise, they also discard questions that are too difficult. After analyzing the data from the beta test, CompTIA has a good idea of which questions to include in the question pool to use on the actual exam.

Test Structure

CompTIA announced that the new test will be a standard, multiple-choice exam. Most questions will have only a single correct answer, while others will have multiple correct answers, in which case, the question will include a note such as "select TWO." You should visit the CompTIA Web site to check on the status of the exam before you take it. The CompTIA Web site is **www.comptia.org**. While there, take the practice exams posted at their site.

e x a m

ⓦatch
An interesting and useful characteristic of the standard test is that questions may be marked and returned to later. This helps you manage your time while taking the test so that you don't spend too much time on any one question.

Remember, unanswered questions count against you. Assuming you have time left when you finish the other questions, you can return to the marked questions for further evaluation.

The standard test also marks the questions that are incomplete with a letter "I" once you've finished all the questions. You'll see the whole list of questions after you finish the last question. The screen allows you to go back and finish incomplete items, finish unmarked items, and go to particular question numbers that you may want to look at again.

Question Types

The A+ exams consist entirely of multiple-choice questions, but the computer may present the test questions on the examination in a number of ways, as discussed here. We provide this information primarily for reference. CompTIA states that the current exam is multiple-choice based.

True/False   Everyone is familiar with True/False type questions, but due to the inherent 50 percent chance of guessing the right answer, you will not see any of these on the A+ exam. Sample questions on CompTIA's Web site did not include any True/False-type questions.

Multiple Choice   A+ exam questions are of the multiple-choice variety. Below each question is a list of four or five possible answers. Use the available radio buttons to select the correct answer from the given choices. Some questions will have more than one correct answer, in which case, the number of correct answers required is clearly stated.

Graphical Questions   There are two types of graphical questions. The first type incorporates a graphical element to the question in the form of an exhibit to provide a visual representation of the problem or present the question itself. These questions are easy to identify because they refer to the exhibit in the question and there is also an Exhibit button on the bottom of the question window. An example of a graphical question might be to identify a component on a drawing of a motherboard.

They call the second type of graphical question a hotspot, and it actually incorporates graphics as part of the answer. These types of questions ask the examinee to click a location or graphical element to answer the question. Instead of selecting A, B, C, or D as your answer, you simply click the portion of the motherboard drawing where the component exists.

Free Response Questions   A test can present another type of question that requires a *free response*, or type-in answer. This is a fill-in-the-blank-type question where a list of possible choices is not given. You will not see this type of question on the A+ exams.

Study Strategies

There are appropriate ways to study for the different types of questions you will see on CompTIA A+ certification exams. The amount of study time needed to pass the exam will vary with the candidate's level of experience. Someone with several years experience might only need a quick review of materials and terms when preparing for the exam.

Others may need several hours to identify weaknesses in their knowledge and skill level, and work on those areas to bring them up to par. If you know that you are weak in an area, work on it until you feel comfortable talking about it. You don't want to be surprised with a question knowing it was your weak area.

Knowledge-Based Questions   Knowledge-based questions require that you memorize facts. The questions may not cover knowledge material that you use on a daily basis, but they do cover material that CompTIA thinks an IT professional should be able to answer. Here are some keys to memorizing facts:

- ■ **Repetition**   The more times you expose your brain to a fact, the more it sinks in and your ability to remember it increases.
- ■ **Association**   Connecting facts within a logical framework makes them easier to remember.
- ■ **Motor Association**   It is easier to remember something if you write it down or perform another physical act, like clicking the practice test answers.

Performance-Based Questions   Although the majority of the questions on the CompTIA A+ exams are knowledge-based, some questions are performance-based scenario questions. In other words, they actually measure the candidate's ability to apply one's knowledge in a given scenario.

The first step in preparing for these scenario-type questions is to absorb as many facts relating to the exam content areas as you can. Of course, actual hands-on experience will greatly help you in this area. For example, it really helps in knowing how to install a video adapter if you have actually done the procedure at least once. Some of the questions will place you in a scenario and ask for the best solution to the problem at hand. It is in these scenarios that having a good knowledge level and some experience will help you.

The second step is to familiarize yourself with the format of the questions you are likely to see on the exam. The questions in this study guide are a good step in that direction. The more you are familiar with the types of questions the exam can ask, the better prepared you will be on the day of the test.

The Exam Makeup

To receive the A+ certification, you must pass both the CompTIA A+ Essentials exam and one of the other three exams, 220-602, 220-603, or 220-604. For up-to-date information about the number of questions on each exam and the passing scores, check the CompTIA site at **www.comptia.org**, or call the CompTIA Certification office nearest you.

The CompTIA A+ Essentials Exam

The Essentials exam consists of eight domains (categories). CompTIA lists the percentages as follows:

1.0 Personal Computer Components	21%
2.0 Laptop and Portable Devices	11%
3.0 Operating Systems	21%
4.0 Printers and Scanners	9%
5.0 Networks	12%
6.0 Security	11%
7.0 Safety and Environmental Issues	10%
8.0 Communication and Professionalism	5%

The CompTIA A+ 220-602 Exam

The CompTIA A+ 220-602 exam consists of eight domains (categories). CompTIA lists the percentages as follows:

1.0 Personal Computer Components	18%
2.0 Laptop and Portable Devices	9%
3.0 Operating Systems	20%
4.0 Printers and Scanners	14%
5.0 Networks	11%
6.0 Security	8%
7.0 Safety and Environmental Issues	5%
8.0 Communication and Professionalism	15%

The CompTIA A+ 220-603 Exam

The CompTIA A+ 220-603 exam consists of six domains (categories). CompTIA lists the percentages as follows:

1.0 Personal Computer Components	15%
2.0 Operating Systems	29%
3.0 Printers and Scanners	10%
4.0 Networks	11%
5.0 Security	15%
6.0 Communication and Professionalism	20%

The CompTIA A+ 220-604 Exam

The CompTIA A+ 220-604 exam consists of five domains (categories). CompTIA lists the percentages as follows:

1.0 Personal Computer Components	45%
2.0 Laptop and Portable Devices	20%
3.0 Printers and Scanners	20%
4.0 Security	5%
5.0 Safety and Environmental Issues	10%

Signing Up

After all your hard work preparing for the exam, signing up will be a very easy process. Prometric or VUE operators in each country can schedule tests at authorized test centers. You can register for an exam online at **www.2test.com** or **www.vue.com/comptia** or by calling the Prometric or VUE Test Center nearest you. There are a few things to keep in mind when you call:

1. If you call during a busy period, you might be in for a bit of a wait. Their busiest days tend to be Mondays, so avoid scheduling a test on Monday if at all possible.

2. Make sure that you have your social security number handy. The test center needs this number as a unique identifier for their records.

3. You may pay by credit card, which is usually the easiest payment method. If your employer is a member of CompTIA, you may be able to get a discount, or even obtain a voucher from your employer that will pay for the exam. Check with your employer before you dish out the money.

4. You may take one or both of the exams on the same day. However, if you take just one exam, you have only 90 calendar days to complete the second exam. If more than 90 days elapse between tests, you must retake the first exam.

Taking the Test

The best method of preparing for the exam is to create a study schedule and stick to it. Although teachers have probably told you time and time again not to cram for tests, there just may be some information that just doesn't quite stick in your memory. It's this type of information that you want to look at right before you take the exam so that it remains fresh in your mind. Most testing centers provide you with a writing utensil and some scratch paper that you can utilize after the exam starts. You can brush up on good study techniques from any quality study book from the library, but some things to keep in mind when preparing and taking the test are:

1. Get a good night's sleep. Don't stay up all night cramming for this one. If you don't know the material by the time you go to sleep, your head won't be clear enough to remember it in the morning.

2. The test center needs two forms of identification, one of which must have your picture on it (for example, your driver's license). Social security cards and credit cards are also acceptable forms of identification.

3. Arrive at the test center a few minutes early. There's no reason to feel rushed right before taking an exam.

4. Don't spend too much time on one question. If you think you're spending too much time on it, just mark it and go back to it later if you have time.

5. If you don't know the answer to a question, think about it logically. Look at the answers and eliminate the ones that you know can't possibly be the answer. This may leave you with only two possible answers. Give it your best guess if you have to, but you can resolve most of the answers to the questions by process of elimination. Remember, unanswered questions count wrong whether you know the answer to them or not.

6. No books, calculators, laptop computers, or any other reference materials are allowed inside the testing center. The tests are computer based and do not require pens, pencils, or paper, although, as mentioned above, some test centers provide scratch paper to aid you while taking the exam.

After the Test

As soon as you complete the test, your results will show up in the form of a bar graph on the screen. As long as your score is greater than the required score, you pass! The testing center will print and emboss a hard copy of the report to indicate that it's an official report. Don't lose this copy; it's the only hard copy of the report made. The testing center sends the results electronically to CompTIA.

The printed report will also indicate how well you did in each section. You will be able to see the percentage of questions you got right in each section, but you will not be able to tell which questions you got wrong.

After you pass the Essentials and one other exam, you will receive an A+ certificate by mail within a few weeks. You are then authorized to use the A+ logo on your business cards, as long as you stay within the guidelines specified by CompTIA. Please check the CompTIA Web site for a more comprehensive and up-to-date listing and explanation of CompTIA A+ benefits.

If you don't pass the exam, don't fret. Take a look at the areas where you didn't do so well, and work on those areas for the next time you register.

Once you pass your exams and earn the title of CompTIA A+ certified technician, your value and status in the IT industry increases.CompTIA A+ certification carries an important proof of skills and knowledge level that is valued by customers, employers, and professionals in the computer industry.

Exam Readiness Checklists

The following four tables—one for the Essentials exam and one for each of the other exams—describe the A+ objectives and where you will find them in this book. The table shows each objective with a mapping to the coverage in the Study Guide. There are also three check boxes labeled Beginner, Intermediate, and Expert. Use these to rate your beginning knowledge of each objective. This assessment will help guide you to the areas in which you need to spend more time studying for the exam.

CompTIA A+ Exam 601: Essentials

Exam Readiness Checklist

Official Objective	Study Guide Coverage	Ch #	Pg #	Beginner	Intermediate	Expert
Personal Computer Components (601: 1.0)						
Identify the fundamental principles of using personal computers (1.1)	Identifying system components, understanding their functions, and explaining basic computer concepts [motherboards and CPUs]	1	4			
Identify the fundamental principles of using personal computers (1.1)	Identifying system components, understanding their functions, and explaining basic computer concepts [components other than CPUs and motherboards]	2	48			
Install, configure, optimize, and upgrade personal computer components (1.2)	Adding, Removing, and Configuring Personal Computer Components	3	108			

Exam Readiness Checklist

Official Objective	Study Guide Coverage	Ch #	Pg #	Beginner	Intermediate	Expert
Identify tools, diagnostic procedures, and troubleshooting techniques for personal computer components (1.3)	Troubleshooting PCs	4	166			
Perform preventive maintenance on personal computer components (1.4)	Preventive Maintenance Techniques	4	199			
Laptops and Portable Devices (601: 2.0)						
Identify the fundamental principles of using laptops and portable devices (2.1)	Introduction to Portable Computers	5	224			
Install, configure, optimize, and upgrade laptops and portable devices (2.2)	Installing and Upgrading Laptops	5	242			
Identify tools, basic diagnostic procedures, and troubleshooting techniques for laptops and portable devices (2.3)	Troubleshooting Laptops and Portable Devices	6	268			
Perform preventive maintenance on laptops and portable devices (2.4)	Preventive Maintenance for Laptops and Portable Devices	6	286			
Operating Systems (601: 3.0)						
Identify the fundamentals of using operating systems (3.1)	Operating System Fundamentals	7	304			
Identify the fundamentals of using operating systems (3.1)	Disk and File Management	9	402			
Install, configure, optimize, and upgrade operating systems (3.2)	Installing, Configuring, Optimizing, and Upgrading Operating Systems	8	348			
Identify tools, diagnostic procedures, and troubleshooting techniques for operating systems (3.3)	Troubleshooting Windows	10	454			
Perform preventive maintenance on operating systems (3.4)	Performing Preventive Maintenance for Windows	10	499			

Exam Readiness Checklist

Official Objective	Study Guide Coverage	Ch #	Pg #	Beginner	Intermediate	Expert
Printer and Scanners (601: 4.0)						
Identify the fundamental principles of using printers and scanners (4.1)	Understanding Printers and Scanners	11	522			
Identify basic concepts of installing, configuring, optimizing, and upgrading printers and scanners (4.2)	Printer and Scanner Technologies	11	533			
Identify tools, basic diagnostic procedures, and troubleshooting techniques for printers and scanners (4.3)	Troubleshooting Printers and Scanners	11	552			
Networks (601: 5.0)						
Identify the fundamental principles of networks (5.1)	Understanding Computer Network Basics	12	584			
Install, configure, optimize, and upgrade networks (5.2)	Installing and Configuring Networks	13	630			
Identify tools, diagnostic procedures, and troubleshooting techniques for networks (5.3)	Troubleshooting Networks	14	690			
Security (601: 6.0)						
Identify the fundamental principles of security (6.1)	Computer Security Fundamentals	15	735			
Install, configure, upgrade, and optimize security (6.2)	Implementing Security	16	790			
Identify tools, diagnostic procedure, and troubleshooting techniques for security (6.3)	Troubleshooting Security	16	834			
Perform preventive maintenance for computer security (6.4)	Preventive Maintenance for Security	16	839			
Safety and Environmental Issues (601: 7.0)						
Describe the aspects and importance of safety and environmental issues (7.1)	Maintaining a Safe Work Environment	17	860			

Exam Readiness Checklist

Official Objective	Study Guide Coverage	Ch #	Pg #	Beginner	Intermediate	Expert
Identify potential hazards and implement proper safety procedures, including ESD precautions and procedures, safe work environment, and equipment handling (7.2)	Maintaining a Safe Work Environment	17	860			
Identify proper disposal procedures for batteries, display devices, and chemical solvents and cans (7.3)	Disposing of Computer Waste	17	878			
Communication and Professionalism (601: 8.0)						
Use good communications skills including listening and tact/discretion, when communicating with customers and colleagues (8.1)	Communications	18	900			
Use job-related professional behavior including notion of privacy, confidentiality and respect for the customers and customers' property (8.2)	Professionalism	18	917			

CompTIA A+ Exam 602: IT Technician

Exam Readiness Checklist

Official Objective	Study Guide Coverage	Ch #	Pg #	Beginner	Intermediate	Expert
Personal Computer Components (602: 1.0)						
Install, configure, optimize, and upgrade personal computer components (1.1)	Adding, Removing, and Configuring Personal Computer Components	3	108			

Exam Readiness Checklist

Official Objective	Study Guide Coverage	Ch #	Pg #	Beginner	Intermediate	Expert
Identify tools, diagnostic procedures, and troubleshooting techniques for personal computer components (1.2)	Troubleshooting PCs	4	166			
Perform preventive maintenance of personal computer components (1.3)	Preventive Maintenance Techniques	4	199			
Laptops and Portable Devices (602: 2.0)						
Identify fundamental principles of using laptops and portable devices (2.1)	Introduction to Portable Computers	5	224			
Install, configure, optimize, and upgrade laptops and portable devices (2.2)	Installing and Upgrading Laptops	5	242			
Use tools, diagnostic procedures, and troubleshooting techniques for laptops and portable devices (2.3)	Troubleshooting Laptops and Portable Devices	6	268			
Perform preventive maintenance on laptops and portable devices (2.4)	Preventive Maintenance for Laptops and Portable Devices	6	286			
Operating Systems (602: 3.0)						
Identify the fundamentals principles of operating systems (3.1)	Operating System Fundamentals	7	304			
Identify the fundamentals of using operating systems (3.1)	Disk and File Management	9	402			
Install, configure, optimize, and upgrade operating systems (3.2)	Installing, Configuring, Optimizing, and Upgrading Operating Systems	8	348			
Identify tools, diagnostic procedures, and troubleshooting techniques for operating systems (3.3)	Troubleshooting Windows	10	454			
Perform preventive maintenance on operating systems (3.4)	Performing Preventive Maintenance for Windows	10	499			

Exam Readiness Checklist

Official Objective	Study Guide Coverage	Ch #	Pg #	Beginner	Intermediate	Expert
Printer and Scanners (602: 4.0)						
Identify the fundamental principles of using printers and scanners (4.1)	Understanding Printers and Scanners	11	522			
Install, configure, optimize, and upgrade printers and scanners (4.2)	Printer and Scanner Technologies	11	533			
Identify tools, basic diagnostic procedures to troubleshooting printers and scanners (4.3)	Troubleshooting Printers and Scanners	11	552			
Perform preventive maintenance of printers and scanners (4.4)	Preventive Maintenance for Printers and Scanners	11	565			
Networks (602: 5.0)						
Identify the fundamental principles of networks (5.1)	Understanding Computer Network Basics	12	584			
Install, configure, optimize, and upgrade networks (5.2)	Installing and Configuring Networks	13	630			
Use tools and diagnostic procedures to troubleshoot network problems (5.3)	Troubleshooting Networks	14	690			
Perform preventive maintenance of networks, including securing and protecting network cabling (5.4)	Preventive Maintenance for Networks	14	718			
Security (602: 6.0)						
Identify the fundamentals and principles of security (6.1)	Computer Security Fundamentals	15	735			
Install, configure, upgrade, and optimize security (6.2)	Implementing Security	16	790			
Identify tools, diagnostic procedures, and troubleshooting techniques for security (6.3)	Troubleshooting Security	16	834			
Perform preventive maintenance for computer security (6.4)	Preventive Maintenance for Security	16	839			

Exam Readiness Checklist

Official Objective	Study Guide Coverage	Ch #	Pg #	Beginner	Intermediate	Expert
Safety and Environmental Issues (602: 7.0)						
Identify potential hazards and implement proper safety procedures, including power supply, display devices, and environment (7.1)	Maintaining a Safe Work Environment	17	860			
Communication and Professionalism (602: 8.0)						
Use good communications skills, including listening and tact/discretion, when communicating with customers and colleagues (8.1)	Communications	18	900			
Use job-related professional behavior, including notion of privacy, confidentiality, and respect for the customers and customers' property (8.2)	Professionalism	18	917			

CompTIA A+ Exam 603: Remote Support Technician

Exam Readiness Checklist

Official Objective	Study Guide Coverage	Ch #	Pg #	Beginner	Intermediate	Expert
Personal Computer Components (603: 1.0)						
Install, configure, optimize, and upgrade personal computer components (1.1)	Adding, Removing, and Configuring Personal Computer Components	3	108			
Identify tools, diagnostic procedures, and troubleshooting techniques for personal computer components (1.2)	Troubleshooting PCs	4	166			
Perform preventive maintenance on personal computer components (1.3)	Preventive Maintenance Techniques	4	199			

Exam Readiness Checklist

Official Objective	Study Guide Coverage	Ch #	Pg #	Beginner	Intermediate	Expert
Operating Systems (603: 2.0)						
Identify the fundamental principles of using operating systems (2.1)	Operating System Fundamentals	7	304			
Identify the fundamental principles of using operating systems (2.1)	Disk and File Management	9	402			
Install, configure, optimize, and upgrade operating systems (2.2)	Installing, Configuring, Optimizing, and Upgrading Operating Systems	8	348			
Identify tools, diagnostic procedures, and troubleshooting techniques for operating systems (2.3)	Troubleshooting Windows	10	454			
Perform preventive maintenance for operating systems (2.4)	Performing Preventive Maintenance for Windows	10	499			
Printers and Scanners (603: 3.0)						
Identify the fundamental principles of using printers and scanners (3.1)	Understanding Printers and Scanners	11	522			
Install, configure, optimize, and upgrade printers and scanners (3.2)	Printer and Scanner Technologies	11	533			
Identify tools, diagnostic procedures, and troubleshooting techniques for printers and scanners (3.3)	Troubleshooting Printers and Scanners	11	552			
Networks (603: 4.0)						
Identify the fundamental principles of networks (4.1)	Understanding Computer Network Basics	12	584			

Exam Readiness Checklist

Official Objective	Study Guide Coverage	Ch #	Pg #	Beginner	Intermediate	Expert
Install, configure, optimize, and upgrade networks (4.2)	Installing and Configuring Networks	13	630			
Identify tools, diagnostic procedures, and troubleshooting techniques for networks (4.3)	Troubleshooting Networks	14	690			
Security (603: 5.0)						
Identify the fundamental principles of security (5.1)	Understanding Security Fundamentals	15	735			
Install, configure, optimize, and upgrade security (5.2)	Implementing Security	16	790			
Identify tools, diagnostic procedures, and troubleshooting techniques for security issues (5.3)	Troubleshooting Security	16	834			
Perform preventive maintenance for security (5.4)	Preventive Maintenance for Security	16	839			
Communication and Professionalism (603: 6.0)						
Use good communications skills, including listening and tact/discretion, when communicating with customers and colleagues (6.1)	Communications	18	900			
Use job-related professional behavior, including notion of privacy, confidentiality, and respect for the customers and customers' property (6.2)	Professionalism	18	917			

CompTIA A+ Exam 604: Depot Technician

Exam Readiness Checklist

Official Objective	Study Guide Coverage	Ch #	Pg #	Beginner	Intermediate	Expert
Personal Computer Components (604: 1.0)						
Install, configure, optimize, and upgrade personal computer components (1.1)	Adding, Removing, and Configuring Personal Computer Components	3	108			
Identify tools, diagnostic procedures, and troubleshooting techniques for personal computer components (1.2)	Troubleshooting PCs	4	166			
Perform preventive maintenance of personal computer components (1.3)	Preventive Maintenance Techniques	4	199			
Laptops and Portable Devices (604: 2.0)						
Identify fundamental principles of using laptops and portable devices (2.1)	Introduction to Portable Computers	5	224			
Install, configure, optimize, and upgrade laptops and portable devices (2.2)	Installing and Upgrading Laptops	5	242			
Identify tools, diagnostic procedures, and troubleshooting techniques for laptops and portable devices (2.3)	Troubleshooting Laptops and Portable Devices	6	268			
Printer and Scanners (604: 3.0)						
Identify the fundamental principles of using printers and scanners (3.1)	Understanding Printers and Scanners	11	522			
Install, configure, optimize, and upgrade printers and scanners (3.2)	Printer and Scanner Technologies	11	533			
Identify tools, diagnostic methods, and troubleshooting procedures for printers and scanners (3.3)	Troubleshooting Printers and Scanners	11	552			
Perform preventive maintenance of printer and scanner problems (3.4)	Preventive Maintenance for Printers and Scanners	11	565			

Exam Readiness Checklist

Official Objective	Study Guide Coverage	Ch #	Pg #	Beginner	Intermediate	Expert
Security (604: 4.0)						
Identify the names, purposes, and characteristics of physical security devices (4.1)	Understanding Security Fundamentals	15	735			
Install hardware security (4.2)	Implementing Security	16	790			
Safety and Environmental Issues (604: 5.0)						
Identify potential hazards and implement proper safety procedures, including power supply, display devices, and environment (5.1)	Maintaining a Safe Work Environment	17	860			

Part I

Personal Computer Components

1

Personal Computer Components— Unit 1

Tthis chapter, along with Chapter 2, introduces you to basic computer concepts, including how to identify common components. Familiarity with the components, as well as a good working knowledge of their function, will allow you to work comfortably with most types of computers, in spite of different layouts or new component designs. Chapter 1 provides the purposes and technologies of PC cases, motherboards, and CPUs. Chapter 2 explores PC power supplies, cooling systems, memory, storage devices, adapter cards, display devices, input devices, ports, and cables.

CERTIFICATION OBJECTIVE

■ **601: 1.1** *Identify the fundamental principles of using personal computers.*

The new CompTIA A+ 2006 exams have quite a bit of overlap, meaning that some identical or nearly identical objectives appear in two or more of the exams. This objective is the exception, because the CompTIA Essentials exam, identified here as 601, is the only exam to include this objective. Consider this the most basic of the basic knowledge for a computer professional working with PCs. It contains a large number of subobjectives, and it spans two chapters in this book, reflecting the weight and importance of this objective. Master the topics in these two chapters to build a foundation for your knowledge to pass all the A+ exams.

on the
Ö o b
Safety first! Throughout this book, you will be asked to install and remove components on a PC system. Therefore, you must thoroughly understand two areas before opening the cover of a computer: electrostatic discharge (ESD), which can kill your computer, and high voltage (inside the power supply and monitor), which can kill you. For complete power protection and safety procedures, read Chapter 17 first.

Introduction to Personal Computers

This chapter, along with Chapter 2, provides an overview of PC components. Once you have a good feeling for how the parts of a computer system work together, you will be on the road to becoming a PC technical professional. This knowledge will aid you in all the technical tasks ahead of you. It is easier to identify, troubleshoot, and replace a failed component when you understand the function of that component and how it interacts with the rest of the PC hardware. This chapter's coverage is not intended to be comprehensive, merely a place to begin.

The basic computer system that sits on your desktop may look like Figure 1-1, but it is an extremely complicated piece of equipment. Literally thousands of different simultaneous operations are occurring in the process of doing even one seemingly simple piece of work. As a computer technician, you do not really need to be overly concerned about the actual inner workings of these components, but it will be helpful to understand what they do. The following sections will briefly outline how the CPU, memory, controllers, and other components work together to provide end users with a system they can use to accomplish their work. In fact, beyond the basic computer system, the selection of components and peripherals added to a personal computer help to make it the tool that an individual user needs for work or play.

on the **job**

Before you open a computer case, be sure to turn the power supply off and unplug any power cords. Then, to prevent damage to the system, equalize the electrical charge between your body and the components inside your computer. If nothing else, touch a grounded portion of your computer's chassis. A better option is to place the computer on a grounded mat, which you touch before working on the PC. You could also wear an antistatic wrist strap.

Warning: do not use an antistatic wrist strap when working with high-voltage devices, such as monitors and laser printers.

FIGURE 1-1

A typical PC

The PC Case

The typical PC user only knows his computer by its most visible components—the display (also called the monitor), the keyboard, the mouse, and the box that houses the main system, called the *case*. Usually constructed of metal and plastic in varying proportions, cases are also available in acrylic. Other terms for the case are chassis, cabinet, tower, box, or housing. In fact, some old-time techs will call it the CPU, a usage we do not support, as this is a preferred term for the processor, not for the entire system. If you purchased your computer from a major computer store, or from a manufacturer, such as Dell, your computer's case has a logo of the manufacturer showing prominently. If you had your computer custom made, it may have no branding information, or may have only the name of the case manufacturer.

When purchased separately, a typical PC case includes the power supply, cooling system, a slot behind each expansion card position, slot covers over the expansion slots, available external ports, and a selection of cables. The back of most PC cases today includes a panel of I/O ports, each connected to circuitry on the motherboard, and slots that give access to the back of expansion cards (see Figure 1-2).

Just as you should not judge a book by its cover, you should not judge a computer by its case. A simple case may hide a very powerful computer. Within the computer

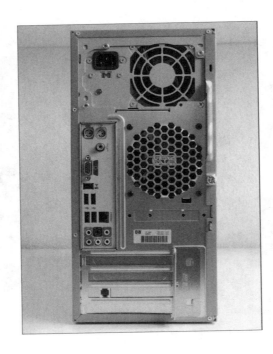

FIGURE 1-2

A PC case from the back showing a panel of ports and expansion slots gaming community it is very popular to create highly personalized cases, a practice called case modding (modifying). These cases may have internal lighting, colorful cable covers, and transparent sides. The computers in them may even be liquid cooled. But the typical PC technician is not concerned with these fancy variants, and you will not be tested on case modding on the A+ exam. We will return to the mundane and examine the purpose and features of a computer case, as well as the common sizes.

on the
Job

Computer case knowledge is not included in the A+ exam objectives for the Essentials (220-601) and 220-602 exams. It is included in this book as useful on-the-job information.

Along with the major computer manufacturers, such as Dell and Hewlett-Packard, there are several companies noted for their cases, including Antec, ASUS, Lian Li, and Thermaltake.

Purpose and Features

The purpose of a PC case is to hold all the basic components, to protect those components from dust and dirt, to cool the components, and to provide noise reduction. This last is not a high priority with most common cases, but cases are available that provide noise dampening using heavier materials, insulation, quieter power supplies, and quieter cooling fans.

A case typically comes with a power supply, cable management systems, and mounting locations for the motherboard, drives, and other internal components. A case will also provide connectors on the outside of the case for USB, IEEE 1394, and multimedia ports. (Learn more about the standards for USB and IEEE 1394 in Chapter 2.) A high-quality case comes with premium features such as a large, quiet power supply; easy-to-remove exterior body panels; and easy-to-use hard drive bays with features such as shock absorption. Similarly, better models will have a feature to make the job of installing a motherboard easier, such as a removable tray to hold the motherboard.

Case Form Factors

PC cases come in form factors to match motherboard form factors, such as ATX, BTX, micro ATX, and NLX. These will be described later in this chapter. A case form factor must take into consideration the location of the motherboard-based components, so that these components can be accessed. For instance, the case needs to have exterior openings for the adapter cards and port connectors that are built into the motherboard. It must also position drive bays so that they will not interfere with any motherboard components. A case also accommodates the standard power supply formats, described in Chapter 2. A case, motherboard, and power supply must be matched, or the motherboard and power supply may not even fit in the case.

Case Categories

Most PC cases fall into one of two categories: tower and desktop. A tower is designed to stand on a desk or floor with its largest dimension oriented vertically. A desktop is designed to sit on a desk with its largest dimension oriented horizontally. In a tower, the motherboard is normally mounted vertically, and in a desktop, the motherboard is mounted horizontally.

Case Sizes

Case sizes are not standardized, nor are the names manufacturers give the various sizes. Quality and features vary, so bigger is not always better. When quality is comparable, then, as size and features expand, so will the prices for PC cases. The following paragraphs describe these sizes, including rough dimensions for each size.

Full Tower

If you need a super-size PC, the *full tower* is the case for you. Cases sold as full towers stand between two and three feet tall and contain many 3.5" and 5.25" drive bays to hold both hard and optical drives. It is difficult to imagine running out of space with a full tower. It is also hard to imagine an individual needing a case this big. This size is rare in the consumer PC market.

Mid-Tower

The *mid-tower* case is just slightly smaller than most full-tower cases—the actual size depends on the manufacturer. This is the more realistic case for someone needing lots of drive bays and room to work when installing and removing components. Expect three or more of each of the two sizes of drive bays (3.5" and 5.25"). This is still an uncommon size in the consumer PC market, but a choice for someone who wants lots of space for expansion.

Mini-Tower

A very popular case, the *mini-tower* is the case you see enclosing most brand-name PCs. At 14 to 15 inches tall, a mini-tower can sit on a desk without causing a complete eclipse of ambient light. It can also be placed in a cabinet (with proper ventilation) or on the floor. Typically, a mini-tower contains one 3.5" bay and two 5.25" bays, but it may include more of each, especially the larger bays. However, the use of the prefix "mini" does not guarantee that a case will be small. Cases labeled "mini-tower" can be over 17" tall!

Desktop

The classic horizontally oriented *desktop case* has become less popular in recent years. This case is generally about 14" wide and 5" tall. It typically has a single 3.5" drive bay and a single 5.25" drive bay. Do not expect it to cool as well as tower cases, and its horizontal orientation generally requires more desk surface. It is common to set the monitor on top of the desktop PC case, which negatively affects the cooling efficiency. This configuration is also an ergonomic disaster for many users, causing neck pain from looking up at the monitor.

Low Profile

The *low-profile case* is a scaled-down version of the desktop case, also called "slimline." It reduces the amount of desktop space required but also has limited space for expansion, and not just in the scarcity of expansion slots. This case cannot accept full-height expansion cards, so a riser card is necessary before you can install a full-height card. In fact, many computers with low-profile cases are not upgradable, unless you are replacing the hard drive or upgrading the memory. Cooling can be a problem in these tiny cases. Several manufacturers offer low-end models in these cases, but this size is not as common or as popular as the mini-tower case.

Motherboards

The foundation of every PC is the motherboard. Each internal and external PC component connects, directly or indirectly, to the *motherboard*. The motherboard, also referred to as the *mainboard*, the *system board*, or the *planar board*, is made of fiberglass, typically brown or green, and with a meshwork of copper lines. These "lines" are the electronic circuits through which power, data, and control signals travel. A group of these wires, assigned a set of functions, is collectively called a bus (described later in this chapter). This section focuses on types of motherboards and their typical integrated components. You will also learn about the differences between the motherboard's communication busses and the types of systems they allow you to use.

on the **!** o b
If you work with experienced PC technicians, read trade publications, or visit technical Web sites, you will probably see the term "mobo" used in place of motherboard.

Form Factors

A motherboard *form factor* defines the type and location of components on the motherboard and the power supply that will work with each form factor. There are several motherboard form factors, each with different layouts, components, and specifications. Most motherboards are restricted to using only a few types of processors and memory. Personal computer motherboards have evolved over the past quarter century and continue to do so. Although motherboards can vary from manufacturer to manufacturer, Intel Corporation, a major manufacturer, has developed several form factors over the years, including the early AT and NLX form factors, and the later ATX and BTX. Each of these has size variations, such as the smaller microATX and microBTX form factors. We will discuss their sizes, typical components, and prevalence next.

Full AT and Baby AT

The *Full AT* and *Baby AT* motherboard form factors—actually two sizes of the AT standard—are the early predecessors to today's motherboards. We mention them here only for a bit of historical context. The *AT (Advanced Technology)* motherboard standard was introduced in 1984 to hold the new (at that time) Intel 80286 processors. Measuring approximately 12 by 13 inches, it supported the 80286 and older processors. The original AT form factor, known as "Full AT" after the introduction of the smaller Baby AT motherboard, measured about 8.5 by 13 inches. This motherboard had only the keyboard port built in—expansion cards were required for all other I/O. There were also problems with the AT form factor; for example, the processor sockets were in the front of the motherboard and interfered with full-length expansion cards. The AT motherboards were long from front to back, and therefore installed components interfered with access to the drive bays.

on the job *Manufacturers continued to make the Baby AT through the 1990s, with updates to support newer technologies in CPUs and newer peripheral support, such as USB.*

exam

watch   *NLX is a very old form factor that you may never encounter on the job. However, it is listed in the exam objectives for the 2006 A+ Essentials, so be sure to remember it and its place in the scheme of things. The AT form factor is not listed in the exam objectives.*

NLX

Predating the ATX form factor (described in the following section), *NLX* was an Intel standard for motherboards targeted to the low-end consumer market. It was an attempt to answer the need for motherboards with more components built in, including both sound and video. These motherboards became obsolete very quickly, in part because they were built around a very old expansion bus, the ISA bus, which had some severe limits that later bus designs overcame.

ATX

The *ATX (Advanced Technology eXtended)* motherboard standard was released by Intel Corporation in 1996 and is the most commonly used form in PCs. The ATX motherboard measures approximately 12" wide by 9.6" from front to back, which keeps it from interfering with the drive bays, as was a problem with the AT motherboards. The processor socket is located near the power supply, so that it will not interfere with full-length expansion boards. Finally, the hard and floppy drive connectors are located near the drive bays (see Figure 1-3).

When first introduced, the ATX motherboard included integrated parallel and serial ports (I/O ports) and a mini-DIN-6 keyboard connector. ATX boards also have built-in multimedia support accessed through a game port, as well as mini-audio ports for speaker, line-in, and microphone port. Manufacturers have modified the ATX standard to support newer technologies, such as USB, IEEE 1394, PCI, and PCIe. A rear panel provides access to the onboard I/O ports.

A typical ATX motherboard will contain up to four memory slots for the latest RAM types, support for BIOS-controlled power management, Intel or AMD CPU sockets, both IDE and SATA drive controllers, and support for USB and IEEE 1394.

BTX

Introduced in 2003 by Intel Corporation, the BTX motherboard form factor is the successor to the ATX standard. This standard is a major departure from ATX and offers improved cooling efficiency and a quieter computer.

An ATX motherboard with the CPU located in the back next to the power supply

SCENARIO & SOLUTION

How do ATX and BTX motherboards differ?	The BTX is a newer design that provides better cooling through the positioning of components on the motherboard, and quieter operation because it does not require as much fan power.
What is the most commonly used motherboard type?	ATX (or its variants) remains the most commonly used motherboard type.
Which motherboard form is typically the largest?	The standard BTX motherboard is larger than the ATX motherboard.

Seeking to improve the airflow through the computer, Intel moved the CPU to the front of the motherboard, placing it next to the intake vent and fan. Therefore, the CPU is the first component cooled by incoming air. Similarly, the chipset is positioned in line with the CPU so that airflow passing over the CPU then passes over the chipset before exiting the case. Other motherboard components benefit from the efficient cooling of this redesign.

You may wonder how a motherboard design can contribute to a quieter computer. A motherboard designed for efficient cooling needs fewer fans. Since fans are just about the noisiest component in a computer, having fewer fans contributes to quieter computing.

BTX boards come in three sizes, BTX (or standard BTX), Micro BTX, and Pico BTX. Table 1-1 gives a comparison of these three sizes.

e x a m
ⓦatch   *Although there are many variants, most of today's computers still use the ATX motherboard and its variants.*

TABLE 1-1		Approximate Size
Motherboard Size Comparison	ATX	12" × 9.6"
	Mini ATX	11.2" × 8.2"
	Flex ATX	9" × 7.5"
	Standard BTX	12.8" × 10.5"
	Micro BTX	Up to 10.4" × 10.5"
	Pico BTX	8.0" × 10.5"

Motherboard Components

The components built into a motherboard include sockets for various PC components, including the CPU, and built-in components such as video adapters, various ports, and the chipset.

Memory Slots

The motherboard will have from one to four slots or sockets for system memory. Depending on the vintage and the manufacturer of the motherboard, the memory sockets for DRAM are *SIMM* (*Single Inline Memory Module*), *DIMM* (*Dual Inline Memory Module*), and *RIMM*. SIMM is the oldest technology, and you will not see these sockets in new PCs. The current standards are DIMM and RIMM. Both of these physical memory slot types move data 64 bits at a time. DIMM sockets for desktop or tower PCs may have 168 pins, 184 pins, or 240 pins. RIMM sockets for non-portable PCs have 184 pins. Chapter 2 includes more information on DIMM and RIMM and other RAM technologies. DIMM and RIMM sockets for portable computers are yet another story, as you will learn in Chapter 5.

Processor/CPU Sockets

Every motherboard contains at least one CPU socket, and the location varies from one motherboard standard to another. Some motherboards even contain sockets for more than one type of CPU.

A common CPU socket type is a zero insertion force (ZIF) socket, which is square, has a retention lever, and accommodates a certain number of pins to match certain CPUs that have a *pin grid array* (*PGA*), which means it has columns and rows of pins. Learn more about how processors attach to motherboards in Chapter 3.

External Cache Memory

The motherboard may have sockets for external cache memory used by the CPU. See the discussion of cache memory later in this chapter, under the heading "Processor/CPU."

Bus Architecture

The term *bus* refers to pathways that power, data, or control signals use to travel from one component to another in the computer. Standards determine use of the wires in the various bus designs. There are many types of busses, including the processor bus, used by data traveling into and out of the processor. The address and data busses are both part of the processor bus. Another type of bus is the memory bus, which is located on the motherboard and used by the processor to access memory. In addition, each PC has an expansion bus of one or more types.

Expansion Bus Types and Slots

The bus standards for input/output (I/O) devices in PCs have evolved along with the PC over the last quarter century. The following bus types are those that you can expect to see in PCs today.

on the

Job *The terms* bus, system bus, *and* expansion bus *are interchangeable. A bus refers to either a system bus or an expansion bus attached to the CPU. PC expansion busses, such as PCI, attach through a controller that attaches to the system or expansion bus.*

PCI   The most common expansion bus architecture in PCs is *peripheral component interconnect (PCI)*, which was released in 1993. The PCI bus transfers data in parallel over a data bus that is either 32 or 64 bits wide. Over the years, there have been several variants of the PCI standard, and data transfer speeds vary, depending on the variant and the bus width. The original 32-bit PCI bus ran at 33.33 MHz with a transfer rate of up to 133 megabytes per second (MBps). PCI is a local bus, meaning that it moves data at speeds nearer the processor speeds.

The variants on the original PCI bus include PCI 2.2, PCI 2.3, PCI 3.0, PCI-X, Mini PCI, Cardbus, Compact PCI, and PC/104-Plus. These substandards vary in signaling speed, voltage requirements, and data transfer speed. Mini PCI and Cardbus brought PCI to laptops, requiring entirely different connectors to save space. Read more on these two busses in Chapter 5.

PCI slots are 3 ⅜ " long and are typically white. PCI cards and slots are not compatible with those of other bus architectures. Although initially developed for video cards, PCI cards are also available for networking, SCSI controllers, and a large variety of peripherals.

PCIe   PCIe *(peripheral component interconnect express)*, an entirely new expansion bus architecture, uses serial communications rather than parallel communications, as well as different bus connectors. Also called *PCI Express* and *PCI-E,* it will replace PCI and is incompatible with PCI adapter cards. While PCIe programming is similar to PCI, the new standard is not a true bus that transfers data in parallel, but a group of serial channels. Data transfers at 250 MBps per channel, with a maximum of 16 channels. The number of serial channels they handle describe PCIe connectors, with the designations x1, x4, and x16 indicating one, four, and sixteen channels respectively. On the motherboard, a PCIe x1 connector is approximately 1½" long, while PCIe x2 is about 2" long, and PCIe x16 is close to 4" long. The combined transfer rate for PCIe x16 is 4 GB second. Figure 1-4 shows a black PCIe x16 connector at the top and three white PCI connectors below it on the motherboard.

exam
watch

You don't need to know the full specifications of standards, such as PCI and PCIe, but you should understand the basics of each standard. For instance, know *that PCI and PCIe are both expansion bus interfaces, and remember that PCIe is the newer of the standards.*

FIGURE 1-4   Comparison of PCIe x16 and the older PCI bus connectors

AGP   AGP (*accelerated graphics port*) is a local bus designed for video only. Because this architecture provides a direct link between the processor and the video card, and gives the graphics adapter direct access to main memory, it is a "port" rather than a bus. It runs at the speed of the processor's memory bus. AGP is available in 32-bit and 64-bit versions. Figure 1-5 shows a motherboard with a brown AGP connector above two white PCI connectors.

There is normally only one AGP slot on a motherboard, and it looks very similar to PCI slots, but it is not compatible with PCI cards. To use AGP, the system's chipset and motherboard must support it. The AGP architecture also includes an AGP controller, which is typically a small, green chip on the motherboard. AGP cards typically run four to eight times faster than PCI. They are rated as 2X, 4X, or 8X. 64-bit 8X AGP

FIGURE 1-5   An AGP connector

transfers data to the display at up to 2 GB second. Fast cards can run in slow AGP slots; however, they will only run at the speed of the AGP port. AGP Pro is a name given to various modified AGP cards with performance enhancements targeted to the very high-performance market. PCIe is fast replacing AGP.

Drive Interface Standards

The preceding I/O bus architectures are for attaching video and other expansion cards to the computer. Next, we will look at the types of connectors you will find on a motherboard for installing hard drives and optical drives. These include EIDE/PATA, and SATA. In Chapter 2 we will discuss SCSI, another interface standard for drives, as it is not usually built into the motherboard.

EIDE/PATA   When it comes to circuitry for connecting drives to a PC, several generations of the *ATA (Advanced Technology Attachment)* standards, now called the *Parallel AT Attachment (PATA)* interface, are often lumped together under the old term *IDE (Integrated Drive Electronics)*, a standard for drives with the controller circuitry mounted on the drive itself. The later versions of IDE are called *Enhanced IDE*, or *EIDE*.

When you open up a PC and see wide ribbon cables, these are usually connecting EIDE drives to the PATA interface. If you follow one of these ribbon cables from a hard or optical drive to the motherboard, the PATA connector label may be "EIDE controller 01" or "EIDE controller 02." Never mind that EIDE is about the drives, and PATA is about the interface for these drives. Even in the latest motherboard, you may see these connectors labeled "IDE 1" and "IDE 2," as shown in Figure 1-6, in which the long PATA connector on the right, labeled "IDE 1," sits next to four SATA drive interface connectors that are replacing PATA. We will discuss SATA, shortly.

Whatever you choose to call it, PATA was used for hard drives and optical drives for many years. The truth is that it is just an interface between the drive and the computer. It is not truly controlling the drive, which a circuit board on the drive itself does.

Technicians have long detested the wide ribbon cabling used for these connectors because it blocks airflow, and it can sometimes be difficult to get unwieldy ribbon connectors tucked into a case without crimping them when closing the case. Space-saving rounded cables are available, but we still see mostly ribbon cables. PATA cables cannot be more than 18 inches in length, and PATA does not support hot swapping. To replace a drive, you must shut down the computer. While EIDE drives may advertise transfer rates above 80 megabytes per second, in reality the PATA interface limits these drives due to protocol overhead and the fact that PATA shares the PCI bus with all other PCI devices.

FIGURE 1-6

A connector labeled IDE 1 is the long, vertically oriented connector on the right, next to four SATA connectors.

exam
ⓦatch
Are you confused yet? The terms IDE, EIDE, ATA, and PATA are all used interchangeably. IDE and EIDE should refer to the drives, while ATA and PATA refer to the interface. In practice, even manufacturers label the PATA motherboard connectors "EIDE" or "IDE." The A+ objectives only mention EIDE and PATA. Remember, PATA is the older technology for interfaces for hard and optical drives. The newer technology is SATA.

ATAPI   ATAPI (*ATA Packet Interface*) is a standard used to connect drives with removable media to the PATA interface. These drives include optical drives (CD and DVD) and tape drives. Refer to Figure 1-6 and you will notice a large ribbon cable on the right. It is connected to (and partially obscuring) the connector labeled IDE 2. In this computer, this cable connects to a DVD drive using the ATAPI standard.

SATA   A new, faster interface for EIDE drives is *SATA (Serial ATA)*. While there are converters that will allow conventional EIDE drives to be connected through this interface, new drives are manufactured especially for this interface.

SCENARIO & SOLUTION	
What are the most common bus architectures in use today?	PCI and PCIe
What drive interface standard is replacing PATA for hard drives?	SATA
What standard, also used by other expansion cards, is replacing AGP for video?	PCIe

PCs now come with both PATA and SATA connectors on the motherboard. For the technician, the main advantage of this interface is that it uses thinner cabling. SATA uses slender cables that can be up to 39.4 inches long. SATA also supports hot swapping, which PATA does not support. The SATA standard calls for faster speeds than PATA—currently between 150 MBps and 300 MBps.

Chipset

A critical component of the motherboard is the *chipset*. When technicians talk about the chipset, they are usually referring to one or more chips designed to work hand in glove with the CPU. One part of this chipset, referred to as the *Northbridge*, controls communications between the CPU and other critical motherboard components. These are the system RAM and the PCI, AGP, and PCIe busses. Another portion, the *Southbridge*, manages communications between the CPU and such I/O busses as USB, IDE, PS2, SATA, and others.

Firmware

Firmware refers to software instructions, usually stored on ROM chips. Firmware exists on most PC components, such as video adapters, hard drives, network adapters, and printers. These instructions are always available, so they are not reprogrammed every time the computer is started.

BIOS

One type of computer firmware is the BIOS *(basic input/output system)*. The BIOS is responsible for informing the processor of the devices present and how to communicate with them. Whenever the processor makes a request of a component, the BIOS steps in and translates the request into instructions that the component can understand.

Older computers contained a true read-only BIOS that could not be altered. This meant that one could not add new types of components to the computer because the BIOS would not know how to communicate with them. Because this seriously limited users' ability to install a new type of device not recognized by the older BIOS, *flash BIOS* was introduced. Now, the flash BIOS can be electronically upgraded (or flashed) so that it can recognize and communicate with a new device type.

Usually you can obtain the flash program from the Web site of the motherboard manufacturer. The upgrade process typically requires you to copy the flash program to a floppy disk and start the system in DOS mode for the upgrade to work properly.

There are companies that specialize in manufacturing BIOSes for PC manufacturers, and many PC and/or motherboard manufacturers make their own BIOSes. Phoenix Technologies, LTD, and Award are companies that made their mark as BIOS manufacturers.

on the
① o b

It is very important that you follow the directions given by the manufacturer when performing a flash upgrade. If done incorrectly, the system can become inoperable and need a replacement BIOS chip from the manufacturer.

CMOS

Another important type of firmware is CMOS (*complementary metal-oxide semiconductor*). The CMOS chip retains settings such as the time, keyboard settings, and boot sequence. (We describe these settings in more detail in Chapter 3.) The CMOS also stores interrupt request line (IRQ) and input/output (I/O) resources that the BIOS uses when communicating with the computer's devices. The CMOS chip is able to keep these settings in the absence of computer power because of a small battery, which is usually good for from two to ten years.

on the
① o b

If the system repeatedly loses track of time when turned off, you probably need to replace the battery. This is usually a simple process, requiring opening the case and exchanging the old battery for a new one.

You can view and modify the computer's CMOS settings by entering the computer's Setup program during bootup. When booting up the computer, watch the screen for instructions such as "Press CTRL-S to access Startup Configuration" or "Press DELETE to enter Setup." You will only have about three seconds to enter the appropriate key combination from the time such a message first displays. You can configure the length of this delay in the CMOS settings, which we discuss in more detail in Chapter 3.

on the
①ob

Interestingly, the term "CMOS settings" is a bit of a misnomer. When people talk about the computer's CMOS, or its settings, they are referring to the items described in the preceding discussion. However, a CMOS is really just a type of physical chip. CMOS chips do a variety of things other than retaining CMOS settings. In fact, many processors are actually CMOS chips.

BIOS and CMOS Roles in the Boot Process

When the computer is started (booted up), the BIOS runs a *power-on self-test (POST)*. During the POST, the BIOS checks for the presence and function of each component it is programmed to manage. It first checks the processor, then the RAM, and then system-critical devices such as the floppy drive, hard drive, keyboard, and monitor. It then tests non-critical components such as CD-ROM drives and the sound card.

Next, the BIOS retrieves the resource settings from the CMOS and assigns them to the appropriate devices. Then the BIOS processes the remaining CMOS settings, such as the time or keyboard status (for example, whether the number lock should be on or off). Finally, the BIOS searches for an operating system and hands control of the system over to it. The CMOS settings are no longer required at this point, but the BIOS continues to work, translating communications between the processor and other components.

on the
①ob

The BIOS contains basic 16-bit drivers for accessing the needed hardware during bootup, such as the keyboard, floppy disk, hard disk, or any other device needed during a bootup.

EXERCISE 1-1

Viewing System Settings in CMOS

1. Restart your computer, and remain at the keyboard.
2. As the computer starts up, watch for a message at the bottom of the screen telling you to press a specific key or key combination in order to enter Setup.
3. Press the key or key combination indicated.
4. Spend time viewing the settings, but *do not* make any changes.
5. When you have finished, use the key combination indicated on the screen for exiting without saving any changes.

Riser Card/Daughter Card

There are two types of *riser card*. The first type, also called a *daughter card*, is a specially designed circuit board that connects directly into a motherboard and adds no additional functionality on its own. Rather, it extends the expansion bus and allows added expansion cards in a different orientation. The riser card is installed perpendicular to the case and may include several expansion slots. An expansion card inserted into a riser card is on the same plane as the motherboard. Riser cards are available for the standard bus architectures, such as AGP, PCI, and PCIe. Ironically, you will find riser cards both in the largest network servers and in the smallest of low-profile desktop computer cases.

In the case of network servers, the use of a riser card allows the addition of more cards than the standard motherboard allows. Otherwise, the additional expansion boards would increase the size of the motherboards beyond the size of even the large cases used for servers.

At the other extreme are the scaled-down low-profile computers, which cannot accommodate most expansion cards because the case height is so low. The riser card allows one or more expansion cards to be installed and does not require a full-height case.

The second type of riser card is a small expansion card containing multiple functions. The two standards for this type of riser card are AMR and CNR. Both of these standards add multiple functions at low cost.

AMR

AMR (Audio Modem Riser), introduced in the late 1990s, allows for the creation of lower-cost sound and modem solutions. The AMR card plugs directly into a special slot on the motherboard and utilizes the CPU to perform modem functions, using up to 20 percent of the available processor power for this purpose. The advantage of this is the elimination of separate modem and sound cards without tying up a PCI slot in newer computers. The AMR card connects directly to a telephone line and audio output devices. One of the shortcomings of AMR was that it was not Plug and Play.

ACR

ACR (Advanced Communications Riser) is a standard introduced in 2000 by AMD, 3Com, and others to supersede AMR. It uses one PCI slot and provides accelerated audio and modem functions as well as networking, and it supports multiple Ethernet NICs. With ACR, one telephone jack could be used for both modem and telephone jack. The ACR PCI slot is blue, and the pin orientation is the reverse of the standard PCI slot.

CNR

The first *CNR (Communication Network Riser)* card was introduced in 2000. Similar to AMR except that it does support Plug and Play, CNR also supports LAN in addition to audio, modem, and multimedia systems. The CNR card plugs directly into the motherboard, thus eliminating the need for separate cards for each capability and reducing the cost of expansion cards.

Processor/CPU

A personal computer is more than the sum of its parts. However, the most important part, without which it is not a computer, or even a useful tool, is the CPU (*central processing unit*), also called the *processor*. The following is an overview of CPUs, their purposes and characteristics, manufacturers and models, and technologies.

Purposes and Characteristics

In a PC, the central processing unit (CPU) is the primary control device for the entire computer system. The CPU is simply a chip containing a set of components that manages all the activities and does much of the "heavy lifting" in a computer system. The CPU interfaces, or is connected, to all of the components such as memory, storage, and input/output (I/O) through busses. The CPU performs a number of individual or discrete functions that must work in harmony in order for the system to function.

Additionally, the CPU is responsible for managing the activities of the entire system. The CPU takes direction from internal commands that are stored within the CPU as well as external commands that come from the operating system and other programs. Figure 1-7 shows a very simplified view of the functions internal to the CPU. It is important to note that these functions occur in all CPUs regardless of manufacturer.

CPU Technologies

There are a number of technologies employed in a CPU, based on both standards and proprietary designs, which are constantly changing. The following describes common technologies used by CPUs.

Simple functional
diagram of a CPU

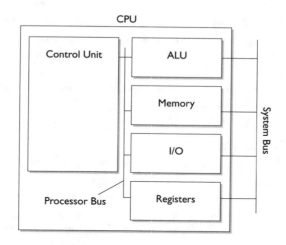

Control Unit

The *control unit* shown in Figure 1-7 is primarily responsible for directing all
the activities of the computer. It also manages interactions between the other
components in the computer system. In addition, the control unit contains both
hardwired instructions and programmed instructions called microcode. See the
explanation later in this chapter on microcode.

Busses

Notice in Figure 1-7 that there are several pathways between components in the
CPU. These are busses, used for special purposes such as moving data from internal
memory to the control unit. The *internal bus* of the CPU is usually much faster than
external busses used on the system. Other busses connect the CPU to the external
devices. The *front side bus* connects the processor to system memory and the video
adapter. These busses do not usually connect directly to external busses, such as PCI,
except through a device called a controller.

ALU

The *arithmetic logic unit (ALU)* is responsible for all logical and mathematical
operations in the system. The ALU receives instructions from the control unit.

The ALU can take information from memory, perform computations and comparisons, and then store the results in memory locations as directed by the control unit. An additional type of ALU, called a *floating-point unit (FPU)* or *math coprocessor,* is frequently used to perform specialized functions such as division and large decimal number operations. Most modern microprocessors include an FPU processor as part of the microprocessor.

Registers

The ALU and control unit communicate with each other and perform operations in memory locations called *registers*. A register is a location, internal to the microprocessor, used as a scratch pad for calculations. There are two types of registers used in modern systems: dedicated registers and general-purpose registers. Dedicated registers are usually for specific functions such as maintaining status or system-controlled counting operations. General-purpose registers are for multiple purposes, typically when mathematical and comparison operations occur.

Memory

Computer memory provides the primary storage for a computer system. The CPU will typically have internal memory (embedded in the CPU) used for operations, and external memory, which is located on the motherboard. The important consideration about memory is that the control unit is responsible for controlling usage of all memory. You will find a more detailed discussion about memory in Chapter 2.

Cache

Cache memory in a computer is usually a relatively small amount of expensive, very fast memory used to compensate for speed differences between components. The cache memory you hear about the most is between the CPU and the main memory. A CPU moves data to and from memory faster than the system RAM can respond. You might think that the solution is to install fast RAM as system RAM, but this would make a PC too expensive. Therefore, main system memory is most often a type of RAM known as DRAM, and cache memory is the faster and more expensive SRAM. Only a relatively small amount of memory is required for cache as compared to system memory. You will learn more about these types of RAM in Chapter 2.

Cache memory runs faster than typical RAM and is able to "guess" which instructions the processor is likely to need, and retrieve those instructions from RAM or the hard drive in advance. Cache memory can also hold preprocessed data, such as out-of-order processing or data used by a game or an applications program.

Typical applications may require frequent processing of the same instructions. For example, a game may have repeatedly-called video instructions. Newer processors can even create a "decision tree" of possible future instructions and store these in the cache, allowing rapid access to information or instructions by the CPU. Even when generating the tree, some instructions are preprocessed and stored in case the specific branch of logic is followed, and those instructions do not have to be reprocessed again. Intel has this down to an art, and the processors are generally correct in the tree they create.

Internal cache memory, more commonly called *L1 cache* or *Level 1 cache*, resides within the processor itself. *External cache memory*, called *L2 cache* or *Level 2 cache*, resides external to a CPU's core. At one time, external cache memory was only on the motherboard, but today's processors usually have L2 cache installed on the same chip as the processor, but electronically separated from the inner workings of the process. Beginning with the Itanium CPU, Intel offers a new level of external cache memory that resides on the motherboard, called *L3 cache (Level 3 cache)*. It measures in megabytes, whereas L1 and L2 cache most often measure in kilobytes. The use of cache memory with CPUs has greatly increased system performance.

Controllers

The CPU also contains a number of interfaces or controllers to access devices and busses. One of the primary functions of a controller is to free up control unit time by performing routine or clearly identified tasks. A typical microprocessor will have a controller interface to slow-speed devices such as serial data connections, high-speed interfaces connected to a computer bus, and connections to dedicated registers containing report status. These controllers will also typically interface to other controllers on a bus for specific types of operations. The details of this are not important for the A+ exams, but they have a huge impact on system performance because they relieve the control unit of unnecessary work.

Programs

The rubber meets the road with programs. The CPU has a large number of coded instructions and programs used to provide instructions on how to handle specific requests. Some of these programs are hardwired into the CPU, while others can be configured as the need arises. Hardwired programs may include the specific method by which data moves from a memory location to a register, how the status of the processor is stored, what specific steps need to occur when an error happens, and hundreds of other activities. Without these programs, the CPU will not know how to respond when powered on. These programs are very complicated and form the basic characteristics of the operation of the CPU. Additionally, most CPUs allow changes to these micro-programs by the manufacturer or operating system provider. In this manner, you can upgrade a CPU without physically replacing it.

Hyperthreading

A *thread*, or thread of execution, is a portion of a program that can run separately from other portions of the program. A thread can also run concurrently with other threads. *Hyperthreading,* also known as *simultaneous multithreading (SMT)*, is a CPU technology that allows two threads to execute at the same time within a single execution core. This is considered to be partially parallel execution. Intel introduced hyperthreading in the Pentium 4 Xeon CPU.

Multicore CPUs

The most visible change in CPUs in recent years has been the introduction of CPUs with more than one core on the same chip. The first of these were *dual-core* CPUs containing two CPU cores. We know of quad-core CPUs in development, and binary progressions of eight-core and beyond are sure to follow.

What is the attraction of these multicore CPUs? Server computers have long been available with multiple CPUs, so why not simply install two or more single-core CPUs on the same motherboard? The answer to both questions is that two cores on the same chip can communicate and cooperate much faster than two single-core processors. A dual-core CPU can simultaneously process two threads in true parallel execution.

At this writing, dual-core CPUs are not listed in the A+ 2006 exam objectives.

In recent years, both AMD and Intel have brought out CPUs with multiple cores on the same chip, beginning with dual-core processors. Newer high-end consumer models from both manufacturers include such dual-core processors.

CPU Clock Speed

The *clock speed* of a CPU is the speed at which it can potentially execute instructions. In older CPUs this was measured in millions of cycles per second, or megahertz (MHz);

more recent CPUs are so fast that they are measured in billions of cycles per second, or gigahertz (GHz). A CPU of a certain type and model may be available in a range of clock speeds. All other features being equal, the CPU with the faster clock speed will be more expensive.

However, when comparing different models of CPUs, the faster clock speed alone will not determine the fastest CPU. Manufacturers use a wide variety of technologies to speed up CPUs. For example, the number of clock cycles required for completing the same operation can vary between CPU models. To the end user, the perceived speed of a PC, or lack of it, may involve other aspects of the total design of the computer, such as the cache size, the amount and speed of the RAM, and the speed of the hard drive.

Throttling

A major problem arises as processor, memory, and other motherboard components become both more powerful and smaller: overheating. This occurs despite efforts to mitigate this problem with heat sinks, fans, and other cooling techniques built into the design of the chips themselves. *Throttling*, or thermal throttling, is a feature that causes the CPU to lower its speed in order to reduce its temperature. In the extreme, a processor will actually turn itself off in order to protect the system from the harmful effects of overheating. Throttling is a feature of the Pentium 4 and newer Intel processors, as well as recent processors in the AMD line. It is common in processors used for notebook computers.

Overclocking

Overclocking is the practice of forcing a CPU or other computer component to run at a higher clock rate than the manufacturer intended. PC hobbyist and gamers often overclock their systems to get more performance out of CPUs, video cards, chipsets, and RAM. The downside to this practice is that overclocking produces more heat and can cause damage to the motherboard, CPU, and other chips, which may explode and/or burst into flames.

Microcode

Microcode (also called a *microprogram*) is one of many low-level instructions built into the control unit of a CPU. An example of an instruction might be the command to fetch information from memory. People often call microcode "hardwired" because you cannot change it.

In January 1997, Intel released a CPU similar to the Pentium but with an improved instruction set called *multimedia extensions (MMX)* as part of its microcode for handling graphics and other multimedia. All Pentium family CPUs released since then include the MMX instruction set.

VRM

A voltage regulator module, or VRM, is a chip or tiny circuit card used to condition the power to the CPU and reduce it from the 5 volts of the motherboard to the lower voltage (3.3 volts or less) of the CPU. Modern CPUs in PCs inform the motherboard of the voltage they require and may not require a VRM.

Manufacturers and Models

There are many CPU manufacturers, but the prevailing ones in the personal computer market today are Intel Corporation and AMD (Advanced Micro Devices, Inc.). Intel received a huge boost when IBM selected their 8088 processor for the original IBM-PC in 1981. For over a decade AMD produced "clones" of Intel CPUs under a licensing agreement granted to them at a time when Intel's manufacturing capacity could not keep up with the demand for CPUs. Eventually this agreement ended, and, since 1995, AMD has designed and produced their own CPUs. Both companies manufacture more than CPUs, but their competition in the CPU market gets more attention in the trade and business press, as AMD has emerged as the only significant competitor to Intel. The following discussion includes a sampling of CPU models from both manufacturers, and avoids mention of CPU models designed specifically for the laptop market. Learn about those CPUs in Chapter 5.

Intel

Over time, both manufacturers have released a number of CPU models. Intel's have ranged from the Intel 8086 (released in 1978) to the latest generation of the Pentium family of processors, including those with "Pentium" in their name as well as the Celeron, Xeon, and Itanium brands. The following subsections discuss the common processors.

exam
watch
It is good for any computer professional to understand the differences between the CPU models. However, the objectives for the CompTIA A+ exams covered by this Study Guide do not include specific CPU models, only the manufacturers and the technologies of CPUs, which we covered in an earlier section.

Intel Pentium Family

The word "Pentium" that is attached to several generations of Intel processors gets its name because Intel considered this first model to be the fifth generation of Intel chips. With three of the earlier generations—286, 386, and 486—they used the initial number in the model to indicate the generation. They dropped this convention with the fifth generation because they ran into legal problems trademarking a simple number. Like any family, the Pentium has many members. The Pentium Pro marked the beginning of the sixth generation, while the Pentium 4 brought in the seventh generation, and the Itanium is the beginning of the eighth generation. What follows is a brief description of the major models in these generations.

Pentium CPU Models   The Intel Pentium CPU, first released in March 1993, began a long dynasty of Intel processor models that continued through the Pentium Pro, Pentium II, Pentium III, and Pentium 4. The first model included *superscalar* processing, meaning that it was capable of parallel processing, so it could process two sets of instructions at the same time. Intel made numerous advances in each new model, increasing the speed and the number of transistors per chip.

Pentium processors in general have a 64-bit data bus, meaning that the processor can receive or transmit 64 bits at a time.

The majority of Pentium models to date have a 32-bit register (internal data bus), which is the on-board storage area in the processor. Newer models have 64-bit registers. Many computer professionals base the label "64-bit CPU" on the size of the register. Therefore, although many Pentium models are called 64-bit, only those with 64-bit registers actually earn that title.

All Pentium CPUs include L1 cache memory and, beginning with the 1997 introduction of the Pentium II, most models included onboard L2 cache of varying sizes. The Pentium III (1999) brought advances in many areas, including enhanced support for multimedia and a faster L2 cache.

Early Pentium processors had a 32-bit address bus, for addressing up to 4 GB of memory, and later Pentium models have a 36-bit address bus, theoretically allowing them to use up to 64 GB of RAM, although this capability has only recently been supported in motherboards.

The Pentium 4 (P4) processor, released in 2000, includes all of the features of the Pentium III plus a few more. The chip went through a redesign that includes a new architecture called the NetBurst microarchitecture. Where older Pentiums pretty much topped out at 1 GHz, the P4 works at much faster speeds and it can exceed speeds of 2 GHz on the desktop. Intel states that NetBurst allows for future processor speeds of up to 10 GHz.

The P4 also includes a number of new instructions and, interestingly enough, a smaller L1 cache than a Pentium III. You would think this would make the system slower, but, in reality, system performance improves. The speed increases because the cache refreshes or updates more efficiently when smaller cache sizes are used. The L2 cache on the original Pentium 4 is 256 KB, but it operated at a faster speed than its predecessor. Subsequent Pentium 4 models have larger L2 caches.

Celeron   The Intel *Celeron* CPUs are consumer-level CPUs designed to have most of the features of the latest Pentium but with lower levels of certain features, such as L2 cache and clock speed, than the premium processors in each model generation. The first Celeron was a budget-level Pentium II. At this writing, the latest Celeron models are the Celeron Ds based on the Pentium D CPU.

Xeon   You can consider the Intel *Xeon* CPUs as the opposite of the Celerons. The Xeon chips are high-end CPUs for the server market. Based on the current Pentium model, beginning with the Pentium II Xeon, these CPUs have several enhancements not found in the same generation of Pentium. The most compelling for server manufacturers has been the multiprocessor support that allows identical Xeon chips to work extremely well together. Server systems utilize sets of two, four, eight, or more of these chips. After dropping "Pentium" from the name, Xeon models were manufactured with even more improvements, including 64-bit registers and support for L3 (Level 3) cache on the motherboard.

Itanium   Not a true member of the Pentium family, the *Itanium* line grew out of collaboration between Intel and Hewlett-Packard. Designed solely for the high-end server market, Intel introduced the first Itanium CPU in 2001. Although it is downwardly compatible with operating systems and code written for the previous Intel (and AMD) CPU architecture, referred to as x86, such software ran more slowly on the early Itanium than it did on the Intel and AMD x86 CPUs. To access the full power of the Itanium you must use an operating system and other software optimized to take advantage of its features.

Subsequent Itanium models, such as the Itanium 2, have greatly improved performance and better acceptance by server manufacturers. In addition to HP (of course), they include Bull, Fujitsu, Hitachi, NEC, Silicon Graphics, and Unisys. In July 2006, Intel introduced the dual-core Itanium CPU, with more power and far less power consumption than previous models. At this writing, two quad-core designs are in the works.

Intel introduced the Pentium D series of multicore CPUs in 2005. The Pentium D target is desktop computers. It has the distinction of being the last CPU series to carry the "Pentium" name. Other recent multicore Intel CPUs include the Intel Core 2 series of desktop processors, and the high-end Pentium Extreme Edition, targeted at high-end workstations and servers.

on the
!
ⓘ o b

Although the Pentium models have long contained a 36-bit address bus, computer manufacturers generally did not use the additional wires in the address bus to address memory. Therefore, many computers that include these processors support only 32-bit addressing and can use only up to 4 GB of system RAM memory. Some implementations, such as the IA-32 Intel Pentium 4 (including Celeron and Xeon models), use the 36-bit address bus, allowing up to 64 GB of addressable memory. This also depends on motherboard support.

AMD

Former employees of Fairchild Semiconductor founded Advanced Micro Devices, Inc., in 1969. They manufacture a large variety of products based on integrated circuits. AMD CPU lines include Athlon, Opteron, Turion 64, Sempron, and Duron. As with Intel, we'll first look at older CPU lines before describing the newer lines.

K5 and K6 CPU Lines AMD designed the *K5* processor, and released it in 1995. It competed directly with the Pentium, with a 64-bit data bus, a 32-bit register, and a 32-bit address bus. The main difference between the Pentium and the K5, other than the supported speeds, is the use of L1 cache. The Pentium had up to 512 KB, whereas the K5 supported only 8 KB.

Around the time of the release of the Intel Pentium II processor, AMD released its own sixth-generation processor, the *K6*. This processor supported speeds from 166–266 MHz. As with most processors, the K6 had a 64-bit data bus, a 32-bit register, and a 32-bit address bus. It also included between 256 KB and 1 MB of L1 cache, but it did not include an on-board L2 cache.

Duron AMD released the *Duron* CPU in 1999 and positioned it to compete with the Intel Celeron in the economy grade PC market. A sixth-generation CPU, the first Duron supported speeds between 700 and 800 MHz.

Athlon The *Athlon*, introduced in 2000 as the upscale CPU to the Duron's low-end market, was a sixth-generation CPU; AMD later introduced a seventh-generation CPU, the Athlon XP, with many performance improvements. The Athlon line continued to evolve through the generations, to the Athlon 64, a 64-bit processor, which can run both 32-bit and 64-bit operating systems.

Opteron Introduced as an eighth-generation CPU, this first CPU in the *Opteron* line has a 40-bit address bus, and it can run both 32-bit and 64-bit operating systems. It is moving toward a true 64-bit address bus and has AMD-developed performance enhancements.

EXERCISE 1-2

Identifying Your Processor

1. Right-click the My Computer icon.

2. Select Properties.

3. Read the information in the General tab to determine your processor type.

CERTIFICATION SUMMARY

Common computer components include the processor, memory, storage devices, and input and output devices. All of these devices have specific functions, and your familiarity with them will help you to determine when to upgrade or replace a component.

This chapter described general characteristics of motherboard components and form factors, CPU technologies used by Intel Corporation and Advanced Micro Devices (AMD), motherboard forms, and CMOS settings. You must use a motherboard that supports the selected CPU and RAM and ensure that the CMOS will support the installed components. Motherboards have many integrated functions. This chapter introduced many of the technologies on which you may be tested on the A+ exams. A good knowledge of these concepts is also important when you are repairing or upgrading a computer system. Chapter 2 will continue with an explanation of other important PC components.

TWO-MINUTE DRILL

Here are some of the key points covered in Chapter 1.

The PC Case

❑ The computer case is the container that houses and protects the PC motherboard, power supply, and other components.

❑ A computer case is constructed of metal, plastic, and even acrylic.

❑ Cases come in a variety of sizes that are not standardized. They include full tower, mid-tower, mini-tower, desktop, and low profile.

❑ A case fits a certain motherboard form factor and comes with a power supply.

Motherboards

❑ All components, including external peripherals, connect directly or indirectly to the motherboard.

❑ The most common type of motherboard in current computers is the ATX form factor, updated since its 1996 introduction to support newer onboard components.

❑ The BTX standard, introduced in 2003 by Intel Corporation, provides improved cooling efficiency and quieter operation.

❑ Both the ATX and BTX form factors come in a variety of sizes.

❑ The most common types of bus architectures are PCI, PCIe, and AGP.

❑ PCI, PCIe, and AGP bus architectures are "local" because they connect more directly with the processor.

❑ The chipset is now one to three separate chips on the motherboard that handle very low-level functions relating to the interactions between the CPU and other components.

❑ Basic input/output system, or BIOS, is firmware that informs the processor of the hardware that is present and contains low-level software routines for communicating with and controlling the hardware.

❑ The CMOS chip is non-volatile RAM, supported by a battery. CMOS stores basic hardware configuration settings, such as those for drives, keyboards, boot sequence, and resources used by a particular component.

Processor/CPU

❏ The CPU is a chip that is the primary control device for a PC.

❏ The CPU connects to all of the components, such as memory, storage, and input/output through communications channels called busses.

❏ CPU components include the control unit, busses, the arithmetic logic unit (ALU), memory, controllers, and L1 and L2 cache.

❏ Hyperthreading is a technology that allows a CPU to execute two threads at the same time within a single execution core. Intel introduced hyperthreading in the Pentium 4 Xeon CPU.

❏ A dual-core processor contains two processing cores and can process two threads simultaneously, performing true parallel execution.

❏ Thermal throttling of a processor is a feature that causes it to lower its speed in order to reduce the temperature of the CPU to protect itself from the harmful effects of overheating. Recent Intel and AMD processors perform throttling.

❏ Intel Corporation and AMD (Advanced Micro Devices, Inc) are the two top manufacturers of PC CPUs.

❏ Intel has many models that have grown from the Pentium line, including the Pentium Pro, Pentium II, Pentium III, and Pentium 4. They also have the Celeron line, which is a generally downscale version of the current Pentium CPU, and the Xeon, which is a more upscale version of the current CPU line. At this writing, the Itanium is the newest line of CPUs.

❏ AMD CPU lines include the old K5 and K6 lines, which were followed by the Athlon, Opteron, Turion 64, Sempron, and Duron.

SELF TEST

The following questions will help you measure your understanding of the material presented in this chapter. Read all of the choices carefully because there might be more than one correct answer. Choose all correct answers for each question.

The PC Case

1. What is the purpose of a PC case?
  A. To block all airflow to the motherboard
  B. To house the monitor and keyboard
  C. To hold, protect, and cool the basic PC components
  D. To process data

2. This feature varies among cases, and depends on heavier materials, insulation, and quieter fans.
  A. IEEE 1394
  B. Easy-to-remove exterior body panels
  C. Easy-to-use hard drive bays
  D. Noise reduction

3. Which statement is true?
  A. A case, motherboard, and power supply must match, or the motherboard or power supply will not fit in the case.
  B. Any power supply will fit into any case.
  C. Any motherboard will fit into any case.
  D. The position of drive bays is not a consideration, since the motherboard is flat.

4. This is the case size on most brand-name PCs.
  A. Full tower
  B. Mid-tower
  C. Mini-tower
  D. Low profile

Motherboards

5. Which of the following statements is true?
  A. The motherboard must always be in a horizontal position.
  B. Each internal and external PC component connects to the motherboard, directly or indirectly.

    C. The "lines" on the motherboard provide cooling.

    D. A system board is an unusual motherboard variant.

6. Which of the following describes a motherboard form factor?

    A. The size and color of a motherboard

    B. The processor the motherboard supports

    C. The type and location of components and the power supply that will work with the mother-board, plus the dimensions of the motherboard

    D. Mid-tower

7. The variants of which motherboard form factor continue to be widely used, in spite of a new standard from Intel?

    A. Baby AT

    B. NLX

    C. BTX

    D. ATX

8. How many memory slots does a typical motherboard have?

    A. Four to six

    B. Three to eight

    C. One to four

    D. None

9. Which statement defines Northbridge?

    A. A chipset component that controls communications between the CPU; the PCI, AGP, and PCIe busses; and RAM

    B. A chipset component that controls communications between the CPU and I/O busses

    C. A component that saves configuration settings

    D. The system setup program itself

10. Which statement most accurately describes the relationship between the computer's BIOS and CMOS?

    A. The CMOS uses information stored in the BIOS to set computer configurations, such as the boot sequence, keyboard status, and hard drive settings.

    B. The BIOS configuration settings are stored on the battery-supported CMOS chip so that they are not lost when you turn the computer off.

    C. The CMOS uses information stored in the BIOS to communicate with the computer's components.

    D. They perform the same functions, but the BIOS is found only in newer computers.

11. Communication Network Riser (CNR) is similar to AMR except for the following.

   A. It provides modem functions but is not Plug and Play.

   B. It provides audio functions.

   C. It provides LAN functionality and is Plug and Play.

   D. It provides wireless networking.

12. Which of the following describes a difference between PCI and PCIe?

   A. PCIe is only used for graphics adapters, PCI is used by a variety of adapters.

   B. PCI uses parallel data communications, PCIe uses serial communications.

   C. PCIe uses parallel data communications, PCI uses serial communications.

   D. PCIe is only used for graphics adapters, PCI is used by a variety of adapters.

13. This type of bus connector is only used by video adapters, and it is being phased out in favor of PCIe.

   A. PCI

   B. NIC

   C. AGP

   D. USB

Processor/CPU

14. Which of the following most accurately describes a function of the CPU's cache memory?

   A. To store instructions used by currently running applications

   B. To provide temporary storage of data that is required to complete a task

   C. To anticipate the CPU's data requests and make that data available for fast retrieval

   D. To store a device's most basic operating instructions

15. What component in a CPU is responsible for all logical and mathematical operations?

   A. ALU

   B. Processor

   C. Control unit

   D. Bus

16. What CPU component contains microcode?

   A. ALU

   B. Processor

   C. Control unit

   D. Bus

17. What type of memory is very fast and too expensive to use as system RAM, but is used as cache memory?

A. DIMM

B. RIMM

C. DRAM

D. SRAM

18. What is the data bus width of all Pentium-class processors?

A. 32-bit

B. 36-bit

C. 64-bit

D. Each Pentium processor has a different data bus width.

19. Which Intel CPU initiated the fifth generation and began an entire dynasty of Intel processors?

A. Athlon

B. Opteron

C. Pentium

D. Celeron

20. The Intel CPU technology that allows two threads to execute at the same time within a single execution core.

A. Hyperthreading

B. Throttling

C. Overclocking

D. Microcode

LAB QUESTION

It is nearly impossible to stay up-to-date on PC technologies. However, a good technician checks out certain reliable Web sites when making a decision about the features of a new PC. Assume that you want to brush up on the very latest in CPUs in preparation for purchasing a new PC for use in a home office. Use an Internet browser to connect to Intel's site (www.intel.com) and to AMD's site (www. amd.com) and check out the latest CPU models. At each site, find one or more CPU models offered for "personal computers." Write down these model names in the space provided:

_____

_____

_____

_____

(continued...)

Then compare the CPU models you found with the CPUs offered in consumer-level PCs by either newspaper advertisements from "brick and mortar" stores, or by online retailers.

	Computer Model	CPU Model	Dual-Core?	Price
AMD-based desktop PC				
AMD-based notebook				
Intel-based desktop PC				
Intel-based notebook				

SELF TEST ANSWERS

The PC Case

1. ☑ C. The purpose of a PC case is to hold, protect, and cool the basic PC components.
   ☒ A is incorrect because the design of a case will allow for proper airflow over the motherboard. B is incorrect because the monitor and keyboard are located outside the typical case. D is incorrect because processing data is the function of the CPU, one of the components located on the motherboard within a case.

2. ☑ D. Noise reduction is a feature that depends on heavier materials, insulation, and quieter fans.
   ☒ A, IEEE 1394, is incorrect because it is not a feature of PC cases, although cases will often have exterior ports that connect to circuitry supporting these features on the motherboard. B is incorrect because easy-to-remove exterior body panels do not rely on heavier materials, insulation, and quieter fans. C is incorrect because easy-to-use hard drive bays do not depend on the items listed.

3. ☑ A. A case, motherboard, and power supply must match, or the motherboard or power supply will not fit in the case.
   ☒ B and C are both incorrect because each case is designed to fit certain power supplies and motherboards. D is incorrect because even though the motherboard itself is flat, the components on the motherboard take up varying amounts of vertical space, and therefore, the position of drive bays is a consideration.

4. ☑ C. Mini-tower is the case size on most brand-name PCs.
   ☒ A, full tower, is incorrect because this very large case is uncommon in the consumer PC market. B, mid-tower, is incorrect because it is also uncommon in the consumer PC market. D, low profile, is incorrect; although this is a consumer-oriented case size, it is only for the low end and is not as common as the mini-tower.

Motherboards

5. ☑ B. Each internal and external PC component connects to the motherboard, directly or indirectly.
   ☒ A is not true because the motherboard can be oriented in whatever position the case requires. C is not true because the lines on the motherboard do not provide cooling but carry signals and are part of various busses installed on the motherboard. D is not true. System board is simply another name for motherboard.

6. ☑ **C.** The type and location of components and the power supply that will work with the motherboard, plus the dimensions of the motherboard.
    ☒ **A** is not correct because, while size may be part of a form factor, color has nothing to do with the form factor. **B** is incorrect because the processor the motherboard supports is not, by itself, a description of a form factor. **D** is incorrect because mid-tower is a case size, not a motherboard form factor.

7. ☑ **D.** ATX. This form factor has had a long run with motherboard manufacturers, even after the introduction of the BTX form factor.
    ☒ **A** is incorrect because Baby AT is a very old form factor that had too many problems with cooling, and the location of components interfering with drive bays. **B**, NLX, is incorrect for the same reasons as Baby AT. **C**, BTX, is incorrect because it is the newest form factor discussed in this chapter, and it has not yet truly replaced the ATX form factor.

8. ☑ **C.** One to four. This is the range of memory slots in a typical motherboard.
    ☒ **A**, **B**, and **D** are all incorrect because they do not give the correct range of number of memory slots found on a typical motherboard.

9. ☑ **A.** A chipset component that controls communications between the CPU; the PCI, AGP, and PCIe busses; and RAM is the correct answer.
    ☒ **B** is incorrect because it describes the Southbridge (a chipset component that controls communications between the CPU and I/O busses). **C** is incorrect because it describes CMOS memory. **D**, the system setup program itself, is incorrect because this program is found in the system BIOS.

10. ☑ **B.** The BIOS configuration settings are stored on the battery-supported CMOS chip so that they are not lost when you turn the computer off—this is the correct answer.
    ☒ **A** is incorrect because it is the CMOS, not the BIOS, that stores computer configurations. **C**, that CMOS uses information stored in the BIOS to communicate with the computer's components, is incorrect because this is the opposite of the actual relationship between the BIOS and CMOS. **D** is incorrect. The CMOS and BIOS do not perform the same functions, and both are found in all PCs, old and new.

11. ☑ **C.** It provides LAN functionality and is Plug and Play.
    ☒ **A** is incorrect because it does both things. **B** is incorrect because both CNR and AMR provide audio functions. **D** is incorrect because CNR does not provide wireless functions.

12. ☑ **B.** PCI uses parallel data communications, PCIe uses serial communications is correct.
    ☒ **A** is incorrect because both are used by a variety of expansion cards. **C** is incorrect because the very opposite is true. PCIe uses serial data communications, and PCI uses parallel data communications. **D**, that PCIe is only used for graphics adapters but PCI is used by a variety of adapters, is incorrect because both are used by a variety of expansion cards.

13. ☑ **C.** AGP is correct because this video-only bus connector is being replaced by PCIe.
    ☒ **A** is incorrect because, although PCI is also being phased out and replaced by PCIe, is it not only for video adapters. **B**, NIC, is incorrect because this stands for a type of expansion card, a network interface card, not a bus connector. **D**, USB, is incorrect because this is a peripheral bus, not a bus connector on the motherboard in which an expansion card is installed.

Processor/CPU

14. ☑ **C.** A function of a CPU's cache is to anticipate the processor's data requests and make that data available for fast retrieval.
    ☒ **A**, to store instructions used by currently running applications, and **B**, to provide temporary storage of data that is required to complete a task, are incorrect because these are both functions of RAM memory. **D**, to store a device's most basic operating instructions, is incorrect because this is a function of a device's ROM memory.

15. ☑ **A.** The ALU is the CPU component that is responsible for all logical and mathematical operations.
    ☒ **B**, processor, is incorrect because this is just a synonym for CPU. **C**, control unit, is incorrect because this is the component responsible for directing activities in the computer and managing interactions between the other components and the CPU. **D**, bus, is incorrect because a bus is just a pathway between components in the CPU.

16. ☑ **C.** The control unit is correct because it contains microcode.
    ☒ **A**, ALU, is incorrect because it does not contain microcode but receives instructions from the control unit. **B**, processor, is incorrect because this is just another name for CPU. **D**, bus, is incorrect because this is just a group of wires used to carry signals.

17. ☑ **D.** SRAM is correct. Static RAM is fast and expensive. It is used as cache memory because relatively small amounts are required.
    ☒ **A**, DIMM, and **B**, RIMM, are both incorrect because they are each a type of slot and a type of packaging for sticks of DRAM. **C**, DRAM, is incorrect because it is dynamic RAM, which is much slower and cheaper than SRAM.

18. ☑ **C.** All Pentium-class processors have a 64-bit data bus. This means that 64 bits can enter or leave the processor at a time.
    ☒ **A**, 32-bit, is incorrect because while older processors have 32-bit data buses, all Pentiums have 64-bit data buses. Pentiums, however, do have a 32-bit register (internal bus). **B**, 36-bit, is incorrect. No Intel CPU has a 36-bit data bus, although some Pentium-class processors have a 36-bit memory address bus. **D** is incorrect. Although Pentium CPUs do differ in memory address bus width, they all have the same data bus width: 64 bits.

19.   ☑   **C.** Pentium. This CPU marked the beginning of the fifth generation of Intel CPU and spanned several more generations before the name "Pentium" was dropped from CPU model names.

☒   **A**, Athlon, and **B**, Opteron, are both incorrect because they are AMD CPUs.

D, Celeron, is incorrect because it is a consumer-level version CPU line and was not the first fifth-generation CPU.

20.   ☑   **A.** Hyperthreading is the CPU technology that allows two threads to execute at the same time within a single execution core.

☒   **B** is incorrect because throttling is the CPU technology that causes the CPU to lower its speed in order to reduce its temperature. **C**, overclocking, is incorrect because this is the practice of forcing a CPU or other computer component to run at a higher clock rate than the manufacturer intended. **D**, microcode, is incorrect because it is the name for the low-level instructions built into a CPU.

LAB ANSWER

At this writing, on their "Personal Computing" page, Intel features two dual-core CPU models: the Intel Core 2 Duo and the Centrino Duo mobile.

At this writing, AMD does not have a separate "personal computing" page, but they do list "Solutions" on their main page, which includes several categories with a CPU product family for each. The Business category solution is the AMD Opteron, while the Digital Media & Entertainment category lists the AMD Turion 64 as the solution. The Do-It-Yourself category offers the AMD Athlon as the CPU solution, while the Gaming category offers the AMD Sempron as the solution.

	Computer Model	CPU Model	Dual-Core?	Price
AMD-based desktop PC	HP Pavilion Media Center A1520N Desktop	AMD Athlon 64 X2 3800+	Yes	$699.98 after rebates (including display)
AMD-based notebook	Compaq Presario	AMD Turion 64 X2 TL-50	Yes	$759.99 after rebates
Intel-based desktop PC	HP Pavilion Media Center A1530N Desktop PC	Pentium D Processor 820	No	$599.99 after rebates (excluding display)
Intel-based notebook	Fujitsu Lifebook Notebook	Intel Core Duo Processor T2300E	Yes	$1099.99 after rebates

2

Personal Computer Components—Unit II

T

his chapter is a continuation of the survey of PC concepts and components begun in Chapter 1. Chapter 1 provides the purposes and technologies of PC cases, motherboards, and CPUs. You also learned about specific examples of each component. In this chapter you will continue along the same vein and explore PC power supplies, cooling systems, memory, storage devices, adapter cards, display devices, input devices, and ports and cables.

CERTIFICATION OBJECTIVE

■ *601: 1.1*   *Identify the fundamental principles of using personal computers*

Recall that this objective appears only in the 601 exam, but it provides the basis for the other A+ exams. These objectives are very important—the 601: 1.0 domain, Personal Computer Components, comprises 21 percent of the test questions in exam 601.

Power Supply

A *power supply* or *power supply unit (PSU)* is the component that provides power for all components on the motherboard and internal to the PC case. Every PC has an easily identified power supply; it is typically located at the back of the computer's interior, and it is visible from the outside when you look at the back of the PC. You will see the three-prong power connector, a label, and sometimes a tiny switch. Figure 2-1 shows the interior of a PC with a power supply on the top left. Notice the bundle of cables coming out of the power supply. These supply the power to the motherboard and all other internal components. The power supply has several very important functions.

Voltage

The power supply is responsible for converting the *alternating current (AC)* voltage from wall outlets into the *direct current (DC)* voltage that the computer requires. In an alternating current circuit, the flow of electrons changes direction, alternating polarity. In a direct current circuit, the flow of electrons is one way. The power supply accomplishes this task through a series of switching transistors, which gives rise to the term *switching mode power supply*.

The power supply, shown in the upper left, is usually located in the back of the computer case.

Another function of the power supply is to ensure that the computer receives the proper amount of voltage. Typical North American wall outlets provide about 110–120 VAC (volts AC), which is also expressed as ~115 VAC. However, computers require considerably smaller direct current (DC) voltages: ±12, ±5, or ±3.3 VDC (volts DC). Elsewhere in the world, standard power is 220–240 VAC. Power supplies manufactured for sale throughout the world will have a switch on the back of the power supply for selecting the correct input power setting. Figure 2-2 shows the back of a power supply with the switch for selecting 115 VAC or 240 VAC. It is the tiny red slide switch positioned below the power connector, officially called an IEC-320 connector.

e**x**a**m**

watch   *Make sure you are familiar with the voltages required by computer components: ±12, ±5, or ±3.3 VDC.*

FIGURE 2-2

The back of a power supply, with the IEC-320 power connector and the power selection switch

The wattage appears on the left side of this label, under the word "output."

Wattage

How big a power supply do you need? First, we are not talking about physical size, but the amount of wattage a power supply can handle. Wattage (W) is the amount of volts and amps required by a device. Figure 2-3 shows the label on a power supply. Notice that this is a 300-watt power supply. While just a few years ago power supplies ranging from 230 to 250 watts were considered more than adequate for PCs, today you will find many modestly priced PCs with 300-watt or greater power supplies. 500-watt power supplies are used in high-end computers.

If a device label does not state the number of watts required, simple math will give you the answer. All you need is the volts and amps, which you should find printed on the device somewhere. Once you have these two numbers, multiply them together and you will have the wattage of the device.

Checking Out the Wattage on PCs and Other Devices

1. Look at the back of a PC and find the label on the power supply, and record it.
2. Do the same on other devices that are available to you, such as the displays, printers, and scanners.
3. Similarly, check out the wattage on non-computer devices in the classroom or at home.

Fan

Yet another function of a power supply is to dissipate the heat it and other PC components generate. Heat buildup can cause computer components (including the power supply) to fail. Therefore, the power supply has a built-in fan that cools the components inside the case.

AC Adapters

Another form of power supply is an AC adapter used with portable computers and external peripherals. We describe AC adapters in Chapter 5. Flip forward to Chapter 5 now if you would like to know more about this type of power supply.

Form Factors

Like motherboards and cases, computer power supplies come in a variety of sizes and configurations. The most commonly used is referred to as the *ATX power supply,* used in most case sizes, except the smallest, which have low-profile power supplies for the low-profile cases, and the largest, which have jumbo-sized power supplies for the full-tower cases.

Power supplies have both dedicated cables for supplying power directly to the motherboard, and other cables for supplying power directly to internally installed peripherals—mainly various drives. The cables for peripherals have *Molex connectors* and *miniconnectors.* The Molex and miniconnectors each have four wires and provide 5 and 12 volts to peripherals. Molex connectors are the most commonly used, while floppy drives use the miniconnector. Figure 2-4 shows a power splitter cable with a single Molex connector on one end and miniconnectors on the other. The form factor of the power supply determines the motherboard it works with and the type of connector used for the motherboard.

FIGURE 2-4

A power splitter cable with a single Molex connector and two miniconnectors

AT

The AT power supply, like the AT motherboard, preceded the ATX form factor. The AT power supply differs from the newer standard by requiring two connectors for the motherboard. These connectors, P8 and P9, provide only ±12 V and ±5 V power to the motherboard, unlike newer power supplies, which also have ±3.3 V output. The fans in AT power supplies blow exhausted air out of the case, drawing it in through vents on the front of the case.

exam

ATX

The design of an ATX power supply lets it pair with an ATX motherboard. Its fan blows exhausted air out of the case to cool components. This form factor has a single 20-pin connector for the motherboard, called the P1 connector. Newer ATX power supplies that follow the *ATV12V* standard will also have an additional connector—with four wires, for 12 V. This is the *P4 12V* connector. You can also use ATX power supplies with BTX motherboards.

ATX power supplies and motherboards work together to provide a feature called *soft power*. Soft power allows software to turn off a computer rather than only using a physical switch. Most PCs have soft power. A computer with soft power enabled has a pair of small wires leading from the physical switch on the case to the motherboard. Usually, a system setting exists that controls just how this feature is used. For safety's sake, you should always consider soft power as being on, because when you have enabled software power, turning the power switch off means that, although the computer appears to be off, the power supply is still supplying ±5 volts to the motherboard. That means that you can never trust the on-off switch. Some PCs come equipped with two power switches. One is in the front, and you can consider it the "soft off" switch. The other is on the back of the case, in the power supply itself, and this is the "real off" switch.

on the

ⓙob   *A motherboard with soft power is never off, even when the switch on the front of the PC is in the "Off" position. There is always a ±5 V charge to the motherboard from the power supply. The only way to ensure that there is no power is to unplug the power supply from a power source. Always do this before opening a PC case.*

Proprietary Power Supplies

In response to the demands of PC-based servers and gamers, power supply manufacturers have added proprietary features beyond those in the standards. You can find power supplies that offer special support for the newest Intel and AMD CPU requirements, and greater efficiency, which saves on power usage and reduces heat output.

Cooling Systems

The more powerful PCs become, the more heat is generated within the case. Heat is your PC's enemy, and it should be yours, too. An overheated CPU will fail. Rather than allow heat to cause damage, Pentium 4 and newer CPUs use thermal throttling, as described under the section titled "Throttling" in Chapter 1. These CPUs and other components will slow down so that they produce less heat before any damage occurs. Manufacturers have struggled to keep ahead of the heat curve and provide sufficient cooling for the entire system. These methods involve fans, heat sinks, thermal compounds, and even liquid cooling systems.

CPU and Case Fans

Early PCs relied on the design of the PC case and the power supply fan to provide all the cooling for the interior. These PCs had vents in the front through which the power supply fan pulled air, and exhausted the air out the back. Today, we usually employ additional methods, but the power supply fan is still an important player in cooling the PC. It is very common to see a fan mounted directly over the CPU, as shown in Figure 2-1, in which the *CPU fan* is clearly visible in the center of the photo.

One or more case fans may also supplement a power supply fan. A *case fan* is a fan mounted directly on the case, as opposed to a power supply fan, which is inside the power supply. Refer back to Figure 2-1 and notice the black case fan on the left, just below the power supply. Systems that do not come with a case fan may have mounting brackets for adding one or more case fans.

Heat Sinks

Another device that works to cool hot components is a *heat sink*. This is usually a passive metal object with a flat surface attached to the component, a chip, for instance. The exposed side of a heat sink has an array of fins used to dissipate the heat.

Look for the heat sink that is partially visible at the bottom of Figure 2-1. A combined heat sink and fan may even attach directly to a chip.

Thermal Compounds

A special substance, called *thermal compound*, *thermal paste*, or *heat sink compound*, increases the heat conductivity between a fan or heat sink and a chip. The most common is a white, silicone-based paste, but there are also ceramic-based and metal-based thermal compounds that create a bond between the chip and the fan or heat sink, increasing the flow of heat from the chip.

Liquid Cooling Systems

If you have recently browsed through the motherboards for sale on the Internet or on display at a large electronics store, you have already seen at least one *liquid cooling system*. There are various types ranging from sealed liquid cooling systems that transfer heat from several components, to active systems that include actual refrigeration units.

Case Design

The design of each case allows for maximum airflow over the components. Part of this design is the placement of vents on the front or side of the case, positioned either to bring in fresh air or to exhaust air. If this airflow is disturbed, even with additional openings, the system may overheat. Therefore, be sure that all the expansion slot openings on the back of the PC are covered. The expansion card's bracket covers each one that lines up with an occupied expansion slot. A metal *slot cover* covers an empty slot in order to preserve the correct airflow.

Memory

Memory, a computer's temporary working space, is one of the most important, but perhaps most misunderstood, computer components. Computer novices often talk about memory when they mean hard drive storage space. Hard drive space is "permanent" storage in which the data consists of magnetized spots within the surface of the recording medium within the hard drive, and it remains there long after you turn the power off. The memory consists of computer chips in which the data resides, but only for as long at the computer remains powered up.

Furthermore, computers use several types of memory, each with a different function and different physical form. Typically, when people discuss memory, they are referring to *random access memory*, or *RAM*, so called because data stored in RAM is accessible in any (random) order. Most of the memory in a PC is RAM. However, some very important memory is read-only memory, or ROM. Chapter 1 describes the various types of RAM memory slots found on motherboards and also describes one important example of ROM found in all PCs—the BIOS. In this section, you will first explore the relationship between the CPU and the main RAM in a PC. Then you will learn about RAM technologies.

Functional Overview of RAM and ROM Usage

When a user makes a request, the CPU intercepts it and organizes the request into component-specific tasks. Many of these tasks must occur in a specific order, with each component reporting its results back to the processor before it can complete the next task. The processor uses RAM to store these results until they can be compiled into the final result(s).

RAM also stores instructions about currently running applications. For example, when you start a computer game, a large set of the game's instructions (including how it works, how the screen should look, and which sounds must be generated) is loaded into memory. The processor can retrieve these instructions much faster from RAM than it can from the hard drive, where the game normally resides until you start to use it. Within certain limits, the more information stored in memory, the faster the computer will run. In fact, one of the most common computer upgrades is to increase the amount of RAM. The computer continually reads, changes, and removes the information in RAM. It is also *volatile*, meaning that it cannot work without a steady supply of power, so when you turn your computer off, the information in RAM is lost.

Although *read-only memory*, or *ROM*, has an important function, it is rarely changed or upgraded, so it typically warrants less attention by most computer users. Unlike RAM, ROM is read-only, meaning the processor can read the instructions it contains, but one cannot use ROM to store new information. As described in Chapter 1, firmware is stored on ROM chips. ROM on peripheral devices maintains the device's basic operating instructions. A PC's system ROM stores the system's basic operating instructions, low-level device drivers, the power-on self-test program, and the system setup program.

RAM Technology

Not all RAM is the same. Over time, RAM technology has improved, changed form, and been used for specialized components. We discuss the most common types of RAM here.

SRAM

Static RAM (SRAM) (pronounced "ess-ram") was the first type of RAM available. SRAM can be accessed within approximately 10 nanoseconds (ns), meaning that it takes only about 10 ns for the processor to receive requested information from SRAM. While SRAM is very fast, compared with DRAM, it is also very expensive. For this reason, PC manufacturers typically use SRAM only for system cache. As you learned in Chapter 1, cache memory stores frequently accessed instructions or data for the CPU's use.

DRAM

Dynamic RAM (DRAM) (pronounced "dee-ram") chips, developed to combat the restrictive expense of SRAM, provide much slower access than SRAM chips but can store several megabytes of data on a single chip (or hundreds of megabytes, and even gigabytes, when they are packaged together on a "stick"). Every "cell" in a DRAM chip contains one transistor and one capacitor to store a single bit of information. This design makes it necessary for the DRAM chip to receive a constant power refresh from the computer to prevent the capacitors from losing their charge. This constant refresh makes DRAM slower than SRAM, and causes the DRAM chip to draw more power from the computer than an SRAM chip. Because of its low cost and high capacity, manufacturers use DRAM as "main" memory in the computer. The term DRAM typically describes any type of memory that uses the technology just described. However, the first DRAM chips were very slow (~80–90 ns), so faster variants have been developed. The list of DRAM technologies is quite large and continues to grow. We will limit the discussion to SDRAM, RDRAM, DDR, and DDR2.

SDRAM   *Synchronous dynamic RAM*, or SDRAM, runs at the speed of the system bus (up to 100–133 MHz). However, as faster system bus speeds developed, faster types of DRAM, such as RDRAM, DDR, and DDR2, replaced SDRAM. SDRAM is used only in systems that support it, and that have 168-pin DIMM sockets on the motherboard. The 168-pin SDRAM module has two notches.

RDRAM   The Pentium 4 has a much faster front side bus than previous processors, requiring faster RAM. One answer to this need is *RDRAM (Rambus Dynamic RAM)*, which gets its name from the company that developed it—Rambus, Inc. RDRAM uses a special Rambus channel that has a data transfer rate of 800 MHz, and one can double the channel width, resulting in a 1.6 GHz data transfer. You can only use RDRAM in computers with special RDRAM channels and slots, called RIMM slots, that will not accept other types of memory sticks. RDRAM RIMM sticks for desktops have 184, 232, or 326 pins. The difference is in the data bus width of the RAM stick. 16-bit RIMMs have 184 pins, 32-bit RIMMs have 232 pins, but 64-bit RIMM uses a 326-pin connector.

DDR   People often call *double-data rate (DDR) SDRAM* simply "DDR RAM." It doubles the rate of speed at which standard SDRAM can process data. That means DDR is roughly twice as fast as standard RAM.

The JEDEC Solid State Technology Association (once known as the Joint Electron Device Engineering Council [JEDEC]) defines the standards for DDR SDRAM. There are two sets of standards involved here—one for the module (the "stick") and another for the chips that populate the module. The module specifications include PC-1600, PC-2100, PC-2700, and PC-3200. This new labeling refers to the total bandwidth of the memory, as opposed to the old standard, which listed the speed rating (in MHz) of the SDRAM memory—in this case, PC66, PC100, and PC133. The numeric value in the PC66, PC100, and PC133 refers to the MHz speed at which the memory operates.

Table 2-1 shows the standards for the individual chips on a stick of DDR SDRAM. A PC-3200 DDR SDRAM module populated with DDR-400 chips can operate at 3.2 gigabytes per second. Each stick or module specification pairs the stick with chips of a certain chip specification. Table 2-2 shows the bandwidths achieved with standard stick/chip combinations.

A stick of DDR memory is a 184-pin DIMM module with a notch on one end so that it can only fit into the appropriate DIMM socket on a motherboard. It requires only 2.5 V compared to SDRAM's requirement of 3.3 V.

TABLE 2-1	Chip Specification	Effective Clock Speed
JEDEC Speed Standards for DDR-SDRAM Chips	DDR-200	100 MHz
	DDR-266	133 MHz
	DDR-333	166 MHz
	DDR-400	200 MHz

TABLE 2-2	DDR Module Specification	DDR Chip Specification	Bandwidth
Maximum Bandwidth of Combined DDR Modules and Chips	PC-1600	DDR-200 (100 MHz)	1.6 GB/second
	PC-2100	DDR-266 (133 MHz)	2.133 GB/second
	PC-2700	DDR-333 (166 MHz)	2.667 GB/second
	PC-3200	DDR-400 (200 MHz)	3.2 GB/second

DDR2   *Double-data-rate two (DDR2) SDRAM* is replacing the original DDR standards, now referred to as *DDR1*. DDR2 can handle faster clock rates than DDR1, beginning at 400 MHz.

As with DDR1, there are specifications for the chips, as well as the modules. Table 2-3 shows the standards for the individual chips on a stick of DDR2 SDRAM, while Table 2-4 shows the bandwidths achieved with standard DDR2 stick/chip combinations.

DDR2 sticks are only compatible with motherboards that use a special 240-pin DIMM socket. The DDR2 DIMM stick notches are different from those in a DDR1 DIMM. A DDR2 DIMM only requires 1.8 V compared to 2.5 V for DDR1. Manufacturers of motherboards and processors were slow to switch to support for DDR2, mainly due to problems with excessive heat. Once manufacturers solved the problems, they brought out compatible motherboards, chipsets, and CPUs for DDR2.

TABLE 2-3	Chip Specification	Chip Operating Speed	I/O Clock Speed
JEDEC Speed Standards for DDR2-SDRAM Chips	DDR2-400	100 MHz	200 MHz
	DDR2-533	133 MHz	266 MHz
	DDR2-667	166 MHz	333 MHz
	DDR2-800	200 MHz	400 MHz

TABLE 2-4	DDR2 Module Specification	DDR2 Chip Specification	Bandwidth
Maximum Bandwidth of Combined DDR Modules and Chips	PC2-1600	DDR2-400 (200 MHz)	3.2 GB/second
	PC2-2100	DDR2-533 (266 MHz)	4.267 GB/second
	PC2-2700	DDR2-667 (333 MHz)	5.333 GB/second
	PC2-3200	DDR2-800 (400 MHz)	6.4 GB/second

SCENARIO & SOLUTION

Which type of memory is responsible for...?	Solution
Storing low-level drivers and programs, as well as the system setup program?	system ROM
Providing temporary storage for application files?	RAM
Storing frequently accessed instructions or data for the CPU's use?	cache

VRAM

Video RAM (VRAM) is a specialized type of memory used only with video adapters. The video adapter is one of the computer's busiest components, so, to keep up with video requirements, many adapters have an on-board microprocessor and special video RAM. The adapter can process requests independently of the CPU and then store its results in the VRAM until the CPU retrieves it. VRAM is fast, and the computer can simultaneously read from it and write to it. The result is better and faster video performance. Because VRAM includes more circuitry than regular DRAM, VRAM modules are slightly larger. The term video RAM refers to both a specific type of memory and a generic term for all RAM used by the video adapter (much like the term *DRAM*, which is often used to denote all types of memory that are dynamic). Faster versions of video memory have been recently introduced, including *WRAM*, which includes a technique for using video RAM to perform Windows-specific functions to speed up the OS.

Operational Characteristics

Among the operational characteristics of DRAM modules, regardless of the type, are memory banks, error-checking methods, and single-sided versus double-sided.

Memory Banks

The *bit width* of a memory module is very important; the term refers to how much information the processor can access from or write to memory in a single cycle. A *memory bank* represents the number of memory modules required to match the data bus width of the processor. For example, consider a computer with a Pentium 4 processor with a 64-bit data bus. You want to install 4 GB of RAM. You could add two 2 GB memory modules or four 1 GB memory modules. Each memory module would take a single memory bank.

exam
ⓦatch

A memory bank refers to a match between the processor's data bus width and RAM's bit width. If you are using a CPU with a 64-bit data bus, one 64-bit DIMM or one 64-bit RIMM makes a full bank. If you are working with an older motherboard with RIMM sockets, four 16-bit RIMMs or two 32-bit RIMMs make a full bank. The term memory bank does not refer to the slots used to attach the RAM modules to the motherboard.

When dealing with processors from the Pentium family, it is not difficult to determine how much memory you need to create a full bank, since they each have a 64-bit data bus. However, you might have to work with older processors and older types of RAM. Use the formula in Exercise 2-2 to calculate the number of memory modules you need to install in your computer.

EXERCISE 2-2

Calculating the Memory Bank Size

1. Determine the data bus width of the processor in your computer (64 bits for the Pentium family, higher for some newer processors).

2. Determine the bit width of the memory module. DIMMs are 64-bit, and older RIMMs are 16-bit and 32-bit, while the newest RIMMS are 64-bit.

3. Divide the processor's data bus width (Step 1) by the memory's bit width (Step 2). The number you get is the number of memory modules you must install to create one full bank.

Memory Error Checking

Earlier you learned that RAM memory is volatile, which should bring you to realize that memory could be error-prone. The fact is that modern memory modules are very reliable, but there are methods and technologies that one can build into RAM modules to check for errors. We'll look at two of these methods: parity and error-correcting code (ECC).

Parity   In one type of memory error checking, called *parity*, every eight-bit byte of data is accompanied by a ninth bit (the parity bit), which is used to determine the presence of errors in the data. There are two types of parity: odd and even.

In *odd parity*, the parity bit is used to ensure that the total number of 1s in the data stream is odd. For example, suppose a byte consists of the following data: 11010010. The number of 1s in this data is 4, an even number. The ninth bit will then be a 1, to ensure that the total number of 1s is odd: 110100101.

Even parity is the opposite of odd parity; it ensures that the total number of 1s is even. For example, suppose a byte consists of the following data: 11001011. The ninth bit would then be a 1 to ensure that the total number of 1s is 6, an even number.

Parity is not failure-proof. Suppose the preceding data stream contained two errors: 101100101. If the computer was using odd parity, the error would slip through (try it; count the 1s). However, creating parity is quick and does not inhibit memory access time the way a more sophisticated error-checking routine would.

DIMM is 64 bits wide, but parity-checking DIMM has 8 extra bits (1 parity bit for every 8 data bits). Therefore, a DIMM with parity is 64 + 8 = 72 bits wide. While parity is not often used in memory modules, there is an easy way to determine if a memory module is using parity because it will have an odd number of chips. A non-parity memory module will have an even number of chips. This is true, even if the module only has two or three chips in total.

If your system supports parity, you must use parity memory modules. You cannot use memory with parity if your system does not support it. The motherboard manual will define the memory requirements.

exam

ⓦatch   *Memory parity versus non-parity is an exam objective for the A+ Essentials 2006 exam, so be sure that you understand the concepts involved.*

on the ⓙob   *Be aware that the majority of today's computer systems do not support memory that uses parity. However, other computing devices use parity. One example of parity use is in some special drive arrays, called RAID 5, mostly found in servers. Therefore, it is useful to understand the basics of parity.*

ECC   *Error-correcting code (ECC)* is a more sophisticated method of error checking than parity, although it also adds an extra bit per byte to a stick of RAM. Software in the system memory controller uses the extra bits to both detect and correct errors. There are several algorithms used in ECC.

Single-Sided vs. Double-Sided

The DIMM and RIMM modules discussed in this chapter come in both single-sided and double-sided versions. Single-sided modules have chips mounted on just one side, while double-sided modules have chips mounted on both sides. Most memory sticks are single-sided because there are incompatibility problems with the double-sided modules and motherboards.

Storage Devices

The function of all storage devices is to hold, or store, information, even when the computer's power is off. Unlike information in RAM, files kept on a storage device remain there unless the user or the computer's operating system removes or alters them. Many types of storage devices are available, including floppy drives, hard drives, optical (CD and DVD) drives, tape drives, USB and IEEE 1394 external hard drives, and solid-state devices. Note that this list includes both removable and fixed (non-removable) devices.

Floppy Disk Drives

A 3.5-inch *floppy disk drive*, also referred to as a *FDD*, reads data from a removable floppy disk and provides a good method for transferring data from one machine to another. A *floppy disk* contains a thin internal plastic disk, capable of holding magnetic charges. A hard plastic protective casing, part of which retracts to reveal the storage medium inside, surrounds the disk. A thin layer of magnetic material coats the disk. The back of the disk has a coin-sized metal circle used by the drive to grasp the disk and spin it. Inserting a floppy disk into a computer's drive causes the drive to spin the internal disk and retract the protective cover. An articulated arm moves the drive's two *read/write heads* back and forth along the exposed area, reading data from and writing data to the disk. Each head reads and writes to one side of the disk.

Floppy drives are fast disappearing from PCs. Most new consumer models do not have built-in floppy drives. If you need one, consider buying an inexpensive external USB floppy drive, like that pictured in Figure 2-5.

3.5-inch floppy disks can hold 1.44 MB (high density) or 2.88 MB (extra high density) of information. The most commonly used such disk is the 1.44 MB capacity disks. Floppy drives are limited in the types of disks they can access. A 1.44 MB drive can access either a 1.44 MB or the old format called double density, which had a capacity of only 720 KB per disk. A 2.88 MB floppy drive can read all three 3.5-inch disk densities.

FIGURE 2-5

An external
floppy disk drive
with its USB
interface

Hard Disk Drives

A *hard disk drive*, also referred to in documentation as *HDD*, stores data in a similar
fashion to a floppy drive, but it typically is not removable and has a different physical
structure (see Figure 2-6). A hard drive consists of one or more hard platters, stacked
on top of but not touching one another. The stack of platters attaches through its
center to a rotating pole, called a *spindle*. Each side of each platter can hold data and
has its own read/write head. The read/write heads all move as a single unit back and
forth across the stack.

FIGURE 2-6

The internal
structure of
a hard disk

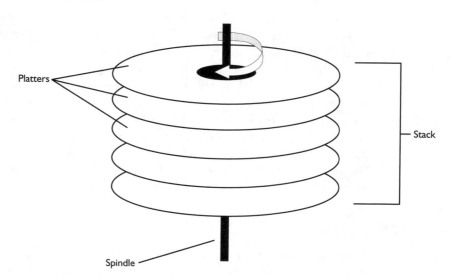

An internal hard
drive system

Hard drives are available in a wide range of capacities and can hold much more data than a floppy disk. Most new hard drives now have a capacity between 40 GB and several hundred gigabytes.

A hard disk drive usually resides inside the computer case in a drive bay that does not have any external access. Figure 2-7 shows a hard disk system designed for internal installation.

All other things being equal, an internal hard drive system is much less expensive than an external hard drive system. The need to provide both an individual case and a power supply for an external hard drive accounts for the cost difference. An exception to the latter is a USB hard drive, which gets its power from the PC through the USB connection. Figure 2-8 shows two external hard drives. The large one has a capacity of 300 GB and connects to a PC using either USB or IEEE 1394. The smaller drive has a capacity of 8 GB and uses a USB connection, but it only measures 2" by 2.5"!

Optical Disk Drives

Optical disk drives have come a long way since the 1980s. There are now two general categories of optical drives and the media (disk) they use—CD and DVD. In addition, some drives can only read one or both of these disk types, and other drives

FIGURE 2-8

Two external
hard drives

can both read and write to one or both of these disk types. Are you confused yet? When it comes to understanding these drives, it is best to start with the discs they use, and then look at the drives.

A typical optical disk of any type is, well, disk-shaped and made of polycarbonate. The standard disk is approximately 4.75 inches (12 cm), but there are minidiscs that measure about 3.125 inches (8 cm). The surface is smooth and shiny with one labeled side and one plain side (there are exceptions to this single-sided form). The data, music, or video is stored on the disk using very small depressed and raised areas, called *pits* and *lands*, respectively. A protective transparent layer covers them. A laser beam reads the data from the disk. Optical storage offers an interim step between the portability of a floppy disk and the capacity of a hard drive. You can access data much faster from an optical disk than you can from a floppy disk, but more slowly than from a hard drive. Optical disk capacity is hundreds of times greater than a diskette, but generally much smaller than commonly available hard disks.

Now that you know what they have in common, we will drop the term "optical disk" and talk about these disks in the terms you normally use, which is CD or DVD.

CD-ROM, CD-R, CD-RW

The CDs (compact disks) sold at retail containing music (audio CDs) or software (data CDs) are CD-ROM (*Compact Disk–Read-Only Memory*) disks, meaning that they are only readable; you cannot change the contents. There are other CD media and drive types, a few differences in capacities, and as the technology has matured, the drives have become faster.

CD Drives and Media CD music players can usually only play music disks. A CD drive in a computer that can play music CDs and read data CDs, but cannot write to a CD, is a CD-ROM *drive*. The next level up includes CD drives that can write to, as well as read from, CDs. A CD-R *(CD-record)* drive can write once to each specially designed CD-R disk. There are two types of CD-R disks. One type holds 650 MB of data or 74 minutes of audio, while the other holds 700 MB of data and 80 minutes of audio. The oldest CD-R drives only supported the first format, while the next generation CD-R drives support both formats.

A newer technology made CD-R drives obsolete—CD-RW *(CD-rewritable)* drives, which can write either to CD-R disks (once only) or to specially designed CD-RW disks. What distinguishes CD-RW drives from CD-R drives is that these newer drives can write more than once to the same portion of disk, overwriting old data. This is not possible with CD-R drives.

CD-ROM, CD-R, and CD-RW drives can play or read from all three types of disks, although there can be problems with the very old CD-ROM drives reading some newer CD disks.

CD Drive Speeds The first CD drives transferred data at 150 KBps, a speed now called "1x." CD drives are now rated at speeds that are multiples of this speed and have progressed through 72x, which is 10,800 KBps. The appropriate name, such as CD-ROM, CD-R, and CD-RW, will describe a CD drive, and it may be followed by the speed rating, which may be a single number, in the case of a CD-ROM, or, in the case of a CD-RW will be three numbers such as 52x24x16x. In this case, the drive is rated at 52x for rads, 24x for writes, and 16x for rewrites.

DVD-ROM, DVD-R, and DVD-RW

Video storage uses digital versatile disks (DVDs) extensively, and they have grown in use for data storage.

DVD Drives and Media   DVD disks are the same physical size as CD disks but have a higher storage capacity. There are several other differences. While CDs only store data on a single side, DVDs come in both a conventional *single-sided (SS) DVD* and a *dual-sided (DS) DVD* variant that stores data on both sides requiring that it be turned over to read the second side.

In addition, the format on each side may *be single-layer (SL)* or *dual-layer (DL)*. While the SL format is like that of CDs in that there is only a single layer of pits, DL format uses two pitted layers on each data side; each layer having a different reflectivity index. The DVD package label shows the various combined features as *DVD-5, DVD-9, DVD-10,* and *DVD-18.* Therefore, when purchasing DVD disks, the labeling is very important to understand the capacity of the disks. Table 2-5 shows DVD capacities based on the number of data sides and the number of layers per side.

Regardless of the actual format, we use the term "DVD." However, the original DVD encoding format for video, used for movies, is *DVD-Video.* DVD music disks sold at retail are *DVD-Audio* disks. An encoding format designed for data is *DVD-RAM.* Most disks that are not, strictly speaking, DVD-Video or DVD-Audio are all lumped together as DVD-Data disks, even if they contain video.

When it comes to selecting DVD disks based on the ability to write to them, you have a selection equivalent to CD disks. The DVD disks sold at retail containing video or software are *DVD-ROM* disks, meaning that they are only readable; you cannot change the contents. DVD-ROM has a maximum capacity of 15.9 GB of data. Similarly, some DVD drives in PCs can only read DVDs.

There are six standards of recordable DVD media. The use of the "dash" (-) or "plus" (+) has special significance. The dash, used in the first DVD recordable format and seen as *DVD-R* and *DVD-RW,* indicates an older standard than those with the plus. DVD-R and DVD-RW are generally compatible with older players. DVD-R and DVD+R media are writable much like CD-Rs. DVD-RAM, DVD-RW, and DVD+RW are writable and rewritable much like CD-RW. When shopping for a DVD drive or a PC that includes a DVD drive, you will see the previously described types combined as DVD+R/RW, DVD-R/RW, and simply DVD-RAM. Drives will also be labeled with the combined + and -, showing that all types of DVD disks can be used: DVD±R/RW.

TABLE 2-5	DVD Type	Capacity
DVD Capacities	DVD-5 (12cm, SS/SL)	4.37 GB data, or over two hours of video
	DVD-9 (12cm, SS/DL)	7.95 GB data, or over four hours of video
	DVD-10 (12cm, DS/SL)	8.74 GB data, or over four and a half hours of video
	DVD-18 (12cm, DS/DL)	15.90 GB data, or over eight hours of video

DVD Drive Speeds DVD drive speeds are expressed in terms similar to those of CD drives, although the spin speed of a 1x DVD drive is three times that of a CD 1x. In fact, a 1x DVD drive transfers data at 1352.54 KB/second, which is faster than a 9x CD drive. When looking at advertisements for DVD drives or PCs that include DVD drives, you will see the combined drive types, as listed in the preceding section, followed by a combination of drive speeds, depending on the drive's operating modes. For instance: "DVD+R/RW 40x24x40x" indicates the three speeds of this drive for reading, writing, and rewriting because each drive has a different potential speed for each type of operation.

However, you need to read the manufacturer's documentation to know the order. As a general rule on DVD drives, reads are fastest, writes may be as fast, or a bit slower than reads, and rewrites are the slowest operation. Table 2-6 shows the read/write transfer rates of a selection of DVD drive speeds along with the equivalent CD drive speeds. Notice that DVD drives leave CD drives behind at the DVD 8x speed.

on the job

Because CDs and DVDs have no protective covering, it's important to handle them with care. Scratches, dust, or other material on the CD surface can prevent data from reading correctly. Because data is located on the bottom side of the CD, always lay the CD label-side down.

High-Definition DVDs At this writing, there are two new competing formatting standards for high-definition video on DVD. They include the *HD-DVD* standard, supported by Toshiba, and the *Blu-ray* standard, supported by Sony Corporation. Like the Betamax versus VHS standards competition of several decades ago, those manufacturers and consumers who bought Betamax were out in the cold when VHS became the winning video tape standard.

TABLE 2-6	Drive Speed	Data Transfer Rate, MB/second	Equivalent CD Transfer Rate
DVD Drive Speeds and Data Transfer Rates Compared to CD Drive Speeds	1x	1.32	9x
	6x	7.98	54x
	8x	10.57	N/A
	10x	13.21	N/A
	12x	15.85	N/A
	16x	21.13	N/A
	18x	42.26	N/A

The first DVD machines that can read one or the other high-definition format are very, very expensive, and probably only one will win out. After that, mass production of high-definition DVDs will use only the winning standard. People won't buy a $1000 machine they cannot use to view new movies!

Which standard will win? You may know the answer to that by the time you read this book. Once there is a winning standard, the number of high-definition DVD readers for the audio/visual market will increase and come down in price, and you will see reasonably priced high-definition DVD drives for PCs.

Currently HD-DVD disks have a capacity of 30 GB, and Blu-ray disks hold either 25 GB or 50 GB. Movie titles available in Blu-ray format were on the 25 GB disks until November 2007, when the first title appeared on 50 GB disks. Development of Blu-ray continues, with capacities of 100 GB and 200 GB announced to date.

The high-definition competition may have a different outcome than that between the old Betamax and VHS standards. As of this writing, it appears consumers will be able to buy one DVD for their favorite movie, but on this one DVD the movie will be available in three DVD formats: each of the two high-definition standards as well as the old DVD video format. Stay tuned!

Tape Drives

A *tape drive* is a data storage device used for backing up data from computers. It uses special removable magnetic data tapes. People often choose tape drives for data backup because the media is relatively inexpensive and long lasting for archiving data. Because data must be stored sequentially on tape, it has a very slow seek time for accessing individual files. However, newer tape drives can write data to tape at transfer rates that compare well to hard drive speeds.

While tape drives are available in the consumer market, they most often back up large server systems, in which case specialized equipment can be used to combine tape drives with auto-loaders that automatically select tapes for use and store filled tapes in tape libraries. High-end tapes can store hundreds of gigabytes per tape.

Solid-State Storage

Up to now, the storage devices we have looked at use magnetic or optical technologies and media. A growing category of storage devices uses integrated circuits, rather than one of these other technologies. Generically called *solid-state storage*, these devices have no moving parts and use large-capacity, *non-volatile memory*. Non-volatile means that it does not require power to keep the stored data intact. Although these devices do not yet compare to hard drives in their storage capacity, there are many uses for these very lightweight devices, even with maximum capacity in the low gigabyte range. There are many names for these devices, some generic, and some trademarked. The text that follows describes some common uses for solid-state storage.

On rare occasion, non-technical PC users embrace a new computer device as quickly as the cognoscenti do. One such device is the small storage device we know by various names, such as *thumb drive*, *flash drive*, or *jump drive*. A thumb drive is very lightweight and small—it really is about the size of a thumb—and it is not a "drive" in that it does not contain a moving disk. In fact, there are no moving parts. These devices most often have a USB interface (explained later in this chapter) and can theoretically hold up to 64 GB of data. When plugged into your computer, it appears as an ordinary drive with a driver letter assigned to it (see Figure 2-9).

The term *flash memory* often describes other removable solid-state storage devices, commonly used in personal data assistants (PDAs) to store data and in digital cameras to store photos. A prolific photographer will carry several of these devices, swapping out full cards with empty ones. While many cameras come with software and cables for transferring the photos from the camera's memory card to a computer and/or printer, another method does not require either cable or software. In this method, you remove the card from the camera and insert it into a special slot on the PC or printer. There are several flash memory card form factors using various solid-state technologies, and with trademarked names. These include CompactFlash, SmartMedia, MMC, and Memory Stick. Figure 2-10 shows a CompactFlash card.

FIGURE 2-9

A USB flash drive

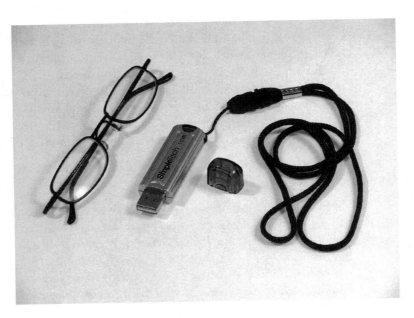

Yet another solid-state storage standard is the *SD (Secure Digital) Card*. Its features go beyond the security against illegal copying, implied in its name. SD Cards are high capacity (2, 4, and 8 GB) yet tiny, at 32 mm × 24 mm × 2.1 mm, and they support high-speed data transfer. SD cards are in portable devices, such as digital video recorders, digital cameras, handheld computers, audio players, and cell phones.

Figure 2-11 shows the front panel of a PC with a variety of flash memory slots. If these aren't built into your PC, and you require some or all of them, you can buy bus cards or external devices to add these interfaces to your PC.

Adapter Cards

An *adapter card* or *expansion board* is a printed circuit board installed into a PC's expansion bus to add functionality. Although also simply called an "adapter," this usage is confusing, because it also applies to a plug-like device that contains a simple circuit for changing one set of signals to another, like a serial-to-USB adapter. An adapter card is actually a controller containing sophisticated circuitry of an entire device. Examples of common adapter cards include those for controlling video, multimedia, I/O interfaces, networking, and modem communications. As you read about these types of devices, keep in mind that PC motherboards contain more and more of these functions and they no longer need an adapter card added to the expansion bus. The functions, however, remain as described in the following sections devoted to each of the most common adapter cards.

Video Adapter Cards

A *video adapter* card controls the output to the display device. This function may be built into the motherboard of a PC, or it may be provided through an adapter card installed into the PCI expansion bus, an AGP connector, or a PCIe connector. Learn more about video adapters later in this chapter.

Multimedia Adapter Cards

In the early 1990s, the term "multimedia PC" was used to describe a PC with a stereo sound card and a CD-ROM drive. Today this is less than the minimum configuration for the most basic consumer PC from a major manufacturer. Today's multimedia PC brings not just music and photos to the user, but support for sophisticated games and integration with home electronics. A savvy user may effortlessly connect a PC to digital cameras (still and video), television, PDAs, and much more. Special versions of Windows—Microsoft Windows XP Media Center and Microsoft Windows Vista Home Premium, which includes Windows Media Center—are aimed at this more advanced multimedia PC and the consumers who desire these features.

PC manufacturers have created multimedia PCs to meet this need. They often have the words "Media Center" in their product name or description. Multimedia capabilities in PCs can now include enhancements to allow users to store and edit media data such as photos, music, and videos, and to watch and record TV thanks to a tuner integrated into the PC.

The PC now includes these multimedia capabilities through specialized components, either installed on separate adapter cards or integrated into the motherboard with appropriate connectors on the front or back of the case.

I/O Adapter Cards

An important characteristic of any peripheral is how it communicates. PCs have evolved, and, with the invention of more and more input/output devices, manufacturers have continued to integrate these new capabilities into the motherboard. There was a time when mouse, serial, and parallel I/O cards had to be added to the expansion bus because these basic I/O standards were not integrated. Today, serial and parallel interfaces (described later in this chapter, under "Ports and Connectors") are built into the motherboard, but due to decreased use of these interfaces, they are often disabled and do not have external connectors. They will eventually disappear from ordinary PCs. While your PC has various I/O technologies built in, you may still wish to add an adapter card to give you additional ports. We'll describe these I/O technologies, including serial, parallel, USB, IEEE 1394, and SCSI, in this chapter.

Communications Adapters

We have used the term "communication" many times in this and the preceding chapter, mostly in talking about communication between components within the PC. Now we will talk about the communication devices that connect a PC to a network, whether it is a local area network (LAN) or the Internet. Once again, the motherboards of most PCs now have these functions built in, and it is not usually necessary to add an adapter card to a computer for communications.

Network Communications

There are few PC users who do not require network communications. On the job, a typical desktop PC is connected to a LAN, which in turn may be connected to a larger private network and, ultimately, to the Internet. At home you may connect two or more PCs, via a LAN connection, to share a DSL or cable modem Internet connection. The network adapter in the PC may be an Ethernet wired network adapter or a wireless adapter, depending on whether you wish to connect to a wired Ethernet LAN or a wireless LAN.

Most desktop PCs come standard with an Ethernet network adapter installed, either on the motherboard, or as an expansion adapter. Laptop computers now usually come with both an Ethernet adapter and a wireless adapter. If you need wireless to your desktop PC, you will need to add it as an internal bus adapter card or as an external USB network adapter. We will save the larger discussion of networking for Chapters 12,13 and 14.

Modem Communication Adapters

A modem, so named for its combined functions of **mod**ulator/**dem**odulator, allows computers to communicate with one another over existing phone lines. An internal modem may be built into the motherboard, or it may be an adapter card in the expansion bus. An external modem connects to a port on the computer, either serial or USB. Whether internal or external, a modem connects to a regular telephone wall jack using the same connector as a phone.

This type of modem is an analog modem, as opposed to the data communication devices used to connect to a cable network or to phone lines for DSL service. "Modem" is actually a misnomer for the devices used on cable or DSL networks because the signals involved are all digital, and therefore there is no need to modulate or demodulate the signal. However, because they are physically placed between the computer and the network, much as a modem is, manufacturers use the term modem.

Video Adapters and Displays

The quality of the image you see on a PC display depends on both the capabilities and configuration of the two most important video components: the display and the video adapter.

Video Adapters

The *video adapter* controls the output from the PC to the display device. While the video adapter contains all the logic, and does most of the work, the quality of the resulting image depends on the modes supported by both the adapter and the display. If the adapter is capable of higher-quality output than the display, the display limits the result. In this section, we will first explore video modes and the bus interfaces used by video adapters, and introduce display types later in this chapter.

Video Modes

Very basic video modes are text and graphics. As a PC boots up, and before the operating system takes control, the video is in text mode and can only display the limited ASCII character set. Once the operating system is in control, drivers for the video adapter and display load and a graphics mode that can display bitmapped graphics is used. Today there are video modes that support millions of colors. There have been several video modes since the introduction of the first IBM PC in 1981. However, we will limit the discussion to the video graphics modes you can expect to encounter in business and homes today.

VGA *Video graphics array (VGA)* is a video adapter standard introduced with the IBM PS/2 computers in the late 1980s. VGA uses analog signals to the display, rather than the digital signals used by the two preceding video standards, CGA and EGA. The analog signal is capable of producing a far wider range of colors than the previous digital signals.

VGA is old technology today, because we have gone far beyond this in capabilities, but some software packages still list it as a minimum requirement for installing the software. VGA has a maximum resolution (number of pixels) of 720 × 400 in text mode and 640 × 480 in graphics mode. The first number is the number of columns, while the second number is the number of rows. VGA can produce around 16 million different colors but can display only up to 256 different colors at a time. Another term for this color setting is "8-bit high color." VGA *Mode* most often consists of a combination of 640 × 480 pixels display resolution and 16 colors.

Beyond VGA   In the past two decades, video standards have advanced nearly as fast as CPU standards. *Super video graphics array (SVGA)* is a term first used for any video adapter or monitor that exceeded the VGA standard in resolution and color depth. But improvements to SVGA's early 800 × 600–pixel resolution now come in various resolutions, including 1024 × 768, 1280 × 1024, and 1600 × 1200. While SVGA also supports a palette of 16 million colors, the amount of video memory present limits the number simultaneously displayed. This is also true of the newer video standards.

And so it goes; as fast as new standards are developed and adopted by manufacturers, they are modified and improved upon. Table 2-7 gives a summary of screen resolution and color density typical of the listed video standards. Keep in mind that the best resolution and color density you will see on your display depends on the capabilities of

TABLE 2-7	A Selection of Video Standards and the Resolution, Color Palette, and Color Density of Each		
Name	**Maximum Graphics Resolution**	**# of Colors in Palette**	**# of Colors Displayed Simultaneously in Standard Color Density**
VGA (Video graphics array)	640 × 480	Over 16 million	16
XGA (eXtended graphics array)	640 × 480 or 1024 × 768	Over 16 million	65,536 or 256
SVGA (Super video graphics array)	800 × 600 or 1600 × 1200	Over 16 million	Over 16 million*
SXGA (Super XGA)	1280 × 1024	Over 16 million	Over 16 million*
SXGA+ (Super XGA Plus)	1400 × 1050	Over 16 million	Over 16 million*
UXGA (Ultra XGA)	1600 × 1200	Over 16 million	Over 16 million*
WUXGA (Wide UXGA)	1920 × 1200 (wide screen)	Over 16 million	Over 16 million*

*Actual number of simultaneous colors depends on the video adapter and the amount of video memory installed.

both the video adapter and display. We will discuss aspect ratio, refresh rates, and other display features later in this chapter under the "Displays" topic.

Interfaces

When purchasing a video adapter, it is important to pay attention to the interface between the video adapter and the computer so that you select one you can install into your PC. If the motherboard contains a video adapter, it still accesses one of the standard busses in the computer. Our experience is that many brand-name PCs have a separate video card. In which case, the video adapter installs into one of three types of bus connectors: PCI, PCIe, or AGP. We discuss these bus types in Chapter 1. You will find the current version of the video standards mentioned here available with any of these interfaces.

Displays

The function of a PC video *display* device is to produce visual responses to user requests. Often called simply a display or *monitor*, it receives computer output from the video adapter, which controls its functioning. The display technology must match the technology of the video card to which it attaches. You have learned about video display technologies, so now we will explore the two main types of displays, the connectors used to connect a display to the video adapter, and display settings. Until just a few years ago, most desktop computers used cathode ray tube (CRT) monitors. Today, flat panel displays (FPDs) outsell CRTs. This is true both for computer displays and for televisions.

CRT

A cathode ray tube (CRT) monitor is bulky because of the large cathode ray tube it contains. A CRT uses an electron gun to activate phosphors behind the screen. Each dot on the monitor, called a pixel, has the ability to generate red, green, or blue, depending on the signals it receives. This combination of colors results in the total display you see on the monitor. CRT monitors are available in a wide array of color depths and resolutions.

Flat Panel Displays

A *flat panel display (FPD)* is a computer display that uses liquid crystal or plasma technology and does not require the bulk of a large picture tube. The screen enclosure can be as thin as one to two inches. Because plasma technology is generally much more expensive than liquid crystal technology, which greatly outsells plasma, we will not discuss it in this book.

LCD Technologies   Early liquid crystal displays (LCDs) did not have picture quality equal to CRTs, but they have improved so much that they now compete with and outsell CRTs. They require much less power than CRTs. The first LCD panels, called *passive matrix displays*, consist of a grid of horizontal and vertical wires. At one end of each wire is a transistor, which receives display signals from the computer. When two transistors (one at the x-axis and one at the y-axis) send voltage along their wires, the pixel at the intersection of the two wires lights up.

Active matrix displays are newer and use different technology, called *thin-film transistor (TFT)* technology. Active matrix displays contain transistors at each pixel, resulting in more colors, better resolution, a better ability to display moving objects, and the ability to view it at greater angles. However, active matrix displays use more power than passive matrix displays.

LCD Display Resolution   An LCD panel has hardwired pixels, with a set of RGB (red/blue/green) dots for each pixel. Therefore, each LCD display has a native resolution beyond which it cannot operate. In addition, if you set an LCD at a lower resolution, the image degrades. For this reason, always set an LCD display at its native resolution, as stated on the box and in the display documentation.

LCD Contrast Ratio   *Contrast ratio*, the difference in value between a display's brightest white and darkest black, is an area in which the early LCD displays could not compete with CRTs. However, today, even moderately priced LCD displays offer a contrast ratio of 500:1 or greater, which is excellent.

Display Aspect Ratio

The *aspect ratio* of a display is the proportion of the width to the height. For instance, a traditional CRT monitor has a width to height aspect ratio of 4:3. LCD panels come in the traditional 4:3 aspect ratio as well as in wider formats, of which the most common is 16:9, which allows viewing of wide format movies. When viewing a widescreen movie video on a 4:3 display, it shows in a *letterbox*, meaning that the image size reduces until the entire width of the image fits on the screen. The remaining portions of the screen are black, creating a box effect. Figure 2-12 shows an LCD display with a 16:9 aspect ratio.

FIGURE 2-12

An LCD display with a 16:9 aspect ratio

Display Connectors

For nearly two decades technicians only needed to work with one video display connector—the DB-15. Now there are other options to go with newer technologies. Learn about common display connectors. Figure 2-13 shows the back of a video adapter with three connectors: (from left to right) DVI, S-Video, and DB-15.

DB-15

The DB-15 connector used on video adapters for connecting to traditional CRT monitors and some LCD displays has three rows of five pins. The connector on the monitor cable is male, while the connector on the video adapter (the computer end) is female. A male port or connector has pins, and a female port or connector is a receiver with sockets for the pins of the male connector. This connector transmits analog signals from the video adapter to a CRT, which is an analog device.

DVI

LCD displays use a digital signal. While video adapters actually store information digitally in video RAM, they have long included circuitry that converts the digital signal to analog for output to CRT displays. Therefore, LCD displays that connect to these traditional video adapters (as distinguished by the DB-15 connector on

FIGURE 2-13

DVI, S-Video, and DB-15 connectors on a video adapter card

the LCD's interface cable) must include circuitry that reconverts the analog signal back to digital! We call such a display an analog LCD display (in spite of its digital nature).

Now that LCD displays have a greater market share than CRTs, you will find displays that do not perform the digital-to-analog conversion. Such a display, called a *digital LCD display*, has a special *digital video interface (DVI)* connector that accepts the digital signal. Match this type of display with an adapter card with a DVI connector.

HDMi

High-definition multimedia interface (HDMi) is a recent interface standard for use with DVD players, digital television (DTV) players, set-top cable or satellite service boxes, and other devices. It combines the audio and video signals into an uncompressed signal and has a bandwidth of up to 5 GB/second. One specially designed cable with an HDMi connector is all you need now between a compatible video device and the TV. Previously, several cables were required.

Type A HDMi is backward compatible with the DVI standard as implemented in PC video adapters and displays. Therefore, a DVI video adapter can control an HDMi monitor, providing an appropriate cable is used. However, the audio and remote control features of HDMi will not be available. Eventually, HDMi will be integrated into media center PCs, replacing DVI.

Composite Video

The next time you watch television, take a close look at the image. You will notice variations in both brightness and color (unless you are watching a black and white TV!). The traditional transmission system for television video signals, called *composite video*, combines the color and brightness information with the synchronization data into one signal. While television sets have long used separate signals, called *luminance* (brightness) and *chrominance* (color), they received composite signals, and had to separate out the luminance and chrominance information. Errors in separating the two signals from the composite signal would result in on-screen problems, especially in complex images.

Component Video Signals

Component video is a video signaling method in which analog video information is transmitted as two or more discrete signals. Two general types of component video are RGB Video and S-Video. The DVI and HDMi interfaces described previously are replacing these component-signaling interfaces.

RGB Video *RGB video* is a simple type of component video signal that sends three separate signals: red, green, and blue using three coaxial cables. There are variations on RGB component signaling, based on how the synchronization signal is handled. The SVGA RGB signaling method was widely used for PC displays before DVI and HDMi came along.

S-Video *Super-Video*, more commonly called *S-Video*, refers to the transmission of a video signal using two signals. These two signals are luminance, represented by a Y, and chrominance, represented by a C. The luminance signal carries the black and white portion of video, or brightness. The chrominance signal carries the RGB color information, including saturation and hue. Further, the chrominance signal can be broken into multiple channels for improved speed and color that is more precise. S-video ports are round to accommodate a round plug with four pins.

Display Settings

You can adjust a variety of display settings. You will find some of these settings, such as vertical hold, horizontal hold, and refresh rate, only on a CRT display, while others, such as resolution, apply to both CRT and LCD displays. Some settings are only available to you from a special menu built into your display. This menu is independent of your operating system, and you access it through buttons mounted on the monitor, as long as the monitor is powered up, regardless of the presence or absence of a PC. Other settings are accessible from within the Display applet in Windows.

V-Hold/H-Hold

The *v-hold* setting, also known as *vertical hold,* is a CRT display setting found on the menu built into a CRT. Like CRT televisions, this setting holds the image vertically on the screen. If this setting is only slightly out of adjustment, the screen image will be stationary, but out of position vertically. If this setting is badly out of adjustment, the image will dynamically roll vertically. Similarly, *h-hold,* or *horizontal hold,* is a CRT-only setting that holds the image horizontally.

Vertical Position/Horizontal Position

The built-in menu on a LCD display will have the *vertical position* setting, which adjusts the viewable area of the display vertically, while the *horizontal position* setting adjusts the viewable area of the display horizontally.

CRT Refresh Rate

The *refresh rate* of a display is a significant setting for a CRT display. On a CRT, this refers to the *vertical refresh rate*, which is the rate per second at which an image appears on the tube. The video adapter drives this setting. If you are running Windows, you can see the refresh rate of your display in the Advanced Settings in the Display applet. Exercise 2-3 explains how to find this setting. In order to avoid eyestrain, a CRT display should refresh at a rate above 60 Hertz (Hertz is a rate of repetition in cycles per second). On some CRTs, you may need to reduce the resolution to achieve an adequate refresh rate.

EXERCISE 2-3

Modifying Display Settings

1. Open the Display applet by right-clicking on the desktop and selecting Properties from the context menu.
2. Select the Settings tab. Notice the current Screen resolution.
3. Click Advanced.
4. In the Advanced dialog box, select the Monitor tab.
5. On the Monitor page notice the screen refresh rate and write down the value. Is it greater than 60 Hertz? If not, first ensure that the box labeled "Hide modes that this monitor cannot display" is checked, and then use the drop-down box. If a setting is available that is higher than 60 Hertz, select it. Click OK on this page and on the Settings page.
6. Do the settings work? Is there a noticeable difference?
7. If necessary, return the display to its original settings.

Do not confuse refresh rate with the number of images (frames) per second. A traditional movie projector runs at 32 frames per second. A human eye can detect flicker in a movie if it runs at a rate close to or less than 20 frames per second.

on the Job *Selecting a refresh rate higher than the CRT can support can cause damage to the display.*

LCD Response Time

While you will find a refresh rate setting in Windows for an LCD display, it is still a video adapter setting. On LCD displays, the closest equivalent to a CRT's refresh rate is *response time*, the time in milliseconds (ms) it takes for a single pixel to go from the active (black) to inactive (white) state and back again. This setting is not adjustable, so you will not find it in the LCD's built-in menu or in Windows. It is a feature that a manufacturer will list with the other specifications of the model. The response time, now commonly in the single digits, is a best-case scenario under controlled testing. A low number is desirable because the lower the number the faster the response time. If your LCD display occasionally seems to blur moving images, the display has a slow (high number) response time.

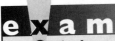

Display Resolution

As you learned earlier in this chapter, resolution is the displayable number of pixels. A CRT display may easily support several different screen resolutions. If you have a CRT, you can play with this setting, along with others, until you have the most comfortable combination of resolution, color density, and refresh rate. On a LCD display, you should keep this setting at the native mode of the display.

Color Quality

The Color Quality setting in the Display applet allows you to adjust the number of colors used by the display. Also called color depth, it may be expressed in terms of 16 bits or 32 bits.

SCENARIO & SOLUTION

A video adapter will have a connector for one of these three busses.	PCI, AGP, or PCIe
What aspect ratio is desirable on an LCD intended for viewing wide-format videos?	16:9
Three settings you will find in the Display applet.	Resolution, refresh rate, and color quality

Input Devices

An input device sends signals into a computer. The two most common input devices are the keyboard and a pointing device.

Pointing Devices

A *pointing device* is an input device used to manipulate a pointer and other items on the computer display. The *mouse* is by far the most popular pointing device. Users learn mouse operations quickly; the movement of a mouse over a surface translates into movement of the pointer. Buttons on the mouse allow the user to perform operations such as selecting items and running programs. Another popular pointing device is the trackball, a device that is generally larger than a mouse but remains stationary, so it requires less desk space. The user moves the pointer by rolling a ball mounted in the trackball device. A trackball will also have two or more buttons that you use like the buttons on a mouse.

Keyboard

For the vast majority of PC users, the *keyboard* is their primary input device. There are several types of keyboards, including 84- and 101-key designs. Newer keyboards might include a variety of additional keys for accessing the Internet, using Microsoft Windows, and other common functions. Some keyboards even include a pointing device, such as a mouse or touch pad.

There are also several keyboard layouts. The key set on an ergonomic keyboard's physical form factor (see Figure 2-14) is split in half and each half slants outward to provide a more relaxed, natural hand position. The layout of the keys themselves

FIGURE 2-14

Ergonomic keyboard with a different structure from a conventional keyboard

FIGURE 2-15

QWERTY and
Dvorak keyboard
layouts

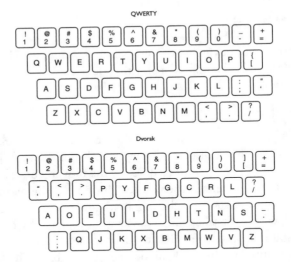

can also vary, regardless of the form factor. Typical English language keyboards (even ergonomic keyboards) have a QWERTY layout, named after the first six letters on the second row of the keyboard. The Dvorak keyboard has an entirely different key layout (shown in Figure 2-15) and allows faster typing speeds.

Ever wonder why the QWERTY keyboard is laid out the way it is, and why it's not laid out in alphabetical order? Christopher Sholes invented the keyboard in the late 1800s, and he arranged the keys in alphabetical order. However, because early typewriters were prone to jam keys, Sholes then created the QWERTY layout, positioning the letters to avoid jams.

In the 1930s, August Dvorak redesigned the keyboard layout so that the most commonly used characters are in or closest to the home row and the strongest fingers can access them. This layout allows for faster typing speeds, less hand strain, fewer typing mistakes, and less overall "finger travel." Typing speeds on a Dvorak keyboard can reach about 100–120 words per minute—double the rate most people can achieve on a QWERTY keyboard. Unfortunately, the Dvorak keyboard has been slow to catch on. It is exceptionally difficult to learn and accurately use both layouts, so most people stick to the old QWERTY standby that they learned in school.

Bar Code Reader

On nearly every item you buy, every package you ship, and the membership cards you carry, there is a small rectangular image with a unique pattern of black bars and white space. This is a *bar code*, which is a code that contains information appropriate to the type of use. On a product, it will contain inventory and pricing information. On your library card, it will identify you as a dues-paying member. A *bar code reader* is a device used to read the bar code. The design of the reader must match the type of code on the item it scans in order to interpret it. The bar code reader uses a laser beam to measure the thicknesses of the lines and spaces. This information converted to digital data and transferred to a computer. At the grocery store, the computer is in the cash register, which tallies up your total and sends inventory information to a central computer.

Multimedia

There is a variety of multimedia input devices for PCs. The short list includes Web video cameras, digital still cameras, MIDI devices, and microphones.

Web and Digital Cameras

A Web camera, or Webcam, is simply a digital video camera, used to broadcast images (usually live) over the Internet. While the Web camera as a PC peripheral has not lived up to the predictions of widespread adoption of a decade ago, it is still an inexpensive and easy-to-use addition to a PC, providing the visual component for meetings and other business communications, as well as entertainment and security functions.

MIDI

A *MIDI musical device* is a synthesizer keyboard that connects to a PC through the special MIDI port. This allows musicians and budding musicians to input their music for mixing and to convert it to musical notation.

Microphones

As a PC peripheral, a microphone gives a remote meeting attendee a voice at the meeting. The latest voice recognition programs allow a user to dictate entire documents with a very low error rate.

Biometric Devices

Biometric devices provide greater authentication security than the simple method of using a username and password. With the appropriate biometric device and security software, a biometric device identifies a user by some measurement from their body, such as a fingerprint or a scan of the retina of their eye.

Touch Screen

The *touch screen* display for PCs has been around for over 20 years. Using a touch-sensitive surface to accept input from the user, this type of device allows the user to touch areas on the screen rather than use a mouse. Most handheld computers use touch screen displays, and PC touch screens operate in some special circumstances, such as shopping kiosks.

Cables, Connectors, and Ports

This section introduces you to a number of basic peripheral installation concepts, such as cable and connector types, as well as communication methods. This information will allow you to determine the pros and cons of various connection methods.

Cables

Cables physically connect components and are responsible for transmitting signals between them. Cables transmit electronic signals and can come in a wide variety of physical forms. Straight-pair cables consist of one or more metal wires surrounded by a plastic insulating sheath. *Twisted-pair cables* consist of two or more sheathed metal wires twisted around each other along the entire length of the cable to help avoid interference. A covering plastic sheath surrounds these wires in turn. *Coaxial cables* contain a single copper wire surrounded by several layers of insulating plastic and a woven wire sheath that provides both physical and electrical protection. Figure 2-16 illustrates some common cable types.

FIGURE 2-16

Common cable types used in computer installations

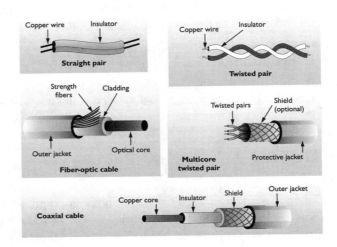

Ports and Connectors

There is a great variety of connector and port types among peripheral devices, and different devices use different cable/connector combinations. For example, the straight-pair cable for a printer has a different connector than the straight-pair cable for a monitor. It is important to make the distinction between a connector and a port. Typically, the term *connector* refers to the plug at the end of a cable, and *port* refers to its place of attachment on a device. Even though we refer to connectors and ports, bear in mind that the port is also a connector. The following sections contain descriptions of some common connector types.

Serial: RS-232

While many of the peripheral interfaces described in this book use serial communications, the classic serial port of a PC, the *RS-232 port*, complies with the Recommended Standard-232 (RS-232) set of standards in its circuitry, cabling, and connector design. Like all serial communications, RS-232 transfers data serially, one bit at a time.

RS-232 serial communication has a maximum speed of 115 kilobits per second (Kbps). In early PCs, the RS-232 port used a 25-pin male D-Shell connector, but because it did not use all the pins, the 9-pin male D-Shell connector that has nine pins in two rows (five in one row and four in the other) replaced it. Also called a DB-9 (D-Shell-9) connector, all D-Shell connectors have this same trapezoidal shape (see Figure 2-17). These were most commonly used for serial devices such as mice and external modems.

Parallel

In parallel communications, multiple wires simultaneously transmit one bit per wire, in parallel. All other things being equal, this results in faster data transfers for large packets. The parallel interface for peripherals found on PCs in the 1980s was

A female DB-25 connector (top) and two male DB-9 connectors (bottom)

unidirectional, so a computer could send data to a device, such as a printer, but the device could not send information back to the computer. In addition, the transfer rate was 150 kilobytes per second (150 KBps).

The IEEE 1284 standard, which supports bidirectional communication and transfer rates of up to 2 MBps, corrected the shortcomings of the old parallel interface in 1991. If you buy a parallel cable today, this standard will be prominently displayed on its packaging. Modern parallel interfaces in PCs and parallel devices follow this standard but also support the previous implementations. A PC's built-in parallel port now has several modes of operation, configurable through the system settings menu. These modes include standard parallel, bidirectional parallel, ECP, and EPP. All but standard parallel are bidirectional.

At one time, external drives and other devices used the parallel interface, and it was the "gold standard" for PC printers. Today, most common external peripherals use USB or IEEE 1394, because both achieve faster speeds, both are Plug and Play, and they each use slender cables as opposed to bulky parallel cables.

The parallel port connector is a D-Shell connector with 25 pins or sockets—13 in one row and 12 in the other. Until recently, most computers included one female DB-25 parallel connector. You can see an example of a DB-25 connector in Figure 2-17. On the device end is a 36-pin connector, sometimes referred to as a Centronics 36-pin connector.

SCSI

Manufacturers rarely build *Small Computer System Interface (SCSI)* into consumer-level PC motherboards, and they are even less likely to do so in the future. Developed by the American National Standards Institute (ANSI), and simply referred to as SCSI (pronounced "skuzzy"), this standard has been used for both internal and external hard drive and optical drives, as well as external devices such as printers, modems, scanners, and most other types of peripherals.

SCSI systems differ from non-SCSI systems in several ways. To begin with, SCSI devices are all attached to and controlled by a SCSI controller in a *daisy chain*, meaning that each SCSI device participates in moving data, as it typically comes with both input and output connectors so that another device can be connected to the SCSI bus through the previous device. Figure 2-18 shows several external devices on a SCSI chain. We describe configuration of host adapters and SCSI devices in Chapter 3.

In PCs, the SCSI controller is usually an adapter card, called a "SCSI host adapter," installed in the expansion bus. This adapter card will typically have

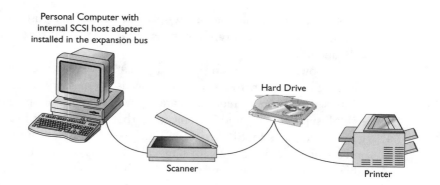

Three devices on
a SCSI chain

Personal Computer with
internal SCSI host adapter
installed in the expansion bus

Hard Drive

Scanner

Printer

a connector on the board for connecting an internal SCSI device, and a connector on the back of the board for connecting an external SCSI device. For several years, SCSI enjoyed popularity for high-end devices, such as hard drives, optical drives, and scanners. It was the disk controller of choice for many expensive servers, but it has had stiff competition in recent years from technologies that improved on the old PATA standard (described in Chapter 3), and more recently, Serial ATA technology (also described in Chapter 3) for drive interfaces is replacing SCSI.

There are several implementations of SCSI, with speeds of up to 320 MBps, described in Chapter 3. Until recently, SCSI systems all used a parallel interface to the computer. For the traditional parallel SCSI interface, there are four different connectors, including 50-pin Centronics (it resembles the device end of a parallel cable), 50-pin HD D-type, 68-pin HD D-type, and a 25-pin D-Shell identical in appearance to a parallel port. More recently, a serial interface has been used with SCSI—a marriage of SCSI and Serial ATA called *Serial Attached SCSI (SAS)*.

USB

The *Universal Serial Bus (USB)* interface has become the interface of choice for PCs, making both parallel and serial ports obsolete, and even replacing SCSI and IEEE 1394 (discussed next). PCs manufactured in the last several years have at least one USB port (it is rare to have only one) and high-end PCs literally bristle with USB connectors located conveniently on the front, as well as the back, of the PC case.

USB is an external bus that connects into the PC's PCI bus. With USB, you can theoretically connect up to 127 devices to your computer. There are currently two major versions of the USB standard. The low-speed .9, 1.0, and 1.1 versions transmit data up to 12 Mbps, while the high-speed 2.0 version transmits data at speeds up to 480 Mbps. You can attach a low-speed device like a mouse to either version, but some devices require, or run best, when attached to a USB port that is up to the 2.0 standard.

Low-power devices, such as flash drives, receive power through the USB bus, while USB devices with greater power needs, such as large external hard drives, printers, and scanners, require separate power supplies that plug into wall sockets.

USB supports Plug and Play, meaning that the computer BIOS and operating system recognizes a USB device, and the operating system automatically installs and configures a device driver (if available). Always check the documentation for a USB device, because many require installation of the device driver before the device is connected. USB ports also support *hot swapping*, which means that you can attach devices while the computer is running, and they are recognized and used immediately.

If a PC has too few USB ports for the number of USB devices a user wishes to connect, the easiest fix is to purchase an external USB hub and connect it to one of the PC's USB connectors. In fact, you can add other hubs and devices in this way. While the USB standard allows for daisy chaining of devices, manufacturers do not support this capability because they prefer to use hubs connected to the USB controller and daisy-chained. There is a limit of five levels of hubs, counting the root hub. Each hub can accommodate several USB devices, possibly creating a lopsided tree. USB supports different speeds on each branch, so there can be devices of varying speeds in use. Figure 2-19 shows a PC with an internal root hub. Connected to this hub are a USB keyboard and another USB hub. Several devices connect to the first USB hub, including yet another hub, which in turn has several devices connected. This configuration is common today. In fact, both authors of this book have a similar number of hubs and devices, only with more printers.

A USB port is rectangular, and acts as a receiver for a USB type-A connector measuring 1/2" by 1/8" (see Figure 2-20). A plastic device in the port holds the four wires. This, together with a similar plastic device in the connector, polarizes the connectors, which keeps the two from being connected incorrectly. The connector on the device end of a USB cable is a square type-B connector. There are also two variations of mini-USB connectors, found on USB digital cameras. All sizes of USB connectors include four wires. Most devices clearly identify USB ports and cable connectors with a fork-shaped symbol.

IEEE 1394/FireWire

Like USB, the *IEEE 1394* standard is an external serial bus that connects to the internal PCI bus. It is commonly called *FireWire*, which is Apple's trademarked name, but other manufacturers call it i.link or Lynx. For simplicity, we will call it FireWire.

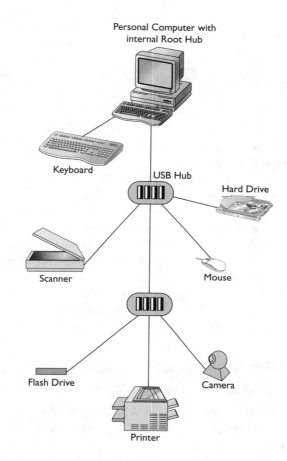

Today, PC motherboards have FireWire support built in, and often have one or
two external FireWire connectors. Like SCSI, each FireWire device can be used to
daisy-chain more devices. A single FireWire port can support up to 63 daisy-chained
devices. Therefore, adding additional ports to the computer itself is not usually

necessary, although you may add them by installing an expansion card. No single cable in a 1394 port can be longer than 4.5 meters.

Originally, the FireWire standard allowed for faster data transfer than the USB 1.0 standard. Therefore, FireWire was the interface of choice for external devices that required high-speed data transfers, such as video cameras, hard drives, and DVD players. After the release and adoption of the USB 2.0 standard, the two bus standards were close in maximum speed, although FireWire performed better in head-to-head tests, providing higher sustained speeds than USB, which communicates in bursts. The original standard, now called IEEE 1394a, supports speeds up to 400 Mbps. In 2003, the IEEE released the 1394b specification, with cable distances of up to 100 meters and top speeds of 800 Mbps, 1,600 Mbps, and 3.2 Gbps. A significant limit is that one 1394a device in a chain will cause any 1394b devices to operate at the lower speed. In addition, while 1394b is generally downward compatible with 1394a, 3.2 Gbps is only available with special hardware that is not downward compatible with 1394a devices.

A standard six-pin FireWire port is about 1/2 inch long; with one squared end and one three-sided end, that guarantees a correct connection of a cable connector. As with USB, the wires connect to a plastic device. Alternatively, you will find smaller four-wire ports, especially on laptops. Most devices clearly identify FireWire ports and cable connectors with a Y-shaped symbol.

RJ11

A *registered jack (RJ)* connector is rectangular in shape and has a locking clip on one side (see Figure 2-21). The number designation of an RJ connector refers to its size rather than to the number of wire connections within it. RJ11 connectors contain either two or four wires and usually attach phone cables to modems and to phone jacks in the wall.

FIGURE 2-21

RJ11 connectors
and cable shown
on a modem card
(left side)

RJ45

RJ45 connectors are slightly larger than RJ11 connectors and contain eight wires.
RJ45 connectors most commonly attach twisted-pair cables to Ethernet network
cards. An RJ45 port is similar to an RJ11 port—only wider. Figure 2-22 shows an
RJ45 port, labeled "Ethernet."

BNC

The acronym BNC for the name of this connector is the subject of some debate, and
there seems to be no consensus as to the origin of its name. What matters is that you
can recognize one when you see it. BNC connectors attach coaxial cables to BNC
ports. The cable connector is round and has a twist-lock mechanism to keep the
cable in place. BNC connectors have a protruding pin that corresponds to a receiver
socket in the port. The type of BNC connector formerly used in computer local area
networks cannot connect your television to the cable outlet in the wall.

FIGURE 2-22

The RJ45 port on
this PC is labeled
"Ethernet." It is
just to the right
of the bottom
two USB ports.

SCENARIO & SOLUTION

Early PCs frequently used these two ports for peripherals, but newer technology is replacing them.	Serial and parallel
These two common communications ports are similar in shape, but one is larger.	RJ11 and RJ45
Two external serial bus standards common on PCs today.	USB and IEEE 1394

PS/2/Mini-DIN

DIN connectors get their name from Deutsche Industrie Norm, Germany's standards organization. Most (but not all) DIN connectors are round with a circle or semicircle of pins. The mini-DIN connector, or more accurately, the mini-DIN-6 connector, gets its name from the fact that it is smaller than a customary DIN-6 keyboard connector. Mini-DIN connectors most commonly connect PS/2 style (Personal System/2) mice and keyboards, so people often refer to mini-DIN connectors as PS/2 connectors. Look back at Figure 2-22 to see two mini-DIN connectors at the top of the panel, one for a keyboard, and another for a mouse.

Multimedia

The types and functions of multimedia ports on PCs increase every year. The Musical Instrument Digital Interface (MIDI) port has been around for almost the entire history of the PC, while you will see a variety of audio ports on almost any consumer-level brand-name PC.

MIDI   A MIDI musical device such as a synthesizer keyboard uses a MIDI port on the PC. A MIDI device will also require an additional piece of equipment, in the form of a box connected between the PC and MIDI device. Alternatively, a joystick can use the MIDI port, although USB joysticks are available. A MIDI port uses a female DB-15 connector that has only two rows of pins, as opposed to the DB-15 connector used for analog video. The MIDI cable is coaxial.

Audio/Video Ports   The typical PC comes with a minimum of three color-coded audio ports, or "jacks." Pink identifies a microphone input port, green identifies a speaker output port, and blue is the auxiliary port. Additional audio ports may be present for additional audio channels, in which case, look for these identifying colors: white for left speaker, red for right speaker, and yellow for composite video. All of these use the 1/8" single-pin mini audio port *plug*, a few generations removed from the larger single-pin RCA phone (as in earphone) connector. Some handheld devices use the 3/32" sub-mini audio port. All of these single-pin plugs come in mono versions and stereo versions. Look for a single black ring around a mono plug and two black rings around a stereo plug. This applies to all of the plugs described previously.

The consumer version of S/PDIF (Sony/Philips Digital Interface) uses a single-pin RCA phone jack, for transferring digital audio from CD and DVD players to amplifiers and speakers.

CERTIFICATION SUMMARY

In addition to the PC case, motherboard, and CPU described in Chapter 1, other common components include the power supply, cooling systems, memory, storage devices, display devices, input devices, and the parts that allow communication: cables, connectors, and ports.

Identifying the components and their functions is the first step in becoming a computer professional. Some components, such as power supplies, have more than one function. For instance, since power supplies provide the DC voltages required by various other components, they produce heat. Therefore, each power supply has a fan that dissipates the heat the power supply creates, as well as contributing to cooling the entire system. In most PCs, this is not enough, so additional methods are used to keep PCs cool enough for the components to function safely.

While PC component technologies are ever changing, understanding the basics of the components and their functions today will help you to understand newer technologies as they are introduced.

It is important to understand how components connect to a PC. Chapter 1 describes the relationship between the CPU and motherboard, along with built-in components. In addition, there are wide varieties of cables that connect components to a PC. The physical form of the cable, and the connectors and ports used with a cable, depends on the purpose and design of the device or devices that use the cable.

✓ TWO-MINUTE DRILL

Here are some of the key points covered in Chapter 2.

Power Supply

❑ A power supply provides power for all components on the motherboard and those internal to the PC case.

❑ The power supply fan blows exhausted air out of the case, drawing it in through vents on the front of the case, to cool both the power supply and other components.

❑ Power supplies come in form factors to match motherboards and cases.

Cooling Systems

❑ PCs usually require additional cooling systems beyond the power supply fan.

❑ PC cooling systems include well-designed case ventilation, CPU and case fans, heat sinks, thermal compounds, and liquid cooling systems.

Memory

❑ SRAM is very fast and very expensive and is used for L2 cache in most systems.

❑ DRAM is slower than SRAM. It is less expensive, has a higher capacity, and is the main memory in the computer.

❑ DRAM technologies include SDRAM, RDRAM, DDR, and DDR2.

❑ Specialized RAM for video adapters is called VRAM.

❑ You must install DIMMs and RIMMs in full memory banks so that their total bit width matches the width of the processor's data bus.

❑ Most memory modules do not perform error checking. Some older memory modules use an error-checking method called parity, and others may use a more complex method called ECC.

Storage Devices

❑ Data is stored permanently on storage devices such as floppy disk drives, hard disk drives, optical drives, tape drives, and flash drives. Each of these drives offers different capacities and portability.

❑ While you can use any writable storage device for data backups, tape drives are designed exclusively for this purpose.

Adapter Cards

❑ An adapter card is a printed circuit board that installs into a PC's expansion bus to add functionality.

❑ The need for adapter cards has diminished as PC motherboards contain more functions.

❑ There are numerous types of adapter cards, including (but not limited to) those for video, multimedia, I/O, and communications.

Video Adapters and Displays

❑ The video adapter controls the output from the PC to the display device.

❑ A video adapter may be built into the motherboard or be a separate circuit board that plugs into a PCI, AGP, or PCIe connector.

❑ The two general PC display types are CRT and LCD. LCD displays are replacing CRT displays.

❑ Display connectors include DB-15 for CRTs and analog LCD displays, and DVI and HDMi for digital LCD displays.

❑ Composite video combines the information for brightness and color into one signal, while component video delivers the brightness and color information in at least two separate signals.

❑ Some display settings, such as v-hold/h-hold (for CRTs) and vertical position/ horizontal position (for LCDs), are only available through a menu on the display itself.

❑ Response time is an LCD feature that is not controllable through any menu settings.

❑ Display resolution is a setting that you can control through Windows.

Input Devices

❑ Common input devices include pointing devices (mouse, trackball), keyboard, and multimedia devices.

❑ Less-common input devices include bar code readers, biometric devices, and touch screens.

Cables, Connectors, and Ports

❑ Common electronic cables include straight-pair, twisted-pair, and coaxial.

❑ Serial devices transmit one bit at a time; parallel devices transmit more than one bit at a time.

❑ Common connectors and ports include serial, parallel, SCSI, USB, RJ11, RJ45, BNC, PS/2 (mini-DIN), and multimedia.

SELF TEST

The following questions will help you measure your understanding of the material presented in this chapter. Read all of the choices carefully because there might be more than one correct answer. Choose all correct answers for each question.

Power Supply

1. Which statement is true?
   A. A power supply converts wattage to voltage.
   B. A power supply converts voltage to wattage.
   C. A power supply converts AC to DC.
   D. A power supply converts DC to AC.

2. What main power connector goes between an ATX power supply and an ATX motherboard?
   A. P3
   B. P1
   C. P2
   D. P4

Cooling Systems

3. Give three locations for PC cooling fans.
   A. Power supply, memory module, and case
   B. Display, power supply, and CPU
   C. Power supply, CPU, and hard drive system
   D. Power supply, CPU, and case

4. This special substance is placed between a CPU and CPU fan to increase heat conductivity.
   A. Liquid cooling
   B. Thermal compound
   C. Metallic foil
   D. Heat sink

Memory

5. Cache memory uses which type of RAM because of its speed?
   A. DRAM
   B. VRAM

    C. DIMM

    D. SRAM

6. RDRAM can use only this type of slot on a motherboard.

    A. RIMM

    B. SIMM

    C. DIMM

    D. DRAM

7. This type of RAM module can run at clock rates of 400 MHz and higher and uses a special 240-pin DIMM socket.

    A. DDR1

    B. SDRAM

    C. DDR2

    D. VRAM

Storage Devices

8. This is a component in a hard drive system that reads and writes data.

    A. Spindle

    B. Head

    C. Platter

    D. Cable

9. Name the rotating shaft to which a hard drive's platters attach.

    A. Head

    B. Cable

    C. Pin

    D. Spindle

10. Name two common interfaces for external hard drives.

    A. IDE and SATA

    B. Serial and parallel

    C. USB and IEEE 1394

    D. Coaxial and twisted pair

11. This DVD type stores 15.9 GB of data, or over eight hours of video.

    A. DVD-18

    B. DVD-9

    C. DVD-10

    D. DVD-5

Adapter Cards

12. Which of the following is not an I/O technology?

    A. Serial

    B. USB

    C. IEEE 1394

    D. P1

13. Name a common communications adapter card used to connect PCs to a LAN or to a DSL or cable modem.

    A. Network adapter

    B. Modem

    C. USB

    D. Serial

Video Adapters and Displays

14. This type of display device takes up less desk space and replaces an older technology that uses more power.

    A. CRT

    B. LCD

    C. ATX

    D. USB

15. A media center PC may have this newest type of digital video connector, which allows one cable to replace several used previously.

    A. DVI

    B. DB-15

    C. HDMi

    D. Component

16. This type of video interface transmits video signals using two signals, Y and C.

    A. S-Video

    B. VGA

    C. Component

    D. Composite

Input Devices

17. Name the most common pointing device.
- A. MIDI
- B. Trackball
- C. Mouse
- D. Keyboard

18. Name the most commonly used English language keyboard layout.
- A. Dvorak
- B. QWERTY
- C. Ergonomic
- D. Flat

Cables, Connectors, and Ports

19. A device with this interface comes with both input and output connectors, so that it can connect through a daisy chain to a controlling host adapter.
- A. USB
- B. Serial
- C. Parallel
- D. SCSI

20. This type of external bus interface allows up to 127 devices (theoretically) to be connected.
- A. Parallel
- B. Serial
- C. USB
- D. IEEE 1394

LAB QUESTION

A coworker asked you to help him select an external hard drive. While some external hard drives have both USB and IEEE 1394 interfaces, he has narrowed his choices down to two hard drives: one with only a USB 2.0 interface and one with a brand new, very high-speed, IEEE 1394b interface. His computer has several USB 2.0 ports and one 1394b port with one slow device attached to it. Write a few paragraphs on the pros and cons of these two choices and provide your own recommendation.

SELF TEST ANSWERS

Power Supply

1. ☑ **C.** A power supply converts AC to DC.
   ☒ **A**, a power supply converts wattage to voltage, is incorrect. **B**, a power supply converts voltage to wattage, is incorrect. **D**, a power supply converts DC to AC, is incorrect. It does just the opposite.

2. ☑ **B.** P1 is the main power connector used between an ATX power supply and an ATX motherboard.
   ☒ **A**, P3, is incorrect because the chapter mentioned no such connector. **C**, P2, is incorrect because the chapter mentioned no such connector. **D**, P4, is incorrect because this is a four-wire 12 V connector used in addition to the P1 connector.

Cooling Systems

3. ☑ **D.** Power supply, CPU, and case are three locations for cooling fans in PCs.
   ☒ **A**, power supply, memory module, and case, is incorrect because a memory module is not a location for PC cooling fans. **B**, display, power supply, and CPU, is incorrect because the display is not a location for cooling fans in PCs. **C**, power supply, CPU, and hard drive system, is incorrect because the hard drive system is not a location for cooling fans in PCs.

4. ☑ **B.** Thermal compound is placed between a CPU and CPU fan to increase the heat conductivity.
   ☒ **A**, liquid cooling, and **C**, metallic foil, are incorrect because they are not between the CPU and CPU fan. **D**, heat sink, is incorrect because, while a heat sink may be attached to a CPU, either by itself or in combination with a CPU fan, this is not applied between the CPU and CPU fan.

Memory

5. ☑ **D.** SRAM is the type of RAM used for cache memory because of its speed.
   ☒ **A**, DRAM, is incorrect because this is slower than SRAM. **B,** VRAM, is incorrect because although it is fast, this type of RAM is used on video adapters. **C**, DIMM, is a RAM connector/slot type, not a type of RAM.

6. ☑ **A.** RIMM is the type of slot on a motherboard that can only be used by RDRAM.
   ☒ **B**, SIMM, and **C**, DIMM, are incorrect because they cannot be used by RDRAM. **D**, DRAM, is incorrect because it is a type of RAM, not a type of slot.

7. ☑ **C.** DDR2 is the type of RAM module that can run at clock rates of 400 MHz and higher and uses a special 240-pin DIMM socket.

    ☒ **A**, DDR1, is incorrect because it uses a 184-pin DIMM socket, not a 240-pin DIMM socket. **B**, SDRAM, is incorrect because it attaches to video adapters, not to memory slots on the motherboard. **D**, VRAM, is incorrect because it mounts on a video adapter, not in a DIMM socket.

Storage Devices

8. ☑ **B.** The head is a component in a hard drive system that reads and writes data. There is one head for each platter side.

    ☒ **A**, spindle, is incorrect because this rotating pole holds the platters in a hard drive. **C**, platter, is incorrect because this component holds the data. **D**, cable, is incorrect because a cable connects a device to a computer but does not read data from a hard drive.

9. ☑ **D.** The spindle is the rotating shaft to which a hard drive's platters are attached.

    ☒ **A**, head, is incorrect because this component reads and writes data. **B**, cable, is incorrect because a cable connects a device to a computer and is not a rotating shaft. **C**, pin, is incorrect because it is a component of a cable plug, not the rotating shaft in a hard drive.

10. ☑ **C.** USB and IEEE 1394 are two common interfaces for external hard drives.

    ☒ **A**, IDE and SATA, are incorrect because these are common interfaces for internal hard drives (Chapter 1), not for external hard drives. **B**, serial and parallel, are not common interfaces for external hard drives. The standard serial interface is not fast enough. Parallel was used at one time, but it has been replaced by newer, faster Plug-and-Play interfaces. **D**, coaxial and twisted pair, are types of cables and not interfaces for external hard drives.

11. ☑ **A.** DVD-18 stores 15.9 GB of data, or over eight hours of video.

    ☒ **B**, DVD-9, is incorrect because it only holds 7.95 GB data, or over four hours of video. **C**, DVD-10, is incorrect because it only holds 8.74 GB data, or over four and a half hours of video. **D**, DVD-5, is incorrect because it only holds 4.37 GB data, or over two hours of video.

Adapter Cards

12. ☑ **D.** P1 is not an I/O technology, but a type of power connector.

    ☒ **A**, serial, **B**, USB, and **C**, IEEE 1394, are incorrect because they are I/O technologies.

13. ☑ **A.** A network adapter is a common communications adapter card used to connect PCs to a LAN or to take advantage of a DSL or cable modem Internet connection.

    ☒ **B**, modem, is incorrect because, while it is a communications adapter card, it is used for a dial-up connection, not for a LAN connection. **C**, USB, is incorrect because it is an I/O interface, not a communications adapter. **D**, serial, is incorrect because it is I/O interface, not a communications adapter, although some external modems can connect to a serial port.

Video Adapters and Displays

14. ☑ **B.** LCD displays take up less desk space and replace an older (CRT) technology that uses more power.
    ☒ **A**, CRT, is incorrect because it takes up more desk space than an LCD display and uses more power. **C**, ATX, is incorrect because it is a motherboard and power supply form factor, not a type of display. **D**, USB, is incorrect because it is an I/O interface.

15. ☑ **C.** HDMi is correct because it is the newest digital video connector and it allows one cable to replace several used previously.
    ☒ **A**, DVI, is incorrect because it is not the newest digital video connector but is being replaced by the HDMi connector on newer media center PCs. **B**, DB-15, is incorrect because it is an analog video connector for CRTs. **D**, Component, is incorrect because it is not a single connector; it requires several cables and plugs.

16. ☑ **A.** S-Video transmits video signals using two signals, Y and C.
    ☒ **B**, VGA, is incorrect because it does not transmit Y and C signals. **C**, Component, is incorrect because DVI and HDMi are replacing component video standards, such as RGB Video and S-Video. **D**, Composite, is incorrect because this type of video interface uses a single signal.

Input Devices

17. ☑ **C.** Mouse is the most common pointing device.
    ☒ **A**, MIDI, is incorrect because it is not a pointing device but an interface for a joystick or musical instrument. **B**, trackball, is incorrect because it is not the most common pointing device, although it may be the second most common. **D**, keyboard, is incorrect because it is not a pointing device.

18. ☑ **B.** QWERTY is the most commonly used English language keyboard layout.
    ☒ **A**, Dvorak, is incorrect because although it is an English language keyboard layout, it is not the most commonly used one. **C**, Ergonomic, is incorrect because this is a form factor design that either QWERTY or Dvorak layouts could use. **D**, Flat, is incorrect because it does not describe a keyboard layout.

Cables, Connectors, and Ports

19. ☑ **D.** SCSI devices each come with an input and output connector so that each device can connect through a daisy chain to a controlling host adapter.

☒ **A,** USB, is incorrect because USB devices do not come with input and output connectors (although the original standard did allow for daisy-chaining). **B,** serial, and **C,** parallel, are incorrect because serial and parallel devices do not come with input and output connectors so that each device can connect through a daisy chain to a controlling host adapter.

20. ☑ **C.** USB is a type of external bus interface that allows up to 127 devices (theoretically) to be connected.

☒ **A,** parallel, and **B,** serial, are incorrect because they do not allow up to 127 devices to be connected. **D,** IEEE 1394, is incorrect because it allows only up to 63 devices to be connected.

LAB ANSWER

First explain to the coworker that when an IEEE 1394a device and an IEEE 1394b device share the same bus they would both operate at 1394a speed. Then ask if the IEEE 1394b device runs at 800 Mbps, 1,600 Mbps, or 3.2 Gbps. Although the IEEE 1394b specification allows for speeds of up to 3.2 Gbps, this speed is only available with special hardware that is not downward compatible with 1394a devices.

As for the USB device my coworker has found, is it USB 2.0? This may be a silly question for a new device, since we assume that all new USB hard drives come with the faster USB 2.0 interface. However, it is the questions we don't ask that come back to haunt us. If the drive is a USB 2.0, recommend that he purchase the USB drive to avoid the potential problems with the IEEE 1394b drive.

3

Installing and Upgrading PCs

T

his chapter describes and demonstrates how to install and replace common components. With a little practice, you will be capable of performing these tasks on most personal computers, in spite of different layouts or new component designs.

You will also find tips on how to optimize personal computers, as well as procedures for upgrading common components in them.

We install many PC components, such as the processor, power supply, and RAM, through simple physical attachment to the computer. That is, physical installation is all that is required to make the component functional. Other components may need changes to system settings or have OS-level drivers installed to become functional.

Many of the components discussed here conform to some type of standard, which means that you can replace them with other components made by a different manufacturer that conform to that same standard. You can use the skills discussed here on practically any desktop PC.

on the !
Ø o b

Whenever you install or replace a computer component that involves opening the case, you must turn the computer's power off and ensure that you follow the electrostatic discharge (ESD) procedures discussed in Chapter 17. All the exercises described in this section assume that you have taken steps to protect yourself and the computer from harm, as described in Chapter 17.

CERTIFICATION OBJECTIVES

■ **601: 1.2   602: 1.1   603: 1.1   604: 1.1**   *Install, configure, optimize, and upgrade personal computer components*

In this chapter, CompTIA expects you to understand the procedures for adding, removing, and configuring internal storage devices, motherboards, power supplies, CPUs, memory, and adapter cards. In addition to installing the hardware components, you should understand how to install device drivers. Also be prepared to describe how to adjust hardware settings. All network-specific installation and configuration issues will be presented in Chapter 13.

Installing Motherboards, CPUs, and Memory

Installing and upgrading a motherboard requires that you understand the CPU models that will work with the motherboard, as well as the appropriate type of memory compatible with both the motherboard and the amount of memory it can handle. Therefore, we address these three topics together in this section.

Selecting a Motherboard, CPU, and Memory Combination

In Chapter 1, you learned that there are several motherboard form factors, each with different layouts, components, and specifications. Each motherboard is unique in terms of the memory, processor, and type and number of expansion slots it supports. In other words, you cannot tell which components a motherboard supports solely by knowing the form factor of motherboard. Therefore, you must always check the manufacturer's documentation before you select a motherboard and the components you wish to install on it. Any motherboard manual contains a list of installed and supported components, such as CPUs and memory.

CPU Sockets

When selecting a CPU, it is important to make sure that it is compatible with the type and speed of the motherboard. Motherboards can typically use only one or two processor models and can usually handle only two or three different processor speeds.

The two major CPU manufacturers, Intel and AMD, each offer, at any given time, only a few current processor lines, but numerous processor models within each line. One of the many differences between the individual processor models is how the processor attaches to the motherboard, referred to as the socket.

At this writing, the majority of processors from both manufacturers use some variation of pin grid array (PGA) socket, meaning that the processor has a square array of pins (numbered in the many hundreds) that insert into a matching socket on the motherboard. In most cases, the word "socket" is used. In many cases, but not in all, a number that indicates the number of pins in the array follows the word "socket." For instance, some AMD processors have 939 pins and use "Socket 939." Read the motherboard and CPU documentation very carefully to be sure that the CPU and socket match, because there are many versions of PGA sockets.

Furthermore, the CPU socket on the motherboard will usually have a mechanism to make it easier to install the CPU without damaging pins. The most common method involves a lever on the side of the socket that you raise to open the socket. To use this type of socket, commonly called a *zero insertion force (ZIF)* socket, position the CPU with all pins inserted in the matching socket holes. Then close the lever, which lets the socket contact each of the CPU's pins. In all cases, do not count on these simple instructions, but follow those provided in the manuals that come with the motherboard and CPU.

Memory Sockets

By knowing a CPU's address bus width, you will know the maximum system RAM capacity it can access. The minimum amount of memory to install is best determined by considering the requirements of the operating system to be installed and how the computer will be used. We will address this in Chapter 8.

In addition, by knowing the CPU's data bus width, you will know how many RAM modules you must install at a time to create a full memory bank. Before purchasing a motherboard, ensure that it has the proper RAM and CPU slots, and that the CMOS settings are appropriate for your needs.

A motherboard must support both the technology and the form factor of a memory module, such as SIMM, RIMM, or DIMM. The system must also support the data width of the memory as well as its method of error correction. Today's typical motherboard has DIMM or RIMM memory sockets. If you work on older PCs with processors predating the Pentium 4, you may see SIMM sockets. Your choice of memory modules will depend on what type of memory the motherboard supports. Here is a brief description of each type.

SIMM   As outdated technology, SIMMs are included here only because they were so common that you will run into them if you work on older PCs. Single inline memory module (SIMM) sockets were produced in two sizes to accommodate either 30-pin or 72-pin SIMM memory modules. Thirty-pin SIMMs are 8-bit, meaning that data can be transferred into or out of the module 8 bits at a time. The other form you may run into are the 72-pin SIMM sockets, which are 32 bits wide, slightly shorter than DIMM sockets, and usually colored white with small metal clips.

DIMM   Dual Inline Memory Module (DIMM) sockets look similar to SIMM sockets but are longer and often dark in color with plastic clips at each end. DIMM sockets for PCs come in three sizes: 168-pin for SDRAM sticks, 184-pin for DDR1 RAM, and 240-pin for DDR2 RAM sticks. You do not have to install DIMMs in pairs.

RIMM   The *Rambus Inline Memory Module (RIMM)* socket is specifically for use with RDRAM. The motherboard must have the special RIMM sockets and other support for this type of RAM. In spite of having a 64-bit data bus that matches the bus width of most new processors, RIMMs must be installed in pairs of equal capacity and speed because RDRAM has a dual-channel architecture. This means that the specially designed Northbridge alternates between two modules to increase the speed of data retrieval. You cannot leave unused RIMM sockets empty. Any unused socket pairs must have a specially designed pass-through device called a C-RIMM (continuity RIMM). The C-RIMM must be installed into each unused RIMM socket in the same manner in which the RIMM RDRAM is installed.

RIMM sockets look just like DIMM sockets but are keyed so that only RIMM modules can be inserted. They are also proprietary, generally more expensive, and less common than DIMMs. The 184-pin RIMMs with a 16-bit data path and the 232-pin, 32-bit RIMMs are readily available. The newest RIMMS are 64-bit RIMMs with 326-pin connectors.

SIMMs are not listed in the A+ exam objectives, but be sure you understand DIMMs and RIMMs, because they are exam objectives.

Replacing a Motherboard

Because most components attach physically to the motherboard, this can be one of the most time-consuming replacements. If you are replacing one motherboard with another of exactly the same brand and version, you should make notes about any BIOS settings and jumper and switch settings (more on jumpers and switches later) for the old motherboard in case you need to change them on the new board. Once you have done this you are ready for the real work.

on the **job**   *When it comes to replacing a motherboard versus building an entirely new system from scratch, it may be easier to do the latter, because you can buy all the pieces at once from one source and request their help and guarantee that all the components will play nicely together.*

Installing a Motherboard

When installing a motherboard, you should follow the instructions in the motherboard manual. Whether you are installing a new motherboard or replacing one, the motherboard manual is your most important tool. In addition to listing the components supported, the typical motherboard manual includes instructions on installing the motherboard in a case, and installing components, such as the CPU, memory, and power supply. The motherboard manual will explain how to set appropriate switches on the motherboard and how to attach all the various related cables.

EXERCISE 3-1

Removing an Old Motherboard

1. If you haven't done this already, power down and unplug the PC's power cord.
2. Remove all expansion cards and cables from the motherboard.
3. If the drives and/or the drive bays interfere with access to the motherboard, remove them.
4. Remove any screws or fasteners attaching the motherboard to the case, lift the board out of the case, and put it aside. Be sure to carefully save any screws you remove.

The first three steps of Exercise 3-2 describe a recommended procedure for handling a motherboard, which applies to any circuit board. The remainder of Exercise 3-2 includes general steps for installing a motherboard. It assumes that BIOS, CMOS, CMOS battery, and chipset have come preinstalled on the motherboard (as is customary). Always check the instructions packed with the motherboard or other component.

EXERCISE 3-2

Proper Handling and Installation of a Motherboard

1. Before unpacking a new motherboard, ensure that you have grounded your body properly. One method is to wear an antistatic safety wrist strap, as described in Chapter 17.

2. Hold the board by its edges and avoid touching any component on it. Always avoid touching module contacts and IC chips.

3. Place the board on a grounded antistatic mat (described in Chapter 17) or on the antistatic bag that came with the board (unless the instructions recommend against this).

4. Install the CPU and memory on the motherboard, per manufacturers' instructions.

5. Follow the motherboard manual's instructions for setting any switches on the motherboard and pay attention to instructions for how to attach stand-off screws, which keep the motherboard from touching the metal floor or wall of the case. Now you are ready to install the board.

6. To place the new (or replacement) board in the computer, line it up properly on the chassis screw holes, and fix it into place.

7. Attach the power and drive connectors as well as connectors to the correct ports on the case.

Upgrading a CPU

Upgrading a CPU is a major undertaking but may not be impossible if you believe that your processor is the only thing holding back performance on your computer. It all depends on the motherboard. With a little research, you may find that all you need to do is change the speed of the motherboard, since most motherboards support more than one speed for a particular CPU.

If you find that a new CPU is both necessary and possible, be sure to consult the manufacturer's documentation for your motherboard to determine which processor and speeds it supports. In most cases, you will need to configure the board for the new speed or model using a set of jumpers.

Removing a CPU

How you remove an installed CPU depends on the type of socket. Once again, read any manuals available for your motherboard or computer. You may need to consult the manufacturer for more information. If the socket is a zero insertion force (ZIF) socket, follow the instructions in Exercise 3-3. No doubt the processor will have a heat sink and/or fan attached to it. If possible, remove the processor without removing these attachments. However, if they interfere with the mechanism for releasing the processor, you may need to remove them.

on the *Job* *The processor will be very hot when you first turn off a PC. You will lose skin if you touch a hot CPU chip, and it will hurt! Always allow at least five minutes for the chip to cool before you remove it.*

EXERCISE 3-3

Removing a PGA Processor from a ZIF Socket

1. Lift the socket lever. You might have to move it slightly to the side to clear it from a retaining tab.
2. Pull out the processor. Because this is a ZIF socket, there should be no resistance when you remove the CPU.
3. Set the CPU on an antistatic mat or place it in an antistatic bag.

Installing a CPU

Follow the instructions in the manuals for the motherboard and the CPU. To install a processor into a ZIF socket, ensure that you raise the lever, line up the pins, and place the processor in the socket, but do not force it. Make sure the processor properly seats in the socket, and then lower the lever so that the socket grips the CPU pins.

Optimizing a System with RAM

One function of RAM is to provide the processor with faster access to the information it needs. Within limits, the more memory a computer has, the faster it will run. One of the most common and effective computer upgrades is the installation of more RAM.

In addition to main system memory, most PCs can use another type of RAM, called cache memory. The CPU accesses cache memory chips even faster than it does regular RAM, so their presence can help speed up the computer. Generally, the more cache a computer has, the faster it will run. Formerly, L1 cache was located on the processor and L2 cache was on the motherboard. However, most new processors have both Level 1 and Level 2 cache on the board. At this time, a few processors have external cache called L3 that may be on the motherboard. So, depending on the vintage and configuration of the motherboard and CPU, there may be special sockets available for adding more L2 or L3 cache. Again, check the documentation!

Installing and Removing Memory

The installation or removal of memory modules is similar for SIMMs, DIMMs, and RIMMs. The following sections describe the specifics of each type of socket. Before you begin, take steps to protect against static electricity damage to the memory modules and motherboard, as described in Chapter 17.

SIMM Modules

Follow the steps in Exercise 3-4 to install and remove a SIMM module.

EXERCISE 3-4

Installing and Removing a SIMM

1. Line up the SIMM's connector edge with the appropriate-sized slot on the motherboard, keeping the SIMM at a 45-degree angle to the slot.

2. After inserting the SIMM into the slot as far as it will easily go, gently rotate the SIMM upright until it clicks into place. Note that a SIMM will fit in a slot only one way. If you have trouble installing the SIMM, reverse its orientation in the slot.

3. To remove a SIMM, pull outward on the slot's retaining clips. The SIMM should fall to a 45-degree angle. Remove the SIMM.

DIMM and RIMM Modules

The technique for installing DIMM and RIMM modules is identical, as shown in Exercise 3-5. Socket keys for DIMM and RIMM modules are different, however, so even if the number of pins is the same, you will not be able to install one into the socket for the other. As you will see, this technique is slightly different from a SIMM. The biggest difference is that you hold the DIMM or RIMM module upright, and do not position it at an angle for installation.

EXERCISE 3-5

Installing and Removing a DIMM or RIMM Module

1. Align the DIMM or RIMM with the slot, keeping the module upright, so that the notches in the module line up with the tabs in the slot.

2. Gently press down on the DIMM or RIMM. The retention clips on the side should rotate into the locked position. You might need to guide them into place with your fingers.

3. To remove a DIMM or RIMM, press the retention clips outward, as shown in Figure 3-1, which lifts the module slightly, then lift the module straight up.

Configuring and Optimizing a Motherboard

Motherboards commonly have jumpers and switches used to configure components. These often enable or disable a feature. A *switch* is a very tiny slide that indicates two states. If two or more switches are together, they can be used together to represent binary values of settings. A *jumper* is a small connector that slides down on a pair of pins jutting up from a circuit board. There are often multiple pins side by side, and a jumper joins a pair of them.

CMOS Settings

The most common way to optimize a motherboard is to modify the BIOS setup configuration, also called the CMOS settings. Literally, hundreds of settings are available in different computers; we discuss only the most common ones here.

FIGURE 3-1

Removing a
DIMM

The choices available and the methods for selecting them may vary from one BIOS manufacturer to another. The best reference for using the BIOS setup menus is the user manual that came with your PC, or the motherboard manual.

To access the computer's CMOS settings, closely watch the computer screen at startup. Following the POST, a message appears indicating the proper key sequence you should use to enter the CMOS settings program. This key combination varies among computers but is typically F2, DELETE, or CTRL-ALT-ESC. In most systems, the message will appear for only three to five seconds, and you must use the indicated key combination within that allotted time.

Note also that CMOS setting programs differ from each other. Some allow you to use the mouse, and some only the keyboard. Furthermore, the names of the settings might also be slightly different. Use the program's Help feature for information about how to navigate through the program and save or discard your changes. It's a good idea to make notes about the current CMOS settings before you change them, in case you need to change them back. Although this won't work in all computers, you can try the procedure in Exercise 3-6 to print out the CMOS settings.

EXERCISE 3-6

Backing Up the CMOS Settings

1. Restart the computer and watch the screen closely for the correct key or keys to press.

2. Enter the CMOS-setting program using the specified key combination.

3. Do not make any changes to the settings.

4. If there is a printer connected to the PC's parallel port, ensure that the printer is turned on and online. Then simply press the PRINT SCREEN key on the keyboard to print the current screen. On some printers, you may need to press a button on the printer to have each page form feed. Although this will not work in all systems, it can provide you with a handy hard copy of the CMOS settings.

5. Repeat this procedure for all the settings screens.

6. Press the correct key or keys to exit Setup without making any changes. This is often the ESC key.

FIGURE 3-2

The main menu
screen for a
CMOS Setup
utility

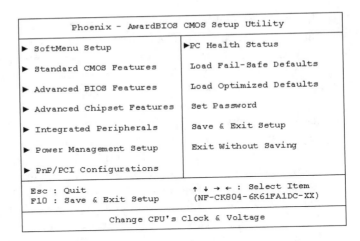

```
                Phoenix - AwardBIOS CMOS Setup Utility

     ▶ SoftMenu Setup            ▶PC Health Status

     ▶ Standard CMOS Features      Load Fail-Safe Defaults

     ▶ Advanced BIOS Features      Load Optimized Defaults

     ▶ Advanced Chipset Features   Set Password

     ▶ Integrated Peripherals      Save & Exit Setup

     ▶ Power Management Setup      Exit Without Saving

     ▶ PnP/PCI Configurations

     Esc : Quit                   ↑ ↓ → ← : Select Item
     F10 : Save & Exit Setup      (NF-CK804-6K61FA1DC-XX)

                  Change CPU's Clock & Voltage
```

If the procedure in Exercise 3-6 does not work on your computer, you can purchase a third-party CMOS backup program, or resort to using pen and paper to write down the settings. You can also use a digital camera to photograph the screens. Figure 3-2 shows a sample BIOS main menu screen.

Parallel Port Settings   You can use the CMOS settings to configure the system's parallel port(s). In newer computers, however, most parallel ports support the IEEE 1284 standard, meaning that the port is bidirectional and the OS can automatically configure it. You may need to change the CMOS settings to set the parallel port mode. For example, many parallel ports run in *unidirectional mode* by default. This means that peripheral devices attached to the port can receive but cannot send data. The CMOS settings might refer to this mode as "Transfer only." However, some parallel devices send communication signals back to the computer. These devices require a *bidirectional mode* (also called Standard mode on some machines).

Newer devices take advantage of faster IEEE 1284 bidirectional modes, called ECP or EPP modes. *Enhanced capability port (ECP) mode* allows access to special features in the PC called DMA channels and is approximately ten times faster than regular bidirectional mode. ECP mode is for printers and scanners. *Enhanced parallel port (EPP) mode* offers the same performance as ECP but is for use with parallel devices other than printers and scanners.

Another CMOS parallel port setting is enable/disable. You can use this feature to instruct the computer to use or ignore the parallel port. Disabling the port temporarily can be useful when troubleshooting, or when the port is in conflict with another component. You might also need to disable the on-board parallel port if it has stopped working. Disabling it will allow you to install an additional (non-integrated) parallel port.

COM/Serial Port   Like the parallel port, you can use the CMOS settings to configure the COM port(s). However, in newer systems, the OS accomplishes this. You can also use the CMOS settings to enable or disable the COM port.

Boot Sequence   The boot sequence CMOS setting relates to the order in which the BIOS will search devices for an OS. The default setting on most computers is A: or Floppy, then C: or Hard Disk, and finally CD/DVD drive. Figure 3-3 shows a CMOS Setup menu in which the boot order is selected as "First Boot Device," "Second Boot Device," and "Third Boot Device." You can change this order so that the computer looks first on the hard drive or CD/DVD and finally, or not at all, on the floppy disk. This is particularly helpful in keeping boot sector viruses from a floppy disk from infecting the computer. For the past several versions, the Windows operating systems have come on bootable CDs, without requiring booting from a floppy disk first, and when installing a new operating system on a brand new computer, it is important that the boot sequence includes the optical drive. If the system already has an OS on it, you will need to ensure that the order places the optical drive before the hard drive.

Floppy Drive   The CMOS settings program contains options for the configuration and use of the floppy drive. You can enable or disable the use of the motherboard's integrated floppy disk controller by selecting the appropriate option.

FIGURE 3-3

Advanced BIOS
Features menu

```
          Phoenix - AwardBIOS CMOS Setup Utility
                  Advanced BIOS Features

    Quick Power on Self Test    Enabled          Item Help
  ▶ Hard Disk Boot Priority     Press Enter
    First Boot Device           Floppy
    Second Boot Device          Hard Disk
    Third Boot Device           CDROM
    Boot Other Device           Disabled
    Boot Up Floppy Seek         Disabled
    Boot Up NumLock Status      On
    Security Option             Setup
    MPS Version Ctrl For OS     1.4
    OS Select For DRAM > 64MB   Non-OS2
    Delay For HDD (Secs)        0
    Full Screen Logo Show       Enabled


  ↑↓:Move Enter:Select +/-/PU/PD:Value F10:Save ESC:Exit F1:General Help
  F5: Previous Values F6: Fail-Safe Defaults F7: Optimized Defaults
```

You might want to disable the controller so that you can use an expansion controller card instead.

You can also configure the floppy drive controller so that a diskette cannot boot the computer. If you don't plan to boot from a floppy, removing the floppy drive from the boot order will speed up the overall boot sequence. If you later find you need to boot from the floppy drive, simply change the CMOS settings accordingly.

Hard Drive Settings   You can use the CMOS settings to set the type and capacity of each hard drive installed in the system. You should set the type to Auto. This setting instructs the BIOS to read the type and capacity from the drive. However, very old systems require that you manually enter the type and capacity (tracks, sectors, and cylinders) of each drive. You can also use the Autodetect feature to force the BIOS to search for and identify all hard drives in the system. Use this option when a second drive is added to the system, or when the hard drive has been upgraded.

Memory   You do not have to configure RAM capacities. Simply install RAM in the computer and the BIOS automatically counts it at startup. However, you can use the CMOS settings to enable or disable the memory's ability to use parity error checking (although you can use this setting only if the RAM supports parity). Warning—if you enable the CMOS parity option but are not using memory that supports parity, the computer will not boot properly.

e x a m

w a t c h   *The BIOS calculates RAM capacity at startup—the CMOS settings do not configure it.*

Date and Time   While it is simpler to change the time and date settings from within Windows (or other operating systems), you can use the CMOS settings program to set the computer's real-time clock. The OS will use the date and time that you set here, as will any applications that are date or time aware.

Passwords   While we do not generally recommend using this feature, most CMOS settings programs allow you to set passwords on the computer. This is separate from a password required by your operating system or network. A user password can be set to allow or restrict the booting of the system. A supervisor password can be set to allow or restrict access to the CMOS settings program itself, or to change user passwords. Some systems (typically newer ones) include both password options; older systems typically include only supervisor-type passwords, required both to boot the system and to enter the CMOS settings program.

You must be especially careful with supervisor passwords. If you forget the CMOS password, you can't even get into the CMOS program to change or disable the password. Fortunately, most systems that have the CMOS password feature include a "clear password" jumper on the motherboard. The user manual or motherboard manual will document this. If you forget the CMOS password, you can open the computer and set the jumper to remove the password. If there is no jumper for clearing the password, you can clear the entire contents of the CMOS by temporarily removing the battery. However, this is a last resort, because it will cause you to lose all but the default settings.

on the job

Unless you have very high security requirements, do not set either type of password in CMOS, because this only creates unnecessary inconvenience to the user and to the person supporting the PC. One situation in which such system-level passwords are commonly set is in a computer lab.

Plug-and-Play BIOS All modern PC BIOSes are Plug and Play, and the CMOS settings program includes some options for configuring it. One option is Plug and Play Operating System. When enabled, this setting informs the BIOS that the OS will configure Plug-and-Play devices. Another Plug-and-Play option allows you to enable or disable the BIOS configuration of Plug-and-Play devices.

Replacing or Upgrading BIOS

The function of the BIOS is to translate communications between devices in the computer. The BIOS is able to do this because it contains the basic instruction set for those device types. This is required only for certain system devices, such as hard disk drives, floppy disk drives, memory, I/O ports, etc.

When to Upgrade the BIOS

If you install a device with which the computer seems unable to communicate, you might need to upgrade or replace the existing BIOS. It is important to understand that this is not necessary for a new device, but for an entirely new device type, and that it requires communications with the computer at a low level even before operating system–level drivers are installed. You do not need to upgrade the BIOS to use a new mouse or printer.

We think of hard drives as being a single type, but to the BIOS, there are many types of hard drives, and the size of the hard drive makes a difference to the BIOS.

Consider a scenario in which you install a new many-gigabyte hard drive that the system will not recognize, and it won't allow you to manually enter or select that size in CMOS setup. In this case, you must upgrade the BIOS.

You will also want to upgrade to a BIOS version that is appropriate to the operating system you are installing.

Upgrading the BIOS

Most computer BIOSes today are actually Flash BIOS chips that can be electronically upgraded using software from the BIOS manufacturer. The most common way to add support for a new device type is by "flashing" the BIOS. You will need to contact the manufacturer of your computer or of the BIOS to obtain the program and instructions for doing this.

In general, you turn the computer off, insert the manufacturer's floppy disk, and restart the computer. The disk contains a program that automatically "flashes" (updates) the BIOS so that it can recognize different hardware types or perform different functions than it could before.

on the **Job**   *The months before the year 2000 were a busy time for replacing and upgrading BIOS chips. Many BIOSes could not recognize any year later than 1999 and would have interpreted 2000 as 1900. This problem, called the Y2K bug, meant that these BIOSes had to have their basic instruction set flashed so that it included recognition of the year 2000 and later. In some computers, the manufacturer no longer supported the BIOS, so it couldn't be flashed. Instead, people had to replace these chips physically.*

Adding, Configuring, and Removing Power Supplies

When building a new computer, a power supply usually comes with the computer case. However, power supplies in existing computers do fail from time to time, and you can replace them using the procedure outlined in Exercise 3-7.

Selecting a Power Supply

When replacing a power supply, be sure to use one that is of sufficient wattage, is of the correct form factor, and that has the appropriate power connectors for the motherboard. Do not just check out the number of pins required for the connectors, but the actual pin-outs required. A pin-out is a diagram of the purpose of each wire in a connector.

The ATX (P1) power supply connector for older ATX motherboards is a 1-piece, 20-pin keyed connector. The biggest confusion at this time is between various 24-pin power supply connectors. Many motherboards for recent multicore Pentium 4 and Athlon 64 processor models require two connectors, often described as ATX12V 2.0. These connectors include a 24-pin main connector and a 4-pin secondary connector. However, some newer motherboards require EPS12V connectors, which include a 24-pin main connector, an 8-pin secondary connector, and an optional 4-pin tertiary connector.

Removing a Power Supply/Installing a Power Supply

Recall that power supplies can still hold a charge when turned off, especially if you have used only the soft-power switch. Before removing even a failed power supply, be sure to unplug it from the wall outlet. To avoid the danger of electric shock, do not wear an antistatic wristband while working with power supplies. Exercise 3-7 provides basic steps for removing an old power supply and installing a new power supply.

EXERCISE 3-7

Replacing a Power Supply

1. Turn off the power and remove the power connector from the wall socket.
2. Remove the power connector(s) from the motherboard, grasping the plastic connector, not the wires.
3. Remove the power connectors from all other components, including hard, floppy, and CD-ROM drives.
4. Using an appropriately sized screwdriver, remove the screws that hold the power supply to the PC case. Do not remove the screws holding the power supply case together!
5. Slide or lift the power supply away from the computer.
6. Reverse these steps to install a new power supply.

Adding, Configuring, and Removing Cooling Systems

As a rule, the typical PC comes with a cooling system adequate for the standard components delivered with the PC. Once you start adding hard drives, memory, and additional expansion cards, you should give some thought to supplementing the existing cooling system. How far you go with this depends on just how much you have added to the PC.

An overheated computer will slow down, thanks to new built-in technology that senses the temperature of the motherboard and slows down the processor when the temperature exceeds a certain limit. This reduces the heat the processor puts out. In the extreme, overheating can damage PC components. The other side of this is that modern cooling systems also use heat sensors and will adjust their performance to keep the system cool. New power supply and case fans will change speed to match the temperature. In most PCs, if the power supply fails, the PC will not boot up at all.

Common Sense First

Before you consider spending money on a new cooling system, make sure that you are not impairing the installed cooling systems. Begin by ensuring that the PC case is closed during operation, that all slot covers are in place, and that airflow around the case is not obstructed by being installed in an unventilated space. Also, check to see if ribbon cables are interrupting the flow of air inside the case. Use plastic ties to secure cables out of the way. Correct these problems before spending money supplementing the cooling system.

Additionally, open the case and give the interior of the PC a good vacuuming before you spend money on upgrading the cooling system. Excessive dust and dirt on components will act as an insulator keeping the heat from dissipating and causing a computer to overheat, which in turn can cause it to slow down, stop operating, or permanently damage it. Learn more about vacuuming a PC in Chapter 4.

Selecting an Appropriate Cooling System

When should you consider upgrading the cooling system in your PC? If you are using the PC only for office applications, and you have added several heat-generating components, such as hard drives or adapter cards, then you should consider upgrading the cooling system. If your PC at home or at work needs to operate in an extreme environment, such as in an un-air-conditioned garage, you should do all you can to increase the cooling capabilities of the PC. If you are a computer gamer with a highly customized PC, you have no doubt put a great deal of thought into the cooling system. If not, shame on you.

Case Fan

New PCs often come with both a power supply fan and a separate case fan. Perhaps you can simply upgrade the present case fan. Also, check to see if the PC has an empty bay or bracket for a case fan. A case fan is a very inexpensive upgrade, cheaper than a latte and muffin at your favorite coffee shop. The only requirement is a bracket or bay in the case that will accommodate a case fan, and the appropriate power connector.

When shopping for a case fan, you will need the dimensions of the fan bay (usually stated in millimeters), rated voltage, and power input. Features to compare are fan speed in revolutions per minute (RPM), airflow in cubic feet per minute (CFM), and noise level in decibels (dbA). The fan speed and airflow reflect the fan's effectiveness for cooling. The noise level is an important consideration, because fans and drives are the only moving parts in a PC and generate the most noise. Look for fans with a noise decibel rating in the twenties or below. Additionally, check out the power connector on new case fans. Many come with a Molex connector that can connect directly to the power supply, and some have a special connector that must connect directly to the motherboard. Figure 3-4 shows a 100 mm–wide case fan with a Molex connector.

CPU Fan/Heat Sink

If you are installing a CPU, then you will also need to install a cooling system for the CPU. Today's processors often require a fan/heat sink combination. Often, the cooling system and the CPU are packaged together, making the choice for you. Pay attention to the power connector for the fan, and locate the socket for this connector

FIGURE 3-4

A case fan

on the motherboard ahead of time. It is unlikely that you will replace an existing CPU fan and/or heat sink, unless the CPU fan has failed. Even then, considering the complexity of it, and the danger of damaging the CPU, it may be easier to replace the entire CPU if the same or similar model is available.

Liquid Cooling Systems

The most difficult and the most expensive cooling system upgrade is a liquid cooling system. These come built-in on many high-end motherboards aimed at the gamer market. A search of gamer sites on the Internet will turn up after-market cooling systems. At this point, this type of cooling system is not something you can expect to run into in PCs used for business applications.

Installing and Configuring a Cooling System

When installing a new cooling system, be sure to read the documentation for the new components as well as for the motherboard, if appropriate. Assemble the components required and follow good practices for avoiding damage to the computer or injuring yourself. Turn the computer's power off, disconnect the power cord, and ensure that you follow the electrostatic discharge (ESD) procedures discussed in Chapter 17.

When installing a new case fan, affix the fan to the case in the appropriate bracket or bay, using the screws that came with the case or the fan itself. Connect the power connector and any required motherboard connectors.

When installing a heat sink and/or fan on a CPU, be sure to apply thermal compound according to the instructions, and carefully connect the heat sink or fan using the clip provided. Plug the fan into the appropriate power socket on the motherboard.

Removing a Cooling System

If a cooling system fails or is inadequate, you will need to remove it from the PC. In that case, turn the computer's power off and ensure that you follow the electrostatic discharge (ESD) procedures. Then reverse the steps for installing the component, unplugging power and motherboard connectors, unscrewing mounting screws, and lifting it out of the case.

SCENARIO & SOLUTION

I would like to build a PC. Is it best to shop for the best price on each component (motherboard, CPU, memory, etc.) from several sources?	No. The best strategy, especially if you are new to this, is to buy all the components from one source and get a guarantee that they will work together.
I read that I might have to upgrade my BIOS before installing the next Windows operating system? Does this mean I have to replace the physical BIOS chip?	You probably will not have to do something this drastic. Most BIOSes today are actually flash BIOS chips that can be electronically upgraded using software from the BIOS manufacturer.
The PC I want to build will be used mostly for running standard office productivity software. Should I consider a water-cooled system?	Generally, a water-cooled system would be overkill in a PC running standard office productivity software.

Adding, Configuring, and Removing Storage Devices

Replacing storage devices is a common task because drives with their moving parts are one of the most common areas of computer failure. Adding more storage is also a common upgrade. Fortunately, since most drives are standardized, they can be recognized by any PC and don't need special configuration.

Optimizing a PC with Storage Devices

Adding more storage to a PC is often a necessity when the user plans to store large amounts of data files, especially graphic files. As more and more people acquire digital cameras, their space needs for storing photo collections increases. The general choices include internal and external storage.

Selecting an Appropriate Internal Storage Device

Internal drives are less expensive than external drives but require more skill to install. The internal hard drives you are most likely to install in a PC are EIDE drives. These will connect to PATA or SATA drive interfaces on the motherboard. If you are adding an optical drive, it will most likely use the ATAPI standard to connect to the PATA interface.

The computer's BIOS will usually recognize these drives. In the simplest cases, all one needs to do to make a hard drive or a CD-ROM drive functional is to physically install it in the computer. However, there are a few configuration issues with drives on the PATA interface, as opposed to those on the SATA interface. When you have a choice, you should choose SATA drives over PATA drives because of these configuration issues with PATA, and the other advantages of SATA, such as higher speeds, thinner cables, and support for hot swapping drives. The drives physically have the same appearance until you look at the back of the drives and see the new connectors for power and data.

The following sections describe alternative drive installations, including how to configure and install multiple drives in a single system.

Installing Drives on PATA Channels

The typical PC motherboard has two PATA hard drive controller channels. That is, the motherboard has connectors for two ribbon cables. Each PATA channel supports two drives. Therefore, you can install four drives, in total, on the standard two PATA channels. One of the motherboard connectors is the primary connector, and the other is the secondary connector. Unfortunately, manufacturers use several conventions for labeling them on the motherboard, such as Primary and Secondary (see Figure 3-5), IDE1 and IDE2, or EIDE1 and EIDE2. If there is only one drive present, it must connect to the primary channel.

Configuring and Installing Drives on a PATA Channel

The on-board drive controller for an EIDE hard drive receives commands to the drive and controls the action of the drive itself. The technology incorporated in EIDE and ATA devices allows one controller to take over the function of an additional drive.

FIGURE 3-5

The primary and secondary PATA controller connectors on the motherboard

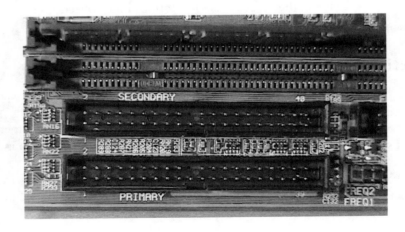

The controlling drive is the *master drive*, while the second drive it controls is the *slave drive*. PATA channels support one master and one slave drive on each channel.

If only one drive is present on a channel, it must be a master drive. The master drive on the first channel is the primary master. The slave drive on the first channel is the primary slave. Similarly, the master drive on the second channel is the secondary master, and the slave drive on the second channel is the secondary slave.

In most cases, a slave drive will work only if a master drive is present. A master can function without a slave drive present. Before you install an EIDE drive on a PATA channel, you will need to configure it for its master or slave role. Do this by setting jumpers on the back of the drive. Most EIDE drives have a label that shows the master and slave jumper settings. Figure 3-6 shows a drive with two white jumpers over two pairs of pins. This position, according to the drive's label, indicates that it is the master drive. Moving these two jumpers to the two right-most pairs of pins would configure the drive for the slave role.

In many cases, it doesn't matter which is which. That is, there is no real performance difference between master and slave drives. However, as with most computer configurations, there are some exceptions. When using a mixture of old and new hard drives within the same system, set the newer drive as the master and the older drive as the slave. This setting is a good idea because newer drives can recognize and communicate with older drives, but the reverse isn't true. An older drive's controller will typically be unable to control the newer drive.

It is important to note here that PATA channels can support a mixture of EIDE and ATAPI (optical) drives. How do you determine which drive should be the master and which should be the slave?

FIGURE 3-6

The back of an EIDE drive, showing two white jumpers over two pairs of pins

When using a hard drive and CD-ROM drive together in a master/slave configuration, always set the hard drive as the master and the CD-ROM as the slave because the CD-ROM's controller is unable to take control of the hard drive. Additionally, some (but not most) older *optical* drives work only as slaves, and you simply cannot configure them as master drives. To create a master/slave configuration, follow the steps in Exercise 3-8.

PATA uses flat ribbon cables or (rarely) round cables. There are two important differences between the flat ribbon and the round cables—price and cooling. The round cables are currently more expensive, but they are superior to the 2" wide flat cables in that they allow better airflow. Both types of PATA cables normally come with three 40-pin connectors—one on either end and one in the middle. One end connects to the PATA channel connector on the motherboard, while the other two connectors plug into the drives. If the system has only one hard drive, attach it to the end of the ribbon cable. The red stripe along the length of the cable represents pin 1. Make sure that this stripe aligns with pin 1, as indicated on both the hard drive and on the channel connector on the motherboard.

Early PATA cables had just 40 wires, but newer cables have 80 wires, although they still have the same 40-pin connectors. The extra wires ensure better signal quality through grounding that shields against interference.

Some drives have a jumper setting called *cable select*. If this setting is used, the position of the drive on the cable will automatically determine the drive's role. If the drive is on the end of the cable, it is the master drive, and if it is on the middle of the cable, it is the slave drive.

EXERCISE 3-8

Choosing a Master

1. Determine which drive will be the master.
2. Locate the master/slave jumper pins and jumpers.
3. Use the information on the drive label to determine which jumper settings to use for a master or slave (or cable select) configuration.
4. Use the jumper(s) to set this drive as a master (or cable select).
5. Secure the drive to an available drive bay.
6. Align the red stripe on the cable with pin 1 on the primary channel connector of the motherboard; attach the cable. Then attach the connector on the far

end of the cable to the master drive, also ensuring that the red stripe on the cable aligns with pin 1 on the drive.

7. Locate an available Molex connector at the end of a cable coming from the power supply, and connect it to the drive.

8. To install a second drive on the same channel, follow the instructions in the previous steps, but set the drive's jumpers to the slave setting. Figure 3-7 shows the completed installation of two drives on one channel. Notice that both drives connect to the same ribbon cable.

Optical Drives

The physical installation and removal of an internal CD-ROM or DVD drive is the same as that for hard and floppy drives except that it must be installed into a bay with a front panel that allows access to the drive for inserting and removing discs. The optical drive also requires the connection of a sound cable to the sound card.

Additionally, a DVD drive may need to connect to a decoder card using separate cables. Normally, the BIOS will automatically recognize the CD or DVD drive. Or it may be necessary to enable the device in the BIOS settings. If the computer doesn't recognize or can't communicate with the new drive, you need to load a driver for it. Learn about installing device drivers in Chapter 8.

on the
Ĵob

You can usually install hard drives and other devices on their sides with no impact on operation or performance. Never install a hard drive upside down.

FIGURE 3-7

The finished installation of two hard drives on the same PATA channel

Installing Drives on SATA Channels

Each SATA device has its own dedicated channel and does not require the setting of jumpers as is required for devices on a PATA channel. Simply connect one end of the SATA data cable to a SATA channel and connect the other end to the drive's data connector. Additionally, SATA devices may come with two power connectors on the drive. If so, one accepts a standard 4-pin Molex connector from the power supply, while the other accepts a special 15-pin SATA power connector. This is an "either-or" situation. Only connect to one of these power connectors. If both are used the drive will be damaged. Exercise 3-9 provides general instructions for installing a SATA drive. Be sure to follow the instructions in the manual for your motherboard and drive before installing a SATA drive. Figure 3-8 shows a SATA data cable alongside a SATA power cable.

EXERCISE 3-9

Installing a SATA Drive

1. Secure the drive to an available drive bay.
2. Locate an available SATA connector on the motherboard or on a SATA expansion card. Plug in one end of the SATA cable (it is keyed so that it cannot be installed incorrectly).
3. Locate an available power connector at the end of a cable coming from the power supply, and connect it to the drive. Figure 3-9 shows an installed SATA drive connected to a SATA channel on the motherboard. Notice the three open SATA channels.

FIGURE 3-8

A SATA data cable connector (left) next to a SATA power connector

FIGURE 3-9

Installed SATA
drive (top)
connected to
SATA channel
on motherboard
(bottom left)

Internal Floppy Disk Drives

Floppy drives have gone from being a necessity in the early IBM PC to being considered as useless as a rotary-dial phone. For this reason, you will rarely see a floppy drive in a new PC. Due to space limitations, they vanished from most laptops years ago.

Installing an Internal Floppy Disk Drive

Most modern motherboards still have an integrated floppy drive controller. Therefore, if you desire to add an internally installed floppy drive to a new computer, you just need to obtain a floppy drive and the cabling. Before installing the drive, be sure to turn off the PC and disconnect the power cord.

Internally mounted floppy drives are installed in a fashion similar to hard drives, with one major difference—the floppy drive must be installed into a bay with a front panel that allows access to the drive for inserting and removing floppy disks. Most PC cases still come with this bay. Locate the bay, slide the drive into the drive bay, and fasten it with the retaining screws.

A floppy drive uses a flat ribbon cable that measures $1\frac{5}{8}$ inches wide with 34-pin connectors on both ends. This cable is keyed to only insert one way, with the red edge lined up with pin 1 of the floppy connector on the motherboard, and similarly lined up with pin 1 on the drive connector. Attach the floppy drive to the end of the ribbon cable; this drive will be assigned drive letter A.

As it is highly unlikely that you will need to install even one floppy drive into a computer, it is even less likely that you will install a second one. However, in that very unlikely situation, you would need a 34-pin ribbon cable with three connectors. In that case, the floppy drive connected to the middle connector is assigned the drive letter B.

Once the drive is in place and the ribbon cable is connected, locate a power cable coming from the power supply that has a plug that fits the floppy drive. This is usually a 4-pin miniconnector.

Removing a Floppy Disk Drive

To remove a floppy drive, disconnect the power and ribbon cables, unfasten the retaining screws, and then slide the drive out of the bay.

The red stripe on a ribbon cable indicates pin 1.

Installing and Configuring SCSI Devices

SCSI systems allow you to attach more devices to the computer than the common EIDE/PATA systems do, but less than USB or IEEE 1394. By installing a SCSI host adapter, you can attach 7, 15, or 31 additional devices in the computer, depending on the type of SCSI host adapter you are using. SCSI systems are typically much faster than non-SCSI systems. However, SCSI systems have the disadvantage of being more expensive than EIDE systems and more difficult to configure. In most cases, people use SCSI systems when speed or the ability to support a large number of devices is a priority. Additionally, like SATA, modern SCSI systems support hot swapping. When cost and ease of use are factors, EIDE systems are generally preferred.

Other devices attach to the controller in a daisy-chain configuration, described in Chapter 2. Each external SCSI device has two ports: one port receives the cable from the device before it in the chain, and one port attaches the next device in the chain. An internal SCSI device may have only one port that requires a special cable for daisy-chaining other internal devices.

Types of SCSI Systems

Like many other computer standards, SCSI systems have evolved and improved over time. Newer SCSI standards are backward compatible with older standards, so older devices are installable in newer systems.

The T10 SCSI committee of the *InterNational Committee on Information Technology Standards (INCITS)* frequently upgrades the SCSI standard. INCITS (pronounced "insights") is in turn accredited by ANSI. Information on the current standards and revisions of SCSI are available at www.t10.org. The following sections briefly describe these standards, and Table 3-1 summarizes their characteristics.

SCSI-1 The first SCSI standard named simply SCSI was released in 1986, and its name only changed to *SCSI-1* when the SCSI-2 standard was released. SCSI-1 has an 8-bit bus, meaning it can support up to eight devices, including the controller. It supports speeds up to 5 MBps, using a data transfer method called single-ended (SE) transfer, which uses one wire to transmit each data signal.

Without standardized device commands, many early SCSI-1 devices were not compatible with each other. The maximum length of the entire SCSI-1 chain was

TABLE 3-1	SCSI Variants and Their Characteristics			
Type	**Variant**	**Bus Width (bits)**	**Max Throughput (MBps)**	**Data Transfer Method(s)**
SCSI-1	n/a	8	5	SE
SCSI-2	n/a	8	5	SE or HVD
SCSI-2	Fast SCSI-2	8	10	SE or HVD
SCSI-2	Wide SCSI-2	16	10	SE or HVD
SCSI-2	Fast Wide SCSI-2	16	20	SE or HVD
SCSI-2	Double Wide SCSI-2	32	40	SE or HVD
SCSI-3	Ultra SCSI-3 (Fast-20)	8	20	SE or HVD
SCSI-3	Wide Ultra SCSI-3	16	40	SE or HVD
SCSI-3	Ultra-2 SCSI (Fast-40)	8	40	HVD or LVD
SCSI-3	Wide Ultra-2 SCSI	16	80	HVD or LVD
SCSI-3	Ultra-3 (Fast 80 or Ultra 160)	16	160	LVD
SCSI-3	Ultra320	16	320	LVD

only 6 meters, and if this length was exceeded, signal interference would cause devices to malfunction.

SCSI-2 The *SCSI-2* standard, released in 1994, includes a standardized device command set and support for more devices. Other improvements included sophisticated device termination (termination is described later), and the ability to send more than one command to a single device at once.

SCSI-2 supports the old SE data transfer method, as well as *high-voltage differential (HVD)* data transfer. Using HVD, a SCSI-2 device sends each data signal over a pair of wires in a manner that resists interference. This allows SCSI-2 systems to support much greater cable lengths. SCSI-2 systems can use either SE or HVD, but the two data transfer methods cannot exist on the same SCSI system (the host adapter and all the devices connected through the SCSI chain), because you risk damaging the SE device. Luckily, HVD SCSI devices were used only on high-end server computers, so you may never run into this problem.

on the **❶**ob *The cables and connectors for SE look just like those for HVD. Therefore, if you find yourself working with SCSI devices, double-check the documentation so that you do not mistakenly put SE and HVD devices on the same chain and risk damaging the SE device.*

There are five variants of SCSI-2: SCSI-2, *Fast SCSI-2*, *Wide SCSI-2*, *Fast Wide SCSI-2*, and *Double Wide SCSI-2*. The main differences between these types are their bus widths and transmission speeds, summarized in Table 3-1. SCSI-2 supports cable lengths up to 6 meters. Fast SCSI-2 has a maximum cable length of 3 meters for SE and 25 meters for HVD. Both Wide and Fast Wide SCSI-2 can support up to 16 devices, including the controller, and have a maximum cable length of 3 meters for SE and 25 meters for HVD.

The final variant, Double Wide SCSI-2, is essentially two Fast Wide systems in one. It supports a 32-bit bus and speeds up to 40 MBps. However, this variant is rarely used, and it is excluded from subsequent SCSI standards.

SCSI-3 *SCSI-3* became a standard in 1996, and it has undergone many revisions and changes. SCSI-3 is really a series of smaller standards rolled up into a single set of standards. There are currently a number of SCSI-3 variants. *Ultra SCSI*, also called *Fast-20*, is an 8-bit system that can support speeds up to 20 MBps. The Ultra SCSI system's bus width can be doubled to 16 bits (*Wide Ultra SCSI*), resulting in a total throughput of 40 MBps. Like SCSI-2, Ultra SCSI can use either SE or HVD technology. Ultra SCSI supports a maximum cable length of 3 meters if four or fewer devices are attached, and 1.5 meters if more than four devices are attached.

Ultra-2 SCSI, also called *Fast-40*, provides a 40 MBps data throughput on an 8-bit system and 80 MBps on a 16-bit system (*Wide Ultra-2 SCSI*). Ultra-2 marks the first use of the *low-voltage differential (LVD)* data transfer method and the removal of support for the SE transfer method. Components that use LVD technology require less power to operate and can operate at higher speeds. LVD also allows Ultra-2 SCSI systems to support cable lengths up to 12 meters.

Ultra-3 SCSI, also referred to as *Fast-80* or *Ultra160*, is available only as a 16-bit system and supports data throughput of 160 MBps. Ultra-3 SCSI systems support LVD technology only and are the first to support up to 32 devices. Their maximum cable length is 12 meters. Ultra320 SCSI is a 16-bit system that supports speeds up to 320 MBps.

Configuring SCSI

Configuring the SCSI host adapter and each device on a SCSI chain requires paying attention to a special address for each called a *SCSI ID*. In addition, each SCSI chain must physically terminate, or the entire chain will not function. The following describes the proper procedures for addressing and terminating SCSI devices so that conflicts do not occur.

Addressing SCSI Devices   You must allocate a special address called a SCSI ID to each SCSI device in a chain. All communications between the computer and a SCSI device go through, and are managed by, the SCSI controller. You must configure each device in a SCSI system so that it can communicate with the controller but not interfere with other SCSI devices in the system. If two devices share an ID, an address conflict will occur. The controller will not be able to distinguish the conflicting devices, and it is likely that neither device will work.

Although computers can support more than one SCSI system, no two devices in a *single* SCSI chain can have the same SCSI ID address. Some SCSI devices are hard-wired to use one of only two or three IDs; others might use any available ID. If the device supports Plug and Play, the system will automatically assign it an available ID address. Other devices require manual address configuration. On some devices, this configuration is via jumpers on the device. An ID address is assigned to other devices electronically using a setup program on the device's ROM chip.

Some SCSI devices that require address assignment through jumpers will indicate, by a label on the device, which setting to use.

Proper addressing can prove challenging, so it is best to work out an addressing "plan of action" before implementing addresses. For example, suppose a SCSI system will include a printer that must use ID 2, a scanner that can use either ID 2 or 4, and a modem that can use ID 4 or 5. Without knowing the address requirement of the printer, the scanner could be configured to use ID 2 and the modem to use ID 4. When it comes time to install the printer, you'll have to reconfigure the ID addresses of all other components.

The priority of ID addresses is also important. In 8-bit SCSI systems, addresses range from 0 to 7. Higher ID addresses have a higher priority on the chain. Because the SCSI controller is such an important part of the system, it usually has ID 7 assigned.

For 16-bit and 32-bit systems, the priority of ID addresses is a bit more complex. In short, addresses increase in priority within each octet, and each successive octet has a lower overall priority than the one before it (see Figure 3-10). That is, IDs 8–15 have a lower priority than 0–7. In a 16-bit system, the order of priority, from lowest to highest, is 8, 9, 10. . .15, 0, 1, 2. . .7. Using the same principles for a 32-bit system, 7 has the highest priority, and 24 has the lowest.

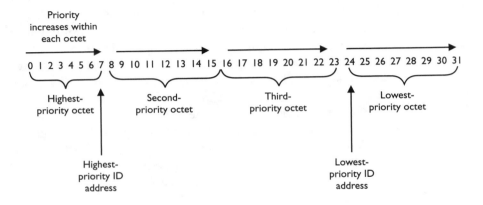

FIGURE 3-10

SCSI ID priorities

If two SCSI devices try to send data at the same time, permission to transmit will go to the device with the highest-priority ID, and the other device will be made to wait. Incidentally, "at the same time" means within 0.24 microseconds!

SCSI System Termination   Equally important is the proper termination of the SCSI system. Improper termination can result in the total or intermittent failure of all devices in the SCSI chain. Signals to a device at the end of the chain must pass through all the devices in between. Because of this unique setup, special terminators, or *terminating resistors*, must be present to ensure that signals at the end of the chain are absorbed rather than bounced back along the chain. In some cases, the resistor fits into the unused second port on the last SCSI device in the chain. In other cases, the SCSI device will include an on-board terminator, made active by using the appropriate jumper setting.

Whether the SCSI chain is strictly internal or strictly external, the last device and the controller must have terminators. Finally, if the SCSI chain is a mixture of both internal and external devices (which is not recommended), both the last external and last internal devices on the chain are terminated.

on the
Job

Many SCSI controllers include internal and external connectors for devices. We recommend that a single SCSI controller not use both the internal and external connections. This may allow more devices to be connected, but it may cause performance issues with the controller. SCSI controllers seem to work most efficiently when seven or fewer devices are connected.

SCSI Cabling

SCSI systems employ a variety of cable types. The specific cable type depends on the SCSI type, the device type, and whether the device is internal or external. Furthermore, each cable type might have a different connector. Until recently, SCSI systems all used a parallel interface to the computer. We will describe those first, and then we will describe the connectors for Serial Attached SCSI (SAS).

8-Bit Systems   All 8-bit SCSI systems use 50-pin cables, called *A-cables*. Internal A-cables are 50-pin ribbon cables, which resemble IDE hard drive ribbon cables (Figure 3-11). External A-cables have either 50-pin Centronics connectors (for 5 MBps systems) or 50-pin high-density connectors (for greater-than-10 MBps systems). Figure 3-12 shows three different A-cable connector types.

FIGURE 3-11

An internal
SCSI A-cable
connector

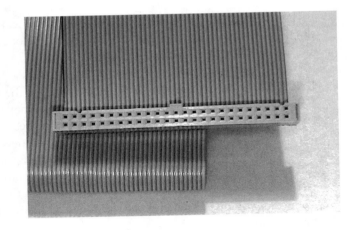

FIGURE 3-12

Internal and
external A-cable
connectors

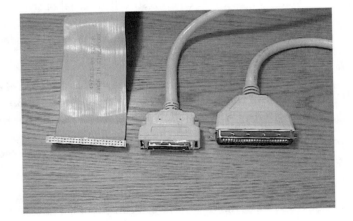

16-Bit Systems   All 16-bit systems use 68-pin cables, also known as *P-cables*. Before the introduction of the P-cable, 16-bit systems used an A-cable/B-cable combination. Internal P-cables are ribbon cables with 68-pin connections, and external P-cables have a 68-pin high-density connector.

32-Bit Systems   Although new SCSI specifications no longer support 32-bit systems, you might be required to work on an older one. All 32-bit systems use a 68-pin P-cable and a 68-pin Q-cable or one 110-pin L-cable.

e x a m
w a t c h

An even larger variety of SCSI cable and connector types are available than are discussed here. The list of possible combinations is beyond the scope of this book. The information that you should know for the A+ exam is the following: 8-bit systems use 50-pin cable, 16-bit systems use 68-pin cables, and 32-bit systems use 110-pin cables. Internal cables (for any numbers of pins) have the same type of connector as hard drive ribbon cables. External cables (for any numbers of pins) are typically Centronics connectors in older systems and high-density connectors in newer systems.

Serial Attached SCSI   Serial Attached SCSI (SAS) targets the server market, not the desktop PC market. However, like many such technologies, it will probably filter down to the desktop, but it will take time before this happens. Currently, although most new PCs have SATA connectors built in, before a SAS device can be added to a PC, a special SAS host adapter card must be installed.

Connecting an External SCSI Device

Exercise 3-10 contains the basic steps that you must perform whenever you install an external SCSI device. Read the documentation for each device carefully before connecting a device, because you perform some steps described here differently, or skip them altogether, for some devices.

EXERCISE 3-10

Installing External SCSI Devices

1. *Attach the device to the chain.* If the new device will be the last in the chain, use its cable to attach it to the device that is currently last in the chain. If the device will be between two existing devices, disconnect them from each other and attach them both to the new device.

2. *Terminate the SCSI chain.* Perform this step only if the new device is at the end of the chain. If the device has an on-board terminator, select the proper jumper setting to enable. If not, place a terminator plug in the unused port on the device.

3. *Set the SCSI ID.* If this is a Plug-and-Play device, the ID assignment is automatic. Simply restart the computer and skip the remaining steps. If you must configure the ID manually and/or electronically, restart the computer and run the device's Setup program (this will also load the driver, so you can skip the next step). To set the ID manually using a jumper, consult the manufacturer's documentation and make the proper jumper setting.

4. *Load the device's driver.* Restart the computer and insert the floppy disk or CD that came with the device. Run the Setup or Install program.

Removing an Internal Storage Device

To remove an internal storage device of any type, check the documentation for the device. Exercise 3-11 provides general steps that will work for all types of internal storage devices.

EXERCISE 3-11

Removing a Drive

1. Remove the power supply and ribbon cables from the back of the drive. Ensure that you grasp the plastic connector, not the wires themselves. If the connector doesn't come out easily, try gently rocking it lengthwise from side to side (never up and down) while you pull it out.

2. Remove the restraining screws that attach the drive to the drive bay. These are usually located on the sides of the drive. Be sure to carefully save any screws you remove.

3. Slide the drive out of the computer.

Installing and Removing an External Storage Device

External storage devices come in many types and sizes. That was not true ten years ago, when external storage was limited to optical drives or conventional hard drives using SCSI or parallel interfaces. These drives were expensive and cumbersome. The SCSI drives came with all the complexity of configuring SCSI devices and required a SCSI bus adapter. Some of the drives also required special drivers.

SCENARIO & SOLUTION

I want to attach ten SCSI devices to my computer. Which type of SCSI should I use?	You need to use a type that supports at least a 16-bit bus. These include any of the Wide SCSI or the Ultra-3 SCSI-3 types. From a performance perspective, you may want to add a second SCSI controller.
I added a SCSI scanner to the middle of my SCSI chain. Should I terminate it?	Do not terminate it. Only terminate devices at the end of each chain.
Which ID should I assign to the SCSI controller?	Assign the SCSI controller the ID with the highest priority. This is ID 7, regardless of how many IDs your SCSI system supports.
I added another device to the end of the SCSI chain, and now none of the devices works. What's wrong?	The new device might have an ID conflict with another device. However, because none of the other devices is working, there are two other likely causes: the new device was not terminated properly, or it causes the chain to exceed the maximum cable length.

Today, the market is practically flooded with inexpensive external storage devices of all types and sizes. In addition, back then, external optical drives were popular because they did not come standard in PCs, and especially not in laptops. Today, with one or two optical drives standard in new PCs, the demand for external optical drives is down, but the need for external hard drives and solid-state drives has grown, and so have the choices.

Most flash memory drives come with a USB interface, and external hard drives have USB and/or IEEE 1394 interfaces. Traditional hard disk drives also come in a full range of sizes from the low gigabytes to several hundred gigabytes. The tiny 2" format drives, like the thumb drives, do not need power supplies; they will draw their power from the USB interface. The more conventionally sized drives require their own power supplies and will need to be plugged into the wall outlet. Besides that one issue, all of these drives are so simple to use that they hardly need instructions. Plug one in and your Windows OS (unless it is very old) will recognize the drive, assign it a drive letter, and include it in the drive list in My Computer. You can browse the contents of the drive and manage data on the drive using the Windows Interface.

You do need to take care when removing a USB or IEEE-1394-connected hard drive. I know many people who simply unplug their thumb drive when they finish with it, but they risk losing their data or damaging the thumb drive. There is an important step you should take in Windows before the drive is disconnected: click on the Safely Remove Hardware icon in the tray area of the taskbar and select the external storage device from the list that pops up. This will notify the operating system that the device is about to be removed so the operating system "stops" the device. If there are open files, Windows may issue a message that the device cannot be stopped. Wait until the status message declares that it is safe to remove the device (Windows will turn off the LED on a thumb drive), and then unplug it from the USB or IEEE 1394 port.

Preparing a Hard Disk for Use

Fresh from the factory a hard disk comes with its disk space divided into concentric tracks, each of which is divided into equal-sized 512-byte sectors. This is the physical format of the disk. The first physical sector on a hard disk is the master boot record (MBR). Within this sector lies a 64-byte partition table, which defines special boundaries on the hard disk, called *partitions*.

The first step in preparing a hard disk for use is to create one or more partitions, the areas of a disk that contain logical drives. The second step is to format the drive. Many hard drives, especially external hard drives, come prepartitioned and preformatted.

Partitioning a Hard Disk Drive

Most operating systems include the partitioning step in a menu-driven process of the installation program, so that anyone who can answer a few simple questions can at least succeed in creating a partition on which to install the OS. In addition, each operating system, such as Windows XP and Windows Vista, comes with a partitioning program you can use after installing the operating system on a PC. This program allows you to partition any additional drives you add to the computer. Figure 3-13 shows the Windows XP Disk Management program, a part of the Computer Management console. A newly installed hard drive shows as Disk 1. The OS recognized it but has not yet partitioned it. Therefore, the space is shown as "unallocated." Right-clicking on the rectangle representing the hard drive space brings up a menu with the option to create a new partition.

Formatting a Hard Disk Drive

You can format each partition with the logical structure required by a file system. This logical format is often simply called *format*. Once you have created the partition, use the appropriate utility to format the drive, which in most operating systems today, requires selecting the *file system*. This is because Windows and other operating systems support more than one file system. The Partition Wizard in Windows XP

FIGURE 3-13

The Windows XP
Disk Management
program, showing
a newly installed
unpartitioned
hard drive

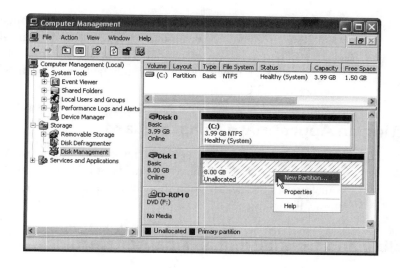

creates and formats the new partition, based on the users' answers to questions the
wizard poses.

A file system is the logical structure on disk that allows the operating system
to save and retrieve files. Chapter 8 will go into detail on the types of file systems
available in Windows, and how to organize files in this logical structure.

Adding, Configuring, and Removing Adapter Cards

Even with the large number of features built into PCs, technicians need to know how
to add new adapter cards to PCs in order to add new functionality to the PC. Installing
an adapter card is a non-trivial task, requiring that you open up the case and install
the card in an available expansion port. For this reason, give careful thought to your
decision. What function do you need to add? Must you use an adapter card to add this
function, or is this something you can add by purchasing a device with a USB or IEEE
1394 connection? These options are much more desirable than installing an adapter
card, if you have a choice. Sometimes, however, an expansion card will provide better
bandwidth, as in a network adapter, or performance, as in a sound card.

Do you simply need more USB or IEEE 1394 ports? Then, in the case of USB,
simply plug one or more USB hubs into your existing USB ports. IEEE 1394 devices
usually come with ports that allow the device to participate in a daisy chain. On the
other hand, does your computer not have one of these types of ports, or are the ports
it has outdated? Some USB devices refuse to work on older USB ports. In that case,
you will need to add a new USB adapter card to upgrade to the new version.

Are you replacing the on-board video adapter with an enhanced video adapter? Are you adding an adapter that will support two monitors, often called dual-headed video adapters? There is no way to avoid installing an adapter to solve these problems.

As new or better technology comes available, you will need experience installing adapters into a PC.

Selecting an Appropriate Adapter Card

When selecting an adapter card, you must do your homework. First determine what expansion ports are available (there may not be a port available) in the PC in which you will install the card. Then shop for the adapter card that both fits your needs and physically fits in your PC.

Installing and Configuring an Adapter Card

Once you have selected the adapter card that meets your needs, you will need to install it in the PC. Exercise 3-12 provides general steps for installing an adapter card. Before you begin, check the documentation for both the adapter card and the motherboard, and note any variations from this general procedure.

Removing an Adapter Card

Before removing an adapter card, be sure that you have an antistatic bag in which to store the removed adapter card. Then, to remove it, simply reverse the steps in Exercise 3-12.

EXERCISE 3-12

Installing an Adapter Card

1. Turn the computer off, unplug it, and ensure that you carry out proper ESD procedures, as described in Chapter 17.
2. Remove the slot cover for the appropriate expansion slot, and position the adapter card upright over the slot (see Figure 3-14).
3. Place your thumbs along the top edge of the card and push straight down. If necessary, rock the card along its length (never side to side).
4. Secure the card to the case using the existing screw hole of the removed slot cover.

Installing an
adapter card

Adding, Configuring, and Removing Displays

An easy and satisfying PC upgrade is a new video display. In most cases, this will not require replacing the video adapter, since even the most standard video adapter in recently manufactured PCs provides excellent output. Perhaps you have used the same bulky CRT display for several years, keeping it even after upgrading the system unit, because of the large price you paid for it ten years ago. Now may be the time to reclaim lost desk space by upgrading to a new flat panel LCD display.

Additionally, many PC tasks are so much easier with two displays. Therefore, you might not be replacing a display, but augmenting it with a second display, so that you can spread your desktop windows across the real estate of two monitors.

Selecting an Appropriate Display Device

Where many of us have skimped in the past is on the display, and at the current low prices of high-quality flat panel displays, it seems like a no-brainer to upgrade your PC and your user experience with a large FPD display that takes up very little desk space. Use the information provided on displays in Chapter 2 to select a new display. Pay attention to the video connector(s) available on your PC.

Installing and Configuring a Display Device

In order to install a CRT monitor or a flat panel display, simply connect the display's cable to the proper connector on the computer and plug in the power cord.

Removing a Display

In order to remove a display, power down the computer and the display, unplug the display from the power outlet, and disconnect the display data cable from the computer.

Adding and Removing Input Devices

In this section, you will examine input devices and how to add, configure, and remove them.

Selecting an Input Device

An input device is a device that allows you to give data to your computer programs. This is critical, since without data there is no reason to compute. Select the input devices to suit your needs, whether you need a basic input device, such as a keyboard and mouse, or a specialty input device, such as a scanner.

Basic

You can, and often do, provide data to programs from disks, but the basic input devices are the keyboard and mouse, described in Chapter 2.

Specialty

There are several specialty input devices. The touchpad is an input device often found on laptops. We describe touchpads in Chapter 5.

Other input devices, such as a stylus or light pen, usually couple with a specialized device. For instance, you use a stylus with a digitizing tablet, or in the case of Tablet PCs, a combined display/digitizing tablet. Learn more about digitizing tablets and Tablet PCs in Chapter 5. A light pen is an input device that uses a light-sensitive detector to select items on a specialized CRT display.

A scanner is an input device that scans images into your computer. Learn more about scanners in Chapter 11. A digital camera is also an input device when it is connected to your computer for downloading photos. The flash memory in a camera is usually seen as a removable drive to the OS; specialized software usually comes with the camera to aid in the transfer of photos to the PC.

Multimedia

Of the various multimedia input devices, the joystick is the most common, as it is an input device used with many video games. The position of the joystick translates into movement of objects on the screen, while one or more buttons add other functions, such as firing weapons or painting bullet holes.

Musical Instrument Digital Interface (MIDI) is a standard that allows musical instruments to communicate with computers and with other instruments. MIDI keyboards and controllers input sound digitally into a computer. These devices have been around for decades, but updated versions include new features and interact better with PCs.

Installing and Removing an Input Device

The installation and configuration required for an input device depends largely on the interface. Most input devices use standard interfaces and connectors. For instance, keyboards and mice come with mini-DIN (also known as PS/2) or USB connectors. Most keyboards and mice will work without the need for add-on device drivers. The standard mouse and keyboard drivers installed into the operating system will be sufficient. To access non-standard features of a keyboard or mouse, however, you will need to install and configure a device driver.

Some input devices, especially keyboards and mice, come with a Bluetooth wireless interface, described in Chapter 5. This short-range radio frequency interface allows devices to communicate over very short distances. Some input devices come with an infrared interface. Bluetooth and infrared require a transceiver device on the computer. Sometimes this device is built into portable computers, but one must be added to desktop PCs and other computers that do not have the built-in Bluetooth or infrared interface.

When you buy a Bluetooth keyboard and/or mouse, it will come with a transceiver device to attach to the computer, which in most cases connects through a USB port. After installing the Bluetooth transceiver, a Bluetooth keyboard or mouse will function like a more conventional keyboard or mouse.

More and more input devices come with a USB interface and are Plug and Play. Even some devices that traditionally had a dedicated interface, such as keyboards and mice, now often come with a USB interface. Another example is the use of USB by MIDI devices. In spite of the variety of devices using USB, installation and removal is simple, because of the use of this Plug-and-Play interface. As always, we remind you to read the manual before installing any device.

CERTIFICATION SUMMARY

This chapter led you through the processes required to install, upgrade, and configure PC components. You learned the important issues for selecting each type of component. For example, whether you are building a system from scratch or just upgrading one or more components, you need to so through a selection process to ensure that the components will function well together. For this, use the knowledge gained in Chapters 1 and 2 about the basic technologies and features of the components. Then, follow the appropriate step-by-step exercise provided in Chapter 3 for the component you are installing. Never fail to read all the appropriate documentation for both a component and the PC or, specifically, the motherboard.

✓ TWO-MINUTE DRILL

Here are some of the key points covered in Chapter 3.

Installing Motherboards, CPUs, and Memory

❑ Select motherboard, CPU, and memory modules that are compatible with each other by researching the specifications of each.

❑ A motherboard must support both the technology and the form factor of a memory module, such as SIMM, RIMM, or DIMM.

❑ When installing a motherboard, follow the instructions in the motherboard manual.

❑ The ability to upgrade an existing CPU depends on the limits of the motherboard.

❑ One of the most common and most effective PC upgrades is the installation of more RAM.

❑ The CMOS settings program enables you to alter the behavior and configuration of many of the PC's components.

Replacing or Upgrading BIOS

❑ An old BIOS may not be able to recognize a new type of device and may need to be upgraded.

❑ BIOSes today are very rarely replaced. Rather, upgrade them through a process called BIOS flashing. This process upgrades the firmware on the BIOS.

Adding, Configuring, and Removing Power Supplies

❑ Replace a failed power supply.

❑ Select a power supply that is of the correct form factor for both the motherboard and the case, and select one that has sufficient wattage for the components you expect to have in the PC.

❑ Older ATX motherboards used a 20-pin ATX (P1) connector to provide power. Some recent motherboards require two ATX12V 2.0 connectors—one is a 24-pin main connector, and the other is a 4-pin secondary connector. Other newer motherboards require EPS12V connectors, which include a 24-pin main connector, an 8-pin secondary connector, and an optional 4-pin tertiary connector.

Adding, Configuring, and Removing Cooling Systems

- ❑ An overheated PC will slow down, stop functioning altogether, or become damaged.
- ❑ The typical PC comes with a cooling system adequate for the standard components delivered with it.
- ❑ Supplement the cooling system when adding hard drives, memory, and additional expansion cards, or if the PC must function in a hot environment.

Adding, Configuring, and Removing Storage Devices

- ❑ EIDE drives come with either a PATA interface or a SATA interface.
- ❑ Most computers have two PATA channels that can each support two EIDE or ATAPI drives.
- ❑ Each PATA channel can have one master device, or one master and one slave device, and you must configure each device on a PATA channel for its role on the channel.
- ❑ Only one SATA device connects to each SATA channel, so there are no configuration issues.
- ❑ While most new PCs do not come with floppy drives, most motherboards have a single channel for floppy drives, which can handle up to two floppy drives.
- ❑ Normally, manufacturers do not build SCSI systems into the typical PC. If you want to add SCSI devices to a PC, you need to install a SCSI bus adapter.
- ❑ There have been a huge number of SCSI standards and variants, and most of them use special parallel connectors of various sizes. There are newer SCSI devices that will connect to SATA channels, but they also need a special host adapter.
- ❑ Various external storage devices, such as those with USB or IEEE 1394, are available today. These devices are truly Plug and Play, and once one is plugged in, the system recognizes it and assigns it a drive letter.
- ❑ To remove one of these external devices, use the Safely Remove Hardware icon on the tray area of the Windows taskbar to stop the device, and only after it is stopped, unplug it.
- ❑ To prepare a hard drive for use you must first partition it, and then format it for a specific file system.

Adding, Configuring, and Removing Adapter Cards

❑ Select an adapter card that will add the functionality you need and that also fits an available expansion port on the motherboard.

❑ Read the documentation for the adapter card and the motherboard before installing the card.

Adding, Configuring, and Removing Displays

❑ Upgrade from a CRT to an LCD to gain more desk space.

❑ Add a second display in order to spread the Windows desktop across the real estate of two displays.

SELF TEST

The following questions will help you measure your understanding of the material presented in this chapter. Read all of the choices carefully because there might be more than one correct answer. Choose all correct answers for each question.

Installing Motherboards, CPUs, and Memory

1. How can you determine which CPU and memory modules to use with a certain motherboard?
    A. No problem. All ATX motherboards accept all Intel and AMD CPUs and DIMM1 memory modules.
    B. Each motherboard is unique; check the documentation.
    C. Check the CPU documentation.
    D. Check the RAM module documentation.

2. Which of the following is true of "Socket 939"? Select all that apply.
    A. It is a term used to describe all PGA CPU sockets.
    B. It is the socket for DIMM2 memory modules.
    C. It is the socket for DIMM1 memory modules.
    D. It describes a PGA CPU socket with 939 pins.

3. A common name for a PGA socket that uses a lever for safely aligning and installing a CPU.
    A. Socket 736
    B. ZIF
    C. Xeon
    D. Athlon

4. If you know a CPU's address bus width, you know this.
    A. The width of a memory bank
    B. The form factor of the CPU
    C. The maximum amount of RAM the CPU can access
    D. The minimum amount of memory that must be installed

5. Which of the following must you do before installing a DIMM module?
    A. Open the retention clips on the socket and tilt the DIMM at a 45-degree angle to the socket.
    B. Open the retention clips on the socket and align the DIMM module with the socket.
    C. Close the retention clips on the socket and tilt the DIMM at a 45-degree angle to the socket.
    D. Close the retention clips on the socket and align the DIMM module without tilting.

Replacing or Upgrading BIOS

6. Which of these events could require flashing the BIOS?

    A. The BIOS does not recognize a new hard drive.

    B. A new mouse does not work.

    C. A new printer does not work.

    D. The monitor goes blank.

7. The BIOS chip in a PC is actually this type of chip, which software can upgrade.

    A. CMOS

    B. Flash BIOS

    C. RDRAM

    D. CPU

Adding, Configuring, and Removing Power Supplies

8. Which power supply connector(s) is likely to be used by a new ATX variant motherboard and a Pentium 4 CPU.

    A. ATX (P1)

    B. ATX 5V 2.0: 24-pin main and 4-pin secondary

    C. ATX 12V 2.0: 24-pin main and 4-pin secondary

    D. ATX (P2)

9. Select all the items below that should be considered when selecting a new power supply.

    A. Wattage

    B. CPU

    C. Form factor

    D. Power connectors

10. What equipment should you never use when working with a power supply?

    A. Screwdriver

    B. Connectors

    C. Motherboard

    D. Antistatic wrist strap

Adding, Configuring, and Removing Cooling Systems

11. In response to rising temperatures inside a PC, the CPU will take this action.
    A. Slow down
    B. Turn off the fan
    C. Speed up
    D. Reboot

12. Which of the following could impair the functioning of the installed cooling system? Select all that are correct.
    A. Keeping the case open during PC operation
    B. Removing slot covers behind empty expansion slots
    C. Vacuuming the interior
    D. Dirt and dust

13. Adding this cooling component is an easy and cheap cooling system upgrade.
    A. Liquid-cooling system
    B. Fan
    C. CPU heat sink
    D. CPU fan

Adding, Configuring, and Removing Storage Devices

14. Which one of the following statements about EIDE/PATA hard drive configurations is true?
    A. Before a master drive will function properly, a secondary drive must be present on the cable.
    B. The master drive must attach to the ribbon cable using the connector closest to the mother-board.
    C. The term for any hard drive on the secondary controller is *slave*.
    D. A slave drive cannot work in the absence of a master drive.

15. You are planning to install a hard drive and an optical drive using the PATA interface in a new system, as the only drives. Which of the following is typically a valid drive configuration for you to use?
    A. Install the hard drive as a primary master and install the optical drive as a secondary master.
    B. Install the optical drive as a primary master and the hard drive as a primary slave.
    C. Install the optical drive as either a primary master or a secondary slave.
    D. Install the optical drive anywhere, as long as the hard drive is a secondary master.

16. Your computer has three hard drives installed—two on the primary PATA controller and one on the secondary PATA controller. You are planning to install a fourth drive without changing the roles of the existing drives. Which of the following accurately describes the procedure you should follow?

    A. Enter the new drive's type and capacity in the CMOS settings, set the drive's jumper to the slave position, and install it on the available connector on the ribbon cable.

    B. Set the drive's jumper to the slave position and attach it to the ribbon cable. Restart the computer and enter the new drive's letter in the CMOS settings.

    C. Enter the new drive's drive letter in the CMOS settings. Set the drive's jumper to the secondary position and attach it to the ribbon cable.

    D. Set the drive's jumper to the slave position and attach it to the ribbon cable.

17. What makes the installation and configuration of SATA drives easier than PATA drives?

    A. No need to configure master/slave, because it is automatic with SATA.

    B. The SATA cables are much thinner than PATA.

    C. No need to configure master/slave, because each drive has its own channel.

    D. SATA drives are physically smaller.

18. Which of the following SCSI IDs has the highest priority on a SCSI chain?

    A. 1

    B. 7

    C. 15

    D. 24

Adding, Configuring, and Removing Adapter Cards

19. You have just purchased a new scanner that requires the latest version of USB, but your USB ports are only at USB 1.1. What is a good solution?

    A. Buy a new computer.

    B. Buy a converter for the scanner so that it can use a parallel port.

    C. Install a USB adapter card with the latest version of the USB standard.

    D. Exchange the scanner for one with a parallel interface.

Adding, Configuring, and Removing Displays

20. What is a benefit of adding a second display to a Windows PC?

    A. More physical desktop space

    B. Less physical desktop space

C. Lower power bills

D. More Windows desktop space

LAB QUESTION

A user asked you to build a PC for daily use. This user plans to use standard business applications under the latest version of Windows. In addition, she will use it to store and edit digital photos, so she has asked for 600 GB of total hard drive space and ability to use two video displays. She is also requesting two 17" LCD displays. She would like a tower case in order to have room for expansion, insulation to minimize noise, and a power supply that is more than adequate for the beginning configuration. She also requests two USB ports and one IEEE 1394 port on the front of the case, at least two USB ports and one IEEE 1394 port on the back of the case, as well as two DVD drives, both capable of reading and writing both CD and DVD discs. Her budget is $1800. Price out just the hardware for a complete system, based on components for this user. Then, use the following table and provide it in a list form, showing the description and price for each component.

Component	Description	Price
Motherboard		
CPU		
RAM		
Hard drives		
Case		
Video adapter		
DVD drives		
Displays		
Total		

SELF TEST ANSWERS

Installing Motherboards, CPUs, and Memory

1. ☑ **B.** "Each motherboard is unique; check the documentation" is correct.

    ☒ **A** is incorrect because it states that all ATX motherboards accept all Intel and AMD CPUs and DIMM1 modules. Each motherboard is unique in the components it will support. **C** is incorrect because checking the CPU documentation will not tell you if the motherboard itself will support this CPU. **D**, check the RAM module documentation, is incorrect because this will not tell you if the motherboard itself will support this RAM module.

2. ☑ **D.** That it describes a PGA CPU socket with 939 pins is correct.

    ☒ **A** is incorrect because each PGA socket style has a unique name. **B** is incorrect because "Socket 939" is not the socket for DIMM2 memory, but for a CPU. **C** is incorrect because "Socket 939" is not the socket for DIMM1 memory, but for a CPU.

3. ☑ **B.** ZIF (zero insertion force) is the name commonly used for a CPU socket with a lever for safely aligning and installing a CPU.

    ☒ **A**, Socket 736, is incorrect because it would describe a single socket style, not necessarily a ZIF socket. **C**, Xeon, is incorrect because this is the name of an Intel CPU line. **D**, Athlon, is incorrect because this is the name of an AMD CPU line.

4. ☑ **C.** The maximum amount of system RAM the CPU can access is correct. For instance, a 32-bit address bus can address a maximum of 4 GB of system RAM.

    ☒ **A**, the width of a memory bank, is incorrect because the data bus width determines this, not the address bus width. **B**, the form factor of the CPU, is incorrect because the address bus only affects RAM addressing, not the physical form of the CPU. **D**, the minimum amount of memory that must be installed, is incorrect because this is determined by the needs of the operating system and how the computer is to be used.

5. ☑ **B.** To open the retention clips on the socket and align the DIMM module with the socket is correct because DIMM modules will not install at an angle, as SIMM models did.

    ☒ **A** is incorrect because you must install DIMMs in an upright position. **C**, close the retention clips on the socket and tilt the DIMM at a 45-degree angle to the socket, is incorrect because you cannot insert a module if the clips are closed, and you do not insert a DIMM at an angle to the socket. **D**, close the retention clips on the socket and align the DIMM module without tilting, is incorrect, only because you cannot insert a module if the clips are closed.

Replacing or Upgrading BIOS

6. ☑ **A.** That the BIOS does not recognize a new hard drive is an event that could require flashing the BIOS.

    ☒ **B** is incorrect because a non-working mouse is not an event that would require flashing the BIOS. **C** is not correct because you would not flash the BIOS to fix a printer. **D** is not correct because you would not flash the BIOS to fix a monitor that went blank.

7. ☑ **B.** Flash BIOS chips are BIOS chips that software can upgrade.

    ☒ **A** is not correct because CMOS is not a BIOS chip, although a special CMOS chip stores system settings. **C** is incorrect because RDRAM is a type of RAM, not a BIOS chip. **D** is incorrect because a CPU is a processor, not a BIOS chip.

Adding, Configuring, and Removing Power Supplies

8. ☑ **C.** ATX 12V 2.0: 24-pin main and 4-pin secondary is correct, although new motherboards may also use EPS12V connectors, or connectors that were not in use at the time of this writing.

    ☒ **A**, ATX (P1), is incorrect because this is an old connector used in the early ATX motherboards. **B**, ATX 5V 2.0: 24-pin main and 4-pin secondary, is incorrect as far as the "5V" is concerned. **D**, ATX (P2), is incorrect because the chapter did not mention it as a power supply connector.

9. ☑ **A, C,** and **D.** You should consider wattage, form factor, and power connectors when selecting a new power supply.

    ☒ **B**, CPU, is incorrect because, although its wattage requirements are important, the CPU itself is not an issue when selecting a power supply.

10. ☑ **D.** You should never use an antistatic wrist strap when working with a power supply.

    ☒ **A**, a screwdriver, is incorrect because it may be necessary to remove the screws holding a power supply to the case. **B**, connectors, is incorrect because you must work with the connectors from the power supply to the motherboard and other components. **C**, motherboard, is incorrect because you may need to work with the power supply connectors on the motherboard.

Adding, Configuring, and Removing Cooling Systems

11. ☑ **A.** In response to rising temperatures inside a PC, the CPU will slow down.

    ☒ **B**, turn off the fan, is incorrect because this would make the PC even hotter. **C**, speed up, is incorrect because this would create more heat. **D**, reboot, is incorrect because this is not an intended action by the CPU if it senses rising temperatures.

12. ☑ **A, B,** and **D.** A and B, keeping the case open during PC operations and removing slot covers, disturb the airflow designed into the case. D, dirt and dust, act as insulation and reduce the cooling ability.

    ☒ **C,** vacuuming the interior, is incorrect because this will remove dirt and dust from components, improving the efficiency of cooling.

13. ☑ **B.** Fan is correct, as this is an easy and cheap cooling system upgrade, as long as there is a place to mount the fan in the case and power is available.

    ☒ **A,** liquid cooling system, is incorrect because this is the most difficult and most expensive cooling system upgrade. **C,** CPU heat sink, is incorrect because it would not be easy, although it may be cheap, unless the CPU is damaged in the process. **D,** CPU fan, is incorrect because it would not be easy, although it may be cheap, unless the CPU is damaged in the process.

Adding, Configuring, and Removing Storage Devices

14. ☑ **D.** A slave drive cannot work in the absence of a master drive is correct. If a drive is a slave and there is no master present, the slave drive will not be able to communicate.

    ☒ **A** is incorrect because a master drive can be alone on a PATA channel, and "secondary drive" is not a correct term, although "secondary channel" is a correct term. **B** is incorrect because it states that the master drive must attach to the ribbon cable using the connector closest to the motherboard. The opposite is true. The master drive must be installed at the end of the ribbon cable. **C,** the term for a hard drive on a secondary controller is slave, is also incorrect. The primary controller and the secondary controller can each have a slave drive, as long as a master drive accompanies each.

15. ☑ **A.** Install the hard drive as a primary master and install the optical drive as a secondary master. This is most common, although you could also install the hard drive as primary master and the optical drive as a primary slave.

    ☒ **B** and **C** are incorrect because they suggest installing the optical drive as a primary master AND hard drives cannot be slaves to optical drives. **C** is also incorrect because it suggests installing the optical drive as the secondary slave, but slave drives must be accompanied by a master drive on the same channel. **D** is incorrect because the only hard drive must be a primary master.

16. ☑ **D.** Set the drive's jumper to the slave position and attach it to the ribbon cable. In most cases, the computer will automatically recognize it when the computer is started up.

    ☒ **A** is incorrect because it suggests setting the new drive's capacity and type before physically installing it in the computer. **B** and **C** are both incorrect because they suggest manually entering the drive letter of the new drive, which is unnecessary because the computer will automatically assign letters to the drives when it is restarted.

17. ☑ **C.** There is no need to configure master/slave, because each drive has its own channel.
    ☒ **A** is incorrect because there is simply no notion of the master and slave roles with SATA. **B** is incorrect because although it is true that the SATA cables are thinner, this is not what makes them easy to install and configure. **D** is incorrect because it is not true that the SATA drives are smaller than PATA, and even if it were true, smaller drives would not necessarily be easier to install and configure.

18. ☑ **B.** 7 is the SCSI ID with the highest priority on a single SCSI chain.
    ☒ **A** is incorrect because 1 would come after 7, 6, 5, 4, 3, and 2. **C** is incorrect because 15 would come after 7, 6, 5, 4, 3, 2, and 1. **D** is incorrect because 24 would have the very lowest priority on a 32-bit SCSI system.

Adding, Configuring, and Removing Adapter Cards

19. ☑ **C.** Install a USB adapter card with the latest version of the USB standard is correct.
    ☒ **A** is incorrect because buying a new computer is not necessarily the solution to a single outdated component on a PC. **B**, buy a converter for the scanner so that it can use a parallel port, is incorrect because you do not know that this is even possible with the scanner, or that the PC has a parallel port. **D**, exchange the scanner for one with a parallel interface, is incorrect because you do not know that such a scanner is available, or if the PC has a parallel port.

Adding, Configuring, and Removing Displays

20. ☑ **D.** More Windows desktop space is correct because you can spread your desktop out onto two separate displays.
    ☒ **A**, more physical desktop space, is incorrect because the opposite is true. **B**, less physical desktop space, is incorrect because it is a disadvantage, not a benefit, of adding a second display to a Windows PC. **C**, lower power bills, is incorrect because it will cost more to power two displays than one display.

LAB ANSWER

Answers will vary. We priced out the following system:

Component	Description	Price ($)
Motherboard	ABIT KN8 ATX Motherboard	79.99
CPU	AMD A64 X2 3800+ Socket 939	299.99
RAM	DDR 2 GB 3200 Dual Kingston	179.99
Hard drives	2 Maxtor SATA hard drives, 300 GB each, at 139.99 each.	279.98
Case	Antec P150 Super Quiet Mini-tower with 430-watt high-efficiency power supply and 3-speed 120 mm fan. It has two USB ports on the front, and four on the back. There is one IEEE 1394 port on the front, and one on the back.	159.99
Video adapter	ATI Radeon X1300Pro with 256 MB video RAM and PCIe interface with two connectors	129.99
DVD drives	2 Plextor ATAPI DVD-RAM drives @ 89.00	178.00
Displays	2 17" Viewsonic VA703 17" LCD FPD displays at 149.99 each	299.98
Total		**1607.91**

4

Troubleshooting and Maintenance for PCs

The most common procedures you will perform as a computer technician are troubleshooting and resolving computer problems. The more familiar you are with a computer's components, the easier it will be for you to find the source of a problem and implement a solution. Build your comfort level by studying Chapters 1, 2, and 3, and with ongoing experience.

In this chapter, you will first learn troubleshooting theory, and then you will progress to basic diagnostic procedures and troubleshooting techniques, practice isolating PC component issues, discover the appropriate troubleshooting tools, and become proactive with common preventive maintenance techniques.

CERTIFICATION OBJECTIVES

■ **601: 1.3   602: 1.2   603: 1.2   604: 1.2**   *Identify tools, diagnostic procedures, and troubleshooting techniques for personal computer components*

For the A+ exams, CompTIA requires that you understand troubleshooting theory, procedures, and techniques. First learn the theory, and then learn how to apply the theory using techniques and procedures appropriate to the symptoms and identified problem area.

Troubleshooting Theory and Techniques

Troubleshooting is the act of discovering the cause of a problem and correcting it. It sounds simple, and if you watch an experienced technician, it may appear so. However, troubleshooting PC problems requires patience, instincts, experience, and a methodical approach. In this section, we will explore troubleshooting theory and techniques for a methodical approach. You will need to acquire the experience on your own, and you will find that your experiences will hone your instincts.

Although we urge you to take a methodical approach, early in the process you will want to take one action that may shortcut the entire process: restart the computer. Do this sooner rather than later. This very popular "single solution" often works for a variety of reasons, mostly software-related. However, it may just be a short-term solution, and the problem may recur. Therefore, unless you are very pressed for time, consider going through the more methodical process described here even after a reboot seems to have resolved the problem.

Theory

When faced with a computer-related problem, resist the urge to jump right in and apply your favorite all-purpose solution, confident that it will work. Rather, take time to do the following:

1. Before making any changes as part of the troubleshooting process, verify that there is a recent set of backups of the user's data. If you find that none is available, perform backups of data (at minimum) and the operating system. We discuss backup techniques in Chapter 9.

2. Assess a problem systematically, and use a strategy of dividing large problems into smaller components for individual analysis. What looks like a big problem is much easier to handle when broken down into smaller pieces.

3. Verify even the obvious, determine whether the problem is something simple, and make no assumptions. Do not even assume that the computer is plugged in, that it is powered on, and that all peripherals are securely connected.

4. Research ideas and establish priorities. Once your research has turned up possible solutions, prioritize the order in which you will apply them, beginning with the easiest to apply.

5. Always have a pad and pencil or a PDA with which to document your actions, findings, and outcomes. It is human nature to skip this step, but do not skip it—even if the documentation is simply informal notes. These will come in handy in the future when confronted with similar problems.

Diagnostic Procedures and Troubleshooting Techniques

Perform diagnostic procedures in a logical order: identify the problem and then analyze it to determine whether it is hardware or software. Then apply troubleshooting techniques appropriate to the problem type.

Identify the Problem

Even when the problem seems obvious to you, gather as much information as you can about the computer and its peripherals, applications, operating system, and history. This will help you clearly identify the problem.

Examine the Environment   Ideally, you will be able to go on site and see the "patient" computer in its working environment. Much of the information you gather in that case will be from your own observations. Whether you go on site, or diagnose a problem over the phone, be sure to question the user. If you cannot go on site, you may be able to diagnose and correct software problems remotely, using remote desktop connection, a method you will practice in Chapter 9. The prize you are looking for is the cause of the problem, which is often a result of some change either in the environment or directly to the computer.

If you are performing onsite troubleshooting, notice your surroundings. They might give you a clue as to a problem's cause, and if you notice a situation that could cause problems, you can correct it to prevent future problems. Consider the following procedures:

1. Take notice of the room's environment, such as the temperature and humidity. Most computer components do not work well in the presence of heat. Furthermore, very high or low humidity can cause condensation or electrostatic discharge, respectively, both of which can lead to problems. A safe humidity level is between 50 and 80 percent.

2. Be aware of nearby devices, such as fans, electrical panels, and fluorescent lights, which could cause electromagnetic interference (EMI).

3. Look at the way components plug into wall outlets, and determine if too many plugs overburden the outlets.

4. Check cable connections. For example, do people have to step over a cable to get to the printer? Such an arrangement can lead to a loose cable connection.

5. Finally, notice the way that people use the computer. Look for inappropriate or rough handling of the equipment. If the user "bangs" on the keys, you will have a good clue as to the cause of a faulty keyboard. In addition, some users tend to triple- and quadruple-click icons on the screen in an attempt to hurry things along. This practice can lead to computer lock-ups.

on the
ī o b

A good rule of thumb when troubleshooting a system that is not functioning properly is to always perform a visual inspection of all cables and connectors. Make sure that all connections are proper before you invest any time in troubleshooting a system.

Question the User: What Has Happened?   One of the best sources for determining the cause of a problem is the person who was using the computer when the failure occurred. While taking note of the environment, your first question to the user should be, "What happened?" This question will prompt the user to tell you about the problem—for example, "The printer will not work." Ask for specific descriptions of the events leading up to the failure, and the symptoms the user experienced.

Do other devices work? This will help you isolate the problem. If one or more other devices do not work, you know you are dealing with a more serious, device-independent problem.

Ask about the device's history. Did this device ever work? If the user tells you that it is a newly installed device, you have a very different task ahead of you than if the user tells you it has worked fine until just now. The former indicates a flawed installation, while the latter points to a possible failure of the device.

If the user mentions an error message, ask for as much detail about the error as possible. If the user cannot remember, try to recreate the problem. Ask if this is a new or old error message, and if the computer's behavior changed after the error. For example, the computer might issue a warning that simply informs the user of some condition. These types of messages might not affect performance. If the error code points to a device, ask device-related questions. For example, the error message might have stated that an optical drive was not accessible.

The Event Logs in Windows XP save many error messages, so if the user cannot remember the error messages, check the Event Logs. Learn more about the Windows Event Logs in Chapter 9.

o n   t h e
Ü o b
Sometimes customers are reluctant to give you all the details of the problem because they do not want to be embarrassed or held responsible for it. Maybe the problem occurred after they installed new hardware or software. Be respectful of the customer, making sure you that treat the customer in a manner that encourages trust and openness about what may have occurred. Every encounter with a user requires that you practice good communications skills and professionalism. In Chapter 18 you will learn the importance of these skills and how to apply them every day.

Question the User: What Has Changed?   You should also find out about any recent changes to the computer or the surroundings. Ask if there is a recently installed new component or application. If so, has the feature or device worked at all since the new installation? The answer to this question could lead you to important information about application or device conflicts. For example, if the user tells you that the audio has not worked since a particular game was loaded, you can suspect that the two events—the loading of the new game and the audio failure—are related.

e **x** a m
Ⓦ a t c h   *For the exam, make sure you understand that you must work to establish a good rapport with the user. You want to make sure that you know about any expansion or upgrades the customer has tried to make. When troubleshooting, remove these upgrades first.*

Analyze the Problem

When you have determined what the problem is—its symptoms, not its cause—try to replicate the problem and begin an analysis. That is, if the user says the printer will not work, have them send another print job to the printer. Watch closely as they perform the task. Take note of any error messages or unusual computer activity that they may not have noticed. Observation will also give you a chance to see the process from beginning to end. Looking over the user's shoulder (so to speak) gives you a different perspective, and you may see a mistake, such as an incorrect printer selection or the absence of an entry in the Number of Pages to print field.

Vendor Documentation   As you work to pinpoint the source of the problem, check out any vendor documentation for the software or hardware associated with the problem. This may be in the form of hard copy or information posted on the vendor's Web site.

Hardware or Software   From your observations, and the information you gather from the user, you may be able to pinpoint the cause of the problem. It may be obvious that a device has failed if the device itself will not power up. If the source of the problem is not yet apparent, you need to narrow down the search even further by determining whether the problem is hardware or software related. We consider a hardware problem to include the device as well as its device drivers and configuration. Software problems include applications, operating systems, and utilities.

One of the quickest ways to determine if hardware or software is at fault, is to use Windows Device Manager, which will indicate any conflicting or "unknown" devices. If Device Manager offers no information about problems, it does not mean that there is not a hardware problem; it only means that Windows has not recognized one. You will work with Device Manager in Chapter 9. For now, Exercise 4-1 shows you how to open Device Manager and look for problem devices.

EXERCISE 4-1

Troubleshooting with Device Manager

1. Right-click the My Computer icon and select Properties.

2. In the System Properties dialog box click the Hardware tab and then click the Device Manager button.

3. In the Device Manager window, you will see the devices on your computer organized under types of hardware, such as Computer, Disk drives, Display adapters, DVD/CD-ROM drives, and Human Interface Devices.

4. If Windows detects a problem with a device, the device type is expanded to show the devices. In the case of a device with a configuration problem, you will see an exclamation mark on both the type icon and the device icon. When Windows recognizes a device but does not understand its type, it places the device under a type named "Other devices," and you will see a question mark, as shown in Figure 4-1.

Potential Causes   Compile a list of potential causes, and if any of them has a simple solution, apply those first. If that does not solve the problem, investigate the other items on your list.

Iterative Troubleshooting

Troubleshooting is an iterative process. If you take certain steps and reach a dead end, you go back and retrace your steps, only with a different focus. Perhaps you were in error when you identified the problem as either software or hardware, and you need to go back and reevaluate the symptoms.

FIGURE 4-1

A problem device will have a question mark or exclamation mark in Device Manager.

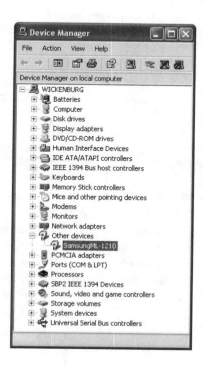

Expect Multiple Problems

Problems can come in multiples. If you have swapped out a suspect component with a new component, and it works, you may have discovered the problem. You can then make the switch permanent, and be finished with it. However, you may have more than one problem. For example, a video system may have both a bad adapter card and a bad display.

If you swap the display with a known good replacement and get no response, you might assume that the display is not the cause of the problem and reconnect it. Do not do that, because if the adapter was at fault, when you get it working, there will still not be any video if the display is also faulty.

on the
ⓘob *Be prepared to accept that you may be fighting more than one problem. However, multiple problems may not closely relate to each other, unlike our example of the video adapter and display problem.*

Working your way into the computer, swap out each component with a working one. This includes the problematic device and any cables attached to it. If the device is external, try plugging it into another port, or try attaching a different device to the suspect port. If the device is internal, switch it to another expansion slot. Do not be afraid to take most of the expansion cards out of the system to establish whether you have one or more problems. You can reinstall them one at a time until the problem recurs.

If you still have not solved the problem, look at the underlying hardware within the computer. That is, test components that are responsible for the computer's performance as a whole, including the BIOS, CMOS battery, processor, RAM, and the system board.

Troubleshooting Software Problems

You can use several techniques to troubleshoot software problems. Begin with restarting the computer, which you may have already done. Restarting the computer releases resources that a device or application needs, but which another device or application is tying up. Restarting the computer also forces the operating system to reestablish the presence of existing devices and clear information out of its memory. If rebooting the computer does not solve the problem, you should then try to narrow the source to a single program and look at minimum requirements, updates, and compatibility. If all of these check out, try uninstalling and reinstalling the software.

Pinpointing the Problem Application   A number of applications can use most hardware devices. Therefore, you can narrow the search by trying to access more than one type of device from the suspect application, or by using more than one application to access the suspect device.

Suppose, for example, that a user was unable to scan an image using a particular scanning program. Use a different application to access the scanner. If it works, you can conclude that the scanner is physically sound and turn your attention to the software as the problem.

If you have determined that the problem is software related, and the problem still exists after a reboot, turn your attention to the application's configuration. Most applications or utilities include a Preferences, Tools, or Options feature, through which you can configure its operation and the devices it can access.

Minimum Requirements   Check to make sure that the computer meets the application's minimum requirements. It is possible that the computer simply will not support the application.

Updates   Check the application manufacturer's Web site for patches and updates. Perhaps this user is experiencing a problem caused by a flaw in the application. Most manufacturers release patches that can remedy discovered problems.

Compatibility   You may also find that a software product works on an older operating system but not in a newer system. Verify that the software that is causing the problem will run on the version of the operating system you are running. This situation is especially common with older computer games. In Chapter 9 you will learn a technique for running such an application in Windows XP.

Flawed Installation or Damaged Application Files   If none of your other efforts solve the problem with an application, then uninstall and reinstall it. This will solve problems that are a result of corrupted application files. This damage may have occurred during or since the original installation of the application. Use the Uninstall utility that came with the application, or use the Windows Add/Remove Programs utility. When reinstalling the application, use its installation utility, often referred to as a setup program.

After the installation is complete, be sure to install any updates for this application by connecting to the manufacturer's Web site, and to Microsoft's update site, in case there is a Windows component that needs updating for this application. You will learn more about updating Windows in Chapter 9.

Exercise 4-2 provides a Step-by-Step guide to troubleshooting.

EXERCISE 4-2

Troubleshooting Step-by-Step

1. Gather as much information from the customer as you can, including symptoms, error messages, computer history, and the user's actions at the time of the failure.

2. Try to reproduce the problem, taking note of any error messages or unusual system activity. Check the Windows Event Logs, if necessary.

3. Determine whether the problem is hardware or software related. Do this by watching error messages, using Device Manager, and accessing the hardware using a variety of applications. (The remainder of this exercise assumes that the problem is hardware related.)

4. Check that an appropriate device driver has been loaded and configured for the device.

5. Test the device by using it in another computer, or by using a known good device in its place.

6. Continue testing and checking all components in the subsystem, working your way into the computer.

7. Reduce the computer to a minimum configuration, removing components that are not critical. Restart the computer. Are there any problems now? Add one component at a time until you have isolated the problem component.

8. Finally, test the computer's most basic components, such as the BIOS, system board, memory, and processor.

Evaluate Results

After applying a solution, evaluate the results. Is it successful? Good, but do not walk away yet. When you believe you have solved the problem, always do a restart of both the device (if appropriate) and computer. Then have the user test the fix, not only doing the function that failed in the first place, but also opening commonly used applications and confirming that everything is working.

This is a very important step. Our experience has been that once you touch a user's computer, even though you solve a problem, they will associate you with the next thing that goes wrong, and you will receive a call stating that "such and such" has not worked since you were there, even though "such and such" does not relate to any changes you made. So, be sure to have the user test everything in your presence and confirm that everything is working.

If your solution seems to have negatively affected anything, be sure to take additional steps to correct the problem. You may find yourself back in the troubleshooting loop.

Document Troubleshooting Activities and Outcomes

Take notes as you work. Then once you have resolved the problem, review the notes, and add any omissions. Sit down with the user and use your notes to review what you did. This is your statement to the user that you made certain changes. You should be clear that you made no other changes to the system.

Afterward, these notes, whether informal or something that is entered into a help desk database, will be useful in the future when you encounter the same or similar problems.

SCENARIO & SOLUTION

What should I do as part of the troubleshooting process before making any changes to a computer?	Verify that there is a recent set of backups; if one does not exist, perform a backup of data and the operating system.
Why should I question the user before jumping in with solutions?	To learn what happened and what has changed.
You have found a solution, applied it, and successfully tested it. What is the final step you need to take?	Document the troubleshooting activities and outcomes.

Troubleshooting PC Component Problems

This section discusses procedures for troubleshooting common component problems. For each component problem, we describe symptoms and causes and provide solutions.

Procedures

When troubleshooting PC components, first do all that you can without opening up the PC. If you do not find the source of the problem and a potential solution through non-intrusive methods, then you will have to open up the PC. Follow these steps, which will take you from the least intrusive to the most intrusive.

1. Check for proper connection (external device).
2. Check for appropriate component.
3. Check installation: driver and settings.
4. Check proper component seating (internal adapter card, memory, etc.).

Video

A computer's video system contains a number of components, so it can be a bit tricky to diagnose and resolve problems. Another difficulty in resolving display problems is that without a working display, you cannot see the OS or BIOS settings in order to remedy the problem. You must replace LCD displays; they cannot be repaired except by highly trained professionals at great cost.

The Computer Continues to Beep at Startup and Will Not Boot Properly

This is an indication of a missing display or a faulty video card. First, check to ensure proper attachment of the display to the video card. Next, check video card function. Because there is no display, you cannot check the driver settings. If the video adapter is not integrated into the motherboard, and if you have a spare computer, install the adapter in another computer to determine if the adapter is functioning. If it is not, replace it.

Complete Lack of Picture

If the display shows nothing at all, and the computer does not issue a beep code, the first thing you should do is move the mouse or press a key on the keyboard. This will reactivate the system if the screen is blank because of a screen saver or power mode setting that causes it to go blank after a specified time period.

If moving the mouse does not solve the problem, check the video system components. Start with the display's connection to power and ensure that it is turned on. Check the data cable and verify that none of the pins on the connector are bent, and straighten them if necessary. Also, ensure that the brightness is set at an adequate level.

You can determine if the display itself is at fault by swapping it with a known good one. If the new display works in the system, you can assume that the original display is the problem. Before replacing a display, you should have it checked by a trained technician. Since displays can be expensive, it would not be prudent to dispose of one if it is possible to have it replaced or professionally repaired at a reasonable cost. Chapter 17 will describe proper disposal of PCs and components.

Once you have eliminated a display as a cause, check for proper seating of the video card in the expansion slot. AGP cards, especially earlier ones, do not seat easily. Press the card firmly (but not too hard) and listen for an audible click to tell you the card seats properly.

Install a different video card in this computer. Doing so might allow you to view the OS so that you can remove a faulty video card configuration, if it exists. Some newer motherboards include an integrated video adapter. If this is one, look for a jumper setting to disable the on-board video and use an adapter card. If this option is not available, you may need to replace the motherboard.

Flickering Display

Flickering may be a symptom of a faulty display. But before you jump to that conclusion, check to see if there is a motor or a fluorescent light very close to the display. Users often have fluorescent lights in their office cubicles, and many add small fans to cool their workspace. Either of these can cause flickering, which goes away as soon as you remove or turn off the motor or fluorescent light. If possible look on the other side of the wall partition, where you might find a source of EMI, such as an electrical panel. If you cannot remove the source from the display, move the display away from the source.

An inappropriate refresh rate setting can also cause flickering. A rate too low for the video system you are using can cause the display to flicker. On a Windows-based system, you can access the Control Panel's Display icon, and choose a different refresh rate. Replace the display with another to see if the problem still exists.

on the
ⓘob
The standard refresh rate for CRT displays is 75 Hz. Older displays may not work at this rate but may require a refresh rate of 60 Hz. An older display will usually blank out if run at faster speeds.

Screen Elements Duplicated All Over the Screen

Repeated screen elements are more common in older video systems. This problem is due to the use of an improper resolution setting for your video system. This setting results in multiple copies of the same image, including the mouse pointer, all over the screen. To solve this problem, go into the Display settings and reduce the resolution setting. This task can be difficult because more than one mouse pointer appears on the screen, making it nearly impossible to work with the mouse. To navigate through the appropriate screens, we suggest you use the keyboard.

e x a m

w a t c h *For the exam, as well as on the job, remember that a CRT display can hold enough charge to injure you seriously, even if it has been unplugged. Never wear an antistatic wrist strap when working with a display, and never open the display's case.*

Do Not Try This at Home or Work

A CRT or FPD display is not usually field-serviceable, so have a technician check it out, and if it is truly beyond repair, replace it rather than try to repair it. One reason for this is that it would typically cost more in labor and parts to fix a display than it would to buy a new one. Another reason not to attempt any repair yourself, and probably the most important one, is that displays can hold enough electrical charge to cause serious personal injury, even when they have been unplugged for an extended time. When a display needs replacing or upgrading, turn off the computer, unplug the display, and replace it with the new one.

e x a m

w a t c h *You can expect questions about the dangers of high-voltage devices and antistatic straps on the exam.*

Power Supply

Power supplies can experience either total or partial failures, resulting in inconsistent or displaced symptoms. However, you can identify a few common symptoms of power supply failure to pinpoint the problem; we discuss those symptoms here. When the power supply fails, replace it. Never try to open or repair a power supply, because it can hold enough charge to injure you seriously.

e x a m

w a t c h *For the exam, as well as your own safety, remember that, like displays, power supplies can cause serious personal injury. Never open the case of a power supply!*

Nothing Happens When the Computer Is Turned On

A few things can cause a total lack of activity at system startup. These include a bad processor or memory, but the most likely suspect is the power supply.

When the power supply stops working, so does the computer's fan, which is typically the first thing you hear when you turn the computer on. Therefore, if you do not hear the power supply fan at startup, suspect a power supply problem, and turn off the computer immediately. Some power supplies will shut down if the fan is not working.

Once the computer is off, try cleaning the fan, using an antistatic vacuum or static-free cloth. Because the fan draws air in through the case, it can also draw in dust, lint, or hair that can cause the fan to stop rotating. If cleaning does not resolve the problem, you must replace the entire power supply.

If the problem is not so easily isolated to the power supply fan because the system simply will not turn on, try removing all power supply connections to internal components, and turning the PC back on. The fan on the power supply should run. If it does not, this is a clear indication that the power supply has malfunctioned and you must replace it.

If the fan is not at fault, check to make sure that the power supply connects properly to an electrical outlet. In addition, check the power selector (on the back of the computer between the power cord connection and the on/off switch) to ensure that it has the right setting for your geographic region (North American [115 volts] or European [230 volts]).

Also, check to ensure the power cables attach properly to the motherboard and other necessary devices, including the computer's power button.

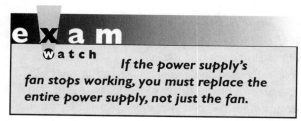

on the **Job** *Since you can switch many power supplies to use either 120 or 230 volts (European standard), verify that someone did not change the setting to the wrong voltage setting.*

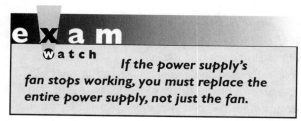

exam

ⓦ**atch** *If the power supply's fan stops working, you must replace the entire power supply, not just the fan.*

The Computer Reboots Itself, or Some Components Sporadically Stop Working

A computer with a bad power supply may reboot itself without warning. If the power supply provides power to only some devices, the computer will behave irregularly; some devices will seem to work, while others will work only part of the time or not at all. Check to make sure that all power plugs connect properly.

Inadequate cooling will cause components to overheat, in which case they might work sometimes but not others, and very commonly, an overheated computer will simply shut itself off or spontaneously reboot. Try cleaning the power supply fan. If this does not solve the problem, replace the power supply or consider adding another case fan, if one will fit in your computer.

Missing Slot Covers

Believe it or not, the removable slot covers at the back of the computer are not there solely to tidy up the appearance of the computer. They keep dust and other foreign objects out of the computer, and if you leave the slot covers off, you run the risk of allowing dust to settle on the internal components, especially the empty expansion slots (which are notoriously difficult to clean). Missing slot covers can also cause the computer to overheat. The design of the computer places the devices that generate the most heat in the fan's "line of fire." Missing slot covers means the cooling air's path through the computer could be changed or impeded, resulting in improper cooling of the components inside.

Noisy Fan

There are more cooling fans inside a computer than the one on the power supply. Today's computers have one (slot) or two (SEC) cooling fans on the CPU. There can also be one or more strategically placed cooling fans inside the case.

When a fan begins to wear out, it usually makes a whining or grinding noise. When this happens, replace the fan, unless it is inside the power supply. In that instance, replace the entire power supply. Opening the power supply is dangerous, and the time spent on such a repair is more valuable than the replacement cost of a power supply.

POST Audio and Visual Errors

When a computer starts up, the BIOS performs a POST (power-on self-test) to check for the presence and status of existing components. A visual error message on the screen, or a series of beeps, typically indicates errors found during the POST. These visual and audible error codes can differ from BIOS to BIOS, so it is best to consult the manufacturer's documentation for the meaning of each code. However, some BIOS error codes are "common" because most machines use them.

For example, most error codes in the 1** series, such as 120 or 162, indicate a problem with the system board or processor. It is rare to see a 1** error code, since most system board and processor errors are serious enough to prevent the computer from issuing the error code at all.

Memory errors detected by the POST are typically indicated by a 2** error, and keyboard errors are indicated by a 3** error. Fortunately, a brief description of the problem accompanies most visual error codes. Again, consult the documentation for your specific BIOS, because these messages can often be cryptic (for example, "213: DMA arbitration time-out").

Some BIOSes use a series of beeps rather than a visual message to indicate a POST error. Typically, one beep indicates that all components passed the POST. This does not mean that there are no problems in the computer; it simply means that none of the components has a problem detected by the BIOS. When the BIOS issues an audio error code, carefully count the beeps and note whether they are long or short. Again, consult the BIOS documentation for the proper meaning of each code, because these differ from system to system. For example, one BIOS might indicate a video problem by issuing eight short beeps, while another might use one short and two long beeps.

e x a m
ⓦatch
While some manufacturers have their own error codes, these codes often are in addition to the original codes discussed here. For the exam, and for real life, memorize the basic meaning of the codes in the 1**, 2**, and 3** range.

CPU

In most cases, CPU problems are fatal, meaning that when there is such a problem, the computer will not boot at all. However, you should be aware of some nonfatal error indicators. As described, 1** error codes are typical of processor problems.

If you turn the computer on, and it does not even complete the POST or it does nothing at all, and you have eliminated power problems, there might be a problem with the processor. The solution to a processor problem is to remove the offending component and replace it with a new one. A persistent error indicates a possible problem with the slot or socket that the processor uses to connect to the motherboard. In this case, you need to replace the motherboard. Check the warranty on the system before taking any action, since it should cover a failure of the motherboard.

on the
❶ob
Considering the low prices of PCs, if you encounter a CPU or motherboard problem on a computer not covered by a warranty, consider replacing the entire system.

Recall the CPU throttling topic in Chapter 1. A slow computer can be a symptom of overheating, because it may indicate that the CPU has reduced its clock speed due to overheating. A processor that has activated thermal throttling will run slower. Why is the computer overheating? Dust? Blocked vents? Failed cooling fan? Check out these possibilities and remedy any that you find.

CMOS

Problems associated with the CMOS chip include lost or incorrect settings. Lost settings occur when the CMOS battery begins to lose power. You will generally be informed of this problem by a 1** error message at startup, or by a prompt to enter the correct time and date. When this happens, replace the battery.

Incorrect CMOS Settings

Incorrect CMOS settings can have many incarnations because there are CMOS settings for a great variety of system elements, including hard drives, floppy drives, the boot sequence, keyboard status, and parallel port settings. An incorrect setting will manifest as an error relating to that particular device or function, so it can be difficult to pinpoint the CMOS as the source of the problem. However, when you need to change or update the CMOS, enter the CMOS settings at startup, make the appropriate change(s), save the new setting(s), and restart the computer.

System Clock Problems

A computer that does not maintain the date and time when powered off probably has a low CMOS battery. Because these batteries only last between 2 and 10 years, you are likely to have to replace a computer's battery before the computer becomes obsolete. To replace the battery properly, follow the steps in Exercise 4-3. Note that although this procedure cannot be followed in all computers, it applies to most recent computers.

EXERCISE 4-3

Replacing the CMOS Battery

1. Enter the computer's Setup program (described in Chapter 3) and save a copy of the CMOS settings by one of the methods you learned in Chapter 3.

2. Turn off the computer and remove the cover, ensuring that you carry out the proper ESD procedures.

3. Locate the CMOS battery on the motherboard.

4. Slide the battery out from under the retaining clip. The clip uses slight tension to hold the battery in place, so there is no need to remove the clip or bend it outward.

5. Note the characteristics on this battery that indicate its orientation when installed, and install the new battery the same way.

6. Restart the computer. Enter the system's Setup program and restore the CMOS setting you recorded in Step 1.

Memory

As with CPUs, physical damage or failure of memory is fatal, meaning that when there is such a problem, the computer will not boot at all. However, you should be aware of some nonfatal error indicators. As described, 2** error codes are typical of memory problems.

If you turn on the computer and it does not even complete the POST or it does nothing at all, and you have eliminated power problems, there might be a problem with the main memory. The solution to a memory problem is to remove the offending component and replace it with a new one. If the error persists, the memory might be in a damaged slot or socket on the motherboard. In this case, replace the motherboard, or the entire PC.

On a final note: the computer does not report some RAM errors at all. That is, if an entire memory module does not work, the computer might just ignore it and continue to function normally without it. At startup, watch the RAM count on the screen (if BIOS configuration allows this) to ensure that the total amount matches the capacity installed in the machine. If this amount comes up significantly short, you probably have to replace a memory module.

watch

Memory failures may not cause a system to appear to malfunction at all. Most modern systems will simply ignore a malfunctioning memory module and normal operations will continue. The user may note performance loss, which is a key symptom of a memory module failure.

Input Devices

A number of different symptoms are associated with input devices, especially mice. They provide a common source of computer problems. Fortunately, most procedures to resolve such problems are quite simple. Now look at two common mouse-related problems.

The Pointer Does Not Move Smoothly Across the Screen

A common mechanical mouse or trackball problem is irregular movement of the pointer across the screen. Some mice even appear to hit an "invisible wall" on the screen. These symptoms indicate dirty rollers, in the case of a traditional mouse or trackball, or dirt on the lens of an optical mouse or track ball. This problem is very common because, as the mouse moves across a desk or table it picks up debris, which is then deposited on the internal rollers. You may still need to clean an optical or electronic motion-sensing track ball or mouse, but they are proving to be much more reliable than the older mechanical mouse. To clean mouse rollers, follow the steps in Exercise 4-4. To clean a trackball, simply remove the ball, and wipe the socket with a soft static-free cloth.

on the
Óob

The most common problem with a mechanical mouse is irregular movement due to dust buildup on the rollers.

EXERCISE 4-4

Cleaning a Mouse

1. Unplug the mouse and turn it upside down. If it is an optical mouse, follow the instructions in Step 2. If it is a mechanical mouse, follow the instructions beginning in Step 3.

2. Use a soft lint-free cloth to wipe off the bottom of the mouse. Skip to Step 10.

3. Remove the retaining ring (usually by twisting it counter-clockwise).

4. Invert the mouse so that the ball drops into your hand.

5. If the ball is dirty or sticky, clean it with warm soapy water and rinse it thoroughly.

6. Locate the rollers inside the mouse (see Figure 4-2). There are typically two long black rollers and one small metallic roller.

FIGURE 4-2

The internal rollers in a mechanical mouse

7. Use your fingers to remove the "ring" of dust from each roller, taking care not to let any material fall further into the mouse.

8. If the rollers are sticky, or if Step 7 is insufficient to clean the rollers, use a cotton swab dipped in isopropyl alcohol to clean them.

9. When finished, replace the mouse ball and retaining ring, ensuring that they are securely in place.

10. Plug the mouse back in. If it is a USB mouse, you can plug it in with the computer running, but the computer must be turned off before you plug in a mouse that uses a serial port or an AT mouse port.

11. With the computer running, test the mouse in Windows.

The Pointer Does Not Move on the Screen

The problem could be that the mouse driver is either corrupted or missing altogether. If you suspect a missing driver, you need to load the driver manually from the Setup disk that came with the mouse.

 on the Job

While PCs provide a dedicated Mini-DIN connection for the mouse, USB connectors are very common on pointing devices.

If there is no driver disk, try simply restarting the computer. Most mice are Plug and Play, so the OS might automatically detect your mouse and load the appropriate driver for it at startup. If you suspect that a mouse driver does exist but is corrupted, use Device Manager or the Mouse icon in Control Panel to remove the existing driver and reload it. Learn about working with Device Manager in Chapter 9.

Adapter Cards

If you must replace or upgrade an adapter card, follow the steps in Exercise 3-12 in Chapter 3. If the adapter card is a video card, ensure that the replacement card has the correct interface. Video cards currently come with a choice of interfaces: PCI, AGP, and PCIe. If your computer supports both PCI and AGP (a common configuration until recently), purchase an AGP card, as it will give better performance than a PCI card. In newer computers both PCI and PCIe connectors will be present, and AGP may also be present. In this case, PCIe is the best choice.

Motherboard

In many cases, when a motherboard fails, it causes a fatal error that prevents the computer from booting properly. However, if the BIOS is able to run a POST, it might report a problem with the motherboard as a 1** error. Unfortunately, as with a BIOS failure, you cannot use one symptom or set of symptoms to immediately pinpoint the motherboard as the point of failure.

A faulty motherboard can cause many different symptoms, and can even cause it to appear that a different component is at fault. This is because a motherboard problem might manifest in one particular area, such as a single circuit or port, causing a failure of a single device only. For example, if the video card's expansion slot on the motherboard stops working, it will appear that there is a problem with the display system. In this case, you are likely to discover the motherboard as the point of failure only after checking all other components in the video system. Later in this chapter, you will learn about a tool called a POST card that you can use to detect a problem with a motherboard or other components.

Hard Drives

Many things can go wrong with a hard drive, each of which can result in a number of different symptoms, so it can be difficult to determine the cause of the problem. You should replace a hard drive that begins to develop corrupted data before all the information stored on it is lost. In Chapter 9 you will learn about using specialized utilities to correct problems with data on the hard drive, including corrupted and fragmented files. We discuss the most common hard drive symptoms and problems in the sections that follow.

The Computer Will Not Boot Properly

When you start a computer, you might receive a POST error message with an error code in the 1700 to 1799 range. You could also get a message stating that there is no hard drive present. Typically, these errors are not fatal, and you can still boot the computer using a special boot (floppy) disk.

This error means that the computer does not recognize, or cannot communicate with, the hard drive. First, restart the computer and go into the CMOS settings. In the BIOS drive configuration, ensure that it lists the proper hard drive type. If not, enter the appropriate settings, or use the system's hard drive detection option.

If the BIOS settings are correct, and the drive still will not work, or if the BIOS cannot detect the hard drive, there could be a cabling problem. To check on cabling and other physical configuration, perform the steps in Exercise 4-5.

EXERCISE 4-5

Troubleshooting a Drive Failure

1. Turn off power to the computer and open the case.

2. If the drive connects to a PATA channel, ensure that it has the proper master or slave setting.

3. Check to see if the drive is attached to a SCSI controller, which may be the source of the problem. In this case, locate another computer with an identical working controller and swap the problem drive into the second computer.

4. Check for secure attachment of the data and power cables. Check the hard drive ribbon cable to ensure that the red stripe aligns with pin 1 on both ends.

5. If possible, replace the ribbon cable with a known good one.

6. If the cables, jumpers, and BIOS settings all check out, the problem is with the drive itself and you must replace it.

The Computer Reports No Operating System

Once the BIOS finishes the POST, it looks for the presence of an OS on the hard drive. If the BIOS does not find a special OS pointer in the drive's master boot record, it assumes that no OS exists. If you have not yet installed an OS, you must do so at that point. If an OS exists but is not accessible, refer to Chapter 9 for steps to take to recover from this situation.

When troubleshooting a disk boot problem, it may be helpful to unplug all other devices not needed for the boot process, and that are using the same interface (PATA or SATA). If the system boots with these devices disconnected, it may help you isolate the problem. You can reconnect them one at a time until you find the problem device.

Optical Drives

CD-ROM and DVD drives are functionally similar, so use similar methods to install or troubleshoot them. A common problem with either of these devices is that the computer will report it cannot read the disc. First, check to ensure you inserted the disc the correct way. The label must be facing up so the drive can access the data on the underside of the disc. Next, visually inspect the disc. Scratches or smudges may prevent the computer from reading the disc.

To rule out the media as the cause, try more than one disc in the optical drive. When you experience problems reading more than one disc in an optical drive, cleaning the lens may solve the problem.

If the drive is the problem, check Device Manager to ensure the computer recognizes it. Reload the device's driver if necessary, and check its system resources. If the problem persists, check the ribbon cable connection and jumper setting. Try the drive in another computer to confirm or rule it out as the cause of the problem.

Floppy Drive Failures

A floppy drive can fail in a number of ways, so there are a number of different symptoms to be aware of. Fortunately, most floppy failures stem from the disk, not the drive itself. Whenever you encounter a floppy drive failure, the first thing you should do is determine if the disk is at fault. The easiest way to do this is to eject the disk and insert another. If the problem goes away, the disk, not the drive, is the source of

e x a m

w a t c h

The floppy disk, rather than the drive, is the cause of most floppy errors. Never touch the surface of the floppy disk (under the metal sliding cover) and do not attempt to clean a floppy disk. It is possible to clean the read/write head of the floppy drive.

the problem. If you must have the information on a particular disk that is giving you trouble, try gently pulling the metal cover back and letting it snap back into place a few times, then reinsert the disk in the drive and try to access the data again. You can also try to use the disk in a different drive.

"Please Insert a Disk into Drive A:" Error Message

If you click the A drive in My Computer or Windows Explorer and receive a message that reads: "Please insert a disk into drive A:" it means the drive cannot detect a floppy disk. The most common reason for this error is simply that there is no disk inserted in the drive, or you did not insert the disk all the way. Check to make sure that there is a disk inserted. If there is, remove the disk and try pulling the metal cover back a few times to loosen it; if the drive cannot pull the cover back, it cannot access the data on the disk.

"Error Writing to Disk" Message

One of the most common symptoms of a floppy drive problem is a message stating that there is an error reading from or writing to the disk. This type of message typically indicates that the floppy drive controller is communicating properly with the computer but simply cannot access disk information. First, try to access a different disk, to rule out the original disk as the cause of the problem. If you determine that the problem is drive rather than disk related, try cleaning the drive's read/write heads, as described later in this chapter.

If the drive still cannot access a disk after cleaning, and you can read the floppy in another system, the problem lies within the drive itself, and you must replace it. A cheap and easy solution is to purchase an external floppy drive with a USB interface.

Floppy Drive Light Will Not Go Off

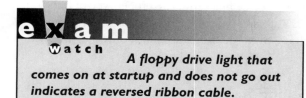

A floppy drive light that comes on at startup and does not go out indicates a reversed ribbon cable.

A floppy drive light that will not go off indicates an incorrectly attached data cable. This problem can occur immediately after installing a floppy drive, with or without a floppy disk in the drive. Turn the computer off, remove the computer's cover, and reattach the cable the right way. Remember, you must align the red stripe on the cable with pin 1 on the system board and on the drive.

"Invalid Drive" Error When Accessing the Floppy Drive

When you see this error, and any time the computer does not recognize the presence of the floppy drive, it means that the drive is not communicating properly with the computer. Turn the computer off and remove the cover. Make sure that the ribbon cable is present and properly and firmly attached. Next, check the connection to the power supply. When you are satisfied that the drive is connected properly, restart the computer and access the CMOS settings program. Ensure that the correct floppy drive configuration is present in the BIOS settings. If the computer still does not recognize the floppy drive, try replacing the cable. If that does not fix the problem, replace the drive with a working drive.

USB Devices

Many common peripherals are now available with a USB interface. We have found this Plug-and-Play interface to be the least troublesome of any we have worked with in the past. However, you may encounter problems with these devices. One handy tool for diagnosing problem USB ports and devices is a USB loopback plug, discussed later in this chapter. The sections that follow describe some common problems you may encounter with USB devices.

USB Device Seems Not to Have Power

Low-power USB devices get their power from the USB system or, more specifically, from the root or external hubs. Other devices require external power and come with their own power supplies that switch on separately from the computer. If such a device has a power switch or button, make sure it is in the on position. If this is a new installation, check the documentation and packaging to be sure an external power cord was not overlooked. Next, make sure the data cable is securely connected. You should also check to make sure that the device plugs into the proper type of hub. You can plug "low-powered" USB devices into any type of USB hub, but "high-powered" devices (USB 2.1 or greater), which use over 100 milliamps, must only plug into self-powered USB hubs.

USB Keyboard Not Functioning

The BIOS typically controls the keyboard's drivers and resources. When you install a USB keyboard, you must inform the BIOS so that it will hand keyboard control to the USB system. Enter the CMOS settings at startup and ensure that the USB keyboard option is turned on and that the BIOS provides a generic driver for USB keyboards. On an older computer, this option may not exist, in which case, you might need to upgrade the BIOS to use a USB keyboard.

"USB Device Is Unknown" Message, or the Device Is Not Functioning

A message stating that the USB device is unknown, or the device simply does not work, means the computer cannot communicate with the device. First, make sure that the device is properly attached and is receiving power, and try switching it to another port. Make sure that the device's cable is less than five meters long. Although most USB devices are Plug and Play, the operating system may not have the specific driver for the device. Make sure that a driver for this device is loaded.

Check to make sure that the device is using the proper communications mode. On startup, the USB controller assigns an ID to all devices and asks them which type of data transfer (interrupt, bulk, or continuous) they will use. If a device is set to use the wrong type of transfer mode, it will not work. Finally, check the device by swapping it with a known good one.

e**x**a**m**

ⓦ**atch**   *Some USB devices require installation of the driver before connecting the device to a USB port. This is especially true of USB printers. If you plug in the device before installing the driver, you may not be able to use the device until you uninstall the driver, disconnect the device, reinstall the driver, and reconnect the device. Be sure to read the documentation before installing any device.*

None of the USB Devices Will Work

If none of the USB devices work, you could have a problem with the entire system or just the USB controller. First, make sure that your OS is USB compliant, such as Windows 98, Windows Me, Windows 2000, Windows XP, or Windows Vista. Next, make sure that the number of devices does not exceed 127, and that no single cable length exceeds five meters. The USB system is also limited to five tiers or five hubs in a single chain. Check the cable length and cable connections, especially from the root hub to the first external hubs. A loose connection will prevent all devices on the external hub from functioning.

If the problem is not in the USB physical setup, turn your attention to the USB hub. In an older, pre–Windows XP OS, make sure that a proper driver has been loaded for it and that it does not have a conflict with another device. You should also check the BIOS for USB support, to determine if you can even use USB in this system. You may also want to uninstall the USB hub or controller driver. When you restart the system, the operating system will notify you to reinstall these drivers. This may fix the problem.

SCSI Devices

The most common problems with SCSI devices involve incorrect installation or configuration. This is more common than failure of the device itself. If the problem occurs immediately after installation, begin by checking all connections. Then check the two usual suspects: SCSI chain termination and SCSI device ID. Refer back to Chapter 3 if you need help with these two issues.

SCENARIO & SOLUTION

The computer does not maintain the date and time when it has been powered on. What should I do?	Replace the CMOS battery.
What should I do with a computer that keeps rebooting itself?	Test the power supply. You may need to replace it.
What should I do when the mouse pointer does not move smoothly on the screen?	Clean the mouse or trackball device.

Troubleshooting Tools

Troubleshooting tools fall into two categories: software or hardware tools, although you will find that sometimes software and hardware work together for troubleshooting, as in the case of the POST card. Software and hardware diagnostics are described in the sections that follow.

Software Tools

You will find handy software troubleshooting tools built into the operating system, through third-party sources, and built into the system BIOS of your PC and the BIOSes of certain components.

Alternate OS Startup Options

One of the most useful tools you can bring with you to a customer's site is knowledge of the operating system's alternate startup options. You will learn about these in Chapter 9. Additionally, under some circumstances, a specialized startup (boot) floppy disk or optical disk is handy. Alternate startup options and some boot disks will allow you to start the computer in a state of minimal devices and files, so that you can locate an offending device or file before it causes the computer to halt or crash (see Chapter 9 for details on using these options).

Utilities

We lump various non-application programs under the category of utility software. There are several such software tools that you should use, beginning with antivirus and antispyware software. These can either be commercial products or free, and you will learn about them in Chapter 16. Other important software, including the installation software for your operating system and for various applications, also comes into play when you are troubleshooting. You will learn more about these in Chapter 9. Then there are the recovery utilities—some built into Windows, and others available through third parties. The Windows recovery options are introduced in Chapter 9. On the job you also will use diagnostic utilities from a variety of sources—once again, some come with Windows, but the more advanced come from third-party vendors.

BIOS and Component Self-Tests

Another tool available to you is knowledge of how your system BIOS, and the BIOSes of various components, behave during the POST at bootup, especially in the case of a failure. Earlier in this chapter you learned about system BIOS.

Other components, such as PATA or SCSI hard drives, will also issue error codes if they have a serious problem. Watch for these codes whenever starting up a computer.

Hard Drive Software Diagnostics Test

You do not normally think about your hard drive having its own BIOS, but it does, and this BIOS, much like the PC's system BIOS, will perform a diagnostics test as the hard drive is powered up. If it discovers a problem, it will display an error message. This should appear immediately after your system POST as a 17** error. In addition, you can obtain hard drive diagnostics utilities from the manufacturer of the hard drive, and from third-party sources. These utilities come in handy when the hard drive does work but is having data errors or performance (slowness) issues and you have exhausted all other avenues.

The Hardware Toolkit

In order to be completely prepared for any onsite computer problem, you would have to equip yourself with every type of cable, connector, battery, or driver that any component might need. Since you cannot do this, you should stick to the basic troubleshooting tools, utilities, and devices described here.

Basic Tools

You may purchase a basic computer technician's toolkit, or assemble the components yourself. Figure 4-3 shows some of the tools you should carry with you at all times on the job.

Following is a list of components you should have in your kit:

- An array of Phillips and flathead screwdrivers, as well as nut drivers of varying sizes.

FIGURE 4-3

An assortment of
basic tools

FIGURE 4-3

An assortment of
basic tools

- An extending extractor, also called a *parts grabber*. This pen-sized tool has a plunger at one end. When pressed, the plunger causes small, hooked prongs to extend from the other end of the tool. These are useful for retrieving dropped objects, such as jumpers or screws, from inside the computer. Be very careful not to touch any circuitry when using one of these.
- A flashlight for illuminating dark places.
- A small container for holding extra screws and jumpers (a slide film case works well).
- An antistatic wrist strap to use when working on any component except the power supply, monitor, and laser printers (see Chapter 10). Attach the alligator clip to the PC's frame and wrap the wrist strap around your wrist. Use your less-favored wrist for this so that the cable does not interfere. Figure 4-4 shows an antistatic wrist strap.

FIGURE 4-4

An antistatic
wrist strap

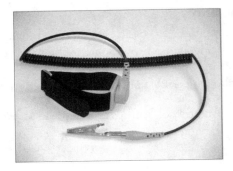

- An antistatic mat. While this will not fit into your toolkit, it is something that should be available at any PC technician's workbench. An antistatic mat (or grounding mat) placed on the bench reduces the risk of electrostatic discharge for components placed on it. An antistatic mat placed on the floor provides the same protection for anyone standing on the mat.

- A multimeter may seem like an advanced tool, but it will be indispensable in determining power problems from a power outlet or from the power supply. A *multimeter* is a handheld device used to measure the resistance, voltage, and/ or current within computer components (see Figure 4-5). The most common multimeter use is to determine if a circuit or cable measures infinite resistance, which means that there is a break somewhere in the line. You can also use a multimeter to check that the power supply is generating the appropriate voltage, or that a motherboard component is receiving the proper current.

Specialized Diagnostic Toolkits

Various vendors sell comprehensive toolkits for PC hardware and software diagnostic tools. Prices for these toolkits can range from a few dollars to many hundreds of dollars. The differences are in the software and hardware included in the kit, and the number of features available.

FIGURE 4-5

A simple
multimeter

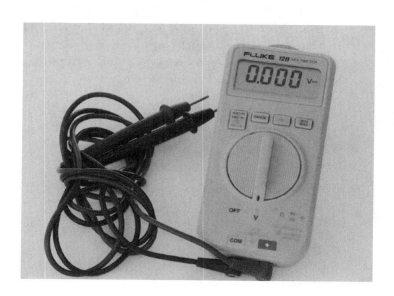

Diagnostics Software

Some diagnostic kits come with a boot floppy disk or CD disc that will boot any IBM-compatible computer regardless of the operating system. Because they bypass the operating system, these diagnostic programs can probe your hardware for problems by testing ports, drives, busses, CPUs, memory, and other components. Some diagnostic software requires specialized hardware to perform these tests.

In addition to diagnostics, these kits often provide software used for preventive and restorative measures. For instance, a kit may contain software for backing up CMOS settings, and recovering important system information from the hard drive so that you can restore the drive after damage to system information. Other software may diagnose and repair other types of damage to disks.

Diagnostics Hardware

The medium-to-high-priced kits will include diagnostics hardware such as loopback plugs and POST cards.

Loopback Plugs   Hardware in a diagnostics kit may include loopback plugs for various common ports. Loopback plugs are available for any common PC port type. Some come with light-emitting diodes (LEDs) that can show the results of various tests. Others are very simple and depend on running software on the PC to conduct tests and show you the results. Figure 4-6 shows three basic loopback plugs that came with software. These three are for serial ports (both 9-pin and 25-pin) and parallel ports. These are falling out of use, since serial and parallel ports are disappearing from PCs.

An example of a loopback plug for a more common port is a USB loopback plug. Once one of these plugs connects to a USB port, the diagnostics software can test both the port and the cable used to connect to the port. With a USB loopback plug, you may be able to

- Check if a USB port is powered.
- Test the port's ability to send and receive data.
- Detect USB error rates.
- Measure transmission speed.
- Detect retransmitted data.
- Test the port's stability during long periods of transmission.
- Test self-powered USB hubs.
- Check USB cabling.

Three loopback
plugs: one 9-pin
serial plug, one
25-pin serial plug,
and one 25-pin
parallel plug

POST Cards   A POST card is an adapter card for checking the POST process that
you install into an expansion slot in a PC. This is one of those rare times when you must
power up the PC with the case open. When you power up the PC you watch a small
two-character light-emitting diode (LED) on the card. In addition to the LED display,
POST cards may also have additional indicator lights. You can interpret the POST
card's findings using the manual that comes with it.

Cleaning Products

There is a variety of cleaning products for PCs. The following list includes some of
the most common.

- Disposable moistened cleaning wipes. These are useful for cleaning optical
  discs and most plastic, metal, and glass exterior surfaces, such as display screens.
- Antistatic display cleaner. This type of product contains a gentle cleansing
  liquid that, when used with a soft cloth, can remove dust and dirt from
  display screens.

SCENARIO & SOLUTION

You carry your troubleshooting toolkit into a client's site. It includes tools in what two very broad categories?	Both software tools and hardware tools.
You believe there is a problem with a component of the motherboard, but swapping out cards has not isolated it, and you do not or cannot remove other components from the motherboard. What should you do?	Consider purchasing a POST card, if you can justify the cost. Alternatively, take the computer to a technician who is experienced in using one. This card will run a variety of tests on the motherboard and isolate the problem.
Digging deeper into your toolkit, you pull out a small device to test the functionality of the USB ports on the PC. What is it?	A USB loopback plug.

- ■ Canned compressed air. This allows you to direct a blast of clean air onto or into your computer. We describe use of this type of product later in the chapter.

- ■ Antistatic vacuum cleaner. This specialized type of vacuum cleaner usually has a conductive path to ground to protect against causing electrostatic discharge damage to a computer during use. These are not cheap, running hundreds of dollars, but are worth having when you are responsible for many PCs.

- ■ Liquid cleaning compound. Keep on-hand a non-abrasive cleaning compound that will not leave a residue. Isopropyl alcohol is a good example.

CERTIFICATION OBJECTIVES

■ **601: 1.4   602: 1.3   603: 1.3   604: 1.3** *Perform preventive maintenance of personal computer components*

While preparing for the CompTIA A+ exams, be sure to study and practice preventive maintenance techniques. CompTIA understands that good preventive maintenance will cut down on the time spent solving problems.

Preventive Maintenance Techniques

The old adage, an ounce of prevention is worth a pound of cure, applies to computers as much it does to the human body. Take time to schedule and perform preventive maintenance on the PCs for which you are responsible. This includes regular visual and audio inspections, driver and firmware updates, and cleaning of components.

Visual and Audio Inspection

Frequent visual inspections will alert you to problems with cables and connections. This is true of your own personal computer as well as other people's computers. Make yourself consciously look at a computer for connection problems and environmental problems. Things change. You may discover that you have inadvertently piled papers on top of a powered USB hub in a corner of your desk, and it is getting hot. You may find that a computer or peripheral moved, and the data cable or power cables are stretched to the point of nearly coming out of the sockets.

An audio inspection involves listening for a noisy fan or hard drive. A squealing fan or hard drive may be a sign of a pending problem. Correct it before you lose use of the fan or hard drive. Clean and/or replace the fan. Immediately back up a hard drive that makes an unusual noise, and take steps to replace it.

Driver and Firmware Updates

Keep current on driver and firmware updates. When you move from an old computer to one with a newer operating system, or upgrade the operating system on an existing computer, obtain new device drivers from the manufacturers. Similarly, when you upgrade to a new operating system, you may need to update the firmware, which, as you learned earlier, means flashing the system BIOS and sometimes the BIOS on devices. We cover driver updates in Chapter 10.

Use of Cleaning Materials

Regular cleaning of computer components can extend a computer's life and prevent problems. For example, by regularly cleaning the power supply and case fans, you can ensure that they properly cool the computer's internal components, preventing a slowdown of the system and potential damage to components.

Removing Dust and Debris from the System

One of the most common reasons to clean a computer is to remove dust buildup. Recall that the power supply's fan draws air out of the computer. Outside air comes in through ports and is distributed over the internal components, bringing with it dust. Because dust can cause ESD (electrostatic discharge) and lead to overheated components, it is important to clean the inside of the computer regularly. Pay particular attention to the system board, the bottom of the computer chassis, and all fan inlets and outlets. Of course, make sure you power down the computer before you start cleaning it.

Using Compressed Air   One of the easiest ways to remove dust from the system is to use compressed air to blow the dust out. Compressed air comes in cans roughly the size of spray-paint cans. Typically, liquid Freon in the can compresses the air and forces it out when you depress the can's nozzle. Tilting or turning the can upside down can cause Freon release. Avoid this because liquid Freon can cause freeze burns on your skin and can damage the computer's components.

Also, be aware of where you are blowing the dust. That is, make sure you are not blowing the dust off one component only to have it settle on another. You can also use compressed air to blow dust out of the keyboard, expansion slots, and ports. Use only canned compressed air, not high-pressure air from a compressor.

Using a Vacuum   Another common method for removing dust is to vacuum the computer or device. This has the advantage of removing dust without allowing the dust to settle elsewhere. It is best to use a special handheld vacuum that allows you to get into smaller places and clean the computer without accidentally hitting and damaging other internal components. Take the nozzle out of the computer, and move the vacuum cleaner away before turning it off.

Using a Lint-Free Cloth   Finally, you can use a lint-free cloth to wipe off dusty surfaces. Avoid using the newer dust cloths that work by "statically attracting" dust. Remember, static is harmful to the computer.

Liquid Cleaning Compounds

A liquid cleaning compound, such as isopropyl alcohol, can come in handy for cleaning gummy residue from the surface of the PC case or from a peripheral. Manufacturer's instructions may also suggest using this for cleaning components inside the PC or other device, but only do this per the manufacturer's instructions.

Ensuring a Proper Environment

Extremes of heat, humidity, and dust are damaging to PCs. Therefore, the best operating environment for a PC is a climate-controlled room with a filtration system to control these three enemies of electronics. If a PC must operate in a hostile environment that exposes it to extremes of any of these, consider spending money on a PC case that will provide better ventilation and filtration. You may find the actual temperature and humidity extremes listed in the user's or technical manual for a PC or component. Look for "Operating Environment." A recommended operating environment is in the range of 50 to 90 degrees Fahrenheit (10 to 32 degrees Centigrade) with relative humidity between 50 percent and 80 percent. A rough guideline: if you are not comfortable, the PC is not either.

Maintenance of Components

Computer components will last longer and function better with some basic and regular maintenance. Learn these simple tasks for maintaining display, power, input, and storage devices.

Display Devices

To maintain a display device, begin by providing it with a well-ventilated location. Use a dry lint-free cloth to remove dust from the display screen, and use an antistatic display cleaner to remove grime. Spray a small amount onto a soft cloth, and then wipe dirt from display screens.

Power Devices

Maintenance of power supplies includes regular vacuuming of the power supply fan and any installed case fans. Ensure that cables do not block the airflow within the PC. This will protect both the power supply and other internal components from overheating.

At a minimum, use surge protectors to protect all computer equipment. A *surge protector* (also called a surge suppressor) may look like an ordinary power strip, except that it protects equipment from power fluctuations. Your PC's power supply will also do this for power fluctuations of up to 600 V, but it will eventually fail if it is the first line of defense. Therefore, plug your PC into a surge protector that has a protection rating of more than 800 joules. (A joule is a unit of energy.) Look for a surge protector that carries the Underwriters Laboratories label showing that it complies with UL standard 1449. This is the least expensive power protection device.

Surge Protectors   Do not just buy the minimum—buy the best power protection you can afford, and that should include protection from both power fluctuations and power outages. Devices that protect from power outages are more expensive than a simple surge protector, but they have come down in price as more manufacturers introduced more consumer-level versions of these devices.

Standby Power Supply (SPS)   One type of device that protects against power outages is a *standby power supply* (SPS). This device contains a circuit that detects a power outage and switches to battery power, which is run through an *inverter,* a device that changes the battery's direct current to the alternating current required by your computer's power supply. The shortcoming of an SPS is that it may not switch fast enough to protect the computer from powering down. This is a standby power protection device, since it does not switch to the alternative power (battery) until there is an outage. Most SPS devices also provide surge protection. An SPS is more expensive than a surge protector but less expensive than the next level of protection.

Uninterruptible Power Supply (UPS)   Another type of device is an *uninterruptible power supply* (UPS), which is an *online power protection device*. A computer or other device plugged into a UPS is truly isolated from the ultimate power source, because during normal operation, it runs directly off the battery through an inverter, rather than switching to the battery only after a loss of power. This is the most expensive type of power protection.

Whether you have an SPS or a UPS, once line power to the protection device is off, your computer is running on the battery, which has a limited lifetime. This lifetime varies by device and by how much power the computer draws. So, unless the power comes back on within a short period of time, consider that you have a window of just minutes to save your data and to power down the computer. For this reason, some of these devices include a data cable and software. When installed, and the UPS or SPS senses a power outage, the software warns you to shut down. If no one is at the keyboard to respond, it will automatically save open data files, shut down the operating system, and power down the computer before the SPS or UPS itself runs out of battery power.

on the ❗️job *Some manufacturers give an "SPS" product a name of "UPS," in which case, look for the words "standby" meaning that it is actually an SPS, or "online" meaning that it is a true UPS.*

Input Devices

For input devices, such as keyboards, mice, and trackball devices, schedule frequent cleaning. For the keyboard, this involves vacuuming the crevices between the keys.

Simply turning a keyboard upside down over a wastebasket and shaking it will remove a surprising amount of dust and debris, depending on the environment and the habits of the user. You may need to protect a keyboard in a dirty environment, such as an auto repair shop, with a special membrane cover that allows use of the keyboard, but keeps dirt, grease, solvents, and other harmful debris out of it. You can find such covers on the Internet or in computer supply catalogs under the category of keyboard protector. For devices that are rarely used, consider using dust covers that remain on the device until needed.

Storage Devices

Common storage devices also require regular maintenance for better performance. The following paragraphs describe simple tasks for maintaining hard drives, optical drives, and floppy drives.

Hard Drives   Hard drive maintenance includes running a utility called a disk defragmenter or disk optimizer to reorganized fragmented files on disk. Do this on a regular basis, perhaps once a week on a drive in which many new files are saved and old files deleted. Chapter 9 will explain the details of this problem and the utilities that resolve the problem.

Optical Drives   Commercially available CD-ROM cleaning and repair kits are readily available to restore CDs or clean the lens. Make sure you follow the directions in these kits, as improper use may cause more problems than they solve.

Floppy Drive Maintenance   You can purchase floppy drive cleaning kits at many computer retail or parts stores. Typically, the kit includes a cleaning solution and what looks like a regular floppy disk. In most cases, you apply the cleaning solution to the disk and insert the disk in the drive. Then the drive cleans the read/write heads as they try to access the disk.

Thermally Sensitive Devices

Many components within a PC are thermally sensitive. These components should only operate within the recommended operating environment, as stated previously in this chapter. Transporting a PC, or thermally sensitive devices, requires that you be aware of the environment. For instance, if you live in a cold climate and bring a new PC home when it is 20° F below zero, be sure to let it sit and acclimate before plugging it in and turning it on. If it feels cold to the touch when you unpack it, this

---

SCENARIO & SOLUTION

You have isolated a performance problem to your hard drive, but you would like to run more diagnostics tests to be sure. What programs should you look for?	Look for a hard drive diagnostics program from the drive's manufacturer, or obtain a third-party hard drive diagnostics program.
You are visiting a customer whose computer is running slow. It is in a fabric store that generates a great deal of dust and fibers. In addition to your basic tools, what should you take along?	Be sure to take a vacuum—an antistatic vacuum, if possible. The slowness may be from overheating due to dust and fibers covering the internal components.

---

acclimation time should be several hours because as it warms up some condensation will occur on internal components, and the PC needs time to dry out!

In addition, be sure to follow the procedures described earlier in this chapter for cleaning dust and dirt from inside the PC to avoid heat buildup and allow sufficient airflow around the PC and its peripherals.

Thermally sensitive devices include

- Motherboards
- CPUs
- Adapter cards
- Memory
- Printers

CERTIFICATION SUMMARY

As a computer technician, you will be required to locate and resolve the source of computer problems. If you have a good knowledge of the functions of the computer's components, you will quickly be able to troubleshoot problems that occur.

However, there are other telltale signs of failed components. For example, you can use POST error codes to determine the cause of a problem. Although the troubleshooting procedures differ from component to component, and even for different problems within the same component, many of the procedures involve cleaning the component, ensuring that it is properly attached to the computer, or finally, replacing the component.

Understanding troubleshooting theory, and taking a structured and disciplined approach, will not only help you to arrive at a solution but will help you to quickly resolve similar problems in the future. When trying to determine a problem's source, gather as much information about the problem as you can, and try to reproduce the problem. Next, determine if this is a hardware problem or a software problem. If it is a software problem, check the application's configuration or try uninstalling and then reinstalling it. If the problem is hardware related, identify the components that make up the failing subsystem. Starting with the most accessible component, check for power and proper attachment to the computer. Check the device's configuration and presence of a device driver. Finally, swap suspected bad components with known good ones.

Remember that every problem has a resolution, whether it is simply reattaching a loose cable, changing an application's settings, or replacing a component or the computer itself. As a computer technician, you have the responsibility for determining which course of action is the most appropriate for each computer problem you face.

TWO-MINUTE DRILL

Here are some of the key points covered in Chapter 4.

Troubleshooting Theory and Techniques

❑ Perform backups of data and the operating system before making any changes.

❑ Assess a problem systematically, and divide large problems into smaller components to analyze individually.

❑ Verify even the obvious, determine whether the problem is something simple, and make no assumptions.

❑ Research ideas and establish priorities.

❑ Always document your actions, findings, and outcomes.

❑ Perform diagnostic procedures in a logical order.

❑ Identify the problem and analyze it to determine whether it is hardware or software. Then apply troubleshooting techniques appropriate to the problem type.

Troubleshooting PC Component Problems

❑ Procedures should move from least intrusive to most intrusive, checking the following: proper connections, appropriate components, drivers, and settings, and component seating of internal devices.

❑ When troubleshooting a video or audio problem, start with the most accessible component, check to ensure that it is getting power, and that it properly connects to the computer.

❑ Never open the power supply or try to replace the fan; rather, replace the entire power supply when the fan stops working.

❑ POST error codes, such as 1**, 2**, and 3**, can indicate system board, memory, or keyboard failures, respectively.

❑ Most CPU problems are fatal, which requires replacing the CPU or system. Check your warranty if you suspect a problem with the CPU, since it may require replacing the motherboard.

❑ Incorrect CMOS settings can affect a variety of system components. Check and correct these problems by running the system setup and changing the settings.

❑ CMOS batteries last from two to ten years. A computer that does not maintain the date and time when it has been powered off is a symptom of a failed battery.

❑ Most system board, processor, and memory errors are fatal, meaning that the computer cannot properly boot up.

❑ The most common mouse problem is irregular movement, which can be resolved by cleaning the internal rollers of a mechanical mouse or the bottom surface of an optical mouse.

❑ Motherboard errors can be the most difficult to pinpoint and, due to the cost and effort involved in replacement, should be the last device you suspect when a subsystem or the entire computer fails.

❑ Replace a hard drive that begins to develop corrupted data before all the information stored on it is lost.

❑ Most floppy drive problems are with the media (floppy disks) rather than with the hardware. If you find a floppy drive problem that cannot be easily corrected, consider replacing it with an external USB floppy drive.

❑ USB device problems may involve power connections for external devices that require external power. Consider using a USB loopback plug to diagnose a stubborn USB problem.

❑ Problems with SCSI devices, beyond failure of the device itself, most often involve termination of the SCSI chain and SCSI device ID.

Troubleshooting Tools

❑ Arm yourself with appropriate troubleshooting tools, including software and hardware tools.

❑ If you must service a large number of PCs, consider investing in a specialized diagnostic toolkit.

❑ Acquire and learn how to use appropriate cleaning products, such as cleaning wipes, antistatic display cleaner, canned compressed air, an antistatic vacuum cleaner, and non-abrasive cleaning compounds, such as isopropyl alcohol.

Preventive Maintenance Techniques

❑ Schedule regular preventive maintenance, such as visual and audio inspections, driver and firmware updates, cleaning, and verifying maintenance of a proper environment.

❑ Schedule regular maintenance for various components, such as displays, power devices, and drives. Protect thermally sensitive devices with regular cleaning, and by ensuring that there is proper airflow.

SELF TEST

The following questions will help you measure your understanding of the material presented in this chapter. Read all of the choices carefully because there might be more than one correct answer. Choose all correct answers for each question.

Troubleshooting Theory and Techniques

1. When faced with a large, complicated problem, what strategy should you use?
   A. Call in a high-level service technician.
   B. Divide a large problem into smaller components to analyze individually.
   C. Replace the entire system.
   D. Check the warranty.

2. What should you do before making any changes to a computer?
   A. Turn off the computer.
   B. Use a grounding strap.
   C. Restore the most recent backup.
   D. If there is no recent backup of data and/or the operating system, perform a backup.

3. What are two methods you should employ for identifying a problem?
   A. Examine the environment.
   B. Question the user.
   C. Vacuum the computer.
   D. Read the label on the back of the power supply.

4. You want to narrow down the source of a problem to one of what two broad categories?
   A. Power or data
   B. Operating system or application
   C. Motherboard or component
   D. Hardware or software

5. How do you narrow down the problem to one hardware component?
   A. Remove the data cables.
   B. Run specialized diagnostics.
   C. Swap each suspect component with a known good one.
   D. Restart the computer.

6. What should you do if you are unsure if a problem is limited to the single application that was in use at the time the problem occurred?
   A. Remove and reinstall the application.
   B. Upgrade the application.
   C. Perform the actions that resulted in the problem from more than one application.
   D. Upgrade the driver.

7. What should you have the user do as part of evaluating the solution? Select all that apply.
   A. First, restart the computer and device (if appropriate).
   B. First, disconnect the problem component.
   C. Test the fix and all commonly used applications.
   D. Print out the user manual.

Troubleshooting PC Component Problems

8. The following is a recommended set of troubleshooting procedures. Which two things should you do first? Which thing should be last?
   A. Check proper component seating (internal adapter card, memory, etc.).
   B. Check for proper connections.
   C. Check for appropriate components.
   D. Check drivers and settings.

9. Your video display is blank. Which of the following should you do first?
   A. Swap the display with a known good one.
   B. Replace the video adapter with a known good one.
   C. Check the power and data cables.
   D. Check the seating of the video adapter.

10. A customer reports that the computer spontaneously reboots and sometimes will not start at all. Furthermore, even when the computer does start, there is not as much fan noise as before. What is the likely cause of these problems?
    A. The power supply
    B. The system board
    C. The processor
    D. The RAM

11. Your computer consistently loses its date/time setting. Which procedure will you use to solve the problem?
  A. Replace the battery.
  B. Flash the battery using a manufacturer-provided disk.
  C. Use the computer's AC adapter to recharge the battery.
  D. Access the CMOS setting programs at startup and select the low-power option.

12. Which component is typically associated with a 3** BIOS error code?
  A. Motherboard
  B. Keyboard
  C. Processor
  D. RAM

13. Which of the following symptoms is not caused by a RAM error?
  A. The POST cannot be conducted.
  B. When you turn on the computer, nothing happens.
  C. The system reports that there is no operating system.
  D. The BIOS reports a 2** error.

14. A user reports that the mouse pointer does not move smoothly across the screen. Which of the following is most likely to remedy the problem?
  A. Reinstall the mouse driver.
  B. Ensure that the mouse cable connects securely to the computer.
  C. Replace the mouse with a trackball. Ensure that there are no IRQ conflicts between the mouse and another device.
  D. Clean the mouse.

15. Which of the following should you do first when you receive this error: "Please insert a disk into drive A:"
  A. Make sure that there is a floppy disk in the drive.
  B. Ensure that the floppy ribbon cable is attached properly.
  C. Make sure that the floppy drive is properly configured in the BIOS settings.
  D. Clean the floppy disk.

16. You have just finished building a computer. You notice that when you turn on the computer, the floppy drive light comes on and will not go off. What should you do?
  A. Insert a different disk into the drive.
  B. Reverse the ribbon cable on the drive.

C. Swap the drive with another one.

D. Nothing.

17. You played a game on the computer about an hour ago and closed the game when you were finished. In the meantime, you opened a word processor, sent a print job to the printer, and then closed the application. When you tried to restart the game, nothing happened. Which of the following should you do first?

A. Obtain a manufacturer's patch for the game.

B. Troubleshoot the printer.

C. Restart the computer.

D. Reinstall the game.

Troubleshooting Tools

18. Which of the following is an advanced hardware diagnostics tool that is inserted into an expansion slot?

A. POST card

B. Loopback plug

C. Video adapter

D. Nut driver

Preventive Maintenance Techniques

19. Which cleaning product blows dirt and dust out of PC components?

A. Antistatic display cleaner

B. Canned compressed air

C. Liquid cleaning compound

D. Antistatic vacuum cleaner

20. Which of the following power protection devices is considered an "online" power protection device?

A. Power strip

B. Surge protector

C. SPS

D. UPS

LAB QUESTION

A customer who has a specialized sound card installed in an expansion slot has complained about a problem in playing a music file. He tells you that the computer seemed to run the file, but produced no sound, even though it worked properly yesterday. Although you do not know it at first, the problem is that the sound card's expansion slot has failed because of a broken circuit. Describe the steps you will perform, in the proper order, to determine that this is the cause of the problem. Also, discuss how you will resolve the problem.

SELF TEST ANSWERS

Troubleshooting Theory and Techniques

1. ☑ **B.** To divide a large problem into smaller components to analyze individually is the correct answer. The smaller problems will be easier to resolve, and eventually you will solve the bigger problem.
   ☒ **A,** call in a high-level service technician, is incorrect. While this may become necessary, take the steps recommended in this chapter first to save time and money. **C,** replace the entire system, is incorrect because you have not made enough effort yet on the problem to do something so drastic. **D,** check the warranty, is incorrect because you have not yet even narrowed the problem down to the source.

2. ☑ **D.** If there is no recent backup of data and/or the operating system, perform a backup. This is correct because you do not want to risk losing the user's data.
   ☒ **A,** turn off the computer, is incorrect because it is rather irrelevant, although after taking care of the backup you may want to restart a computer. **B,** use a grounding strap, is incorrect because until you have narrowed the cause down, you do not know if this will be necessary. You must do a backup before you reach this point. **C,** restore the most recent backup, is incorrect because you have no idea if this is even necessary at this point.

3. ☑ **A,** examine the environment, and **B,** question the user, are two methods for identifying a problem.
   ☒ **C** is incorrect because vacuuming the computer seldom helps to identify the problem. **D,** reading the label on the back of the power supply, won't help to identify the problem, unless it is a brand-new computer that has never been run.

4. ☑ **D.** Hardware or software are the two broad categories of problem sources.
   ☒ **A,** power or data, is incorrect because, while you may have problems in these areas, they are not the two broad categories of problem sources. **B,** operating system or application, is incorrect because these are both types of software, and software is just one of the two broad categories of problem sources. **C,** motherboard or component, is incorrect because these are both types of hardware, and hardware is just one of the two categories of problem sources.

5. ☑ **C.** To swap each suspect component with a known good one is correct because this will narrow down a hardware problem to one component.
   ☒ **A,** remove the data cables, is incorrect because, while this may be part of removing a component, this alone will not help you narrow down the problem to one component. **B,** run specialized diagnostics, is incorrect because they lead to general areas, not specific components. **D,** restart the computer, is incorrect because restarting will not indicate one component, although it might cause the problem to disappear.

6. ☑ **C.** To perform the actions that resulted in the problem from more than one application is correct. If the problem only occurs in the one application, then focus on that application.

☒ **A,** remove and reinstall the application, is incorrect because, while this may be a fix for the problem, you must first determine that the problem only occurs with that application before doing something so drastic. **B,** upgrade the application, is incorrect because, while this may be a fix for the problem, you must first narrow it down to the one application. **D,** upgrade the driver, is incorrect because, while this may be a solution, you must first narrow down the cause to specific hardware before upgrading the driver.

7. ☑ **A.** First, restart the computer and device (if appropriate) and **C.** Test the fix and all commonly used applications. These are both correct. The user should do this to be sure that the fix works and to assure the user that the changes you made were not harmful.

☒ **B,** first, disconnect the problem component, is incorrect because without the problem component you cannot evaluate the solution. **D,** print out the user manual, is incorrect because that has little to do with evaluating the solution.

Troubleshooting PC Component Problems

8. ☑ The correct order is **B,** check for proper connections, and **C,** check for proper components.

☒ **D,** check installation drivers and settings, and **A,** check proper component seating. While the first three may be out of order without much problem, opening up the PC to check proper component seating should be the last because you want to perform the least intrusive steps first.

9. ☑ **C.** Check the power and data cables is correct because it is the least intrusive action. If this does not resolve it, check the brightness setting, and then continue to A, D, and B, in that order.

☒ **A,** swap the display with a known good one, is incorrect because this is more trouble than simply checking the cables. **B,** replace the video adapter with a known good one, and **D,** check the seating of the video adapter, are incorrect because these very intrusive actions should wait until you have performed less intrusive actions.

10. ☑ **A.** The power supply is the most likely cause of these symptoms. When a power supply begins to fail, it often manifests in a number of different, sporadic symptoms. If the power supply's fan stops working, the computer will overheat and spontaneously reboot itself. If the components are still excessively hot when the system restarts, the computer may not start at all.

☒ **B,** the system board, **C,** the processor, and **D,** the RAM, are all incorrect. Failure of these components does not cause the specific set of symptoms mentioned in the question. A RAM failure will not cause the computer to reboot (unless *all* the RAM fails). While an overheated processor could cause the system to reboot, it would not be associated with the lack of noise from the power supply fan.

11. ☑ **A.** You should replace the battery. When the computer "forgets" the time and date, it is most likely because the CMOS battery, which normally maintains these settings, is getting low and must be replaced.

☒ **B** is incorrect because it suggests flashing the battery. This procedure (flashing) applies to the upgrade of a BIOS chip, not a CMOS battery. **C** is incorrect because it suggests recharging the battery with the computer's AC adapter. Although this procedure will work with a portable system battery, you cannot recharge CMOS batteries with an AC adapter. **D** is incorrect because it suggests selecting a "low-power" option in the CMOS settings program. Any low-power setting in the CMOS settings refers to the function of the computer itself, not to the CMOS battery. You cannot adjust the amount of power the CMOS chip draws from its battery.

12. ☑ **B.** The keyboard is typically associated with a 3** BIOS error code. When the computer is started, the BIOS performs a POST, which checks for the presence and function of certain components. If a keyboard error, such as a missing cable or stuck key, is detected, the BIOS typically reports a 3** error code.

☒ **A**, motherboard, and **C**, processor, are incorrect because these errors, if detected by the BIOS, are typically indicated by a 1** error code. **D**, RAM, is incorrect because memory errors are typically associated with 2** error codes.

13. ☑ **C.** The system reports that there is no operating system. The OS resides on the hard drive and, following the POST, the BIOS looks for the OS, loads it into memory, and gives it control. If the computer reports a missing OS, it means either that one does not exist on the hard drive, that it cannot be read from the hard drive, or that the computer cannot communicate with the hard drive. This message is not associated with a memory error.

☒ **A**, **B**, and **D** are incorrect because these are all typical symptoms of bad memory. If the memory has totally failed, the BIOS cannot conduct or complete the POST and might not even be able to initiate the processor. This might make it appear that the computer does absolutely nothing when it is turned on. Non-critical memory errors can be indicated by a 2** error code.

14. ☑ **D.** Cleaning the mouse is most likely to remedy the problem of a mouse pointer that does not move smoothly on the screen.

☒ **A**, reinstalling the mouse driver, is incorrect because if the mouse does not have a proper driver, it will not work at all. Driver problems for any device will cause that device to stop functioning altogether, or to work sporadically. **B**, ensuring that the mouse cable connects securely to the computer, is also incorrect. If the mouse connector is not plugged into the computer, there will be no response from the mouse at all. If the mouse connector is loose, the operation of the mouse could be sporadic, working at some times, and not working at all on other occasions. **C**, replacing the mouse with a trackball, is also incorrect. While this may actually resolve the problem caused by a dirty mouse, it is more extreme than cleaning the mouse.

15. ☑ **A.** Make sure that there is a floppy disk in the drive. This error indicates that the drive did not detect a disk. The most common reason for receiving this error is simply that a disk is not inserted, or is not inserted all the way.

    ☒ **B**, ensure that the floppy ribbon cable is attached properly, and **C**, make sure that the floppy drive is properly configured in the BIOS settings, are both incorrect. You should suspect a ribbon cable or BIOS setting problem only if the computer cannot communicate with the floppy drive. **D**, clean the floppy disk, is incorrect because although this message is used to indicate a problem accessing the disk, you may cause more problems by trying to clean the disk.

16. ☑ **B.** You should reverse the ribbon cable on the drive. A floppy drive light that will not go out is a sure indicator of a ribbon cable that has been reversed in the drive's port. Make sure that you align the cable's red stripe with pin 1 on both the floppy drive's port connector and the socket on the motherboard.

    ☒ **A**, insert a different disk into the drive, is incorrect because the floppy light remaining on will occur at startup, with or without a disk present in the drive. **C**, swap the drive with another one, is incorrect because there is probably no need to do so. Reverse the ribbon cable on the drive first. **D** is incorrect because it suggests that you should do nothing. However, when the stated condition occurs, the ribbon is on backward, and the drive will not work.

17. ☑ **C.** You should restart the computer. In some cases, applications can use computer resources, such as memory or processor time, and will fail to release them, even when the application is closed. By restarting the computer, you will remove the application from memory and cause it to release any system resources.

    ☒ **A**, obtain a manufacturer's patch for the game, and **D**, reinstall the game, are incorrect because you typically use these procedures when an application contains corrupt or improper instructions. Since the game worked originally, this is not likely the case. Furthermore, it is typically more time-consuming to install a patch or reinstall an application than it is to reboot the system. **B**, troubleshoot the printer, is incorrect because the printer is also an unlikely suspect in this case. It is not impossible for the printer to be the cause of this problem, but troubleshooting the printer is more time-consuming and less likely to resolve the problem than simply restarting the computer.

Troubleshooting Tools

18. ☑ **A.** POST card is correct. You must install this into an expansion slot. Then when the computer is booted up, it performs advanced diagnostics and displays the results on an LED and through indicator lights.

    ☒ **B and D** are incorrect because, while these are examples of hardware tools, neither can be inserted into an expansion slot. **C**, video adapter, is incorrect because this is not a hardware diagnostics tool but a common PC component.

Preventive Maintenance Techniques

19. ☑ **B.** Canned compressed air is the cleaning product used to blow dirt and dust out of PC components. The drawback to this is that it can blow dirt and dust into components, and if used improperly, the liquid Freon within the can will spill onto skin or computer components, causing injury or damage.

    ☒ **A**, antistatic display cleaner, and **C**, liquid cleaning compound, are both incorrect because these are wet cleaning products used to wipe off the screen and other surfaces. **D**, antistatic vacuum cleaner, is incorrect because it draws the dust in, rather than blowing it. This more expensive product is really preferred for cleaning out a PC.

20. ☑ **D.** UPS is correct. This is the only true online power protection device.

    ☒ **A**, power strip, is incorrect because this provides no power protection whatsoever. **B**, surge protector and **C**, SPS, are incorrect because neither of these alone is an online power protection device in the way that a UPS is, providing full-time power from the battery.

LAB ANSWER

1. On arrival at the customer's site, take note of potential problem-causing environmental factors, such as the temperature and humidity.

2. Ask the customer about the computer's history. For example, ask whether this has occurred before, or if a new device or application was installed.

3. Have the customer try to play the sound file again. Watch for irregular system activity, the presence of error messages, and other on-screen indicators, such as a visual volume control on the screen.

4. Check that the speakers are receiving power and that the volume is set at a sufficient level. (You might choose to do this before the preceding step, since it is so easy and quick to check.)

5. Make sure that the speakers connect securely to the sound card.

6. Try to play a different sound file to determine if the first sound file is corrupt. In this particular case, the second sound file should cause the same result as the first.

7. Try to play a sound file in a different application. Do not use the original sound file, because both the file and the original application file could be at fault. Again, considering the actual cause of the problem, the result should be the same. This indicates (but does not prove) that the original application and sound file are not at fault.

8. Restart the computer, and then try to have the system produce sound again. This might resolve the problem if the sound card's configuration was improperly loaded the first time or if another application is using a resource the sound card or application needs.

9. At this point, you should have determined that this is a hardware problem, not a software problem. Swap the speakers with known good ones.

10. Swap the speaker cables with known good ones.

11. Check the configuration of the sound card. Look for a resource conflict or a bad or missing driver. You can use Device Manager to access this. Given the actual cause of this problem, you should see nothing to indicate a configuration error. However, you might want to remove the sound card's driver, and then reinstall it, just to rule it out as the cause.

12. Turn the computer off, remove the case, use an appropriate grounding method, and ensure that the sound card seats properly in the expansion slot.

13. At this point, you can try to either install the card in another expansion slot or swap the sound card with a known working one. If you swap the card first, turn the computer back on, configure it, and then try to play a sound file. If you try the original card in another slot first, you will have located the source of the problem (the expansion slot).

14. To determine why the slot has failed, you can use a multimeter to test its ability to receive signals. In this case, you would find that the bad circuit offers infinite resistance, indicating a break in the circuit.

15. To resolve this problem, you can continue to use the original sound card in an alternate expansion slot. However, if you need all the slots for other components, you will probably end up replacing one of the devices with an external one (to free up a slot) or replacing the entire motherboard. If you don't need to use all the slots, you might put a piece of tape over the bad slot with a note on it indicating that the slot is bad so someone else doesn't waste time trying to use a bad slot.

Part II

Laptops and Portable Devices

5

Using and Supporting Laptops and Portable Devices

I n recent years there has been an increase in growth, year-to-year, in laptops sales versus desktop PC sales. Laptops comprised 50.9 percent of PC sales in the U.S. in 2005, due to lower prices, higher performance, and the availability of wireless networks. This figure does not include large sales to corporations or direct sales from computer companies. Laptop sales were not expected to pass desktop sales until 2008. These trends guarantee that most PC technicians will need to understand laptop-specific technologies.

CERTIFICATION OBJECTIVES

■ **601: 2.1   602: 2.1   604: 2.1**   *Identify the fundamental principles of using laptops and portable devices*

For the CompTIA exams be sure that you can describe portable computer form factors, peripherals, expansion slots, ports, connectors, power and electrical input devices, and other technologies that may not be exclusive to portable computers but are commonly found on them. These include LCD technologies and input devices.

Introduction to Portable Computers

A portable computer is any type of computer that you can easily transport and that contains an all-in-one component layout. In addition to the size difference, portable computers differ from desktop computers in their physical layout.

Finally, although portable computers are functionally similar to desktop computers, they are primarily proprietary and tend to use specialized components that are generally miniaturized versions of those described in Chapters 1 and 2. Repairing portable systems usually requires a skill set beyond what is necessary to service desktop PCs.

Portable computers fall into two broad categories: laptops and handhelds. In this chapter and in Chapter 6 we will focus on laptops, the most common of portable computers.

Laptops and Notebooks

A laptop, like other portable computers, is a small, easily transported computer. Laptops generally weigh less than 7 pounds, can fit easily in a large bag or briefcase, and have roughly the same dimensions as a 1- to 2-inch thick stack of magazines.

Laptops computers have an all-in-one layout in which the keyboard, and often the pointing device, are integrated into the computer chassis and an LCD display is in a hinged lid. Typically, laptops open in the same manner as a briefcase. The top contains the display, and the bottom contains the keyboard and the rest of the computer's internal components. Laptops use liquid crystal display (LCD) displays, and they use small credit-card-sized specialized integrated circuit cards, called PC Cards, rather than the expansion cards used in PCs.

Additionally, a laptop has a built-in battery allowing it to be used for short periods without an outside power source. The battery life of a laptop depends on the battery and how the laptop is used, but under normal use, it will last from two to six hours.

Truly designed for the mobile lifestyle of many users today, some laptops, called ultra-portables, weigh less than three pounds, and they may even give up features to keep the weight down and maintain the highest battery life. The typical laptop user also has a desktop PC at the office.

People purchase other laptops as full-featured desktop replacements in which performance is more important than battery life. These have large screens and weigh in at over seven pounds.

Often "laptop" is used interchangeably with "notebook." Initially, people called most portable computers laptops because they could fit comfortably on the user's lap, although early laptops were a little heavy to do this comfortably. As technology improved, laptops became smaller and smaller, and the term notebook came into use to reflect this smaller size. Throughout the remainder of this book, we will use the term laptop to describe any computer categorized as either a laptop or notebook.

Laptops based on the Intel IBM-compatible platform can run the same operating systems as desktop PCs. Most laptops come with Windows installed, but you can also find laptops with Linux installed, or install it yourself. Additionally, Apple Computers has switched to an Intel platform, although not a strictly IBM-compatible platform.

Handheld Computers

Handheld computers come in a variety of types. The most common are personal digital assistants (PDAs), but many cell phones now have PDA functions built in and people call the fanciest of these smart phones. There are also specialized handheld computers developed for specific job functions.

Personal Digital Assistant (PDA)

A personal digital assistant, known more commonly as a PDA, is a portable computer small enough to fit in your hand, and it is also referred to as a "palmtop" computer. Because it is so small, a PDA does not have the functionality of a laptop or desktop computer. In other words, a typical PDA allows you to perform only a small number of functions.

The two most common operating systems used in PDAs today are the Microsoft Pocket PC operating system and the Palm operating system. In general, these two operating systems do not support interchangeable applications, though most PDA software manufacturers now support both platforms.

One of the most common uses for a PDA is as an organizer used to keep track of appointments and record addresses, phone numbers, and notes. Many PDAs also allow you to plug into a fax machine to send faxes, or to connect wirelessly to a network to send e-mail or access the Internet.

PDAs are too small to include a regular keyboard layout, so the primary input device is a small stylus, shaped like a pen, which you use to press small keys on a virtual keypad, tap the screen to select items, or write data on the screen. PDAs are entirely proprietary, non-serviceable by regular technicians, and they differ from one another in their technology and functions. Therefore, although you should be aware of their existence, you shouldn't expect to see many questions about PDAs on the A+ exam.

Specialized Handheld Computers

There is a variety of handheld computers, each dedicated to a single purpose. For example, you may see employees in grocery stores using specialized handheld computers to take inventory counts. These devices often include wireless communications with a central computer in order to update the central inventory database.

Laptop Hardware

Because laptops are largely proprietary, motherboards and other components are not interchangeable between brands. Not only are they proprietary by manufacturer, their internals can be very different from model to model from the same manufacturer. Therefore, you must return most laptops to the manufacturer to be repaired or upgraded. This section introduces you to some laptop-specific components and describes installation procedures, where applicable.

Motherboard

While laptops run standard PC operating systems and applications, the motherboards do not comply with the form factor standards found in PCs. The miniaturization required for laptops has inspired manufacturers to come up with largely proprietary motherboard form factors. Motherboards (also called processor boards) contain specialized versions of the components you would expect to find in a desktop PC, such as the CPU, chipset, RAM, video adapter (built-in), and expansion bus ports.

CPU

Both Intel and AMD have a number of CPUs designed especially for laptops. Intel includes the word "mobile" in some model names, and simply uses an "M" in other model names. AMD currently uses an "M" in the model name. These chips include the Intel Pentium 4-M and the AMD Athlon XP-M.

Both manufacturers include special mobile computer technologies in their mobile CPUs, such as power-saving and heat-reducing features, and throttling that lowers the clock speed and supply voltage when the CPU is idle. We described throttling in Chapter 1.

Just as there are different sizes of laptops, there are different models of mobile processors. These include high-performance models requiring more power that are appropriate for desktop replacement, and CPUs that run at lower voltage and reduced clock speeds to give the best battery life. The latter CPUs may have "Low Voltage" or "LV" in the model name. Many mobile CPUs support Wi-Fi wireless networking. Learn about wireless networking in Chapter 12.

Video Adapter

As in a desktop PC, a video adapter controls a laptop's video output. Typically, the video adapter for a laptop is integrated into the motherboard and is not upgradeable. In most cases, a faulty video adapter requires manufacturer replacement of the motherboard.

Display

A laptop has an LCD display screen integrated into the "lid" of the case. In addition to the features discussed in Chapter 2, an LCD screen installed in a laptop also requires an internal inverter to convert the DC current from the power adapter or battery to the AC current required by the display.

e x a m

w a t c h *The three main components of the video system in a laptop include the LCD screen, the inverter, and the built-in video adapter.*

Memory

Laptop memory modules come in small form factors, the most commonly used is Small Outline DIMM (SODIMM), which are about half the size of DIMM modules.

SODIMM modules initially had 30 pins, and the next generation had 72 pins. These had a data bus width of 8 bits and 32 bits, respectively, per module. Over the years, SODIMM modules have improved their data width progressing through form factors with 100, 144, and 200 pins. Notches prevent you from installing a module in the wrong orientation to the SODIMM memory slot. The 200-pin SODIMM in Figure 5-1 measures $2\frac{5}{8}$ " wide. Table 5-1 shows the width at which data can be transferred for each of these form factors.

Another type of laptop memory module is Small Outline RIMM (SORIMM), which comes in 120-pin and 160-pin forms.

MicroDIMM, a RAM module designed for subcompact and laptop computers, is half the size of a SODIMM module and allows for higher density of storage.

TABLE 5-1	Number of Pins per SODIMM Module	Data Bus Width
The Data Bus Width of SODIMM Modules	30	8-bit
	72	32-bit
	100	32-bit
	144	64-bit
	200	64-bit

FIGURE 5-1

A 200-pin SODIMM module

Hard Drives

Laptop hard drives are typically 2.5" wide versus the 3.5" hard drive currently widely used in desktop PCs (see Figure 5-2). The interface typically is either PATA or SATA. There are also hard drives that you can install into the PC Card expansion bays.

Peripherals

Laptops can use just about any external peripheral that a PC can use, unless it relies on inserting a full-sized expansion card. You can attach a full-sized external display to a laptop and any printer or scanner that can use one of your laptop's interfaces, such as USB, FireWire, or one of the PCMCIA interfaces discussed a little later in this chapter.

We discussed common PC peripherals in earlier chapters, and printers and scanners are the topics of Chapter 10. Therefore, we'll now discuss those peripherals that are specifically designed for laptops: port replicators, docking stations, and those that fit into specialized media/accessory bays.

FIGURE 5-2

A 2.5" laptop hard drive shown next to a 3.5" PC hard drive

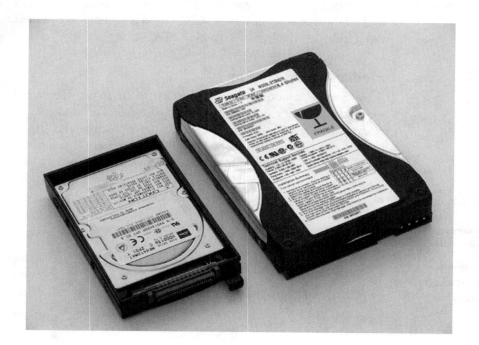

Port Replicators and Docking Stations

The typical laptop owner uses a laptop while in transit but has a "base of operations" office. This is typically where the user will use external devices, such as keyboards, printers, displays, and mice. The user must connect and disconnect these components every time he or she returns to or leaves the office with the laptop.

A device called a port replicator can make this task less time-consuming by providing a permanent connection to these external devices. A port replicator is a device that remains on the desktop with external devices connected to ports on it. When a port replicator plugs into a laptop, each of the ports on the replicator passes communications through to the appropriate port on the laptop, usually through a special proprietary port.

A more advanced and more expensive alternative to the port replicator is a docking station, which provides more advanced enhancements for a laptop. In addition to the ports normally found on a port replicator, a docking station may include full-size expansion slots, and drives. Figure 5-3 shows a laptop and a docking station.

The port replicators and docking stations of the past were proprietary—often only fitting one model of laptop. If the manufacturer did not make one of these devices to fit your laptop—and you wanted one—you had no options. Now you can easily find an inexpensive "universal" USB-based port replicator or docking station that interfaces with the laptop via a USB port.

Media/Accessory Bay

To save space, a laptop may contain a media bay, a compartment that holds a single media device that can be switched with another. For instance, you may switch an optical drive, a secondary hard drive, or a floppy drive into and out of a single bay, but you can use only one device in the bay at a time. Figure 5-4 shows a media bay and two drives that you can alternate in the bay. This type of bay, also called an accessory bay, is now used less frequently, since so many accessories and drives are available with USB or FireWire interfaces.

FIGURE 5-3

A laptop sitting next to a docking station

A media bay in a laptop, with two drives that one can swap using this bay

Memory Card Reader

Some laptops come with a built-in flash-memory card reader. Since there are several formats for these solid-state storage devices (see Chapter 2), you should be sure that your laptop supports the format you use, such as CompactFlash cards.

Expansion Slots

Laptops come with specialized, small form factor, expansion slots. The most common expansion slots are those based on standards developed by the Personal Computer Memory Card International Association (PCMCIA), an organization that creates standards for laptop computer peripheral devices. All the standards described here support hot swapping, meaning devices can be plugged in and removed while the computer is running. A service called socket services running in the operating system on the laptop detects when a card has been inserted. After socket services detects a card, another service, called card services, assigns the proper resources to the device.

PC Card

The early standard developed by PCMCIA was referred to at first simply as the "PCMCIA" interface. The credit card–sized cards that fit into this interface, sliding in from slots on the side of a laptop, were called PCMCIA cards, but eventually the name changed to PC Card. The earliest interface and cards used a 16-bit interface.

CardBus

Eventually the standard was modified to use a 32-bit parallel PCI bus, which is known as CardBus. In fact, the CardBus allows 32-bit burst mode transfers, but only 16-bit memory transfers (for memory devices) and 16-bit I/O transfers for network cards, modems, and other I/O devices.

PC Card and CardBus Types

The cards that fit into the PC Card interface, including both PC Card and CardBus cards, measure 85.6 mm long by 54 mm wide. The three types vary in thickness: Type I measures 3.3 mm thick, Type II measures 5.0 mm thick, and Type III measures 10.5 mm thick. Figure 5-5 shows a Type II PC Card.

The PC Card slots are downward compatible. A Type III card can only fit in a Type III slot, while you can use a Type II card in either a Type II or a Type III slot, and a Type I card in all three. They all have 68 pins, fit into the PC Card sockets, and only vary in thickness. It is the thickness and the circuitry that fits into each size that dictates the type of device that will use each PC Card type. Table 5-2 lists the PC Card types and the devices that would use each type.

Additionally, there is a physical distinction between the older 16-bit PC Card and a CardBus PC Card. When comparing the two types of cards, look at the area

FIGURE 5-5

A Type II PC Card with a cable to attach to a network

TABLE 5-2	Type	Device
The Kinds of Devices That Use Each Type of PC Card	I	Solid-state memory cards
	II	I/O devices: modems, network interface cards
	III	Rotating mass storage hard drives

above the connector. On a 16-bit card, this is smooth, while on the newer CardBus PC Card there is a gold grounding strip that usually has 8 bumps. You can insert a 16-bit PC card into a 16-bit slot or a CardBus slot, but the CardBus PC Card can only be inserted into a CardBus slot.

PC Card and CardBus Voltages

There are voltage differences among PC Cards. Some operate at 3.3 V, while others operate at 5.0 V. A PC Card interface that can only operate at 5.0 V will have a key along one edge of the connectors that prevents cards that can only operate at 3.3 V from insertion into the slots. Some cards, and some PC Card interfaces, can operate at either voltage. All of this voltage variation applies only to the older PC Card interface. The CardBus PC Card interface only operates at 3.3 V.

EXERCISE 5-1

Using Device Manager to View a CardBus Controller

You can use Device Manager to discover the standard supported by a PCMCIA slot in your laptop.

1. Open the Start menu and right-click My Computer to display the context menu.
2. Select Properties.
3. In the System Properties dialog box, select the Hardware tab.
4. On the Hardware page, click the Device Manager button.
5. Scroll through the list until you find the PCMCIA Adapters node. Then click the plus (+) sign next to this node to expand it.
6. You will then see the PCMCIA-supported standard, as shown in Figure 5-6.

FIGURE 5-6

Device Manager
shows the
CardBus adapters
for a laptop.

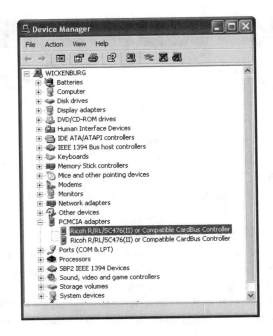

ExpressCard

Laptops are currently moving to the most recent PCMCIA standard—ExpressCard, which comes in two interfaces: the PCIe (PCI Express) interface, at 2.5 gigabits per second, and the USB 2.0 interface, at 480 megabits per second. ExpressCard is incompatible with either PC Card standard. To begin with, the ExpressCard interface does not have actual pins, but instead has 26 contacts in a form referred to as a beam-on-blade connector. Although all ExpressCard modules have the same number of contacts (also called pins), there are currently two sizes of modules: Both are 75 mm long and 5 mm high, but they vary in width. The form factor known as ExpressCard/34 is 34 mm wide, while ExpressCard/54 is 54 mm wide. ExpressCard/34 modules will fit into ExpressCard/54 slots.

ExpressCard supports a variety of device types, including the following:

- LAN and WAN adapters
- FireWire
- SATA
- USB hubs
- Serial and parallel I/O adapters
- Television tuners

- Video capture cards
- Solid-state storage
- Micro–hard drive storage
- Micro-optical storage
- SmartCard devices
- Biometric security sensors

ExpressCard technology is not just for laptops. In the not-too-distant future, you will find the ExpressCard interface built into desktop PCs and tied into the PCI Express bus or USB hub. Ironically, this will occur because the devices are smaller than PC Card devices.

Mini–Expansion Slots

Some laptops also have one or more special mini–expansion slots inside the case. The two most common are based on the full-sized PCI and PCIe expansion bus found in a desktop PC. The first is Mini PCI, and the latest is PCIe Mini Card. These use scaled-down versions of the cards used in desktop PCs and also require opening up the case to install or remove a card. Laptops that use these Mini Cards usually provide a small removable door, often attached with a screw, so they are not intended to be installed and removed frequently, like the PC Card, CardBus, or ExpressCard devices.

Mini PCI   Mini PCI is a standard based on PCI (see Chapter 1). The biggest difference (although there are others) is that Mini PCI is much smaller than PCI—both the card and the slot. Mini PCI has a 32-bit data bus. If a Mini PCI slot has been installed on a laptop, it is usually accessible via a small removable panel on the bottom of the case. A Mini PCI card measures 61 mm by 51 mm.

e x a m
ⓦ a t c h   *Remember, PC Card, CardBus, and ExpressCard all have slots you can access without opening up the computer. Mini PCI and PCIe Mini Card use bus connectors that you must access by opening up a small covering over the connector.*

PCIe Mini Card

A newer standard for Mini Cards is replacing the Mini PCI standard. That is the PCIe Mini Card specification, which provides much faster throughput with a 64-bit data bus. A PCIe Mini Card, at 30 mm by 51 mm, is half the size of a Mini PCI card. Small is good!

Communication Connections and Appropriate Uses

Several communications technologies, which differ in the media they use and the effective range of the signal, are in use on portable computers. They may be built into the motherboard; installed in a Mini Card port (Mini PCI or PCIe Mini Card);

inserted as a card in a PC Card, CardBus, or ExpressCard slot; or come in the form of an external device connected through a USB, FireWire, or other port.

Wireless Communications

Wireless devices use radio waves or infrared light waves. The major wireless technologies support a range of distances from one meter to many miles. Those wireless devices that communicate over the shortest distances create a personal area network (PAN). Other types of wireless devices have a range in the hundreds of feet and work in a wireless local area network (WLAN). When you need to communicate wirelessly through your laptop over miles, you need a cellular wireless device.

Infrared   One technology that allows you to create a personal area network for your devices to communicate with your laptop is infrared. These devices use infrared light waves to communicate with each other through infrared transceiver ports. Some laptops and PDAs come with ports that comply with the Infrared Data Association's (IrDA) data transmission standards. IrDA is an organization that creates specifications for infrared wireless communication. You can also add IrDA devices to a system by installing an infrared adapter. Any two IrDA-enabled devices can communicate with each other. The drawback to this type of communication is the very short distance supported (one meter) and the fact that it relies on line-of-sight, so the ports on the communicating devices must be directly facing one another with nothing in the way.

Microsoft Windows (9x, Me, and 2000, as well as XP) supports Plug and Play for IrDA infrared devices. IrDA infrared devices support a maximum transmission speed of 4 Mbps.

Bluetooth   Bluetooth is another wireless standard for use in a PAN. Bluetooth devices use radio waves, rather than physical connections, to communicate with each other. Some laptops come with a Bluetooth adapter built in. If not, you can purchase one—often along with one or more wireless devices that use the Bluetooth standard. A popular peripheral package is a Bluetooth adapter with a Bluetooth keyboard and mouse. Many newer cell phones have Bluetooth built in for use with wireless headsets, and for communicating with a Bluetooth-enabled computer to share the phonebook and other data stored in the phone.

While we think of Bluetooth as mainly a very short distance communications standard, there are actually three classes of Bluetooth, each with its own power requirements, and each with a power-dependent distance. Class 1 Bluetooth devices have a distance limit of about 100 meters, while Class 2 is limited to about 10 meters,

and Class 3 is limited to one meter. The usage described in this chapter is Class 3.

Older Microsoft Windows operating systems do not support the Bluetooth standard, but Windows XP does.

Wi-Fi

Most new laptops today come with a Wi-Fi radio frequency networking adapter built in. The built-in adapters will usually have an invisible antenna, integrated into the screen lid. For those laptops without built-in Wi-Fi, a variety of Wi-Fi adapters are available in PC Card form or as an External USB device.

Wi-Fi is actually a group of wireless networking standards that are much more suited for wireless LAN than Bluetooth is because they provide a stronger, faster connection and a level of security not possible with Bluetooth. We will describe Wi-Fi in more detail in Chapter 12.

Cellular WAN   For those who need to connect a laptop over great distances to another network, such as the Internet, cellular WAN may be the answer. The major cellular telecommunications providers now offer a variety of options for data communications over the cellular networks, but unlike Wi-Fi, this is not built into laptops. If you wish to connect your laptop to the Internet via one of these services, you need to contact a cell provider, sign up for the service, and buy a cellular adapter from that provider. You cannot use one cellular data service's adapter for service from another provider. You also must be sure that the card they offer is of a type (PC Card, CardBus, ExpressCard, etc.) that will work in your laptop.

Wired Communications

When it comes to wired communications, the choices are the same as those for a desktop PC—dial-up modem and Ethernet. Most laptops have adapters for both of these built in.

Dial-up Modem   For those who require a dial-up connection to the Internet, most laptops come with an integrated dial-up modem. The only part of the modem visible on the outside of the case is an RJ11 connector (described in Chapter 2). All you need is a land-based phone line and the services of an ISP. Learn how to configure a dial-up connection in Chapter 9.

Ethernet   Most laptops now come with a built-in Ethernet adapter for connecting to a wired network. The only part of a built-in Ethernet adapter visible on the outside of the case is an RJ45 connector (described in Chapter 2).

Power and Electrical Input Devices

Laptops come with two source of electrical input. For portability, a laptop comes with a battery that will support it when not plugged into a power outlet. These rechargeable batteries have a battery life without recharging in the range of 5 to 8 hours at best and tend to last only a few years. They are also quite expensive.

Batteries

When not plugged into a wall outlet, a laptop computer gets its power from a special rechargeable battery. The typical laptop today has a *lithium ion (Li-Ion) battery*. You may also run into Nickel Metal Hydride (NiMH) batteries in older laptops. Li-Ion batteries use newer technology than NiMH, are smaller and lighter, and produce more power. When purchasing a laptop today, your battery choice may run to the number of cells in the battery—6-cell, 8-cell, or 12-cell.

You must recharge laptop system batteries when they run down, and this is the job of the AC adapter, which plugs into a regular electrical outlet. The adapter recharges the battery while the portable is operating. However, if you are not near a wall outlet when the battery's power fades, you will not be able to work until you replace the battery with a fully charged one or until AC power is available again.

DC Controller

Most portable computers include a *DC controller*, which monitors and regulates power usage. The features of DC controllers vary by manufacturer, but typically, they provide short-circuit protection, give "low battery" warnings, and can be configured to automatically shut down the computer when the power is low.

AC Adapter

The *AC adapter* (the "brick" or "wall wart") is your laptop's power supply that is plugged into an AC power source. Like the power supply in a desktop PC, it converts AC power to DC power. Figure 5-7 shows an AC adapter for a laptop. The AC adapter is also responsible for recharging the battery. If you must replace an external adapter, simply unplug it and attach a new one from the laptop manufacturer that matches the specifications of the one it is replacing. Furthermore, since AC adapters have varying

FIGURE 5-7

A laptop AC
adapter

output voltages, never use an AC adapter with any laptop other than the one it was made for. Previously, laptop power supplies were set to accept only one input power voltage. Now, many laptop AC adapters act as *auto-switching power supplies*, detecting the incoming voltage, and switching to accept either 120 or 240 VAC.

Input Devices

As with a PC, the primary input devices for a laptop are the keyboard and a pointing device. Take a closer look at keyboards and other input devices designed for portability.

Keyboard

Due to size constraints, the built-in keyboard in a laptop has thinner keys that do not travel as far vertically as those on traditional keyboards do and thus do not give the same tactile feedback. A laptop keyboard will have the alphanumeric, ENTER keys, function keys (F1, F2,…F12), and some of the modifier keys (SHIFT, CTRL, and CAPS LOCK) in the same orientation to one another as on a full-sized keyboard. But you will find many of the special keys—the directional arrow keys and the INSERT, DELETE, PAGE UP, and PAGE DOWN keys—in different locations.

A laptop keyboard usually does not have the separate numeric keypad that is available on most external keyboards. Rather, the keypad function integrates into the alphanumeric keys, and small numbers on the sides of keys or in a different color on the top of each key tell what they are. As you know, each alphanumeric key normally produces two characters—one when pressing the key alone, and another when pressing the key with the SHIFT key. To enable some of these keys to create yet a third character, you must press the FN key while pressing the keys in the embedded keypad. This key enables the special functions for a laptop keyboard.

If you do a great deal of number entry work and feel more comfortable using a more traditional numeric keypad, consider buying a separate one and attaching it to your laptop.

Pointing Devices

When shopping for a new laptop, you can expect to find a built-in pointing device on all the most popular models. After experimenting with a variety of such devices, most manufacturers have settled on the *touchpad*, which is a smooth rectangular panel sitting in front of the keyboard. Move your finger across the surface of the touchpad to move the pointer on the display, and then use the buttons next to the touchpad as you would use buttons on a mouse or trackball. Alternatively, you can tap the touchpad in place of clicking a button.

Other pointing devices you may encounter on laptops are variations of a *pointing stick*, which is a very tiny joystick-type device that usually sits in the center of the keyboard, sometimes between the G, H, and B keys. Barely protruding above the level of the keys, this pointing device usually has a replaceable plastic cap for traction and two buttons located in the front of the keyboard. You operate a pointing stick by pushing it in the direction in which you want to drive the on-screen pointer. IBM's version of the pointing stick is the *TrackPoint*. Although Lenovo now owns the IBM laptop and PC business, you can still see the red-tipped TrackPoint on their laptops (as of this writing).

Touch Screen

You won't typically find a touch screen input device on laptops, but it is the main input device for most handhelds. A touch screen is a display screen that includes a touch-sensitive panel. Using your finger, or a small slender plastic or metal rod called a *stylus* or *pen*, you touch the screen and point to objects, much as you use a mouse.

Digitizing Tablet

A *digitizing tablet* or *digitizer* is another input device that uses a stylus. Available as an external device, a digitizer uses touch screen technology and is usually at least the size of a sheet of paper. The primary use of a digitizer is for creating computerized drawings; it is, for this reason, also called a *graphics tablet*. A *Tablet PC* is a laptop in which the display is an integrated digitizer that swivels around so that it sits on

SCENARIO & SOLUTION

I plug my laptop into a CRT, printer, and keyboard every time I return to the office. Is there an easier way to do this?	Yes. Plug each of these devices into a port replicator and leave them there. To access the devices, simply attach your laptop to the port replicator.
When I'm in the office, I'd rather use my laptop than my desktop because it is faster. What can I do to access from my laptop the better peripherals that my desktop has?	Your laptop might be able to use a full docking station. This device will allow your laptop to access most devices that a desktop can access.
I want to access a USB scanner with my laptop. My docking station doesn't have a USB port, but my colleague's does. How do I use my colleague's docking station?	You will not be able to do this if your colleague's docking station is proprietary to his laptop model, and if you have a different laptop model. However, if the docking station is one of the newer universal docking stations, you may be in luck.

top of the keyboard, concealing the keyboard for drawing. While a stylus would seem like the primary input device for this type of computer, expect an integrated keyboard, if not an integrated pointing device, for users who find it handy to use a mouse. These choices allow the user to use the mode that fits the current task, such as writing a memo using the keyboard, surfing the Internet using a mouse, and creating drawings using a stylus on the tablet.

CERTIFICATION OBJECTIVES

■ **601: 2.2   602: 2.2   604: 2.2**   *Install, configure, optimize, and upgrade laptops and portable devices*

In the A+ exams CompTIA will test your knowledge of how to install and upgrade components in laptops. The limited space in a portable computer poses several problems. One is that the display and input devices are built in and users often want to have external versions of these. The other is that you are limited in options for upgrading internal components, such as memory, hard drives, and specialized bus cards (PC Card/CardBus/ExpressCards). Be prepared to select appropriate components for a laptop upgrade.

Installing and Upgrading Laptops

Because laptops are proprietary, the integrated components are very difficult to upgrade, and you are limited to using the components that came with the system. However, because of their compact size, many portable components, such as the keyboard and pointing device, can be difficult to use. For this reason, most laptops allow you to attach easier-to-use desktop devices, for times when you are not in transit.

Keyboards

The built-in keyboards on portable PCs have greatly improved over the last two decades, but for a variety of reasons users often wish to use an external keyboard. A user who uses the numeric keypad may add an external keyboard for this convenience. Some people simply prefer the tactile feel of certain external keyboards (some IBM keyboards come to mind) and will add the external keyboard when they are not traveling with the portable. Ergonomically, it is more comfortable to sit further from the screen, and an external keyboard will allow you to do just that.

It is simple to add an external keyboard to your laptop—you simply plug it in. The trick is buying a keyboard with the correct connector. Most new laptops have done away with the mini-DIN keyboard connector. However, they all have USB ports. The newer the laptop, the more USB ports it will have. To attach a full-size keyboard to a USB port, simply plug in the keyboard. Some portables will disable the on-board keyboard. In others, this is still fully functional when the external keyboard is plugged in.

Mouse

Most portables do not come with a mouse. Instead, they use pointing devices such as pointing sticks or touchpads. Because these devices are small and can be difficult to use, many portable computers allow you to attach a full-sized desktop mouse. If the mouse uses a PS 2/mini-DIN connector, turn off the portable, attach the mouse to the port in the back, and then restart the system. It is not necessary to turn the portable off first if the mouse connects to a USB port. Some portables will automatically disable the onboard pointing device when an external pointing device is connected.

on the job   *With the availability of USB devices, it is convenient to add a USB mouse and keyboard to your system, and you can add or remove them as needed. This allows the use of a full-sized keyboard when you are not traveling.*

Docking Stations

If you have a docking station or port replicator for your laptop, how you connect it will depend on the type of interface it has. A proprietary docking station or port replicator may have a special connector that uses a special port on the laptop, but they will only connect to the models they fit. It may also have a locking device that secures it to the laptop.

If you have one of the universal docking stations, all that is required is a standard USB port, in which case, you connect it as you would any USB device.

In both cases, be sure to read the documentation that comes with the docking station or port replicators.

PC Card/CardBus/ExpressCards

The various small playing card–like devices that install in the PC Card, CardBus, or ExpressCard slots are all Plug and Play, and you can install them without opening up the computer. You simply slide the card into the appropriate slot, pushing it in until it feels firmly seated (see Figure 5-8). Recall that PC Cards and CardBus cards have pin and socket connectors, while the ExpressCards have contacts in a beam-on-blade configuration. Once properly installed, the card should not wiggle when gently tapped. When removing one of these cards, look for a small button next to each card that releases it from the socket.

FIGURE 5-8

A PC Card being installed in a portable computer

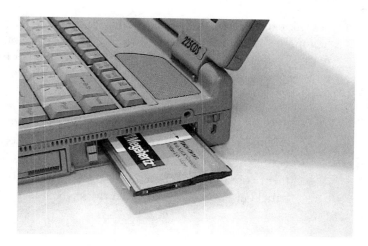

FIGURE 5-9

Installing a RAM
module in a
portable system

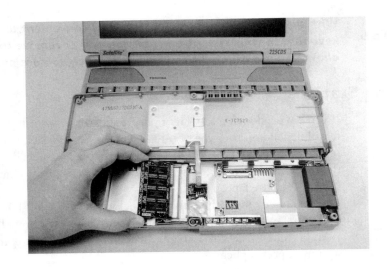

Memory Upgrades

You can add additional RAM to a portable system in a number of ways. Some
systems include extra RAM slots within the chassis. This type requires you to open
the computer's case and place the RAM module in an available slot (see Figure 5-9).
The most common laptop RAM slots take SODIMM modules.

EXERCISE 5-2

Installing SODIMM Memory

For this exercise, you will need a module of SODIMM memory appropriate for your
laptop, the user's manual, the new module in an antistatic bag, and a small non-
magnetic screwdriver for opening the case. If you do not have a new module, simply
remove a module that is already installed, and reinstall it. In this case, you will need
to have an antistatic bag.

1. Turn off the computer and all external devices.
2. Ground yourself using one of the methods described in Chapter 17.
3. Following the instructions in the computer user manual, open the compartment containing the SODIMM slots. This is most often behind a back access
   panel but may be located under the keyboard.

4. Your laptop may have one or two memory slots. Look for numbers near any open slots and fill the lowest numbered slot first.

5. If you are replacing memory, remove the modules or modules being replaced. To remove a module, press down on the retaining clips located on the sides, and then lift the edge of the module to a 45-degree angle and gently pull it out of the slot, being careful to hold it by its edges, and not touch the contacts or chips.

6. Place the old module in an antistatic bag. Remove the new module from its antistatic bag, being careful to hold it by its edges, and not touch the contacts or chips.

7. Align the notch of the memory module with that of the memory slot and gently insert the module into the slot at a 45-degree angle. Gently rotate the module down flat until the clamps lock it in place (see Figure 5-9).

8. Before closing the memory compartment, power up the computer and, if necessary (according to the user manual), configure it in BIOS setup, although this is not normally required.

9. Do a normal startup into Windows, and check the System Properties applet in Control Panel to see if the new memory was recognized.

10. Shut down the computer and close up the memory access panel.

Another way to add more RAM to your portable is to use a memory card of the correct PCMCIA form for your laptop. The choices are PC Card, CardBus PC Card, or ExpressCard, all of which we described earlier in this chapter.

No matter how you add memory to your laptop, you may notice that the memory count during bootup does not quite add up to the total installed. If this is the case, your laptop may be using some of your system RAM for the use of the video adapter. Any video adapter needs to use RAM for temporary storage of the rendered images it sends to the screen. Considering how often images may change on your screen, this memory is quite busy, so it must also be fast.

Most video adapters have their own, very fast, memory, and since video cards actually contain a processor and other circuitry that actually creates the images, your main CPU is only required to provide input to the video adapter. That's all fine, until you look at integrated video adapters, such as those found on laptop motherboards. Rather than providing memory separately to the video adapter, laptop manufacturers will often use a portion of the system memory for the video adapter function. This means, for instance, that a laptop with 2 GB of memory installed has 64 or 128 megabytes less memory for the operating system to use. Memory used in this way is *shared video memory*.

FIGURE 5-10

Removing a hard
drive from a
laptop computer

Hard Drives

Replace a hard drive only with another of the same type from the same manufacturer. After you power down the computer, use the same precautions you would use with a PC case before proceeding. Usually, you can remove a small plastic cover on the bottom of the laptop to access the hard drive. Slide the drive out (see Figure 5-10), then replace it with a new drive, and replace the cover.

Batteries

Due to the necessity for changing the battery, most portables allow easy access to it. In many cases, the battery fits into a compartment on the bottom or in the side of the computer. If this is the case, remove the battery compartment's cover, slide the old battery out, and slide the new one in (see Figure 5-11). There may be a release mechanism to let you remove the battery.

Some laptops allow multiple batteries to be contained in the system, although you may have to swap out another component, like an optical drive, to have two batteries installed simultaneously. While this adds battery usage time, it also increases the weight of the system.

Fortunately, most portable systems give you plenty of notice before the battery goes completely dead. Many systems include a power-level meter that allows you to see the battery's charge level at all times. Other systems give you a visual warning when the battery's power dips below a certain level.

FIGURE 5-11

Installing a
battery in a
compartment on
the underside of
a laptop

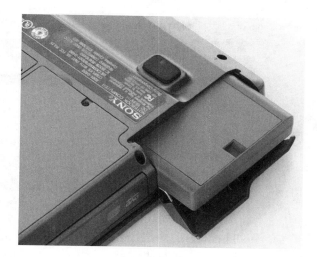

The useful life of a battery is usually only a few years, so expect to need to replace a laptop battery as it approaches two years of age.

Peripherals

When installing or removing standard peripherals, such as printers, cameras, keyboards, and scanners, use the same precautions you would use if the peripheral were attached to a desktop PC. Read the documentation for each device before taking any action.

You can simply power down a printer or scanner of any type before unplugging the interface cable. Learn more about printers and scanners in Chapter 11.

Most devices today are Plug and Play, in that they are recognized by the operating system, their drivers can be automatically located and installed, and the device and driver can be configured by the OS. Another issue is whether or not a device is hot swappable. Some, but not all, Plug-and-Play devices are hot swappable.

Hot-Swappable Devices

Hot-swappable devices can be safely installed and removed while a computer is up and running. Hot-swappable devices include most devices that use a USB, FireWire, PC Card, CardBus, or ExpressCard interface. USB devices, however, often require that you install the driver before the device is connected.

FIGURE 5-12 An example of a list of items displayed after clicking the Safely Remove Hardware icon

FIGURE 5-13

The Safe
To Remove
Hardware
message

You should not remove even hot-swappable devices out without regard to open programs and files. The best way to remove a storage or communications device is to first open the Safely Remove Hardware icon in the tray area of the taskbar. This icon resembles a PC Card. Simply click the icon and you will see a list of hardware. Figure 5-12 shows a list that includes a USB storage device (a flash drive, in this case), a FireWire hard drive, and a USB network adapter. Clicking once on the device you wish to remove will result in the operating system stopping the device, if possible. Then you will see a balloon message indicating that it is safe to remove the device (Figure 5-13). You may remove the device at this point. If the operating system is not able to do this, it will display a different message, stating that it was unable to stop the device.

Non-Hot-Swappable Devices

Non-hot-swappable devices may still be Plug and Play but cannot be removed or installed without doing damage to the system. These devices require that you shut the computer down before removing or installing them. The most common of these are any cards that you install into the case of the laptop by opening it up.

Configuring Power Management

Current laptop technology has come a long way from the days of using nearly standard PC components modified mainly for size, not for power management and heat dissipation. Nearly every component in a modern laptop has some sort of power management feature. Many, like the hard drive, will power down when not in use. CPUs and other circuitry will draw less power when they have less demand for their services. Displays will power down when there has been no activity from the mouse or keyboard for a certain period. If a component is not drawing power, it is not creating heat, so power management and cooling go hand-in-hand.

To support the power management features in laptop hardware requires that the system BIOS, the chipset, the operating system, and device drivers be aware of these features and be able to control and manage them. This is *power management*.

Several standards and practices have come together for power management. They include an alphabet soup of standards called SMM, APM, and ACPI. In addition, there are power features that you can implement through Windows that depend on SMM, APM, and ACPI. We discuss all of these in the sections that follow.

System Management Mode

For the past twenty years, Intel CPUs have included a group of features called *System Management Mode (SMM)*. Other CPU manufacturers have followed suit. SMM allows a CPU to reduce its speed without losing its place, so to speak, so that it does not stop working altogether. In addition, a CPU using SMM mode triggers power saving in other components. The next step was to create system BIOSes and operating systems that could take advantage of SMM.

Power Management Standards

The answer to how to involve the BIOS and OS in power management came in two steps. First, Intel developed the *Advanced Power Management (APM)* standard in 1992, and later they improved on this with the *Advanced Configuration and Power Interface (ACPI)* standard in 1996.

APM

Advanced Power Management (APM) defines four power-usage operating levels: Full On, APM Enabled, APM Stand By, and APM Suspend. Details of these operating levels are not important, as they are now a subset of the next standard, ACPI.

ACPI

Advanced Configuration and Power Interface (ACPI) includes all the power-usage levels of APM, plus two more. It also supports the soft-power feature described in Chapter 2. ACPI defines how to configure this feature in the BIOS settings. The seven power-usage levels of ACPI, called *power states*, are described in Table 5-3.

TABLE 5-3		The ACPI Power States

Power State	Substate	Description
G0 Working	N/A	The computer is fully on and all devices function. Optionally, some devices will be in a low-power mode, depending on operating system and device settings.
G1 Sleeping	S1 Stand By	The CPU throttles down (not entirely off) and some devices turn off. The entire system state is saved in RAM memory. The system appears off.
G1 Sleeping	S2 Stand By	The same as S1, but the CPU powers off. Resuming from this state takes a few seconds longer than from S1, but it saves more power.
G1 Sleeping	S3 Stand By	Similar to S2, but the processor and *most* devices power off. This saves even more power, but takes several seconds to resume. This is the Windows Stand By mode.
G1 Sleeping	S4 Hibernate	Everything powers down after the system state and all contents of RAM are saved to disk. Provides the most power saving, but takes the longest time to resume.
G2 Soft off	N/A	The system powers down, but a soft-power state is enabled in the BIOS, maintaining a charge to the motherboard so that the system powers up faster.
G3 Mechanical off	N/A	The system powers down, but a soft-power state is not enabled. The system receives no power. This state is usually initiated by a special switch on the back of the power supply.

Configuring Power Management in Windows

Getting the most out of your laptop battery depends on how you manage the use of the battery's power. You can use the power options in Windows to minimize the power usage of components, such as the display and hard drive. You can put the entire system into one of two special "sleep" modes called Stand By and Hibernate.

Using Stand By vs. Hibernate

Imagine that you are a business traveler waiting to board a commercial jet. You arrive at the airport in plenty of time and find yourself at the departure gate with 90 minutes to spare. Is this wasted time? No. You open your laptop, complete a report on your trip, and begin to create an expense request. You are not quite finished with this task when it is time to board. Rather than completely shut down your computer, you can put it into a sleep mode that will preserve your open files, just as they are. Once you have done that, you slip the machine into your carry-on case and board the plane.

Once settled in your seat, you open your laptop, and within seconds, you are back where you left off. Learn more about these two sleep modes, called Stand By and Hibernate, now.

on the **job**

If your computer is connected to a UPS that includes a data cable and software, you may be required to turn Hibernate on. In this case, if there is a power outage, the UPS software will put your computer into Hibernate mode after a configurable length of time (before the UPS battery runs out of power).

Stand By *Stand By* is a sleep mode that is available on any computer that supports ACPI power management. Stand By conserves power while saving your desktop in RAM memory in a work state. While it appears that the computer is off, you will notice the power indicator light is on. When you wish to resume, you simply press the power button. Your desktop either appears immediately, or after you log on, if your computer is configured to require a logon.

Stand By requires first that your computer support ACPI power management. It also requires a power source to work because it does not completely shut down. So in the scenario described previously in which the laptop is running on battery, if the battery runs out of power, any data saved for Stand By mode, and not saved to disk, will be lost.

Configure Stand By mode in the Power Options applet in Control Panel. You can set it to occur automatically after a specified period of mouse and keyboard inactivity, or you can simply select Stand By from the Shutdown menu.

Hibernate *Hibernate* is a sleep mode that uses hard drive space to save all the programs and data that are in memory at the time you choose this mode. The computer then completely shuts down, requiring no power while it is hibernating.

exam

watch *CompTIA's published objective 2.2 of the 220-601 exam, under Configure Power Management, uses the following language: "Identify the difference between suspend, hibernate, and Stand By." However, "suspend" is simply another term for "Stand By."*

Like Stand By, Hibernate allows you to stop work on your computer but quickly pick up where you left off. It takes slightly longer to go into and out of hibernation.

Configure Hibernate mode from the Hibernate tab of the Power Options applet. Simply click to place a check in the box next to Enable Hibernate. Now Hibernate will appear at the bottom of the Power Schemes page, and as an option under the Power buttons settings on the Advanced page of the Power Options applet (see Figure 5-14).

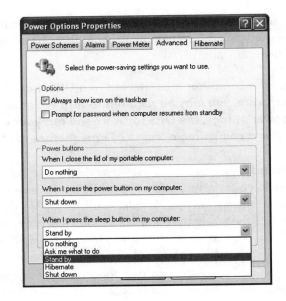

Configuring Low Battery Options

Would you like to know when your battery is low? Most laptops will do this for you, and Windows allows you to configure an alarm notification when the battery is low and when it is critically low. Windows' default low battery level is 10 percent battery life, while 8 percent battery life is the default critical level. You may change either or both of these settings, and you may also define a warning action for each.

A smart configuration will issue a warning sound for low and for critical, and place the computer into Stand By or Hibernate (better choice) when the critical level is reached.

EXERCISE 5-3

Configuring Power Settings

You can configure power options for your computer whether you have a laptop or not. If you do not have a laptop, you will simply not see the battery options. Open the Start menu and select Control Panel.

1. If Control Panel shows dozens of icons in the main window, move to Step 3. If it only shows ten icons in the main window, it is in Category view. In this case, select Switch to Classic View on the left.

2. Double-click the Power Options icon.

3. In the Power Options Properties dialog box, first make note of the current settings, so that you can return to these settings.

4. Now use the drop-down box under Power Schemes to select each scheme in turn and notice the changes in the values in the Settings area at the bottom of the page (see Figure 5-15). When you have viewed the schemes, return this page to its original settings.

5. Select the Alarms tab, if it is available. Note the settings for Low Battery Alarm and for Critical Battery Alarm. Click the Alarm Action button under each of these and view the settings.

6. Select the Power Meter tab, if available, and notice current power status.

7. Select the Advanced tab and notice the group of settings on the bottom under Power Buttons. Use the drop-down box to view the options under each of the settings. Do not change any settings.

8. Select the Hibernate tab and notice the Hibernate setting and the amount of disk space available and the amount required to hibernate.

9. Click Cancel to close the Power Options Properties without making any changes.

FIGURE 5-15

On a laptop the Power Schemes page shows settings for when it is plugged in, as well as for when it is running on batteries.

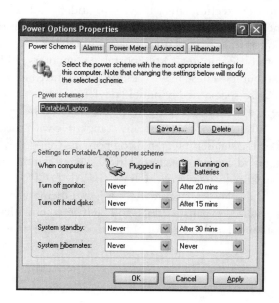

SCENARIO & SOLUTION

I use my laptop at work, taking it with me from meeting to meeting in order to take notes. How can I avoid the hassle of waiting for it to power up at the beginning of each meeting?	When you power down, select Stand By.
When traveling, I would like to save all my work and desktop when I shut down, and have the laptop start up with my work state exactly as it was when I stopped. How do I achieve this, plus conserve as much battery life as possible?	Enable Hibernate in the Power Options applet in Control Panel, and then when you are ready, select Hibernate from the Turn Off Computer dialog box.
How do I get my laptop to alert me with an audio alarm when the battery gets to 12 percent battery life?	Open the Power Options applet, select the Alarms tab, and ensure that a check is in the box under Low battery alarm. Position the slider at 12 percent. Click the Alarm Action button and place a check in the Sound Alarm box.

CERTIFICATION SUMMARY

Most PC technicians will need to understand laptop technologies because use of these portable computers has increased—both in the workplace and in homes. Laptops, also called notebooks or notebook computers, are not the only type of portable computer. Other portable computers fall into the category of handheld computers. These may be PDAs with limited functionality compared to a PC. There are also specialized handheld devices used in a variety of fields. A common such device is used for taking inventory in retail stores.

While laptops are basically compatible with the Intel IBM-compatible architecture, they use smaller integrated components that do not conform in form and size with the standard components found in PCs. Laptop motherboards are usually proprietary. With specialized versions of the Intel and AMD CPUs, integrated video adapters, integrated LCD display screens, small form-factor memory modules, physically small hard drives, specialized expansion slots, and built-in communications adapters, laptops are self-contained and pack a lot of functionality in a small package.

✓ TWO-MINUTE DRILL

Here are some of the key points covered in Chapter 5.

Introduction to Portable Computers

❑ A portable computer is any type of computer you can easily transport and that has an all-in-one component layout.

❑ A laptop (or notebook) computer is a small, easily transported computer that can run the same operating systems as a desktop PC, with an integrated display in a hinged top.

❑ A handheld computer fits in the palm of the hand and runs a specialized operating system and applications.

Laptop Hardware

❑ Internal and integrated laptop hardware, such as the display, keyboard, pointing device, motherboard, memory, hard drives, and expansion bus, have special scaled-down form factors.

❑ Laptops can use most standard PC peripherals.

❑ Port replicators and docking stations provide permanent connections for external devices used in the laptop user's office.

❑ A laptop may have a media/accessory bay holding a single device that you can switch with another device that fits in the bay.

❑ Laptops contain specialized expansion slots, such as PC Card, CardBus, ExpressCard, Mini PCI, and PCIe Mini Card.

❑ Laptops often come with built-in communications adapters; including Wi-Fi and Ethernet for LAN connections, IrDA infrared and Bluetooth for PAN connections, and modems for dial-up connections. You can add a cellular adapter to a laptop.

❑ A laptop comes with two sources of electrical power: a rechargeable battery and an AC adapter.

❑ A laptop comes with an integrated, scaled-down keyboard, and often (but not always) with an integrated pointing device, such as a touchpad or pointing stick. You can add an external keyboard or external pointing device, if desired.

❏ A handheld computer usually has a touch screen as its main input device. The user uses a finger or stylus to touch objects on the screen.

❏ A Tablet PC is a laptop in which the display is an integrated digitizer that uses touch screen technology but is usually at least the size of a sheet of paper. A tablet also includes an integrated keyboard.

Installing and Upgrading Laptops

❏ Many laptops come with a touchpad or pointing stick integrated into the keyboard, but most people find them more difficult to use than a standard mouse or trackball and use external full-sized keyboards and pointing devices.

❏ The manner used to attach a docking station or port replicator depends on the connector. Some have proprietary connectors and locking devices to secure the connection, so you should attach the device per the manufacturer's instructions.

❏ Universal docking stations and port replicators have USB interfaces and therefore are connected and removed in the same manner as other USB devices.

❏ When installing a PC Card, CardBus, or ExpressCard, slide the card into the correct slot until it feels firmly seated. When removing a card, look for and press the small button next to the card that releases it from the socket.

❏ You can add memory to a laptop in the form of SODIMM or SORIMM modules installed into slots inside the case. It can also be added in the form of a PC Card, CardBus, or ExpressCard.

❏ A laptop hard drive can be replaced, but only by one that matches the manufacturer's requirements.

❏ Laptops are designed to allow changing of the battery—in both normal usage using a spare, or when the useful life of the battery ends and it must be replaced.

❏ Most standard peripherals connect to a laptop using the same techniques used for desktop PCs.

❏ Hot-swappable devices can be installed and removed while a computer is up and running. You should first stop storage devices using the Windows Safely Remove Hardware taskbar icon.

❏ Non-hot-swappable devices may still be Plug and Play, but cannot be removed or installed without doing damage to the system.

Configuring Power Management

❏ You can configure laptops that comply with the ACPI power management standards through the operating system to shut down the display, the hard drive, and even the entire system when there has been a period of inactivity and/or when the battery is low.

❏ The BIOS, the chipset, and the operating system must support power management features.

❏ Stand By is a sleep mode that conserves power while saving your desktop in RAM memory in a work state. In Stand By mode, the processor and most devices are powered off.

❏ Hibernate is a sleep mode that uses hard drive space to save all the programs and data that are in memory at the time you choose this mode. The computer then completely shuts down, and requires no power while it is hibernating.

SELF TEST

The following questions will help you measure your understanding of the material presented in this chapter. Read all of the choices carefully because there might be more than one correct answer. Choose all correct answers for each question.

Introduction to Portable Computers

1. What are the two broad categories of portable computers?
   A. LCDs
   B. Handhelds
   C. Laptops
   D. PC Cards

2. A laptop typically opens like what common business accessory?
   A. Pager
   B. PDA
   C. Briefcase
   D. Headphone

3. What built-in component allows laptop use for short periods without an outside power source?
   A. Keyboard
   B. Touchpad
   C. Pointing stick
   D. Battery

Laptop Hardware

4. What is the common name for a handheld computer used to keep track of appointments and to record addresses, phone numbers, and notes?
   A. Notebook
   B. Laptop
   C. PDA
   D. Pocket PC

5. Which of the following is often included in the model names of CPUs specifically designed for laptops? Select the two best answers.
   A. M
   B. Portable

    C. Mobile

    D. Wireless

6. A laptop component used to convert the DC power from the power adapter or battery to the AC power required by the LCD display.

    A. Inverter

    B. Converter

    C. Power switch

    D. Generator

7. The most common laptop memory module, which is a scaled-down version of a type of full-sized PC memory module.

    A. SORIMM

    B. MicroDIMM

    C. SODIMM

    D. DIMM

8. Which is a common width of a laptop hard drive?

    A. 2.5"

    B. 5"

    C. 3.5"

    D. 1"

9. Which of the following allows you to attach nearly any type of desktop component to a portable computer?

    A. Port replicator

    B. Enhanced port replicator

    C. Extended port replicator

    D. Docking station

10. A compartment in some laptops, which can hold one media device (secondary hard drive, optical drive, floppy drive, etc.) that you can swap with another device. Select the two names for this type of compartment from the following list.

    A. Slot

    B. Media bay

    C. USB port

    D. Accessory bay

11. What organization has produced standards commonly used for laptop expansion slots?
    A. IEEE
    B. Intel
    C. AMD
    D. PCMCIA

12. What two card standards come in types labeled Type I, Type II, and Type III?
    A. PC Card
    B. CardBus
    C. ExpressCard
    D. PCIe Mini Card

13. Which two wireless communications standards are used between a laptop and nearby devices that are within one meter?
    A. Cellular
    B. Wi-Fi
    C. Bluetooth
    D. Infrared

14. A battery type commonly used in recently built laptops.
    A. Lithium ion
    B. AC adapter
    C. DC controller
    D. Nickel Metal Hydride

15. This group of keys is usually a separate area of a desktop keyboard, but it is often integrated into the alphanumeric keys on a laptop keyboard.
    A. Function keys
    B. Directional arrow keys
    C. Numeric keys
    D. Numeric keypad

16. What are two types of built-in pointing devices often found on laptops?
    A. Trackball
    B. Pointing stick
    C. Keyboard
    D. Touchpad

17. Where in Windows can you configure a low battery alarm for a laptop?

    A. Power Options in Control Panel

    B. System Properties in Control Panel

    C. Battery Options in Control Panel

    D. BIOS setup

18. What is the name for system memory used by the video adapter and therefore unavailable to the operating system?

    A. VRAM memory

    B. SODIMM memory

    C. Shared video memory

    D. SRAM memory

Installing and Upgrading Laptops

19. What is the term that describes a device that you can safely install and remove while a computer is up and running?

    A. Plug and Play

    B. Hot-swappable

    C. Stoppable

    D. Removable

20. What is the name of the taskbar icon you should use to stop a USB flash drive before removing it from a Windows computer?

    A. Security Center

    B. Volume

    C. Safely Remove Hardware

    D. My Computer

LAB QUESTION

You were asked to help a neighbor buy and configure a new laptop. It must weigh under six pounds and have four integrated USB ports. Since his camera uses CompactFlash memory cards, he would like a card reader for this format, and the other standard flash cards for future use. When he travels, he will use the laptop for e-mail, for writing short reports, and for a small amount of Internet research, but he will be without AC power for only brief periods.

In his home office, he will use this as a desktop and will want to be able to attach an external monitor, keyboard, and a USB hub to accommodate his two printers, scanner, and camera. He would like an external floppy drive that he will only use in his home office. He needs Wi-Fi wireless for getting online while traveling. At home, he will connect via an Ethernet port to his broadband modem and attach an external display, which, together with the built-in LCD, will give him two displays. At home, he also needs an external keyboard and trackball.

He will use stereo headphones for listening to his CD collection and presentations over the Internet. He wants to be able to watch and record television so that he can experiment with some of the multimedia features in Windows Media Center. The laptop should have a DVD/CD burner, and a built-in webcam is on his wish list, as is 2 GB of memory and at least a 120 GB internal hard drive. He hates messing with plugs, so he wants all his stay-at-home peripherals attached in a way that he only has to worry about one or two plugs to attach his laptop.

This computer should be powerful enough that it won't bog down when it is simultaneously doing such common tasks as running a virus scanner and reading a DVD. He also needs a large capacity external hard drive. He wants the latest version of Windows and the Microsoft Office Basic Suite and an Internet security suite. His budget is $3000.

Check out laptops online or in a computer store and come up with an appropriate computer for his needs and under his budgeted amount. Then write a brief description of this computer and any additional components you wish to recommend.

SELF TEST ANSWERS

Introduction to Portable Computers

1. ☑ **B** and **C.** Handhelds and laptops are correct because these are the two main categories of portable computers.

☒ **A**, LCDs, is incorrect because LCDs are a type of display screen, not a category of portable computers. **D**, PC Cards, is incorrect because these cards plug into special slots in a laptop and are not a category of portable computers.

2. ☑ **C.** Briefcase is correct because a laptop opens like a briefcase.

☒ **A**, pager, **B**, PDA, and **D**, headphone, are incorrect because, while all of these are common business accessories, none of them opens in the same manner that a laptop does.

3. ☑ **D.** Battery is correct because it provides power to the laptop when not plugged into AC power.

☒ **A**, keyboard, **B**, touchpad, and **C**, pointing stick, are all incorrect because, while they may be built into a laptop, they do not make it possible for a laptop to be used for short periods without an outside power source.

Laptop Hardware

4. ☑ **C.** PDA is the common name for a handheld computer used to keep track of appointments and to record addresses, phone numbers, and notes.

☒ **A**, notebook, is incorrect because this is the name for a small laptop, not for a handheld computer. **B**, laptop, is incorrect because a laptop is a portable computer, but not as small or limited as a handheld. **D**, Pocket PC, is incorrect because this is an operating system for a handheld computer, not the computer itself.

5. ☑ **A.** and **C.** M and mobile are both correct, as these are often included in names of CPUs designed for laptops (and other portable computers).

☒ **B**, portable, and **D**, wireless, are both incorrect because they are not commonly used in model names for CPUs designed for laptops.

6. ☑ **A.** Inverter is correct. This component converts DC power to the AC power required by an LCD panel.

☒ **B**, converter, is incorrect because a converter does just the opposite, converting AC power to DC power. **C**, power switch, is incorrect because the power switch simply turns the main power on and off to the laptop. **D**, generator, is incorrect because this is not a component of a laptop. A generator generates power using an engine powered by a fuel such as gasoline or diesel.

7. ☑ **C.** SODIMM is correct because this is the most common memory module. SODIMM is a scaled-down version of the DIMM memory module.

    ☒ **A,** SORIMM, is incorrect because, while this is a type of memory module for laptops, it is less commonly used. **B,** MicroDIMM, is incorrect because this is half the size of SODIMM and is used in handheld computers. **D,** DIMM, is incorrect because this is a full-sized memory module for desktop PCs.

8. ☑ **A.** 2.5" is correct because this is the most common width of a laptop hard drive.

    ☒ **B,** 5", is incorrect because this is a very large size not used in laptops. **C,** 3.5", is incorrect because this is also a large size that is not used in laptops but is common in desktop PCs. **D,** 1", is incorrect (at this writing) because it is not a size commonly used in laptops, and if it is available at all at this time, it would physically not have sufficient data capacity.

9. ☑ **D.** A docking station allows you to attach nearly any type of desktop component to a portable computer. The docking station can remain on the desk with all the desired devices installed or plugged into it. To access these devices, simply plug the portable into the docking station.

    ☒ **A,** port replicator, and **B,** enhanced port replicator, are incorrect because they do not allow access to the number and variety of devices that a docking station does. **C,** extended port replicator, is incorrect because this is not a real type of portable system component.

10. ☑ **B and D.** Media bay and accessory bay are correct as names for the compartment in some laptops used for swapping between one device and another.

    A, slot, is incorrect because that is the socket a circuit card plugs into. **C,** USB port, is incorrect because that is the term for a USB socket into which a USB cable plugs.

11. ☑ **D.** PCMCIA is correct because the Personal Computer Memory Card International Association has developed the most commonly used laptop expansion slot standards.

    ☒ **A,** IEEE, is incorrect because, although this organization does create standards, they have not produced standards commonly used for laptop expansion slots. **B,** Intel, and **C,** AMD, are incorrect because they are CPU manufacturers, not standards organizations.

12. ☑ **A and B.** PC Card and CardBus are the two card standards that come in types labeled Type I, Type II, and Type III.

    ☒ **C,** ExpressCard, and **D,** PCIe Mini, are incorrect because they are entirely different form factors from the cards that are labeled Type I, Type II, and Type III.

13. ☑ **C and D.** Bluetooth and infrared are two wireless communications standards used between a laptop and nearby devices that are within one meter.

    ☒ **A,** cellular, is incorrect because this technology can be used to connect a laptop to the Internet. **B,** Wi-Fi, is incorrect because this connects a laptop to a local area network (LAN).

14. ☑ **A.** Lithium ion is the battery type commonly used in recently built laptops.
☒ **B**, AC adapter, is incorrect because this is the laptop's power supply that plugs into an AC power source. **C**, DC controller, is incorrect because this is not a battery type but a laptop component that monitors and regulates power usage. **D**, Nickel Metal Hydride, is incorrect because this is a type of battery more common in older laptops.

15. ☑ **D.** Numeric keypad is correct because this group of keys often integrates into the alphanumeric keys in order to save space.
☒ **A**, function keys, is incorrect because these are usually in their normal position across the top of the keyboard. **B**, directional arrow keys, is incorrect because these are often (but not always) separate on the laptop keyboard. **C**, numeric keys, is incorrect because these are usually in their normal position in the row immediately below the function keys.

16. ☑ **B and D.** Pointing stick and touchpad are two types of built-in pointing devices often found on laptops.
☒ **A**, trackball, is incorrect because, while it is sometimes built into a laptop, the pointing stick and touchpad are used more often. **C**, keyboard, is incorrect because, while this is an input device, it is not a pointing device.

17. ☑ **A.** Power Options in Control Panel is the location where you can configure a low battery alarm for a laptop.
☒ **B**, System Properties in Control Panel, is incorrect because you cannot configure a low battery alarm here. **C**, Battery Options, is incorrect because there is no such applet in standard Windows. **D**, BIOS setup, is incorrect because this is not in Windows, but at the system level of the computer.

18. ☑ **C.** Shared video memory is the name for system memory used by the video adapter and therefore unavailable to the operating system.
☒ **A**, VRAM memory, is incorrect because this is a type of memory installed on a video adapter (Chapter 2). A video adapter with VRAM installed does not need to use system memory. **B**, SODIMM memory, is incorrect because, while this is the physical memory module used in most laptops, the portion of this memory used by the video adapter is what we are looking for. **D**, SRAM memory, is incorrect because this is a type of RAM used only for cache memory.

Installing and Upgrading Laptops

19. ☑ **B.** Hot-swappable is the term that describes a device that you can safely install and remove while a computer is up and running.
☒ **A**, Plug and Play is incorrect, although hot-swappable devices are also Plug and Play. **C**, stoppable, is incorrect because this is not the correct term, although many devices can be stopped in Windows. **D**, removable, is incorrect because this does not fully describe the ability in the question.

20. ☑ **C.** Safely Remove Hardware is the taskbar icon that should be used before removing a USB flash drive from a Windows computer.

☒ **A,** Security Center, is incorrect because this will not allow you to stop a USB flash drive. **B,** Volume, is incorrect because this is the name of an icon used to open the volume control program. **D,** My Computer, is incorrect because this is not a taskbar icon, and you don't use it to stop a USB flash drive.

LAB ANSWER

Answers will vary. A computer that would fit the customer's needs at this writing is a Dell XPS M1210, selling at a base price of $1199, with Windows Media Center installed. The features are as follows:

- ❑ Under 5 pounds
- ❑ 4 USB ports
- ❑ RJ45 Ethernet port
- ❑ RJ11 Modem port
- ❑ 15-pin monitor connector
- ❑ S-Video connector
- ❑ Component Video
- ❑ S/PDIF digital audio out
- ❑ 5-in-1 removable memory card reader
- ❑ 120 GB SATA hard drive
- ❑ Audio jacks: stereo headphones/speakers miniconnectors
- ❑ Wireless Wi-Fi 802.11a/g
- ❑ An external 4-port mini–USB 2.0 hub
- ❑ External USB mouse
- ❑ External floppy drive
- ❑ External 320 GB hard drive
- ❑ Expansion dock
- ❑ Microsoft Office Basic Suite
- ❑ Norton Internet Security suite
- ❑ Total price: $2496 (before tax and shipping)

6

Troubleshooting and Preventive Maintenance for Laptops

A s with desktop computers, the most common procedures performed by most computer technicians on laptops are troubleshooting and resolving problems. Understanding the technologies of PCs in general, as presented in Chapters 1, 2, and 3, as well as troubleshooting theory, diagnostic techniques, procedures, and use of tools, are all required to work with laptop computers.

In addition, you must understand the technologies that are either unique to laptops and other portable computers or are just more common in these devices than in desktop computers. Chapter 5 introduced you to these technologies. In this chapter you will explore special problems you may encounter related to these technologies.

CERTIFICATION OBJECTIVES

- **601: 2.3   604: 2.3**   *Identify tools, diagnostic procedures, and troubleshooting techniques for laptops and portable devices*

- **602: 2.3**   *Use tools, diagnostic procedures, and troubleshooting techniques for laptops and portable devices*

CompTIA expects you to understand and apply your knowledge of troubleshooting theory and techniques to the special area of laptops and portable devices. The emphasis is on laptops.

Troubleshooting Laptops and Portable Devices

Laptop computers and other portable devices are much more difficult and costly to repair than desktop PCs. To make matters worse, they are also much more likely to need repairs due to physical damage. Because laptops are "portable," they are placed in harm's way more often than the typical desktop computer. It's easy for the busy traveler to drop one, bang it into things, and so on, all of which can cause damage.

Laptops are vulnerable to the same power problems that plague desktop PCs, but they have a group of problems that are unique to laptops. When it comes to troubleshooting laptops, you will use the same skills and procedures you learned in Chapter 3. In addition to the problem areas you learned about in that chapter, this chapter examines the laptop-specific problems you may encounter when working with AC adapters and batteries, displays, input devices, and built-in wireless adapters.

Power Problems

Laptop-specific power problems involve the rechargeable batteries and the external AC power adapters that put the portability into laptops.

AC Adapter Power Problems

AC adapter problems fall into two categories: damage or failure of the original AC adapter, and damage to the computer due to use of the wrong AC adapter. To understand these problems, we will consider the requirements for the correct AC adapter in terms of voltage, amperage, and polarity, and then look at power-related problem scenarios.

How Amperage and Voltage Can Affect Performance   Never, under any circumstances, casually substitute another AC adapter for the one that came with your laptop unless you are absolutely sure it will not do harm to your computer. Look on the underside of your computer where you should find a label describing the power requirements (see Figure 6-1). The most important features you are looking for are the DC input voltage, amperage, and polarity requirements.

DC input may be in the neighborhood of 19.5 volts, 2.15 amps. Volts indicate the pressure of the electrons, while amps (amperes) is a measurement of the volume of electrons, also called current.

Labels on the laptop and the AC adapter show the positive or negative polarity of the laptop power connector, which must be compatible with the polarity of the connectors on the AC adapter's plug (see Figure 6-2).

Now look for a label on the AC adapter and ensure that the output from this device and the polarity of its connector match those of the laptop (see Figure 6-3). Connecting an adapter that does not meet the laptop's requirements will cause damage to the laptop. Depending on just which parameter is wrong, and in which direction, you may destroy the power components in the laptop, or the laptop motherboard and its components.

Some power adapters include an automatic circuit breaker that trips when it detects an input power overload. This works just like the circuit breaker in your

---

FIGURE 6-1

A label on the back of a laptop shows its power requirements.

NOTEBOOK COMPUTER
DC 19.5V⎓

The laptop
power connector
is labeled for
polarity.

home; you need to reset it before it allows power through again. With some AC adapters, you do this simply by unplugging the adapter for a few minutes before reconnecting it. Some laptops have a reset button that you may use. If so, unplug the power cord, remove the battery, and follow the instructions to press the reset button. Then reinstall the battery, plug in the power cord, and turn on the computer.

What about those internal components? When the power comes into the laptop, it passes through circuits on the motherboard to voltage regulators. These are typically 5 volts, 12 volts, 3.3 volts, and whatever voltage the CPU requires. The voltage regulators connect to capacitors, which maintain a steady voltage as demand goes up and down. Finally, power is distributed to the components.

Power to the LCD display is handled separately, using an inverter, as described in Chapter 5.

e x a m
ⓦatch
Be sure that you understand the function of an AC adapter and the difference between amperage and voltage.

Battery Problems

Like the average car owner, the typical laptop owner doesn't worry much about the battery until it is a problem. On a daily basis, that means watching the battery indicator, and recharging the battery when it gets low. Make sure that the battery is inserted properly and is charging. If a battery fails to fully charge and is about two years or older, you may need to replace the battery.

The label on
an AC power
adapter

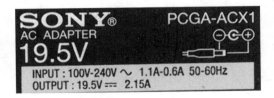

Rechargeable batteries have a limited lifetime, beyond which their ability to hold a charge diminishes until they cannot hold a charge at all.

If a newer battery fails, check your warranty. You may be entitled to a replacement battery from the manufacturer. If the battery is one that has only two or three connections you can test it with a multimeter set to read DC volts. A reading much less than the battery rating probably indicates a bad battery. Unfortunately, many laptop batteries have multiple power connectors and no guidance as to which connectors should provide what power, so it is very difficult to test them. Sometimes the laptop's manual will indicate the voltages at the various terminals, but not always.

Power-Related Scenarios

Understanding the basics of AC adapters and batteries will serve you well, when you are faced with symptoms pointing to power problems. The most obvious is when the laptop will not power up. As you learned in Chapter 3, you should always approach troubleshooting systematically and be sure you observe all the symptoms.

If a laptop will not power up at all when plugged into an AC power source, suspect the AC power adapter. But before you go down that road, first ask "What has changed since it last successfully started up?" If there have been changes to the hardware, then remove any new hardware devices installed since it last started up normally. This is especially true of memory modules.

If it starts up after removing any new hardware, then check with the manufacturer of the new hardware and/or with the manufacturer of the laptop. The hardware may be incompatible with the laptop.

If no new hardware was added since the last time the laptop started up normally, check out one of the usual suspects: an external monitor. Do you hear normal fan sounds from your laptop? If you are using an external monitor, keyboard, and mouse with the laptop screen shut, the computer may be powering up, but because no image appears on the external monitor, you may have jumped to the conclusion that the computer failed. Troubleshoot the monitor.

- Is it simply in sleep mode?
- Is it turned off?
- Is the contrast or brightness control set too dark?
- Is it connected? Is it powered up?

If you are using the laptop's integrated display, use similar questions to eliminate it as the problem area.

If you have eliminated new hardware or display problems, continue through the following list of actions until you have either found the source of the problem, or resolved it and the computer starts normally.

■ Make sure that the AC adapter is the one that came with your computer. Using the wrong AC adapter can damage your laptop or other device.

■ An AC adapter may (but not always) have an indicator light to show that it is receiving power. Check for this light on the adapter as a way to verify that it is receiving AC power from the power source.

■ Check that the adapter is securely plugged into the laptop and directly into a working power outlet (without an extension cord or other device), and that the power switch is turned on. Check the power indicator light on the laptop to see that it is receiving power.

■ Check that *all* power cords are firmly connected. One that is easy to overlook is the cord that goes from the outlet to the AC adapter.

■ Make sure there is no sign of damage to any power cable. If there is, replace the cable, or the entire device if the cable is not removable.

■ Another way to verify that your AC adapter is or is not working is to swap it with another identical power supply. If the laptop works with the swapped AC adapter, then you have isolated the problem to the AC adapter.

■ Use a multimeter and test the computer end of the AC adapter cable to check the output that the computer is receiving. It should be producing the DC voltage specified on the label, or very close to it (see Exercise 6-1 and Figure 6-5).

■ If the laptop is plugged into a power strip or a power protection device, such as a surge protector, SPS, or UPS, ensure that the device is plugged in and the power to this device is turned on. If the circuit breaker in the power strip has tripped, you may need to reset it.

■ Check indicator lights on a power strip or power protection device to see if it has failed. If this device is suspect, unplug the computer from it and plug the laptop directly into a wall outlet and attempt to turn it on again.

■ In order to protect itself and the computer, an AC adapter may turn itself off after detecting a power overage. This depends on the design of the AC adapter. Check your user manual for how to reset the AC adapter.

■ If you suspect that the power outlet is bad, test it first the simple way by plugging another device, such as a lamp, into it. You may also check it with a multimeter

FIGURE 6-4

A multimeter
testing the power
from the input
line to the AC
adapter

by inserting the probes into the socket and checking the voltage. Typical voltage
in the United States is 110–130 volts (see Figure 6-4).

■ If you have not been able to isolate the problem after performing the preceding
checks, disconnect the AC adapter and remove the battery. Wait an entire
minute, and then reinstall the battery and reconnect the AC adapter. Then
turn on the power and see if it starts.

■ If it still fails to start up, disconnect the
AC adapter and remove the battery. Leave
the battery out but close the compartment
door if there is one, and reconnect the AC
adapter to both the laptop and the power
outlet and try to start the computer again.

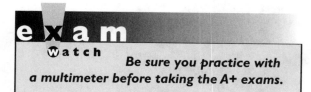

EXERCISE 6-1

Using a Multimeter to Test an AC Adapter

In this exercise you will verify the DC power output of an AC adapter. For this exercise, you will need a multimeter, and an AC adapter with a single plug on the computer end.

1. Unplug the AC adapter from the laptop, but leave it plugged into the wall outlet.

2. Examine the label on the AC adapter and write down the voltage output. Note the polarity and write down which is positive and negative: the tip of the plug versus the outside of the plug.

3. Set the multimeter to "Volts DC."

4. Place the positive probe on the positive portion of the plug, and the negative probe on the negative portion of the probe (see Figure 6-5).

5. The voltage should be close to that shown in the AC adapter label, or just one or two volts more.

FIGURE 6-5

A multimeter testing the output of an AC adapter

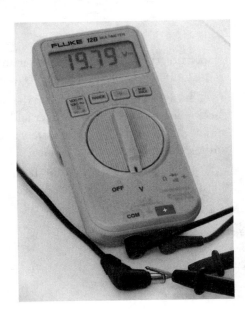

SCENARIO & SOLUTION

I powered up my laptop, but nothing appears on the external display, although I can hear fan noises from the laptop. What should I check first?	Check the display. Look to see if the external display is in sleep mode, powered off, disconnected from the laptop, or has the contrast or brightness control set too dark. Toggle the display mode keys on the laptop.
My laptop will not turn on at all, and the AC adapter power indicator LED is off. What should I do?	Check the AC power source by plugging a lamp into it.
My laptop is two years old, with its original battery. This battery no longer holds a charge. What should I do?	Consider replacing the battery. It may be at the end of its life. If you have an extended warranty, a battery replacement may be included.

Other Startup Problems

A laptop can fail at startup for reasons other than loss of power. Failure can be due to a variety of causes, including both hardware and software. In this section, we will look at hardware errors, limiting our examination of software errors to those errors related to BIOS setup. Learn about startup problems related to Windows operating systems in Chapter 9.

Laptop Fails at Startup

- If a laptop fails after you have added a new peripheral, remove the peripheral.
- If a laptop fails, and you have eliminated power as a problem, remove all peripherals and add them back one at a time, attempting to restart after each addition.
- If you cannot isolate the problem, it may be a failure of the motherboard or one of its integrated components. Laptops are not user-serviceable. Check your warranty to see if the suspected component is still under warranty. If you purchased an extended warranty that is still in effect, this is the time to use it.
- If you do not have a warranty in effect but have a problem that persists that you cannot solve, check with the manufacturer. The easiest way to do this is to locate their Web site and research problems associated with your laptop. You may discover that your laptop is part of a recall, involving the component that has failed.

on the job

While we emphasize that you should have a laptop serviced by the manufacturer or authorized service center, it is not always practical to do so. If your laptop does not have a warranty, and you feel it is worth the extra effort, check out local or Web-based repair services. Some businesses even specialize in replacement LCD panels for many laptop models. If you choose to go this route, know that there are no guarantees that the repair will be worth the cost, or that it will be successful, especially if you choose to do the repair yourself.

Laptop Fails During POST

If Windows fails to start and a text-mode screen displays, do not panic. A problem was detected during the power-on self-test (POST). Simply read the information on the screen and follow any instructions. In the example shown in Figure 6-6 the BIOS hardware monitor found a problem, and the message on the error screen directs you to enter the Power setup menu to see the details. Perhaps the hardware monitor detected a high temperature in the CPU or motherboard, which can indicate a failing cooling fan that is allowing the system to overheat.

on the job

This scenario can also occur on a desktop PC.

FIGURE 6-6

An error detected during the POST

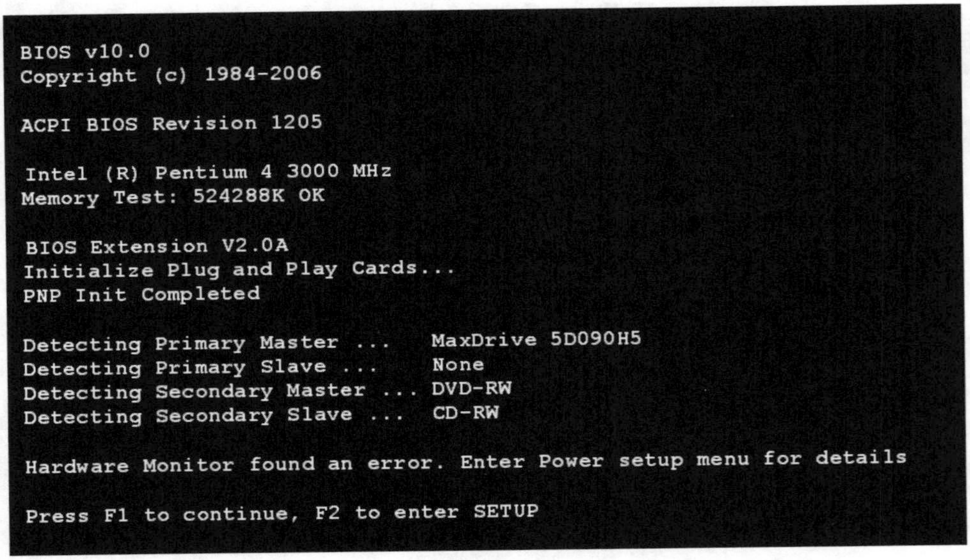

```
BIOS v10.0
Copyright (c) 1984-2006

ACPI BIOS Revision 1205

Intel (R) Pentium 4 3000 MHz
Memory Test: 524288K OK

BIOS Extension V2.0A
Initialize Plug and Play Cards...
PNP Init Completed

Detecting Primary Master   ...   MaxDrive 5D090H5
Detecting Primary Slave    ...   None
Detecting Secondary Master ...   DVD-RW
Detecting Secondary Slave  ...   CD-RW

Hardware Monitor found an error. Enter Power setup menu for details

Press F1 to continue, F2 to enter SETUP
```

System Instability

System instability is a term used for a large number of symptoms, with an even larger number of causes. For our purposes, system instability includes one or more of the following symptoms:

- Desktop looks normal on the monitor, but the system does not respond to mouse clicks or keyboard input. This is also described as a system "hang."
- Desktop icons are missing or incomplete.
- The screen changes very slowly in response to mouse or keyboard actions.
- The hourglass pointer (indicating that a program is busy) stays on the screen, even when the pointer is over a different open window. Normally, the hourglass will only appear when the pointer is within the busy application.
- It takes a very long time for a new window to open.

These problems are usually associated with software causes, which we describe in Chapter 9. However, some hardware problems can cause them.

For instance, if the system hangs when attempting to use an optical disk (CD or DVD), remove the disk and wait a few minutes to see if the system recovers. Then try to close the window for the program that was trying to access the disc. This may be an audio or video player, or it may be Windows Explorer. If you are successful, open the Start menu and select Turn Off Computer. In the Turn Off Computer dialog select Restart. Then clean the disc, and, after the computer has restarted, insert it again and attempt the same operation.

If you are not successful in closing the windows, press CTRL-ALT-DELETE, which brings up Task Manager. On the Applications tab look for the program that was trying to access the optical drive. You may find that this program will show as "not responding." Try to stop the program that was attempting to access the optical disc. If you are successful, select Shut Down from the Task Manager menu or open the Start menu and select Turn Off Computer. In the Turn Off Computer dialog select Restart. Then clean the disk and after the computer has restarted insert it again and attempt the same operation.

If you are not successful in shutting down the application and cannot restart the computer through the Start menu, open Windows Task Manager and select Shut Down from the main menu.

If the system does not respond to any of these actions, you will have to power it down using the power button. This normally requires holding the button in for several seconds until the computer shuts off. After a pause, restart it. Then insert

SCENARIO & SOLUTION

I upgraded the memory in my laptop with a new SODIMM module. Now the laptop fails to power up at all. What should I do?	Remove the SODIMM module and power up again. If it powers up without the new module, it may be a defective or incompatible module.
My laptop failed before loading Windows. There is plain text on my screen. What should I do?	Simply read the information on the screen and follow any instructions.
In the middle of working, my system became unresponsive, with an hourglass pointer. What should I do?	If the pointer remains as an hourglass, even when positioned over other windows, press CTRL-SHIFT-ESC to open the Task Manager and try to stop the unresponsive application.

the cleaned optical disk in the drive and attempt to read it again with the same program. If this causes the same problem as before, you will have to follow the same procedures to shut down and restart. You have now determined that the problem is not the disk, but perhaps the program you were attempting to use.

To make sure that it is not the optical drive itself, insert a different disk of the same type and try to access it with the original program.

Display Problems

When a laptop LCD display fails, first assure yourself that it is not a power problem (see the preceding section) then eliminate the simple causes:

- Move the mouse or press a key on the keyboard to ensure that the problem is not simply in a power-saving configuration (described in the preceding section) or the wrong screen mode.
- Is the laptop switched to external monitor only? The vast majority of laptops have an adapter for an external monitor and the ability to switch the output from the built-in LCD display to the external display. This is usually accomplished by pressing and holding the FN key and pressing the function key that doubles as the display mode toggle key, changing the video output from the inboard LCD display to an external monitor. Press this key combination once and wait a second to see if it makes a difference. If not, press again and wait to see if the display turns on. There are usually three states for this key: integrated LCD only, external display only, and both.

Once you have eliminated simple causes, check for the following areas.

Damaged Wiring

The wires for a laptop LDC panel must pass through the hinge of the lid. Therefore, in some cases the wiring comes loose at this point. This can cause a dim or blank display. Manufacturers of conventional laptops have generally solved the wire-through-the-hinge problem, but some Tablet PCs still have problems with this. The hinge on a Tablet PC is more complex than on a standard laptop, because it must allow for the lid to both open and rotate into "tablet" position covering the keyboard so the user can hold the PC like a physical clipboard. The manufacturer, or a qualified repair center, must correct these problems.

Temperature Problems

Is the laptop operating in a very hot or very cold room? The liquid crystal material within an LCD panel also makes it sensitive to extremes of hot and cold. If a display that is exposed to temperature extremes goes blank, move the laptop to a heated or air conditioned room with a moderate temperature and wait an hour before trying it again. If the display appears to work correctly after adjusting the temperature, take steps to avoid the problem in the future.

If you must transport a laptop in extremely cold or extremely hot conditions, do not power it up until you can place it in a room with a moderate temperature and allow it to warm up or cool down.

If you must use a laptop in an inhospitable environment, consider running it with an external CRT display, which is not as susceptible to problems from temperature extremes. With the display mode set to external only, you will not have to deal with the display problems. However, prolonged exposure to temperature extremes may permanently damage the laptop display.

Blank Window

If the laptop powered up normally, and Windows started normally, but when you tried to run a video you could hear the sound, but no image appeared in the video window, it could be that the display resolution is set too high for the video. Correct this by opening up the Display applet, and changing the screen resolution setting on the Settings page.

Backlight Problems

The backlight in a laptop LCD screen consists of several components. These include fluorescent tubes, positioned at the top, sides, and sometimes behind the screen, and a white diffusion panel behind the LCD that scatters the light evenly. The fluorescent tubes are thinner than a pencil and very fragile. For this reason, if a laptop has been dropped or handled roughly, one or more of these tubes can break, causing the display to dim or go totally dark.

Pixilation Problems

Most laptops now use active matrix LCD screens, described in Chapter 2, and therefore have special pixilation problems related to the LCD technology. These screens have three transistors per pixel, one transistor each for red, green, and blue. The transistors turn on and off to create a combination of colors. When a transistor is turned off permanently (not by design, but through failure), it shows a dark spot on the screen, called a dead pixel. Another, nearly opposite problem is lit pixel (also called a stuck pixel). This occurs when a transistor is permanently turned on, causing the pixel to constantly show as red, green, or blue. When pixels contiguous to each other are all in this lit-pixel state, they show as the color derived from their combination.

on the job

Before you decide that you have a defective LCD panel, be sure to wipe it clean with a soft, antistatic cloth.

You may have bad or lit pixels on your LCD display without noticing it because the dead pixels do not show when displaying an image with dark colors in the defective area, and lit pixels may not show when displaying an image showing the colors that result from the dark pixels. Also, a few defective pixels are considered normal, since it is nearly impossible to find an LCD panel without a few. It is a problem if there are many bad pixels together that cause the image to be distorted or unreadable. To test for dead or lit pixels, follow the steps in Exercise 6-2.

EXERCISE 6-2

Testing for Pixilation Problems

While there are many sophisticated ways to test an LCD display for pixilation problems, our favorite is this quick and easy test. Try this on any LCD panel you currently own and the next time you are shopping for a laptop.

1. Open the Display applet in Control Panel: locate an empty area of the desktop, right-click, and select Properties.
2. Select the Desktop tab. In the Background box scroll to the top of the list and select None.

3. In the color box to the right, click the spin arrow and select white. Select OK to close the dialog box.

4. Press and hold the Windows key and the D key to close all open windows.

5. If the taskbar is still visible, take action to make it auto-hide by right-clicking on an empty area of the taskbar and selecting Properties. In the Taskbar And Start Menu Properties dialog box, click to place a check mark in Auto-Hide The Taskbar. Click OK to close the dialog box.

6. Now examine the screen, looking for areas that are not white. These may appear as the tiniest dot, about the size of a mark made by a fine-point pen on paper. Black dots indicate dead pixels, while any other color indicates a lit pixel.

7. When you have completed the test, open the Display applet and return your desktop to its previous settings.

Video Adapter Problems

The easiest way to test the integrated video adapter in a laptop is to plug in an external monitor and see if it works. Plug it in, power it up, and wait a minute. If nothing appears on the screen, press the FN key and the display mode toggle key. If you have the same problems with the external monitor, then you have isolated the problem to the video adapter. Check your warranty to see if this is covered. If it is covered, then take the steps to have the laptop serviced by the manufacturer or an authorized repair site. If not covered by warranty, you must decide if the laptop is worth taking it to a repair center at your or your company's cost.

Input Devices

If you have problems with an external mouse, refer back to Chapter 4, where we described some common problems and solutions. There are certain problems with the specialized laptop input devices such as touchpads, digitizers, and the integrated keyboard.

Touchpad

Touchpad problems fall into two categories: problems with the touchpad functionality and problems with accidental use of the touchpad.

Problems with Touchpad Functionality   Sometimes the touchpad will fail to work or control of the pointer through the touchpad will become erratic. In these cases, restart the computer and try it again. This often takes care of the problem. If it occurs frequently, make note of the application software in use at the time. There may be an incompatibility with the touchpad driver and the application. Check the laptop manufacturer's Web site for any updates to the touchpad driver.

Problems with Accidental Use of the Touchpad   The touchpads on laptops cause problems for some users who cannot seem to avoid unintentionally resting their hands on the touchpad, or brushing their hands or fingers over it when using the keyboard. This can cause a variety of problems, depending on what application is open and has the focus at the time. For instance, while the user is typing into the document, the pointer may suddenly jump to another part of the page and the typed text suddenly will be inserted where it does not belong. Or text may be deleted and overwritten, or applications opened or closed without the user intending. The result is confusing to the user who is not aware of touching the touchpad.

Check the Mouse applet in Control Panel, which opens the Mouse Properties dialog box. On a laptop with a touchpad, this should include settings to control how the touchpad works. Check for a setting that controls the sensitivity of the touchpad, so that it does not respond to light, accidental contact. One such setting may be found under a Tapping tab in a section labeled Typing. Selecting Tap Off When Typing will disable the touchpad while keys are pressed, and provides for a configurable delay after the last key is hit. Manufacturers use different terminology for this, so you will have to look for it and experiment.

If nothing else works, disable the touchpad and attach a more conventional pointing device, such as a mouse or trackball. For the user who travels, this means one more piece of equipment to take along, but it may be well worth the trouble to avoid this annoyance. Check the laptop's documentation to find out how to disable the touchpad; in fact, some laptops have a switch next to the touchpad to disable it. If you cannot disable the touchpad, just tape a piece of card stock over it as a means of mechanically disabling it.

Keyboard Failure

Most laptops come with small, integrated keyboards. Some laptop keyboards include a pointing device such as a pointing stick or touchpad. Unfortunately, because keyboards are integrated into laptops, they are not easily replaced, and the entire computer must usually be sent back to the manufacturer when part or all of a keyboard fails.

Keyboard Usage Issues

The laptop keyboard typically has several functions that are not included in a desktop keyboard. We mentioned some of these in Chapter 5. For instance, some keys normally have special functions when combined with the FN key. Laptop keyboards present special problems, first because they have more functions than desktop keyboards and second because these functions are squeezed into a smaller space.

Problems with laptop keyboards often result from users not remembering that they have turned a certain feature on or off (recall the display mode key problem discussed previously), or have accidentally pressed a combination of keys that enables or disables some function.

When using a laptop for the first time, familiarize yourself with the special function keys. Close all open applications before using any of these key combinations. At the very minimum, be sure to click on an empty area of the desktop so that your keystrokes do not affect an open application.

A few common keys and their associated problems are described next. The names provided here are not standard, and keys with similar functions may have different names.

Display Mode Key   Problems with the display mode key were described earlier in this chapter. Any time the display is blank, and you can clearly hear the fan and see indicator lights, press the display mode key combination to eliminate this as the cause of the problem. When you first attach an external display, it should be automatically detected and used, but if not, try toggling the display mode key. The display mode key usually has a symbol resembling a video screen.

Speaker On/Off Key   Another common special key is the SPEAKER ON/OFF key. Some laptop keyboards identify the speaker key by a speaker icon with an "X" over it. This may appear in blue on one of the function keys, such as the F3 key. When the FN key is combined with the SPEAKER ON/OFF key, it toggles the speaker on and off. This is handy on a trip when you want to quickly turn off the speaker so that you do not bother your fellow travelers. The problem comes in when you either forget that you toggled the speakers off or you accidentally toggled them off. Therefore, if you believe the inboard speakers are not working, first look for the SPEAKER ON/OFF key.

Speaker Volume Key   Similarly, some laptops include a SPEAKER VOLUME key. When the FN key is combined with the SPEAKER VOLUME key and either the up (↑) or right (→) arrow key, the volume will increase. To decrease the volume, press the FN key and the SPEAKER VOLUME key along with either the left (←) or down (↓) arrow key. This changes the speaker volume at the hardware level, bypassing Windows' volume control. Therefore, if you have no sound, and using the Windows volume control has no effect, try turning the volume up using the SPEAKER VOLUME key.

Display Brightness Key   The DISPLAY BRIGHTNESS key may appear as a sun icon on one of the function keys. Pressing the FN key and this key plus either the up (↑) or right (→) arrow key will cause the display to get brighter. Pressing the FN key and the DISPLAY BRIGHTNESS key plus either the left (←) or down (↓) arrow key will cause the display to get darker.

e x a m

ⓦatch   *Pay special attention to the problems caused by the portability features of a laptop, such as the special FN keys that change modes for the display, speaker, and other components. If these modes are changed, it may appear that there is a more serious problem.*

Digitizer Problems

Digitizers are strange but wonderful devices. While they are not just for laptops, an entire class of laptop, the Tablet PC, includes a display that is both an LCD panel and a digitizer tablet—hence the name. The main device for using the tablet as a digitizer is the stylus, a pen-shaped device described in Chapter 5.

When using a digitizer, the user draws or writes on the tablet with the stylus and can even select "ink" of various colors and textures with which to draw. When the user is writing, a handwriting recognition program converts the writing into a text document, but the handwritten page is also saved as a graphic.

Problems with digitizers often involve the use and appearance of the ink while working in various applications.

Problems that are common to all applications can be resolved by updating the digitizer driver. Many, but not all, Tablet PCs use the Wacom driver, as they are the major manufacturer of digitizer tablets—both free-standing and those that are integrated into Tablet PCs. FinePoint is another digitizer manufacturer.

Digitizer problems associated with only one application, or two or more from the same manufacturer, need to be resolved through the application. Sometimes an update will take care of the problem.

A damaged or defective stylus may cause other digitizer problems. Whereas on a handheld computer you can use anything from a pen to your finger to work with a touch screen, on a digitizer, you must use a stylus that sends a signal to the digitizer, giving it the position of the stylus on the tablet. The stylus, therefore, must have power somehow, either by a battery or by an outside source like a USB port.

Further, the stylus used with a digitizer or Tablet PC must be compatible with the digitizer. When it comes to replacing a stylus, the general rule is that a Wacom stylus will work with any digitizer or Tablet PC using the Wacom tablet, and similarly the FinePoint stylus will work with FinePoint digitizers and Tablet PCs using the FinePoint digitizer.

Digitizer tablets are subject to radio frequency interference, which can cause distortion of the created image. Some digitizers have additional insulation to block this interference. If you are having problems writing or drawing on a tablet, try to move it away from any possible sources of interference and try it again.

Wireless Problems

Wireless problems specific to laptop computers come in two main categories: antenna problems and interference problems.

Antenna Problems

Many laptops today come with built-in wireless Wi-Fi network adapters, each with a built-in antenna, which is usually located in the lid. While this antenna may be adequate in many instances, it lacks the flexibility and power of some add-on external antennas. Attaching an external antenna to a built-in adapter is nearly impossible. Therefore, to increase the signal range, you may need to disable the built-in Wi-Fi adapter and replace it. On most new laptops, there is a switch to turn off the internal Wi-Fi adapter. The replacement should then be either a PCMCIA card with a special connector for an external antenna or a USB Wi-Fi card with an antenna at the end of the USB cable. The latter is preferred, since the USB cable allows you to position the antenna for better wireless reception. Several manufacturers make such a USB Wi-Fi card and antenna.

Interference Problems

Interference problems are not limited to laptops. However, using a Bluetooth device with a laptop that also has a Wi-Fi adapter introduces a conflict, because both of these wireless standards use the same radio band, 2.4 GHz. You may have to choose which wireless devices you will use; or when you will use them. Since Bluetooth works only for very short distances, it is used for keyboards, pointing devices, printers, and headphones. Wi-Fi connects to a local area network, and in many cases, connects through that network to the Internet. You may need to choose between uninterrupted Wi-Fi access, or wireless connections between your local devices and the laptop.

SCENARIO & SOLUTION

When I am typing on my laptop, the pointer seems to jump all over the document. How can I prevent this from happening?	This is a common problem when a hand or finger contacts a touchpad while you are typing. If the laptop has a touchpad, try to turn it off or tape a piece of cardboard over it and use an external pointing device.
I attached an external display to my laptop, but after I powered it up, no image appeared on the external display, only on the integrated display. What have I done wrong?	Try toggling the display mode key to make the laptop use the external display.
My laptop has a built-in Wi-Fi adapter. How can I improve my wireless signal to my laptop?	An external USB Wi-Fi adapter gives the most flexibility in positioning an antenna for better signal reception.

CERTIFICATION OBJECTIVE

- **601: 2.4**   *Perform preventive maintenance on laptops and portable devices*

    In this section, prepare for the CompTIA A+ exams by learning the correct preventive maintenance and care practices for laptops and portable devices. Use these in addition to the preventive maintenance techniques and practices introduced in Chapter 4.

Preventive Maintenance for Laptops and Portable Devices

In general, laptops and desktop PCs have much in common. Therefore, the preventive maintenance information in Chapter 4 applies to laptops and other portable devices. However, there are certain issues that are either unique to portable computers or more common to them because they use certain technologies not used in most desktop PCs. The following sections cover these issues. While we discuss laptops specifically, most of these issues also apply to other portable devices.

Transporting and Shipping a Laptop

Portability is the key feature of any laptop. However, moving sensitive equipment is fraught with opportunity for damage. Therefore, when transporting a laptop, always use a proper carrying case or bag to protect it from damage. Select a case that feels comfortable to carry because a laptop is something that you should normally keep with you whenever you are traveling.

When purchasing a case, try it out in the store with the laptop in it. Look for a case with a wide, padded, adjustable shoulder strap. You will also want adequate compartments for any accessories, such as the AC adapter, an extra battery, a pointing device, and compartments to carry a few optical discs and a flash drive.

People tend to overstuff their laptop bags with books and other equipment. The danger in this practice is that it will put enough pressure on the back of the laptop display to crack the glass on the LCD panel. Therefore, refrain from packing bulky or non-essential items in the laptop case, even if you must use a second carrying case for books and other items.

Never check a laptop as baggage unless you pack it in a case especially designed to protect it while it is being treated like, well, baggage. This will not be your typical laptop carrying case, but a metal case with molded foam padding to protect it.

If a laptop must be shipped via a package service or the U.S. Postal Service, do not pack it in its carrying case, because this will not be adequate. Nothing beats the original packing material and box. Always save these, because you never know when you may have to ship the laptop for service, in which case manufacturers recommend that you ship it in the original box.

Never leave a laptop in a vehicle for extended periods, especially when the laptop is powered on. This is because even in mild weather, on a sunny day, the interior temperature can climb into a range that could damage the laptop. The LCD display is especially sensitive to temperature extremes. Extreme cold can also damage the laptop.

Cooling Issues

There are several cooling issues specific to laptops. The fact that a laptop has a great deal of circuitry in a very small space makes it more likely to overheat and compounds the problem. All but the LCD display is in the bottom of the laptop case, and this small area contains a great deal of heat-generating equipment. Therefore, you should pay attention to the work environment and consider supplemental cooling, when possible.

The Work Environment

When operating a laptop, be sure that there is adequate ventilation around the laptop. Using your laptop while on the go means that you must often improvise a workspace. In fact, you may see travelers who simply unzip the case and run the laptop while it is still nestled in the case. The problem with this practice is that air vents are blocked, which can cause the laptop to overheat. Ideally, when operating, a laptop should never be placed on soft, conforming surfaces like couches, beds, or even laps.

Another issue, especially for the mobile laptop user, may be air quality. A project manager on a construction site may necessarily expose her laptop to all the dirt and dust of a construction site, whether working out of a pickup truck or an on-site office. Since this cannot be avoided, this user should have the inside of the laptop cleaned frequently, and keep it powered off, closed, and in its case when it is not in use.

Supplemental Cooling

Supplemental cooling for a laptop can come in the form of a special laptop stand that holds the laptop off the surface of the desk to allow airflow underneath. This alone will help, but these stands also often contain one or more fans. The laptop's USB hub powers some of these, while others require 110 V power and therefore have a power adapter. If you plan to use this device while traveling, look for the lightest one you can find, which means you want to avoid one with an AC adapter. If this device will remain on your office desktop, then weight is no problem, and you should buy the one that you judge will be most effective.

Be sure you understand how to protect a laptop during storage, transportation, and shipping.

Hardware and Video Cleaning Materials

When it comes to cleaning the laptop case and display, treat a laptop just like a desktop PC. Follow the suggestions and instructions in Chapter 4 for materials and techniques to use.

CERTIFICATION SUMMARY

Laptops and other portable computers have much in common with desktop PCs. However, the form factors and technologies that make these computers portable also make them vulnerable to certain problems. When troubleshooting problems with portable computers, a computer technician must apply the same procedures and techniques presented in Chapter 4. In addition, he must also understand the special problems associated with laptops and other portables.

When it comes to preventive maintenance, a similar approach is required. Everything that applies to desktop PCs also applies to portable computers. In addition, there are certain issues that are either unique to portable computers or more common to them because they use technologies not used in most desktop PCs. Therefore, the technician must apply these special preventive maintenance and care procedures to portable computers.

✓ TWO-MINUTE DRILL

Here are some of the key points covered in Chapter 6.

Troubleshooting Laptops and Portable Devices

❑ Laptop-specific power problems involve rechargeable batteries and the external AC power adapters that put the portability into laptops.

❑ AC adapter problems fall into two categories: damage or failure of the original AC adapter, and damage to the computer due to using the wrong AC adapter.

❑ The AC adapter voltage, amperage, and polarity must match those required by the laptop.

❑ A battery that is not properly inserted or charged, an old battery that can no longer hold a charge, or defective new batteries can cause battery problems.

❑ If a laptop fails to power up when connected to an AC power source, suspect the AC adapter.

❑ Before troubleshooting for an AC adapter problem, remove any hardware devices that were installed since the laptop last powered up normally.

❑ Eliminate other usual suspects, such as an external monitor that is in sleep mode or not powered up.

❑ If using the laptop's integrated display, eliminate it as the source of the problem.

❑ Once you eliminate other simple causes, proceed to troubleshoot the AC adapter.

❑ If a laptop fails, and you have eliminated power as the source of the problem, remove all peripherals and add them back one at a time until you have isolated the cause to one device.

❑ Check with the manufacturer if you are unable to solve the problem. It may be covered by warranty, or may be part of a recall that will resolve the problem.

❑ Like a desktop PC, if a laptop fails at POST, you may have to enter the Setup mode to discover the cause and possibly apply a solution.

❑ Software generally causes system instability, which Chapter 9 addresses.

❑ Hardware can cause some instability problems. For instance, if a system hangs when attempting to use an optical disc, remove the disk and wait a few minutes to see if the system recovers. Then clean the disk and reinsert it.

❑ If system instability keeps you from closing applications and Windows itself, try opening Task Manager and closing the program listed as "not responding."

❑ If you suspect a problem with an optical disk or drive, insert a different disk to determine whether it is the disk or the drive.

❑ A laptop display may appear to have failed because the display mode function key has switched it to external monitor only. Try pressing the display mode key combination to change the mode.

❑ The wires for a laptop LCD panel must pass through the hinge of the lid, and therefore the wiring can come loose at this point. Contact the manufacturer or authorized repair center for help with this problem.

❑ The LCD panel in a laptop and other portable devices is vulnerable to temperature extremes, in which case it may go blank. Remove it from exposure.

❑ When running a video, if the sound works, but the window in which the video is to run is blank, reduce the screen resolution and run the video again.

❑ The fluorescent tubes that backlight the LCD screen in a laptop are fragile and can break if the laptop has rough handling. This will cause the display to dim or go totally dark.

❑ Most LCD panels (laptop or external) have a few dead or lit pixels. Large numbers of these can distort areas of the screen. If you find this is the case, contact the manufacturer for a replacement LCD panel.

❑ To isolate a display problem to the video adapter, attach an external display and see if there is still a failure to display. Display adapters are built into laptops, and if one has failed, then you must contact the manufacturer or an authorized dealer.

Preventive Maintenance for Laptops and Portable Devices

❑ The portability of laptops also makes them more vulnerable to damage than a desktop computer.

❑ Use a proper carrying case for transporting a laptop.

❑ A laptop should not be shipped as baggage, but if it must, be sure to pack it in an adequate case, preferably a metal case with molded foam padding to protect it.

❑ Save the original carton and packing material in case you need to ship the laptop to have it repaired.

- ❏ Never leave a laptop in a vehicle for extended periods.
- ❏ The very compactness of laptops makes them vulnerable to overheating.
- ❏ Be sure to provide adequate ventilation. If this is not possible, consider buying supplemental cooling in the form of a laptop stand with one or more fans installed.
- ❏ If you must use the laptop in a dirty, dusty environment, power it off, close it, keep it in its carrying case when not in use, and have it cleaned frequently.
- ❏ Clean the laptop case and display surfaces as described in Chapter 4.

SELF TEST

The following questions will help you measure your understanding of the material presented in this chapter. Read all of the choices carefully because there might be more than one correct answer. Choose all correct answers for each question.

Troubleshooting Laptops and Portable Devices

1. What two components must be checked when a laptop experiences power problems?
   A. LCD panel
   B. AC adapter
   C. Power-on self-test
   D. Battery

2. When replacing an AC adapter for a laptop, match these three characteristics.
   A. Volts, amps, and polarity
   B. Volts, amps, and current
   C. Inverter, converter, and generator
   D. AC, DC, and amps

3. There are several of these power components on a motherboard. They manage the current required for internal components at 5 volts, 12 volts, 3.3 volts, and whatever voltage is required.
   A. Generator
   B. Inverter
   C. Converter
   D. Voltage regulator

4. You watch the battery indicator in Windows to determine when this is needed.
   A. Replacement
   B. Recharging
   C. Rebooting
   D. Testing

5. A laptop plugged into an AC power source will not power up. What component should you suspect as the source of the problem, assuming the power source is working?
   A. Battery
   B. LCD panel
   C. AC adapter
   D. Keyboard

6. What is a simple way to test an AC power outlet?

   A. Use an inverter.

   B. Plug in a converter.

   C. Plug a generator into the outlet.

   D. Plug a lamp into the outlet.

7. What action will some AC adapters take when they detect a power overage?

   A. Turn on

   B. Automatically restart

   C. Shut down

   D. Beep

8. When testing the power output of an AC adapter, what should you set your multimeter to test?

   A. Volts DC

   B. Volts AC

   C. Amps

   D. MHz

9. What should you do if your laptop fails to start up after you have installed a new memory module?

   A. Reboot.

   B. Power off and power on.

   C. Remove the memory module and restart.

   D. Update the device driver.

10. What should you do if a laptop fails during the POST?

    A. Restart.

    B. Return it to the manufacturer.

    C. Remove the battery.

    D. Read the information on the screen and follow any instructions.

11. What term is used for a variety of symptoms, one of which is a system "hang"?

    A. POST

    B. System instability

    C. Reboot

    D. System failure

12. What can you do if a system is unresponsive and you cannot close any open windows normally?
    A. Turn off the power switch.
    B. Use Task Manager to stop the unresponsive program.
    C. Unplug the computer.
    D. Remove the battery.

13. What is a simple cause for a blank display?
    A. Broken fluorescent lamp
    B. Power saving mode
    C. Damaged wiring
    D. Temperature extremes

14. How do you bring a display screen out of power saving mode?
    A. Move the mouse or press a key.
    B. Unplug the laptop.
    C. Reset the AC adapter.
    D. Press CTRL-ALT-DELETE.

15. Your laptop was left in your car for several hours while visiting Minnesota in winter. What should you do?
    A. Power it up in the car and run it on battery.
    B. Allow it to warm up before turning it on.
    C. Replace the battery.
    D. Clean the display screen.

16. After you dropped your laptop, you powered it up and the display screen is blank, although you can hear the fan. What may be the problem?
    A. Pixilation problems
    B. Temperature extremes
    C. Failed touchpad
    D. Broken fluorescent tubes

17. What can cause tiny black dots that are always in the same place on the screen, while the rest of the LCD display shows an image correctly?
    A. Lit pixels
    B. Damaged wire
    C. Dead pixels
    D. Backlit pixels

18. Your stylus will no longer write to your digitizer on your Tablet PC. Changing the batteries did not help. What can you use as a replacement for the stylus?

   A. The stylus from a handheld computer

   B. Any digitizer stylus

   C. A stylus from the manufacturer of your digitizer tablet

   D. A ballpoint pen

Preventive Maintenance for Laptops and Portable Devices

19. How should you prepare a laptop to ship via UPS?

   A. Pack it in a laptop case.

   B. Pack it in its original box and packing material.

   C. Remove the LCD panel and pack it in a case.

   D. Clean the LCD panel.

20. What should you do for a laptop that seems to run hot, in addition to having it cleaned and keeping it in a well-ventilated area?

   A. Turn off the display and use an external display.

   B. Purchase a laptop stand.

   C. Close some applications.

   D. Turn down the brightness of the display.

LAB QUESTION

The Lab Question in Chapter 5 had you research a laptop computer to fit a certain set of requirements. Using that specific model (or if you did not complete that lab, select a laptop model) research the terms of the standard warranty (free with the purchase). Then list these terms.

SELF TEST ANSWERS

Troubleshooting Laptops and Portable Devices

1. ☑ **B and D.** The AC adapter and the battery are the two components that must be checked when a laptop experiences power problems.

   ☒ **A,** LCD panel, is not correct because this would not be what you would check when troubleshooting a power problem. **C,** power-on self-test, is not correct because if power is off, the self-test will not occur.

2. ☑ **A.** Volts, amps, and polarity is correct. These must match between the AC adapter and the laptop.

   ☒ **B,** volts, amps, and current, is not correct. Although volts and amps is correct, and current is often used in place of amps, the third requirement, polarity, is missing. **C,** inverter, converter, and generator, is incorrect because an inverter is a device that converts DC current to AC current, a converter is a device that converts AC current to DC current, and a generator is a device that creates electrical current. **D,** AC, DC, and amps, is incorrect. Only one of these, amps, is one of the characteristics that should match between a laptop and an AC adapter.

3. ☑ **D.** A voltage regulator is the device found on a motherboard that manages the current required for internal components, providing the different voltage levels required by different components.

   ☒ **A,** generator, is incorrect because it is a device that generates electricity, usually from gasoline, propane, or diesel fuels. **B,** inverter, is incorrect because it converts AC to DC, typically for battery charging. **C,** converter, is incorrect because it converts DC to AC, typically for the use of devices requiring AC power.

4. ☑ **B.** Recharging is correct because this is what you do when the battery indicator in Windows says that the battery is low.

   ☒ **A,** replacement, is incorrect because the battery indicator does not explicitly tell you when to replace the battery. **C,** rebooting, is incorrect because the battery indicator does not tell you when to reboot the computer. **D,** testing, is incorrect because the battery indicator does not tell you when to test the battery.

5. ☑ **C.** The AC adapter is the component you should suspect as the source of a problem if a laptop that is plugged into an AC power source will not power up.

   ☒ **A,** battery, is incorrect because if the laptop is plugged into an AC power source, it does not need the battery to power up. **B,** LCD panel, is incorrect because, although a failed LCD panel will make the laptop appear to be turned off, the laptop should still power up if it can receive power. **D,** keyboard, is incorrect, since this has nothing to do with the laptop's ability to power up.

6. ☑ **D.** Plug a lamp into the outlet is correct, as this is a simple way to test an AC power outlet.
☒ **A,** use an inverter, is incorrect because this device uses DC power as its input and therefore cannot be used to test an AC power outlet. **B,** plug in a converter, is incorrect because although a converter uses AC power as its input, this is not a simple test, as a lamp is more common than a converter. **C,** plug a generator into an outlet, is incorrect because most common generators convert a fuel, such as diesel or gasoline, to AC power. You would not plug one into an AC outlet.

7. ☑ **C.** Shut down is the action some AC adapters take when they detect a power overage.
☒ **A,** turn on, is incorrect because this is not the action of an AC power adapter when a power overage is detected. **B,** automatically restart, is incorrect because this action would not protect the AC adapter or the computer from damage from a power overage. **D,** beep, is incorrect because this, in itself, would not protect the AC adapter or the laptop.

8. ☑ **A.** Volts DC is correct because the AC adapter converts volts AC to volts DC (output).
☒ **B,** Volts AC, is incorrect, because the AC adapter converts volts AC to volts DC (output). **C,** amps, is incorrect because, although many multimeters can measure amps, in this case you want to measure volts. **D,** MHz, is incorrect because this is not something most multimeters measure. MHz has been mentioned in this book as a measurement of CPU speed.

9. ☑ **C.** Remove the memory module and restart is the correct answer, since this is what has changed since the computer last successfully powered up.
☒ **A,** reboot, is incorrect because this will not change anything in this case. **B,** power off and power on, is incorrect because this would also not change anything. **D,** update the device driver, is incorrect because memory does not require a device driver.

10. ☑ **D.** Read the information on the screen and follow any instructions is the correct answer, because the POST may have detected a problem, in which case it will provide an error message.
☒ **A,** restart, is incorrect, although you may be instructed to do this by the message on the screen. **B,** return it to the manufacturer, is incorrect because this is a drastic step to take when you have not tried to discover the problem. **C,** remove the battery, is incorrect because you have no indication that this is the problem.

11. ☑ **B.** System instability is the term used to describe a variety of symptoms.
☒ **A,** POST, is incorrect because this is the acronym for the power-on self-test and is not related to a system hang. **C,** reboot, is incorrect because this is the term for restarting a system and is not related to a system hang. **D,** system failure, is incorrect because this term describes a complete breakdown, not the group of symptoms that fall under system instability.

12. ☑ **B.** Use Task Manager to stop the unresponsive program.
☒ **A,** turn off the power switch, is incorrect. Although this may be necessary, you should try a less drastic measure first. **C,** unplug the computer, and **D,** remove the battery, are both too

drastic for the problem described. At most, you will turn off the power switch after trying to shut down the application and shut down Windows and failing.

13. ☑ **B.** Power saving mode is a simple cause for a blank display. Always check for a simple cause first.

☒ **A**, broken fluorescent lamp, is incorrect because while it can cause a blank display, it is not a simple cause. **C**, damaged wiring, is incorrect for a similar reason. **D**, temperature extremes, is also a possible cause, but not a simple one.

14. ☑ **A.** Move the mouse or press a key is correct because this will bring a display screen out of power saving mode.

☒ **B**, unplug the laptop, is incorrect because this will not bring the display out of power saving mode. **C**, reset the AC adapter, is incorrect because this will not bring the display out of power saving mode. **D**, press CTRL-ALT-DELETE, is incorrect because this will not bring the display out of power saving mode.

15. ☑ **B.** Allow it to warm up before turning it on is correct because running it in extremely cold temperatures can damage it, especially the display.

☒ **A**, power it up in the car and run it on battery, is incorrect because running the laptop in the extreme cold can damage it. **C**, replace the battery, is incorrect because there is no indication that this is necessary. **D**, clean the display screen, is incorrect because this will not address the problem of the temperature extremes.

16. ☑ **D.** Broken fluorescent tubes is correct because the backlight consists of fluorescent tubes.

☒ **A**, pixilation problems, is incorrect because this would not make the screen go blank. **B**, temperature extremes, is incorrect because temperature was not mentioned in the question. **C**, failed touchpad, is incorrect because this would not make the screen go blank.

17. ☑ **C.** Dead pixels can cause tiny black dots that are always in the same place on the screen.

☒ **A**, lit pixels, is incorrect because these do not show up as black dots. **B**, damaged wire, is incorrect because if a wire to the LCD panel is damaged, the symptoms include flickering or complete failure. **D**, backlit pixels, is incorrect because pixels, as part of the LCD screen, are always backlit.

18. ☑ **C.** A stylus from the manufacturer of your digitizer table is correct.

☒ **A**, the stylus from a handheld computer, is incorrect because this is a passive device, and a digitizer requires a stylus that uses radio frequency signals to transmit its coordinates on the tablet. **B**, any digitizer stylus, is incorrect because it may not be compatible if it is not made for the tablet. **D**, a ballpoint pen, is incorrect because, like the stylus from a handheld device, this is a passive device, not capable of transmitting the correct radio signals to the digitizer.

Preventive Maintenance for Laptops and Portable Devices

19. ☑ **B.** Pack it in the original box and packing material is correct.

☒ **A**, pack it in a laptop case, is incorrect because this will be inadequate. **C**, remove the LCD panel and pack it in a case, is incorrect because you should never remove the lid. **D**, clean the LCD panel, is incorrect because this in no way prepares the laptop for shipping.

20. ☑ **B.** Purchase a laptop stand is correct because this will allow air to circulate underneath, and many stands also have one or more fans.

☒ **A**, turn off the display and use an external display, is incorrect because the heat is usually generated in the bottom of the laptop case. **C**, close some applications, is incorrect because this has not proven to have any significant effect on the heat generation. **D**, turn down the brightness of the display, is also incorrect because this has also not proven to have any significant effect on heat generation and does not affect the main case of the laptop, where the most heat is generated.

LAB ANSWER

The standard warranty for the Dell XPS M1210:

- ❏ 90-day coverage for hardware support for defects in materials and workmanship
- ❏ One year of e-mail, chat, or telephone-based hardware support
- ❏ At-home service available (after phone-based troubleshooting)
- ❏ Online troubleshooting available to customers with broadband connections in select situations
- ❏ "How To" for XP operating system
- ❏ System configuration restore

Part III

Operating Systems

7

Operating System Fundamentals

L ike many people you may have used a computer for much of your life, and you know how to open windows, navigate folders, download files, and run programs. With such proficiency, you may wonder why you need to study the operating system.

Using an operating system is far different from supporting an operating system. Just as driving a car does not guarantee that you fully understand internal combustion engines or automatic transmissions, using a computer does not guarantee that you understand it, nor that you are prepared to be a technician who must install, configure, optimize, and troubleshoot an operating system.

This chapter, and the three that follow, will lead you on a journey of understanding, but they do not require you to be a systems programmer who understands the programming code of the OS. You only need a sharp mind, good powers of observation, and patience. This chapter describes operating system fundamentals, the first layer in your foundation of understanding. Chapter 8 describes the tasks involved in installing, configuring, and optimizing operating systems. Chapter 9 will give you practice working with Windows file management as well as the use of Windows utilities, and in Chapter 10 you will apply the troubleshooting theory you learned in Chapter 4 to Windows operating systems.

CERTIFICATION OBJECTIVES

■ **601: 3.1   602: 3.1   603: 2.1**   *Identify the fundamental principles of using operating systems*

Beginning with the 2006 exams, CompTIA no longer separates their A+ exams by operating system and hardware. All four of the 2006 exams released to date include hardware, and all but one of these includes operating system topics. The exception is exam 220-604, which targets the depot or bench technician, who needs very little operating system knowledge. For this job title the operating system objectives covered in the A+ Essentials exam (220-601) should be sufficient.

We have spread coverage of the topics in the preceding certification objectives over two chapters. This chapter includes all of the topics under those objectives, with the exception of *Identify concepts and procedures for creating, viewing, managing disks, directories, and files in operating systems.* Chapter 9 presents that topic.

Major Operating Systems

In this section you will learn the purpose of operating systems, the differences among the three most common operating systems, and the reasons for revision levels.

The Purpose of Operating Systems

The purpose of an operating system (OS) is to control all of the interactions between the various system components, human interactions with the computer, and network operations for the computer system. It accomplishes this by building an increasingly complex set of software layers between the lowest level of a computer system (the hardware) and the highest levels (user interactions). From a user perspective, this means that the user either points, types, or displays data using a device under the control of the OS system.

The OS is also responsible for managing the computer's files in an organized manner, and allowing the user to manage data files. The OS keeps track of the functions of particular files, and calls or runs those files when needed. Furthermore, the OS is responsible for maintaining file associations so that files launch in the proper applications.

Additionally, the OS is responsible for managing the computer's disks, keeping track of how each disk (and portion of each disk) is identified, and managing the use of the disk space.

Differences Between Major Operating Systems

The major current desktop operating systems include Windows, the Mac OS, and Linux. Each of these operating systems performs the basic OS functions. There was a time when there was a wide gulf between the capabilities of Windows and the other two OSs. This gap is now mostly closed, and today the greatest differences lie in their interfaces, which, ironically, now also have more commonalities than differences. At one time they were very different from each other visually, but today they each offer a graphical user interface (GUI), a user interface that takes advantage of the video system's graphics capabilities for manipulating graphic elements that represent objects and tasks. Among the three major OSs, the GUIs are so similar that an experienced user of one of these GUIs can easily switch to another with only a short period of adjustment required.

e x a m
⑩atch

Three of the released CompTIA A+ exams, 601, 602, and 603, include operating systems as a major objective domain. At present, all three of these exams require knowledge of Microsoft Windows 2000, Microsoft Windows XP Professional, Microsoft Windows XP Home, and Microsoft Windows XP Media Center. Microsoft Windows Vista is not as yet included in the objectives for these exams.

Apple Mac OS X

One characteristic of the Mac OS sets it apart from Windows or Linux: it only runs on computers manufactured by Apple Computer Company. As a proprietary product, the Mac OS and Apple Computer combination offers better integration of the OS and the hardware because it lacks the incompatibility problems of the other major operating systems, which must work with computers from a myriad of manufacturers.

This close integration between the OS and hardware gives generally better performance and stability than Windows does, but it comes at a higher purchase price, which is part of the reason the Mac OS is still a minor player in the personal computer arena. Apple computers have a very loyal base of users in various walks of life; for many years Apple Macintosh computers were the preferred computers for graphic artists.

Mac OS X (ten) is currently the most recent version of this OS, but it has had several major revisions, including Cheetah (OS X v10.0), Puma (OS X v10.1), Jaguar (OS X v10.2), Panther (OS X v10.3), Tiger (OS X v10.4), and Leopard (OS X v10.5). Releases of the first five occurred between March 2001 and April 2005. At this writing Leopard is projected to be released in October 2007. Figure 7-1 shows the Mac OS X desktop.

Until Tiger, OS X ran solely on Apple computers with the PowerPC CPU. Tiger runs on two platforms, the traditional Apple/IBM PowerPC platform, as well as an Apple platform built around Intel CPUs.

Linux

Linux is an operating system modeled on the venerable UNIX operating system and named in honor of its original developer, Linus Benedict Torvalds. It began as a project in 1991 while Torvalds was a student at the University of Helsinki in his native Finland. He invited other programmers to work together to create an open-source operating system for modern computers. They created Linux using a powerful programming language called C, along with a free C compiler developed through the

FIGURE 7-1 The Mac OS X desktop

FIGURE 7-1 The Mac OS X desktop

GNU project called GNU C Compiler (GCC). Linux has continued to evolve over the years from programmers all over the globe testing and upgrading its code.

Long a text-only operating system (see Figure 7-2), Linux now includes GUI shells that make Linux look and act very much like Windows or the Mac OS. Figure 7-3 shows one of the many Linux GUI shells.

The biggest nontechnical difference between Linux and Windows is its price and how it is distributed. Anyone can get a free copy of Linux on the Internet, and publishers often insert disk-based copies in popular computer books and magazines.

FIGURE 7-2

Linux character mode showing the prompt at which you enter commands

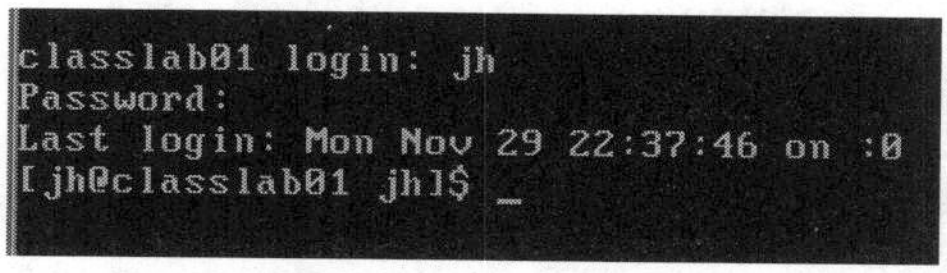

```
classlab01 login: jh
Password:
Last login: Mon Nov 29 22:37:46 on :0
[jh@classlab01 jh]$ _
```

FIGURE 7-3   Linux with a GUI shell

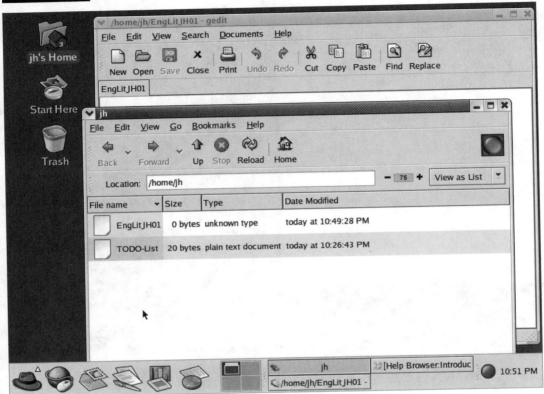

Commercial versions of Linux, which are very inexpensive when compared with the cost of other powerful operating systems, are also available from a variety of vendors who provide the Linux code free and only charge for the extras, such as utilities, GUI shells, and documentation. At this writing, the most popular Linux vendors are Red Hat and Novell, both of which offer special Linux software bundles for desktop computers as well as for servers. In fact, Linux is the operating system on a very large number of Internet Web servers.

Linux has become a popular OS in certain circles. Teachers have adopted Linux for their PCs, especially for teaching systems programming skills to students. They also can participate in the global community that has built up around it. This community invites Linux users and developers to contribute modifications and enhancements, and it freely shares information about Linux and Linux-related issues.

Until several years ago there were very few Linux-GUI-based suites of office applications for the ordinary user. However, an increasing number of software companies are writing new desktop applications or modifying existing ones for Linux. While Microsoft has long dominated the home and business desktop, Linux is making significant inroads because of the price and security issues.

on the Job   *If you need to find a suite of general business applications to run under Linux, use your favorite Internet search engine and search on "linux office suites." You will find a variety of suites—both free and for a modest price. With further research you will find reviews of some of these to help you find an office suite that works for you.*

Linux will run on an older PC and generally requires much less in the way of CPU power, memory, and disk space.

While Windows still has a much greater share of the PC market, Linux is gaining ground from Windows, since it now has more business applications available than previously. Linux also has a reputation for being more secure, perhaps because the much smaller market share it has on the desktop makes it a smaller target for those who write malicious code.

Microsoft Windows

Microsoft Windows, in its many versions, is the most widely used PC operating system for home and business. Of the two competitors to Windows, Linux comes closest to threatening the Windows dominance. One hurdle to the Linux movement is that no one person or company is responsible for the underlying Linux code, as opposed to Windows, a product of Microsoft. There is also a broad base of people trained and experienced in supporting Windows desktops. However, the latter is changing, as there is now a great deal of training available for Linux and there are several certifications, including the CompTIA Linux+ certification.

For now, technicians should be prepared to work with the Windows operating systems, including the most current desktop operating systems: Windows 2000 (see Figure 7-4), Windows XP (see Figure 7-5), and Windows Vista (being released as this book is being written).

For your future, you should be prepared to keep your knowledge of operating systems up-to-date and watch for any major movement toward alternatives to Windows on the desktop. Company decision makers are looking at the total cost of ownership issue with Windows versus Linux, and yes, versus Mac.

FIGURE 7-4   The Windows 2000 desktop

32-Bit vs. 64-Bit Operating Systems

Operating systems tie closely to the CPUs on which they can run. Therefore, we often use CPU terms to describe an operating system's abilities. For instance, the latest Intel CPUs each have a 64-bit register, meaning that the CPU can manipulate code or data in chunks up to 64 bits, and there are 64-bit operating systems that take advantage of this feature.

Just a few years ago, most of the Pentium-class CPUs had 32-bit registers. There was some confusion caused by the fact that these same CPUs had data buses 64 bits

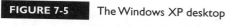

FIGURE 7-5   The Windows XP desktop

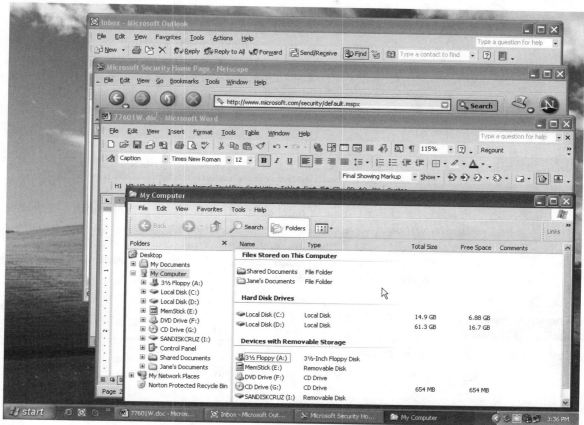

wide, meaning that they could move data into and out of the CPU in 64-bit chunks. But at its core, such a CPU was still a 32-bit CPU.

A 32-bit operating system can run on a 64-bit CPU, but a 64-bit operating system cannot run on a 32-bit CPU.

Windows 2000 was a 32-bit operating system. Windows XP comes in both 32-bit and 64-bit editions. Most of the Windows XP editions are 32-bit except for a special version, Windows XP Professional x64 Edition.

A 64-bit operating system requires 64-bit applications. For this reason there has not yet been a mass movement of users to 64-bit OSs.

Operating System Revision Levels

Computer hardware technology does not stand still, and therefore, operating systems must change to keep up. Each of the major operating systems is fairly modular, so that incremental updates can make some changes to the existing OS. In Microsoft terminology, an update contains one or more software fixes or changes to the operating system. Some updates add abilities to the OS to support new hardware, and some resolve problems discovered with the operating system. More and more, this second type of update is required to fix security problems. A *patch* is a software fix for a single problem.

At one time these updates, whether for functional or security problems, were issued without a predictable timetable. In recent years, Microsoft has assigned the second Tuesday of each month as the release day for updates. This is widely called "Patch Tuesday."

A service pack is a bundle of patches or updates released periodically by a software publisher. Windows service packs are major milestones in the life of a Windows operating system. Some devices and applications will require not simply a certain version of Windows, but also a certain service pack. Follow the steps in Exercise 7-1 to view the version information for Windows.

EXERCISE 7-1

Viewing the Version Information

Here is an easy way to determine the version and service pack level for Windows.

1. Open My Computer.
2. Open the Help menu in My Computer and select About Windows.
3. This will display the About Windows dialog box listing the version information as well as the service pack level, as shown in Figure 7-6.

Windows has had many major revisions, which are repacked and branded. The revisions of Windows for the desktop in the last several years include Windows 2000, Windows XP, and Windows Vista. Each revision, also called a version, of Windows has significant changes to the core components of the operating system, as well as a distinctive and unifying look to the GUI.

Microsoft released Windows 2000 in 2000, and followed it with Windows XP in 2001. There was a wait of over five years before they released the next version—Windows Vista.

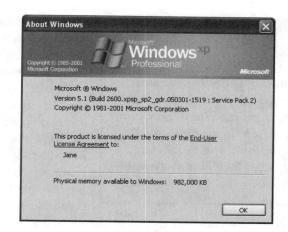

FIGURE 7-6

The About
Windows
dialog box

Further, each revision of Windows comes in a variety of editions, each including the core OS plus special features that distinguishes it as a separate product targeted to a certain type of end user. Windows XP editions included in the CompTIA A+ exams are

- Windows XP Home Edition
- Windows XP Professional Edition
- Windows XP Media Center Edition

e x a m

ⓦatch *While the CompTIA exam objectives are specific about the editions of Windows XP included in the objectives, they only list Windows 2000 without specifying an edition. For study purposes, look at Windows 2000 Professional Edition,* *and remember that Windows 2000 and Windows XP have many things in common. The biggest differences between the two in the test will involve the GUI and recovery options (discussed in Chapter 10).*

System Requirements

Each revision or version of an operating system has specific requirements for the level of CPU, amount of memory, and amount of free hard disk space. To determine if it will run on your existing computer, check the system requirements listed on the package and published on the Web site.

exam
ⓦatch   *The major differences in
the three competing operating systems
involve the platforms on which they will
run. Windows runs on the Wintel platform,
Mac OS only runs on the Apple PowerPC
or Apple Intel platform, and Linux runs
on several platforms, including the Wintel
platform.*

You can almost always count on the system requirements being greater as you move from one version to another, as from Windows XP to Windows Vista.

There is also the issue of the computer platform on which a given OS will run. A computer platform is the hardware architecture, including the CPU, BIOS, and chipset. The Mac OS runs only on the Apple family of computers, but the family is now divided into two platforms: the Apple/IBM PowerPC platform, and the Apple/Intel platform. Linux comes in versions for various platforms. Many versions of Linux will run on the same platform as Windows. This is the Microsoft/Intel platform with a range of CPUs (Intel and AMD), BIOSs, and chipsets compatible with Microsoft OSs. Some call this the "Wintel" platform.

Application and Hardware Compatibility

When introducing an operating system in a new, branded revision, we have a transition. This occurred between Windows 98 and Windows XP and is currently occurring between Windows XP and Windows Vista. Not everyone immediately embraces the new OS, and replaces their old OS with the new one. There are many reasons for this.

One reason for not moving immediately to a new operating system is the system requirements, discussed previously. It is clear that an individual who has Windows at home for e-mail and casual Internet browsing may be working on a computer that is way below the minimum requirements for a newly introduced OS. This user will weigh the benefits against the costs of upgrading or replacing a computer just to have the features of the new OS. Likewise, businesses will not simply reflexively upgrade to the new OS until they have a compelling reason.

Another reason for not moving to the new OS is compatibility. There are several faces to the compatibility issue. First of all there is hardware compatibility. The BIOS on an older PC may not support critical features of the new OS. We saw this in 2001 when Windows XP was introduced. Some manufacturers offered free BIOS upgrades on some of their models. But those with incompatible computers, and no way to upgrade the BIOS, either stayed with their installed version of Windows or bought an entirely new PC for the new OS.

Hardware compatibility can extend to peripherals. You may find that your trusty old printer or scanner does not have a driver that will work in the new OS, and the manufacturer has no intention of creating a new driver. This is a less expensive compatibility problem.

The last type of compatibility problem is between the OS and application programs. Individuals and users need to take a close look at what applications will be compatible with the new OS. Is an incompatible application indispensable to the user? Large organizations have often delayed upgrading to a new OS until they could either find a way to make the critical old applications run in the new OS or find satisfactory replacements that would work in the new OS.

In the case of Windows, Microsoft has provided a utility that will allow you to test your computer and hardware for compatibility. This program, called Upgrade Advisor, has separate versions for testing a Windows computer before upgrading to Windows XP or Windows Vista.

The Upgrade Advisor comes on the installation disc for each of these operating systems, but you can also download it from the Internet before buying the new OS. Check out the Windows XP or the Windows Vista site to locate the Upgrade Advisor for that version of Windows.

After testing the hardware and the software, the program produces a report providing valuable information and recommendations or tasks that you need to perform before installing the next version of Windows. The report may also show tasks to perform after the installation. You may find the tasks required to make a computer meet the compatibility and minimum system requirements are too expensive to perform on an older computer.

Exercise 7-2 provides the steps for acquiring and running the Windows Vista Upgrade Advisor. Chapter 9 includes details on the practice of upgrading an existing OS with a new OS.

EXERCISE 7-2

Running Upgrade Advisor

You can see if your Windows XP computer hardware and application software will be compatible with Windows Vista. You will need a broadband Internet connection to successfully complete this exercise. If the URL in Step 1 no longer exists, search www.microsoft.com for "vista upgrade advisor" and go to that link.

1. Open your Internet browser and point it to www.microsoft.com/windowsvista/getready/.

2. Look for a Download link on this page titled Windows Vista Upgrade Advisor and click this link.

3. The File Download dialog box will open with a security warning. Click Save.

4. When the Save As dialog box opens, select the Desktop and click the Save button in this dialog.

5. When the download completes, locate the file on the desktop and double-click it to run the Advisor.

6. When the Upgrade Advisor completes, it will display a task list similar to the one in Figure 7-7. Print this out or save it.

Windows Vista Business Task List

Task list:

Edition	Current System Configuration	
Windows Vista Business	CPU:	Intel(R) Pentium(R) 4 CPU 2.66GHz
	Memory:	1024.00 MB
	Hard Disk Drives:	"C" - 3.75 GB Free (15.00 GB Total)
		"D" - 13.88 GB Free (17.50 GB Total)
		"H" - 53.50 GB Free (149.00 GB Total)

Things you need to do before installing Windows Vista

• Please visit <u>Windows Update</u> to download all the latest critical updates for your system before installing Windows Vista.

System			
Issue Type	Category	Action Required	Explanation
	Hard drive"C:"	Before you install Windows Vista, create additional free hard disk space	You need 15 gigabytes (GB) of free hard disk space to install Windows Vista. Your hard disk currently has 3.75 GB of free space. Do one of the following: - Upgrade your hard disk to increase its capacity. - Remove unwanted files to create additional free hard disk space.

SCENARIO & SOLUTION

I need an inexpensive operating system that will run on the Wintel platform. I am a student studying operating systems and programming. What OS should I consider?	Linux is inexpensive and has been adopted by many teachers for students learning system programming skills.
I have installed Linux on an old PC, but now I do not know where to find office applications that will run on it.	There are plenty of applications for Linux. Use an Internet search engine to find available Linux office suites.
I have found an application I would like to buy and install on my PC, but it requires Windows XP Service Pack 2. How can I determine the service pack level?	In My Computer open the Help menu and select About. This will display the version information required.

Common Windows Components

This section provides an overview of the primary Windows components, including the graphical user interface, file systems, registry, and virtual memory.

Graphical User Interface

Windows provides a graphical user interface that the user can navigate using either a mouse or keyboard. As with most common GUIs, including those for the Mac OS and Linux shells, the Windows GUI uses the desktop metaphor. The main Windows screen, called the desktop, has containers for your work like a physical desk does. These containers, called folders, are organized in Windows in a hierarchical fashion. This allows for easy access to the commonly used files and programs using a mouse for point-and-click operations.

The Windows desktop has a variety of graphical objects in addition to folders, including the mouse pointer, icons, shortcuts, dialog boxes, windows, buttons, toolbars, menus, and the taskbar. All of these do not appear at the same time, or at least they are not on the desktop at the end of a standard installation of Windows. You encounter and use these icons as you navigate in Windows using your mouse and keyboard.

An icon is a tiny graphic image representing applications, folders, disks, menu items, and more. A shortcut is an icon that represents a link to any object that an icon can represent. Activating a shortcut (by double-clicking on it) is a quick way to access an object or to start up a program from the desktop without having to find the

Microsoft
Word

actual location of the object on your computer. You can represent a single object, like a program file, by more than one shortcut, and a shortcut can be placed on the desktop, taskbar, and other places within the Windows GUI. Shortcut icons are often (but not always) distinguished by a small bent arrow and have a title below the icon, like the Microsoft Word shortcut icon shown here.

Taskbar

By default, Windows displays a horizontal bar across the bottom of the desktop. This is the taskbar. The Windows XP taskbar, shown in Figure 7-8, includes (from left to right) a Start button, the Quick Launch toolbar, buttons for currently running programs, and at the far right, the systray, also called the notification area or system tray. Programs and some hardware devices use the systray to display status icons. These

icons may represent devices, such as a network adapter, or software, such as a battery meter, antivirus program, and so on. Pausing the mouse pointer over one of these icons will cause a rectangular status box to pop up, as shown here.

Another type of pop-up box, a message balloon, will pop up near the notification area for events relating to one of the icons. The Wireless Network Connection status message shown here is a good example.

The Quick Launch bar is an optional toolbar that can be added to the taskbar. Add this through the properties dialog box for the taskbar. You can launch any shortcuts on the Quick Launch bar with a single click without having to first open the Start menu.

You can reposition the entire taskbar by simply moving the pointer to an "empty" taskbar area and dragging it to a new position, such as at the top of the desktop, or

vertically positioned at either side. You can also resize the taskbar by dragging just an edge of it until it is the desired size.

The Windows XP taskbar option, Lock The Taskbar, locks the taskbar in place so that you cannot move it—at least, not until the option is turned off. Turn it on or off by right-clicking the taskbar and selecting or deselecting Lock The Taskbar from the context menu, shown at left.

FIGURE 7-8   The Windows XP taskbar

Start Menu

The Start button on the taskbar opens a very important menu, called the Start menu. This menu has areas containing shortcuts and submenus. It is the central

tool for finding and starting a variety of programs in Windows. The Start menu in Windows 2000, shown here, is a single column list of folders and programs, and by default, there are a number of shortcuts on the Windows 2000 desktop.

The Windows XP default desktop contains only one shortcut—the Recycle Bin, while the Start menu contains the former desktop icons (and more) arranged in a two-column format. The right column serves the purpose of the single column in Windows 2000, containing a fairly standard set of icons that you can configure through the Start menu Properties dialog box. An arrow on an icon indicates that you can expand the item to display the contents or submenus.

Windows 2000 contains a Shut Down option at the bottom of the Start menu, which will open a dialog box from which you can select further options for logging off or shutting down your computer.

At the bottom of the Windows XP Start menu there is a bar containing two choices: Log Off and Turn Off Computer. The Log Off option will log off the currently logged-on user. Selecting Turn Off Computer will open the Turn Off Computer dialog box, shown here, which will give you three choices: Standby, Turn Off, or Restart. If hibernation is enabled, the middle button will be labeled Hibernate.

If an update was downloaded to your Windows XP computer, but not yet installed, the Turn Off Computer dialog box will display as shown at left, with the Microsoft Security Center icon positioned over the Turn Off button, and a message will instruct you to click Turn Off to install the updates. If you choose this, do not power off the computer, because it will turn off automatically after the updates are installed.

Pinned Items List On the top left of the XP Start menu is the pinned items list, shown at right, with shortcuts to Windows Update and programs for browsing the Internet and using e-mail. The shortcuts in the pinned items list remain there unless you choose to remove or change them.

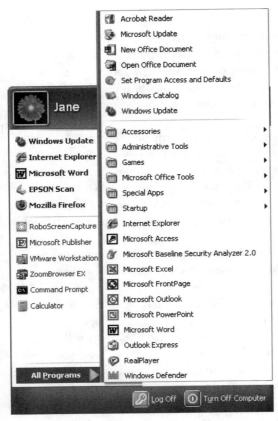

To add additional shortcuts to the pinned items list on your Windows XP computer, right-click any shortcut and choose Pin To Start Menu. To remove an item from this list right-click it and choose Unpin From Start Menu.

Recently Used Programs List   In the Windows XP Start menu, a separator line marks the end of the pinned items list and the beginning of the recently used programs list. This list contains shortcuts to recently run programs. You can change the number of items in this list through the Start menu Properties dialog box.

Programs/All Programs   In Windows 2000, the Programs menu item has an icon showing a folder with an overlapping program icon. This indicates that it is a folder containing links to programs and other folders containing programs. In Windows XP the All Programs menu item serves the same function but does not have an icon, as you can see here. Click this Start menu shortcut to open a menu with a list of programs and program categories. When you install a new application in Windows, it will usually add a folder or program icon to this menu.

Windows Explorer

Windows has a very important GUI component, the program EXPLORER.EXE. This program supports the entire Windows GUI. So, as long as the GUI is running, which means as long as you are able to work in Windows, this program is loaded into memory. Once in the Windows GUI, if you call it up, it opens a window, called Windows Explorer, for browsing your local disks and files. Open Windows Explorer from the Accessories menu of All Programs or by entering **explorer** in the Start | Run dialog box.

Personal Folders

The Start menu contains shortcuts to your personal folders. In Windows XP these titles are My Documents, My Recent Documents, My Pictures, My Music, and My Computer. The exact folders displayed will depend on how you have configured the Start menu using the Properties dialog box.

My Documents contains data files you create. Many applications will, by default, save their data files in this location. My Recent Documents contains shortcuts to recent data files, no matter where you saved the files. My Music contains audio files. My Video contains video files, such as movies. My Pictures is the default location for graphic files, such as photo files from digital cameras. Some applications with special file types will create their own folders under My Documents. Each of these icons on the Start menu points to a folder created as part of the user's personal folders, giving the user a ready-made folder structure for organizing data files of many types.

In Windows 2000 the Documents icon on the desktop points to the user's personal data folders.

My Computer

My Computer is a shortcut on the desktop in Windows 2000 and on the Start menu in Windows XP. It opens the My Computer folder in Windows Explorer, displaying file folders, hard disk drives, and removable storage on the local computer. The actual objects shown depend on the computer's configuration. Clicking the Folders button on the toolbar will change the view from the default view with a task pane on the left and a contents pane on the right to a two-pane view showing a folder hierarchy in the left pane and the contents of the currently selected folder on the right. In the first view you can select an action from the task pane on the left, or open a folder or drive on the right. In Folder view, you can see the entire folder hierarchy on the left while browsing folders in the right pane (see Figures 7-9 and 7-10). Use My Computer when you need to work with disk folders beyond those available through your other personal folders, for instance to access folders on a removable drive.

Control Panel

Control Panel is a Windows folder that contains numerous applets you can use to adjust the configuration of many different aspects of the OS. Windows 2000 has a Settings shortcut on the Start menu. Click this to select Control Panel and other options for configuring Windows. These other options are simply links to applets

FIGURE 7-9

My Computer
with the task
pane on the left

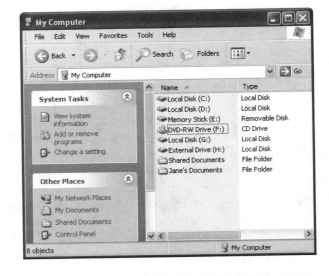

FIGURE 7-10

My Computer
with a folder pane
on the left

within Control Panel. Windows XP does not have the Settings menu, but it has Start menu shortcuts for Control Panel and the Printers and Faxes applet.

Windows XP introduced a new view for Control Panel called Category view. This view displays far fewer icons by lumping them into categories—Appearance and Themes, Network and Internet connections, and so forth. Some of these icons represent several applets, while some, such as Add or Remove Programs, represent a single applet.

FIGURE 7-11

Windows XP
Control Panel

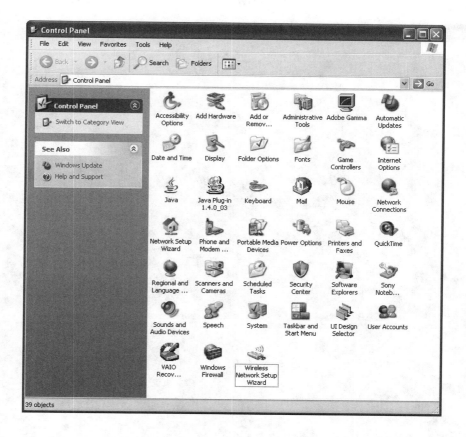

Many experienced Windows users prefer the former view, now called Classic view, which lists the individual applets. Suit yourself. It is easy to switch between these views using a link in the task panel in the left pane. Figure 7-11 shows the Windows XP Control Panel folder in Classic view. Most of the Control Panel applets are common for all installations of Windows XP, but the presence of some depend on the devices and components installed.

Command Prompt

The command prompt in Windows is a place in which commands can be entered in a simple character-mode interface. You can enter certain commands, such as IPCONFIG, DIR, ATTRIB, COPY, XCOPY, and PING, at the command prompt. You will find a shortcut to the command prompt at Start | All Programs | Accessories. Our preferred method for opening a command prompt in Windows is to enter the command **cmd** in the Start | Run dialog box.

FIGURE 7-12   The Windows XP command prompt

You will practice working at the command prompt in Chapter 9. Figure 7-12 shows the command prompt in Windows XP.

Network Neighborhood and My Network Places

The Start menu icon labeled Network Neighborhood in Windows 2000, or My Network Places in Windows XP, opens a folder containing shortcuts to network locations on the LAN or the Internet. If the task list is visible, it includes tasks appropriate for working with network locations, such as Add A Network Place, View Network Connections, View Workgroup Computers, and Set Up A Home Or Small Office Network.

File Systems

A file system includes operating system code as well as a structure created on disk for saving and organizing files. Windows 2000 and Windows XP support several file systems, including FAT16, FAT32, and NTFS. The NTFS file system is the most advanced, including features for keeping files secure from unauthorized access. You will learn more about Windows file systems in Chapter 8.

Registry

The registry, introduced in Windows 95, is one of the several technical features of Windows that has made it easier to configure and support. Ironically, it is also one of the most complicated and least understood features of Windows. The ordinary user is rarely aware that the registry exists, but support personnel need to understand the purpose of the registry. In this section, you will learn about the registry—its role in Windows and how to view the registry.

The Registry Defined

The Windows registry is a database of all Windows configuration settings for both hardware and software. As it is starting up, Windows reads information in the registry that tells it what components to load into memory and how to configure them. After startup, the OS writes any changes into the registry and frequently reads additional registry settings as different programs are loaded into memory. The registry includes settings for

- Device drivers
- Services
- Installed application programs
- Operating system components
- User preferences

Created when Windows is installed, the registry continues to be modified as you configure Windows and add applications and components.

The best way to change the registry is indirectly, using various tools in the GUI, such as Control Panel applets. You should directly edit the registry only when you have no other choice. We will discuss this in Chapter 10.

on the
job *Two great places to get additional information on the registry are the Microsoft site (www.microsoft.com) and the WinGuides site (www.pctools .com/guides/).*

Automatic Registry Changes

Any change to the operating system or installed applications will result in a change in the registry. The registry will automatically change when

- Windows starts or shuts down
- During Windows Setup (which is run more often than you may think)
- Changes are made through a Control Panel applet
- A new device is installed
- Any changes are made to the Windows configuration
- Any changes are made to a user's desktop preferences
- An application is installed or modified with user preferences

exam

Watch *Be sure you understand that virtually all administrative tools, such as the Control Panel applets, handle registry administration for you, at least in the area of safely making changes to the registry.*

Viewing the Registry

You can view and edit the registry with the registry editor. Its program file, REGEDIT.EXE, is located in the folder in which the operating system is installed (C:WINDOWS or C:\WINNT), but it does not have a shortcut on the Start menu. This is for a very good reason: it should not be too easy for the casual user to find and run this program. Learn how to open and explore the Registry Editor in Exercise 7-3.

Until Windows XP there were two separate Registry Editor programs, REGEDIT .EXE, which came with Windows 9x, and REGEDT32.EXE, which first appeared in Windows NT. Windows 2000 had both of these as separate programs with some differences in capabilities and user interface. Windows XP has a single Registry Editor program that can be called up by using either executable name: REGEDIT or REGEDT32.

EXERCISE 7-3

Using the Registry Editor

Open Regedit from the Run box, and then explore the registry.

1. Click Start | Run.

2. In the Run box type **regedit** and click OK.

3. The first view of the registry will show the subtree folders on the left. Click the plus sign next to each folder to see the folders and data it contains, which will appear in the contents pane to the right (see Figure 7-13).

4. Do not click in the contents pane. Do not make any modifications because they will be immediately recorded in the registry.

5. Click the Exit button to the top right of the Registry Editor window.

You can navigate the registry with your mouse in the same way you navigate any disk folder, by opening and closing folders. Each folder represents a registry key, an object that may contain one or more settings as well as other keys. The top five folders are root keys, often called subtrees in Microsoft documentation. Each of these subtrees is the top of a hierarchical structure.

A subkey is a key that exists within another key. The settings within a key are called value entries. When you click the folder for a key, it becomes the active key in Regedit. Its folder icon opens, and the contents of the key show in the right pane (see Figure 7-14). Table 7-1 gives an overview of the information stored within each subtree of the registry.

on the job

To describe a registry location, use a notation that shows the path from a subtree down through the subkeys, similar to that used to describe file and folder locations on disk: HKEY_LOCAL_MACHINE\SYSTEM\ CURRENTCONTROLSET\CONTROL.

FIGURE 7-13

The registry subtrees

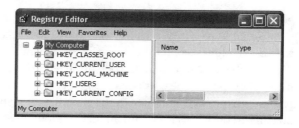

FIGURE 7-14 Registry components

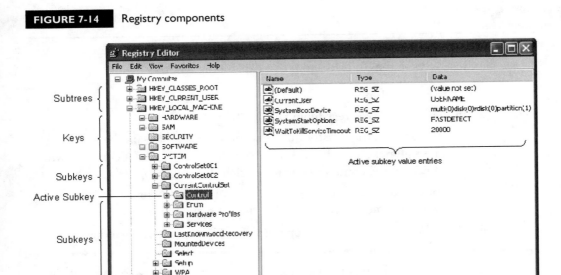

Virtual Memory

Windows allows us to have several programs open in memory at the same time. We call this multitasking, and this feature, combined with large program and data files, means that it is possible to run out of physical RAM in which to keep all the open programs. When a Windows computer is running low on memory available for the operating system and any loaded applications, it will use and manage a portion of disk space as if it were RAM.

Virtual memory is the use of a portion of hard disk as memory. Windows uses a special paging file, PAGEFILE.SYS, to allocate disk space for virtual memory. By default, Windows creates this file in the root of C: and sets the size to one and a half times the installed physical RAM. Swapping is the act of moving data and code between this file and RAM, and therefore the paging file is also called the swap file.

It is thanks to virtual memory that things do not come to a screeching halt whenever we run out of memory for the operating system and all the applications we have open. Much of the data and program code not needed in the current application will move into the swap file. The user is generally unaware of this process. When you switch to a program that has code or data in the swap file, there may be a slight delay while the OS prepares to bring this back into memory after moving other data to the virtual memory space on disk.

TABLE 7-1	Subtree	Description
Contents of Registry Subtrees	HKEY_LOCAL_MACHINE	This subtree contains the detected hardware, software, and hardware configuration information, along with security settings and the local security accounts database.
	HKEY_CLASSES_ROOT	This subtree contains the relationships (called associations) between applications and file types defined by file extension. Information here is used for object linking and embedding (OLE) and special objects called COM objects. This subtree is actually all the information located in HKEY_LOCAL_MACHINE\Software\Classes.
	HKEY_CURRENT_CONFIG	This subtree contains the configuration information for the current hardware profile, a set of changes (*only* changes) to the standard configuration in the Software and Systems subkeys under HKEY_LOCAL_MACHINE.
	HKEY_CURRENT_USER	This subtree contains the user profile for the currently logged-on user, which consists of the NTUSER.DAT file for the user along with any changes since logon.
	HKEY_USERS	This subtree contains all user profiles that are loaded in memory, including the profile of the currently logged-on user (also shown under HKEY_CURRENT_USER), the default profile, and profiles for special user accounts used to run various services. Except for the default profile, each is labeled with a security ID (SID), a unique string of numbers preceded by S-1-5 that identifies a security principal in a Windows security accounts database.

SCENARIO & SOLUTION

The pinned items list on my Start menu contains a program I no longer want in this list. How can I remove it?	Right-click the item and choose Unpin From Start Menu.
I have Windows XP. How can I store my data files in an organized folder structure to make it easy to find the files?	The folder structure for this is already set up in Windows XP. You access these folders through the Start menu shortcuts that begin with "My."
I never seem to run out of memory, even though I often have many programs open at once. Why is this?	This is because Windows uses virtual memory, disk space that is used and managed like RAM memory, storing the code and data for open applications that are not currently needed.

Operating System Files

A quick look in the Windows folders containing the operating system will tell you that this operating system has hundreds, if not thousands of files. It would be a daunting task to have to memorize all of these by name and function, but that is not necessary. Just learn about the most critical files—those required to start up the operating system. These include three groups of files: boot files, system files, and registry files. All of the other files are other Windows components, device drivers, and applications files that make it possible to work the way you want in Windows. In this section you will learn about the boot, system, and registry files required for Windows to start up.

Make sure that you are familiar with the role of these files and where they are located.

Windows Boot and System Files

Windows is a very large and complicated OS, and for it to function, many files have to be brought into memory while the OS is starting up. These include boot files, which reside in the root of drive C:, and system files that reside in folders below the folder in which you install Windows. The boot files are the very first files of the operating system that are loaded into memory during startup. All of the boot files are important, but one of them, NTLDR, plays a critical role, loading the other OS components into memory and finally giving control to one of the system files. Table 7-2 lists the boot files with a brief description of each.

TABLE 7-2	Filename	Location	Description
Windows Boot Files	BOOT.INI	C:\	Contains the OS Selection menu
	Bootsect.dos	C:\	Only present when a computer is configured to dual-boot between Windows 2000 or Windows XP and Windows 9x or DOS
	NTBOOTDD.SYS	C:\	SCSI device driver (rarely needed)
	NTDETECT.COM	C:\	Hardware detection program
	NTLDR	C:\	Windows operating system loader started by the OS loader program in the boot sector of C:

By default, many of the files listed in Table 7-2 are hidden from view in My Computer/Windows Explorer. You can view the boot files in My Computer, but first, look at your current view settings and modify them, as necessary, to display the boot files on the root of C:. Exercise 7-4 will guide you through this process so that you may see these files.

EXERCISE 7-4

Using My Computer to View the Boot Files

You may view the boot files, but be very careful not to delete or alter any of these files.

1. Open My Computer and look at the contents of the root of C:. Are NTLDR and NTDETECT.COM visible? Can you see the filename extensions on the files that are visible? If you can answer yes to both questions, do not make changes to your view settings but skip to Step 3. If no, go to Step 2.

2. Select Tools | Folder Options. On the View page, select Show Hidden Files And Folders and deselect two boxes: Hide Extensions For Known File Types and Hide Protected Operating System Files. Then click OK to close the Folder Options dialog box.

3. Confirm that you can see NTLDR and NTDETECT.COM and that file extensions are visible. Many other files will also be visible.

4. After viewing the files close My Computer.

The system files are critical components of an operating system that generally stay in memory while the operating system is running. When you install Windows and allow it to install the system files into the default location, Windows 2000 system files are installed into C:\WINNT, and Windows XP system files are installed into C:\Windows. Because the location of the system files can vary, depending on the version of Windows and the choices made by the person installing, Microsoft often uses the variable *systemroot* to represent the full path to this location, including the drive letter. Table 7-3 lists the Windows system files used by Windows at startup, their locations, and descriptions. Notice that the paging file is listed here, but it is installed in the top level (root) of C:, not in *systemroot*.

TABLE 7-3	Filename	Location	Description
Windows System Files	CSRSS.EXE	*systemroot*\SYSTEM32\	The user-mode portion of the Windows subsystem.
	Device driver files	*systemroot*\SYSTEM32\ DRIVERS	For example: acpi.sys, disk.sys, ftdisk, and hundreds of others.
	HAL.DLL	*systemroot*/SYSTEM32	Hardware abstraction layer software provided by a computer manufacturer as a software layer between the hardware and the OS, hiding (abstracting) the details and making all systems appear the same to the OS.
	pagefile.sys	C:\	The file used by the virtual memory manager.
	SERVICES.EXE	*systemroot*\SYSTEM32	Service controller contains code for several services.
	SMSS.EXE	*systemroot*\SYSTEM32	Session manager initializes drivers and services.
	Win32k.sys	*systemroot*\SYSTEM32\	The kernel-mode portion of the Windows subsystem.

EXERCISE 7-5

Using My Computer to View the System Files

You may view the system files, but be very careful not to delete or alter any of these files.

1. Open My Computer and look at the contents of the root of C:. Are NTLDR and NTDETECT.COM visible? Can you see the filename extensions on the files that are visible? If you can answer yes to both questions, do not make changes to your view settings, and continue with Step 2. If not, go back to Exercise 7-4 and complete Steps 1 and 2.

2. Using the Location information in Table 7-3, browse to the folders containing the various system files and locate the system files. Do not double-click any of these files, and do not delete or move them. Doing so could make Windows unstable or unusable.

3. After viewing the files close My Computer.

Registry Files

The registry is loaded into memory during startup and remains in memory while Windows is active. Although considered a single entity, the registry is actually stored in a number of binary files on disk. A binary file contains program code, as opposed to a file containing data, such as word processing data. The Windows registry files include the following:

- **SYSTEM**   This file contains information used at startup, including a list of device drivers to be loaded, as well as the order of their loading and configuration settings. Other information includes the starting and configuring of services, and various operating system settings.
- **SOFTWARE**   This file contains configuration settings for software installed on the computer.
- **SECURITY**   This file contains the local security policy settings for the computer.
- **SAM**   This is the local security accounts database containing local user and group accounts and their passwords. SAM is an acronym for Security Accounts Manager.
- **DEFAULT**   The DEFAULT file contains user desktop settings, called a user profile, used when there is no logged-on user. If your Windows computer requires a logon before you can access the desktop, these settings affect the appearance of the desktop before you log on. Figure 7-15 shows the Log On To Windows dialog box that appears on some computers before logging a user on.
- **NTUSER.DAT**   This file contains the user profile for a single user. These settings include application preferences, screen colors, network connections, and other personal choices. There is a separate NTUSER.DAT file for each user who logs on to the computer, as well as one located in the DEFAULT USER folder. During startup, the other registry files (located in the CONFIG folder) load and configure the operating system. When a user logs on, the settings from that user's NTUSER.DAT file are applied and become part of the current registry. The first time a user logs on to a computer, the NTUSER.DAT file from the DEFAULT USER folder creates the initial profile for the user. The NTUSER.DAT file is in the top-level personal folder for the user.

The default user
profile is used until
a user logs on.

All changes to the registry saved from one session to the next are in these registry files, each file saving data from one part of the registry.

With the exception of the NTUSER.DAT file, these registry files do not have file extensions and are saved in a disk folder named CONFIG. In Windows 2000, the default location of this folder is C:\WINNT\SYSTEM32. In Windows XP and Windows Vista, this location is C:\WINDOWS\SYSTEM32. Figure 7-16 shows the contents of the CONFIG folder in Windows XP Professional.

The NTUSER.DAT registry file is stored in the personal folders for the user. Figure 7-17 shows the personal folders for the user Jane. NTUSER.DAT is located in the top level of the user's personal folders. In this case that is C:\Documents and Settings\Jane.

FIGURE 7-16

The CONFIG
folder contains
most of the
registry files as
well as Event
Viewer log files.

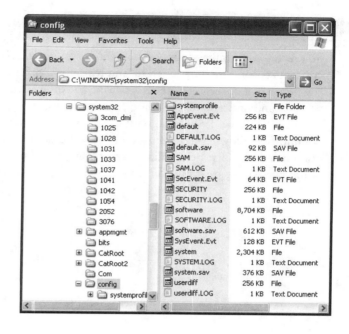

FIGURE 7-17

The NTUSER.DAT
registry file in the
personal folders
for the user Jane

CERTIFICATION SUMMARY

To prepare to install and support computers, you must develop an understanding of the concepts beyond those required to simply use an OS. This begins with understanding the purpose of operating systems, knowing the differences between the major operating systems, and understanding updates, service packs, and revision levels.

Since Windows is the dominant OS for PCs and laptops, learn to identify the common Windows components, especially the GUI elements, file systems, registry, and virtual memory. Be familiar with operating system files required for starting Windows. These are grouped into the boot files, system files, and registry files.

✓ TWO-MINUTE DRILL

Here are some of the key points covered in Chapter 7.

Major Operating Systems

- ❏ An OS controls all the interactions between the various system components, human interactions with the computer, and network operations for the computer system.

- ❏ An OS is responsible for managing the computer's disks and files in an organized manner, keeping track of the functions of particular files that it activates when needed.

- ❏ Microsoft Windows in all its versions is still the most popular OS at home and in business.

- ❏ The other two major OSs, with much smaller market shares, are the Mac OS and Linux.

- ❏ Operating systems tie closely to the CPUs on which they run. Therefore, CPU terms, such as 32-bit and 64-bit, may also describe an OS.

- ❏ Each version of an OS has a certain set of system requirements, which include the computer platform, as well as the amount of RAM and disk space.

- ❏ Each new OS also introduces hardware and software compatibility issues. Some computers may require a BIOS upgrade before you can install a new version of Windows. If this is not available, you will not be able to install the OS on the old computer.

- ❏ A similar issue occurs with application software. If the software publisher does not upgrade the program to run on the new OS, the user may decide not to upgrade.

Common Windows Components

- ❏ Common Windows components include the GUI, file systems, registry, and virtual memory.

- ❏ The Windows GUI includes important elements, such as the taskbar, Start menu, Windows Explorer, My Computer, Personal folders, Control Panel, Command Prompt, and Network Neighborhood.

❏ File systems supported by Windows 2000 and Windows XP include FAT16, FAT32, and NTFS—the most advanced.

❏ The Windows registry stores settings for the OS itself, device drivers, and applications. The OS uses these when it starts up and whenever an application is run.

❏ The registry is updated frequently.

❏ You can view the registry with the Windows Registry Editor, also known by its program filename, REGEDIT.EXE.

❏ When Windows runs low on memory, it will use and manage a portion of disk space as if it were RAM. This is virtual memory, and a special paging file, PAGEFILE.SYS, is used for this purpose.

Operating System Files

❏ There are hundreds of files used by the Windows operating system. The most critical are those required to start up the operating system. These include the boot files, system files, and registry files.

❏ The registry files include SYSTEM, SOFTWARE, SECURITY, SAM, DEFAULT, and NTUSER.DAT.

SELF TEST

The following questions will help you measure your understanding of the material presented in this chapter. Read all of the choices carefully because there might be more than one correct answer. Choose all correct answers for each question.

Major Operating Systems

1. What makes up the layers of an operating system?
   A. Hardware
   B. Software
   C. Memory
   D. Silicon

2. An operating system typically controls what interactions?
   A. Between the system and the human
   B. Between the chair and the keyboard
   C. Between the AC adapter and the wall outlet
   D. Between Windows and Linux

3. Which of the following describe a responsibility of an OS?
   A. Printer cartridges
   B. AC to DC conversion
   C. Disk and file management
   D. Inverters

4. Fill in the blank. A major difference between Windows, Linux, and Mac OS X is the
   _____ on which they run.
   A. Displays
   B. GUIs
   C. Platforms
   D. Mouse pads

5. Which of the following describes the OS code in all but one of the Windows XP editions?
   A. GUI
   B. Multitasking
   C. 64-bit
   D. 32-bit

6. Which of the following best describes system requirements for an OS?

   A. Platform

   B. CPU and amount of RAM and hard disk space

   C. Form factor

   D. Code size

7. Before you install Windows XP (or Windows Vista), you can use this program to determine if your computer has hardware and software that is compatible with the new OS.

   A. Setup

   B. Backup

   C. Upgrade Advisor

   D. Help | About

Common Windows Components

8. The Windows GUI uses this metaphor.

   A. Mouse

   B. Desktop

   C. Taskbar

   D. Task list

9. Folders, mouse pointer, icons, shortcuts, dialog boxes, windows, buttons, etc., are all examples of these components of a GUI.

   A. Pixels

   B. Pictures

   C. Graphics

   D. Objects

10. What is the horizontal bar that is usually across the bottom of the Windows screen?

   A. Taskbar

   B. Start menu

   C. Systray

   D. Menu bar

11. What is the central tool for finding and starting programs in Windows?

   A. Taskbar

   B. Start menu

   C. My Computer

   D. Menu bar

12. By default, what is the only shortcut displayed on the Windows XP desktop?
   A. Start menu
   B. Recycle Bin
   C. My Programs
   D. My Computer

13. What are the usual three buttons on Turn Off Computer dialog box in Windows XP?
   A. Shut Down, Log Off, Restart
   B. Stand By, Shut Down, Restart
   C. Log Off, Turn Off, Restart
   D. Stand By, Turn Off, Restart

14. What is the name for the list of items on the upper left of the Windows XP Start menu?
   A. Recently used programs list
   B. Pinned items list
   C. Quick Launch bar
   D. Task list

15. What Windows component is a database of all Windows configuration settings?
   A. System files
   B. Boot files
   C. Registry
   D. Control Panel

16. What registry subtree tracks relationships between applications and file types defined by file extension?
   A. HKEY_LOCAL _MACHINE
   B. HKEY_CLASSES_ROOT
   C. HKEY_CURRENT_CONFIG
   D. HKEY_CURRENT_USER

17. What is the term that describes disk space used by the operating system when it runs out of physical memory?
   A. Virtual memory
   B. RAM memory
   C. ROM memory
   D. Flash memory

Operating System Files

18. What two groups of files go into memory as Windows is starting up?

    A. Registry and application files

    B. Boot and configuration files

    C. Bootsect.dos and NTLDR

    D. Boot and system files

19. What registry file contains all the settings for a single user?

    A. DEFAULT

    B. SYSTEM

    C. NTUSER.DAT

    D. SAM

20. Which registry file contains information used at startup, including a list of device drivers to load, and the order of their loading and configuration settings?

    A. SECURITY

    B. SOFTWARE

    C. DEFAULT

    D. SYSTEM

LAB QUESTION

If you use more than one operating system on a regular basis, describe some of the similarities and differences you have noticed between two of them. You are not limited to the operating systems described in this chapter. For instance, if you use a handheld computer or Internet-enabled cell phone and use a desktop Windows computer, these are different operating systems. If you have not worked with more than one operating system, find someone who has and interview that person to answer this question.

SELF TEST ANSWERS

Major Operating Systems

1. ☑ **B.** Software makes up the layers of an operating system.
   ☒ **A,** hardware, is incorrect because the operating system itself is entirely software. **C,** memory, is incorrect because although the OS runs in memory, the layers running in memory are composed of software. **D,** silicon is incorrect because this is a physical ingredient in computer hardware components, not a part of an operating system.

2. ☑ **A.** Between the system and the human is correct because these interactions are the main reason we have operating systems.
   ☒ **B,** between the chair and the keyboard, is incorrect because the human resides between the chair and keyboard, and the operating system does not control that interface. **C,** between the AC adapter and the wall outlet, is incorrect because all that resides there is a power cord. **D,** between Windows and Linux, is incorrect because this is not an interaction typically controlled by an operating system.

3. ☑ **C.** Disk management and file management are responsibilities of an OS.
   ☒ **A,** printer cartridges, is incorrect because they are not responsibilities of an OS. **B,** AC to DC conversion, is incorrect because this is the responsibility of a computer power supply. **D,** inverters, is incorrect because this is not an OS responsibility, but a hardware device.

4. ☑ **C.** Platforms is correct because a major difference between Windows, Linux, and Mac OS X consists in the platforms on which they run.
   ☒ **A,** displays, is incorrect because an OS does not run on a display, but on a computer that can use a display. **B,** GUIs, is incorrect because an OS does not run on a GUI; a GUI is a component of an OS. **D,** mouse pads, is incorrect because a mouse pad does not require an OS.

5. ☑ **D.** 32-bit describes the OS code in all but one of the Windows XP editions.
   ☒ **A,** GUI, is incorrect because a GUI is a component of any Windows XP edition. **B,** multitasking, is incorrect because this describes the OS code of all Windows XP editions. **C,** 64-bit, is incorrect because this describes the OS code in only one edition: Windows XP x64 Edition.

6. ☑ **B.** CPU and amount of RAM and hard disk space best describes system requirements for an OS.
   ☒ **A,** platform, is incorrect because this alone does not best describe the system requirements for an OS. **C,** form factor, is incorrect because this describes the dimensions of a hardware device, not the system requirements for an OS. **D,** code size, is incorrect because this just describes the size of the OS code, not the system requirements for the OS.

7. ☑ **C.** Upgrade Advisor is the program that will determine if your computer has hardware and software compatible with Windows XP (or Windows Vista).

☒ **A**, Setup, and **B**, Backup, are incorrect. We have not discussed Setup and Backup as yet, but neither is the program named in this chapter for testing hardware and software compatibility. **D**, Help | About, is incorrect because this is a menu choice in My Computer (and other programs) that will provide version information, not hardware and software compatibility information.

Common Windows Components

8. ☑ **B.** Desktop is the metaphor used by the Windows GUI.

☒ **A**, mouse, is incorrect because this is not a metaphor for the Windows GUI, but a hardware pointing device used with the Windows GUI. **C**, taskbar, is incorrect because, although this is a Windows GUI component, it is not the metaphor used to describe the Windows GUI. **D**, task list, is incorrect because this is part of the Windows GUI, not the metaphor that describes the GUI.

9. ☑ **D.** Objects, such as folders, mouse pointer, icons, shortcuts, dialog boxes, windows, buttons, etc., are components of the Windows GUI,

☒ **A**, pixels, is incorrect because this describes a dot on a display screen, not a component of the OS GUI. **B**, pictures, is incorrect, even though you could call each of the GUI objects a picture. **C**, graphics, is incorrect, even though you could call each of the GUI objects a graphic.

10. ☑ **A.** Taskbar is correct because this is the horizontal bar that is usually across the bottom of the Windows screen.

☒ **B**, Start menu, is incorrect because this is just a small portion on the left end of the taskbar. **C**, systray, is also incorrect because this is just a small portion of the taskbar—located on the far right end. **D**, menu bar, is incorrect because this is a component of a window, not the horizontal bar that is usually across the bottom of the Windows screen.

11. ☑ **B.** Start menu is correct because this is the central tool for finding and starting programs in Windows.

☒ **A**, taskbar, is incorrect because this is only the location of the Start menu and the place that displays buttons for open programs. **C**, My Computer, is incorrect because this is a shortcut on the desktop of Windows 2000 and on the Start menu, which opens to display file folders, hard disk drives, and removable storage on the local computer. **D**, menu bar, is incorrect because this is a component of an open window, not the central tool for finding and starting programs in Windows.

12. ☑ **B.** Recycle Bin is the only shortcut displayed by default on the Windows XP desktop.

☒ **A**, Start menu, is incorrect because it is not a desktop shortcut but is located on the taskbar. **C**, My Programs, and **D**, My Computer, are both incorrect because they are not desktop shortcuts (by default) but are located on the Start menu.

13.   ☑   **B.** Stand By, Shut Down, Restart are the usual three buttons on the Turn Off Computer dialog box in Windows XP.

☒   **A**, Shut Down, Log Off, Restart; **C**, Log Off, Turn Off, Restart; and **D**, Stand By, Turn Off, Restart are all incorrect because they are not the usual three buttons in the Turn Off Computer dialog box.

14.   ☑   **B.** Pinned items list is the name for the list of items on the upper left of the Windows XP Start menu.

☒   **A**, recently used programs list, is incorrect because this is the list that is below the pinned items list on the Start menu. **C**, Quick Launch bar, is incorrect because this is an optional item on the taskbar, not a list on the Start menu. **D**, task list, is incorrect because this is not the name of the list of items on the upper left of the Windows XP Start menu.

15.   ☑   **C.** Registry is the name of the database of all Windows configuration settings.

☒   **A**, system files, is incorrect because, although the registry is part of the system files, the system files include many other files that do not fit the description in the question. **B**, boot files, is incorrect because these files are not used to hold the configuration settings. **D**, Control Panel, is incorrect because this is a special folder in Windows that contains programs for configuring Windows.

16.   ☑   **B.** HKEY_CLASSES_ROOT is the registry subtree that tracks relationships between applications and file types defined by file extension.

☒   **A**, HKEY_LOCAL _MACHINE, **C**, HKEY_CURRENT_CONFIG, and **D**, HKEY_ CURRENT_USER, are incorrect because, while these are registry subtrees, they are not used to tracks relationships between applications and file types defined by file extension.

17.   ☑   **A.** Virtual memory is the term for disk space used by the OS when it runs out of physical memory.

☒   **B**, RAM memory, is incorrect because this is the physical memory. **C**, ROM memory, and **D**, flash memory, are incorrect because the OS uses neither when it runs out of physical memory.

Operating System Files

18.   ☑   **D.** Boot and system files go into memory as Windows is starting up.

☒   **A**, registry and application files, is incorrect because although registry files are brought into memory, application files are not brought into memory as the OS is starting up. **B**, boot and configuration files, is incorrect because although boot files is correct, configuration files is not the other group of files brought into memory as Windows is starting up. **C**, Bootsect.dos and NTLDR, is incorrect because these are individual files, not groups of files.

19. ☑ **C.** NTUSER.DAT is a registry file that contains all the settings for a single user.

☒ **A**, DEFAULT, is incorrect because this registry file contains user desktop settings, called a user profile, used when there is no logged-on user. **B**, SYSTEM, is incorrect because this registry file contains information used at startup, including a list of device drivers to be loaded, and the order of their loading and configuration settings. **D**, SAM, is incorrect because this registry file contains the local security accounts database containing local user and group accounts and their passwords.

20. ☑ **D.** SYSTEM is the registry file that contains information used at startup, including a list of device drivers to load, and the order of their loading and configuration settings.

☒ **A**, SECURITY, is incorrect because this file contains the local security policy settings for the computer. **B**, SOFTWARE, is incorrect because this file contains configuration settings for software installed on the computer. **C**, DEFAULT, is incorrect because this file contains user desktop settings, called a user profile, used when there is no logged-on user.

LAB ANSWER

Answers will vary. There are several possible comparisons, but you may note differences and similarities in working with the various user interfaces and different types of input devices. You may work with an operating system in text mode, such as a version of Linux, in which case you might discuss having to remember cryptic commands. You may work with a computer dedicated to a single purpose, like hospital patient admittance, where you are always in a single application, and quite often, it is not a GUI screen. Even GUI interfaces that at first blush seem very similar have significant differences, especially if you wish to change the configuration of the OS.

8

Installing, Configuring, Optimizing, and Upgrading Operating Systems

I n this chapter, we will examine the successful installation and configuration of Windows 2000 and Windows XP. Whether you are installing from scratch, upgrading, or configuring the system, you must follow certain guidelines and procedures. You will learn basic preparation and installation procedures, as well as post-installation tasks now.

A good time to take the steps for optimizing your OS is soon after installing an operating system. Then you need to develop good habits that keep it optimized and running smoothly, paying attention to the areas of virtual memory, hard drives, temporary files, services, startup, and applications.

CERTIFICATION OBJECTIVES

■ **601: 3.2 602: 3.2 603: 2.2** *Install, configure, optimize, and upgrade operating systems*

The CompTIA exam objectives for installing, upgrading, configuring, and optimizing Windows 2000 or Windows XP involve understanding a variety of scenarios for each of these areas. In this chapter you will explore these scenarios, such as preparing for a clean installation of Windows versus preparing for an upgrade, performing an attended installation versus performing an unattended installation, post-installation tasks, and areas of Windows that you can optimize for better performance.

Installing Windows

Installing a new operating system is not a one-step process. In fact, it occurs in three stages. In the first stage you perform necessary tasks before the installation begins, the second stage is the actual installation, and the final stage includes follow-up tasks. In this section, you will learn the necessary tasks for the first two stages when installing the Windows 2000 and Windows XP operating systems.

Prepare to Install Windows

Prepare to install Windows 2000 or Windows XP Professional by ensuring hardware requirements are met, verifying hardware and software compatibility, determining how to boot into the Windows setup program, and finally, taking the time to understand the difference between activation and registration and how to handle both tasks when it comes time to do them during installation.

Hardware Requirements

Neither Windows 2000 nor Windows XP is a small operating system—in terms of disk space needed for storage, and in term of the CPU and RAM needed to run either of them and the supported programs. The published minimum requirements are not just about compatibility, but about quantity and power; it takes a modern CPU to run these operating systems well. For instance, the minimum requirements for Windows 2000 Professional include: 133 MHz Pentium or higher microprocessor (or equivalent), 64 MB of RAM, a 2 GB hard disk with 650 MB of free space, a VGA or higher resolution video adapter with a compatible monitor, a keyboard, and a Microsoft mouse or compatible pointing device. Additionally, a CD-ROM drive is required if you want to install from the Windows 2000 Professional CD. But these requirements are modest and far less than you will find in the most minimally configured new desktop PC.

You would be very unhappy trying to work on a PC with a minimal configuration because the programs most people choose to run on desktop computers have grown in their processor, storage, and memory requirements. Table 8-1 shows the minimum requirements, as well as our recommended minimums, for installing Windows XP on a typical desktop computer in preparation for daily use by an office professional who is using a productivity suite such as Microsoft Office 2007. As you can see, there is a large difference between minimum requirements and our recommended minimums, which allow a great deal more memory and disk space for working simultaneously in several large programs and for saving large, complex data files.

TABLE 8-1	Minimums for Windows XP Professional	Recommended Minimums for Windows XP Professional
Windows XP Minimums vs. Our Recommended Minimums	Any Intel or AMD 300 MHz or higher CPU	Any Intel or AMD 2.66 GHz or higher CPU
	128 MB of RAM	1 GB of RAM
	1.5 GB of free hard drive space	40 GB of unused hard drive space
	Super VGA video card that supports 800 × 600 resolution or greater	Super VGA video card that supports 1024×768 resolution or greater
	CD-ROM or DVD drive	CD-R, CD-RW, or DVD-R drive

Verify Hardware and Software Compatibility

The Setup programs for both Windows 2000 and Windows XP include a compatibility test of your hardware (clean installation) or hardware and software (upgrade installation).

The Windows Marketplace (formerly the Windows Catalog) is a searchable list of hardware and software known to work with Windows. You can find this Web site at www.windowsmarketplace.com. Once at the Windows Marketplace home page, you can search on specific hardware or software products, or browse through the catalog of hardware and software products known to work with Windows XP.

Disk Preparation

To prepare a hard disk for use, you must first partition it and then format it. Partitioning is the act of creating a partition, also called a volume, which is a portion of a hard disk that can contain both a file system and a logical drive. You assign a drive letter to a partitioned volume, and then you must format it before it is usable. The formatting process is what places the logical structure of a file system on the volume. Read more about partitions in Chapter 9, where you will learn how to use the Disk Management console in Windows to perform many tasks, including partitioning. You will also learn about the FDISK partitioning utility.

If you install Windows 2000 or XP on an unpartitioned hard disk, the Setup program will automatically prompt you to create a partition. You can do both partitioning and formatting during the installation process.

File System Selection

A file system is the means an operating system uses to organize information on disks. Windows 2000 and Windows XP support several file systems, including FAT16, FAT32, and NTFS. Unless you have a special reason for selecting one of the older file systems, you should choose the NTFS file system during installation.

Installation Startup and Source Locations

You can start the Windows 2000 or Windows XP Setup program in two ways. One is by booting into setup from diskette or CD, or you can initiate it without a bootup by calling up the WINNT.EXE (from MS-DOS) or WINNT32.EXE (from Windows) program from the setup source files in the i386 folder on the distribution CDs. This second method requires enough available disk space on the boot drive to copy the Setup files onto the hard drive. It then modifies the bootup settings for the existing OS so that after copying the Setup files the system will restart and boot into Setup.

Boot Media

When installing Windows on a new computer that does not have an OS on the hard drive, you will need to boot into the Setup program. How you do this depends on the computer.

CD   The Windows XP CDs are bootable, and Microsoft no longer includes a program to create a set of setup boot disks. This should not be an issue, because PCs manufactured in the last few years have the ability to boot from CD-ROM. This is a system BIOS setting, usually described as "boot order," controlled through a PC's BIOS-based setup program. While we don't recommend that you modify the system settings on your computer, if you want to boot from the installation CD and find you cannot, you will need to configure the System settings of the PC so you can boot from a CD.

Floppy   In the unlikely event that you cannot configure a PC to boot from CD, you can boot into setup from diskette. Windows 2000 has four setup boot diskettes. Windows XP does not come with setup boot diskettes. Therefore, if you must boot Setup from floppies, you must create a set of six (yes, six!) Windows XP setup boot disks using a program downloaded from Microsoft's Web site.

If you find that you cannot boot from the local optical drive and do not have a floppy drive, consider using an external USB floppy drive. Unless the computer is very old, it will have USB ports, and you should be able to configure the computer to boot from the floppy drive. This will also give you a floppy drive that you can move from computer to computer, as needed.

on the
() o b

If you need to create the setup boot diskettes for Windows XP, connect to www.microsoft.com and search on "310994." This is the number of an article titled "How to obtain Windows XP Setup Boot disks" that explains how to create the disks and provides links for several versions of the program to create them.

Network Installation

It is possible to install Windows over a network from a server. A network installation can involve an image installation, an attended installation, or an unattended installation. Any of these network installation methods requires quite a bit of prep work. Here we will describe the steps required for either an attended or unattended network installation. Later, we will address an over-the-network image installation.

To prepare for an attended or unattended network installation, first, copy the Windows source files into a shared folder on the server, then configure the client computer to boot up and connect to the server, and finally start the setup program itself. The actual steps for doing this are extensive, often requiring trained personnel and testing of the procedure.

Attended Windows Installation

There are two main methods of installation: attended and unattended. An installation of Windows XP requires the input of certain unique information for each computer. During an attended installation of Windows 2000 or Windows XP, also called a manual installation, you must pay attention throughout the entire process to provide information and to respond to messages.

Installing Windows 2000 or Windows XP is simple. The Windows Setup Wizard guides you through every step of the process. The onscreen directions are correct and clear, and you will need to make very few decisions. If you are in doubt about a setting, pressing ENTER will likely perform the correct action by selecting a default setting.

Overall, the installation process takes about an hour, and you spend most of that time watching the screen. Feel free to walk away as the installation is taking place, because if it needs input the installation program will stop and wait until you click the correct buttons.

on the !
ɵ o b   *If you are not available to respond to a prompt on the screen during installation, it will only delay completion. Microsoft has improved the Windows XP installation process over that of Windows 2000. Where the Windows 2000 Setup program required frequent input across the entire process, the Windows XP Setup program requires input from you only at the very beginning and at the very end.*

At this point, we assume that you have assured that your computer meets the hardware compatibility and system requirements. The following description is of a clean install, meaning that the partitioning and formatting of the hard disk will occur during the installation. This is the type of installation you would perform on a new computer or on an older computer when you want to have a complete new start. A clean install avoids the potential problems of upgrading, which we will describe later.

Gathering Information

Before you begin an attended installation from a retail version of Windows, gather the information you will need, including the following:

- The Product ID code from the envelope or jewel case of the Windows CD
- A 15-character (or less) name, unique on your network, for your computer
- The name of the workgroup or domain the computer will join
- A password for the Administrator account on your computer
- The necessary network configuration information—ask your network administrator

In addition, gather any device driver disks for the computer and its installed peripherals. You may need to download device drivers from manufacturers' Web sites. It is nice to have these on hand before you start the installation. Windows may have appropriate drivers for all your devices, but if it does not, it may prompt you to provide them. You can do that during installation, or let Windows install minimal generic drivers during the Setup, and wait until after the final reboot at the end of installation to install the correct drivers according to the manufacturers' instructions.

The Installation

Begin the attended Windows installation by inserting the Windows distribution CD and booting the computer. After inspecting your hardware configuration, Windows Setup will show the blue screen of character mode setup and copy files to your computer. When it finishes, it will prompt you to remove the CD and reboot

the system. Windows Setup will start, load system devices, and display the Welcome
To Setup screen shown here. Press ENTER to start the installation.

```
Windows XP Professional Setup

    Welcome to Setup.

    This portion of the Setup program prepares Microsoft(R)
    Windows(R) XP to run on your computer.

        • To set up Windows XP now, press ENTER.

        • To repair a Windows XP installation using
          Recovery Console, press R.

        • To quit Setup without installing Windows XP, press F3.




 ENTER=Continue   R=Repair   F3=Quit
```

Next, the End User License Agreement (EULA) appears. This is your agreement
to comply with your license to use Windows XP Professional, which allows you to
install Windows XP Professional on one computer for each license that you own.
Read the EULA; and press F8 to acknowledge acceptance of the agreement and to
continue.

Windows Setup will display a list of existing partitions and unpartitioned space.
If your hard disk is unpartitioned, you will need to create a new partition by ensuring
that the highlight is on "Unpartitioned space," and then pressing C to create a
partition in the unpartitioned space. On the following screen, shown next, you
can either accept the default size for the partition, or enter a smaller value in the
highlighted box.

```
Windows XP Professional Setup

    You asked Setup to create a new partition on
    4095 MB Disk 0 at Id 0 on bus 0 on atapi [MBR].

        • To create the new partition, enter a size below and
          press ENTER.

        • To go back to the previous screen without creating
          the partition, press ESC.

    The minimum size for the new partition is        8 megabytes (MB).
    The maximum size for the new partition is     4087 megabytes (MB).
    Create partition of size (in MB):     2048

  ENTER=Create    ESC=Cancel
```

The next screen is similar to the one in which you first chose to partition the hard disk, only now you'll select the new partition and press ENTER to install Windows XP on that partition. Then, you need to decide on the file system format for the new partition from the screen shown next. We recommend that you select "Format the partition using the NTFS file system" and then press ENTER. The next screen will show a progress bar while Setup formats the partition.

```
Windows XP Professional Setup

    The partition you selected is not formatted. Setup will now
    format the partition.

    Use the UP and DOWN ARROW keys to select the file system
    you want, and then press ENTER.

    If you want to select a different partition for Windows XP,
    press ESC.

        Format the partition using the NTFS file system (Quick)
        Format the partition using the FAT file system (Quick)
        Format the partition using the NTFS file system
        Format the partition using the FAT file system

  ENTER=Continue    ESC=Cancel
```

Next, Setup copies files to the newly formatted partition, displaying another progress bar. Unless you specify another location, Setup creates a folder named Windows in C:\ into which it installs the OS, creating appropriate subfolders below it. After it finishes copying the base set of files to this location, your computer reboots, and the graphical mode of Windows XP Setup begins. On the left of the screen, uncompleted tasks have a white button, completed tasks have a green button, and the current task has a red button (see Figure 8-1).

On the Regional And Language Options screen, leave the defaults and click Next to accept the default for the way Windows displays numbers, dates, currencies, and time, which is English (United States) for a U.S. distribution of Windows XP. Click Customize if you wish to select other options. Click Next to continue.

On the Personalize Your Software page, enter your name and the name of your school or employer. Next, you must enter a valid product key for Windows XP. You will find this on the CD case containing your copy of Windows XP. Be sure to enter

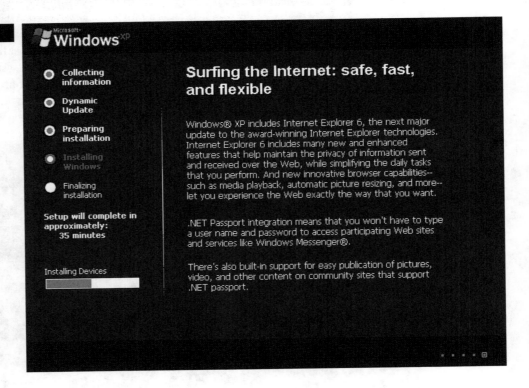

FIGURE 8-1

The graphical mode of Windows XP Setup

it exactly, or you will be unable to continue. We have also learned to write this number directly onto the CD itself, in case it becomes separated from its CD case.

Next, you need to name your computer, which identifies your computer on a network. In addition to a valid name for your computer, you need to create a password for the Administrator user account. This will be the password that allows you to modify and fix the computer. Next, set the date, time, and time zone.

If Setup detected a network card, the network components will install next, and you will have an opportunity to configure the network settings. On the Network Settings page shown next, select Typical Settings, unless told otherwise by your instructor or network administrator. Once the networking elements finish installing, you need to configure the network. Relax—Windows Setup will do most of the work for you. Unless you have specific instructions from your network administrator, the default settings are the preferred choices.

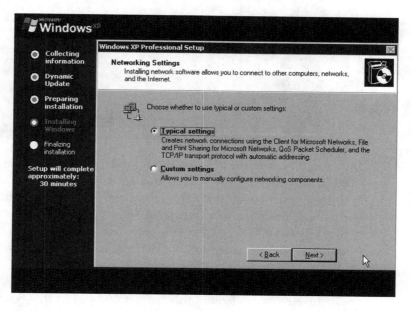

If your computer participates in a domain-based network, you need to set the domain options, shown next. The computer shown here is on a network without a domain, and we have selected the No option and can either accept the default workgroup name of "workgroup" or enter a new name. Click Next and be prepared to wait for several minutes while Windows Setup copies files (again).

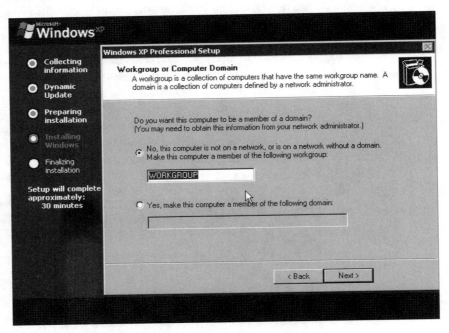

After it copies the files required for the final configuration, Windows XP will reboot. During this reboot, Windows XP determines your screen size and applies the appropriate resolution. This reboot can take several minutes to complete, so be patient. Once the reboot is complete, you must log on as the Administrator. There may be balloon messages over the tray area of the taskbar. A common message concerns the display resolution. Click the balloon and allow Windows XP to automatically adjust the display settings.

Another message reminds you that you have 30 days left for activation. We explain Activation later in this chapter. We suggest that when you do a single install, you test it for a few days before activating it, in case you need to make any significant changes in the hardware. This is because it might appear to the activation program that you have installed on a different computer or made sufficient changes to a computer after product activation to require reactivation. Delaying activation also allows time to work out any problems with network connectivity. If you are not choosing to activate at this time, click the close button of the message balloon. Congratulations! You have completed the Windows XP installation and should have a desktop with the default Bliss background.

SCENARIO & SOLUTION	
How do I boot a computer with an unpartitioned hard drive prior to installing Windows 2000 or Windows XP?	If the computer can boot from the optical drive, place the Windows distribution disc into the drive and start the computer.
How do I create a partition for the new installation of Windows 2000 and Windows XP?	The Setup program will do this during the installation. You will only have to answer a few questions.
How do I start the Setup program?	Setup begins automatically when you boot from the distribution disc. You can also start it from files on the distribution server by running the program WINNT or WINNT32.

Unattended Installation

An unattended installation is one in which the installation process is automated. There are two general types of unattended installations:

- Scripted installation using answer files and Uniqueness Database Files (UDFs)

- An image installation, using the Microsoft Windows 2000 System Preparation tool (Sysprep.exe) and a third-party imaging tool

Scripted Installation

A scripted installation uses scripts that someone has prepared ahead of time. Organizations with large numbers of desktop computers that need identical applications and desktop configurations use this. It requires training and planning by one or more people.

To automate the installation process, you must create special script files to be used by the Windows Setup program (WINNT or WINNT32). These files provide answers to the questions Setup usually asks, so that a person does not have to manually answer these questions during Setup. These two files are the answer file and the Uniqueness Database File (UDF), which are both text files.

The information in the answer file includes common configuration settings for all the computers that will use this answer file. The information in the UDF file provides settings that are unique for each computer. In this file, there is a section for each computer providing the computer name and all unique settings.

o n   t h e
!
Öo b

With a great deal of planning, customization of the script files, and testing,
you can also script the installation of application software into the Windows
installation, to occur at the end of Windows Setup. Microsoft also provides
more elaborate server-based software for distributing Windows OSs, updates,
and applications to desktop computers.

Drive Imaging

In organizations in which the same OS and all the same applications software will
be installed on many desktop PCs, drive imaging is often used. A *drive image* is an
exact duplicate of an entire hard drive's contents, including the OS and all installed
software. The image is applied to one or more identically configured computers. This
is a little tricky, since each installation of Windows XP must have a unique license
and a unique computer name. Therefore, there are tools for creating drive images
that take this problem into account. Microsoft has tools for preparing a computer for
imaging, but they do not have imaging software.

Preparation for Imaging

In general, an imaging program will take an image of an entire hard drive, save it on
a CD or server hard disk, and allow you to apply this image to another computer. To
achieve this, Microsoft recommends certain procedures:

1. Prepare a reference computer. This is a computer on which you install the
   operating system and all the necessary applications. Then, make any configuration changes that will be common to all the computers, such as placement
   of icons on the desktop and addition of network printer drivers.

   All of this is done while logged on as Administrator, so in order to make
   sure that the configuration you have created will apply to ordinary users
   who log on to the imaged computer, you need to copy the settings from the
   Administrator's profile into the Default User profile.

   Once the reference computer is prepared, Microsoft recommends preparing
   the hard drive for imaging. Use the Microsoft Sysprep utility, available in
   \support\tools\deploy.cab on the distribution CD. Running Sysprep on the
   reference computer will remove all settings unique to the reference computer
   and install the Mini-Setup Wizard.

2. Optionally, automate the answers for the Mini-Setup Wizard, which will run
   when a user logs on to a computer that has received this image. This is done

by creating a script file named sysprep.inf. If you plan to have a user answer the Mini-Setup questions, do not create a script file.

3. Use a third-party disk-imaging program to create an image of the reference computer. Available imaging programs include Acronis' True Image, Disk Backup by Paragon Software Group, and Norton Ghost from Symantec. Read the documentation for the disk-imaging program for the exact instructions.

4. Create a software distribution point by creating a shared folder on a distribution server and copying the image onto the server. Some disk-imaging programs include special software installed on the server computer, in addition to the copies of the images. This software manages image distribution.

5. Start the client computer using one of the startup options described earlier. Connect each client computer, over the network, to the software distribution point and deploy the image to the client computer, also called a target computer. Each target computer must have the same disk controller type, such as PATA, SATA, or SCSI.

6. After installing the image on a client computer, restart it and the Mini-Setup Wizard will run. If there is a sysprep.inf file, it will read configuration information out of this file; otherwise, it will prompt the user for the unique information for this computer, including username, computer name, and other information.

Microsoft provides a tool for creating the answer, UDF, and sysprep.inf files. This tool is the Setup Manager Wizard (SETUPMR.EXE), located in the deploy.cab file in the \support\tools folder on the Windows CD.

Upgrading Windows

An upgrade installation of Windows involves installing the new version of Windows directly on top of an existing installation. During an upgrade, Windows reads all the previous settings from the old registry, adapts them for the new registry, and transfers all hardware and software configuration information, thus saving you the trouble of reinstalling applications and configuring your desktop the way you like it.

While you can upgrade Windows with the full retail version of the latest version of Windows, you can buy a special Upgrade version of Windows that is much less expensive. The drawback to this version is that it will only install on a computer with a previous legally licensed version of Windows preinstalled. It will not install on a computer with an empty hard drive.

You must approach a Windows upgrade with caution, because you will first have to determine if there is an upgrade path from the old version of Windows, and you will have to determine if the hardware meets the system and compatibility requirements. Then you will need to complete certain pre-upgrade tasks.

Upgrade Paths

You can upgrade the following operating systems directly to Windows 2000 Professional: Windows 95, Windows 98, Windows NT 3.51 Workstation, and Windows NT 4.0 Workstation.

exam
ⓦatch   *Realistically, a computer so old that it is running Windows 95 or Windows NT 3.51 or 4.0 is probably underpowered for Windows XP. However, objective 3.2 of the CompTIA A+ 220-602 exam states: "Install, configure, optimize, and upgrade operating systems—references to upgrading from Windows 95 and NT may be made," so you should understand the upgrade paths described here.*

Windows XP Professional is directly upgradeable from Windows 98, Windows Me, Windows NT 4.0 Workstation SP5, and Windows 2000 Professional. If a computer has Windows 95 and you wish to upgrade to Windows XP, you must first upgrade to Windows 98.

Similarly, if a computer has a Windows NT version previous to Windows NT 4.0 Workstation SP5, you must first bring it up to this level. This means that if it is only at Windows NT 3.51 Workstation, you must first upgrade it to Windows NT 4.0 Workstation and then update it with Service Pack 5 before upgrading it to Windows XP Professional.

Requirements and Compatibility

The computer must meet the requirements for CPU, memory, and hard disk space before performing an upgrade (see the earlier section "Hardware Requirements"). This is not as daunting as the compatibility requirements.

In our experience, Windows 2000 and Windows XP support a wide range of hardware and software, even on some rather old "no name" computers, but we like to be proactive when planning an installation. This is especially true of an upgrade on a computer with older peripherals and lots of installed applications. You may not have the luxury of time in upgrading a computer—your boss or client may ask you to perform an upgrade now. Fortunately, you can run a compatibility test early in the Windows 2000 and Windows XP installations.

When upgrading a computer from an older version of Windows to Windows 2000 or Windows XP, be sure to pay close attention to compatibility issues, and be ready to resolve any you find. For instance, if a compatibility test shows that the new operating system does not have a driver for your network adapter and you proceed with the upgrade, you will not be able to access the network through the existing adapter. Your solution may be to find a new driver for the adapter that will work with the new OS, or to replace the adapter with one that comes with a compatible driver. Either way, you should find the new driver or purchase the new adapter in advance.

Also, as a precaution, uninstall or disable antivirus and antispyware programs before beginning the upgrade. These have a reputation for interfering with the upgrade. If you are concerned about being vulnerable to viruses during the installation, disconnect from the Internet until after the installation is complete.

The following describes the compatibility tests for Windows 2000 and Windows XP.

Windows 2000 Readiness Analyzer

The Windows 2000 Professional installation program performs a hardware compatibility test before beginning the installation. Although you could rely on this test to ensure that your system meets the compatibility requirements, we don't advise doing so. If it finds incompatible hardware, you'll have to abort the installation and resolve the compatibility issues before proceeding.

As an alternative, you may want to use the Readiness Analyzer, a stand-alone compatibility test for both hardware and software that you can launch from the Windows 2000 CD by running the WINNT32 program with the `checkupgradeonly` switch (`WINNT32/checkupgradeonly`). WINNT32 is the program that starts an upgrade installation from Windows 9*x* or greater. When you run it with the `checkupgradeonly` switch on, it runs the compatibility test without starting the upgrade installation, resulting in an upgrade report on the compatibility of all detected hardware and software.

You can view this report on the screen, or print it. The program saves it in a file called upgrade.txt, although you can choose a different name from within the Readiness Analyzer. Figure 8-2 shows the upgrade report information after we ran the Readiness Analyzer on a computer with a video adapter unknown to Windows 2000 Professional. In a case like this, try to obtain a Windows 2000 Professional device driver from the hardware manufacturer.

on the **job**

The Readiness Analyzer also relies on some outdated information, so don't give up hope if it announces that some component is not compatible with Windows 2000. Check with the manufacturer; you may find that a new driver or patch is available for use under Windows 2000.

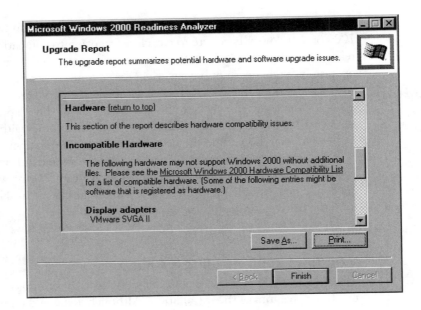

FIGURE 8-2

Readiness
Analyzer upgrade
report

Windows XP Upgrade Advisor

The Upgrade Advisor is the first process that runs on the Windows XP installation CD. It examines your hardware and installed software and provides a list of devices and software known to have issues with Windows XP, and the tasks required to resolve these issues. Be sure to follow the suggestions on this list!

You can also run the Upgrade Advisor separately from the installation. It can run from the Windows XP Professional CD, or, if you want to find out about compatibility for an upgrade before purchasing Windows XP, connect to the Windows XP Compatibility Web page at www.microsoft.com/windowsxp/pro/upgrading/advisor.mspx. Scroll to the bottom of the page, and follow the instructions under "How Do I Use Upgrade Advisor?"

Once, when we ran the Upgrade Advisor, it produced a report that found only one incompatibility—an antivirus program that was only incompatible with the Setup program but was compatible with Windows XP. Therefore, it suggested removing the program before installing the OS, then reinstalling it after installing the OS.

The computer in question was a test computer, so we ignored the instructions just to see what the consequences would be. After the upgrade, Windows XP did not run, and it would not even boot up into Windows XP's Safe Mode (described in Chapter 10). After several hours of trying to fix the installation, we had to wipe the hard drive clean and start from scratch.

In Exercise 7-2 you ran the Upgrade Advisor from the Windows XP site. If you have a Windows XP CD, you can run the Upgrade Advisor from the CD, as described in Exercise 8-1.

EXERCISE 8-1

Running Upgrade Advisor from the Windows XP CD

Before installing Windows XP you can run the Upgrade Advisor from the Windows XP CD. For purposes of this exercise, you can run this on a computer with an earlier version of Windows or one that already has XP installed.

1. Insert the Windows XP CD in the drive.

2. If autorun is enabled, the Welcome to Microsoft Windows XP screen will appear. If this does not appear, select Start | Run, and enter

   `d:\setup.exe`

   where *d* is the drive letter for the optical drive. Click OK.

3. At the Welcome To Microsoft Windows XP screen, select Check System Compatibility.

4. On the following page, select Check My System Automatically.

5. At completion it will list any hardware or software incompatibilities (see Figure 8-3.)

6. If it finds an incompatibility, select the item and click Details for more information. In the case of an incompatible program, you may need to get an upgrade to the program, or replace it entirely.

Pre-Upgrade Tasks

Before you upgrade Windows, there are some tasks we strongly recommend you perform. They include resolving incompatibilities, cleaning and optimizing the hard drive, and backing up data.

Resolving Incompatibility Problems

If the Upgrade Advisor found incompatible hardware or software, take steps to resolve these problems before you upgrade.

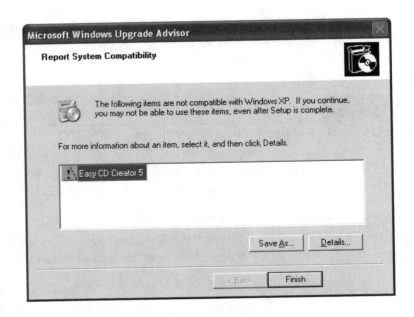

FIGURE 8-3

Upgrade Advisor
finds incompatible
software and
hardware.

Resolving Software Incompatibility   If there is an upgrade for an incompatible application program, obtain it and check with the manufacturer. Upgrade the application before upgrading the OS (unless advised otherwise by the manufacturer).

Remove any programs that will not run in the new OS from the computer before upgrading. There are also programs that interfere with the Windows Setup program but are compatible with the new version after installation. The Upgrade Advisor report will list these, in which case follow the instructions in the Details in the Upgrade Advisor report. You may need to uninstall the program before the upgrade and reinstall it after the new version of Windows runs successfully.

Resolving Hardware Incompatibility   Before upgrading, remove any program from the computer that will not run in the OS. Go to their Web site or phone them. Hardware incompatibility is most often actually just a device driver that is incompatible. The manufacturer may have an updated driver that will work. If so, obtain the driver beforehand and follow the manufacturer's instructions. They may instruct you to wait to upgrade the device driver until after the installation.

If your research shows that there is no way to resolve a hardware incompatibility, remove the hardware in question, and replace it with a component that has a driver that works with the new OS.

Backing Up Data

Back up any data from the local hard drive. Installing a new OS should not put your data in danger, but you just never know. Upgrading makes many changes to your computer, replacing critical system files with those of the new OS. If your computer loses power at an inopportune time, it could become unusable. This is a rare but real danger, especially if the computer is very old.

Besides, surely you need to back up your hard drive. Backup can be as simple as copying the contents of your My Documents folder onto an external hard drive or flash drive, or you may use the built-in Windows Backup program, NTBACKUP .EXE, to back up files to any non-optical drive attached to your computer. Learn more about the Windows Backup program in Chapter 9.

Clean Up the Hard Drive

Before upgrading your computer to a new version of Windows, clean up the hard drive, especially the C: volume. This cleanup should include removing both unwanted programs and unnecessary files. After you perform these two tasks, use the Windows Drive Defragmenter to optimize the remaining space on the hard drive.

Remove Unwanted Programs   Begin your cleanup by removing all unwanted programs. The programs you should look for are those nifty programs you installed on a whim and now find you either dislike or never use. They are all taking up space on the hard drive.

First look in the All Programs/Programs menu for unwanted programs. Many (but not all) have an uninstall shortcut on the same menu with the shortcut that launches the program. Select uninstall, and it should remove the program and solve the problem.

For programs that do not have a shortcut to an uninstall program, open Add/ Remove Programs or Add or Remove Programs (Windows XP) and scroll through the list looking for programs you are sure you will never use. Be careful not to remove updates for Microsoft Office or Windows. When you complete this, leave this applet open while you remove unwanted Windows Components.

Remove Unwanted Windows Components   As you prepare to upgrade to a new version of Windows, you should also consider removing unwanted Windows Components. To do this, open Add or Remove Programs (Add/Remove Programs in Windows 2000) and click the Add/Remove Windows Components button on the left. This will open the Windows Components Wizard (Figure 8-4). The Components

FIGURE 8-4

The Windows
Components
Wizard

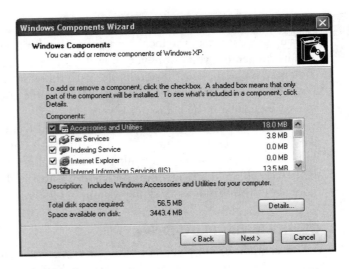

list shows groups of components, as in Accessories and Utilities, and individual components, such as Internet Explorer. To see the individual components in an entry that represents more than one, click Details. This will allow you to select a single component for removal without removing the entire category.

exam

ⓦatch   *Internet Explorer closely integrates with the operating system. Therefore, unless required through very special circumstances, never remove Internet Explorer. What special circumstances?*   *We have never encountered a reason to remove it, but since there are no absolutes in computing, you just never know. Learn more about Internet Explorer and other Web browsers in Chapter 13.*

Remove Unnecessary Files   It's amazing how fast hard drive space fills up. One way is with large data files, especially music, video, and picture files. Another, less obvious way that hard drive space fills up is with temporary files, especially temporary Internet files that accumulate on the local hard drive while you are browsing the Internet.

Windows 2000 and Windows XP have a nifty utility for cleaning up these files—Disk Cleanup. This program will allow you to choose the drive to clean up and the types of files to be removed. Exercise 8-2 will walk you through the steps for using this program.

EXERCISE 8-2

Using Disk Cleanup

Run the Windows Disk Cleanup utility to remove the hundreds of files (mostly temporary) that accumulate on your hard disk while you are browsing the Web, installing updates, and doing other work on your computer.

1. Launch Disk Cleanup from Start | All Programs (Programs in Windows 2000) | Accessories | System Tools | Disk Cleanup.

2. When prompted, select drive C:, as this is where most of these files accumulate. You can go back and clean up other drives later.

3. A small message box will inform you that Disk Cleanup is calculating how much space you will be able to free.

4. After a short delay the Disk Cleanup dialog box will show you how much space you can gain from deleting several types of files (see Figure 8-5).

5. Leave the check in the box next to any file types you wish to delete, and remove the check from any that you do not wish to delete. Select a file type and click View Files to see a list of the files.

6. The item in the Files To Delete list labeled Compress Old Files is a bit odd. This will not delete files but instead compress old files that you have not accessed in some period of time. This will free up more disk space.

7. Once you are satisfied with the files you have selected, click OK, and they are deleted from the selected drive.

Defragmenting the Hard Drive

Over time Windows develops a problem on its hard drives called fragmented files. This will cause the system to be slower at reading files into memory. Disk space divides into chunks called *clusters,* and most files are larger than the size of these clusters, which are generally 4 KB. That is fine, because the OS does not have to save all the pieces of a file into a single location—it can save a file into as many clusters as are required to hold the entire file, and these clusters can be scattered in any location in the logical drive on the disk. This creates a problem, because as you save and then delete files, the clusters in which the deleted files resided become free to use, but they may be scattered among occupied clusters. Therefore, when you save a big file, pieces of it are put all over the disk in these free clusters.

FIGURE 8-5

Disk Cleanup
dialog showing
how much disk
space can be
freed

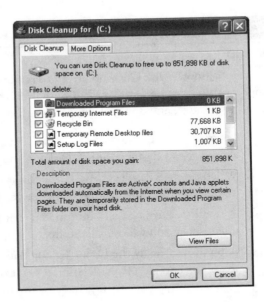

The solution is called defragmenting, and you should do it any time you remove programs and/or delete a large number of files. The tool you will use is the Disk Defragmenting utility found in Windows XP at Start | All Programs | Accessories | System Tools | Disk Defragmenter. You can also start it from Start | Run; enter **dfrg.msc**, and click OK.

In the Disk Defragmenter folder select a drive volume; then click Analyze. After the analysis completes, an Analysis Report dialog box, shown next, will inform you that your volume either does or does not require defragmenting. If it requires defragmenting, click Defragment. It will take a while to complete this process, but when it is completed, you are ready to begin your upgrade to the new OS.

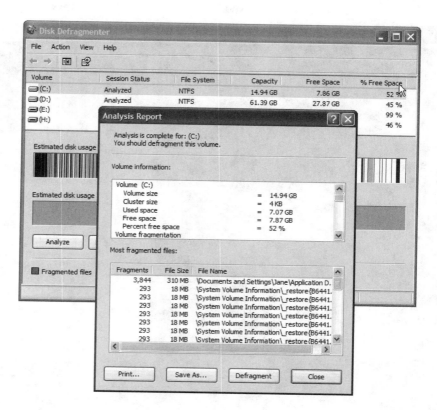

Running an Upgrade

To start an attended upgrade to Windows 2000 or Windows XP, start the existing version of Windows and place the distribution disc into the drive. Wait a minute to see if the Setup program starts on its own. If it does not start, use My Computer to browse to the CD and launch the Setup program. The Setup programs for both versions are similar, and we will use Windows XP in our example.

From the Welcome To Windows Setup screen select Install Windows XP. Setup will detect the existing version of Windows. If it is a version that you can directly upgrade, Setup will show Upgrade in the Installation Type box, as shown in Figure 8-6. Click Next to continue with an upgrade and Setup will continue in the manner of a clean installation, only with fewer interruptions for information, and you will not be prompted to create a new partition for the OS, since that would wipe out the installed OS and programs. If this is from a full retail or upgrade version of Windows XP, you will need to provide the Product Key.

FIGURE 8-6 Windows XP upgrade Setup dialog

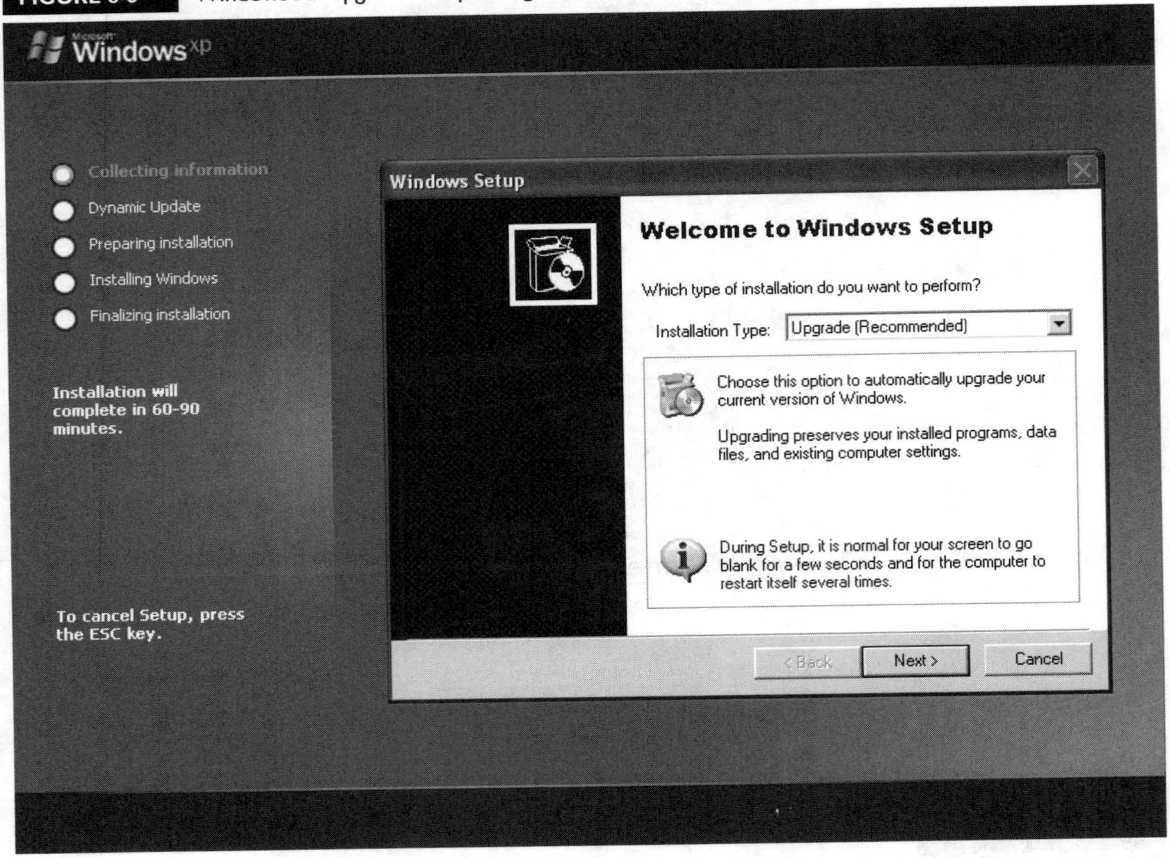

SCENARIO & SOLUTION

I have Windows 2000 running on my computer and would like to upgrade to Windows XP Professional, but the retail version is too expensive. What should I do?	Buy the Upgrade version of Windows XP Professional; it will be much less expensive and will install as an upgrade to Windows 2000.
Windows is prompting me to activate my upgrade of Windows, but I do not want to send personal information to Microsoft. Should I activate Windows?	This is not a problem. While the activation process is mandatory, it does not send personal information to Microsoft.

Post-Installation Tasks

After installing Windows XP, you have a few necessary post-installation tasks. They include verifying network access (assuming connection to a network), registration, activation, and installation of updates. You should complete these tasks before moving on to customizing the desktop for yourself or another user, and performing other desktop management tasks.

Network Configuration

Once you have completed the installation, if the computer is on a network, verify that it can communicate with other computers on the network. If it cannot, you may need to add a device driver for the network adapter and/or configure the network components. Network connectivity is important because this is the best way to download updates to your newly installed operating system—a task you must do as soon as you have Internet access.

Check Network Connectivity

Use My Network Places and see if you can see any computers on the network besides your own. In Windows 2000, this will be on the desktop; in Windows XP it is in My Computer, which is on the Start menu. Only computers with the Server service turned on are visible. (Learn more about the server service in Chapter 13.) Windows XP installation turns this service on by default, so you should see your computer and others on the network.

EXERCISE 8-3

Check Out Your Neighborhood

If your Windows XP computer connects to a network, verify that you can see other computers on the network. Try this:

1. Select Start | My Computer. In My Computer, under Other Places, select My Network Places. If any folders on other computers are shared on your network, you may see them in this view. If you see folders, you have verified network connectivity.

2. Under Network Tasks (in the task pane), select View Workgroup Computers. You should, at minimum, see your computer in the workgroup you specified during installation. The workgroup name appears in the title bar (see Figure 8-7).

3. Under Other Places, select Microsoft Network to see other workgroups on your network. When you have finished, close all open windows.

Adding a Network Adapter Device Driver

If Windows 2000 or Windows XP does not recognize your network adapter, it may not install a driver. Alternatively, it may recognize the network adapter but may not have the appropriate driver in the source directory. In this case, a prompt to provide a new device driver may appear, but we find it is best to wait until after Setup completes to install new drivers.

If you are installing network drivers, or other drivers, after the installation, wait until after the final reboot, and then follow the manufacturer's instructions for installing the device driver(s). Learn more about installing and configuring network components in Chapter 13.

Registration and Activation

In one of the final steps during setup is a prompt for you to register Windows and to activate it. Many people confuse registration and activation. These are two separate operations. Registration informs the software manufacturer (Microsoft in this case) who the official owner or user of the product is and provides contact information such as name, address, company, phone number, e-mail address, and so on, about them. Registration of a Microsoft product is still entirely optional.

Activation, more formally called Microsoft Product Activation (MPA), is a method designed to combat software piracy, meaning that Microsoft wishes to ensure that only a single computer uses each license for Windows XP. Learn more about activation so that you won't be misinformed.

FIGURE 8-7

A workgroup with only one computer showing

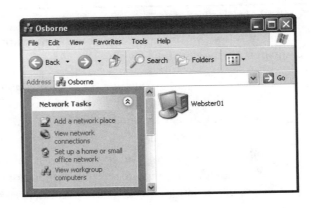

Mandatory Activation Within 30 Days of Installation

Activation is mandatory, but you may skip this step during installation. You will have 30 days in which to activate Windows XP, during which time it will work normally. If you don't activate it within that time frame, Windows will automatically disable itself at the end of the 30 days. Don't worry about forgetting, because once installed, Windows XP frequently reminds you to activate it with a balloon message over the tray area of the taskbar. The messages even tell you how many days you have left, as shown here.

on the **Job**

It is important to understand activation, because Windows XP Professional is not the only Microsoft product requiring activation, and Microsoft is not the only software vendor using an activation process. Rather than a grace period for certain applications, some manufacturers allow you to start up and use the program a certain number of times before failure to activate will disable it. Software purchased with a volume license agreement does not require product activation.

Activation Mechanics

When you choose to activate, the product ID, generated from the product key code that you entered during installation, combines with a 50-digit value that identifies your key hardware components to create an installation ID code. This code must go to Microsoft, either automatically if you have an Internet connection, or verbally via a phone call to Microsoft. Microsoft then returns a 42-digit product activation code.

If you are doing this online, you do not have to enter any codes; it is automatic and very fast. If you are activating over the phone, you must read the installation ID to a representative. There will be a slight delay while they generate the 42-digit activation code at Microsoft. Then the representative will read it back to you while you enter it into the Activate Windows By Phone dialog box.

on the **Job**

If you must activate Windows XP by phone, be sure you are sitting at your computer. Our experience is that you have to do all this in real time, including entering the code while the representative dictates it to you; you cannot write the number down and use it later. Your experience, however, may be different than ours.

FIGURE 8-8

Activation will take just seconds with an Internet connection.

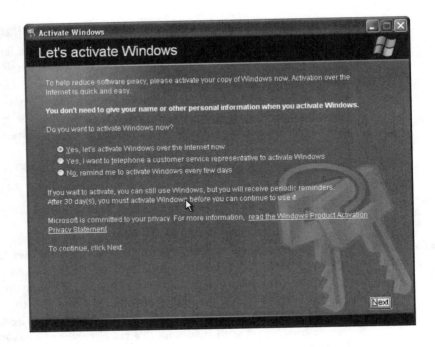

Microsoft Product Activation does not scan the contents of the hard disk; search for personal information; or gather information on the make, model, or manufacturer of the computer or its components. No personal information about you is part of the activation process. Figure 8-8 shows the dialog box that opens when you start activation by clicking on the reminder message balloon.

Reactivation

Sometimes reactivation is required after major changes to a computer. To understand why, you need to understand how MPA creates the 50-digit value that identifies your hardware. This hardware identifier value used during activation, called the "hardware hash," is generated by applying a special mathematical algorithm to values assigned to the following hardware:

- Display adapter
- SCSI adapter
- IDE adapter
- Network adapter media access control address

- RAM amount range (for example, 0–64 MB or 64–128 MB)
- Processor type
- Processor serial number
- Hard disk device
- Hard disk volume serial number
- CD-ROM/CD-RW/DVD-ROM drive

MPA will occasionally recalculate the hardware hash and compare it to the one created during activation. When it detects a significant difference in the hardware hash, you will be required to reactivate, and may be asked to call and confirm the reason for the reactivation. This is their way of ensuring that the product was not installed on a new computer.

Adding new hardware will not necessarily require reactivation, but replacing any components in the preceding list, or repartitioning and reformatting a drive, will affect the hardware hash. We have had to reactivate after making a number of changes to a computer, and again when we decommissioned a computer and installed the licensed retail version of Windows XP that had been used on a different computer. In both instances, we had to do this over the phone because we had to explain the circumstances to the representative.

Updating Windows

As soon as possible after the installation is completed and network connectivity confirmed, connect to the Windows Update site, and update Windows. This is important to do for the sake of stability and improved security. Windows updates have been an important, but often neglected, task for computer users. Typically, Microsoft finds and corrects problems with its software in a timely fashion. Earlier versions of Windows let the users decide when, if ever, to update their computers. To provide a friendlier way to update software, Microsoft has improved their update Web pages.

Windows Update

At one time Microsoft had separate update pages for Windows and Microsoft Office. The Windows Update Web site only checked for and downloaded updates for Windows, and the Microsoft Office Update page only checked for and downloaded updates for Microsoft Office. It does little good to have your OS fully updated but not your Microsoft Office programs.

Now they have combined Windows Update and Microsoft Office Update into one site called Microsoft Update. Microsoft Update checks for updates to both. You can browse to any of these sites, but it is simpler to start the Windows Update program from the Start menu to connect to the Windows Update site.

Every time you connect it will check to see that your locally installed Windows Update software is up-to-date. It will also ask you if you want to install the Microsoft Update software. If you agree to this, it will connect you to the Microsoft Update site whenever you launch the Windows Update program on your computer. Upgrading to Microsoft Update is optional and may be unnecessary if you do not use Microsoft applications. If you do not do this, you will still have to upgrade the Windows Update software whenever necessary.

exam

🐋**atch** *Both the Windows Update and Automatic Update programs require Internet Explorer. Updates to these programs may also require updates to Internet Explorer.*

Automatic Update

So far, we have only considered the Windows Update program, which allows you to interactively connect to an update site. Microsoft also provides a second program, Automatic Update, which you can configure to automatically connect to the Microsoft site and download updates.

Windows XP actually nags you to enable Automatic Update. Soon after installing Windows XP, a message balloon will pop up suggesting that you enable automate updates. If you click this message, the Automatic Updates Setup wizard will run, allowing you to configure the update program.

You do not have to wait to see this message balloon. Simply right-click My Computer (on the Start menu), select Properties, and then click the Automatic Updates tab and select the settings you desire. Then, whenever your computer connects to the Web, it checks the Windows Update page. What happens next depends on the settings you choose. Figure 8-9 shows the Automatic Updates page of the System Properties dialog box.

If you have a slow Internet connection (dial-up), you may want to disable Automatic Updates and opt to use Windows Update to manually connect and download the updates at times that will not interfere with your work. If you have a faster connection, you may elect to have the updates downloaded automatically, and review and select the updates you wish to install. Whichever option you choose, keeping Windows up-to-date should reduce the number of viruses that exploit system flaws.

FIGURE 8-9

Choosing to
enable automatic
updates

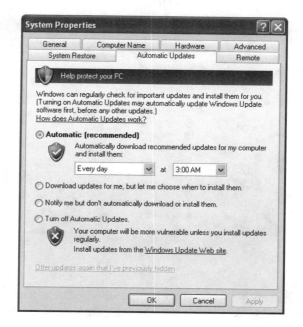

Other Updating Options

In spite of these easy options for updating Windows over the Internet, how you
actually obtain updates will depend on the organization (school or business) where
you install Windows. In some organizations, the IT department may distribute
updates intended for new installations on CD, in order to install them before a
computer is even connected to a network. Other organizations may make them
available on a shared folder on the network.

Updates can bring their own problems. Therefore, many organizations with
IT support staff will test all updates before distributing them to the user desktops.
For individuals and small organizations, it is too time-consuming to set up a test
computer on which to install updates and test them before updating production PCs.
Therefore, they rely on the ability to uninstall an update using the Add or Remove
Programs applet in Control Panel.

You can see a history of the updates installed on your computer in at least two
ways. One is by using the Add or Remove Programs Control Panel applet. Select the
Show Updates option and then scroll down through the list of currently installed
programs and updates until you see the list of software updates (Figure 8-10). This
list begins with the earliest updates and continues through the very latest updates.

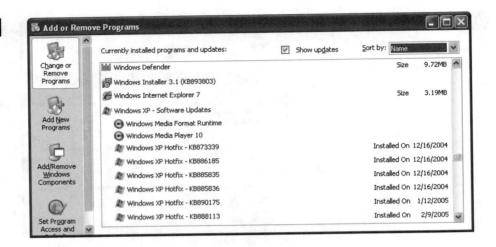

FIGURE 8-10

Add or Remove
Programs shows
the Windows
update history.

Another method for viewing the update history is to connect to either the
Windows Update or Microsoft Update site and select the link to review your update
history.

Install Additional Applications and Windows Components

After installing Windows and updating it, you can install applications, following the
instructions for each application and configuring the application preferences. After
installing each application, update it, also.

Installing New Devices

Installing a new device involves attaching the device and installing the appropriate
device driver. But you do not necessarily do these tasks in that order. Always read
the documentation before installing a new device. For instance, many USB devices
instruct you to install the device driver before connecting the device.

A device driver is program code that allows an operating system to control the
use of a physical device. A manufacturer of a device will create device drivers for
common operating systems and make the drivers available with the device.

Adequate Permissions

In order to install or uninstall device drivers, you must log on as the Administrator or a member of the Administrators group. If you attempt to install a device driver while logged on with a non-administrator account, you will see a message stating that you have insufficient security privileges to install or uninstall a device. However, once it is installed, an ordinary user may disconnect and reconnect the device without restriction.

Attaching Devices

You can attach most Plug-and-Play devices while the computer and the operating system are running. Since most devices today are Plug and Play, this is almost the rule rather than the exception. Always read the documentation.

Vendor-Supplied Installation Programs

Most devices come with a vendor-supplied installation program. If it instructs you to run this program first, it will install the driver and any additional program relating to the device. If the documentation tells you to connect or install the device first, do so before installing the software. In this case, the Found New Hardware balloon will appear over the systray, from which you may launch the Add Hardware Wizard. This program should then configure the device, often prompting you for information.

If the documentation instructs you to install the software first, do so, then, after attaching the device, the Found New Hardware balloon will appear.

Driver Signing

A device driver becomes a part of the operating system with access to the core operating system code. Therefore, a poorly written device driver can cause problems—even system crashes. They have long been a major cause of operating system instability. To prevent this problem, Microsoft works with manufacturers to ensure that driver code is safe to use.

Approved driver files have a digital signature, which is encrypted data placed in a file. The all-encompassing term for this is code signing, and when applied to device drivers it is driver signing. Microsoft began signing all of the operating system code starting with Windows 2000.

When you attempt to install a file, Windows looks for a digital signature. If it finds one, it uses a process called file signature verification to unencrypt the signature data and use the information to verify that the program code in the file was not modified since the signature was added. If it was tampered with, you will receive a warning and can stop the installation.

This does not mean that all unsigned device drivers are bad. If you trust the source of a device driver, you can allow it to install on your computer. You will see a warning

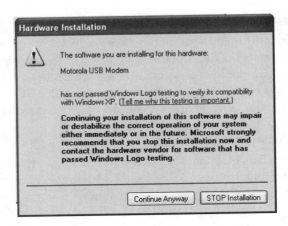

similar to that in Figure 8-11. If you trust the source of the driver, select Continue Anyway.

We strongly recommend that, if you install an unsigned driver, you first back up all your data. When you install an unsigned driver, Windows XP will automatically create a restore point before making any changes to Windows.

If you suspect a problem with the device driver, restore the operating system to the restore point. To do this, open the System Restore utility from Start | All Programs | Accessories | System Restore. Select Restore My Computer To An Earlier Time. Click Next and select the restore point that was created at the time you started the device driver installation.

Windows will not always allow you to install an unsigned driver. Your ability to install unsigned drivers or programs depends on the settings in Driver Signing Options. To get to this dialog box, right-click My Computer, select Properties, click the Hardware page, and then click the Driver Signing button.

You must log on as the Administrator or member of the Administrators Group to make changes to these settings. The three settings are

■ **Ignore** Windows will install drivers and not inform you when code is found not to contain a digital signature.

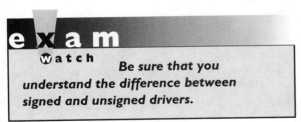

■ **Warn** When Windows detects unsigned code, it will display a warning (see Figure 8-12), and not proceed until you make a decision about using the device or canceling the installation.

■ **Block** Windows will block the installation of unsigned code.

FIGURE 8-12

The Driver
Signing Options
dialog box

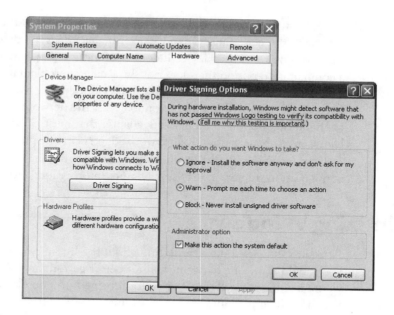

Automated vs. Manual Driver Installation

Most PCs and peripheral devices are fully Plug and Play, as are the Windows operating
systems since Windows 2000. Therefore, when it detects a newly installed device, the
operating system does an automated search for an appropriate device driver. If it finds
one, it installs it and configures the device. You may have to answer a few questions
during the configuration process.

The driver it finds during this automated search may be one that came with Windows
or one that you preinstalled before installing the device. If Windows cannot find a driver
during this automated search, it will prompt you to insert a disk or browse to the folder
containing the driver.

Verifying Driver Installation

After installing a device and its driver and associated utility program, verify the
success of the installation. Do this by checking Device Manager and by testing the
functionality of the new device.

Device Manager   Immediately after installing a new device, open Device Manager
and look for the device you just installed by browsing for the device. If the device is in
the list and does not have a yellow circle with an exclamation mark over its icon, the
system considers it to be functioning properly.

Functionality   You should also test the functionality of the new device. This is because there are times when Device Manager does not detect a problem, but when you try to use the device it does not function properly. This is usually due to a configuration option that does not show up as a problem in Device Manager. An example of this is a network adapter that is functioning okay from Device Manager's point of view but will not allow you to access the network. There are higher-level configuration options for a network adapter that must be correct before it will work. Learn more about configuring network adapters in Chapter 13.

If a device does not work, check the documentation. You may have skipped a configuration step or need to supply more information before it is fully configured.

Optimizing Windows

After installing Windows, and throughout the lifetime of the OS on your computer, you should take time to optimize it for better performance. There are a few areas where making some changes or performing certain housekeeping tasks will decrease the time you must wait for the OS to start up and will increase the speed while you are working. These areas include virtual memory, hard drives, services, and startup.

Virtual Memory

As a rule, Windows manages virtual memory just fine without intervention. We recommend that, with few exceptions, you should not modify the default settings on your computer. As stated in Chapter 7, when you install Windows it sets the size of the paging file, PAGEFILE.SYS, to 1.5 times the size of the installed physical RAM. This is an optimum setting for most uses of desktop or laptop computers.

Modifying the Paging File

There are a few exceptions to the rule we just stated. Sometimes the virtual memory settings need to change to improve performance. An example of this is that some applications (very few) recommend resizing the paging file (swap file) for better performance. It is also possible that such software would also include this resizing in its installation process.

Another time when you might need to modify the size of the paging file is if you add more RAM memory to your computer. Windows will not automatically resize the paging file to go with the new RAM amount. Even so, we don't recommend that you resize the paging file immediately. Your reason for installing additional RAM may have been to meet the requirements of new software, or perhaps to increase the performance of your computer (see Chapter 10). Whatever the reason for the memory upgrade, if you find that your computer seems to be as slow or slower than it was before the upgrade, reconfigure the Virtual Memory.

If you must change the page file size, the Virtual Memory settings on the Advanced page of Performance Options is the place to go. These settings include the size and location of the page file, and the number of page files used. If the present size is less than 1.5 times the size of the installed RAM, select the option for System Managed Size and click Set, followed by OK. The next time you reboot, the size of the paging file will be resized to 1.5 times the size of the physical RAM.

In Exercise 8-4 you will view the Virtual Memory settings on your computer. The default location of the paging file is on drive C:. If you are running out of free disk space on drive C:—and if you have other internal hard drive volumes—consider moving the paging file to another drive that has more free space. It is also possible to have more than one paging file, but this is not normally necessary on a desktop or laptop computer. Never place the paging file on an external hard drive, because it may not be available during startup and this could prevent Windows from starting.

EXERCISE 8-4

Viewing the Virtual Memory Settings

You can easily view the present virtual memory settings for your computer.

1. Right-click My Computer and select Properties.

2. In the System Properties dialog box select the Advanced tab.

3. Under Performance click Settings. In the Performance Options dialog box select the Advanced tab.

4. In the Virtual Memory dialog box click Change to view the virtual memory settings for all the hard drives on your computer (see Figure 8-13).

5. If you made no changes, click Cancel three time to close the three dialog boxes: Virtual Memory, Performance Options, and System Properties.

Figure 8-13 shows a paging file smaller than 1.5 times the installed RAM size. This is because we had upgraded the RAM. After taking this screen shot we selected System Managed Size in the Virtual Memory dialog box, and on the next reboot the paging file increased to 1437 MB. The computer operated faster after this change.

FIGURE 8-13

The Virtual
Memory dialog
box

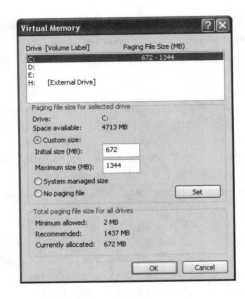

Hard Drives

To optimize your hard drive, take time on a regular basis to uninstall unwanted
programs, run the Disk Cleanup program, and then run the Disk Defragmenter. How
frequently depends on how often you install new programs, how much you browse
the Internet (creating temporary Internet files), and how often you delete and create
new files. Begin with a schedule of once a month, and increase it if you find that
your system seems to slow down whenever it is reading large files.

Services

Windows contains a number of special programs called services. A *service* is code
that becomes part of the operating system, performing some unique function. A
service does not have a user interface; it runs in the background. Windows Setup
installs many services. Not every user needs all of these services, and you can remove
or disable them to improve performance. Removing a service is an advanced task,
which can cause serious problems. We recommend that you first learn about services,
and then if you wish to improve performance, disable selected services.

To see the installed services, open the Administrative Tools applet in Control
Panel and open Services. From this console, shown next, you can disable or enable
services. However, you should never disable a service unless you are sure of the
consequences. You may be disabling a service required for another service called

a dependency. You can view the dependencies of each service by double-clicking the service in the Service console and selecting the Dependencies tab of the Properties dialog box for that service.

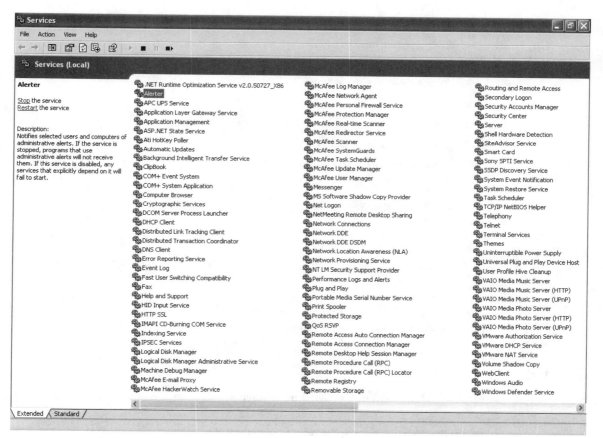

on the job

To place a shortcut to Administrative Tools on your Windows XP Start menu, right-click on an empty area of the taskbar and select Properties. In the Taskbar And Start menu Properties dialog box select the Start Menu tab. On the Start Menu tab click Customize. In the Customize Start Menu dialog box select the Advanced tab, and scroll to the bottom of the list. Under System Administrative Tools select the radio button for Display On The All Programs Menu And The Start Menu. Click OK on that page and on the main page of the Start Menu And Toolbar Properties dialog box.

Services that you can disable on most Windows XP systems without dire consequences (with emphasis on "most" and "dire") include the following:

- Alerter
- Distributed Link Tracking Client (definitely disable if you are not in a Microsoft domain)
- Indexing Service (if you do a great deal of file searches on your local drives, do not disable this service)
- IPSEC Services
- Messenger (this is disabled automatically by Windows XP SP2)
- Portable Media Serial Number
- Remote Registry Service
- Secondary Logon
- SSDP Discovery Service
- Telnet
- Upload Manager
- Wireless Zero Configuration (only disable this is you are not on a wireless network).

If you disable services, do it one-at-a-time and test all of your necessary applications after disabling a single service.

Startup

Windows 2000 and Windows XP tend to have a great many programs that automatically load into memory at startup. Some of these are Windows components, such as services, but too many of them are applications that you install along the way. If you purchased your computer from a retail outlet, or a major PC vendor, you will have a large number of "bundled" applications usually touted as a great value. However, the installers for these companies will configure most of these applications to start up automatically, and this is a problem.

When too many programs are starting up automatically during Startup, you will find yourself waiting several minutes to get to the desktop. One way to optimize Startup so that it occurs faster is to remove unwanted programs and services from Startup.

SCENARIO & SOLUTION

I have installed additional RAM, but Windows does not seem to run any faster. What do I do?	Change the virtual memory settings to System Managed Size, and reboot.
My Windows XP computer came with a large number of bundled programs that I never use. I also dislike waiting so long for Windows to start up. What do I do?	The two may be related. Many of the installed applications may be starting automatically with the OS. Try uninstalling these unwanted applications.

Uninstalling Programs

A quick and easy way to stop programs from starting up automatically is to completely uninstall them. Follow the instruction earlier in this chapter for uninstalling unwanted programs.

Changing Program Startup

What do you do about the automatically started program you do not want to remove from your computer? You just want to stop it from starting up automatically. This is not a trivial task, because a program's startup instructions to Windows can be in one of several locations, including several registry keys, Startup folders, Scheduled Tasks folders, logon scripts, and a file named WIN.INI that is a vestige of early versions of Windows.

When you simply want to stop a program from starting up automatically with Windows, use the MSCONFIG utility. This program shows you the locations of startup instructions and allows you to test the effects of disabling a program's startup before you make it permanent. Learn how to use the MSCONFIG utility in Chapter 10.

CERTIFICATION SUMMARY

There are many decisions to make before installing a new version of Windows. Will this be a clean installation or an upgrade? Will the installation be attended or a fully automated unattended installation? What tasks should you perform before installing or upgrading? What tasks should you perform after installing Windows? Finally, what will improve the startup and running performance of Windows?

All of these questions are important to understand for passing your A+ Certification exams, and for doing your job.

✓ TWO-MINUTE DRILL

Here are some of the key points covered in Chapter 8.

Installing Windows

❏ Installing Windows involves three stages: preparation, installation, and follow-up tasks.

❏ Preparation tasks include verifying that the target computer meets the physical hardware requirements, as well as the hardware and software compatibility requirements.

❏ Select a file system. The recommended file system for Windows 2000 and Windows XP is NTFS.

❏ Plan how to start up Setup, and the location of the source files.

❏ An attended installation requires the presence of a person who can respond to occasional prompts for information.

❏ Scripts that answer the Setup program's questions automate an unattended installation.

❏ A drive image is an exact duplicate of an entire hard drive's contents, including the OS and all installed software.

Upgrading Windows

❏ An upgrade installs the new version of Windows directly on top of an existing installation, transferring all the settings from the old installation into the new one.

❏ An Upgrade version of Windows is cheaper than a full retail version but will only install into a previous installation of Windows.

❏ Windows 95, Windows 98, Windows NT 3.51 Workstation, and Windows NT 4.0 Workstation are all directly upgradable to Windows 2000 Professional.

❏ Windows XP Professional is directly upgradable from Windows 98, Windows Me, Windows NT 4.0 Workstation SP5, and Windows 2000 Professional.

❏ Windows 95 must first be upgraded to Windows 98 before it can be upgraded to Windows XP.

❏ A Windows NT version previous to Windows NT 4.0 Workstation SP5 must first be upgraded to Windows NT 4.0 Workstation and then be updated with Service Pack 5 before upgrading it to Windows XP Professional.

❏ Before upgrading, test for incompatible software and hardware and then resolve any incompatibilities.

❏ Before upgrading, back up all data, clean up the hard drive, and then defragment the hard drive.

Post-Installation Tasks

❏ Test network connectivity and, if necessary, add and configure a network adapter driver.

❏ Within 30 days of installation activate Windows. This is mandatory. You may optionally register Windows at any time.

❏ Making major changes to Windows may cause MPA to require reactivation.

Optimizing Windows

❏ Sometimes the virtual memory settings need to change to improve performance.

❏ One example of when you might change the default virtual memory settings is when you install software that requires that the paging file be larger than it already is.

❏ Another time to modify the virtual memory settings is after installing more RAM, because the system will not automatically modify the paging file to reflect the additional RAM.

❏ Run the Disk Defragmenter utility to optimize your hard drive.

❏ Disable unnecessary services.

❏ Improve the speed of startup by changing program startup behavior or removing unwanted programs with automatic startup.

SELF TEST

The following questions will help you measure your understanding of the material presented in this chapter. Read all of the choices carefully because there might be more than one correct answer. Choose all correct answers for each question.

Installing Windows

1. Which of the following refers to the lowest level of CPU and the minimum amount of RAM and free hard disk space needed to install an OS?
   A. Hardware compatibility
   B. Software compatibility
   C. Hardware requirements
   D. Hardware optimizing

2. What is the order of tasks when preparing a new hard drive?
   A. Format, then partition
   B. Partition, then install OS
   C. Format, then install OS
   D. Partition, then format

3. What is the preferred file system for Windows 2000 and Windows XP?
   A. NTFS
   B. FAT16
   C. FAT32
   D. FAT

4. What are two ways to start the Windows Setup program?
   A. Booting from diskette or booting from CD
   B. Booting into Setup or running either WINNT.EXE or WINN32.EXE
   C. Imaging or scripting
   D. Unpartitioned boot or booting from CD

5. What type of installation requires a person's real-time response to prompts?
   A. Unattended
   B. Image
   C. Scripted
   D. Attended

6. What method of installation places an exact copy of a hard drive containing a previously installed operating system and applications (from a reference computer) onto the hard drive of another computer?

A. Attended

B. Scripted

C. Image

D. Unattended

7. What method of installation runs the Setup program from a distribution server?

A. Local attended

B. Local unattended

C. Image

D. Network

Upgrading Windows

8. What is the upgrade path to Windows XP for a computer running Windows NT 3.51 Workstation?

A. Windows NT 3.51 to Windows NT 4.0 SP5 to Windows XP

B. Upgradable directly to Windows XP

C. Windows NT 3.51 to Windows 2000 to Windows XP

D. There is no upgrade path

9. Which one of the following statements is *not* true?

A. You can upgrade with a retail upgrade version of Windows XP.

B. You can install the upgrade version of Windows XP onto an unpartitioned hard drive.

C. You can upgrade from a upgrade version of Windows XP.

D. You can do a clean install from a retail version of Windows XP.

10. What can you do to check the compatibility of existing hardware and software before starting an upgrade to Windows 2000?

A. Run the Readiness Analyzer.

B. Check the hardware list.

C. Run the Upgrade Advisor.

D. Remove all peripherals.

11. What can you do to check the compatibility of hardware and software before starting an upgrade to Windows XP?
    A. Run the Readiness Analyzer.
    B. Check the hardware list.
    C. Run the Upgrade Advisor.
    D. Remove all peripherals.

12. What should you do before an upgrade if you discover incompatible software or hardware?
    A. Nothing. The incompatibility will be resolved during the upgrade.
    B. Buy a special version of Windows for incompatibility problems.
    C. Resolve the incompatibility before beginning the upgrade.
    D. Repartition and format the hard drive.

Post-Installation Tasks

13. What purpose does Microsoft Product Activation serve?
    A. Product compatibility
    B. Prevention of software piracy
    C. Product registration
    D. Disabling the OS

14. What is the consequence of not completing the activation process for Windows XP?
    A. No consequence.
    B. You will not receive updates.
    C. After 30 days Windows XP will be disabled.
    D. You will not receive e-mails about new products.

15. What task should you do as soon as possible after installation for the sake of stability and improved security?
    A. Upgrade
    B. Activate
    C. Update
    D. Partition

16. What may MPA require if you make too many hardware changes to a Windows XP computer?
    A. Reinstallation
    B. Removal of Windows
    C. Reactivation
    D. Update

17. What is a simple test of network connectivity?

    A. Performing Activation

    B. Locating the new computer in My Network Places

    C. Locating the new computer in My Computer

    D. Adding a network adapter driver

18. To what site does Windows Update connect by default?

    A. The local workgroup

    B. Microsoft Update

    C. Windows Update

    D. Microsoft Office Update

Optimizing Windows

19. What should you do if your computer seems slow when you are saving or retrieving files?

    A. Defragment the hard drive.

    B. Remove unnecessary programs.

    C. Delete unwanted files.

    D. Reboot.

20. What happens to the paging file when you add more RAM memory to a Windows XP computer?

    A. Nothing.

    B. It is automatically resized to 1.5 times the size of the RAM.

    C. It is deleted.

    D. It is automatically resized to one half the size of the RAM.

LAB QUESTION

In a previous chapter you shopped for a laptop computer based on a set of customer requirements. Now you will create a description of a computer configuration (CPU, memory, and hard disk) that you would use to shop for a computer based on the system requirements of the operating system and the office suite you intend to install on the computer. You pick the operating system and the office suite. Write a paragraph describing your choice of software, and then describe the system requirements specified for each of these. Finally, come up with your recommended configuration for a new computer. Be sure to take into consideration extra memory for having many applications open at one time, and sufficient disk space for saving data files.

SELF TEST ANSWERS

Installing Windows

1. ☑ **C.** Hardware requirements are the CPU, minimum amount of RAM, and free hard disk space needed to install an OS.

   ☒ **A,** hardware compatibility, is incorrect because this refers to the actual make and model of the hardware, not the level of CPU and quantity of RAM and free hard disk space. **B,** software compatibility, is incorrect because it does not refer to the CPU, RAM, and free hard disk space. **D,** hardware optimizing, is incorrect because this does not refer to the level of CPU and quantity of RAM and free hard disk space.

2. ☑ **D.** Partition, then format is the correct order for preparing a new hard drive.

   ☒ **A,** format, then partition, is incorrect because it reverses the correct order of tasks when preparing a new hard drive. **B,** partition, then install OS, is incorrect because it skips the formatting step. **C,** format, then install OS, is incorrect because it skips the partitioning step.

3. ☑ **A.** NTFS is the preferred file system for Windows 2000 and Windows XP.

   ☒ **B,** FAT16, **C,** FAT32, and **D,** FAT, are incorrect because none of them is the preferred file system for Windows XP. While there are significant volume size limits for FAT16, the main reason for not using any FAT file system is due to the lack of support for file-level security, which is built into NTFS.

4. ☑ **B.** Booting into Setup or running either WINNT.EXE or WINNT32.EXE are two ways in which the Windows Setup program can start.

   ☒ **A,** booting from diskette or booting from CD, is incorrect because these are two ways to boot into Setup, which is one of the ways to start Windows Setup. **C,** imaging or scripting, is incorrect because these are not methods to start Windows Setup. **D,** unpartitioned boot or booting from CD, is incorrect because unpartitioned boot is not possible and booting from CD is just one way to boot into Setup.

5. ☑ **D.** Attended installation is the type that requires a person's real-time response to prompts.

   ☒ **A,** unattended installation, is incorrect because this type of installation does not require a person's real-time response to prompts. **B,** image, is incorrect because this method replaces Setup altogether. **C,** scripted, is incorrect because you could use this term to describe an unattended installation, which does not require real-time response to prompts.

6. ☑ **C.** Image installation places an exact copy of the operating system and applications (from a reference computer) onto the hard drive of another computer.

   ☒ **A,** attended installation, is incorrect because this does not place an exact copy of a hard drive onto another computer. **B,** scripted, is incorrect because scripting is just part of an installation, not a method of installation. **D,** unattended, is incorrect because this method may or may not include an image.

7. ☑ **D.** Network installation runs the Setup program from a distribution server.
☒ **A,** local attended, **B,** local unattended, and **C,** image, are incorrect because they do not describe a method that calls the Setup program from a distribution server.

Upgrading Windows

8. ☑ **A.** Windows NT 3.51 to Windows NT 4.0 SP5 to Windows XP is the upgrade path to Windows XP for a computer running Windows NT 3.51.
☒ **B,** upgradable directly to Windows XP, and **C,** Windows NT 3.51 to Windows 2000 to Windows XP, are incorrect because neither is the correct upgrade path. **D,** there is no upgrade path, is incorrect because there is one, and it is answer **A.**

9. ☑ **B.** You can install the upgrade version of Windows XP onto an unpartitioned hard drive is correct because this statement is not true. The upgrade version will only install onto a computer with a previous version of Windows already installed and running (and only certain versions are directly upgradable).
☒ **A,** you can upgrade with a retail upgrade version of Windows XP, **C,** you can upgrade from a upgrade version of Windows XP, and **D,** you can do a clean install from a retail version of Windows XP, are all true and therefore are not correct answers.

10. ☑ **A.** Run the Readiness Analyzer is correct because you can run this before upgrading to Windows 2000 to check the compatibility.
☒ **B,** check the hardware list, is incorrect because this was not an option in the chapter, although it could be construed as referring to the old hardware compatibility list, which was not mentioned and was not as effective as the Readiness Analyzer. **C,** run the Upgrade Advisor, is incorrect because this is the name of the compatibility checker for Windows XP. **D,** remove all peripherals, is incorrect because this is extreme unless all the peripherals are hopelessly incompatible.

11. ☑ **C.** Run the Upgrade Advisor is correct because this can run before upgrading to Windows XP to check the compatibility.
☒ **A,** run the Readiness Analyzer, is incorrect because this is the name of the compatibility checker for Windows 2000. **B,** check the hardware list, is incorrect because this was not an option in the chapter, although it could be construed as referring to the old hardware compatibility list, which was not mentioned and was not as effective as the Upgrade Adviser. **D,** remove all peripherals, is incorrect because this is extreme unless all the peripherals are hopelessly incompatible.

12. ☑ **C.** To resolve the incompatibility before beginning the upgrade is the correct action to take before an upgrade if you discover incompatible software or hardware.
☒ **A,** nothing, is incorrect because the incompatibility will not be resolved during the upgrade. **B,** buy a special version of Windows for incompatibility problems, is incorrect because there is

no such version. **D**, repartition and format the hard drive, is incorrect because this is extreme and will void the ability to install an upgrade.

Post-Installation Tasks

13. ☑ **B.** Prevention of software piracy is correct because this is the purpose of Microsoft Product Activation.
    ☒ **A**, product compatibility, **C**, product registration, and **D**, disabling the OS, are all incorrect because they are not the purpose of MPA.

14. ☑ **C.** That after 30 days Windows XP is disabled is the consequence of not completing the activation process for Windows XP.
    ☒ **A**, no consequence, is incorrect because there is a consequence, and it is answer **C**. **B**, you will not receive updates, is incorrect because you will receive updates until Windows is disabled after 30 days of not activating. **D**, you will not receive e-mails about new products, is incorrect because this may be a consequence of not registering.

15. ☑ **C.** Update is correct because you should do this task as soon as possible for the sake of stability and security.
    ☒ **A**, upgrade, is incorrect because this is not a task you should do for the sake of stability and improved security immediately after installing a new OS. **B**, activate, is incorrect because this is not a task you should do for the sake of stability and improved security. **D**, partition, is incorrect because this is not a task you should do for the sake of stability and improved security.

16. ☑ **C.** Reactivation is correct because MPA may require that you reactivate if you make too many hardware changes to a Windows XP computer.
    ☒ **A**, reinstallation, is incorrect because MPA will not require reinstallation if you make too many hardware changes. **B**, removal of Windows, is incorrect because MPA doesn't care if you remove Windows. **D**, upgrade, is incorrect; MPA will only require reactivation, not upgrading, if you make too many hardware changes.

17. ☑ **B.** Locating the new computer in My Network Places is a simple test of network connectivity.
    ☒ **A**, performing activation, is not a simple test of network connectivity, although you will not be able to activate over the Internet if you do not have network connectivity. **C**, locating the new computer in My Computer, is not a simple test of network connectivity, although you should be able to browse to the computer through My Computer. It is not the tool that you would normally use. **D**, adding a network adapter driver, is incorrect because you couldn't perform a simple test of network connectivity if you didn't already have one installed.

18. ☑ **C.** Windows Update is the site to which Windows Update connects by default.

☒ **A,** the local workgroup, is incorrect because this is not something Windows Update connects to. **B,** Microsoft Update, is incorrect because this is not the site to which Windows Update connects to by default. It will connect here after you connect to Windows Update and agree to install Microsoft Update. **D,** Microsoft Office Update, is incorrect because this is not the site to which Windows Update connects by default.

Optimizing Windows

19. ☑ **A.** You should defragment the hard drive if your computer seems slow when you are saving or retrieving files.

☒ **B,** remove unnecessary programs, and **C,** delete unwanted files, are not the action you should take if your computer seems slow when you are saving or retrieving files. However, it is a good idea to do these two things before running Disk Defragmenter. **D,** reboot, simply restarts the computer and has no effect on the speed of the computer.

20. ☑ **A.** Nothing is correct because when you add more RAM memory to a Windows XP computer Windows does not automatically resize the paging file.

☒ **B,** it is automatically resized to 1.5 times the size of the RAM, is incorrect, although this will happen when you install Windows. **C,** it is deleted, is incorrect because installing more RAM will not cause the paging file to be deleted. **D,** it is automatically resized to one half the size of the RAM, is also incorrect because nothing is done to the paging file as a result of installing more RAM.

LAB ANSWER

Answers will vary because the choice of the OS is up to you.

The OS we chose is Windows XP Professional, with minimum requirements of an Intel or AMD 300 MHz or higher CPU, 128 MB of RAM, and 1.5 GB of free hard drive space. We chose Microsoft Office 2007 Professional, which requires Windows XP Service Pack 2 running on a computer with 256 MB RAM or higher, 2 GB of free hard disk space for the installation, a CD-ROM or DVD drive, and a 1024 × 768 resolution or greater video display.

Our conclusion is that we would order a computer with a 2 GHz CPU, 2 GB of RAM, and a 250 GB hard disk drive minimum. In addition, we would order a 17" or larger LCD panel (1024 × 768 resolution or higher) and a DVD±RW optical drive.

9

Disk and File Management

W

hile each GUI operating system has its own methods for allowing you to manage disks and your data files, the Windows OSs have changed very little in file management from version to version. In this chapter, check out Windows disk management theory and practices, file and folder basics, organizing files using folders, creating files, GUI and non-GUI utilities for managing files, and maintenance of files and disks.

CERTIFICATION OBJECTIVES

- **601: 3.1   603: 2.1**   *Identify the fundamentals of using operating systems*

- **602: 3.1**   *Identify the fundamental principles of operating systems*

In this chapter we continue with the A+ operating system fundamental objectives begun in Chapter 7, in which all but one of the topics under the preceding objectives were explored. Here you will learn the disk and file management concepts and practices that you must know for the A+ 601, 602, and 603 exams.

Disk Management

Disk management topics include Windows disk storage types, and partitioning basics. PC technicians need to understand how to prepare a disk for use, and beginning with Windows 2000, this also requires understanding storage types and disk partitioning for the storage type you will work with the most in Windows PCs. Finally, learn about drive letter assignments, mount points, and drive paths.

Disk Storage Types

This section is all about how hard disks are prepared for use. Windows 2000 introduced the concept of disk storage types—dynamic and basic—that Windows XP and Microsoft's newer server and desktop OSs continue to use. The basic storage type is the default disk type of Windows 2000 and Windows XP. Because it is the one you are most likely to use in Windows on desktop computers, we will give only a brief overview and comparison of these two storage types. The remainder of this section dwells on the partitioning and managing of basic disks.

Dynamic Disks

Dynamic storage is a new way to allocate disk space and manage hard disks. Support for dynamic storage began with Windows 2000 and continues in newer Microsoft OSs. Using dynamic storage, a *dynamic disk* has space allocated in volumes, not partitions, and does not have the limits imposed on basic disks.

- There is no limit to the number of volumes on a dynamic disk.
- A volume can extend to include available space on any hard disk in the computer.
- Configuration information for a dynamic disk is located on the disk space beyond the first physical sector. This configuration information is stored outside of any volume on the hard disk.

When you install Windows 2000 or Windows XP, the default disk type is the *basic* disk type. Once the operating system is up and running, you may choose to convert a basic disk to dynamic, but the benefits of dynamic disks really aim at disks on network servers, not desktop computers. In fact, many of the best features of dynamic disks (volume types that support fault tolerance) are not available in Windows 2000 Professional, and only one, disk mirroring, is available in Windows XP. The more advanced features are available only in the Windows 2000 and newer Server products.

on the
job
Leave your options open! In order to convert a disk from basic to dynamic there must be at least 1 MB of unallocated space on the physical disk to hold the disk configuration information. Therefore, when creating partitions on a basic disk, be sure to leave at least 1 MB of unallocated space free.

Basic Disks

Under the Windows OSs beginning with Windows 2000, *basic disks* are those disks using *basic storage* techniques. Basic disks are prepared and managed in the manner of MS-DOS, Windows 9x, and Windows NT. Such disks use the traditional method for creating partitions, including the use of a single partition table per disk, which resides in the first physical sector of a hard disk. The partition table occupies a mere 64 bytes of the 512 bytes in the sector. This sector, called the *master boot record* *(MBR)*, also contains the initial boot program loaded by BIOS during startup. This program, and the partition table, are created or modified in this sector when a disk is partitioned.

If you understood disk partitioning in Windows 9x, then you understand partitioning of basic disks under Windows 2000 and newer versions of Windows, with only a few changes that you will notice in the next section where we discuss partitioning basic disks. Try Exercise 9-1 to view the disk storage type on your computer.

EXERCISE 9-1

Viewing the Disk Storage Type

You can view the disk storage type on your Windows 2000 or Windows XP computer.

1. Log on as an Administrator, open the Start menu, right-click My Computer, and select Manage from the context menu. This will open the Computer Management console.

2. In Computer Management, click the Disk Management folder under the Storage node. After a brief delay, the Disk Management snap-in will appear in the right pane of the console.

3. In Disk Management, look for Disk 0. This normally is your first internal hard disk drive, and the one from which Windows boots. Just below the words "Disk 0" you will see the storage type (see Figure 9-1).

FIGURE 9-1

Disk Management shows the storage type.

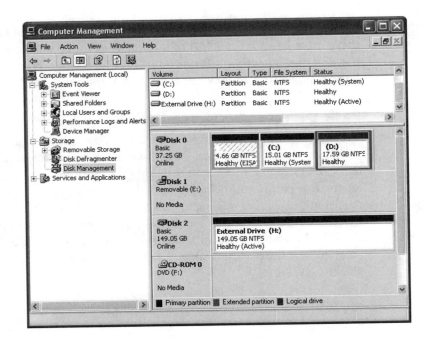

You can convert a disk from basic to dynamic using Disk Management, but this is something you should not do unless you have very good reason. Even on Windows server computers, implementation of fault tolerance in the form of disk mirroring and disk striping with parity is most often done at the hardware level and is invisible to the operating system. In these cases, the disks remain basic disks.

Partitioning Basic Disks

Now that you understand Windows storage types, you can continue to the first step in preparing a basic disk—partitioning. Before a new disk drive is able to save data, you must partition and format it. Partitioning a disk means you divide the disk into one or more areas that you can treat as a separate logical drive, and each may, therefore, get its own individual drive letter. Each logical drive can have a different file system, as explained in the following discussion.

Often, you don't want to divide a hard disk into multiple logical drives, in which case you create a single partition that uses the entire drive.

On basic disks a partition table holds a record of the partition boundaries on a disk. But there are limits to the old type of partition tables, and these limits apply to basic disks. A basic disk is compatible with older operating systems, and it can have up to four partitions. This is true for Windows NT, Windows 2000, and newer OSs. It is not entirely true of older Windows OSs and MS-DOS. The one major difference is that while older versions of Windows (and MS-DOS) used the partition table, they were not capable of using the entire partition table. They could only create and/or use two partitions, and there were even limits to the types of partitions they could use, as explained next.

Partition Types

There are two *partition types* used on basic disks in Windows 2000 and Windows XP. They are primary and extended, of which there can be a maximum of four primary partitions or three primaries, and one extended partition (see Figure 9-2).

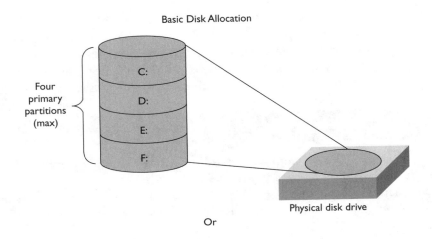

FIGURE 9-2

Basic Disk
Allocation allows
for a maximum of
four partitions.

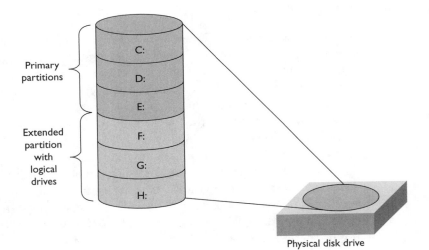

Primary Partitions Each *primary* partition can have only one logical drive assigned to it encompassing the entire partition. Because a computer can only boot from a primary partition that has been marked as active, a Windows PC with basic disks must have at least one primary partition.

Extended Partitions An *extended* partition can have one or more logical drives (each with a drive letter). Older operating systems such as MS-DOS, Windows 3.x, or Windows 9x (including Windows Millennium Edition) could only create two partitions.

The extended partition type was, in a real sense, a fix for the limits of these OSs. Since they could not work with more than two entries in the partition table, Microsoft created this new partition type. An extended partition is divisible into one or more logical drives, each of which has a drive letter assigned. This allows these OSs to work with more than two logical drives on a single hard disk system.

Further, the older operating systems cannot work with more than one primary partition. If a hard drive has two partitions, one must be primary and the other must be an extended partition.

Things have changed. While many new Windows XP computers still come configured with one primary and one extended partition, this is unnecessary, and the second partition should really be a primary partition. It actually takes longer to access data on a logical drive within an extended partition.

Designating the Active Partition

In order for Windows to boot from a partition, that partition must be a primary partition that is marked as active. This is because the startup procedure common to all PCs looks for an *active partition* on the first physical drive from which to start an OS. Installing Windows on a new unpartitioned hard drive creates a primary active partition.

Partition Size Limits

When you partition a drive, the maximum partition size is the lesser of two values: the maximum partition size supported by the hardware or the maximum partition size supported by the file system. The FAT16 file system has a 4 GB partition size limit in

SCENARIO & SOLUTION

You want to have more than four logical drives on a disk. What are your options? What option is preferred?	If you convert the disk to a dynamic disk, you can create more than four logical drives. This is preferred. You can also create three primary partitions and one extended. The three primary partitions would each be a logical drive, and the extended partition can have multiple logical drives.
You would like to divide the space of a single basic disk into four logical drives. Describe the partitions you would create.	Create four primary partitions on a basic disk.

Windows 2000 and Windows XP, and a 2 GB partition size limit in Windows 9x and DOS. The FAT32 file system has a partition size limit of 2 terabytes (2 trillion bytes).

In Windows 2000 and Windows XP the NTFS file system has a partition size limit of 16 exabytes (an exabyte is one billion billion bytes). Now, this is obviously theoretical, because the hardware limit (mostly a BIOS limit) is 137 GB, although the exact number is increasing. If you are working with a computer with a very old BIOS, you may run into a smaller limit.

Logical Drives, Drive Paths, and Mounted Volumes

When it comes to assigning drive letters to primary partitions or logical drives on an extended partition, the 26 letters of the alphabet limit us. In fact, the first two letters, A and B, are reserved for floppy disk drives, and we only have 24 letters for other drives.

Windows assigns drive letters automatically in a specific order. During an upgrade installation, it will preserve the drive letter assignments that existed under the previous version of Windows. The drive letter assignments are in a special database called MountMgr, located in the registry.

During a fresh install of Windows 2000 or Windows XP, the Setup program will assign letter C: to the first primary active partition it detects. It will then assign drive letters (D:, E:, etc.) to the first primary partition on other drives, and then it will assign drive letters to all logical drives in extended partitions. Finally, it will assign drive letters to all the remaining primary partitions. These are in the MountMgr database. Once assigned, these drive letters are persistent until changed in the Disk Management console.

Beyond Drive Letters   Beginning with Windows 2000 this limit extends in two ways. First, if you do not have floppy disk drives, you can assign letters A and B to other drives. Second, a pair of new features called drive paths and mounted volumes allow you to avoid using drive letters in some special cases.

These new features are available on both basic and dynamic disks. This means that a partition (basic disk) or volume (dynamic disk) need not have a drive letter assigned at all but can be "connected" to an empty folder on another logical drive. This connection of a partition or volume to a folder is a *mount point*; the path to the partition or volume is a *drive path*, which requires NTFS on the partition or volume hosting the drive path. A partition or volume can have both a drive letter and one or more drive paths. In My Computer or Windows Explorer, the mount point lists along with local folders, but with a drive icon. Figure 9-3 shows a mount point labeled "Q1-2006"; the contents of the mounted volume show in the right-hand pane.

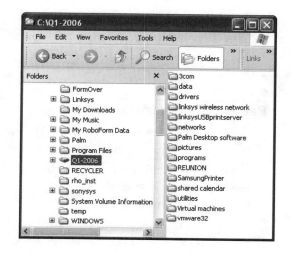

FIGURE 9-3

You can create a
mount point and
drive path in a
Windows 2000
Professional or
greater OS.

Creating a New Partition

With the very large hard disks, often over 250 GB, that come standard in desktop
computers today, we prefer a strategy of dividing the hard disk space into two
partitions. This allows the operating system and applications installed into the
operating system to "own" the system partition, the partition on which the OS is
installed. This also provides a distinct drive or drives that can be devoted purely to
data, making it easier to back up data.

To that end, we plan for our disk space needs ahead of time, deciding on the
portion of the hard disk that should be devoted to the OS and other programs, and
the portion that should be devoted to data. Next, during a clean installation of an
OS, we create a system partition of the size planned.

Immediately after the installation, we perform the essential post-installation tasks.
When these are complete, we create the new partition or partitions and then install
any necessary applications. This order is important if you install applications from
CD-ROM, which is the most common source. If you choose to change the drive letter
of the CD-ROM drive, as shown in Exercise 9-2, it is best to do it before installing
applications, because the setup programs for the applications usually remember the
program installation drive as being the former drive letter of the CD-ROM drive.

Any time you want to modify the application using its installation program, or
the Windows Setup program, it will look for application components at the location
where the source files were located when first installed. If you change the drive
letter of the CD-ROM drive after installing applications from CD, you will have
to manually change the drive path whenever you run an installation program that

requires that remembered location. Exercise 9-2 will walk you through the procedure for changing drive letters and creating a new partition in unallocated space.

EXERCISE 9-2

Creating a New Partition after Installation

This exercise assumes that the disk storage type has not changed from basic since the installation, and that there is unallocated space on the disk.

1. Log on as an Administrator, open the Start menu, right-click My Computer, and select Manage from the context menu. This will open the Computer Management console.

2. In Computer Management, click the Disk Management folder under the Storage node. After a brief delay, the Disk Management snap-in will appear in the right pane of the console.

3. If there is unallocated space remaining on the hard disk, you will see an area labeled "Unallocated" along with the amount of space (see Figure 9-4).

4. Before creating the new partition, change the drive letter of the CD-ROM drive: Right-click on the area labeled "CD-ROM 0" and select Change Drive Letter And Paths from the menu.

5. In the Change Drive Letter And Paths dialog box, select the Change button and then choose a new drive letter for the CD-ROM drive. Click OK, then click Yes in the Confirm box, and keep the Computer Management console open to Disk Management.

6. Right-click in the box labeled "Unallocated," and click New Partition to launch the New Partition Wizard.

7. In the Welcome page of the New Partition Wizard, select the Next button. In the Select Partition Type page, select Primary Partition and click Next. In the Specify Partition Size page, select a partition size that is at least 1 MB smaller than the maximum space. Then click Next.

8. In the Assign Drive Letter page, keep the default drive letter setting (which should now be D:) and click Next.

9. In the Format Partition page, keep the default selection, which will format the drive with NTFS (actually NTFS5), using the Default allocation size (don't change this!), and will name (label) the volume New Volume. Click Next.

10. The Completing The New Partition Wizard page displays a summary of the settings you have selected. Review these settings. If you wish to change any of them, use the Back button to find the page for the setting. Otherwise, click Finish to complete the partitioning.

11. If you watch Disk Management carefully, you will see the unallocated space change to a partition, then the formatting progress will display, and finally it will show as a Healthy volume (see Figure 9-5). Close the Computer Management console when it is complete.

File Management

File management begins with understanding the underlying file system. While most file management tasks remain the same across all the file systems supported by Windows, there are a few features that are not available in all these file systems. Next, learn about files, text file editors, and organizing files into folders in Windows.

File Systems

Windows NT 2000 and Windows XP fully support three file systems: NTFS, FAT16, and FAT32. All three file systems have on-disk components and program code in

FIGURE 9-4

Before creating
a new partition

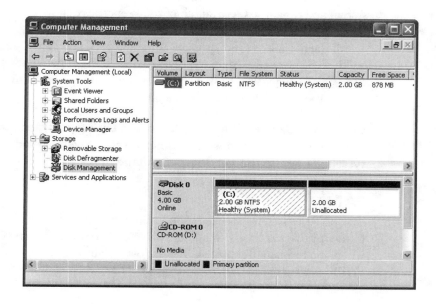

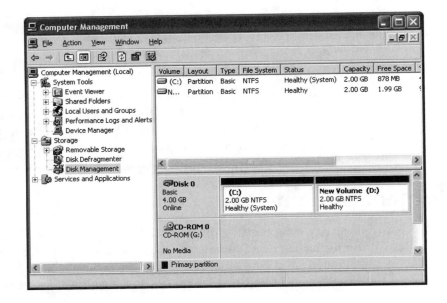

the operating system. In other words, the operating system must have some code in memory that allows it to manage the on-disk components of the file system.

An operating system installs the on-disk components when it formats a disk with a file system. Since you can only format a disk partition with a single operating system at a time, the General tab of the Properties dialog box of a drive will show which file system is on a drive (see Figure 9-6).

All the file systems supported by Windows 2000 and Windows XP (FAT16, FAT32, and NTFS5) can be used on either disk type—basic or dynamic—and on any partition type. Once you partition a basic disk, you may format it with any of these file systems. This is also true of dynamic disk volumes.

on the
Ɉob
Don't confuse disk type with file system. Disk type affects the entire disk underlying the partitions or volumes on the drives. The boundaries of a file system lie within the partition or volume in which it resides.

FAT12

The FAT file system has been around since the early days of MS-DOS. FAT12 is for floppy disks and very small hard drives—too small to worry about today. In fact, when you format a floppy disk in Windows, it automatically formats it with the FAT12 file system.

FIGURE 9-6

The General tab of the Properties of a drive showing NTFS as the file system

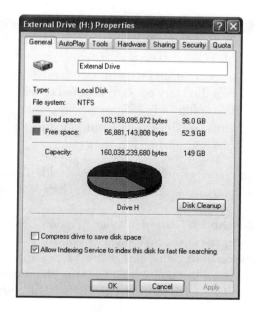

FAT16

FAT16 is the file system used by MS-DOS for hard drives. Windows 95 introduced a modified version of FAT12 and FAT16 called the *virtual file allocation table (VFAT)*. When talking about VFAT in terms of simple file manager, as we are doing here, technicians usually simply call it the "FAT file system."

FAT File System Components   When Windows formats a disk with the FAT file system, it places the FAT file system's three primary components on the disk. These components are the boot record, the FAT table, and the root directory. They reside at the very beginning of the disk, in an area called the *system area*. The space beyond the system area is the data area, which can hold files and subdirectories.

- ■ **Boot Record**   The *boot record* or *boot sector* is the first physical sector on a floppy disk, or the first sector on a partition. The boot sector contains information about the OS used to format the disk, and such file system information as the size of a disk sector, the number of sectors per cluster, and the locations of the FAT table and the root directory.

- ■ **FAT Table**   The *file allocation table (FAT)* is the file system component in which the OS creates a table that serves as a map of where files reside on disk.

■ **Root Directory**   A directory is a place where DOS stores information about files, including a reference to the FAT table so it knows where to find the file's contents on disk. The *root directory* is the top-level directory on the FAT file system, and the only one created during formatting. The entries in the root directory point to files and to the next level of directories. A directory that resides within another directory is a subdirectory. You can continue to create subdirectories within subdirectories, each of which can hold entries for files and subdirectories.

All space beyond the system area holds files and subdirectories. Let's consider how these components are organized and how Windows uses them.

Using the FAT Table   When Windows formats a disk with the FAT file system it divides the entire disk space for one volume (A:, C:, and so on) into equal-sized allocation units called clusters. A *cluster* is the minimum disk space that a file can use, even if the file contains only 14 bytes, and the cluster size is 32,768 bytes. The FAT table has a single entry for each cluster. The entry is a status code, showing whether a cluster is empty, occupied, or damaged. If the entry shows it as occupied, it also indicates whether the file continues in another cluster, by listing the cluster number.

When saving a file to disk, Windows checks the FAT table to find available space and then updates the FAT table entries for the clusters used for the file. When reading a file from disk, DOS reads the FAT table to determine where all the pieces of the file are located.

FAT32

Both Windows 2000 and Windows XP support the FAT32 file system, introduced by Microsoft in a special release of Windows 95. This improved version of the FAT file system can format larger hard disk partitions (up to 2 terabytes) and allocates disk space more efficiently. A FAT32-formatted partition will have a FAT table and root directory, but the FAT table holds 32-bit entries, and there are changes in how it positions the root directory.

The root directory on FAT16 was a single point of failure, since it can only reside in the system area. The FAT32 file system is a bit more flexible about the root directory, allowing the OS to back up the root directory to the data portion of disk, and to use this backup in case the first copy fails.

FAT Cluster Sizes

The numbers 12, 16, and 32 in the names for the different FAT file systems refer to the size of each entry in the FAT table. On a FAT12-formatted floppy disk, each entry is 12 bits long; on a FAT16-formatted drive, each entry is 16 bits long; and on a FAT32-formatted drive, each entry is 32 bits long.

The length of the entry limits the number of entries the FAT table can hold and thus the maximum number of clusters that may be used on a disk. The data space on each disk volume divides up into the number of clusters the FAT table can handle.

FAT16 Clusters   The FAT16 file system is limited to 65,525 clusters. The size of a cluster must be a power of 2 and less than 65,536 bytes (64 KB). This results in a maximum cluster size of 32,768 bytes (32 KB). Multiplying the maximum number of clusters (65,525) by the maximum cluster size (32,768 bytes) equals 2,147,483,658 (2 GB), which is the maximum partition size supported by MS-DOS, Windows 3.*x*, and Windows 9*x*.

Later versions of Windows, including Windows NT, Windows 2000, and Windows XP, have changed these limits slightly and support a maximum cluster size of 65,536 bytes (64 KB). This increases the maximum partition size to 4 GB.

FAT32 Clusters   The FAT32 file system still uses the FAT table and root directory, much as that of FAT16 does, but it addresses certain problems with FAT16. It uses space more efficiently. For instance, whereas FAT16 creates 32 KB clusters on a 2 GB partition, FAT32 uses 4 KB clusters for partitions up to 8 GB.

Because it uses a 32-bit FAT table entry size, FAT32 theoretically supports a partition size of two terabytes (2 TB), but the OS, BIOS, and other hardware limits it to something much smaller than this.

NTFS

Windows 2000 and Windows XP both support an improved version of a file system introduced in Windows NT. This is NTFS, the NT File System. From its beginnings, NTFS has been a much more advanced file system than any form of the FAT file system.

In contrast to the FAT file system, NTFS has a far more sophisticated structure, using a master file table (MFT) that is expandable. This makes the file system adaptable to future changes. In addition, NTFS works like a transaction-based database, in that it sees all file accesses as transactions, and if a transaction is not complete, it will roll back to the last successful transaction. This makes the file system more stable.

In another improved feature, NTFS also avoids saving files to damaged portions of a disk, called bad sectors. Windows will not allow you to format a floppy disk with NTFS, because it requires much more space on disk for its structure than FAT does. This extra space is the file system's overhead. You may format a fairly small hard disk partition with NTFS, but because of the overhead space requirements, the smallest recommended size is 10 MB.

If you choose FAT32 while installing Windows, and you change your mind later, you can convert the file system to NTFS after the installation using the Disk Management console. This is a safe way to convert without deleting any of your existing data. However, you should still take the precaution of backing up the drive before starting the conversion.

NTFS Versions   While we most often simply use the acronym "NTFS" when talking about this file system, Microsoft has released several versions with improvements. NTFS4 (NTFS version 4) is the version that came with Windows NT 4.0. The version of NTFS in Windows 2000 and Windows XP is actually NTFS5. Both versions include file and folder security, and file and folder compression. Microsoft has added several features to NTFS5, some of them fairly technical.

The features of NTFS5 that are most likely to be important to you are the encryption and indexing features. Encryption allows a user to encrypt a file or folder to protect sensitive data. Once a file or folder is encrypted, only someone logged on with the same user account can access it.

The indexing service is part of Windows 2000 and Windows XP and speeds up file searches. If this service is on, indexing of any folder that has the index attribute turned on will occur so that future searches of that folder will be faster.

---

e x a m

watch   On the A+ exams, if the term NTFS is used, assume that the question involves NTFS5, unless it specifically gives the older version or refers to Windows NT 4.0. NTFS5 is the version of NTFS in the Windows versions included in the exam—Windows 2000 and Windows XP.

Security   Finally, NTFS provides folder and file security, which allows you to apply permissions to any file or folder on an NTFS partition. This is one of the most important differences between NTFS and FAT file systems.

The Properties dialog box of each folder and file on a drive formatted with NTFS will have a Security tab (see Figure 9-7) with a Permissions button that brings up a dialog box in which you can assign permissions (Read Only, Full Control, No Access, and so on) controlling user access to the file and folder. Learn more about file and folder security in Chapter 16.

FIGURE 9-7

The Directory
Permissions
dialog box for
a folder

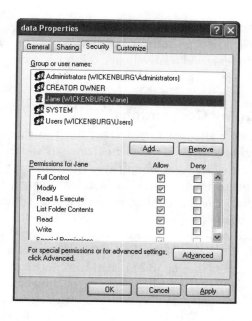

While Windows uses the term folder *and shows a folder icon in the GUI, many of the dialog boxes and messages continue to use the old term* directory *for what we now know as a disk folder. People frequently use these two terms interchangeably. In this book, we generally use* folder *when working in the GUI, and* directory *when working from the command prompt.*

Files

A *file* is information organized as a unit. The author of a file determines just how much information to save in a single file. For instance, the chapter you are reading right now is a single file. We could have chosen to save all of the chapters of this book in a single file, but instead we chose to save them in individual files, because it breaks the information up into more workable "chunks" for us. That's the key to working with information in general—using chunks that you can manage well.

A file saves into a special file on disk called a folder. When you are working in an application, such as a word processor, it will usually have a default folder into which it saves your files, but you can choose to save any file in other folders—you can even create additional folders. You have choices like these when you are working with data files.

As part of managing your files, you'll perform different actions—such as opening, closing, copying, and moving files and folders. File management in the Windows GUI is easy and relatively safe because you can see exactly what files and folders you have selected for a file management operation.

Naming Conventions

MS-DOS and Windows 3.*x* used the 8.3 naming convention, in which the filename could be a maximum of eight characters and the file extension was a maximum of three characters. A *long filename (LFN)* is any file or folder name that breaks the 8.3 file naming convention. Windows now supports LFNs on all file systems on all media, including hard drives, flash drives, optical discs, and even floppy disks.

The directory entries of the FAT file system were built around the 8.3 naming convention. In fact, the directory entries only had room for 8.3 names. Beginning with Windows 95, the FAT file system directory entries were modified to save long filenames (with up to 255 characters, including spaces, which were not allowed in 8.3 filenames) as well as the legacy 8.3 filenames.

When you name a file or folder with a filename that does not comply with this convention, Windows saves both the actual name (as a long filename) and an 8.3 version of the name, called an alias, that consists of the first six 8.3-valid characters, followed by a tilde (~) and a number, beginning with zero (0).

Windows supports long filenames on floppy disks as well as logical drives on hard disks. By default, Windows creates 8.3 aliases for long filenames on both FAT and NTFS partitions.

You can cause problems with this dual filename system if you copy and modify files from the command prompt using the 8.3 filename. This will cause the file to lose its association with the long filename. Then someone working in Windows may not be able to find their long filename files. Be sure to do all your file management in Windows using the GUI rather than the command prompt.

File Attributes

A file attribute is a component of a file or directory entry that determines how an operating system handles the file or directory. In all the variations of the FAT file system supported by Windows the standard file attributes are read-only, archive, system, and hidden. Two other special attributes in all the Windows file systems are volume label, which allows you to give a name to the volume, and directory, which identifies an entry as a directory. The operating system modifies these attributes, as do certain programs such as file backup utilities.

The following are explanations of each of the standard file attributes.

Read-Only Attribute   The read-only attribute ensures that the file or folder will not be modified, renamed, or deleted accidentally. In Windows, if you try to delete a read-only file, you will receive a warning message requiring confirmation.

Archive Attribute   By default, Windows turns on the archive attribute for all files at creation or modification. This marks a file as one that needs backing up. Many backup utilities, including Windows Backup, provide the option to back up only files marked with the archive attribute. A backup program can turn off the archive attribute as it backs up a file. This allows the backup program to do subsequent backups that only back up files with the archive attribute turned on, thus backing up only those files created or modified since the last backup.

System Attribute   The OS, or an application, gives certain files the system attribute automatically, depending on the function. Most system files also get the hidden attribute to keep users from accidentally modifying or deleting them.

Hidden Attribute   A file or folder with the hidden attribute normally will show in My Computer or Windows Explorer, but the Windows Search feature will not list it. If a folder has the hidden attribute, you cannot view the files in the folder using My Computer or Windows Explorer, even if those files are not marked as hidden. However, you can view those files using the Search feature.

Additional Windows File Attributes   The NTFS file system has these original file attributes, listed above, and also additional file attributes. In fact, NTFS saves a file's actual contents as one or more file attributes. The file system allows for future expansion of attributes—making the NTFS file system more expandable.

The General tab of the Properties dialog box for a file or folder will show two of the traditional attributes: read-only and hidden. On an NTFS file or folder the Advanced button will display the status of four attributes: archive, index, compress, and encrypt (see Figure 9-8). Index, compress, and encrypt are special NTFS file attributes. Use the compress attribute on a folder to compress the contents, and use the encrypt attribute to encrypt the contents of a folder. These two attributes are mutually exclusive. You cannot both compress and encrypt, but you can apply one or the other of these attributes to a file or folder.

FIGURE 9-8

The Advanced
attributes

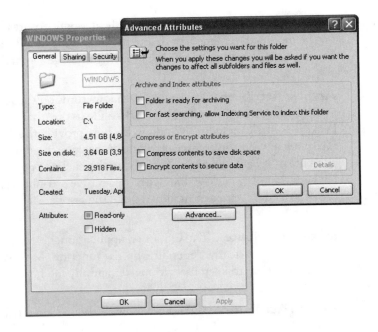

File Types

Windows computers use several file types, including, in broad terms, data files and
program files. Data files contain the data you create with application programs.
Program files (also called binary files) contain programming code (instructions read
by the OS or special interpreters). Program files include those that you can directly
run, such as files with the COM or EXE extension (called executables), and those
that are called up by other programs, such as files with the DLL extension.

Data Files   When it comes to file management, you should only manage data
files. Leave management of program files to the operating system. There are a large
number of data file types. A short list includes

- *Text files,* which most often have the TXT extension
- *Word processing document files* (Microsoft Word and others use the DOC
  extension)
- *Graphic files* (with a variety of extensions, such as BMP, DIB, GIF, JPG,
  and TIF)

- *Database files* (Access uses the MDB extension)
- *Spreadsheet files* (Excel uses the XLS extension)

Program Files   Leave program files where their installation programs place them. Before studying file management of data files, take a brief look at the folder structure created by Windows for the use of the program files belonging to the operating system, add-on components, and applications. They include

- **Documents and Settings**   This folder, located in the root folder of the boot partition, is where Windows 2000 and Windows XP place the personal folders for all users who log on.
- **Windows**   This folder, located in the root folder of the boot partition, is where the Windows operating system is stored. Note that before installing the operating system, the setup program will allow you to give this folder a different name, but we strongly suggest you resist any urge to do this!
- **Program Files**   This folder contains subfolders, where your application programs are typically installed.
- **Fonts**   Here you will find the various fonts installed on the PC. This folder is always a subfolder of the Windows folder and is a special folder.
- **System and System32**   These are subfolders of the Windows folder that are used to store many very important files necessary for the proper operation of Windows. Stay out of these folders unless you are confident that you know what you are doing.
- **Temp**   This is a folder used to temporarily store files, such as those used during the installation of new application programs, and those temporary files created by a program while it is working. This folder often contains out-of-date files left over from an installation operation.

on the
job

The rule for the Temp folder is that any program writing files to it should delete those files when the program is closed. If a program ends abnormally (you tripped over the power cord or the OS hung up), it can't do this important chore. Therefore, it is generally safe to delete files from the Temp folder that are unused in over a week. In practice, we delete all temporary files dated before the last restart.

Hands Off System Files!   *System files* are program files and some special data files that are part of the OS and are very important to the proper operation of Windows.

As you learned in Chapter 7, some are located in the root of drive C:, while others are located in the folder in which Windows is installed. The default name for this folder is WINNT or WINDOWS, depending on the version of Windows. This folder in turn contains many additional folders containing important operating system files.

In Windows 2000 and Windows XP, the default settings for My Computer or Explorer will hide the contents of a folder in which system files and other important files are stored. In Windows XP, if you try to access one of these folders a message will display informing you that these are hidden files (see the illustration). When this occurs, you must take an additional action to view the contents. In Windows 2000, you click a link titled "Show Files"; in XP, you click the words "Show the contents of this folder."

These files are hidden.

This folder contains files that keep your system working properly. You should not modify its contents.

Show the contents of this folder

By default, Windows XP hides the contents of both the root folder and the Windows installation folder, while Windows 2000 hides only the latter. If you decide to make them visible, do not make manual changes to these folders or their contents. Other changes you make to Windows through Control Panel applets and setup programs will alter the contents of these folders.

Some, but not all, files in these folders have the hidden attribute turned on so that Windows hides them, even when you view the folder contents. But when you are studying or troubleshooting an OS, you may want to change this default so that you can see the hidden files. You can change these defaults in My Computer or Windows Explorer if you choose Tools |

e x a m

w a t c h *Hiding the folders in the GUI does not depend on the hidden file attributes. My Computer or Explorer will hide the contents of a folder without regard to the file attributes.*

Folder Options and modify the settings on the View tab. Figure 9-9 shows the settings we use when we want to be able to see all files, including file extensions.

on the
job *Although the default View setting that hides the important operating system files is pretty effective, it does not provide absolute protection for those files. When logged on as an Administrator, you can delete a folder containing those files. You would receive a warning message, but you could choose to ignore the warning.*

Modified View
settings

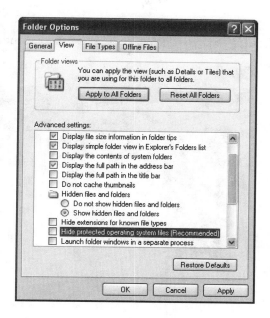

Text File Editors

A type of application called a text editor allows you to create and edit text files using only the simplest of formatting codes (like carriage return, line feed, and end of document codes). A text editor uses only one set of characters and does not use or understand codes for special character fonts or special paragraph formatting.

As a technician or support person, it is helpful to understand text editors and to know how to create and edit text files. The reason is that there are some text files used by the operating system and by certain applications. While these files may not have the standard filename extension (txt) used for text files, you can still use a text editor to view and modify them.

One such file is the BOOT.INI file that you learned about in Chapter 7. This important system file is actually a text file containing startup instructions for Windows. In Chapter 10 you will learn about the contents of this file and how to edit it if required.

Windows comes with two text editors—one, Notepad, is a Windows application. This is the preferred text editor when working in the Windows GUI. Another, Edit, is a DOS application. Compare the two programs, shown next. When you call up Edit in Windows, it is loaded in a text mode window.

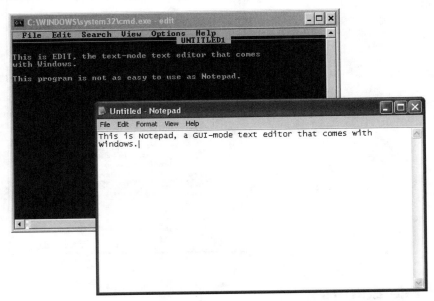

Notepad is a typical Windows GUI application and uses the standard Windows commands and mouse actions. Other applications (WordPad and Microsoft Word) can create and edit text files, but they are primarily word processors, which can create documents with fancy formatting instructions included. To create a text file with a word processor, you must choose to save the file as a text file. Notepad and Edit create only simple text files without the extra formatting.

Organizing Files Using Folders

All information on a computer is stored in files, and typically, you organize those files by separating them into folders containing related files. It's important for you to understand how to organize files and folders properly so that you can easily access important files, and so that you know which files you should not touch. And because even the best file organization won't guarantee that you'll always remember the name of that very important file or even where you saved it, you should practice searching for files.

Any filing system needs a level of organization if it is to be useful. If you use a filing cabinet to hold a number of important documents, most likely you organize those documents into separate file folders and use some sort of alphabetical arrangement of the folders so that you can locate the documents quickly when you need them. Imagine what a difficult time you would have finding your tax-related documents if all year you simply threw everything into a large box and then had to sort through each piece of paper to find the few important ones out of thousands.

In Windows, you do not need to alphabetize your folders; Windows will sort them for you in the GUI. Simply give the folders names that make sense to you. You might simply name a top-level data folder "data." Subfolders below this level should have more meaningful names, perhaps a department name, such as "accounting," or a project or customer name.

As your data files grow in number, you will want to make more folders to organize them more logically. You will soon find that you have created an entire hierarchy of folders. If they are all under one or more top-level folders, this will make it easier to back up. You can select the top folder and have the backup program back up all subfolders and files.

As you work with Windows, you will develop your own filing system. The only caution is to never save data files in the *root folder* (root directory). Oh yes, even on the NTFS file system, we have the notion of the root directory; even though NTFS has a different file system structure on disk. From either the command prompt or the GUI the folder and file organization looks the same across all the file systems. The root folder is at the top level of any drive, and you should never use it for saving data files. In My Computer, when you double-click one of the drive icons, it opens to the root folder, showing the top level.

GUI Techniques

If you are already familiar with Windows GUI techniques and tools for file management, you will be tempted to skip this section. But don't! Take the time to check out the drag-and-drop rules and to practice basic file management tasks.

Mouse Basics   A quick review of mouse usage is in order at this point. A conventional mouse, as well as wheel mice and trackballs, has at least two buttons. Of these two buttons, one is the *primary mouse button*. This is the button used for most mouse-clicking operations and is most often the left button. By default, a single-click with this button will select an object, while a double-click will open a folder, expand a list, launch a program, or open a data file assigned to additional functions.

The *secondary mouse button* is usually the right mouse button, in which case a single-click on most objects causes a context menu to pop up. A right-click and drag will also cause a menu to pop up so that you can select the action of the drag operation.

You can switch the mouse buttons by using the Mouse applet in Control Panel.

Drag-and-Drop Dragging is a basic GUI action in Windows accomplished by selecting a screen object and then, while pressing and holding down a mouse button, moving the mouse to where you want the object to be placed. When you release the mouse button, the object is "dropped" or positioned at the new location. People call this complete operation drag-and-drop. When you perform drag-and-drop on folders and files in Windows Explorer, certain rules apply:

- Pressing CTRL while dragging results in a copy, meaning that the original file remains in the source location, and a copy is made in the target location. This is regardless of the location of the source and target locations (same drive or different drive).

- Dragging an item to another drive also performs a copy of the item.

- Pressing and holding down SHIFT while pressing the left mouse button and dragging a file or folder to another driver results in a move, meaning that, at the end of the operation, the file or folder only exists in the target (destination) location. It is no longer in the source location.

- To actually move a program, you must log on as an Administrator. Windows treats program files differently than data files: when you drag a program file to a new folder, Windows does not move or copy the program file. It creates a shortcut to the program instead.

- Dragging a file or folder while pressing and holding the secondary (often the right) mouse button allows you to choose whether to move, copy, or create a shortcut to the file in the new folder. This is a great technique for those of us who cannot remember which action copies and which action moves.

EXERCISE 9-3

Managing Files and Folders

In this exercise, you will practice some common file management tasks. First you will create a folder, and then you will copy, move, and delete files. Finally, you will open a file from its shortcut and edit it in Notepad.

1. Open the My Documents folder.

2. Position your cursor over an empty area of the Contents pane (right pane) of the window and then right-click. In the context menu, select New | Folder. Name the folder **data1**. Repeat this step to create a folder named **data2**.

3. Double-click the data1 folder to open it, then right-click the Contents pane, and select New | Text Document. Name the document **report1.txt**.

4. If the folder hierarchy is not visible in the left pane of the window, change the view to folder view by clicking the Folder icon on the toolbar.

5. Drag the file report1.txt from the Contents pane, and drop it on the data2 folder in the Folders pane. This moves the file, so that it no longer exists in the data1 folder, as shown in Figure 9-10.

6. Open the data2 folder and confirm that report1 moved to this folder.

7. Press and hold the right mouse button while dragging the file back to the data1 folder. When you release the mouse button over the data1 folder, a context menu pops up that gives you the choice of copying, moving, or creating a shortcut to the file. Select the option to create a shortcut.

8. Expand the data1 folder and double-click the **shortcut to report1.txt**. This is a shortcut to a text file, so double-clicking it causes Notepad to open, because that is the program associated with text files.

9. Now type a few sentences describing what happens when you drag a file from one folder to another folder on the same drive. Then save the file by selecting File | Save. Exit from Notepad.

10. Open the data2 folder and double-click the report1 file. The sentence you typed should be in the file. Exit from Notepad.

FIGURE 9-10

The report1.tif file moved to the data2 folder

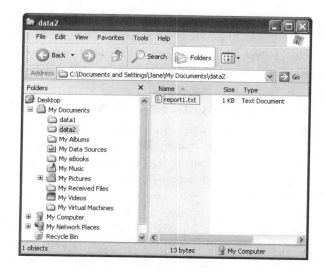

Searching for Files   Windows has a Search utility you can open from the Start menu or from the Search button in My Computer or Windows Explorer. In Windows XP, Search expands to allow you to search for almost anything you want on your computer, and on any network to which it is attached—even on the Internet. The list of items expands to include people, files in online tape backup storage, various types of files, help topics, and more.

Use the size option on a regular basis to find space-hogging files on your drives. For instance, search for files of at least 10,000 KB and then browse through them. Are there large zipped files that you no longer need? Media files you no longer care to see or hear? Delete all the unwanted files. This is a handy "tidying up" technique. This will find files that the Disk Cleanup utility described in Chapter 8 can miss.

The Search utility is a great time-saver for those of us with many drives attached to our computers who occasionally forget where we saved a file (see Figure 9-11).

One of the best uses for Search is to help you find a file when you do not know the filename. As long as you can think of a fairly unique word, phrase, or even number that is within the file, you can locate it using Search.

File Management at the Command Prompt

We strongly suggest that under normal circumstances you not do file management from the command prompt. When doing file management at the command prompt you can only use text-mode commands that give you very little feedback, and a minor typo can result in disaster—often without a clue that you have harmed critical files.

However, as a support person, you might find yourself working at a special command-line interface—either the Recovery Console or Safe Mode with Command Prompt. Use these solely to recover from serious damage to the OS. Therefore, it is valuable for you to have more practice working at the command line. If you have not worked at the command prompt, learn more about it now, and

FIGURE 9-11

The Search utility will allow you to search all local hard drives at once.

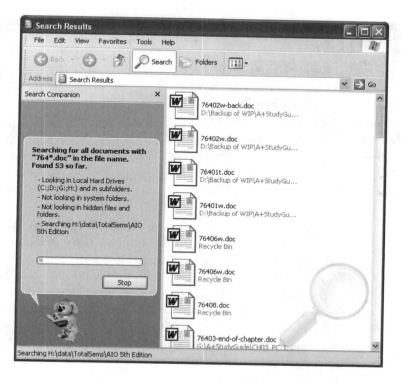

use what you learn when you work with the Recovery Console and Safe Mode with command prompt in Chapter 10.

Background: The Command Prompt in Windows 9x

In Windows 9x, the command prompt that you can select from Start | Programs runs in a DOS virtual machine. A *virtual machine* is a software simulation of a computer—it's a computer within a computer, residing entirely in memory. A *DOS virtual machine* is a virtual machine that is running the DOS operating system.

To start this type of command prompt, you can use Start | Run and then type **command** in the Run box. This has the same effect as the Start | Programs method in Windows 9x, because both call up the DOS command shell (COMMAND.COM), which in turn causes Windows to launch a DOS virtual machine.

The choice from the Programs menu in Windows 98 is MS-DOS Prompt. This is a subtle hint that the program you launch is MS-DOS running in a virtual machine in Windows 98. When you run a program that will only run in MS-DOS, Windows creates a DOS virtual machine in memory. Then, the DOS program can run as if it were running on a real DOS computer.

The Command Prompt in Windows 2000 and Windows XP   In Windows NT, Windows 2000, and Windows XP, the choice you see when you browse through the Start menu hierarchy is command prompt, which reflects a significant difference between these OSs and the Windows 9x OSs. The program that launches when you select the Command Prompt option from the Start menu hierarchy is CMD.EXE. This offers you a full 32-bit, character-mode command prompt that is not a DOS virtual machine with the limits of DOS and doesn't take up nearly as much space in memory when opened.

Figure 9-12 shows the differences between the two methods for opening a command prompt. The command prompt at the top left was opened with Start | Run | COMMAND, which creates a DOS virtual machine, while the command prompt on the right was opened with the Command Prompt option found in the Accessories menu in Windows XP. Notice the lack of long filename support in the DOS virtual machine and the differences in version information seen at the top of each window. In addition, in the CMD version, you can use the UP ARROW key to browse through the list of commands you have entered during that session. This capability is not on by default in the MS-DOS command prompt. Learn more about the Windows command prompt in Exercise 9-4.

FIGURE 9-12

Compare the two methods for opening a command prompt.

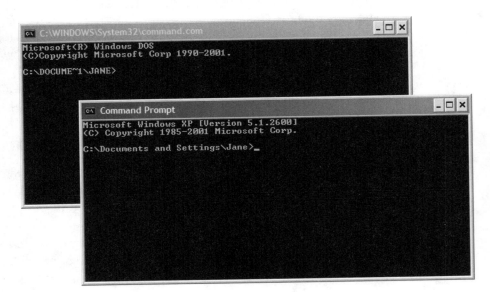

on the
job

From a command prompt you can launch any program that will run in Windows. If the program is a character-mode program, it will run within the command-line interface. If written for DOS, a virtual machine will launch in which to run the program, but you will still remain in the Command Prompt window. If the program is a 32-bit GUI program, it will launch in a separate window.

Creating and Deleting Directories   There are two commands for creating and deleting directories at the command prompt. They are MD (Make Directory) and RD (Remove Directory). Use the DIR (Directory) command to view listings of files and directories. Move around the directory hierarchy at the command prompt using the CD (Change Directory) command. Use two dots together (..) to indicate the directory immediately above the current directory. You can use these in many command-line commands. For instance, if you only want to move up one level, type **cd ..** and press ENTER.

Wildcards can be used from the command prompt. The most useful one is the asterisk (*). Use the asterisk to represent one or more characters in a filename or extension. For instance, enter the command **dir *.exe** to see a listing of all files in the current directory ending with "exe." Using *.* will select all files and directories.

When you are working at the command prompt, the previous commands and messages remain on the screen until they scroll off. To clear this information off the screen, use the clear screen command (CLS). When you want to copy files, there are two basic commands to learn. The one is COPY, which is a very, very old command that does not understand directories. To use this command on files in different directories, you must enter the path to the directory or directories in the command. It helps to first make either the source directory or target directory current before using this command.

The second copy command to know is the XCOPY command. This is a more advanced command that understands directories. In fact, you can tell XCOPY to copy the contents of a directory simply by giving the directory name. The simple syntax for each of these commands is *command from_source to_destination*.

Exercise 9-4 demonstrates the use of these commands as it walks you through creating and removing a directory. You will also move around the directory structure and copy and delete files.

EXERCISE 9-4

Managing Directories and Files at the Command Prompt

Practice working with directories and files from the command prompt. This exercise requires the folders and files you created in Exercise 9-3.

1. Open the command prompt.
2. At the command prompt, type **dir** and press ENTER. A listing of files and directories within the directory displays. If they scrolled off the screen, type the command again with the pause switch: **dir /p**.
3. Type the clear screen command, **cls**, and press ENTER to clear the screen.
4. Change to the My Documents directory by typing **cd my documents** and pressing ENTER.
5. Create a new directory in the MY DOCUMENTS directory. At the command prompt type **md testdata** and press ENTER.
6. Enter the command **dir /ad** to confirm that it created the new folder within the current folder. The switch /ad will only display directories.
7. To make the data2 directory current, type **cd data2** and press ENTER.
8. Copy the report1.txt file to the TESTDATA directory. Type **copy report1 .txt ..\testdata**.
9. Use the more advanced XCOPY command to copy the contents of the DATA1 folder into TESTDATA. Type **xcopy ..\data1 ..\testdata** and press ENTER. Figure 9-13 shows Steps 5–9.
10. Change the current directory to the My Documents directory, which is the parent directory of the data1, data2, and testdata directories. To do this type **cd ..** and press ENTER.
11. Use the DIR command to view the contents of testdata. Type **dir testdata** and press ENTER.
12. To delete the TESTDATA folder, first move into that folder. Type **cd testdata** and press ENTER.
13. Now delete all of the files within that folder. Type **del *.*** and press ENTER.
14. Now the TESTDATA directory is empty, but it is the current directory, and you cannot delete the current directory. Move out of the directory. Type **cd ..** and press ENTER.

15. Now remove the directory. Type **rd testdata** and press ENTER.
16. Confirm that it removed the TESTDATA folder. Type **dir /ad** and press ENTER.
17. Close the Command Prompt window.

Windows Utilities

Windows comes with many utility programs. These are specialized programs that support people and technicians use to configure, optimize, and troubleshoot Windows and networks. Up to this point in the book we have introduced you to some of these utilities, such as Device Manager, Disk Defragmenter, and Disk Management. We even consider the Readiness Analyzer and Upgrade Advisor to be utilities.

FIGURE 9-13

Creating a directory and copying files at the command prompt

SCENARIO & SOLUTION

I want a file moved to a different folder on the same drive, and I do not want to leave a copy of it in the source location. How do I do this?	Using the primary mouse button, drag the file from the source folder to the destination folder. This is a move.
How can I place a copy of a file in a different directory on the same hard drive, leaving the original file in the source location?	Press the CTRL key while using the primary mouse button to drag the file from the source location to the target. The file will remain in the source location and a copy put into the target location.
I can never remember the file copy and move rules. What is one easy drag-and-drop operation that will work for either a copy or move?	Press and hold the secondary mouse button while dragging a file or folder, and when you reach the destination, release the button and select the action you desire from the pop-up menu.

In this section we will look at some of the command-line and GUI utilities that come with Windows. As you continue through the book, you will encounter more of these, where appropriate. In Chapter 10 you will learn certain command-line utilities used in troubleshooting problems in Windows. In the chapters on networking you will use utilities for testing network configuration and connectivity.

Command-Line Utilities

You have already learned to use the most common file management utilities at the DOS prompt. There are a few more used for disk management. Some of these commands have strong roots in MS-DOS but have been updated and modified to run from a Windows command prompt. Some may be traditional DOS commands such as DIR, XCOPY, ATTRIB, DEFRAG, and FORMAT. There are also specialized command-line commands, such as the IPCONFIG and PING commands that you will use in Chapter 12 to view network configuration and to test connectivity, respectively.

One of the handiest commands when you are working at the command prompt is the HELP command, which, when entered alone at the command prompt, gives a list and brief description of commands. A handy trick for a command that sends a great deal of information to the screen, like the HELP command, is the use of the pipe (|) and the MORE filter. Exercise 9-5 will demonstrate the use of the HELP command, the pipe, the MORE filter, and the /? switch that can be used for individual commands. You will also use the DEFRAG command.

EXERCISE 9-5

Working at the Command Prompt in Windows

In this exercise, you will run some simple file management and disk maintenance commands from the command prompt.

1. Open the command prompt.

2. Type the HELP command with the MORE filter: **help | more**, and press ENTER to display a list of commands. As you finish reading each page, press SPACEBAR to display a new page. Continue until you are finished. If you wish to end without viewing all the pages, press the CTRL-C key combination.

3. Check out the syntax for the DEFRAG command by using the /? switch. Type **defrag /?** and press ENTER.

4. Now enter the command to run an analysis of drive (volume) C:. To do this, type **defrag c: -a** and press ENTER. This command returns the analysis results much faster than the GUI version of this program (see Figure 9-14).

5. Close the command prompt.

FIGURE 9-14   Run the DEFRAG command to quickly analyze a disk.

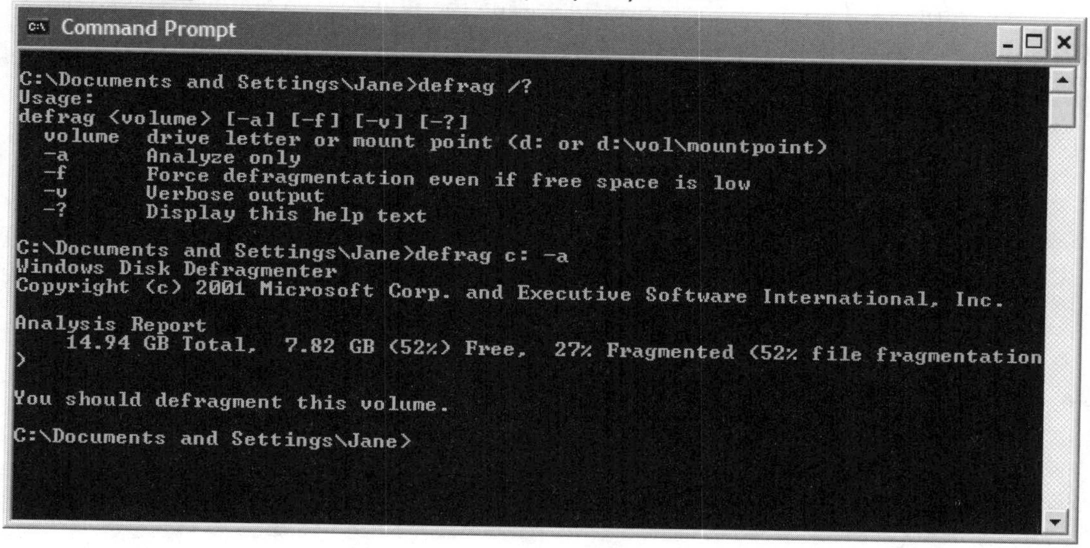

```
Command Prompt                                                    _ □ ✕

C:\Documents and Settings\Jane>defrag /?
Usage:
defrag <volume> [-a] [-f] [-v] [-?]
   volume   drive letter or mount point (d: or d:\vol\mountpoint)
   -a       Analyze only
   -f       Force defragmentation even if free space is low
   -v       Verbose output
   -?       Display this help text

C:\Documents and Settings\Jane>defrag c: -a
Windows Disk Defragmenter
Copyright (c) 2001 Microsoft Corp. and Executive Software International, Inc.

Analysis Report
    14.94 GB Total,  7.82 GB (52%) Free,   27% Fragmented (52% file fragmentation
>

You should defragment this volume.

C:\Documents and Settings\Jane>
```

As you can see, these programs quickly perform a task and then are gone from memory. Other commands, such as EDIT, may start programs that we call applications, which stay in memory, have a user interface, and allow us to do work, such as creating and modifying text or word processing documents, or creating, modifying, and manipulating data with a database.

In addition to these methods of working at the command prompt from within Windows, Windows 9x, Windows 2000, and Windows XP have startup options that allow you to start at a command prompt. Accessing the command prompt in this way is valuable for troubleshooting startup problems. You will have a chance to look at the startup options in Chapter 10.

The Dangers of FDISK and Other DOS Utilities

Some DOS utilities are included in Windows 9x but not in other versions of Windows, either because they don't run in these versions, or because they are considered too harmful to be included. An example of such a program is the FDISK utility, a disk-partitioning program. It cannot run in Windows NT, Windows 2000, Windows XP, or Windows Server 2003, but it is the only disk partitioning tool included with Windows 95 and Windows 98.

Many of us have Windows 98 Startup disks for some troubleshooting tasks. In fact, you can boot up a computer and run FDISK to remove or create hard drive partitions. This is also the danger. FDISK on the Windows 98 Startupdisk is an old partitioning program, and unless you understand how it works, the best time to partition a hard disk for any current version of Windows is when you run Windows Setup to install the OS. Figure 9-15 shows the main menu of the FDISK program.

CHKDSK   The CHKDSK command is the text-mode version of the GUI error-checking program you can access from the Tools page of the Properties dialog for a disk. It checks disks for physical and logical errors.

Running CHKDSK without the /F parameter is like running DEFRAG with the –A parameter—it only analyzes the disk. If errors are found, rerun the command and include the /F parameter. If the volume is in use (as is always the case with drive C:), you will see a message asking if you would like to schedule the volume to be checked during the next system restart. Press Y and ENTER to schedule this.

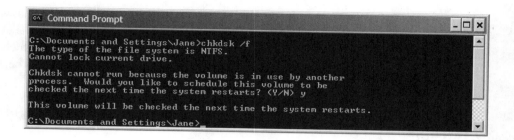

As a technician you will hear about a program called SCANDISK, which was part of Windows 9x. This disk error-checking program is no longer a part of Windows, although CHKDSK has much of the functionality of SCANDISK. There are also third-party utilities that perform disk error checking and repair and are easier to use than CHKDSK.

ATTRIB The ATTRIB command lets you view and manipulate certain file attributes. These attributes are read-only, archive, system, and hidden. As a technician you may encounter a situation in which you need this command.

One scenario is that you may want to modify a file that has the read-only attribute turned on. If this attribute is on you can open and read the file, and even modify it, but you will not be able to save it with the new changes.

FIGURE 9-15

The main menu
of the FDISK
utility

```
                              FDISK Options

    Current fixed disk drive: 1

    Choose one of the following:

    1. Create DOS partition or Logical DOS Drive
    2. Set active partition
    3. Delete partition or Logical DOS Drive
    4. Display partition information


    Enter choice: [1]




    Press Esc to exit FDISK
```

The solution is to turn off the attribute, and this is something that you would normally do in the GUI by deselecting the read-only attribute in the Properties dialog box of the file. However, you may encounter situations in which you need to do this from a command line. Therefore, practice working with the ATTRIB command in Exercise 9-6.

EXERCISE 9-6

Using the ATTRIB Command

Use the ATTRIB command from the command prompt to view and modify attributes.

1. Open the command prompt.
2. Type **attrib** and press ENTER. The list of files will display with one or more letters to the left of the filename. Each letter represents a "turned on" (or set) attribute: R=read-only, A=archive, S=system, and H=hidden.
3. Select a file that only has the archive attribute turned on and turn it off. Type **attrib** *filename* **-a** and press ENTER.
4. Run the ATTRIB command as you did in Step 2 and confirm that the attribute turned off.
5. Turn the archive attribute on. Type **attrib** *filename* **+a** and press ENTER.
6. Close the command prompt.

The one problem may be permissions, which you will learn about in Chapter 16. You may not have sufficient permissions to modify the attributes on a file. For now, remember that you will need to log on as Administrator, or some other member of the Administrator's group, to change the attributes on certain protected files.

FORMAT The FORMAT command will allow you to format a hard drive or floppy disk from a command prompt. Once again, the preferred way is to format from the GUI, where you are less likely to make an error when doing this. The correct GUI tools are the Disk Management console for formatting a hard drive, and My Computer or Windows Explorer for formatting a floppy disk.

Figure 9-16 shows the command for formatting the D: drive. Notice that it does not proceed until you press Y. Press N to cancel. This command will wipe out the contents of the drive. Using the proper syntax, you can format a hard drive with any of the file systems supported by Windows for the target disk.

The FORMAT command gives you a chance to change your mind.

```
C:\WINDOWS\system32\cmd.exe - format d:
Microsoft Windows XP [Version 5.1.2600]
(C) Copyright 1985-2001 Microsoft Corp.

C:\Documents and Settings\Jane>format d:
The type of the file system is NTFS.

WARNING, ALL DATA ON NON-REMOVABLE DISK
DRIVE D: WILL BE LOST!
Proceed with Format (Y/N)?
```

Windows GUI Utilities

There are a number of Windows GUI utilities—we have already explored some in this book. In the area of file management, the backup program NTBACKUP deserves mention here. We will introduce other important GUI utilities later in this book. They include MSCONFIG.EXE, Event Viewer, Task Manager, and System Restore, which you will learn about in Chapter 10. We will introduce Remote Desktop in Chapter 12.

Backing Up Data with NTBACKUP

The data created and stored on computers is far more valuable than the computer hardware and software used to create and store the data. This is true for individuals as well as organizations. For this reason, your backup strategies, the hardware and software used for backup, and the actual habit of backing up are critical to maintaining both data and computers.

In case of the accidental destruction of data and/or the disks containing the data, having a recent backup on removable media can be the difference between personal or professional disaster and the relatively minor inconvenience of taking the time to restore the data. Therefore, most versions of Windows include backup programs. The executable name of the backup program that comes with Windows NT, Windows 2000, and Windows XP Professional is NTBACKUP.EXE. This is also referred to as the Backup Utility and Windows Backup.

Running NTBACKUP opens the Backup or Restore Wizard. You can access it through a shortcut in the System Tools folder, or from Start | Run using the executable name NTBACKUP. The Windows NT version only worked with tape backup systems, and on a rather short list of compatible tape backup systems at that.

Since Windows NT, each version of Windows has improved the backup program—both in capabilities and in the backup media it will use. It will now back up to a tape drive, to a local hard disk, or to a network location that is available as a drive letter (a "mapped" drive).

NTBACKUP is available in Windows 2000 and in Windows XP Professional. By default, it is not included in Windows XP Home. If you find yourself working with Windows XP Home Edition, you may still install Windows Backup if you have the distribution CD.

NTBACKUP and its installation program are located under VALUEADD\MSFT\ NTBACKUP. Simply launch the installation program located in this directory (it has an MSI extension), and NTBACKUP will be installed. If your computer came preinstalled with XP Home, and you do not have the distribution CD, search for this folder on your hard drive, because it may be there, along with the other distribution files.

Also, some excellent third-party backup programs offer additional features and capabilities.

SCENARIO & SOLUTION

I need to back up my data from my Windows XP computer, but I do not have a tape backup system. What can I do?	A tape backup system is not required to use the Backup Utility in Windows XP. If you have the space on another drive on your computer, or on a networked server, you can back up to one of those locations.
I want to turn off the read-only attribute on the BOOT.INI file, but every time I try, I get an error message stating something about permissions. What can I do?	This message means that you do not have sufficient permissions to change this file. You need to log on as Administrator, or another member of the Administrators group, to modify this file. However, do not make any changes to the BOOT.INI file until you are sure you know what you are doing. You will learn more about it in Chapter 10.
I have Windows XP Home Edition, and I cannot find the Windows Backup Utility. What can I do?	If you have the Windows XP Home distribution CD, look in the VALUEADD\MSFT\NTBACKUP folder, where you will find the installation program (it has an MSI extension). Run this program to install Windows Backup.

CERTIFICATION SUMMARY

As a computer support professional, you need to arm yourself with knowledge of operating systems disk and file management. Disk management in Windows 2000 and Windows XP begins with understanding both basic and dynamic storage types. Dynamic disks give you features you would normally use on network servers. Technicians working with Windows desktop PCs should focus on creating the primary and extended partitions on basic disks. Primary partitions are the preferred partition type, and one is required for booting the operating system.

Most file management tasks remain the same across all the file systems supported by Windows. NTFS is the preferred file system for Windows 2000 and Windows XP, providing more advanced file storage features and file and folder security. You should perform file management from the GUI tools, such as My Computer and Windows Explorer, but a technician should be familiar with command-line file management methods for certain troubleshooting scenarios. Learn about file naming conventions, file attributes, file types, and text file editors. Organize files into folders, and learn techniques and rules for moving and copying files in the GUI.

Windows comes with a number of utilities, specialized programs used to configure, optimize, and troubleshoot Windows and networks. A short list of GUI utilities includes Device Manager, Disk Defragmenter, Disk Management, Readiness Analyzer, Upgrade Advisor, NTBACKUP, MSCONFIG, Event Viewer, Task Manager, and System Restore. We introduced some of these earlier in the book and some in this chapter, but you will explore others later in the book.

Command-line utilities also have their place in Windows. Just a few of these include DIR, XCOPY, ATTRIB, DEFRAG, FORMAT, IPCONFIG, PING, and HELP.

✓ TWO-MINUTE DRILL

Here are some of the key points covered in Chapter 9.

Disk Management

❑ Disk management in Windows 2000 and Windows XP begins with the underlying storage type: basic or dynamic.

❑ Dynamic disks have features not available on basic disks; these features are for use on network server computers, not desktop computers, which are the focus of this book and the A+ exams.

❑ Basic disks use the same partition table used by DOS, Windows 3.*x*, Windows 9.*x*, and Windows NT.

❑ A basic disk can have up to four partitions. Either all four partitions can be primary, or the disk can have a combination of up to three primary and one extended partition.

❑ A primary partition has a single drive letter assigned to it, while you can divide an extended partition into multiple logical drives, each with a drive letter.

❑ A PC with one or more basic disks must have at least one primary partition in order to boot Windows.

❑ Windows Setup will create a basic disk with a primary, active (bootable) partition and format the partition with a file system.

❑ After installing Windows, use Disk Management to create or modify additional partitions and to format hard drive partitions.

File Management

❑ Most file management tasks remain the same across all the file systems available in Windows 2000 and Windows XP: FAT12, FAT16, FAT32, and NTFS.

❑ Of these file systems, NTFS is the preferred file system because it works with larger hard drive partitions, is a more stable file system, and offers file and folder security that is not available in the FAT file systems.

❏ Knowing the naming conventions (8.3 and long filenames), common file extensions, and file types is important to file management in Windows.

❏ Windows supports the traditional FAT file attributes of read-only, archive, system, and hidden. It also supports additional file attributes in NTFS, including index, compress, and encrypt.

❏ Never move program files from their folders in Windows. Most users should manage only data files.

❏ By default, Windows hides system files from view in My Computer or Windows Explorer. This does not depend on the hidden file attribute, and you can change it through the View page in the Folder Options dialog box.

❏ You can use text file editors to modify certain text files used by Windows and other programs.

❏ Use My Computer or Windows Explorer to organize data files into folders containing related files.

❏ Learn to use the Windows Search utility to locate misplaced files.

❏ Do not do normal file management from the Command Prompt, but instead familiarize yourself with command-line file management commands for use in extreme troubleshooting scenarios.

Windows Utilities

❏ Windows includes a variety of command-line utilities, some for simple file management, but many others as well. Display a list of command-line utilities with the HELP command.

❏ Command-line disk management utilities include DEFRAG and CHKDSK. FDISK was the partitioning tool that came with DOS and Windows 9x. You can run this from a Windows 9x startup disk, but it is rarely needed now. It is better to partition a disk for Windows 2000 and Windows XP using the Setup program or Disk Management console.

❏ Use the ATTRIB utility to view and modify file attributes.

❏ The FORMAT command will allow you to format a hard disk or floppy disk from the Command Prompt.

❏ NTBACKUP is a backup utility that comes with Windows 2000 and Windows XP.

SELF TEST

The following questions will help you measure your understanding of the material presented in this chapter. Read all of the choices carefully because there might be more than one correct answer. Choose all correct answers for each question.

Disk Management

1. Which disk storage type should you use on a typical Windows desktop PC?
   A. Dynamic
   B. Basic
   C. Primary
   D. Extended

2. Which of the following describes a partition from which Windows can boot?
   A. Primary extended
   B. Active extended
   C. Primary active
   D. Simple extended

3. Which is the tool for creating a partition after installing Windows 2000 or Windows XP?
   A. My Computer
   B. FDISK
   C. Disk Defragmenter
   D. Disk Management

4. How many logical drives are on a typical primary partition?
   A. One
   B. Two
   C. Three
   D. Up to 24

5. What is the partition size limit for the FAT16 file system in Windows XP?
   A. 2 terabytes
   B. 16 exabytes
   C. 2 GB
   D. 4 GB

File Management

6. Which file system supports file and folder security?
   A. FAT12
   B. NTFS
   C. FAT16
   D. FAT32

7. Which file system can you format onto a primary partition? Select only one answer.
   A. NTFS
   B. FAT16
   C. FAT32
   D. All three file systems

8. When you format a floppy disk from within Windows, you normally place which file system on the disk?
   A. FAT16
   B. NTFS
   C. FAT12
   D. FAT32

9. Which of the following file attributes cannot be changed in a file's Properties dialog box?
   A. Read-only
   B. Archive
   C. System
   D. Hidden

10. A user calls with a question: "Several ordinarily hidden files are showing up in My Computer without the warning message." What do you tell her?
   A. Turn on the hidden attribute to make them hidden in the GUI.
   B. The hidden files should be moved to the Recycle Bin.
   C. Hide the files in the GUI by selecting the appropriate option in the My Computer | View menu.
   D. She must be mistaken, hidden files cannot be viewed in My Computer.

11. Which of the following procedures should you use to compress a folder in Windows?
   A. Select the Compress option in Windows Backup.
   B. In the folder's Properties dialog box, select Advanced, and then select the Compress option.

    C. Use the Compress Selected Files option in Disk Management.

    D. Copy the files into the Compressed folder.

12. Which file system supports file compression and encryption?

    A. FAT32

    B. NTFS4

    C. FAT16

    D. NTFS5

13. During Windows XP installation you selected FAT32 as your file system, but after learning about NTFS, you would like to change the file system to NTFS. How can you safely do this?

    A. It is not possible to do this without losing data.

    B. Use the Windows 9x FDISK program.

    C. Convert from within Disk Management.

    D. Use the Convert tool found in System Tools.

14. Which of the following can you use for managing files and folders?

    A. The Display applet in Control Panel

    B. Notepad

    C. My Computer

    D. Disk Management

15. Which of the following best describes the type of files you should not move, delete, edit, or try to manage directly?

    A. Text

    B. Spreadsheet

    C. Program

    D. Data

16. What is a good technique to use if you have trouble remembering which drag-and-drop action moves a file and which action copies a file?

    A. Run XCOPY from the command prompt.

    B. Press SHIFT/DELETE.

    C. Press the primary mouse button while dragging a file.

    D. Press the secondary mouse button while dragging a file.

17. What should you do if you have forgotten where you saved a file?

    A. Use the Search utility.

    B. Use Windows Help.

C. Record file locations on paper.

D. Save all data files in the root folder.

Windows Utilities

18. What command-line command will list the command-line commands and a brief description?

A. DIR

B. HELP

C. PING

D. IPCONFIG

19. What is the correct syntax (command plus switch combination) that will analyze drive C:, looking for file fragmentation, without changing anything on the drive?

A. dir /a

B. help | more

C. defrag c: −a

D. defrag a:

20. What disk error-checking program can you run from the command prompt to do a quick analysis of the disk for physical and logical errors?

A. CHKDSK

B. DEFRAG

C. SCANDISK

D. ATTRIB

LAB QUESTION

You were asked to help the agents in a real estate brokerage firm organize their data files on their new Windows XP computers. You have talked to the agents and determined the applications they use and the files they will create with each. You have created a list of the applications the agents use and the business functions of the data they create with each application. You will create a standard folder hierarchy for use on all the agents' computers.

Application	Business Function(s)
Microsoft Access	Client list database Contractor list database
Microsoft Word	Introductory letters Proposal presentations Offer presentations
PowerPoint	Listing brochures Self-marketing brochures

1. Using this list, design a file management strategy for the agents that will be logical to use and that will make the backup process easier for them. Write a description and justification of this design to present to them.

2. Using your lab computer, create the folders that will be required to fulfill your design.

SELF TEST ANSWERS

Disk Management

1. ☑ **B.** Basic is the disk storage type you should use on a typical Windows desktop PC.
☒ **A**, dynamic, is incorrect because this disk type is more suited for a network server.
C, primary, is incorrect because this is a partition type, not a disk storage type. **D**, extended, is incorrect because this is a partition type, not a disk storage type.

2. ☑ **C.** Primary active describes a partition from which Windows can boot.
☒ **A**, primary extended, is incorrect because it describes two different partition types, not the partition type, primary, marked as active. **B**, active extended, is incorrect because you cannot mark an extended partition as active; only a primary partition can be marked as active. **D**, simple extended, is incorrect because it describes a partition from which Windows cannot boot (and "simple extended" is not a term that is normally used).

3. ☑ **D.** Disk Management is the tool used for creating a partition after installing Windows 2000 or Windows XP.
☒ **A**, My Computer, is incorrect because this is not a tool for creating a partition. **B**, FDISK, is incorrect because this partitioning utility does not run in Windows 2000 or Windows XP. **C**, Disk Defragmenter, is incorrect because this is a tool for defragmenting files on a drive, not for creating partitions.

4. ☑ **A.** One is the number of logical drives on a typical primary partition.
☒ **B**, two, **C**, three, and **D**, up to 24, are all incorrect because a primary partition can only have one drive letter assigned to it.

5. ☑ **D.** 4 GB is the partition size limit for the FAT16 file system in Windows XP.
☒ **A**, 2 terabytes, is incorrect because this is the partition size limit for FAT32 under Windows XP. **B**, 16 exabytes, is incorrect because this is the partition size limit for NTFS under Windows XP. **C**, 2 GB, is incorrect because this is the partition size limit for FAT16 under DOS and Windows 9x.

File Management

6. ☑ **B.** NTFS is the file system that supports file and folder security
☒ **A**, FAT12, **C**, FAT16, and **D**, FAT32, are incorrect because they do not support file and folder security.

7. ☑ **D.** All three file systems is correct because any of these can format a primary partition, as long as it is not too large for the file system.
☒ **A**, NTFS, **B**, FAT16, and **C**, FAT32, are individual and not the correct answer, even

though all of them can be formatted onto a primary partition. However, none of these alone is the full answer, and the question specified that you should select only one answer.

8. ☑ **C.** FAT12 is the file system Windows will apply when it formats a floppy disk.
   ☒ **A,** FAT16, **B,** NTFS, and **D,** FAT32, are all incorrect. All of them take up more room on the floppy disk than FAT12, with NTFS taking up the greatest amount by far. FAT16 and FAT32 take up more room than FAT12 because they have larger FAT tables.

9. ☑ **C.** System is the file attribute you cannot change in the file's Properties dialog box.
   ☒ **A,** read-only, **B,** archive, and **D,** hidden, can all be changed in the file's Properties dialog box.

10. ☑ **C.** Hide the files in the GUI by selecting the appropriate option in the My Computer | View menu.
   ☒ **A,** Turn on the hidden file attribute to make them hidden in the GUI, is incorrect because the hidden file attribute does not control how a file is viewed in the GUI. **B,** the hidden files should be moved to the Recycle Bin, is absolutely the worst thing to do. **D,** she must be mistaken, hidden files cannot be viewed in My Computer, is incorrect.

11. ☑ **B.** In the folder's Properties dialog box, select Advanced, and then select the Compress option.
   ☒ **A,** select the compress option in Windows Backup, is incorrect. **C,** use the Compress Selected Files option in Disk Management, is incorrect because there is no such option in Disk Management. **D,** copy the files into the Compressed folder, is incorrect. Although this is one way to compress files, the question asked how to compress a folder.

12. ☑ **D.** NTFS5 is the file systems that support file compression and encryption.
   ☒ **A,** FAT32, and **C,** FAT16, are both incorrect because they do not support either compression or encryption. **B,** NTFS4, is incorrect because while NTFS4 does support compression, it does not support encryption.

13. ☑ **C.** Convert from within Disk Management.
   ☒ **A,** it is not possible to do this without losing data, is incorrect. The convert tool is normally safe. **B,** use the Windows 9x program, is incorrect because this program does not run under Windows XP and does convert the file system. **D,** use the Convert tool found in System Tools, is incorrect because this tool does not exist in system tools in Windows XP.

14. ☑ **C.** You can use My Computer for managing files and folders.
   ☒ **A,** the Display applet in Control Panel, is incorrect because this is only used to change video and display settings. **B,** Notepad, is incorrect because this is simply a text file editor. **D,** Disk Management, is incorrect because this tool is for managing disk partitions.

15. ☑ **C.** You should not move, delete, edit, or manage program files in any way.
   ☒ **A,** text, is incorrect because it is generally acceptable for a user to manage text files, except

for those that are created and used by the operating system and stored with the boot files or system files. **B**, spreadsheet, is incorrect because this is a type of data file that the user can manage. **D**, data, is incorrect because the user can and should manage data files.

16. ☑ **D.** Press the secondary mouse button while dragging a file. This will cause a context menu to pop up from which you can choose the action you intend.
☒ **A**, run XCOPY from the command prompt, is incorrect because you should avoid doing file management from the command prompt. **B**, press SHIFT/DELETE, is incorrect. **C**, press the primary mouse button while dragging a file, is incorrect because you will not have a chance to select the operation you desire.

17. ☑ **A.** Use the Search utility, which will let you search on filename or contents of a file.
☒ **B**, use the Windows Help, is incorrect, although it will tell you to use the Search utility. **C**, record file locations on paper, is incorrect because this would not be a very smart way to work at a computer. **D**, save all data files in the root folder, is incorrect because this is not recommended and would be like dumping a bunch of letters in a pile rather than organizing them and putting them in file folders.

Windows Utilities

18. ☑ **B.** HELP is the command that will list the command-line commands and a brief description.
☒ **A**, DIR, is incorrect because this command displays a list of files and directories. **C**, PING, and **D**, IPCONFIG, are incorrect because these are commands used to view network configuration and connectivity.

19. ☑ **C.** defrag c: -a is the command that will analyze drive C:, looking for file fragmentation, but it will not change anything on the drive.
☒ **A**, dir /a, is incorrect because this will only display a list of all the directories within the current directory. **B**, help | more, is incorrect because this will display a list of command-line commands with a brief description. **D**, defrag a:, is incorrect because the question asked the syntax for analyzing drive C: and this command would defrag drive A:.

20. ☑ **A.** CHKDSK is the disk error-checking program that you can run from the command prompt to do a quick analysis of the disk for physical and logical errors.
☒ **B**, DEFRAG, is incorrect because this command analyzes the disk for fragmentation. With the correct switch DEFRAG will defragment a disk. **C**, SCANDISK, is incorrect because, while this was the Windows 9x disk error-checking command, it is no longer found in Windows 2000 and Windows XP. **D**, ATTRIB, is incorrect because this command displays and manipulates file attributes.

LAB ANSWER

Answers will vary. One possible design is to create a folder named Data at the root level of drive C:. If there is more than one drive partition, we suggest that you create it at the root of the drive that does not contain the operating system. Then within the Data folder, create three folders named Access, Word, and PowerPoint. Within the Access folder, create the following two folders: Clients and Contractors. Within the Word folder, create the following three folders: Intros, Proposals, and Offers. Within the PowerPoint folder, create a folder named Brochures. Within the Brochures folder, create two folders: Listing and Self-Marketing.

This design creates a hierarchical and logical arrangement of the folders all under a single folder. It will make backup easier, because you can simply back up the top-level folder and all of its contents to back up all of the agent's important data.

10

Troubleshooting and Preventive Maintenance for Windows

Y ou are now familiar with the major functions of the Windows operating systems, understand how to install Windows, and know how to manage files and disks. It is time to learn how to troubleshoot common problems. Each new version of Windows has become more stable, with more safeguards against failure. However, Windows is still not impervious to failures and other problems.

Your best troubleshooting tool is knowledge. The previous chapters have given you a strong foundation of knowledge about PCs and the Windows operating system. In this chapter you will learn more about the Windows startup process, and a set of skills and tools for modifying startup failures. You will also learn how to diagnose and solve common operational problems, including instability, Stop errors, application failures, and other problems.

Finally, in order to minimize your risk of problems, and increase your ability to quickly recover from failures, you will learn operating system preventive maintenance.

CERTIFICATION OBJECTIVES

■ **601: 3.3   602: 3.3   603: 2.3**   *Identify tools, diagnostic procedures, and troubleshooting techniques for operating systems*

This objective is broader than it would appear. In addition to the preceding statement, CompTIA includes within this objective the ability to identify basic boot sequences, recognize and resolve common operational problems, and recognize and resolve common error messages.

Understanding and Modifying Windows Startup

Before you can interpret Windows operating system startup failure symptoms, you must understand the normal Windows startup sequence and learn the role of each boot and system file in this sequence so that you can determine at what point Windows startup fails. Then learn to work with BOOT.INI and modify its startup options through the System Properties dialog box.

Windows Startup Phases

The Windows startup process on a desktop PC has several phases:

- Power-On Self-Test
- Initial Startup
- Boot Loader
- Detect and Configure Hardware
- Kernel Loading
- Logon and Plug-and-Play Device Detection

watch *It is essential that you be familiar with the phases and files of the Windows 2000 and Windows XP startup process.*

In the first two phases, the hardware "wakes up" and the BIOS searches for an operating system. Through the rest of the phases the operating system builds itself, much like a building, from the ground up, with more levels and complexity added at each phase. You will learn about these phases in the order in which they occur.

Power-On Self-Test

The power-on self-test phase is common to all PCs. It starts when you turn on or restart a computer. The CPU loads the BIOS programs from a special read-only memory (ROM) chip. The first of these programs include the power-on self-test (POST). The POST tests system hardware, determines the amount of memory present, verifies that devices required for OS startup are working, and loads configuration settings from CMOS memory into main system memory. During the POST, the BIOS briefly displays information on the screen as it tests memory and devices. We described BIOS and CMOS in Chapter 1.

Initial Startup

The initial startup phase is also common to all PCs. In this phase, the BIOS startup code uses CMOS settings to determine what devices can start an OS, and the order in which the system will search these devices while attempting to begin the OS startup process. One common order is A:, then a CD drive, then C:, in which case, the system will look for a bootable floppy disk in drive A:. If one is not there, it will try to boot from a bootable optical disc (if present).

If a bootable optical disc is not present, then the startup code will try to boot from the hard disk, and load the master code record (MBR)—the first sector on a hard disk—into memory. The BIOS loads the executable code from the MBR, giving control of the system to this code, which then uses information in the partition table (also located in the MBR) to find the first sector of the active partition, called the boot sector, which is loaded into memory and called the boot code.

Format places the boot code in the first sector of a partition using any of the Windows file systems. The job of the Windows boot code is to identify the file system on the active partition, find the NTLDR file, and load it into memory.

Boot Loader

During the boot loader phase, NTLDR, the Windows boot loader, takes control of the system, switches the CPU to protected mode, starts the file system (the in-memory code that can read and write an NTFS or FAT volume), reads the BOOT.INI file, and in some cases, displays the OS Selection menu. Windows NT 4.0 displays this menu by default, but Windows 2000 and Windows XP display this menu only if it lists more than one operating system, as is the case in a dual-boot configuration.

on the job

Up to this point, the CPU is in a very limited mode called real mode. This was the mode of the early Intel CPUs in the early PCs. Only when the CPU switches to protected mode can it access memory above 1 MB and support both multitasking and virtual memory. Protected mode refers to the fact that each application's memory space is protected from use by other applications.

If this is a dual-boot computer—one that is capable of booting from two different operating systems—then, if you select Windows 9x or DOS from the OS selection menu, NTLDR loads the boot sector file called BOOTSECT.DOS, and NTLDR is out of the picture for this session. BOOTSECT.DOS contains the boot code for DOS or early Windows versions up through Windows 9x.

The OS Selection menu may show a choice between two versions of Windows, as seen here. When Windows NT, Windows 2000, or Windows XP is selected from the OS selection menu (either automatically as the default, or manually), NTLDR moves to the next phase in the Windows startup process.

```
Please select the operating system to start:

    Microsoft Windows XP Professional
    Microsoft Windows 2000

Use the up and down arrow keys to move the highlight to your choice.
Press ENTER to choose.




For troubleshooting and advanced startup options for Windows, press F8.
```

Detect and Configure Hardware

During the detect and configure hardware phase NTLDR starts NTDETECT.COM, which in turn scans the computer's hardware and passes the resulting hardware list to NTLDR for later inclusion in the registry.

Kernel Loading

During the kernel loading phase NTLDR loads NTOSKRNL.EXE (the Windows kernel or core component) after locating it through the BOOT.INI file. Or, if no BOOT.INI file is present, NTLDR loads the kernel from the default location for this version of Windows. During kernel loading the Windows logo will display, as well as a progress bar, as seen here.

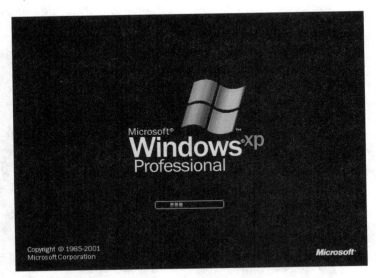

NTLDR then passes the hardware information to the kernel. The hardware abstraction layer file for the system, HAL.DLL, is also loaded into memory. NTLDR loads the SYSTEM portion of the registry and the drivers that are configured (through registry settings) to load at startup. All of this code is loaded into memory but not immediately initialized (made active).

Once all startup components are loaded, the kernel initializes and takes over the startup process. The kernel then initializes the components (services and drivers) required for startup. Once that is accomplished, the kernel scans the registry for other components that were not required during startup, but which are part of the configuration, and then loads and initializes them.

The kernel also starts the session manager (SMSS.EXE), which creates the system environment variables and loads the kernel-mode Windows subsystem code that switches Windows from text mode to graphics mode.

The session manager then starts the user-mode Windows subsystem code (CSRSS.EXE). Just a few of session manager's other tasks include creating the virtual memory paging file (pagefile.sys), and starting the Windows logon service (WINLOGON.EXE), which leads us to the next phase.

exam

W a t c h *Be sure to remember the main files required for starting up Windows 2000 and Windows XP. They are: NTLDR, BOOT.INI, NTDETECT.COM, and NTOSKRNL.EXE.*

Logon

The key player in this phase is the Windows Logon service, which supports logging on and logging off, and also starts the service control manager (SERVICES.EXE) and the local security authority (LSASS.EXE).

At this point, the Log On To Windows dialog box may appear (see Figure 10-1). Depending on how your computer was configured, you may first see the Welcome To Windows, requiring that the user press CTRL-ALT-DELETE before the Log On To Windows dialog box appears. A user enters a user name and password, which the local security authority uses to authenticate the user in the local security accounts database.

on the
job

The actual screen or dialog box that appears before you log on varies with the configuration of your computer. You may not have to enter a user name and password, or you may only need to select a user name from a list. Learn more about the logon process and its role in security in Chapter 15.

Program Startup   A lot of other things happen during the logon phase. Logon scripts run (if they exist), startup programs for various applications run, and non-critical services start. Windows finds instructions to run these programs and services in the following registry locations:

- HKEY_LOCAL_MACHINE\SOFTWARE\Microsoft\Windows\
  CurrentVersion\RunOnce
- HKEY_LOCAL_MACHINE\SOFTWARE\Microsoft\Windows\
  CurrentVersion\Policies\Explorer\Run
- HKEY_LOCAL_MACHINE\SOFTWARE\Microsoft\Windows\
  CurrentVersion\Run

FIGURE 10-1

Logging on to
Windows

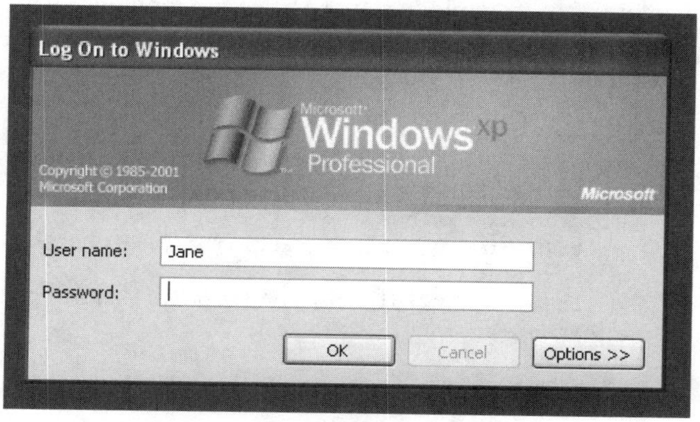

- HKEY_CURRENT_USER\Software\Microsoft\Windows NT\ CurrentVersion\Windows\Run
- HKEY_CURRENT_USER\Software\Microsoft\Windows\ CurrentVersion\Run
- HKEY_CURRENT_USER\Software\Microsoft\Windows\ CurrentVersion\RunOnce

Windows also starts programs located in the following folders:

- *systemdrive*\Documents and Settings\All Users\Start Menu\Programs\ Startup
- *systemdrive*\Documents and Settings*username*\Start Menu\Programs\ Startup

Plug-and-Play Detection   During the logon phase, Windows 2000 and Windows XP perform Plug-and-Play detection, using BIOS, hardware, device drivers, and other methods to detect new Plug-and-Play devices. If it detects a new device, Windows allocates system resources and installs device drivers.

The BOOT.INI File and System Startup Settings

The BOOT.INI file holds important information used by NTLDR to locate the operating system, and in the case of a dual-boot configuration, to display an OS selection menu. In Windows NT, this menu displays by default, even if the system is not dual-boot.

Inside BOOT.INI

Here is an example of a BOOT.INI file for a dual-boot installation in which Windows 2000 is booted from the first partition on the hard disk (C:) and Windows XP is booted from the second partition on the hard disk (D:):

```
[boot loader]
timeout=30
default=multi(0)disk(0)rdisk(0)partition(1)\WINDOWS
[operating systems]
multi(0)disk(0)rdisk(0)partition(1)\WINDOWS="Windows XP Professional"
/fastdetect
multi(0)disk(0)rdisk(0)partition(2)\WINNT="Windows 2000 Professional"
/fastdetect
```

The lines beginning with "multi" provide the location information to NTLDR in a format called an ARC path: `multi(0)disk(0)rdisk(0)partition(1)\WINDOWS`. In brief, this identifies the disk controller, the hard disk on that controller, the partition on that hard disk, and finally, the folder in that partition in which the OS is located.

Following is a more typical BOOT.INI for a Windows XP installation.

```
[boot loader]
timeout=30
default=multi(0)disk(0)rdisk(0)partition(1)\WINDOWS
[operating systems]
multi(0)disk(0)rdisk(0)partition(1)\WINDOWS="Windows XP Professional"
/fastdetect
```

The words that appear in quotes on the lines under the [operating systems] section display on the OS Selection menu. Anything after the quotes is a switch that affects how Windows starts up. For instance, the /fastdetect switch is the default switch used with Windows 2000 and Windows XP. It causes NTDETECT to skip parallel and serial device enumeration. This is a good thing, now that these two types of ports have all but disappeared from PCs.

Another switch that was noticed on Windows XP machines after Service Pack 2 is /NoExecute=OptIn. The NoExecute switch controls the use of Data Execution Prevention (DEP), technologies that help prevent harmful code from running in protected memory locations. The OptIn sub-parameter enables DEP only for the Windows kernel and drivers.

While there are many other BOOT.INI switches, you should not normally need to manually add any to your desktop installation of Windows.

on the Job *Still curious? Learn more about BOOT.INI switches. Point your browser to www.microsoft.com, and search for the article "Available switch options for the Windows XP and the Windows Server 2003 Boot.ini files."*

Modifying System Startup

As a rule, you should not edit the BOOT.INI file directly, but as a PC technician, you may run into a situation in which it is important to know how to edit this file. In Windows 2000 and Windows XP, you can do this though System Properties | Advanced | Startup And Recovery (see Figure 10-2). The settings that modify the BOOT.INI file are in the top of this dialog box, in the System Startup section.

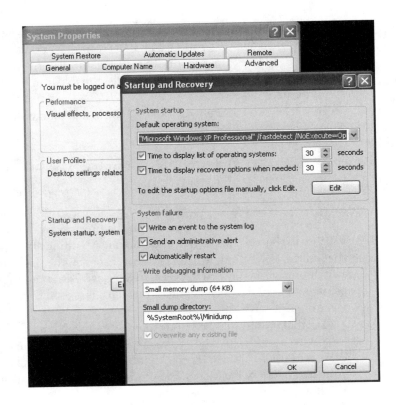

FIGURE 10-2

The System
Startup settings
are saved in the
BOOT.INI file.

A drop-down list lets you choose the default OS in a dual-boot system, and another
setting allows you to set the length of time the OS selection menu displays.

In Windows XP you also have a System Startup setting that controls the length
of time recovery options display, when needed. Plus, you have an Edit button
that opens Notepad with the BOOT.INI file loaded in it for editing. We strongly
recommend that you not directly edit the BOOT.INI file without a great deal of
preparation and/or expert advice.

*Even though the Edit button will open Notepad with the BOOT.INI file loaded
into it, you will not be able to save changes you make unless you remove the
read-only attribute from this file.*

FIGURE 10-3

The BOOT.INI
file on a simple
installation of
Windows XP

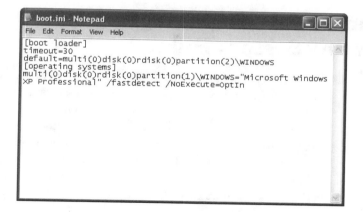

```
boot.ini - Notepad
File  Edit  Format  View  Help
[boot loader]
timeout=30
default=multi(0)disk(0)rdisk(0)partition(2)\WINDOWS
[operating systems]
multi(0)disk(0)rdisk(0)partition(1)\WINDOWS="Microsoft Windows
XP Professional" /fastdetect /NoExecute=OptIn
```

EXERCISE 10-1

Viewing the BOOT.INI File

You can easily view the BOOT.INI file.

1. Right click My Computer.
2. Select Properties from the context menu.
3. Click the Advanced tab.
4. On the Advanced tabbed page locate the section titled Startup and Recovery and click the Settings button located nearby.
5. In the Startup and Recovery page click Edit.
6. View the contents of your BOOT.INI file and compare it with those listed previously and displayed in Figure 10-3.

SCENARIO & SOLUTION

What is the function of NTLDR?	It controls the Windows boot process until the kernel is loaded.
What is the function of NTOSKRNL.EXE?	This is the Windows core (or kernel) component. It loads the operating system, memory management, and other system functions.
What is the function of BOOT.INI?	This text file, located in the root of C:, provides information to NTLDR about the location of the operating system files.

Diagnosing and Repairing Operating System Failures

Operating system failures occur for a variety of reasons, with just a few types of failures, startup, device driver, and application failures, accounting for the majority. In this section, begin by viewing the Advanced Options menu, which gives you alternative ways to start up Windows when you are troubleshooting. Then, work with various recovery tools, including System Restore, Recovery Console, Automated System Recovery, and Emergency Repair Process. Determine which of these tools are available in Windows 2000, which are available in Windows XP, and which are available in both versions of Windows.

Using the Advanced Options Menu

When a Windows computer fails to start up normally, the first thing you should do is make sure there are no disks in the floppy or optical drives, and restart the computer. If it fails on restart, there are several tools and boot methods at your disposal.

The Advanced Options menu gives you several boot methods to use for troubleshooting. Access this menu by restarting the computer and pressing the F8 key to access the OS Selection menu, and then pressing F8 again to access the Advanced Options menu. Figure 10-4 shows the Windows XP version of this menu. There are many options here, including Safe Mode, which allows you to start Windows without some of the components that may be causing the startup failure. Then you can remove, replace, or reconfigure the failed driver or other component.

FIGURE 10-4

Use the Windows XP Advanced Options menu to troubleshoot startup problems.

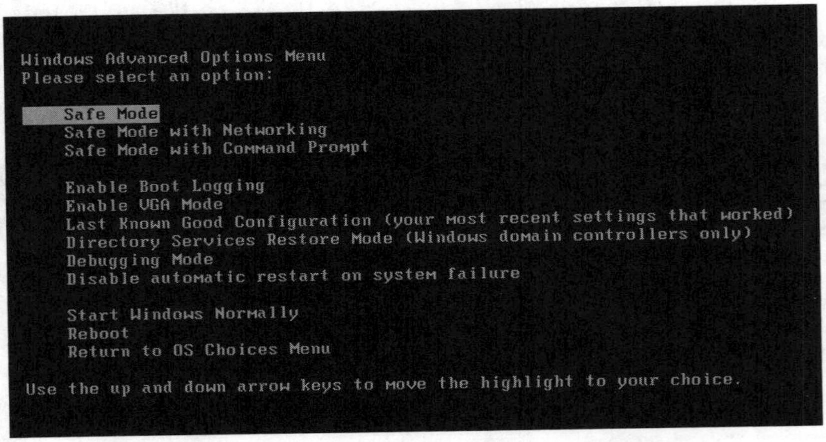

```
Windows Advanced Options Menu
Please select an option:

    Safe Mode
    Safe Mode with Networking
    Safe Mode with Command Prompt

    Enable Boot Logging
    Enable VGA Mode
    Last Known Good Configuration (your most recent settings that worked)
    Directory Services Restore Mode (Windows domain controllers only)
    Debugging Mode
    Disable automatic restart on system failure

    Start Windows Normally
    Reboot
    Return to OS Choices Menu

Use the up and down arrow keys to move the highlight to your choice.
```

If Windows will not start normally, but starts just fine in Safe Mode, work in Safe Mode to determine the source of the problem and correct it. Safe Mode does not disable Windows security. If you must enter a user name and password during a normal startup, you are also required to log on in all three variants of Safe Mode. In Safe Mode, as in normal mode, you can only access those resources for which you have permissions.

Three Safe Mode variants are available from the Advanced Options menu. They are Safe Mode, Safe Mode with Networking, and Safe Mode with Command Prompt.

Safe Mode

This basic Safe Mode starts up without using several drivers and components that Windows normally starts, including the network components. It loads only very basic, non-vendor-specific drivers for mouse, video (VGA.SYS), keyboard, mass storage, and system services, and it displays at a low resolution (see Figure 10-5).

If Windows will not start up normally, but it starts okay in Safe Mode, you know that the problem is with a component that Safe Mode did not start. Networking components do not start in this basic Safe Mode. Therefore, once you determine that Windows will start in Safe Mode, a quick test of networking components is to restart and select Safe Mode with Networking.

FIGURE 10-5

The Desktop displays at a lower resolution in Safe Mode.

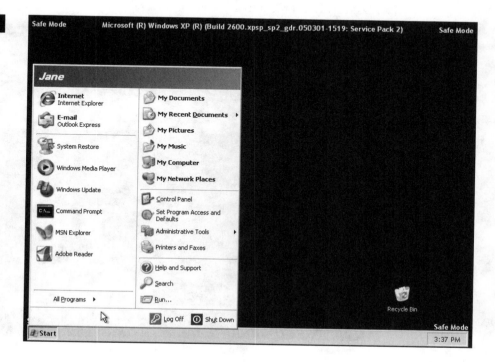

Safe Mode with Networking

Safe Mode with Networking is identical to basic Safe Mode, except that networking components also start. If Windows fails to start in Safe Mode with Networking, after starting in Safe Mode, the problem area is network drivers or components. Use Device Manager to disable the network adapter driver (the likely culprit), and then boot up normally. If Windows now works, replace your network driver.

If this problem occurs in Windows XP immediately after upgrading a network driver, use Device Manager in Safe Mode to roll back the updated driver. In Windows 2000, which does not have this option, remove the device driver. When an updated driver is available, install it. This applies to other device drivers, also—not just network device drivers.

Safe Mode with Command Prompt

This mode is Safe Mode without the GUI desktop, meaning that the Windows GUI EXPLORER is not running. You have only the command prompt, as shown here, from which to run commands and launch Windows administrative utilities. This mode is a handy option to remember if the desktop does not display at all after a normal startup. The most likely causes of this are corruption of either the EXPLORER.EXE program or the video driver.

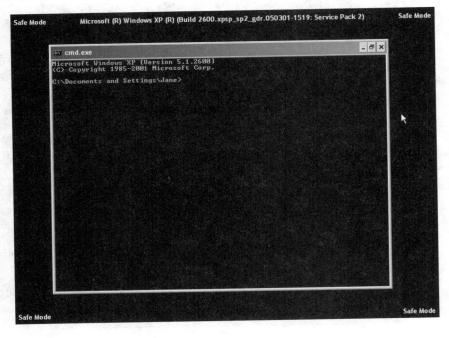

A scenario in which this approach is very valuable is if you had upgraded the video driver in Windows XP immediately before the last reboot. Restart the computer in Safe Mode with Command Prompt and open Device Manager using its command name, DEVMGMT.MSC, from the command line. Then, open the properties for the video adapter and select Roll Back Driver.

On a Windows 2000 computer, you do not have the Roll Back Driver option and would therefore need to use the Last Known Good option, explained a little later in this section.

If you eliminate the video driver as the cause, corruption of the EXPLORER.EXE program may be the problem. Try launching this program from the command prompt. Do not expect the GUI to look like it does when Windows starts normally. If, after starting EXPLORER from the command prompt, you have a recognizable taskbar at the bottom of the screen and you can open the Start menu, EXPLORER is not corrupted, and you will need to continue your troubleshooting efforts.

If you believe EXPLORER is corrupted, you can delete the corrupted version of EXPLORER.EXE and copy an undamaged version. This requires knowledge of the command-line commands for navigating the directory structure, as well as knowledge of the location of the file that you are replacing. The default location of EXPLORER.EXE is C:\Windows. The original compressed file is in the I386 folder of the Windows 2000 or Windows XP CD. From the command prompt use the EXPAND command to expand it. The actual command line would look like this:

```
EXPAND d:\I386\EXPLORER.EX_  C:\WINDOWS\EXPLORER.EXE
```

If you ruled out the video driver and EXPLORER as the source of the problems, launch Event Viewer (EVENTVWR.MSC) and search the System and Application logs for recent errors. Learn more about Event Viewer and Computer Management later in this chapter.

on the
O o b
Launch the Computer Management Console (COMPMGMT.MSC) and you will have several administrative tools in one console.

Enable Boot Logging

When boot logging is enabled, a log of the Windows startup is created in a file named NTBTLOG.TXT and saved in the *systemroot* folder (normally C:\Windows). Boot logging creates an entry in this file for each component as it is loaded into memory. It also lists drivers that were not loaded. An administrator viewing this file can discover what drivers were loaded into memory. Boot logging occurs automatically with each of the three Safe Modes. Enabling boot logging alone from the Advanced Options menu will turn on boot logging and proceed with a normal startup.

Enable VGA Mode

This option starts Windows normally, except that the video mode is changed to the lowest resolution (640 × 480), using the currently installed video driver. It does not switch to the basic Windows video driver, as the Safe Modes do. Restart your computer and select this option after making a video configuration change that is not supported by the video adapter and that prevents Windows from displaying properly, making it impossible to work in the GUI to change the configuration.

Last Known Good Configuration

A parenthetical phrase, "your most recent settings that worked," appears on the line with this choice in the Advanced Options menu. This phrase says it all. Last Known Good (LKG) only lets you restore a group of registry keys containing system settings such as services and drivers. These are the last settings that worked, and you only have a narrow window of opportunity to use LKG—on the first reboot after making a configuration change, and *before* logging on. Therefore, the definition of "settings that worked" is those used the last time you logged on. Once you log on, Windows deletes the former LKG settings, and the new settings with the changes included become the LKG.

If your computer was configured to start up without presenting you with an actual logon dialog box in which you enter your user name and password, then you are automatically logged on at every restart. In this case, once you have restarted and reached the desktop, it is too late to use Last Known Good because a logon has occurred.

Directory Services Restore Mode

This mode is only available in Windows Servers acting as domain controllers.

Debugging Mode

This is an advanced option used to send debugging information about the Windows startup over a serial cable to another computer running a special program called a debugger.

Disable Automatic Restart on System Failure

This is a setting found on the Startup and Recovery page, and accessed through the Advanced page of System Properties. It is located under System Failure and labeled "Automatically restart." If this setting is selected, which is the default for Windows XP, then Windows will automatically restart when there is a system failure.

The problem that can occur if this setting is on, is a situation in which Windows refuses to shut down. In fact, if, every time you try to shut down Windows, it immediately restarts, this is an indication that Windows is failing during the shutdown operation. You may even see the blue screen during shutdown, followed immediately by a restart.

You can change this setting through the System Properties dialog box, or you can temporarily change it by selecting the Advanced menu option Disable Automatic Restart On System Failure. Using the latter option only changes this setting for one reboot. It will revert back on the next reboot.

Start Windows Normally

Use this option to start Windows normally from this menu. You would use this after using F8 to view the Advanced Options menu and deciding to continue with a normal startup. It does not restart the computer. It also does not guarantee that Windows will start normally if there is a problem.

Reboot

This option restarts the computer, acting like a warm reboot (CTRL-ALT-DELETE) from MS-DOS, or like Restart Windows from the Windows Shut Down menu. You may then choose to allow Windows to start normally, or to open the Advanced Options menu with the F8 key.

o n   t h e

❢ⓙ o b

In place of the two options Start Windows Normally and Reboot, Windows 2000 has only one option, Reboot Normally, which behaves like the Windows XP Reboot option.

Return to OS Choices Menu

Under certain circumstances the Advanced Options menu will include the Return To OS Choices menu. When available, selecting this option will return to the OS Choices menu (OS Loader menu).

EXERCISE 10-2

Working in Safe Mode

It is good practice to become familiar with Safe Mode before you have a startup problem.

1. Restart your computer. Press F8 after the POST messages.

2. From the Advanced Options menu, select Safe Mode, and then press ENTER.

3. You might return to the OS selection menu, in which case, you will see the words "Safe Mode" in blue at the bottom of the screen. If there is only one Windows OS listed, simply press the ENTER key. If there is more than one OS displayed, use the UP ARROW or DOWN ARROW key to select one, and then press ENTER.

4. As Safe Mode loads, notice that the screen lists all the drivers and components as they are loaded and started.

5. What you will see next depends on your computer configuration. You may see the full, blue screen with the message "To begin, click your user name," or you may see a small Welcome To Windows message box displayed against a black background with the build version number at the top of the screen and "Safe Mode" in each corner of the background.

6. In either case, follow the instructions to begin or to log on.

7. A Desktop dialog box will inform you that Windows is running in Safe Mode. Select Yes to proceed with Safe Mode.

8. View the desktop, recalling that the standard video drivers are the only ones installed, and some components are not loaded, so the desktop will not look normal, although it will still have the taskbar and even some desktop icons.

9. Explore some of the GUI tools, such as My Computer (see Figure 10-6) and Control Panel.

10. If time permits, restart your computer, and select each of the other two Safe Mode configurations.

11. When you have finished working in Safe Mode, use the Start menu to restart Windows and start up normally.

FIGURE 10-6

Launch Windows utilities and programs in Safe Mode.

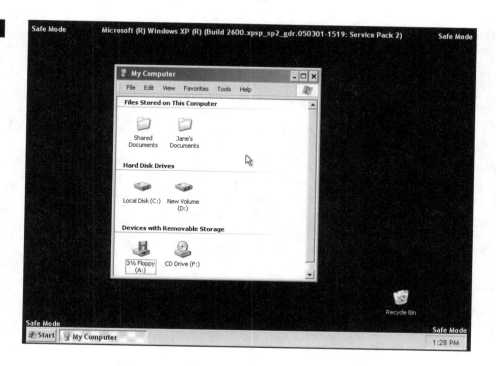

System Restore

If you have ever added the latest software or new device to your Windows computer, only to find that nothing seems to work right after this change, System Restore will come to your aid. You must be able to get into the Windows GUI to use this great recovery tool that first appeared in Windows Me and is not available in Windows 2000. It was improved, and included in Windows XP.

System Restore creates restore points, which are snapshots of Windows, its configuration, and all installed components. Restore points are created automatically when you add or remove software, or install Windows updates, and during the normal shutdown of your computer. You can also choose to force creation of a restore point before making changes. If your computer has nonfatal problems after you have made a change, you can use System Restore to roll it back to a restore point.

During the restore process, only settings and programs are changed. No data is lost. Your computer will include all programs and settings as of the restore date and time. This feature is invaluable for overworked administrators and consultants. A simple restore will fix many user-generated problems.

To restore a Windows system to a previous time point, start the System Restore Wizard. Choose Start | All Programs | Accessories | System Tools | System Restore. Select the first radio button, Restore My Computer To An Earlier Time, and then click Next.

The next screen will show a calendar with restore points. Any day with a boldface date has a restore point. Select a date to restore to, and click Next.

The last screen before restoring the system is a warning. It advises you to close all open programs, and reminds you that Windows will shut down during the restore process. It also states that the restore operation is completely reversible. Thus, if you go too far back in time, you can restore to a more recent date.

You don't have to count on the automatic creation of restore points. You can open System Restore at any time and simply select Create A Restore Point. This is something to consider doing before making changes that might not trigger an automatic restore point, such as directly editing the registry.

System Restore is on by default and uses some of your disk space to save information on restore points. To turn System Restore off or change the disk space usage, open the System Properties applet in Control Panel and select the System Restore tab, where you will find these settings. Disabling System Restore is now a common part of cleaning off many virus infections to make sure that a virus isn't hiding in the restore files, but be aware that turning System Restore off, even for a moment, deletes all old restore points.

Recovery Console

Introduced in Windows 2000, the Recovery Console in both Windows 2000 and Windows XP allows you to recover from a failure of the OS when all else has failed. The Recovery Console is a totally non-GUI command-line interface. If you have the Windows 2000 or Windows XP Professional CD, you can start the Recovery Console by booting from the CD, running Setup and selecting Repair, and then selecting Recovery Console.

However, if you like to be proactive, you can install the Recovery Console on your hard drive so that it is one of your startup options and does not require the Windows CD to run. The steps to do this in Windows 2000 and Windows XP are identical.

Log on as an Administrator, and insert the Windows 2000 or Windows XP Professional CD-ROM. If Autorun starts the Setup program, click No. Then open a Windows command prompt by selecting Start | Run and typing **CMD** into the dialog box. In the command prompt, enter the following command:

```
d:\i386\winnt32 /cmdcons
```

where *d* is your CD drive letter.

Just follow the instructions on the screen. If connected to the Internet, allow the Setup program to download updated files. After the Recovery Console installs, at each restart, the OS selection menu will show your Windows OS (Windows 2000 Professional or Windows XP) and the Microsoft Windows Recovery Console. It may also show other choices if yours is a multiboot computer. When you select the Recovery Console, it will start, and then you will see the Recovery Console command prompt.

Note: As with most command-line interfaces, the previous information stays on the screen until the screen is full.

The cursor is a small white rectangle sitting to the right of the question mark on the last line. If there is only one installation of Windows on your computer, type **1** at the prompt, and press ENTER. If you press ENTER before typing in a valid selection, the Recovery Console will cancel and the computer will reboot. Once you have made your selection, a new line appears on the screen prompting for the Administrator password.

Enter the Administrator password for that computer and press ENTER. The actual password will not display on the screen; asterisks will show in place of the password. The screen still shows everything that has happened so far, unless something has caused an error message. It now looks like Figure 10-7.

Now what do you do? Use the Recovery Console commands, of course. Recovery Console uses many of the commands that worked in DOS as well as some uniquely its own. To see a list of Recovery Console commands, simply enter **help** at the prompt.

FIGURE 10-7	

Microsoft Windows XP Recovery Console

```
Microsoft Windows XP(TM) Recovery Console.

The Recovery Console provides system repair and recovery functionality.

Type EXIT to quit the Recovery Console and restart the computer.

1: C:\WINDOWS

Which Windows installation would you like to log onto
(To cancel, press ENTER)? 1
Type the Administrator password: ********
C:\WINDOWS>
```

To learn more about an individual command, enter the command name followed by /?. Here is a brief description of a few handy commands:

- **DISKPART**   A disk partitioning program
- **EXIT**   Exits the Recovery Console and restarts your computer
- **FIXBOOT**   Writes a new partition table from the backup Master File Table
- **FIXMBR**   Repairs the Master Boot Record (MBR)
- **HELP**   Displays a Help screen
- **LOGON**   Logs on to a Windows installation
- **SYSTEMROOT**   Sets the current directory to the location of the Windows system files—usually C:\Windows

The files that make up the Recovery Console reside on drive C:, making the Recovery Console unavailable if this partition is badly damaged. The Recovery Console shines in the business of allowing an administrator to manually restore registry files, stopping problem services, rebuilding partitions (other than the system partition), or using the EXPAND program to extract uncorrupted files from a CD-ROM or floppy disk to replace corrupted files.

You can reconfigure a service so that it starts with different settings, format drives on the hard disk, read and write on local FAT or NTFS volumes, and copy replacement files from a floppy or CD. The Recovery Console allows you to access the file system, but it is still constrained by the file and folder security of NTFS. Recovery Console is a very advanced tool—definitely not for amateurs!

Automated System Recovery (ASR)

To recover from damage that prevents the operating system from starting up in any way, Automated System Recovery (ASR) is available from the Backup program (NTBACKUP.EXE). ASR replaces the Emergency Repair process of Windows NT and Windows 2000, which depended on restoring a special backup of system settings. ASR, in contrast, uses a backup of the entire system partition (where the OS is installed) and therefore provides a more holistic repair, restoring the entire operating system to a certain point in time.

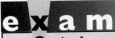

e x a m

ⓦatch   *The CompTIA objectives for exam 601 mention "boot to restore point." The closest you can come to booting to a restore point is by using ASR, which boots up and restores the entire system volume.*

Using ASR requires some planning. You must use the Advanced Mode of the Backup Utility (NTBACKUP.EXE) to create an ASR backup set, which includes an ASR diskette to initiate a bootup into the ASR state, and a system partition backup to media, such as tape, another local hard disk, or a network location that is accessed via a drive letter (a mapped drive).

The Welcome page of the Advanced Mode of the Backup Utility contains the option for running the Automated System Recovery Wizard to create an ASR set.

An ASR backup set does not include a backup of other partitions, nor does it allow you to select data folders. Therefore, your Windows XP Professional backup strategy should include occasional creation of an ASR set, and frequent backups to save data and changes to the OS since the last ASR set.

Automated System Recovery and the Backup Utility are not included in Windows XP Home Edition. However, you can install the Backup Utility (NTBACKUP.EXE) from the Windows XP Home distribution CD. Some computer manufacturers include a custom system recovery tool, but they may not include a backup utility.

Emergency Repair Process

The Emergency Repair Process in Windows 2000 is a carryover from Windows NT. In Windows XP, this awkward, and error-prone, repair process was replaced by Automatic System Recovery.

The Emergency Repair Process requires an up-to-date Emergency Repair Disk (ERD), or recent emergency repair information stored on the local hard disk. In Windows 2000, clicking a button on the Welcome page of the Windows Backup program (see Figure 10-8) will open an Emergency Repair Disk dialog box that

SCENARIO & SOLUTION

Where can I find a variety of boot methods to use for troubleshooting Windows startup problems?	The Advanced Options menu, accessible by restarting the computer, and pressing the F8 key immediately after the POST.
What is the difference between Safe Mode and Safe Mode with Networking?	Safe Mode starts up without using several drivers and components that Windows normally starts, including networking components. Safe Mode with Networking only differs from Safe Mode in that networking components also start.
What is the effect of using the Advanced Options menu choice titled Disable Automatic Restart On System Failure?	Selecting this from the Advanced Options menu disables the automatic restart on system failure for one restart only.

FIGURE 10-8

The Emergency
Repair option
in the Windows
2000 Backup
program.

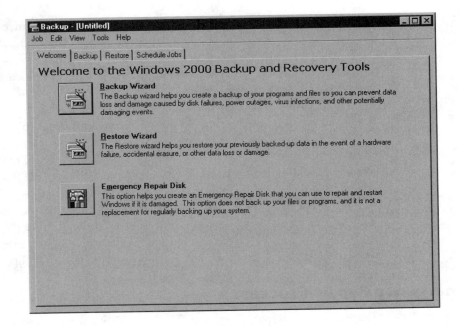

guides you through creating an ERD, including providing an option to also back up
the registry to the Repair directory located in *systemroot*.

To perform an emergency repair, you need the Windows 2000 CD and the most
recent ERD. If you do not have an ERD, the Emergency Repair Process will look for
recent emergency repair information saved to the hard drive.

Boot up to the Setup program. At the Welcome To Setup screen, press R to repair
a damaged operating system. On the following screen, select or deselect the desired
actions in the box, and then press ENTER to continue.

Operational Issues and Symptoms

Operational problems are those that occur while Windows is running, as opposed
to those that occur during startup. These may be instability problems, and they may
involve OS components, including drivers, or application components. Regardless of
the source of the problem, it is important to watch for error messages, and to become
familiar with common error messages.

OS Instability Problems

What does OS instability look like? Instability includes a variety of symptoms such as

- Extreme slowness
- Inability to open programs
- Failure of running programs
- System lockup
- Complete failure of the OS, resulting in a Stop error on a blue screen.

Let's examine some of these symptoms and their potential solutions.

Instability Associated with Hibernate Mode

If you initiate Hibernate Mode, but then interrupt it before the computer completely enters hibernation, the OS may become unstable. If this is the case follow the steps described in Exercise 10-3.

EXERCISE 10-3

Restoring Stability after an Interrupted Hibernate Mode

If your computer shows signs of instability, and you believe that you interrupted Hibernate Mode, take these steps to correct the problem:

1. Close all open applications.
2. Select Start | Turn Off.
3. In the Turn Off Computer box select Turn Off.
4. Turn power off using the power button.
5. Turn power on again, and Windows should start up normally.

Blue Screen Errors

When a system malfunctions due to a fatal error, this results in a text-mode screen with white letters on a blue background. This has the unofficial name of Blue Screen of Death (BSOD), but it is officially a Stop screen. A message, and multiple numbers that are the contents of the registers and other key memory locations, will display. This information is usually not overly useful to a computer technician, but it can provide a great deal of information to developers and technical support professionals as to the nature of the failure. It is a good idea to capture that information before you contact customer support.

A fatal error is one that could cause too much instability to guarantee the integrity of the system. Therefore, when the operating system detects a fatal error, it will stop and display the Stop screen.

Preparing for Stop Errors   To prepare for a Stop error, you should decide how you want your computer to behave after one. You do this by modifying the System Failure settings on the Startup and Recovery page. You can find these settings by opening the System applet in Control Panel, selecting the Advanced tab, and clicking the Settings button under Startup and Recovery.

- **Write An Event To The System Log** causes Windows to write an event to the system log, which is one of several log files you can view using Event Viewer (found under Administrative Tools). We highly recommend this setting, because it means that even if the computer reboots after a Stop screen, you can read the Stop error information that was on the screen in the system log.

- **Send An Administrative Alert** is a setting that sends an alert message to the administrator that will appear on the administrator's screen the next time he or she logs on. This is a useful setting if your computer is part of a domain, to alert a domain administrator.

- **Automatically Restart** is a setting we recommend, as long as you have also selected the first option, which preserves the Stop error information in the system log file.

- **Writing Debugging Information** contains a drop-down list, a text box, and a check box. The drop-down list allows you to control the existence and size of the file containing debugging information. This file, called a dump file, has settings that include None, Small Memory Dump (64KB), Kernel Memory Dump, and Complete Memory Dump. A complete memory dump contains an image of the contents of memory at the time of the fatal error. You can send this file to Microsoft for evaluation of a problem, but this amount of effort and cost (Microsoft charges for these services) is normally only expended on a critical computer, such as a network server. For a desktop computer, a small memory dump should be adequate, unless a support person advises you otherwise. The text box allows you to specify the location of the dump file. The default is %SystemRoot%, which is a variable way of pointing to the folder containing the Windows system files. The default location is C:\Windows. The final setting is the check box labeled "Overwrite any existing file." We recommend you select this option so that large dump files do not accumulate on your computer's hard drive.

Troubleshooting a Stop Error   If you are present when a Stop error occurs, read the first few lines on the screen for a clue. If the system reboots before you can read this information, you can view it in the system log after the reboot. Open Event Viewer and look in the System log of a Stop error.

For example, say the error message looks something like this: "STOP [several sets of numbers in the form 0x00000000] UNMOUNTABLE_BOOT_VOLUME." If you search www.microsoft.com using just the last part of this message (UNMOUNTABLE_BOOT_VOLUME), you may find sufficient information to determine the cause and the action to take by examining the values that preceded it. One possible solution offered is to restart Windows using the Recovery Console, and to run a command from the command line. Now you see the value of understanding how to work with the Recovery Console.

Troubleshooting Applications

Common problems with applications include the failure of an application to start, and problems when running legacy applications in Windows.

Application Fails to Start

Imagine that you have spent days preparing a presentation for work. Your computer is running Windows XP and you have several applications open. The presentation consists of a complex Excel spreadsheet, a Word report, and a PowerPoint slide presentation.

In researching a topic for this report, you locate source information in a file on the Internet. The file is in PDF format. You double-click the file, expecting it to load into the Acrobat Reader program. The hourglass appears briefly, but Acrobat does not start up, and no error message appears. You open the Task Manager, which shows current tasks. You expect to see Acrobat listed with a status of "not responding," but there is no listing for it. The possible problem is that there is not enough memory to run the additional program. The solution is to close one or more applications, and then attempt to open Acrobat.

An Old Application Will Not Run

You have a brand-new Windows XP computer. You need to run a program that worked nicely on your now-defunct Windows 98 computer. Such a program, called a legacy application, was for an older version of Windows.

When you start the program in Windows XP, the legacy application does not run correctly. Maybe the screen doesn't look quite right, or perhaps the program frequently hangs up. To solve this problem, Windows XP allows you to trick the program into thinking that the OS is actually Windows 98 by using compatibility options. You can set these options to modify the environment, called Compatibility Mode, in which the program runs. Do this by running the Program Compatibility Wizard from the Help and Support Center. You can also launch it from the Start | All Programs | Accessories | Program Compatibility Wizard. The wizard saves the settings it creates in the properties of the application's shortcut or program file.

Start the wizard and follow the instructions. You may choose to have the wizard display a list of all installed programs, from which you can select your problem program. Then you can move through the wizard, selecting settings for emulating earlier versions of Windows, and/or modifying the display settings for the program. Then test the program to see if there is an improvement.

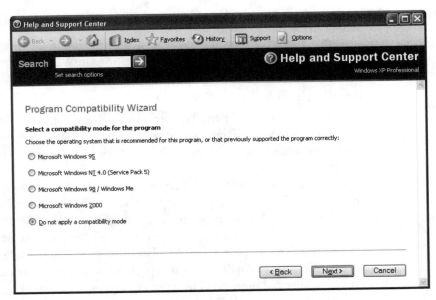

Alternatively, you can set compatibility settings manually. On the Start menu, locate the shortcut for the offending program. Right-click, select Properties, then select the Compatibility tab. On this page, place a check in the box under

Compatibility Mode, and then select Windows 98 in the drop-down list below it. Click OK, and test the program. If it still has problems, go back to the Compatibility page, tweak the Display Settings, and/or turn off advanced text services. If you need help, click the Program Compatibility link at the bottom of the page.

Common Error Messages and Codes

An IT professional must recognize and interpret common error messages and codes. These range from messages that appear during the early stages of a failed startup, through a variety of operational error messages. Once-fleeting messages that were not available after the fact are now logged in many cases, and a knowledgeable person learns where to find them, as you will see in the text that follows. Microsoft also has a system called Windows Reporting, which you can use to resolve Windows problems.

Startup Error Messages

When an OS fails in the early stages of startup, the problem often stems from corruption or loss of essential OS files. If this is the case, you may need to reinstall the OS, but before you do such a drastic step, consider other actions.

Before an OS fails, you may see signs of data corruption, a sign that the disk is about to fail. You should consider running CHKDSK to resolve these problems. You might also want to consider replacing the hard disk before it fails completely. Before you do this, though, boot from a floppy disk, and then try to access and save any salvageable information from the hard drive.

NTLDR or NTDETECT.COM Is Missing   If startup fails, and you see a message that NTLDR or NTDETECT.COM is missing when you boot from your hard disk, simply boot with your Windows startup disk, and copy the missing file from A:\ to C:\.

On a Windows 2000 computer the message "NTLDR is missing" may appear when a floppy disk formatted in Windows 2000, and not configured to start Windows, is left in a floppy drive during startup. Therefore, when you see this message, be sure to first check that there is no disk in the floppy drive.

NTOSKRNL Is Invalid or Missing   The error message "NTOSKRNL is invalid or missing" does not occur too often, but when it does, this message is usually incorrect and misleading because it is highly unlikely that this file is either invalid or missing. What is more likely is that NTOSKRNL is not where NTLDR expects it to be. NTLDR finds this location by reading the BOOT.INI file. If a BOOT.INI file is not present, NTLDR attempts to locate this file in the default location for the version of Windows you are using.

In Windows NT 4.0 and Windows 2000, that location is C:\WINNT32\ SYSTEM32, while in Windows XP, the default location is C:\WINDOWS\ SYSTEM32. If Windows was not installed in the default location, and the BOOT .INI file is damaged or missing, Windows will fail to start and will display the "NTOSKRNL invalid or missing" error.

Similarly, if the BOOT.INI is present but contains incorrect information, NTLDR will look in the wrong location and once again display the error message. If the computer previously started without failure, and if you have a Windows startup disk for the computer, use the disk to start Windows. If Windows starts when using the startup disk, correct the problem by copying the BOOT.INI file to the root of C:. Learn how to create a Windows startup disk later in this chapter.

If Windows does not start properly with the disk, then you have a more advanced problem. It may still relate to the BOOT.INI file, but it may involve a change to the disk partitioning. This is a very advanced problem. If this is the case, research the Microsoft site for articles on the BOOT.INI file and how it describes the path to NTOSKRNL.EXE using an ARC path.

Remove Disks or Other Media   If, when you start up your computer, the message in Figure 10-9 appears, there is a formatted floppy disk in the drive. A disk formatted from XP without having any system files added is only for data storage; it is not intended to be used to start up Windows. Therefore, if it is left in the drive, this message will appear. Simply remove the disk and press any key to restart.

Invalid Boot or Invalid System Disk   There can be several causes for an error message that reads "Invalid system disk" or "Invalid boot disk." This error message is more likely to occur on a Windows 9x computer than on one running Windows 2000 or Windows XP. Here are a few possible causes and their solutions:

- If the message "Invalid system disk" appears after Windows Setup reboots, first check to see if a Windows 95 or Windows 98 startup disk is in the floppy drive. If a floppy disk is in the drive, remove it and restart.

FIGURE 10-9   A message that displays when a floppy disk, formatted in Windows XP, is left in the drive during restart.

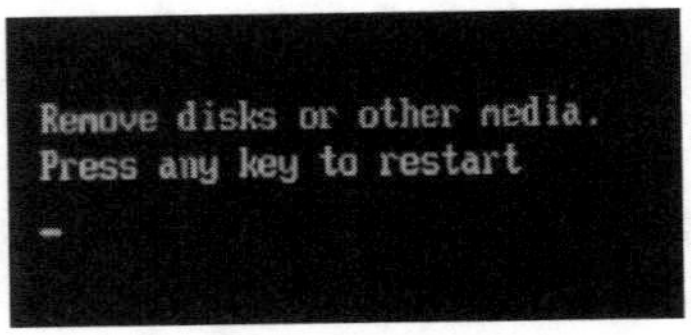

```
Remove disks or other media.
Press any key to restart
_
```

- A boot-sector virus may have infected your computer. Learn more about boot-sector viruses at **support.microsoft.com**.

- Third-party hard drive drivers did not copy to the hard disk during Setup. You will need to obtain updated drivers and follow the manufacturer's instructions. This may require reinstalling Windows.

- Specialized security software is preventing access to drive C:. Check the documentation for the security software.

Inaccessible Boot Drive   This error may show as a blue screen Stop error, in which case, the exact wording is "Inaccessible Boot Device." This fatal error has several possible causes and solutions. Here are just a few:

- A boot-sector virus has infected the computer. Learn more about boot-sector viruses at **support.microsoft.com**.

- A resource conflict exists between the boot controller and another controller. This is most likely to occur after the installation of an additional controller. In that case, remove the controller and reboot. If Windows starts up normally, then troubleshoot the new controller for a configuration that conflicts with the boot controller.

- A configuration conflict exists between SCSI devices. Check the configuration of the SCSI controller in the computer. Once again, this is most likely to occur after adding an additional controller. Remove the new controller and restart. If Windows starts up normally, check the configuration of the two controllers and reconfigure the new controller so that it does not conflict with the boot controller.

- The boot volume is corrupt. If you have eliminated other causes, then remove the boot hard drive system and install it in another computer that has a working installation of the same version of Windows. Configure it as an additional drive, boot into the existing operating system, and then run the CHKDSK program on the hard drive to diagnose and fix errors.

Device Has Failed to Start   If you see the message "Device has failed to start," open Device Manager and double-click the device name to open the device's Properties dialog box. On the General tab, look in the Device Status box for an error code. Troubleshoot in accordance with the error code. You may search the Microsoft Web site for this error code and find a recommended solution.

For instance, Article 310123 contains a list of device error codes and their recommended resolutions. If the driver is corrupted, it may instruct you to uninstall the driver and then click the Action menu in Device Manager and select Scan for hardware changes. This will cause it to reinstall the driver.

Another common solution is to select Update Driver in Device Manager. This will start the Hardware Update Wizard, which will walk you through the process.

Service Has Failed to Start   If you see the message "Service has failed to start," open Computer Management (right-click on My Computer and select Manage). In the Computer Management Console, expand the Services and Applications node and click on Services. In the contents pane, scroll down until you see the service that failed to start and right-click it. From the context menu, click Start. It may take several minutes for the service to start. If it starts normally, without any error messages, then do not take any further steps unless the problem recurs. In that case, you will need to research the problem. Do this by searching the Microsoft site on the service name, adding the word "failed" to the search string.

Device Referenced in Registry Not Found   If you see an error message that a device referenced in the registry was not found, use the instructions given in the earlier section "Device Has Failed to Start" to either update the driver or uninstall and reinstall the driver.

Program Referenced in Registry Not Found   If you see an error message that a program referenced in the registry was not found, uninstall and reinstall the program.

Viewing Error Messages in Event Viewer

In early versions of Windows, error messages were something fleeting that you could not go back and read again. This was a major problem for PC support personnel relying on the user's memory to describe symptoms and messages. In Windows NT, Windows 2000, and Windows XP, error messages are no longer something fleeting that users must write down in order to troubleshoot.

Event logs save most error messages. Become familiar with Event Viewer before a problem occurs, so that you will be comfortable using it to research a problem. Use Event Viewer to view logs of system, security, and application events, paying attention to the warning and error logs for messages you can use to solve problems.

Event Logs   Event Viewer has three standard categories of events: system, application, and security. Other event logs may exist, depending on how Windows is configured. For instance, Internet Explorer 7 creates its own event log. You can open Event Viewer in Windows 2000 and Windows XP Professional by selecting Start | Control Panel | Administrative Tools | Event Viewer. Open Event Viewer quickly from Start | Run in Windows 2000 or Windows XP by using its filename: **eventvwr.msc**.

- The System log records events involving the Windows system components (drivers, services, and so on). The types of events range from normal events, such as startup and shutdown (called information events), through warnings of situations that could lead to errors, to actual error events. Even the dreaded "Blue Screen of Death" error messages show up in the system log as Stop errors. The system log, shown here, is the first place to look when a message indicates failure of a component, such as a driver or service. Double-click an event to see the details, including the actual message that appeared on the desktop in a warning. The message itself may lead you to the solution. Each event also has an ID number. Search the Microsoft Web site for a solution using either a portion of the error message, or the event ID.

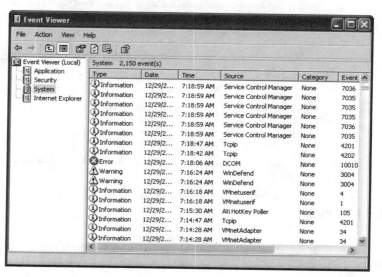

- The application log shows events involving applications. These applications may be your office suite of applications or Windows components that run in the GUI, such as Windows Explorer. When a program error occurs, a special program called Dr. Watson starts automatically and records some application events in the application log. If you see a Dr. Watson error on your screen, you will find the error listed in the application log.

■ Event logs do not record security events by default; therefore, don't be surprised to find an empty Security log. Only after an administrator turns on auditing will security events appear in the Security log, and then it can log several types of events. In Windows 2000 and Windows XP, you can turn on auditing through the Local Security Policy shortcut on the Administrative Tools menu. In the Local Security Setting console, you control auditing through these settings: Security Settings | Local Policies | Audit Policy, shown here. If you have enabled Audit Account Logon Events, the security log will log each successful and/or failed logon attempt. These events will show in the Security log in Event Viewer as "Success Audit" or "Failure Audit." Other settings that affect Security logging are the three policies that begin with "Audit" in Local Security Settings under Security Settings | Local Policies | Security Options.

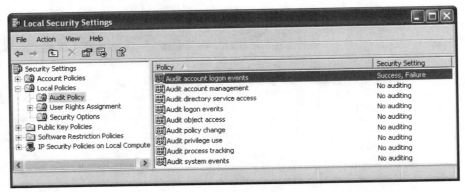

on the job **To learn more about Event Viewer, use the help program from within Event Viewer.**

Configuring and Saving Event Logs Windows 2000 and Windows XP allow you to manage each log file separately. The Properties dialog box for each log file will allow you to configure the maximum size to which each event log may grow, and the action to take when the event log is full (reaches the maximum size). Figure 10-10 shows the properties dialog box for the System log file.

In addition, you may clear each log file, save the log file to view later, open a previously saved log file, and create multiple views of the log files. In Windows XP,

The Properties
dialog box for the
System log file

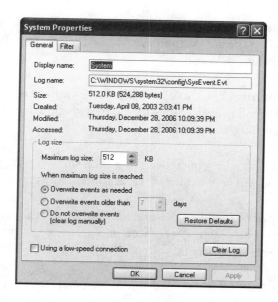

simply right-click a log file to choose one of the following actions from the context
menu that appears when you right-click a log node in Event Viewer:

Open Log File   Use this command to open a previously saved log file.

Save Log File As   Save a log file for future reference.

New Log View   Create a new node in the Event Viewer console, and then use the
View settings to filter the events viewed.

Clear All Events   Use this to clear out the event log; this option prompts you to
save the log file before clearing, but you may also choose to "lose" all the events.

View   This choice brings up the View menu (identical to the list of options from
the View item on the menu bar). This menu allows you to add or remove columns in
the detail pane, view all the records, filter the records that are viewed, display events
from newest to oldest or oldest to newest, find a record based on search criteria, and
customize the view.

Delete This command is only available for any views added beyond the default views of the application, security, and system logs. When used on a user-added view, it *instantly* deletes it!

Rename Use this command after creating a new view of an Event Viewer log (as in the following step-by-step). Otherwise, the new view has a less-than-meaningful name like "System (2)"!

Refresh Logging is occurring even while you are using Event Viewer. This command will update Event Viewer to show any new events recorded in the log files.

Export List Use this command to export the event list to a file for import into a word processor, spreadsheet, or database program. There are four file format choices to choose from, depending on the type of file your application can import.

Properties Use this command to open the properties dialog box of the selected log.

Microsoft Windows Error Reporting

When an application or Windows component fails, you will see a dialog box asking if it should send an error report to Microsoft. If you choose to send a report, it will collect data and send it to Microsoft, and you may receive a solution to the problem. This is the Microsoft Windows Error Reporting (WER) service at work for you. Learn more about this important service.

Collection of Error Reports WER collects information about the application or component involved in the failure. When you choose to send information to Microsoft, this data is sent to Microsoft, where it is used for quality control purposes.

Analysis of Data The WER service analyzes the data, organizing error reports into classifications, or "buckets," for each problem.

watch *The CompTIA A+ exam objectives use the term "Windows Reporting" when referring to Microsoft Windows Error Reporting (WER).*

Providing Solutions If Microsoft has information that will help you to solve the problem, a message displays on your desktop with a link to a page on the Microsoft Web site that may help you with the problem. Sometimes the

SCENARIO & SOLUTION	
What are at least four symptoms of OS instability?	Symptoms include extreme slowness, inability to open programs, failure of running programs, system lockup, and complete failure of the OS.
An application that ran well in Windows 98 frequently hangs in Windows XP. How can I make the program run better in Windows XP?	Run the Program Compatibility Wizard and configure compatibility settings to create an environment for the old application similar to that provided by the old operating system.
Windows fails to start up and the following message displays: NTLDR is missing. What should I do?	Use a Windows startup disk to boot up the computer. If Windows starts up normally, copy the NTLDR file from the floppy disk to the root of drive C:.

linked page has a message that there is no more information on this problem, but other times, the linked page has a step-by-step solution to the problem. Therefore, it is worth using WER in the hopes that Microsoft has a solution to offer.

Using Diagnostic Utilities and Tools

Troubleshooting Windows requires the use of a variety of utilities and tools. In this chapter you have already explored a number of diagnostic tools and utilities. For instance, the Advanced Options menu is an invaluable tool for troubleshooting startup problems, the Recovery Console is a tool for recovering from a total failure, and Automated System Recovery gives you a complete Windows XP operating system backup set, while Windows 2000 relies on the Emergency Repair Process for recovering from a major failure.

In this section you will explore the documentation resources available to you, learn to create startup disks, and define the value of such tools as Device Manager, Task Manager, System Configuration Utility (MSCONFIG), and System File Checker.

Documentation Resources

An IT professional working with Windows operating systems quickly learns to use all the documentation resources available. The best documentation is from reliable sources—Microsoft, as well as certain third-party vendors, and some other organizations. Regardless of the source of the documentation, there are certain features you should look for. While you will still find paper documentation, the best documentation is up-to-date and searchable, which rules out most paper documentation. This includes a locally installed online manual, and Internet-based sources.

The following is an overview of useful documentation resources.

User/Installation Manuals

Most software comes with some documentation. This can range from a simple "Read me" file to a comprehensive hardcopy or disk-based manual with detailed instructions on installing, using, and troubleshooting the software. This last is becoming very rare, and read-me files usually just provide last-minute information about installing or using the software that was not included in the other documentation.

To begin, look for an installation manual, which may be a one-page quick start guide or may be a detailed manual. Check out the documentation before you have a problem with Windows or an application. Keep the paper-based manuals organized in a handy place.

Online Help

Online Help utilities are very common. Windows and most Windows applications include a Help menu on the main toolbar. Online help has come a long way from the simple text files of early PC software, which were often no more than glossaries. Windows Help includes searchable databases with extensive documentation. In fact, the Help utilities for Windows and Windows applications will search the local Help data, as well as the Microsoft Web site, including the Microsoft Knowledge Base at the Microsoft Web site, for answers to your queries.

Windows and most Windows applications will bring up context-sensitive Help when you press the F1 key. This means that it will display help information appropriate to your current operation.

Internet/Web-Based

As mentioned, a search initiated in the Help program in Windows, or most Windows applications, will result in a local search as well as a search of Internet-based sources. Beyond the Help program and the Web sites it searches, learn to search manufacturers' sites and to do Internet searches using your favorite search engine, such as Google. There are also certain sites that function as online encyclopedias, such as Wikipedia.

Training Materials

Be aware of the training opportunities available to you. You might think that when you are in the middle of troubleshooting, you do not want to participate in training. However, training has taken on new meaning with the sources available both within the Windows Help program and on the Microsoft Web site. For instance, Windows Help has Troubleshooters that walk you through troubleshooting common problems.

Try this sometime, and you will find yourself receiving training while solving a problem.

Subscription Support

In addition to free support options, such as online knowledge bases and newsgroups, Microsoft and other vendors offer for-pay support services providing varying levels of access to support help based on a range of prices. Microsoft and most other organizations charge for phone support—either a per-incident charge or as part of a support subscription.

While many organizations subscribe to these plans, others opt to have well-trained personnel who can use the free services of the manufacturers. Many use a combination of employees and subscription services. The downside of this is the expense of employing qualified personnel, but many organizations, especially large corporations, find that a well-trained in-house staff can be cost effective because they can deliver a higher level of service focused on the exact needs of the organization. Many organizations outsource all or part of their IT organization, meaning that they purchase these services from other organizations that provide on-site or remote support of computers and software.

Create Startup Disks

Ask anyone with long experience supporting Windows desktop computers if they use startup disks (actually, floppy disks), and you will probably hear about more than one type of startup disk. They will talk about MS-DOS, Windows 98, Windows NT, Windows 2000, and Windows XP startup disks. The disks allow you to start an operating system either completely, in the case of MS-DOS and Windows 98 startup disks (the latter starting up in MS-DOS), or less completely, as in the case of Windows 2000 and Windows XP startup disks. In all cases, these are handy to have when troubleshooting startup problems. Learn how to create Windows 2000 and Windows XP startup disks.

A large number of files are critical to getting Windows up and running. Have you wondered what can be done if one of those files is damaged? Not knowing how to solve a problem like this could affect your computing career, or at least ruin your day. The Windows 2000 and Windows XP startup disks are similar and can only be used through the detect and configure hardware phases. After that, there must be Windows system files on the hard disk to complete the Windows startup.

You should create a startup disk for each Windows computer that is configured to boot from floppy disk, and the floppy disk should be kept in a safe place where you can quickly access it in the event of a startup failure.

Windows is far too big to fit onto a floppy disk, but you can easily fit the boot files that must be on the system partition (the root of drive C:). Although you cannot reliably use a startup disk for one version of Windows on a computer running another version of Windows, a startup disk should work on most computers running the same version, as long as Windows was installed using default locations. The exception will be if one of the computers has a SCSI controller that requires the use of an NTBOOTDD.SYS file. To keep life simple, create a Windows boot floppy disk on each computer, and keep it handy to that computer.

To create a Windows startup disk for Windows 2000 and Windows XP, first format a floppy disk in Windows. Then copy NTLDR, NTDETECT.COM, BOOT.INI, and (if present) NTBOOTDD.SYS to the floppy disk.

You can use the floppy disk to bypass the Windows boot files in the root of C:. You will find this capability very handy if, when you try to boot normally from the hard disk, an error message indicates that it did not find one of those files. Simply insert the Windows Startup floppy disk in the floppy drive and reboot. A successful reboot will confirm that the problem is limited to the missing file. Copy it from the floppy disk to the root of C:, remove the floppy disk, and reboot the computer.

EXERCISE 10-4

Creating and Testing a Windows Startup Floppy Disk

You can create a Windows startup floppy disk for a Windows 2000 or Windows XP computer that has a floppy drive.

1. Log on as an Administrator, insert the floppy disk into the drive, open My Computer, and right-click the icon for drive A: in My Computer (be careful not to click it before you right-click, or it will not allow you to format).

2. Select Format and click Start in the Format dialog box. Click OK in the Warning box. The formatting may take a few minutes, because floppy drives are very slow (see Figure 10-11).

3. When formatting is complete, close the dialog box and return to My Computer.

4. Expand drive C: and locate the following files: NTLDR, NTDETECT.COM, BOOT.INI, and NTBOOTDD.SYS. Don't be concerned if the last file is not present, as it is present only if needed for certain hard disk controllers. Select them and copy (not move!) them to drive A:.

5. When the files have finished copying, leave the floppy disk in the drive and restart your computer. The restart should work exactly like a normal restart, except it will be slower, and you will hear drive A: work as it reads the boot files from there. After a successful restart, remove the floppy disk, label it "Windows X Startup Disk," where X is the version of Windows used, and set it aside for use if you encounter a problem booting up this computer.

Device Manager

Device Manager is a tool that allows an administrator to view and change device properties, update device drivers, configure device settings, and uninstall devices. Windows XP Device Manager will even allow an administrator to roll back a driver update. Device Manager did not exist in Windows NT, but it has been included in every other version of Windows since Windows 95. Microsoft has worked to improve this utility in each successive version.

In Windows 2000 and Windows XP, Device Manager can be found through the System applet by selecting the Hardware tab and then clicking Device Manager. It is an MMC snap-in and opens up into a separate console window. Only administrators can make modifications in Device Manager in Windows 2000 and Windows XP. Device Manager in Windows XP works almost exactly as in Windows 2000, with some small changes in viewing information, and with the addition of the new Roll

FIGURE 10-11

The Format
dialog box

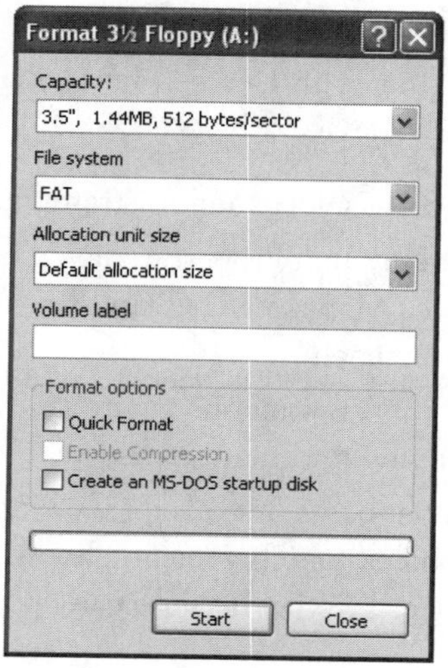

Back Driver button on the Driver tab of the Properties dialog box, as seen here. This feature works on device drivers that were updated with new drivers. It is quite handy for those times when you find the new device driver causes new problems.

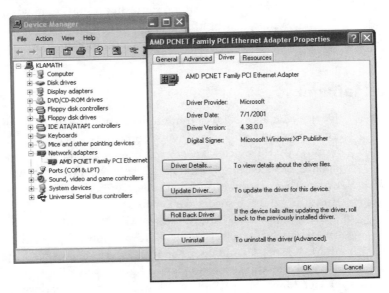

EXERCISE 10-5

Getting to Know Device Manager

Become familiar with Device Manager so that you are prepared to use it to solve problems with device drivers.

1. Log on as a local administrator, and open the System applet in Control Panel.

2. In the System Properties dialog box, select the Hardware tab, and then click Device Manager. The window that opens gives you access to all the devices on the machine.

3. Use the View menu (Figure 10-12) to experiment with various ways of changing information display.

4. You have two options for viewing devices and two options for viewing resources, which you can choose from the View menu. You will normally view devices by type, because this approach is simpler and more understandable.

5. When viewing devices by type, you will see a node for each device type, such as Computer, Disk Drives, and so on. Familiarize yourself with Device Manager by opening the nodes.

6. Click the yellow question mark in the toolbar to open Device Manager Help; and browse through the topics to learn more.

7. Find out how you can print information about a device—a handy trick if you need to give information about a problem device to someone helping you. When you are finished, close all open windows.

Task Manager

Task Manager is another utility that has been improved in each successive version of Windows. The current Task Manager does not resemble the simple tool we used to remove unresponsive programs from memory in Windows 9x, but you can still use it for that same task and more in Windows 2000 and Windows XP. Task Manager is now a very sophisticated program that allows you to end an unresponsive program and do other tasks.

It is important to know how to start Task Manager, and how to stop an unresponsive program. There are two keyboard shortcuts for opening this program. One is CTRL-SHIFT-ESCAPE, which starts up Task Manager directly. Another shortcut is CTRL-ALT-DELETE. If your computer is not configured to use the Security dialog box, Task Manager will open

FIGURE 10-12

Select a view in Device Manager.

at this point. If your computer is configured to use the Security dialog box, that will open, and from there you can click Task Manager. You can also open Task Manager by right-clicking on an empty area of the taskbar and selecting Task Manager from the context-sensitive menu that displays.

Task Manager has several tabbed sheets; the Applications tab is the one from which you view and manage GUI applications. If an application is not responding, and you cannot close the application any other way, open Task Manager, select the non-responding application, and click End Task.

System Configuration Utility (MSCONFIG)

Windows XP includes a System Configuration Utility that allows you to modify and test startup configuration settings without having to directly alter them. The program filename is MSCONFIG.EXE. Therefore, to launch the System Configuration Utility, enter MSCONFIG in the Start | Run box.

on the job *Take time to practice using the System Configuration Utility before you need to use it for troubleshooting.*

This is a great utility to use when you want to stop a program from launching at startup but do not want to search all the possible startup locations, including some legacy locations. For instance, Windows still uses some old files designed for Windows 3.x. These files are SYSTEM.INI and WIN.INI, and they still exist for downward compatibility with very old applications, written for early versions of Windows.

The value of MSCONFIG today is that it will let you test what-if scenarios for startup. For instance, you can temporarily disable the startup of one or more programs using MSCONFIG. When you make such changes from within MSCONFIG and then restart the computer, it will start up and reflect the change you made in MSCONFIG. This allows you to test to make sure that making this change would not negatively affect your computer. Once you have arrived at the desired configuration, you can instruct MSCONFIG to make the change permanent.

You can also use MSCONFIG to start up Windows with a minimal configuration, much like that used by Safe Mode.

e x a m
w a t c h

The CompTIA A+ exam objectives list refers to this utility only by its filename, MSCONFIG.EXE. The title bar for this GUI utility clearly shows its full name, System Configuration Utility. In the multiple-choice questions of the exam, you are most likely to see it referred to by its filename, but be prepared to recognize it by either of these names. Be sure that you understand when to use this utility and both of its names.

System File Checker (SFC)

System files have very privileged access to your computer, and therefore malicious software targets them. At one time system files were fair game for such software, but recent versions of Windows come with protections, both at the file system level and through the use of a service that protects system files.

This service, called Windows File Protection (WFP), maintains a file cache of protected files. If a file is somehow damaged, WFP will replace the damaged file with the undamaged file from the cache. WFP will allow digitally signed files to safely replace existing system files. The files it will allow are those distributed through the following:

- Windows service packs
- Hotfix distributions

- Operating system upgrades
- Windows Update
- Windows Device Manager

WFP will overwrite files introduced into Windows in any other way by using files from the cache.

The System File Checker (SFC) is a handy utility that uses the WFP service to scan and verify the versions of all protected system files after you restart your computer. The syntax for this program is as follows:

```
sfc [scannow] [scanonce] [scanboot] [revert] [purgecache] [cachesize=x]
```

When you run SFC with the /scannow parameter, you will see a message box like the one shown here. If SFC finds any files that do not comply, it will replace them with the correct, signed file from the cache.

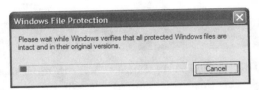

SCENARIO & SOLUTION

How can I be prepared to quickly recover from a corrupted boot file?	Create a Windows startup disk by formatting a floppy and copying the boot files NTLDR, NTDETECT.COM, BOOT.INI, and NTBOOTDD.SYS to the floppy disk.
An application has stopped responding, and I cannot close it. What should I do?	Open Task Manager, select the application in the applications page, and click End Task.
There are programs starting up in Windows, and I would like to stop them. What is a safe way to do this?	Use the System Configuration Utility (MSCONFIG.EXE) to select the program or programs you do not want to start up. Then test it by restarting. Once you are satisfied with the results, you can make the changes permanent through this utility.

CERTIFICATION OBJECTIVES

■ *601: 3.4   602: 3.4   603: 2.4   Perform preventive maintenance on operating systems*

CompTIA requires that you understand preventive maintenance tasks that you should perform on a PC on a regular basis. Preventive maintenance is important to your career, because it can eliminate the danger of certain problems from occurring and limit the amount of time you need to spend troubleshooting preventable problems.

Performing Preventive Maintenance

Preventive maintenance for Windows operating systems includes tasks that either prevent certain problems from occurring or guarantee that you can quickly recover from a problem or disaster with a minimum loss of time or data.

Preventive maintenance tasks include the following: defragmenting hard drives on a regular basis, keeping your operating system and applications updated, backing up the registry before making changes, scheduling OS and data backups, testing your ability to restore backups, and configuring System Restore so that it creates restore points without taking up unnecessary space.

Defragment Hard Drive Volumes

A common, and easily corrected, cause of system slowness is fragmented files. Windows writes files in available space beginning near the outside of the disk platters. Over time, as files are deleted, this leaves open space into which new files can be written, but large files may require more space than is available in the first available contiguous open space. The OS then places what will fit into this space, and seeks the next available space.

This practice causes files—especially large ones—to be fragmented, meaning that the various pieces of one file are in several locations on the disk. Reading or writing a fragmented file takes much longer than it does for the same file written into one contiguous space. Therefore, over time, a system will slow down simply because of the large number of fragmented files on a volume.

A simple preventive task is defragmenting the hard drive. You can do this, using one of the methods described in Chapters 8 and 9. That is, you can use the GUI program, Disk Defragmenter, the command-line program, DEFRAG.EXE, or a third-party defragmenter. Whichever program you use, defrag your hard drive volumes on a regular basis—once a week or once a month.

There are certain tasks you should perform before defragmenting a drive. Because Disk Defragmenter cannot work on the Recycle Bin, consider emptying it before running the program. This will open up more space. It also cannot defrag any open files, so close all other applications before starting Disk Defragmenter. This program also requires 15 percent free space on the drive in which to work as it moves files around. If you start defragmenting when there is insufficient space, it will stop and display an error message. Therefore, before beginning, check on the available disk space on the volume you wish to defrag. You can do this from within the GUI Disk Defragmenter program. Look at the value at the right of the drive to confirm it has more than 15 percent free space before selecting it.

If you find that you do not have enough free space, delete files. Use the Disk Cleanup program to free up adequate space. We describe this program in Chapter 8.

Turn on Automatic Updates

One of the most important preventive maintenance tasks is keeping Windows up-to-date. You learned about Windows Update in Chapter 8. We recommend using the Automatic Updates page in System Properties to configure Windows to connect to the Microsoft site and download updates automatically.

Software Updates

Software updates are also very important. For your Microsoft software, such as Office, you can use either the Microsoft Office Update site or configure Windows Update to connect to Microsoft Update, which will update both the operating system and the installed Microsoft applications.

For non-Microsoft applications, check to see if the application has an automatic update option, and configure it to check for updates automatically. Most applications do have this option.

Back Up the Registry

If you ever make changes to your Registry, it is a very good idea to back it up before you start. One of the easiest ways to save your Registry settings is to use the Export Registry File option from the Regedit program. To do this, launch Regedit by selecting Start | Run, and typing **regedit** in the Open box.

In the Registry Editor select File | Export Registry File from the menu bar to launch the Export Registry File dialog box. Select a filename and location to save your Registry File. If you damage your Registry, you can reload the old registry by selecting File | Import Registry File and selecting the REG file you created.

You can also back up the registry in Windows XP by using the Windows Backup program. Exercise 10-6 will walk you through backing up the registry, which is included with the System State. Make sure that the location to which you plan to back up has at least 500 MB of disk space, because our experience has been that the System State alone is nearly this large.

EXERCISE 10-6

Backing Up the Registry

You can easily back up the Registry.

1. Click Start | Run.
2. In the Run dialog box enter **NTBACKUP** and click OK, or press the ENTER key.
3. In the Backup Utility dialog box select the Backup tab.
4. If necessary, expand the My Computer node, and then click to place a check in the box next to System State. The System State includes the registry and other components (see Figure 10-13). You must select and back them up together.
5. At the bottom of the dialog box click Browse next to Backup Media Or File Name.
6. In the Save As dialog box, browse to the location where you want to save the system state. You can create a folder for the backup, if needed. You can also modify the filename, but do not change the Save As Type.
7. Click Save when you have selected the location and filename.
8. Click Start Backup.
9. In the Backup Job Information dialog box verify that the information is correct. You may want to change the default setting of Append This Backup To The Media to Replace The Data On The Media With This Backup in order to save disk space.
10. When you have made any necessary changes, click Start Backup. If you chose Replace The Data, you will need to respond to a Replace Data warning dialog box before it will proceed.
11. You can follow the progress in the Backup Progress window.
12. When it is complete, close the Backup Utility dialog box, and browse to the backup location to verify that the backup file is there. Notice the size of the file.

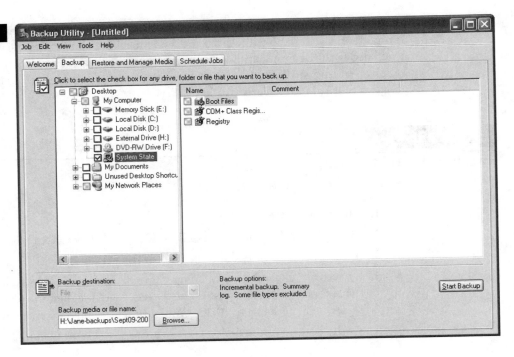

FIGURE 10-13

Select System
State to back up
the registry.

Scheduled Backups

You should perform scheduled backups of your complete system as well as data
files. Perform these backups manually according to a regular schedule, or use the
scheduling option in your backup software.

A backup requires a destination location other than drive C:. Many people back
up to a shared network folder or to an external hard drive. The Windows Backup
Utility does not support backing up directly to an optical disk, but you can do this
in a two-step process. This requires that you have a local or network drive with
sufficient space for the backup. After you complete the backup to the location
selected, copy it to a writable optical disk. This may require extra planning, as you
will not be able to copy a backup file that is larger than the capacity of the optical
disk. For instance, a CD-R only holds 650 MB.

As for the backup program itself, the Windows Backup Utility comes with Windows, and there are third-party backup programs from several vendors that offer more features than the Backup Utility.

Test Restore

If possible, occasionally test your backups by restoring them. Now, you need to be careful when doing this, because if the backup is even minutes old, and you have made changes to files since the backup, you will end up restoring on top of the changed files, and lose your work. Therefore, if possible, test your backups by restoring to another identically configured computer—perhaps one you use for test or training purposes.

Configure System Restore

As you learned in Chapter 7, System Restore is on by default, but it can also be totally disabled. We recommend that you enable it, and tweak the configuration so that it does not take up too much disk space, and so that it is not monitoring drives that do not require the System Restore service. To do this, open the System Properties applet found in Control Panel and click on the System Restore tab. On this page look at the settings under the heading Available Drives. Select a drive and then click Settings.

The default setting is for System Restore to reserve up to 12 percent of each drive for saving restore data. This can be excessive on very large hard drives.

If you have a drive used exclusively for data, turn off System Restore on that drive. Since you normally only use removable hard drives for data, be sure to turn it off for all removable hard drives.

Do not turn it off for the system drive (usually drive C:), because this is the main location of system information and therefore the most important place to save system settings information. Also, turning it off for this drive will cause it to turn off for all drives.

When you finish working with all the available drives, the Available Drives settings should look something like those in Figure 10-14. The drives with System Restore turned on will have a status of Monitoring, while those with System Restore turned off will show a status of Offline. In this case, Offline does not indicate that the drives are not available for normal saving and retrieving of data.

System Restore is turned on for drives C: and D: but turned off for drives G: and H:.

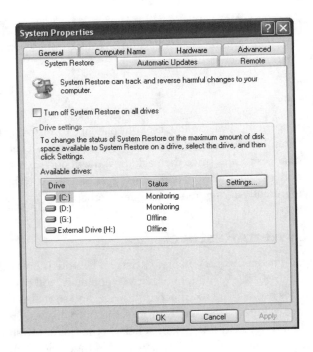

SCENARIO & SOLUTION

My computer seems to run slowly when I am accessing large files. What can I do?	A common cause for such slowness is fragmented files. Run the Windows Disk Defragmenter on your hard drive.
I often forget to run the Windows Update program to connect to the Microsoft site and update my computer. What is the solution?	Use the Automatic Updates page in System Properties to turn on Automatic Updates.
How can I ensure that System Restore is on?	Open the System Restore page in System Properties and make sure that System Restore is on for drive C: and all other permanently attached hard disk drives.

CERTIFICATION SUMMARY

An IT professional must have a foundation of knowledge about Windows in order to troubleshoot common problems. Understanding of the Windows Startup Phases helps in pinpointing the cause of startup failure. The Advanced Options menu offers a variety of choices for modifying startup for troubleshooting. The Safe Modes offered on this menu are invaluable in allowing access to a Windows installation that may otherwise fail during startup.

You also need to understand when and how to use System Restore, the Recovery Console, Automatic System Recovery (ASR), and the Emergency Repair Process. You should recognize operational problems by their symptoms, and understand the common causes and solutions to these problems. Such symptoms include instability, system lock-up, and device driver failure. Know how to troubleshoot a failed application, and how to configure a legacy application to run in a new version of Windows. Recognize common error messages and codes, and understand how to work with Event Viewer and the Microsoft Windows Error Reporting service.

Familiarize yourself with the utilities and tools for troubleshooting. Begin with documentation resources available to you for troubleshooting and training yourself in using and supporting Windows and applications. Create startup disks before you have a failed startup, and practice using Device Manager, Task Manager, System Configuration Utility (MSCONFIG), and System File Checker.

Perform preventive maintenance on Windows computers, including defragmenting hard drive volumes, turning on Automatic Updates for both Windows and applications, backing up the registry, scheduling backups, testing restore, and configuring System Restore.

TWO-MINUTE DRILL

Here are some of the key points covered in Chapter 10.

Understanding and Modifying Windows Startup

❑ The Windows startup phases are Power-on Self-Test, Initial Startup, Boot Loader, Detect and Configure Hardware, Kernel Loading, and Logon.

❑ The BOOT.INI file contains instructions to the NTLDR program that affect where it looks for the OS kernel for loading Windows. When a computer is to boot from more than one Microsoft OS, the BOOT.INI file will contain the locations of the OS files for each, and they will be displayed in the OS Selection menu, from which a user can select an OS to load.

❑ BOOT.INI also contains instructions that affect how a Windows OS is loaded.

❑ The safest way to modify the startup settings in BOOT.INI is through the Startup and Recovery Settings, accessible through the Advanced page of the System Properties dialog box.

Diagnosing and Repairing Operating System Failures

❑ You can access the Advanced Options menu by pressing F8 as the computer is restarting.

❑ The Advanced Options menu contains many alternative ways to start Windows when you are troubleshooting startup problems.

❑ Select from three Safe Mode options to troubleshoot and solve Windows problems. These are Safe Mode, Safe Mode with Networking, and Safe Mode with Command Prompt.

❑ System Restore creates restore points, which are snapshots of Windows, its configuration, and all installed programs.

❑ Restore points are created automatically when you add or remove software, or install Windows updates, and during the normal shutdown of your computer.

❑ You can also force the creation of a restore point before making changes.

❑ If your computer has nonfatal problems after you have made a change, you can use System Restore to roll it back to a restore point.

❑ The Recovery Console allows you to recover from a failure of the OS when all else has failed.

❑ The Recovery Console is a totally non-GUI command-line interface.

❑ Start the recovery console from the Windows 2000 or Windows XP CD, running Setup, and selecting Repair, then selecting Recovery Console.

❑ You can also install the Recovery Console on your hard drive, so that it is one of your startup options and does not require the Windows CD to run.

❑ From within the Recovery Console you can run various special command-line commands to repair system problems.

❑ Beginning with Windows XP, Automated System Recovery (ASR) allows you to create a backup of the system partition, which will include a bootable disk and backup media. Use this to recover from a complete failure when all other options have failed.

❑ The Emergency Repair Process made its last appearance in Windows 2000. This involved the creation of a repair disk, or the saving of repair information on the local hard disk. If the OS failed, you would run the Windows Setup program and select the Repair option.

Operational Issues and Symptoms

❑ Operational problems are those that occur while Windows is running. They include instability and may involve OS components and applications.

❑ Instability problems include extreme slowness, inability to open programs, failure of running programs, system lockup, and complete failure of the OS, resulting in a Stop error.

❑ When an application fails to start, but there are no other obvious symptoms, suspect that there is insufficient memory.

❑ If an old application will not run, and that application was for an earlier version of Windows, use the Program Compatibility Wizard to modify the environment in which the program runs so that it resembles that of the earlier version of Windows. This environment is Compatibility Mode.

Using Diagnostic Utilities and Tools

❑ Documentation Resources for your operating system and other software include quick start guides, installation manual, user manuals, online help, Internet-based sources, and training materials.

❑ Create a startup disk for a Windows 2000 or Windows XP computer by first formatting a floppy disk from within the OS and then copying the boot files to the floppy disk. These include NTLDR, NTDETECT.COM, BOOT.INI, and (if present) NTBOOTDD.SYS.

❑ Become familiar with Device Manager before you need to use it for troubleshooting.

❑ Use Task Manager to stop a program that has stopped responding and cannot be stopped any other way.

❑ Use the System Configuration Utility (MSCONFIG.EXE) to modify startup configuration settings without having to directly alter the settings. You can test startup settings without making them permanent until you are satisfied with the results.

❑ Use System File Checker (SFC) to have the Windows File Protection (WFP) service scan and verify the versions of all protected system files.

Performing Preventive Maintenance

❑ Defragment files on your hard drives on a regular basis to prevent the slowdowns that can result from file fragmentation.

❑ Turn on Automatic Updates for both Windows and your applications.

❑ Back up the registry before making changes for troubleshooting purposes. You can back up the registry by using the Registry Editor, or by using the Windows Backup Utility.

❑ You should schedule regular backups of both the OS and data files using either the Windows Backup Utility or a third-party backup program.

❑ Configure System Restore settings so that it is on for the system drive and any other drives that contain system and program data. Do not turn it on for drives that only contain data.

SELF TEST

The following questions will help you measure your understanding of the material presented in this chapter. Read all of the choices carefully because there might be more than one correct answer. Choose all correct answers for each question.

Understanding and Modifying Windows Startup

1. This startup phase, common to all PCs, tests system hardware, determines the amount of memory present, verifies that devices required for OS startup are working, and loads configuration settings from CMOS into memory.
   - A. Boot loader
   - B. POST
   - C. Detect and configure hardware
   - D. Kernel loading

2. This Windows component supports logging on and off and starts the service control manager and the local security authority.
   - A. SERVICES.EXE
   - B. Windows Logon service
   - C. LSASS.EXE
   - D. NTLDR

3. This file holds information used by NTLDR during the boot loader stage to locate the kernel and other operating system files.
   - A. NTBOOTDD.SYS
   - B. NTDETECT.COM
   - C. NTOSKRNL.EXE
   - D. BOOT.INI

4. What is the safest GUI tool for editing the system startup settings of the BOOT.INI file?
   - A. Notepad
   - B. REGEDIT
   - C. System Properties dialog box
   - D. Automatic Updates

Diagnosing and Repairing Operating Systems Failures

5. Where can you access Safe Mode?
   A. Start menu
   B. Advanced Options menu
   C. Control Panel
   D. Systems Properties

6. In what startup mode should you attempt to start Windows after making a change to the video settings that results in the Windows GUI not displaying properly, making it impossible to work in the GUI?
   A. Software Compatibility Mode
   B. System Restore
   C. Boot Logging
   D. Enable VGA Mode

7. Automated System Recovery (ASR) in Windows XP replaced this recovery option, discontinued after Windows 2000.
   A. Recovery Console
   B. Emergency Repair Process
   C. Startup
   D. System Restore

8. Last Known Good (LKG) only works within a narrow window of opportunity that ends when the following occurs:
   A. A user logs on.
   B. The computer reboots.
   C. The disk is defragmented.
   D. A restore point is created.

9. This Windows XP recovery tool creates a backup of the entire system partition, as well as a boot disk to start the recovery process.
   A. System Restore
   B. Automated System Recovery
   C. Last Known Good
   D. Safe Mode

Operational Issues and Symptoms

10. What can you do if your computer becomes unstable after you interrupt hibernation?

    A. Power off and power up.

    B. Put the computer in Sleep Mode.

    C. Use Hibernate Recovery Mode.

    D. Look for an error message in Event Viewer.

11. How can you control Windows' automatic behavior after a Stop error?

    A. Power off and power up.

    B. Modify System Failure settings.

    C. Open Event Viewer.

    D. Use System Restore.

12. What can cause an application to fail to start without issuing an error message?

    A. A Stop error

    B. Hibernation turned off

    C. Sleep Mode

    D. Insufficient memory

13. What mode can you use to allow a legacy application to run well in Windows XP?

    A. GUI Mode

    B. Legacy Mode

    C. Compatibility Mode

    D. Virtual Mode

Using Diagnostic Utilities and Tools

14. After receiving an error message in Windows, I searched for the error message using the Help program. It failed to find a solution, even though it searched the Microsoft Knowledge Base. Where can I search now?

    A. Locate the paper documentation for Windows.

    B. Call Microsoft's free 24-hour support line.

    C. Search the Internet using the error message.

    D. Locate the Windows Read Me file.

15. To create a startup disk for Windows 2000 or Windows XP, you first format a floppy disk and then copy this group of files to the disk.
    A. System files
    B. Kernel files
    C. Registry files
    D. Boot files

16. If you upgrade a device driver in Windows XP only to find it causes problems, use this feature in Device Manager to return to the old device driver.
    A. Roll Back Driver
    B. Update Driver
    C. Uninstall
    D. Driver Details

17. What GUI tool will you use to stop an application that is not responding to mouse and keyboard commands?
    A. Startup disk
    B. Task Manager
    C. System Configuration Utility
    D. Device Manager

18. What GUI tool will allow you to modify and test Windows startup configuration settings without having to alter them directly? Once you are satisfied, you can use this tool to make the settings permanent.
    A. Device Manager
    B. Safe Mode
    C. Notepad
    D. MSCONFIG

Performing Preventive Maintenance

19. What utility should I run to free up more disk space before using Disk Defragmenter on a drive?
    A. Format
    B. Task Manager
    C. Disk Cleanup
    D. System File Checker

20. What utility includes the registry as part of the System State for purposes of backing up the registry?

    A. REGEDIT

    B. NTBACKUP

    C. MSCONFIG

    D. System File Checker

LAB QUESTION

Describe the differences between the Windows XP recovery tools: System Restore and Automatic System Recovery.

SELF TEST ANSWERS

Understanding and Modifying Windows Startup

1. ☑ **B.** POST is the startup phase, common to all PCs, that tests system hardware, determines the amount of memory present, verifies that devices required for OS startup are working, and loads configuration settings from CMOS into memory. It is also the first startup phase.

   ☒ **A,** boot loader, is incorrect because it is not the startup phase described in the question. Boot loader is the third phase in the startup process. **C,** detect and configure hardware, is incorrect because it is not the startup phase described in the question. It is the fourth phase in the startup process. **D,** kernel loading, is incorrect because it is not the startup phase described in the question. It is the fifth phase.

2. ☑ **B.** Windows Logon service is the component that supports logging on and off and starts the service control manager and the local security authority.

   ☒ **A,** SERVICES.EXE, is incorrect because it is just one of the services started by the Windows Logon service. **C,** LSASS.EXE, is incorrect because that is the local security authority service, just one of the services started by the Windows Logon service. **D,** NTLDR, is incorrect because this is the program in charge of the boot loader stage of Windows startup.

3. ☑ **D.** BOOT.INI is the file that holds information used by NTLDR during the boot loader state to locate the kernel of the operating system.

   ☒ **A,** NTBOOTDD.SYS, is incorrect because this file is the SCSI driver for a Windows system with a SCSI hard disk controller. **B,** NTDETECT.COM, is incorrect because this is the file that is loaded by NTLDR during the detect and configure hardware phase of Windows startup. **C,** NTOSKRNL.EXE, is incorrect because this is the kernel of the Windows operating system that is loaded during the kernel-loading phase of Windows startup.

4. ☑ **C.** The System Properties dialog box is the safest GUI tool for editing the system startup settings of the BOOT.INI file.

   ☒ **A,** Notepad, is incorrect because, although this can be used to edit the BOOT.INI file, it is not the safest GUI tool to use for this purpose. **B,** REGEDIT, is incorrect because this is not a tool for editing the BOOT.INI file, but for editing the registry. **D,** Automatic Updates, is incorrect because this is not a tool for editing the BOOT.INI file, but for having updates automatically downloaded to Windows.

Diagnosing and Repairing Operating Systems Failures

5. ☑ **B.** The Advanced Options menu is the place where you can access Safe Mode. Get to this menu by pressing the F8 key immediately after restarting your computer.

☒ **A**, Start menu, is incorrect because this is not where you can access Safe Mode. **C**, Control Panel, is incorrect because this is not where you can access Safe Mode. **D**, Systems Properties, is incorrect because this is not where you can access Safe Mode.

6. ☑ **D.** Enable VGA Mode is the startup mode you should attempt after making a change to the video settings that result in Windows not displaying properly.

☒ **A**, Software Compatibility Mode, is incorrect because this is not a startup mode for the operating system, but a mode for running a legacy application. **B**, System Restore, is incorrect because this is not a startup mode for the operating system, but a tool for restoring the operating system to a previous point in time. **C**, Boot Logging, is incorrect because this is a startup option that will cause the system to create a log of all components as they are loaded and started.

7. ☑ **B.** Emergency Repair Process is the discontinued Windows 2000 recovery option replaced by Automated System Recovery (ASR) in Windows XP.

☒ **A**, Recovery Console, is incorrect because, while this is a recovery option, it existed for Windows 2000 and has continued for later versions of Windows. **C**, Startup, is incorrect because this is not a recovery option. **D**, System Restore, is incorrect because while it is a recovery option, it did not exist in Windows 2000 but is part of Windows XP.

8. ☑ **A.** A user logs on is the event that terminates the window of opportunity for using Last Known Good.

☒ **B**, the computer reboots, is incorrect because you must restart the computer and press F8 to access the Advanced Options menu from which to select Last Known Good. **C**, the disk is defragmented, is incorrect. This has no bearing on the use of Last Known Good. **D**, a restore point is created, is incorrect because this has no effect on using Last Known Good.

9. ☑ **B.** Automated System Recovery is the recovery tool that creates a backup of the entire system partition, as well as a boot disk to start the recovery process.

☒ **A**, System Restore, is incorrect because this does not create a backup of the entire system partition, nor does it create a boot disk. **C**, Last Known Good, is incorrect because Last Known Good only uses a set of registry keys; it does not back up the entire system partition. **D**, Safe Mode, is incorrect because this is simply a special startup mode, not a backup of the system partition.

Operational Issues and Symptoms

10. ☑ **A.** Power off and power up your computer if it becomes unstable after you interrupt hibernation.

☒ **B**, put the computer in Sleep Mode, is incorrect because it will not correct the problem. **C**, use Hibernate Recovery Mode, is incorrect because there is no such mode discussed in this book. **D**, look for an error message in Event Viewer, is incorrect because, while it is always wise to check the Event Logs while troubleshooting, the recommended action for the problem described is to power off and power up.

11. ☑ **B.** Modify System Failure settings. These can be found in the System Properties dialog box. Click Settings under Startup and Recovery on the Advanced page.

    ☒ **A,** power off and power up, is incorrect because this will only happen automatically if you change the System Failure settings. **C,** open Event Viewer, is incorrect because this does not control Windows' automatic behavior after a Stop error. **D,** use System Restore, is incorrect because this will not alter Windows' automatic behavior after a Stop error.

12. ☑ **D.** Insufficient memory can cause an application to fail to start without issuing an error message.

    ☒ **A,** a Stop error, is incorrect because, while this will only display the Stop error message, it is not necessarily related to the cause of the problem described. **B,** hibernation turned off, is incorrect because this is not related to the problem described. **C,** Sleep Mode, is incorrect because this will not cause the problem described.

13. ☑ **C.** You can use Compatibility Mode to allow a legacy application to run well in Windows XP.

    ☒ **A,** GUI Mode, is incorrect because this is not used to allow a legacy application to run well in Windows XP. **B,** Legacy Mode, is incorrect because this is not the mode described. **D,** Virtual Mode, is incorrect because this is not the mode described.

Using Diagnostic Utilities and Tools

14. ☑ **C.** Search the Internet using the error message is correct.

    ☒ **A,** locate the paper documentation for Windows, is incorrect because this is not as searchable as the Microsoft site, or the Internet. **B,** call Microsoft's 24-hour support line, is incorrect because the Microsoft phone support is a service for which they charge. If it is available to the user, that user will either pay per-incident or be part of a paid subscription plan. **D,** locate the Windows Read Me file, is incorrect because it holds very limited information.

15. ☑ **D.** Boot files is the group of files you copy to a floppy disk to create a Windows 2000 or Windows XP startup disk.

    ☒ **A,** system files, is incorrect because these files are too large to copy to a floppy disk and rely on the work of the boot file to load them into memory from the hard drive. **B,** kernel files, is incorrect because there is actually only one file, not a group, called the kernel, and this cannot be used to create a Windows startup disk for the same reasons given for answer A. **C,** registry files, is incorrect for the same reason given for answer A.

16. ☑ **A.** Roll Back Driver is the feature in Windows XP's Device Manager that will allow you to return to an old device driver after upgrading.

    ☒ **B,** Update Driver, is incorrect because this feature installs an updated driver; it does not remove an updated driver and return to the old driver. **C,** Uninstall, is incorrect because this will completely uninstall the driver for the device. **D,** Driver Details, is incorrect because this will only display information about the driver files.

17. ☑ **B.** Task Manager is the GUI tool used to stop an application that is not responding to mouse and keyboard commands.
☒ **A,** startup disk, is incorrect because this is neither a GUI tool nor the tool to use to stop a non-responsive application. **C,** System Configuration Utility, and **D,** Device Manager, are incorrect because neither is the correct GUI tool to use to stop a non-responsive application.

18. ☑ **D.** MSCONFIG is the tool that will allow you to modify and test startup configuration settings without having to alter them directly.
☒ **A,** Device Manager, is incorrect because this GUI tool works solely with device drivers, not with the Windows startup settings. **B,** Safe Mode, is incorrect because this is simply a startup mode that allows you to troubleshoot and make changes using a variety of tools. **C,** Notepad, is incorrect because this is simply a Windows text editor.

Performing Preventive Maintenance

19. ☑ **C.** Disk Cleanup will free up more disk space to be defragmented.
☒ **A,** Format, is incorrect because this will remove all files from the drive. **B,** Task Manager, is incorrect because this utility will not free up more disk space. **D,** System File Checker, is incorrect because it is not the utility to use for freeing up more disk space.

20. ☑ **B.** NTBACKUP (also known as the Windows Backup Utility) includes the registry as part of the System State for purposes of backing up the registry.
☒ **A.** REGEDIT, is incorrect because, while you can use it to back up the registry, it does not also back up the other components of the System State. **C,** MSCONFIG, is incorrect because this utility cannot back up the registry. **D,** System File Checker, is incorrect because this utility cannot back up the registry.

LAB ANSWER

The two recovery tools System Restore and Automatic System Recovery (ASR) are for two levels of system damage. You can use System Restore after a configuration change causes problems but you are still able to start the operating system and use System Restore to return to a point in time (a restore point). ASR is useful when you cannot start Windows XP Professional in any mode and have determined that the operating system is irretrievably damaged.

Part IV

Printers and Scanners

11

Using and Supporting Printers and Scanners

I t may seem odd to combine the discussion of printers and scanners into one chapter. This is especially true when you consider the relationship of each of these devices to a computer, because they appear to be polar opposites. A scanner is an input device that can copy the contents of a printed page or an image into a computer's memory, while a printer is an output device, capable of producing hard copy of text or graphics from the computer. However, the task of inputting graphic and/or text documents for storage and editing purposes actually has a nice fit with printing those same documents. In fact, this relationship has developed into marrying scanning and printing technologies into "all-in-one" devices that include both scanners and printers within one box.

In this chapter, you will examine printers and scanners separately to understand the types of each in use, and the technologies, components, and consumables involved. You will learn about the typical issues with installing and configuring printers and scanners, the typical upgrading and optimizing options for each type of device, troubleshooting issues, and preventive maintenance.

CERTIFICATION OBJECTIVES

■ **601: 4.1   602: 4.1   603: 3.1   604: 3.1**   *Identify the fundamental principles of using printers and scanners*

CompTIA requires that A+ certification candidates recognize the various types of printers and scanners available for use with PCs, and understand the differences among each of these device types so that you can make purchasing decisions and determine the consumables required for each.

Understanding Printers and Scanners

Printers are the most common peripherals used with PCs. While scanners are not nearly as common as printers, their use by all levels of users has grown in recent years, as prices have dropped and they have become easier to install and use. Therefore, a PC support professional must understand both printer and scanner technologies. This involves understanding how each type of device works, the consumables required, and the various interfaces used between the device and the PC.

Printer Technologies

This discussion of printer technologies covers the types of printers, the medium, and paper feeding technologies.

Types of Printers

There are several types of printers commonly used with PCs. They include impact, laser, inkjet, solid ink, and thermal.

Impact   *Impact* printers include daisy wheel, type-bar, chain, and dot matrix, among others. Like an old-fashioned typewriter, an impact printer has a roller or platen against which a physical impact occurs when a print head strikes an ink ribbon, transferring ink to paper that feeds around the roller. Most of the impact printers listed here are extinct, with the dot matrix printer still holding its own in special uses. The only other of these that you may run into is the daisy wheel printer, which has a wheel of fixed characters, much like a typewriter, that is used to imprint these characters on paper. The only impact printer currently being sold is dot matrix.

The dot matrix impact printer is the original type of printer used with PCs. The most common use for dot matrix impact printers today is for printing multiple-page receipts or forms. In fact, these printers are often referred to as "receipt printers."

Dot matrix printers are so named because they use a matrix of pins to create dots on the paper, forming alphanumeric characters and graphic images. Each pin is attached to a solenoid, which, when activated, forces the pin toward the paper. As the print head (which contains the pins) moves across the page, different pins move forward to strike a printer ribbon against the paper, causing ink on the ribbon to adhere to the paper. Because they create printouts line by line, dot matrix printers are also called line printers. As printers that physically strike the ribbon and paper, dot matrix printers fall into the impact printer category. The impact printing process is often very loud, and the wear-and-tear of the repeated impact makes these printers prone to mechanical failures.

Dot matrix printers do not provide very good resolution. That is, text and images usually appear grainy, and you can usually see each individual printed dot. Furthermore, dot matrix printers are limited in their ability to use color. Most of these printers can use one printer ribbon only (typically black, although you can substitute another color). Although some dot matrix printers can use ribbons with more than one (up to four) colors and/or more than one (up to four) printer ribbons, dot matrix printers are not capable of producing as many color combinations as other printer types.

Laser   Laser printers are printers that use a coherent, concentrated light beam (laser) in the printing process. They are generally faster than other types of printers, provide the best quality, and have the most complex structure and process. Because of the high quality and speed, these are perhaps the most commonly used printers in business environments, especially for shared network printers. Figure 11-1 shows a typical laser printer.

Although some laser printers use slightly different processes, the one described here is the generally accepted order of events that occur in the laser printing process. Note that these events occur in cycles, so it is not as important to know which step is first or last; rather, it is the order of events that is important. For example, some sources list charging as the first step, while others list cleaning as the first step.

exam
ⓦatch

Make sure that you are familiar with the laser print process, especially the order of the stages and what each stage accomplishes. Remember, the stages are in a cycle, so where you begin is not terribly important. For the exam, be sure that you can select the correct order when presented with several choices.

In a laser printer, the drum is made of metal with an electro-photosensitive coating. The drum is actually very slender, more like a tube, with a typical circumference of less than an inch. For this reason, the printing cycle must repeat several times per printout page. Both the drum and the primary corona wire usually are contained within the

FIGURE 11-1

A desktop laser printer

toner cartridge. When a page is to be printed, the paper starts to move and the drum rotates. All the steps that follow occur repeatedly while the paper is moving and the drum is turning.

1. **Charging** In the charging step, the printer's high-voltage power supply (HVPS) conducts electricity to the primary corona wire, a wire that stretches across the printer's photosensitive drum, not touching it, but very close to the drum's surface. The charge exists on the wire, and in a corona (electrical field) around the length of the wire. The voltage passes a strong negative charge to the drum.

on the *Some laser printers use charged rollers rather than a corona wire to pass*
job *voltage to the drum.*

2. **Writing** The photosensitive drum now contains a very high negative charge. In the writing step, the printer's laser beam moves along the drum, creating a negative of the image that will eventually appear on the printout. Because the drum is photosensitive, each place that the laser beam touches loses most of its charge. By the end of the writing step, the image exists at a low voltage while the rest of the drum remains highly charged. The lamp that generates this laser beam is normally located within the printer body itself, rather than in the toner cartridge.

3. **Developing** In this stage, the open cover on the printer's toner cartridge lets toner be attracted to the drum. The toner itself consists of microscopic particles that are attracted to the relatively less negatively charged areas of the drum. By the end of this stage, the drum contains a toner-covered image (in the shape of the final printout).

4. **Transferring** At this point, the paper moving through the printer passes the drum. The transfer corona wire, located within the body of the printer, and very close to the paper as it travels, applies a small positive charge to the paper as it passes through. This positive charge "pulls" the negatively charged toner from the drum onto the paper. The only thing holding the toner to the paper at this point is an electrical charge.

5. **Fusing** The toner itself contains resin, which melts when heated. As the paper leaves the printer, it passes through a set of fusing rollers, heated by a fusing lamp, which press the toner onto the paper, and the hot rollers cause

the toner to melt, or fuse, to the paper, creating a permanent non-smearing image. The fusing components, called the fuser assembly, are normally located within the body of the printer rather than in the toner cartridge.

6. **Cleaning**   There are two parts to the cleaning state. First, when the image on the drum transfers to the paper a cleaning blade (normally located within the toner cartridge) removes residual toner, which drops into a small reservoir or returns to the toner cartridge. Next, one or more high-intensity erasure lamps (located within the body of the printer) shine on the photosensitive drum, removing any remaining charge on that portion of the drum. The drum continues to rotate to step 1 and the cycle continues.

on the !
ⓘo b   *Understanding the laser printing process will help you determine which component is at fault when troubleshooting problems.*

The laser printer is a non-impact printer, because it does not require any form of physical impact to transfer an image to a printout. Because it creates printouts one page at a time (rather than one line at a time), a laser printer is called a page printer.

Laser printers use very small dots of toner, so they are able to provide excellent resolution. They are also able to blend colors into practically any shade. A color laser printer uses four toner cartridges, and the writing and developing stages take place four times (once for each color—black, cyan, magenta, and yellow) before the image transfers to the paper.

SCENARIO & SOLUTION

What is the function of the laser beam generated in a laser printer?	To reduce the printer drum's charge in areas that will later hold toner.
In a laser printer, how does the image get from the drum to the paper?	The transfer corona wire applies a positive charge to the paper. As the paper passes the drum, the negatively charged toner is attracted to the page.
How is the photosensitive drum in a laser printer cleaned?	A cleaning blade removes residual toner from the drum, and an erasure lamp removes any remaining charge from the drum.
What makes the toner in a laser printer stick to the paper?	In a laser printer, when the paper carrying the transferred image passes through the heated fusing rollers, the resin in the toner melts and permanently adheres the toner to the paper.

Laser printers are generally the quietest and fastest printers, but they are also the most expensive to operate. The toner cartridges for a typical non-color desktop laser printer run around $50 and up, but they last for several thousand pages, making these printers inexpensive per page to use. Color laser cartridges are several hundred dollars a set but offer very high quality and also print thousands of pages before you need to replace the cartridges.

Inkjet   The printers we lump together as inkjet printers use several technologies to apply wet ink to paper to create text or graphic printouts. These printers provide much better resolution than dot matrix printers, and many of them create wonderful color output because, unlike dot matrix printers, inkjets can combine basic colors to produce a wide range of colors. Inkjet printers are not nearly as loud as dot matrix printers and are much faster. Figure 11-2 shows an inkjet printer.

The two most popular inkjet printers are the InkJet, developed by Hewlett-Packard, and the Bubblejet, developed by Canon. Epson uses the term "ink jet" (with a space) but it does not appear in the model names of their printers. As described in the text that follows, inkjet and bubblejet printers differ in how they transfer an image to the paper. Beyond the discussion of these differences, however, when we use the term "inkjet" in this chapter it applies to both types of printers as well as others with similar technology.

e x a m

ⓦ a t c h   *Technically, we could lump inkjet and bubblejet printers under the heading of "ink dispersion" printers. However, the A+ exam objectives use the term "inkjet" to cover both technologies.*

The ink cartridge in an inkjet printer contains a small pump that forces ink out of the reservoir, through nozzles, and onto the page. When it comes to these nozzles, there are many. For instance, an Epson Stylus Photo R220 printer has 180 nozzles per cartridge, with one cartridge for each color. Small nozzles make small droplets.

FIGURE 11-2

An inkjet printer

The ink droplets are measured in picoliters. A picoliter is a trillionth (one millionth of a millionth) of a liter. That same Epson Stylus Photo printer has ink droplets that measure 1.5 picoliters.

Bubblejet printers resemble inkjets, but their ink cartridges contain heating elements rather than pumps. When the element is heated, the ink expands and forms a bubble of ink on the nozzle. When the bubble becomes large enough, it "bursts" onto the paper and creates a dot of color. Although this process sounds messy, bubblejets produce very high-quality printouts.

Inkjet printers create printouts line by line, so they are line printers, but their print mechanisms do not make contact with the page, making them non-impact printers.

Inkjet and bubblejet printers are usually inexpensive. The significant costs of these printers are the cartridges. It is not unusual for it to cost between 12 and 25 cents per printed page. So, while these printers are inexpensive to buy, the cost of the consumables (ink) can be quite high.

Solid Ink　There are two types of printers that use solid (rather than liquid) ink. One is dye-sublimation, and the other is a thermal wax printer, which is normally classified as a thermal printer. We will discuss thermal printers after the description of dye-sublimation printers and how they work.

The ink in a dye-sublimation printer is in a solid form, embedded into a roll of heat-sensitive plastic film. The roll contains full-page size areas of solid ink (or dye)—one for each color, normally cyan, magenta, yellow, and often black. The roll of film (also called a dye ribbon roll) rolls past a print head that is normally the width of the paper. The print head presses the film against the paper as the paper passes over a roller that acts much like the platen roller in a typewriter or dot matrix printer. The print head contains thousands of heating elements that vaporize the ink so that it adheres to the paper.

For each page printed out, the dye-sublimation process requires one pass for each color, causing the colors to mix to the desired shade as they adhere to the paper.

Dye-sublimation printers are very expensive, and their use is limited to when high-quality color printing is very important.

Thermal　A thermal printer uses heat in the image transfer process. Thermal printers for PCs fall into two categories: direct thermal printers and thermal wax transfer printers.

In a direct thermal printer a heated print head burns dots into the surface of paper. The paper used in these printers is heat sensitive. Early fax machines used this technology for printing, and direct thermal printers still work as receipt printers in retail businesses.

In thermal wax transfer, printers use a film coated with colored wax that melts onto paper. These printers are similar to dye-sublimation printers but differ in two major ways: the film contains wax rather than dye, and these printers do not require special paper. Thermal wax transfer printers are, therefore, cheaper than most dye-sublimation printers, but the dye-sublimation printers create higher-quality output.

Paper Feeding Technologies

The two most common paper-feeding technologies are friction feed and continuous form feed. A printer using friction feed moves paper by grasping each piece of paper with rollers. All the printer types discussed here can and often do use friction feed.

Inkjet, bubblejet, and laser printers use friction feed to move paper through the printer. Some of these, especially laser printers, use more than one set of rollers to keep the page moving smoothly until ejecting it. In addition to hand-feeding friction-fed printers one page at a time, most printers using this type of feed have some type of tray that can hold many sheets to automatically feed into the printer. This can amount to a few pages in vertical trays, to up to several reams in the large paper feeders of high-end network printers.

Dot matrix printers often are capable of friction feed but also offer continuous form feed. This requires sheets of paper attached to each other at perforated joints. Further, continuous form paper has about a half-inch-wide border at each side that attaches with perforations. This tear-away border has holes that accommodate the sprockets on the tractor feed mechanism, effectively pulling the paper through the printer. When using continuous form feed, you must disable the friction feed.

Checks, receipts, and other forms, including multiple part forms, use continuous form feed paper. Because these forms often have specific areas in which the information must print, a necessary step when inserting this paper into the printer is to accurately align the perforation between each form with a guide on the printer.

Printer Components

The actual printer components vary, depending on the printing and paper feed technology of the printer. However, regardless of the printing technology used, all printers have a certain set of components in common. They include the system board, memory, driver and related software, firmware, and consumables.

System Board

Each printer contains a system board that serves the same purpose as a PC's motherboard. Often referred to simply as a printer board, this circuit board contains a processor, ROM, and RAM. The processor runs the code contained in the ROM, using the RAM memory as workspace, composing the incoming print jobs (in most printers) and storing them while waiting to print them.

Driver

A new printer comes packaged with a disk containing drivers—usually for several operating systems. Like drivers for other devices, a print driver allows you to control a printer through the operating system.

Printer Language

Beyond a driver that physically controls the action of a printer, the computer must also have special software printer language that translates the characters and graphics of your computer-generated document into a form that the printer can compose and print out. Common printer languages include PostScript, Hewlett-Packard Printer Control Language (PCL), Windows GDI, and other vendor-specific printer languages.

Firmware

A printer, like a computer and most devices, has its own firmware code, including BIOS code that contains the low-level instructions for controlling the computer. Printer BIOS code is accessed by the driver, which is installed into the operating system. Another type of firmware code in printers is an interpreter for at least one printer language.

Consumables

Printer consumables include toner, ink, and paper. The printer medium is a consumable that contains the pigment for the image that a printer creates. The medium comes in a special form for the technology and specific to the model of printer. The most common forms are ink ribbon, ink cartridge, and laser printer toner cartridge.

The shelf life of both laser printer toner cartridges and inkjet printer cartridges are similar, and are usually two years from production date, and six months from when the package is first opened (or first put into use).

Used printer consumables can negatively affect the environment and should be disposed of in a manner that is both legal and respectful of the environment. In Chapter 17 you will explore the best methods for disposing of used consumables.

Ink   Ink for printers comes in the form of ink ribbons for dot matrix printers, and ink cartridges for inkjet and bubblejet printers. The medium for a dot matrix printer is an inked ribbon—a fabric ribbon embedded with ink. The medium for inkjet printers is ink, contained in reservoirs. In the case of inkjet printers, this reservoir is part of a small cartridge that also contains the print head that sprays the ink on the paper. Bubblejet printers use cartridges with the ink reservoir that also contains the print head required to heat the ink so that it creates the bubbles that burst onto the paper.

If you search the documentation or the manufacturer's Web site, you can discover the expected yield of a cartridge. The yield of an inkjet cartridge is in the hundreds of pages. For instance, an Epson R220 Photo Printer shows a black ink cartridge yield of 630 pages of text (using the OSI/IEC 10561 letter pattern) and 450 pages for graphic printouts that have 5 percent coverage. The same printer shows a color ink yield of 430 pages with 5 percent coverage per color. If your printouts used more ink per page, then the yield will be much smaller.

on the
Ỉob   *The International Organization for Standardization (ISO) and International Electrotechnical Commission (IEC) developed the ISO/IEC 10561 letter pattern for measuring the throughput of printers. It specifies test patterns for each of the following types of documents: a standard business letter, a spreadsheet, and a graphic pattern.*

Toner   Toner is the medium for laser printers and is normally available packaged within a toner cartridge. The toner consists of fine particles of clay combined with pigment and resin.

The cartridges for many laser printers also contain the cylindrical photosensitive drum, the cleaning blade, and other components, that are also considered consumables, because the entire cartridge together with its contents is normally replaced once the toner is consumed by printing.

There are many companies that take used printer cartridges, recondition the drum and other components, refill the toner reservoir with fresh toner, and offer them at significantly lower cost than manufacturer's fresh cartridges. We have had mixed experience with these "refilled" cartridges. Some refilled/reconditioned cartridges have performed as well as the best brand-name new toner cartridges, while others have produced, at best, low-quality printouts from the beginning.

The brand-name cartridges from your printer's manufacturer will normally produce the highest quality and demand the highest price. We often buy new cartridges from a company that sells both new and reconditioned cartridges. No matter what vendor we use for our toner cartridges, we always buy from one that takes our old toner cartridges for recycling at no cost to us.

The yield of a laser cartridge for a typical desktop monochrome black laser printer is several thousand pages. Numbers such as 6000 are not uncommon.

The yield for a color laser printer generally runs over 1000 pages per cartridge. For instance, the documentation for one model of the Epson color AcuLaser estimates the yield for a standard-capacity black toner cartridge at 4000 pages, while that for each of the standard cyan, magenta, and yellow cartridges is estimated at 1500 pages. The high-capacity color toner cartridges for this printer show an expected yield of 4000 pages.

on the job *When working with laser printers and handling toner cartridges, avoid breathing in the toner powder. While the chemical makeup of laser toner may not be harmful, the super-fine powder form of laser toner poses a hazard to your lungs.*

Paper   With the exception of printers that require tractor-feed paper, most printers can use ordinary copier paper for drafts and everyday casual printing. For the best results, however, consult the printer documentation for the type and quality of paper to use.

CERTIFICATION OBJECTIVES

■ **601: 4.2**   *Identify basic concepts of installing, configuring, optimizing, and upgrading printers and scanners*

■ **602: 4.2   603: 3.2   604: 3.2**   *Install, configure, optimize, and upgrade printers and scanners*

CompTIA requires that A+ candidates understand the steps for installing scanners and both Plug-and-Play and non-Plug-and-Play printers. Once one of these devices is installed, you need to understand where to go in the user interface to configure, optimize, and upgrade it.

Printer and Scanner Technologies

The Plug-and-Play nature of Windows, as well as of printers and scanners, makes installing and configuring these devices quite easy, even for the ordinary PC user. In this section explore the issues related to installing printers and scanners.

Scanner Technologies

A *scanner* is a device that uses optical technology to scan something and process information from the scan. Some scanners interpret symbols, such as UPC codes, while others can copy an image of anything you can place in front of their optics. In most cases, the item to scan is a piece of paper. The technology falls under a large category called optical technology, or technology using light.

Types of Scanners

The vast majority of scanners used with PCs are image scanners. Scanners of another type, bar code readers used in many businesses, large and small, are also discussed here.

Bar Code Readers   While not a common PC peripheral, bar code readers are very common scanners. In most grocery stores bar code readers are part of the checkout station counter, and the checker simply passes each item over this reader with the printed bar code, also called a UPC code, positioned to be read.

In that same grocery store you often see employees in the aisle using handheld bar code readers to scan products for inventory. Package delivery services use bar code readers to track packages from source to destination.

Bar code readers read bar codes, which are patterns of bars of varying widths printed on labels or directly on items. The bar code reader generates a beam of light that the bar code image reflects to a light-sensitive detector. The bar pattern is converted into a numeric code that is transmitted to a computer as data.

Image Scanners   High-end scanners used by publishing companies are usually drum scanners, which we will not address in this book. When talking about a scanner attached to PCs, we usually are referring to an image scanner, which converts a printed image to data for input to a computer. There are two general types of image scanners used today in PCs: handheld scanners and flatbed scanners. A handheld image scanner looks much like a handheld bar code reader. These are far less common than they were several years ago when flatbed scanners were still very expensive. Today, the most common image scanner used with PCs, a flatbed scanner, also called a desktop scanner, can scan high-quality images. A variation on the flatbed scanner is the sheet-fed scanner in which the document moves, while the scan head is stationary.

The technology is very much like that of a bar code reader: the scanner directs a beam of light onto the image, which reflects back to a sensor in the scanner that measures the intensity of the reflected light.

However, bar code readers do not normally need to be concerned with color, while image scanners most often do need to accurately duplicate the colors in an image. For this color image, scanners use filters to separate the colors of the reflected light into red, green, and blue components. These are additive colors, because they can be added together in varying amounts to create all colors. A scanner interprets the depth of colors and stores information about each point on a document in digital form. The computer then interprets it so that the image can be faithfully displayed and printed.

Optical Character Recognition

Without further processing, your computer sees a scanned image as a graphic bitmap image, whether it's a picture or printed text. If you wish to view and edit scanned print images in your word processor, or other program that works with text, then you must convert the scanned image into a data document using specialized software that uses optical character recognition (OCR) software.

OCR software interprets the pattern of dots in the image as words. To do so, it must first isolate a pattern that appears to represent a single character. It then attempts to recognize the pattern and determine what character it represents. This may sound easy, until you consider all the various fonts and treatments we use in our documents.

This book contains body text that is a serif font, meaning that it has small serifs, or tiny lines at the end points of each letter. The chapter titles and section heads of this book are in a sans serif font, meaning that the font does not have these curved lines. Serif and sans serif are two broad categories under which many fonts fall. Each font has its own special design for each character.

The fonts chosen for this book are very readable, but some fonts, such as 𝕺𝖑𝖉 𝕰𝖓𝖌𝖑𝖎𝖘𝖍 font, are difficult for even a human to read and can really confuse an OCR program. Therefore, you should check an OCR-converted scanned document for accuracy.

The Image Scanning Process

In the image scanning process a bar of light moves across a printed page. Light reflects from the page back to the scanner, where it focuses on light-sensitive diodes that convert the light into electricity. Circuitry in the scanner converts the electricity to numeric data and then transmits this data to the computer.

Scanner Components

Scanner components that support the image scanning process include the following:

- **Bulb**   Each scanner has one or more bulbs to generate the bar of light at the core of the image scanning process. These bulbs are the main consumable components and can be expensive to replace—both in the price of the bulb itself and the labor to replace them, since they are often not user serviceable.
- **Lens**   An optical lens focuses the reflected light onto light-sensitive diodes.
- **Light-sensitive diodes**   Diodes convert the reflected light into electricity.
- **Memory**   An image scanner requires RAM memory in which to assemble and process the image, and as storage space for images waiting to transfer to the PC.
- **Firmware**   Like a printer, a scanner has firmware in the form of ROM chips containing the BIOS and other necessary programming code within the scanner for processing images and transmitting them as data to the computer.
- **Driver**   Like all PC peripherals, a scanner requires that a driver be installed on the PC. This enables the PC to communicate with the scanner, and to control the scanning process.
- **Scanner software**   Most scanners come with a variety of software for processing and manipulating the scanned images in the computer.

Scanner-Printer Combinations

When shopping for a scanner or printer, you will soon discover a large number of devices that combine the scanner and printer in one box. These devices physically resemble the ubiquitous conventional copiers that have been common in offices for decades. While it is true that such an all-in-one device can function like a copier—you place an image to be copied on top and the copied image comes out the side—there are significant differences between the old and the new. While an all-in-one device can behave like a stand-alone copier, it shines as a PC-connected device that provides all the functionality of a printer as well as a scanner. That means that you can send output to the printer, and receive digital images from the scanner, while using up the desk space of just one of these devices.

Printer and Scanner Interfaces

There are a number of interfaces for connecting to a printer or scanner. For example, you can configure either of these devices so that it attaches directly to the computer, or indirectly through a network. You can also configure a printer or scanner so that it is accessible to only one person, or to an entire network of people. Printers and scanners use the common interfaces described in Chapter 2, under the section titled "Cables, Connectors, and Ports." Therefore, the following text only surveys usage of each of these interfaces with printers and scanners.

Parallel

For almost two decades after introduction of the IBM PC in 1981, the most common way to attach a printer to a computer was through the computer's parallel port. The parallel interface requires a significant amount of space on the PC case for its 25-pin connector. It also needs an even larger 36-pin Centronics connector on the printer or other device. Top that off with a heavy cable with appropriate connectors on each end. Figure 11-3 shows a parallel port connector on a PC, and Figure 11-4 shows a Centronics connector on a printer. Next to it is a USB port.

FIGURE 11-3

Compare the large 25-pin parallel connector on the back of this PC with each of the other connectors, including the USB connectors at the bottom left.

FIGURE 14-4 This Centronics connector on a printer is nearly 2" wide and contains 36 pins (only 18 are visible from this angle). A USB connector is immediately to the left of it.

The parallel interface dominated for a long time and was the hands-down favorite over another common, but slower, interface—serial—that shared its long history. Where the original RS-232 serial interface transferred data one bit at a time, the parallel interface transfers eight bits at a time (in parallel), but it originally only supported one-way communication. For this reason, it was best suited for early printers, sending print data to the printer, but it could not receive status data from the printer. The speed of the standard parallel port is 150 Kbps.

Today's printers send status data back to the PC, alerting you when you are out of paper, or low on ink or toner. This requires two-way communications.

When you buy a new parallel cable, it will be labeled as compliant with the IEEE 1284 standard introduced in the 1990s. This standard defines a parallel interface that is backward-compatible with the original parallel port in the early IBM PCs. It also introduced five modes of operation:

- **Compatibility mode** Data only travels in one direction—from the PC to the device—in compatibility mode (also called Centronics mode). This mode ties up the PC's CPU, which must poll the printer for handshaking signals and error messages. Speed: 150 Kbps.

- **Nibble mode** Used together with compatibility mode, nibble mode offers limited bidirectional communications. Because this mode depends on software to send each 8-bit byte in two chunks of 4 bits (a nibble), nibble mode uses more CPU cycles than compatibility mode. Its top speed is 50 Kbps.

- **Byte mode** Also called enhanced bidirectional port mode, byte mode, used together with Centronics mode, supports two-way eight-bit data communications with a device. This configuration can communicate at speeds close to 150 Kbps.

- **Enhanced Parallel Port (EPP) mode** Enhanced Parallel Port (EPP) mode offers high-speed, bidirectional speeds of between 500 Kbps and 2 Mbps. This is possible because the parallel interface hardware does most of the work of data transfer, requiring less involvement by the CPU. This mode is not for printers but for network adapters, portable hard drives, and other devices that require high transfer speeds, such as data acquisition hardware used to automatically collect data from special sensors, and readers used in factories, test laboratories, scientific research, and medical equipment.

■ **Extended Capability Port (ECP) mode** The fastest parallel port mode for use with printers and scanners is Extended Capability Port (ECP) mode. Like EPP, ECP requires hardware that supports its features, and like EPP, ECP supports speeds of 500 Kbps to 2 Mbps and bidirectional communications.

on the
job

On some computers and peripherals, you may encounter parallel port modes that are not part of the IEEE 1284 standard. These come with names such as "Fast Centronics Mode" or "Parallel Port FIFO Mode." They offer greater speeds (up to 500 Kbps) but are proprietary and not supported on all parallel devices or computers.

In the past several years, other, faster interfaces have become far more popular than the parallel interface. The most popular of these is USB, discussed later in this chapter. Where it was once considered a given that a parallel port was standard on a new PC, many new computers today, especially laptops, do not come with a parallel port. This omission goes unnoticed by most people because most new printers and scanners do not come with a parallel interface.

Serial

The serial interface, as described in Chapter 2, was once a common printer interface. But even the parallel interface was, and is, faster than the traditional RS-232 serial ports. Therefore, in the days when your choices were limited to serial or parallel, parallel was more popular than serial. The newer USB and IEEE 1394 (FireWire) interfaces are great improvements over the old ones, as they are much faster and they support Plug and Play, which a serial interface does not natively support. Therefore, printers today rarely use a serial interface: in fact, the serial port is disappearing from standard PC configurations.

Universal Serial Bus (USB)

The Universal Serial Bus (USB) is the current dominant printer and scanner interface. As its name implies, data travels one bit at a time over the USB interface. However, as described in Chapter 2, USB is fast, transferring data at up to 480 Mbps. It also requires a very small connector on both ends. The PC end uses a USB type A connector, and the device end of the cable may be either a type A or type B connector, depending on what is required by the device. While printers do not always come with a USB cable, most other USB devices, including scanners, come with the appropriate cable.

While a USB interface can provide a small amount of electrical power from the PC, printers and scanners normally require more power than can be supplied through USB and therefore use an external power supply.

To attach a USB device, simply plug it into a USB external or root hub. There is no need to even turn the computer off for this Plug-and-Play interface, but be sure to read the instructions first, because many USB devices require installing the device driver before plugging in the device.

Figure 11-5 shows a USB cable next to a parallel cable. Compare the thicknesses of these cables, as well as the connectors at the ends of the cables.

IEEE 1394/FireWire

The IEEE 1394 interface is now the second most-common printer and scanner interface after USB. Most low-end printers come with only USB, but many medium- and higher-priced printers offer both interfaces (as well as network interface). As you learned in Chapter 2, IEEE 1394a is the original standard that supports speeds up to 400 Mbps, while the newer IEEE 1394b standard supports speeds of 800 Mbps, 1,600 Mbps, and 3.2 Gbps. Recall that 3.2 Gbps is only available with special hardware that is not downward compatible with 1394a devices.

SCSI

SCSI was never a common interface for printers, and you will rarely find a desktop printer that uses the SCSI interface. The story is slightly different for scanners, for which SCSI was a common interface until about a decade ago.

FIGURE 11-5

A parallel cable on the left and a USB cable on the right

Network

It has long been common to share printers over a network, but networking scanners was problematic. This disparity is due to how each type of device is used. You send output from your computer to a printer, so you don't necessarily need to come in physical contact with the printer device to use it. The issue of what happens to the printed output once it is printed is more of an administrative issue than a computer one.

on the *Printers are one of the most commonly accessed network resources and are*
Job *the cause for a majority of network-related trouble calls.*

As an input device, a scanner requires that the user be present to place the document to copy on the scanner—even a scanner with a document feeder must occasionally be "fed." There are currently some solutions that make networked scanners possible. But the network-scanning model differs from network printing in that you are not sharing a single device but sharing the document imaging and conversion software, which resides on a special server. In this model, multiple scanners can be at various locations on a network, and the scanned images are sent over the network to a specialized server where the image processing and conversion, such as OCR, is performed. These are still not yet practical for most users. Therefore, the remainder of this discussion will be limited to making a printer available over a network.

There are two ways to access a printer on a network.

1. Use a true network printer that contains a network interface card (NIC) and is configured in the same manner as any computer on the network. The printer will act as a print server, accepting print jobs over the network. This network interface can use either wired or wireless technologies. If the printer is powered on and online, it is available to network users.

2. Configure the printer to be a shared resource. A computer with a network connection can share a printer attached to that computer's local interface (parallel, USB, or other). This computer becomes the print server. In this case, you can only access the printer from the network if the computer it is attached to is turned on and has network access.

Wireless

Wireless communications for printers and scanners comes in three possible choices: the very short distance infrared (IrDA) and Bluetooth standards and the 802.11

standards for local area networks. Finding actual implementations of these wireless standards is a bit problematic.

The infrared (IrDA) standard has become less popular for all types of devices because it requires direct line-of-sight, while the Bluetooth standard is wildly popular for hands-free cell phone headsets, but is much less popular for use with printers or scanners. Refer to Chapter 5 for more information on IrDA and Bluetooth.

As mentioned earlier in this chapter, a printer can come with an integrated network adapter, either wired or wireless. We describe details of wired and wireless local area network technologies in Chapter 12.

Installing and Configuring Printers and Scanners

Before installing either a printer or scanner, be sure to follow the manufacturer's instructions. Both types of devices are easy enough to install that the average user can perform this task.

Installing a Printer

Windows controls application-generated print jobs. When you print from an application, it hands the print job over to Windows, and you can continue working in the application. This is a great improvement over earlier operating systems, in which each application had its own print driver and controlled each print job itself. In DOS, when an application was busy printing, nothing else happened. Of course, DOS could only handle a single task at once, and Windows manages many tasks at once.

In Windows, the printing subsystem provides a link between all applications and the printer. You install and configure printers in Windows, which intercepts every print job and sends it to the printer using the defined Windows print settings. In most applications each installed printer appears in a list of printers. To use a particular printer, simply select it from the printer list within the application.

Windows includes extensive Plug-and-Play support for printers. As with other Plug-and-Play devices, Windows automatically detects and configures most printers if they connect to a Plug-and-Play interface such as USB, IEEE 1394, or infrared. Follow the manufacturer's instructions, because you may need to run the installation program that comes with the printer before connecting it to the computer to ensure that the driver is available in Windows before it detects the printer. Then connect the

printer to the computer and turn it on. If the printer uses an infrared interface, this will require turning the printer on and pointing its infrared port at your computer's infrared port. Once Windows detects the printer it will automatically install the printer drivers. You will see a balloon message similar to the one shown here over the tray area of the taskbar.

In the event that you attach a non-Plug-and-Play printer, you will have to install it manually. A non-Plug and-Play printer is most likely to be an old printer, and it is most likely to have a parallel interface. After connecting the printer to a power source and to the PC, power it up and install the print drivers and associated software. In Windows 2000 you will do this by selecting Start | Settings | Printers. In Windows XP select Start | Printers And Faxes. In both you will then select Add Printer, which opens the Add Printer Wizard.

Be prepared to make selections on each page of the wizard. You will need to know the following:

- Is it a local printer or a network printer?
- For a local printer, you will need to know the port it uses.
- For a network printer, you will need to know its location on the network.
- For a local printer and some network printers, to install the printer driver and other software, either select the printer manufacturer and model from a list provided by the wizard or provide a disk or a location for the driver files.
- For the network printer, the printer software may automatically install over the network from the print server.
- Do you wish to give the printer a user-friendly name to better identify it?
- For both local and network printer installation, you will be asked if you want to set the printer as the default printer.
- Do you wish to share the local printer over the network?
- Do you wish to print a test page to confirm proper printer installation and functions?

Exercise 11-1 describes the steps for installing a non-Plug-and-Play printer in Windows XP.

Installing a Non-Plug-and-Play Printer

The Add Printer Wizard in Windows 2000 and Windows XP makes installing a non-Plug-and-Play printer easy, as long as you know the answers to the questions.

1. Follow the manufacturer's instructions for unpacking, preparing, and connecting the printer to the computer.

2. Select Start | Printers And Faxes.

3. In Printers And Faxes select Add A Printer from the Printer Tasks list.

4. In the Add Printer Wizard, read each page and follow the instructions to make a selection from the choices given. Begin by clicking Next on the Welcome page of the wizard (see Figure 11-6).

5. Respond to each page, using the responses you prepared from the list that precedes this exercise. When prompted, choose to print a test page to confirm that the printer installation is working correctly.

6. Click Finish to close the Add Printer Wizard, and it will copy the files, the installation will complete, and the test page will print out.

After successfully installing a printer, the Printers And Faxes dialog box (Printers in Windows 2000) will display. Look for the icon for the new printer.

FIGURE 11-6

Use the Add Printer Wizard to install a non-Plug-and-Play printer.

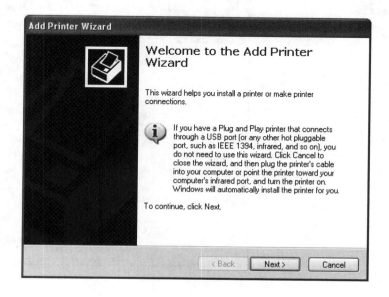

Welcome to the Add Printer Wizard

This wizard helps you install a printer or make printer connections.

If you have a Plug and Play printer that connects through a USB port (or any other hot pluggable port, such as IEEE 1394, infrared, and so on), you do not need to use this wizard. Click Cancel to close the wizard, and then plug the printer's cable into your computer or point the printer toward your computer's infrared port, and turn the printer on. Windows will automatically install the printer for you.

To continue, click Next.

< Back   Next >   Cancel

Testing a Printer for Compatibility

The printer test you perform at the end of printer installation in Windows will test and verify the compatibility of your printer and its software with Windows. The way the Windows printing system works eliminates most problems with incompatibility between individual applications and a printer. However, there are the rare instances in which output from an application does not produce the expected results. Therefore, to further test the compatibility of your applications with the new printer, open each application and print a document to the printer.

Configuring a Printer

In Windows there are two sets of printer settings: Printer Properties and Printing Preferences.

Printer Properties

Open a printer's Properties dialog box to configure settings for both the printer and the documents it creates. Right-click the appropriate printer's icon in the Printers And Faxes dialog box (Printers in Windows 2000) and select Properties. This will open a window similar to Figure 11-7. The tabs may vary, depending on the printer's capabilities and Windows' configuration.

FIGURE 11-7

Configure a printer using the printer's Properties dialog box.

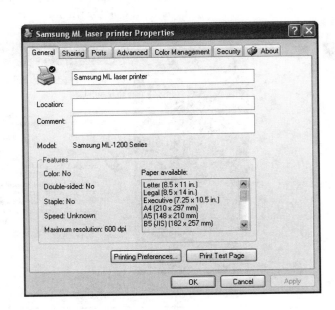

The actual settings vary by printer model, but you will be able to control a variety of settings such as resolution, paper type, color use, and print density. You can also print a test page from this dialog box, and use one or more cleaning and diagnostic modes for the printer.

Windows includes a print spooler, software that stores the print job in memory or on disk until the printer is ready to print it. This is especially important when sending several jobs to a printer at once, as is typical with a network printer. The correct spool settings for a printer will avoid potential problems. These settings are found on the Advanced tab in Windows XP, and through the Details tab in Windows 2000.

Enable spooling by selecting Spool Print Jobs So Program Finishes Printing Faster. The alternative to spooling is to select the Print Directly To The Printer option. If you have enabled spooling, you will be able to decide whether the printer begins printing after the first page is spooled or after the last page is spooled.

You can also select the spool data format. In Windows 2000, find this setting on the Spool Settings page. In Windows XP, this setting is contained in a dialog box that opens from the Print Processor button on the Advanced page of the printer's Properties dialog box, as shown in Figure 11-8.

Enhanced Metafile Format (EMF) is a Windows graphic-rendering language. When you use EMF spooling, the printing application builds an EMF file representing the print job, and Windows sends this file to the printer.

FIGURE 11-8

Select the data type from the Print Processor dialog box in Windows XP.

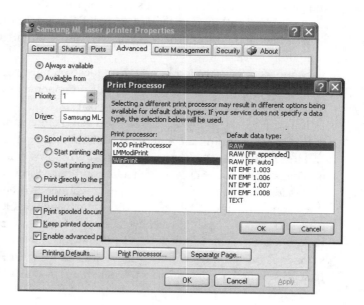

When the RAW data type is used, Windows translates each print job into printer-specific code. It actually takes Windows longer to do this than to create an EMF file. Windows then sends the resulting RAW file to the printer.

The output will look the same with either file format, but not all printers can print EMF print jobs. The printer's installation program will normally select the correct spool data format, and normally you should not select a different format.

Printing Preferences

Another group of options, Printing Preferences, controls how documents are printed, and these settings vary from printer to printer. This is where you select the number of copies, paper orientation, paper source, paper size, paper types, graphic options, output mode (number of pages per side, etc.), print order (front-to-back, back-to-front, etc.), printed overlays, and watermarks. To access printing preferences, right-click a printer in the Printers And Faxes dialog box (Printers in Windows 2000), and select Printing Preferences. This dialog box is also available through the Printing Preferences button in the Properties dialog box.

Installing and Configuring Scanners

Before unpacking a new scanner, locate the documentation for the scanner within the packaging. Look for a parts list, and refer to this while unpacking to confirm that the scanner has all the components listed. Follow the instructions for unpacking the scanner, and position the scanner on a well-ventilated level surface, close to the computer.

Scanners often have a transportation lock you must engage any time you move the scanner. This lock secures fragile internal components from damage by movement. Release this lock once the scanner is in position.

If instructed to install the scanner software before connecting the scanner, do so at this point. Running the scanner installation program copies the device driver files and installs several scanner programs into Windows. The most important of these programs is the one that gives you a user interface for working with the scanner.

In addition to this software, the types of scanner programs installed will depend on the scanner and its capabilities, but this list may include OCR, photo editing, business card, and Adobe Reader. If you have been keeping this computer up-to-date, you will have a newer version of Adobe Reader than what comes on disc packed with the scanner. A freestanding scanner will also include a copy utility, which you can configure to send scanned documents to a printer that is also available to this computer.

Along with the software installed, a complete User's Guide should also copy to your computer with a shortcut on the Start menu or desktop.

Now ensure that all necessary accessories are connected or installed in the scanner, and connect the interface cable to both the scanner and the computer. Connect the power cord to the scanner. Many scanners do not have a power switch. If that is true of the scanner you are installing, it will power up at this point. If the scanner has a power switch, turn it on now. Windows should recognize it at this

point, and a notification balloon will appear over the tray area of the taskbar, as shown here. Windows will automatically install the device driver and configure it with the default settings for the scanner. Another message will state that the new hardware is installed and ready to use.

Once the scanner installation is complete, open the scanner application. For our Epson Perfection scanner, this application is Epson Scan. In this program you can configure the defaults used for scanning all documents, and you can configure different settings for an individual scan.

Use the scanning software to inform the scanner of the document type (reflective or film), the document source and exposure type (photo or document), the image type (color and density), and scanning quality. You can adjust color settings and exposure levels (high and low values), and much more. A scanner will allow you to preview an image on your computer screen before beginning a full scan.

Educating Users

Users should either read the documentation for the printer or scanner they are using, or receive instructions on the care and use of these devices. Determine what each user's responsibilities are, and be sure that they get sufficient instructions or training in the device to do their work.

User Instructions for Printers

Users should know how to turn a printer on, how to load paper into their printer, and how to safely clear paper jams. Be sure to instruct them never to pull paper in the opposite direction in which paper travels through the printer.

Show each user how to change the toner or ink cartridges, and how to interpret the error lights on the printer.

User Instructions for Scanners

Show users how to position documents in a scanner, how to open the scanner software they will need to use, and how to interpret error lights on the scanner. Also show users how to safely wipe the scanner's glass surface, because it does tend to smudge during normal use, and it must be very clean for good scans. Users are less familiar with scanners and may need to get some precautionary advice, such as the following:

- Do not press on the glass surface with any force.
- If you must use error correcting liquid on an original, make sure it is completely dry before placing the document against the glass.
- Be careful not to scratch or damage the glass surface, because a damaged glass surface can decrease the scan quality.
- Never use alcohol, thinner, or corrosive solvent to clean the scanner.
- Be careful not to spill liquid into the scanner mechanism or electronic components.
- Do not spray lubricants inside the scanner.
- Never open the scanner case.

Upgrading and Optimizing Printers and Scanners

After an installed printer or scanner has been in use for some time, you may need to upgrade the driver, or some hardware component. In this section learn about upgrades for both types of devices as well as optimization techniques.

Upgrades

Unlike computers, which you can upgrade in many ways, such as adding memory, installing a large selection of new peripherals, upgrading the ROM BIOS, and upgrading the software, printers and scanners are somewhat limited in how they can be upgraded. We will describe some possible software and hardware upgrades for printers and scanners.

Device Driver and Software Upgrades

Like other software, software associated with printers and scanners calls for occasional upgrades. Drivers are the most frequently upgraded. When an updated driver is available for your printer, follow the manufacturer's instructions to install it. If it comes with its own installation program, run it. Alternatively, the instructions may tell you to use the Update Drivers option in Windows XP. To update a printer driver in this fashion, open the printer's Properties, select the Advanced tab, click New Driver, and follow the instructions in the Add Printer Driver Wizard.

Similarly, to install an updated scanner driver that does not come with its own installation program, open Device Manager and locate the scanner under the Imaging Devices node. Double-click on the scanner to open the Properties dialog box. Select the Driver tab and click Update Driver. Follow the instructions in the Hardware Update Wizard.

Hardware Upgrades

Popular hardware upgrades for printers and scanners are automated document feeders for scanners and larger-capacity paper trays for laser printers. Higher-end devices in both categories are most likely to offer upgrade options. Usually, the manufacturer offers these options.

Another popular hardware upgrade is memory, particularly for laser printers. Adding memory can increase the speed when printing complex documents or graphics. A search of the Internet will turn up many manufacturers of memory upgrades for laser printers.

Firmware Upgrades

Some printers, in particular laser printers, support upgrading of the firmware. This, of course, depends on the manufacturer releasing firmware upgrades. First, determine the firmware version currently in your printer, and then check on the manufacturer's Web site for notices of upgrades. Instructions from the manufacturer will guide you through upgrading the firmware, which you do from your computer.

Optimizing Printer Performance

The average user is happy if a printer is reliable and creates reasonable printouts, but a growing number of users have more discerning tastes and more exacting needs. For them printers offer a variety of optimizing choices.

Tray Selection

If a printer has multiple trays, there are a few ways to optimize the use of these trays. One is to load plain paper in one tray and special stationery in the other tray. Then instruct users on which tray to select for the types of jobs they send to the printer.

Tray Switching

You should use a different strategy when users send a large volume of printing to a multiple-tray printer using just one kind of paper. In this, you set the printer's preferences for tray switching so that it will use the first tray until it is empty, and then automatically switch to the second tray.

Color Calibration

For those who need accurate color printouts, color calibration is a serious consideration. Color calibration is adjustment of the colors on an output device (printer) to match the colors of another output device (display), which, in the best scenario, was previously adjusted to match the original images.

Perhaps a photograph looks great on your display, but the printout does not quite match the displayed colors. If your printer takes special cartridges for photo printing, buy and install a new set of these ink cartridges. If the output is quite lovely but still does not match the color on the display, calibration of both the display and the printer will adjust each for the best color output.

Before calibrating a printer, you place a calibration device that can measure color over the display, and connect it to the computer so that specialized calibration software can access it. This software sends color signals to the display. The software, in communication with the calibration device, compares the color signals sent with the resulting color measured by the device.

Depending on the discrepancies detected and the type of monitor, the color calibration software may create a correction matrix, called an International Color Consortium (ICC) Profile, or recommend settings changes for the display. You use the ICC Profile to adjust the display output to conform to the desired output. The manual changes to the settings also aim to create display output that matches the desired colors.

Next, the color calibration software sends a print job to the printer. Another calibration device (also connected to the computer) measures the color on the printout. The result of this test goes to the calibration software, which creates a calibration profile for adjusting the printer. This test can be run using different paper types, and it creates a different profile for each.

The calibration devices and software are not inexpensive, and there are services that will perform these calibrations for your computer display, printers, and even scanners. The poor man's version of all this work is to experiment with adjusting first the color settings on the display, and then both Printer Properties and Printing Preferences settings until the display and the printer images match. Remember that these settings will be different for each printer. Check out the Printing Preferences, because on many color printers you will find several levels of quality, options for various types of paper, and color enhancement settings. Also, look for advanced settings in Printing Preferences to get even more control over color.

Optimizing a Scanner

Optimizing a scanner for best results includes color calibration, and selecting the best settings for resolution, color density, and file format.

Color Calibration

Color calibration for a scanner may involve software and a supplied color chart. Scan the color chart, and print out the scanned image. Assuming previous calibration of the display and printer, you must now scan the printout. The calibration software calibrates the scanner's color sensing to match the original color chart.

As with a printer, you will find settings in your scanner's software that will allow you to adjust colors. You may have to look for an "Advanced" or "Professional" button, but this will allow you to experiment with settings until you achieve the desired results in your scanned images.

Resolution and Color Density

Your scanner software will allow you to adjust the resolution and color density of the scanned image. Image resolution is in dots per inch (dpi). This setting is important, because a higher resolution provides higher-quality images.

Although the color density setting may not use that exact term, you will recognize it because it uses terms such as 48-bit color, 24-bit color, 16-bit grayscale, 8-bit grayscale, black and white, and other formats. We list these here in descending order from the largest file size to the smallest. If you preview a document, your scanner software should select the best color density and resolution. Check this setting after a preview, and adjust it if necessary.

However, you must still strike a balance, because the higher the resolution and color density, the larger the file, and you will use up disk space at a great rate if you set your resolution higher than you really require.

File Format

Beyond resolution and color density, there are numerous file formats for scanned images. Your first consideration is how you want to use the scanned image, particularly which software you wish to use to view and/or edit the data.

Your second consideration may be the size of the created file. A document that is all text and processed by OCR software will take up very little disk space. If the OCR software saved the file as a text-only file, it will be very small. Saving this same file in Microsoft Word format will make the file larger yet, but still much smaller than many graphic file formats.

There are a huge number of graphic file formats that you can identify by their filename extensions. Determine the file format required before saving a file. Many graphic editing programs will allow you to convert a file to other formats. Some file formats, such as JPEG, create smaller files than others because they compress the data in the file. Here is the short list of graphic file formats with their name and filename extension:

- BITMAP (*.bmp)
- JPEG (*.jpg)
- PDF (*.pdf)
- TIFF *.tif

CERTIFICATION OBJECTIVES

- **601: 4.3   602: 4.3   603: 3.3   604: 3.3** *Identify tools, diagnostic procedures, and troubleshooting techniques for printers and scanners*

A+ certification candidates must demonstrate a knowledge of troubleshooting techniques for printers and scanners, as well as the tools required. They also identify common problems and solutions for both types of device.

Troubleshooting Printers and Scanners

When troubleshooting printers and scanners, apply the same troubleshooting theory used with other computer components. Gather, review, and analyze collected data, and identify solutions to problems. Become familiar with common printer and scanner problems, and use appropriate generic or vendor-specific diagnostic tools, including Web-based utilities.

The Hardware Toolkit

Many tools in your computer hardware toolkit, described in Chapter 4, will come in handy when troubleshooting and maintaining printers and scanners.

Gather Information

Troubleshooting printer and scanner problems is much like troubleshooting other computer problems. Take an organized approach using the following stages:

- **Identify symptoms**   Have the user describe and, if possible, demonstrate the problem to you.
- **Review errors**   Document the error codes issued by the printer or scanner—on the device's control panel (if one exists), in the form of error lights on the device, and on the computer screen. Look for error messages recorded in the System or Application Event Log using Event Viewer.
- **Check for visual indicators**   Look for and interpret error lights on the device.
- **Print or scan a test page**   Try to duplicate the problem yourself, taking note of the application used, the printer or scanner selected from the application, and the results.
- **Cycle power**   Turn the printer or scanner off and then on again. This will give the device a chance to start over again, with memory refreshed. This may solve the problem if the cause was a corrupted data stream.

Review and Analyze Collected Data

From the information you have gathered you can now move on to an analysis that includes these actions:

- **Establish probable cause**   The information may point to a very obvious probable cause, or at least point you in the right direction.
- **Review service documentation**   It never hurts to read the manual, and now that you are armed with information about the problem, the documentation should help you to find the source and solution of the problem.

■ **Review the knowledge base and define and isolate the problem** Go beyond the documentation to other sources, if necessary, and isolate the problem to software or hardware. If it is software, the driver is the usual suspect. If it is hardware, connectivity is the most likely source.

Identify Solutions to Problems

As a result of your review and analysis, you should have identified one or more possible solutions. You can now proceed with these actions:

■ **Define the specific cause and apply a fix** With experience, you will become better at this. Once you have gathered information on the problem and established a probable cause, your familiarity with common problems will allow you to decide if the problem is in that group. In that case, move right to the correct fix for the problem. If, after establishing a cause, you still do not know the solution, you will have to do further research, as defined previously.

■ **Replace consumables as needed** Other than the special light bulb, a scanner does not have consumables like a printer, which cannot work without consumables, such as paper and print cartridges. If you are the one responsible for purchasing and storing these products, it is bad for your career to let these supplies run out.

■ **Verify functionality and get user acceptance of the problem fix** Once you have fixed the problem, be sure to demonstrate to the user that the problem has been solved. If the user is present, have him or her print from at least one application, and depending on how formal your organization is, have the user sign off on the work or at least verbally confirm that he or she is happy with the results. If the user is not present, be sure to leave a professionally worded note that the problem is fixed, and leave at least a sample printout showing that the printer is now working, or leave a scanned document on the user's computer to show that the scanner is now working. In either case, if you can use the job the user was attempting to print or scan, do so.

Common Printer Problems

Once you have gathered information, you can quickly solve the most common printer problems without further analysis. Following are several common problems and their solutions. If the problem does not appear to be one of these common problems, then move on to a more careful analysis of the problem.

Paper Feed Problems

A common printer problem is the mechanics of the paper-feed process. If there is too much paper in a friction-feed paper tray, more than one page can feed through the printer at a time. The extra page can cause problems with the print process itself and can cause jams within the printer. Static electricity within the pages can cause the pages to stick together. Moisture in paper can also cause pages to stick together or not feed properly. To avoid multiple-page feeding problems, reduce the amount of paper you place in the tray and use your thumb to "riffle," or quickly separate, the pages before you load them into the paper tray. This puts air between the pages, and can reduce "static cling."

Successful friction feed depends on paper that is not too thin, not too thick, and with a certain range of moisture content to avoid static build-up. Dust in the printer can cause static to build up and cause friction-feed problems. Worn out friction-feed parts can cause paper jams.

Most paper jams will stop the current print job. If you suspect a paper jam, consult your printer documentation. Normal instructions are to turn off and open the printer. carefully remove any paper jammed in the paper path, following the manufacturer's instructions. Some printers include levers that you can release to more easily remove jammed paper. It is normally necessary to gently pull the paper in the direction the paper normally moves through the printer. Pulling in the opposite direction could damage internal components, such as rollers. This is especially true of the fusion roller in a laser printer. Avoid tearing the paper. If it tears, be sure you locate and remove all pieces from the printer.

If you notice a build-up of dust and debris, unplug the printer's power cord and use an antistatic vacuum or canned compressed air to clean the interior of the printer. Inspect for any broken parts in the paper path. If you find any, you will have to investigate repairing or replacing the printer.

Once you have finished clearing the jam and cleaning the printer (if necessary), reconnect the power cord, turn the printer's power on, and either resume the print job or send another print job. Most printers will not resume operation until you have completely cleared the jam. Many printers also require you to press the reset or clear button to restart the printer.

If the printer continues to jam, try using a different weight paper. Printers work best with a particular weight of paper, and if you use paper that is too thin or too thick, jams can occur more frequently.

Another friction-feed printer problem occurs when pages do not feed into the printer. This is more common in printers that have an upright paper tray. If the stack of paper is too small, the friction rollers might not be able to make contact with the top page.

Tractor feed has its own problems. These feed mechanisms are notorious for feeding paper incorrectly through the printer. The problem is usually caused by misalignment of the paper in the printer. These mechanisms require special paper, in which each piece of paper attaches to the page before it, much like a roll of paper towels. If the perforations between pages of paper do not line up properly, the text for one page will print across two pages. When this happens, look for a paper advance button on the printer that will incrementally advance the paper until it is aligned. If you do not have the documentation for the printer, this may take trial and error.

Another problem with tractor feed occurs when the friction-feed mechanism is not disabled. The most obvious symptom of this problem will be torn paper if the tractor pulls faster than the friction feed, or bunched paper if the opposite condition exists.

Print Quality

Print quality problems are very common with all types of printers. The text that follows lists several common print quality problems and their suggested solutions. When a major repair of a printer seems to be needed, first evaluate the cost benefit of the repair. How much more would it cost to replace the printer than to repair it?

In laser printers, print quality problems are most often (but not always) associated with a component in the toner cartridge. When troubleshooting a print quality problem on a laser printer, swapping the toner cartridge solves many of the problems listed here.

Blank Pages If a dot matrix printer produces blank pages, pay attention to the sound coming from the printer. If you cannot hear the pins striking the page, try replacing the print head. If the pins are striking the page but there is no print, you have a ribbon problem. Check to ensure that the ribbon lines up with the print head. If it does not, move it into position. You may have to find a way to remove slack from the ribbon. You usually do this by removing the ribbon cartridge and manually rewinding the ribbon before reinserting it into the printer. If the ribbon does line up properly but there is no print, the ribbon has probably worn out, and you can resolve the problem by replacing the ribbon. If carbon copies printed on a dot matrix printer are blank or dim, consult the documentation and adjust the distance between the print head and the paper.

If an inkjet printer produces blank pages, the likely suspect is an ink cartridge. Use the printer's software utility to determine the amount of ink left in an ink cartridge. If no such utility came with the printer, remove each cartridge and gently rock it back and forth to determine if there is ink present. If there is not, replace the cartridge. If there is ink, the problem could be clogged nozzles. Follow the printer manufacturer's instructions for cleaning the nozzles in the print head. Software installed with the printer driver usually does this. If it doesn't, check the documentation for a way to initiate this from the controls on the printer. In the extreme, follow the manufacturer's instructions for manually cleaning the cartridge, perhaps with a lint-free cloth slightly dampened with distilled water.

If a laser printer is producing blank pages, suspect some component of the printing process. For instance, a blank page can result if the image is failing to transfer to the paper. This could be a problem with the transfer corona wire. Shut down the printer, disconnect the power cable, open the printer, and inspect the corona wire (consult your manual for its location). You may find dirt or debris (like a staple) shorting out the wire. You may discover that the wire itself is broken, although it would take rough treatment to do this. If you find the wire intact, but debris on it that could be shorting it out, clean the printer, and then try to print again.

It is rare for a cartridge to be the cause of a completely blank page, unless it contains the drum and the drum has failed. If it has, you must replace it. If the drum is part of the cartridge, replace the cartridge. You are more likely to see some of the other problems described next when there is a problem with the cartridge.

Random Speckles on the Page   If any type of printer produces a page with speckles or blotches on it, try cleaning the printer. Ribbon ink, cartridge ink, and toner residue can be within the printer itself and can be transferred onto the paper.

Repeated Pattern of Speckles or Blotches   A repeated pattern on a printout (that is not an intended part of the printout) is also an indication of ink or toner residue in the printer. Clean the printer, paying attention to the feed rollers. If there is a repeated pattern on the printout of a laser printer, suspect the drum. A small nick or flaw in the drum will cause toner to collect there, and it will transfer onto each page in a pattern. In addition, during the cleaning step, some drums lose their ability to drop their charge. The drum has a very small diameter, so this same pattern will repeat several times down the length of the page. In either case, replacing the drum should solve the problem.

A Faint Image from the Previous Page   A ghosted image occurs when an image from a previous page appears on subsequent pages. This occurs only in laser printers, and indicates a cleaning stage failure. The drum might have lost the ability to drop its charge in the presence of light. Replace the drum to resolve the problem. If the drum is not the cause, it could be either the cleaning blade or the erasure lamps. Both the cleaning blade and drum are inside the toner cartridge in many laser printers, so this will be resolved by replacing the toner cartridge. The erasure lamps are always (to our knowledge) in the printer itself, and they are not easy to replace. You will probably have to send the printer back to the manufacturer, or to a specialized printer repair shop.

The Wrong Colors   Assuming this is not an application-related setting, a problem with incorrect colors is almost exclusively limited to inkjet printers. One or more color cartridges may be out of ink, causing the incorrect colors. If the nozzles on one or more of the colors on a color ink cartridge clog, the colors may come out "dirty" or might not be produced at all. Remove the cartridge from the printer and follow the manufacturer's instructions for cleaning the nozzles. This may involve using isopropyl alcohol on a cotton swab to remove dried ink and unclog the nozzles, but do not do this unless it is recommended by the manufacturer. In any type of color printer, if one cartridge gets low, it will not be able to produce the proper shades. To get the desired results in a printout, you may simply need to replace the cartridges.

Smudging   If a dot matrix printer produces a smudged printout, check the pins on the print head. Stuck pins can cause printouts to have a smudged appearance as they continue to transfer ink to the page, even when they do not create a character or image. If this is the case, notify the manufacturer, and replace the print head or the entire printer.

If the output from an inkjet printer appears smudged, the most likely cause is someone touching the printed page before the ink dries. The ink used in inkjet and bubblejet printers must totally dry before it is touched, or it will smear. Most inkjet and bubblejet printers do not use permanent ink, and even after it has dried, these inks will smear if they become wet again.

The heat and pressure of the fusion stage in a laser printer create a smudge-proof permanent printout. Smudged laser printouts are usually the result of a failed fusing stage. Depending on the exact source of the problem, you may need to replace the fusing rollers or the halogen lamp.

e**x**a m
ⓦatch
Remember that whenever you face an unfamiliar print-quality problem in a laser printer, suspect the drum. If this does not solve the problem, use your knowledge of the laser print process to determine which stage (and therefore, which component) has failed.

"Garbage"   Garbled output—often called "garbage"—usually indicates a communications problem between the computer and printer. The most common cause of this is an incorrect or corrupted print driver. Check that this printer is using the correct driver. Look at the printer settings by opening Printers And Faxes from the Start menu. Ensure that the physical printer matches the printer shown in this dialog box.

Next, make sure of firm and proper attachment of the data cable. Try turning the printer off and then back on (it may have simply experienced temporary confusion). Restarting the computer may also solve the problem.

Finally, this problem could be the result of insufficient printer memory. You can test this by trying to print a very small document. If it works, there is a good chance that the original document was too large for the printer's memory. You can add more RAM. Check the documentation to find out how to check on the amount of memory, what type of memory to install, and how to install the memory.

Printer Error Messages

Printers generate a variety of error messages. They often come with their own configuration and monitoring utility installed on your computer when you install the printer driver. We describe some of the more common error messages. Note that these messages could appear on the computer screen or the printer's console, or both. The OS generates some of these messages. Any time you get a printer error message that you do not understand, check the message or error code number in the manufacturer's documentation. You may need to do a search on the manufacturer's Web site, where a more complete list is often available.

Paper Out   A Paper Out message indicates that there is no paper in the printer. If the printer uses a tractor feed, you will need to lift the printer lid, feed the first sheet of the new stack through the paper path, and line up the holes with the feed wheels. As this procedure varies from model to model, consult the manufacturer's documentation.

Adding paper to any printer should only take a few seconds because it does not involve turning off the printer's power. If you are using a tray to feed a friction-feed printer, simply pull out the appropriate paper tray. Fan a stack of fresh paper, and insert it into the tray. If there is a lid for the tray, replace that before inserting the tray into the printer. The error message should go away on its own. If you do not close or insert the tray properly, a Tray Open or Close Tray message may appear. If the printer uses an upright friction feed, follow the steps in Exercise 11-2 to add more paper.

EXERCISE 11-2

Adding Paper to an Upright Friction-Feed Tray

If you have access to a printer with an upright friction-feed tray you can follow these instructions.

1. Release the tray lever at the back of the printer (if so equipped). This will cause the paper tray to drop away slightly from the friction rollers.
2. Place a small stack of paper in the tray, using the paper guides.
3. Engage the tray lever. This will bring the paper closer to the feed rollers.
4. The printer might automatically detect the paper and continue the print job. If not, look for and press the Paper Advance button on the printer. This instructs the printer to detect and try to feed the paper.

The Paper Out message could appear even if there is paper in the tray. Over time the surface of the rollers used to feed the paper may lose their ability to grip and move the paper. This is especially true as the paper becomes low in the tray and the rollers cannot benefit from the pressure of a full stack of paper to grip and feed the paper. Locate the rollers and clean them, first wipe the dust and grime off, and then use isopropyl alcohol to clean any residue that may make the rollers slippery.

I/O Error   An I/O error message can take many forms, including "Cannot communicate with printer" or "There was an error writing to LPT# or USB#." Windows typically reports this message and it indicates that the computer cannot properly communicate with the printer. Start by ensuring that the printer is on. If it is not, turn it on, and then try to print. You might need to restart the computer to ensure that it redetects the presence of the printer.

Next, make sure that the printer data cable firmly and properly attaches to both the printer and the computer, and that a proper driver has been loaded. If you suspect that the driver is corrupt, remove it, and then reload it. Ensure that the driver uses the correct port.

Incorrect Port Mode   An incorrect port mode error applies to parallel ports. Wording of this message may vary, but it indicates that the parallel port the printer attaches to is using the wrong mode. This message usually appears on the computer rather than on the printer. Enter the computer's system setup program, and change the parallel port to the proper mode (unidirectional, bidirectional, or ECP). If the error message does not indicate the correct mode, consult the printer manufacturer's documentation.

No Default Printer Selected   The first printer installed in Windows gets the Default Printer designation. A default printer is the printer that automatically receives a print job when you select the Print command from within a program, but do not specify which printer you want to use. If you install one or more printers after that, the first one will remain the default printer until you change its status. Make the printer you use the most the default printer by opening the Printers And Faxes folder and right-clicking on the desired printer. On the context menu select Set as default printer. The printer icon for the default printer has a small black circle with a white check in it to indicate that it is the default printer, as shown in Figure 11-9. Notice that the icons for some of the printers are grayed out, while others are brighter. The gray icons represent printers that are installed, but not presently online to the computer.

If you delete a default printer, and then install another printer, you will receive a warning message similar to the one shown here.

If there is no installed printer and you attempt to print, Windows will issue the error message "No Default Printer Selected." Once you install at least one printer, this error message is rare in Windows 2000 and Windows XP, but it is not totally extinct. Corrupted printer drivers and utility files can disable the printer and cause this message to appear, but it will probably appear before or after another message that begins "Rundll has caused an error in…" This message will include a filename and will end with "Rundll will now close." If this occurs, attempt to uninstall the printer software, and then reinstall it. If this occurs

FIGURE 11-9

A tiny black circle with a white check mark indicates the default printer.

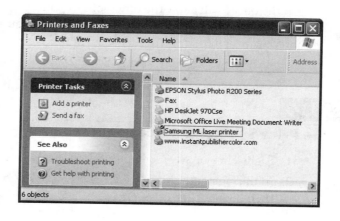

immediately after installing a new printer, contact the manufacturer for another copy of the printer software as the one that came with the printer may be corrupted.

Low Toner or Ink   The Low Toner (or similar) message applies to laser printers only. It appears well before the toner is completely gone, as an early warning. The printer should continue to print normally. You can make the error message go away by removing the toner cartridge and gently rocking the cartridge back and forth. This will resettle the toner. Note, however, that this is not a solution to the problem. The reason for the error is to warn you to replace the toner cartridge soon. Most laser printers will not work at all if the toner cartridge is empty.

When you are using an inkjet, the "Ink low" (or similar) message will appear on your computer screen, or an ink level bar will be displayed. Replace the cartridge.

on the
ỏ o b
When an ink cartridge gets low, you should replace rather than refill it. Each cartridge comes with a new pump or heating element, and new nozzles. By refilling an old cartridge, you are reusing old, possibly worn-out components.

Windows Print Spooler Problems

Sometimes the Print Spooler service stops, and when it does, nothing prints until it is started again. If a print job has failed to print, or has stopped before completing, first check that it is not out of paper, ink, or toner. Check the power cable and status lights. If everything seems to be normal, then open Printers And Faxes (or Printers in Windows 2000) and double-click the printer. This opens the user interface for the print queue from which you can manage jobs the print spooler is holding. Check the status of the print job. If the print job status is Paused, right-click on it and select Restart. If this fails, attempt to cancel the print job. Sometimes canceling the first job in the queue will allow the other jobs to print.

If this does not help, then cancel each job in the queue. If you are not able to restart or cancel jobs in the queue, you will need to restart the Print Spooler service. Follow the steps in Exercise 11-3 to restart this service.

EXERCISE 11-3

Restarting the Print Spooler Service

1. Right-click on My Computer, and select Manage from the context menu.
2. In the Computer Management Console select Services and Applications, and then double-click on Services.

3. In the contents pane, scroll down to Print Spooler.

4. Right-click on Print Spooler and select Restart (see Figure 11-10).

5. If restarting the service failed, then close all open windows and restart. When Windows restarts, the Print Spooler service will restart.

6. Recycle power on the printer.

7. Resend the print jobs to the printer.

Common Scanner Problems

As with most computer components, scanner problems can include hardware and software problems, temporary malfunctions, and fatal errors.

Power Problems

A disconnected or loose power cable is easy to overlook when your crowded desktop has a nest of tangled wires. Always check power connections and power switches. As mentioned earlier in this book, go as far as testing the outlet itself. Once you have corrected or eliminated power problems, move on to other connection issues.

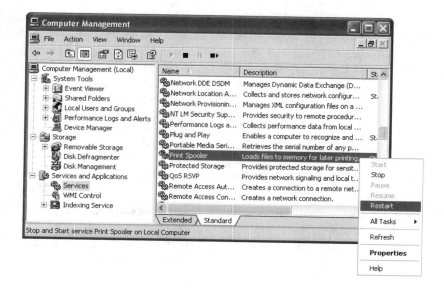

FIGURE 11-10

Right-click the Print Spooler service and select Restart.

Interface Problems

First make sure the scanner is properly connected to the computer. If it is using a parallel port, and it was disconnected, turn the computer off before connecting and testing the scanner. If a scanner connected via the parallel port does not appear to be communicating, restart the computer and enter the system setup program. Look for the settings for the parallel port (LPT1) and verify that the port mode is ECP or bidirectional. If both are available, turn on one, restart the computer, and test the scanner again. If that mode does not work, repeat the cycle to test the other mode.

Scanner Lock

As mentioned earlier, many scanners have a transportation lock that you must engage when moving the scanner to protect fragile components. Refer to the documentation for the location of this lock, and then check to see if this lock was released. If not, unlock it and test the scanner again.

Uninstall and Reinstall Scanner Software

If all connections appear to be correct, it is possible that Windows installed the wrong driver. This can happen if someone connected the scanner to the computer and powered it on before installing the scanner software. If that was the case, it is possible that Windows detected the scanner, but installed the wrong driver—perhaps a driver for an older model by the same manufacturer. This is a very bad beginning for the Windows-to-scanner relationship, and the best solution is to uninstall the scanner software and driver. You can uninstall the driver using Device Manager. Once it is uninstalled, disconnect or power-off the scanner, and install the correct scanner software. If you no longer have the CD or CDs that came with the scanner, download the correct software from the manufacturer's Web site.

Scanner Lamp Problems

Over time, the luminosity of the lamp deteriorates and it cannot create images. Most scanners will detect this problem, stop working, and display an error light or message. A lamp replacement requires opening the case, and, as a rule, you should never open the scanner case. Therefore, this is not a user-serviceable failure. Contact the manufacturer for instructions on where to take the scanner for service.

Scanned Images Look Distorted on the Display

If scanned images do not appear correctly on the display, it may be a display problem, not a scanner problem. The scanner may be scanning with a color density of 24-bit color (16 million color palette), while the display is displaying at a very low color density—as low as 256 colors. Check the Display properties, and make sure the display uses a color density of 24 bits or higher. Only do this if your display adapter can support this density.

CERTIFICATION OBJECTIVES

■ **602: 4.4   604: 3.4**   *Perform preventive maintenance of printer and scanner problems*

CompTIA will test your knowledge of preventive maintenance tasks required to avoid problems with printers and scanners.

Preventive Maintenance for Printers and Scanners

Because of the frequency with which printers and scanners are used, they require almost constant maintenance. Fortunately, the maintenance procedures are usually easy. Consider scheduling regular maintenance, such as cleaning, based on the amount of usage for each printer and scanner. Manufacturers may provide a list of other maintenance tasks, such as vacuuming the ozone filter in laser printers, which should occur along with a regular cleaning, but not at the same frequency.

Maintenance Kits and Page Counts

Some printers—mainly professional-quality and high-production laser printers—have what is called maintenance counts. The printer counts the number of pages printed over the lifetime of the printer, and when this page count reaches a certain number, called the maintenance count (in the hundreds of thousands), a service message will appear on the printer's LED display. This indicates that the printer has reached the end of the expected service life for some of the internal components. When this occurs, you must install the manufacturer's maintenance kit, which consists of replacement parts, after which you must reset the page count so that it can track the expected life of the parts in the new maintenance kit.

If you do not reset the page count, the printer will continue to issue the maintenance warning. Use the manufacturer's instructions for resetting the page count. In the rare instance when you must install a new maintenance kit before the page count reaches the maintenance count, on some models you must reset the maintenance count to match the page count. Then, when the next page is printed, you will receive the maintenance message and can proceed with the maintenance and reset the page count.

Cleaning a Printer

The best thing you can do to prolong the life of a printer and prevent problems from occurring is to clean it regularly. In all printers small particles of paper and other debris can be left behind and cause a potentially harmful build-up. As mentioned earlier, this build-up can hold static, which can in turn damage components through electrostatic discharge (ESD), or cause pages to stick together.

Removing the build-up will also keep the paper path clear, thus reducing paper jams and ensuring that there is no inhibition of moving parts. You can remove dust and particle build-up using compressed air or a vacuum. As you clean the printer, be on the lookout for small corners of paper left behind during the print process, or when you cleared a paper jam.

In an inkjet printer, you should look for and remove ink from the inside of the printer. Ink can leak and cause smudges on the paper. As the ink dries, it can cause moving components or paper to stick. Laser printers can accumulate toner. Remove excess toner using a paper towel or cotton swab.

You can also prevent paper jams and component wear and tear using the proper paper for your printer. Read the documentation for the printer to determine the best paper for the results you desire.

Cleaning a Scanner

The primary reason to frequently clean a scanner is to maintain the quality of images. Smudges and dirt on the glass will contribute to bad images. Be sure to read the scanner's documentation for details on how to clean the scanner. Keeping in mind the manufacturer's instructions, Exercise 11-4 contains generic steps for cleaning a scanner.

EXERCISE 11-4

Cleaning a Scanner

You can avoid having dust and dirt appear in your scanned images by cleaning it regularly.

1. Turn the scanner off (if it has a power switch) and unplug the scanner.

2. Wipe the outside of the case with a dry lint-free cloth, and then dip another cloth in a mild detergent and water and wring it out until it is just damp. Use this second cloth to wipe off any dirt that is clinging to the case.

3. Repeat Step 2 for any external components, such as a document feeder.

4. Use a clean, soft, lint-free cloth to wipe the glass surface free of any loose dust and dirt. If other dirt remains, use a small amount of glass cleaner on a clean, soft, lint-free cloth to remove it, being careful to wipe the surface dry when done.

5. If there are any components, such as a transparency unit, installed under the lid of a flatbed scanner, follow the manufacturer's instructions for cleaning them.

6. Close the scanner.

Ensuring a Suitable Environment

Prevent a myriad of problems with your printer or scanner by providing a suitable environment. Be sure that it is on a level surface, close to the computer to which it is connected, and convenient for the user. Both temperature extremes, and dirt and dust, will negatively affect either type of device. Dirt and dust will affect the quality of scanned documents, and, if they infiltrate the case, can cause heat build-up in any device.

Use Recommended Consumables

For the best results, especially for printers, use the manufacturer's recommended consumables. This includes ink and toner cartridges as well as paper for printers. In the case of the major printer manufacturers, their branded ink and toner products may only be available at premium prices. To save money, consider third-party sources, but be prepared to buy one set of cartridges to test before ordering any quantities.

SCENARIO & SOLUTION

My laser printer produces the same blotch over and over again. What should I do?	Clean the printer, especially the fusion roller. If this doesn't work, replace the drum. If the drum is in the toner cartridge, replace the toner cartridge.
I am careful not to handle the printouts from my inkjet printer, but they are coming out with smudges. What can I do?	Check the paper path. Something may be coming in contact with the page before the ink has had a chance to dry.
Why do printouts from my color inkjet printer have the wrong colors?	The printer is probably low in one or more colors, or has a clogged cartridge nozzle.

CERTIFICATION SUMMARY

This chapter explored printer and scanner issues for IT professionals. The focus of this chapter was the components, procedures, troubleshooting, and maintenance procedures for common printer and scanner types. A variety of printer and scanner types are available to choose from, as well as levels of features and quality.

Dot matrix printers provide the lowest quality, and today they mainly print multiple-part forms. Laser printers, the most expensive, can provide excellent printouts and are the most common type used in offices. For this reason, you are likely to deal with laser printers in businesses more frequently than with other printer types. Inkjet printers are extremely popular as inexpensive desktop color printers.

Bar code scanners are in wide use, but image scanners are the most commonly used type with desktop computers. Flatbed scanners are the most common image scanners used with PCs.

Before installing a printer or scanner, carefully read the manufacturer's instructions. In many cases, you must install the software for the device before connecting the device to the PC.

When working with printer or scanner problems, apply the troubleshooting procedures learned earlier in this book, and familiarize yourself with symptoms and problems common to the printer or scanner. Printers require maintenance to replenish paper and, less frequently, ink or toner. Clean both printers and scanners regularly to ensure high-quality results and to avoid many problems that dirt, dust, and grime can create.

TWO-MINUTE DRILL

Here are some of the key points covered in Chapter 11.

Understanding Printers and Scanners

- ❑ Printers are the most common peripheral used with PCs.
- ❑ Scanners are much less common than printers, but their usage is increasing.
- ❑ Dot matrix impact printers are usually of low quality, use a ribbon, move paper with friction feed or tractor feed, and are most often used for printing multiple-part forms, such as retail receipts.
- ❑ Laser printers use laser light technology in the printing process.
- ❑ The stages of the laser printing process are charging, writing, developing, transferring, fusing, and cleaning.
- ❑ The term "inkjet" refers to printers that use one of several technologies to apply wet ink to paper to create text or graphic printouts. Manufacturers use several names for these printers, including "inkjet," "ink jet," "bubblejet," and others.
- ❑ Printers that use solid ink usually fall under two headings: dye sublimation and thermal wax.
- ❑ Thermal printers use heat in the image transfer process.
- ❑ The two most common paper-feed technologies are friction feed and continuous form feed.
- ❑ The typical printer has a system board, ROM (containing firmware), and RAM memory, as well as various components related to the specific printing technology and paper-feed mechanism.
- ❑ Additional components include the device driver and related software, and consumables in the form of paper, ink ribbons, ink cartridges, or toner cartridges.
- ❑ A scanner is an input device that uses optical technology to scan something and process information from the scan.
- ❑ A bar code reader is a scanner designed specifically for reading patterns of bars of varying widths to interpret as a special UPC code.

❑ Image scanners convert printed images to data for input to a computer, and come as handheld and flatbed devices. The flatbed devices are now more common and provide high-quality results.

❑ A variety of software can process scanned images, depending on the type of image. A scanned document is simply a graphic image, until optical character recognition (OCR) software interprets the patterns on the page into individual characters of a document and processes it so that you can read and edit it using word processing software.

❑ In the image scanning process, a beam of light moves across a printed page and reflects from the page back to the scanner, where it passes through a lens to light-sensitive diodes that convert the light into electricity, which is converted to numeric data.

❑ Scanner components include a bulb, lens, light-sensitive diodes, memory, and firmware. In addition, scanners require drivers and usually come with a variety of software for processing and manipulating the scanned images.

❑ Manufacturers offer products that include a scanner and printer integrated within the same case.

❑ Printer and scanner interfaces include parallel, serial, USB, IEEE 1394/ FireWire, SCSI, network, and wireless.

Installing and Configuring Printers and Scanners

❑ Before installing a printer, be sure to read the manufacturer's instructions. Many printers must have their drivers installed on the computer before the printer is connected and powered up.

❑ Installing a printer in Windows is a simple job, especially for Plug-and-Play printers. Even non-Plug-and-Play printers are easy to install using the Add New Printer Wizard.

❑ After installing a printer, do a test print, and then print from each installed application to ensure compatibility.

❑ Configure a printer through the Printer Properties dialog box, and through the Printing Preferences dialog box.

❑ Before installing a scanner, be sure to read the manufacturer's instructions for unpacking the scanner and installing the software. Some scanners have a transportation lock that must be disengaged before using the scanner.

❑ Many scanners must have their drivers installed on the computer before the printer is connected and powered up.

❑ Educate users on the use and care of printers and scanners.

❑ There are a few common upgrades to printers and scanners, including device drivers and other software, document feeders, memory, and firmware.

❑ Ways to optimize a printer's performance include tray selection for different stationery, and enabling of tray switching.

❑ For the best results, use color calibration of displays, printers, and scanners to adjust the colors of these devices.

❑ Higher resolution and color density will result in higher-quality scanned images, but larger file sizes.

❑ The file format you choose will also affect the file size.

Troubleshooting Printers and Scanners

❑ When troubleshooting and maintaining printers and scanners, use tools from the hardware toolkit described in Chapter 4.

❑ The troubleshooting process for printers is identical to that used for computers. Gather information, review and analyze collected data, identify solutions to problems, and be familiar with common printer and scanner problems.

❑ Common printer problems include those involving paper feed and print quality. Printer error messages on your computer screen or the printer panel will alert you to common problems, such as paper out, I/O errors, and print spooler problems.

❑ Common scanner problems can involve power, the interface, and attempting to use the scanner with the scanner lock engaged.

❑ When power and connections do not appear to be the source of a scanner problem, power down the scanner, and uninstall and reinstall the scanner software.

❑ If the scanner lamp becomes too dim to work, the scanner will stop functioning, and you should contact the manufacturer for lamp replacement, which is usually not a user-serviceable item.

❑ The cause of a scanned image appearing incorrectly on the display may be a display setting that is incorrect for the image. Change the display color density to a greater number of colors, such as 24-bit color.

Preventive Maintenance for Printers and Scanners

❑ Some laser printers track the number of pages printed in a page count, and require that critical components be replaced using a maintenance kit. After installing the maintenance kit you must reset the page count.

❑ Clean each printer and scanner according to the manufacturer's recommendation to avoid poor output and other problems.

❑ Provide a suitable environment for each printer and scanner to avoid problems that dirt and temperature extremes can cause in these devices.

❑ For the best results, use the recommended consumables in printers. This may require using the media and paper provided from the manufacturer, or cheaper substitutes of equal quality from other sources.

SELF TEST

The following questions will help you measure your understanding of the material presented in this chapter. Read all of the choices carefully, because there might be more than one correct answer. Choose all correct answers for each question.

Understanding Printers and Scanners

1. What is a common use for dot matrix printers?
    A. High-quality color images
    B. High-speed network printers
    C. Multiple-part forms
    D. UPC code scanning

2. What type of printer is the most often-used shared network printer in businesses?
    A. Laser
    B. Dot matrix
    C. Thermal
    D. Inkjet

3. In what stage of the laser printing process does a laser beam place an image on the photosensitive drum?
    A. Cleaning
    B. Developing
    C. Charging
    D. Writing

4. Which stage in the laser printing process is responsible for creating a permanent non-smearing image?
    A. Cleaning
    B. Fusing
    C. Transferring
    D. Writing

5. What name is given to the type of printer that applies wet ink to paper?
    A. Laser
    B. Dot matrix
    C. Thermal
    D. Inkjet

6. What is the unit of measure used to describe the size of droplets created by the nozzles in an inkjet printer?

   A. Millimeter

   B. Meter

   C. Picoliter

   D. Liter

7. What are two examples of solid ink technology?

   A. Inkjet and bubblejet

   B. Laser jet and dot matrix

   C. Dye sublimation and thermal wax

   D. Direct thermal and thermal wax transfer

8. What software converts a scanned page of text from graphic format to editable text format?

   A. Copy

   B. OCR

   C. Scanning

   D. Graphics editing

Installing and Configuring Printers and Scanners

9. What Windows GUI tool can you use to install a non-Plug-and-Play printer?

   A. Add Printer Wizard

   B. Device Manager

   C. My Computer

   D. Add or Remove Programs

10. What device in a scanner protects internal components from moving while the scanner is in transit?

   A. OCR

   B. Transportation lock

   C. Lid

   D. Scanning software

Upgrading and Optimizing Printers and Scanners

11. What is the most common software upgrade for a scanner or printer?

   A. Graphics software

   B. Word processing software

C. Firmware upgrade

D. New device driver

12. In addition to printers and scanners, what other device can benefit from color calibration?

A. Memory

B. Display

C. Hard drive

D. Paper tray

Troubleshooting Printers and Scanners

13. What can contribute to static build-up in a printer?

A. Dust

B. Ink

C. Overloaded paper tray

D. Paper jams

14. What component on an inkjet printer may clog with ink?

A. Nozzles

B. Hammers

C. Friction-feed rollers

D. Tractor feeder

15. What is a possible source of a problem causing blank pages to print out on a laser printer?

A. Paper path

B. Transfer corona wire

C. Power supply

D. Paper tray

16. What component in a laser printer could be the source of a repeated pattern of speckles?

A. Fusion roller

B. Drum

C. Toner

D. Primary corona wire

17. When a ghosted image from a previous page occurs on subsequent pages printed on a laser printer, what component is a probable source?

A. Fusion roller

B. Drum

C. Toner

D. Primary corona wire

18. What can cause scanned images to look distorted on a computer display?

A. Display resolution set too low

B. Scanner resolution set too low

C. Display color depth set too low

D. Scanner color depth set too low

Preventive Maintenance for Printers and Scanners

19. What should you do after installing a maintenance kit in a laser printer?

A. Reset the maintenance count.

B. Reset the page count.

C. Reset the printer.

D. Call the manufacturer.

20. What simple maintenance task for both printers and scanners helps maintain high-quality results?

A. Memory upgrade

B. Installing a maintenance kit

C. Calibration

D. Cleaning

LAB QUESTION

Use the Internet to research a color printer for a college department network in which a dozen people will make printouts of documents with a mixture of text and graphics. This printer must print over 15 pages a minute and create output that is suitable for printing instruction manuals used by the school in its chemistry lab. These manuals must be in color, printed double-sided, and printed in small batches, so you need a color printer to create multiple sets of the books. The expected monthly page count is under 10,000 copies. The printer must be under $1000, and the cartridges must not cost more than $1000 a year. A set of toner cartridges must have an expected life of 4000 pages or more, and the cost must be under $400 to keep the cost of toner under ten cents a page. Write a few sentences describing the type of printer you believe is best suited for the job, and then describe the printer model you selected and why you selected it.

SELF TEST ANSWERS

Understanding Printers and Scanners

1. ☑ **C.** Multiple-part forms printing is a common use for dot matrix printers.
   ☒ **A**, high-quality color images, is incorrect because dot matrix printers do not create high-quality color images. **B**, high-speed network printers, is incorrect because dot matrix printers are not high-speed printers. **D**, UPC code scanning, is incorrect because no stand-alone printer can scan.

2. ☑ **A.** The laser printer is the most often-used shared network printer in businesses.
   ☒ **B**, dot matrix, **C**, thermal, and **D**, inkjet, are all incorrect because these types of printers seldom are shared network printers in businesses.

3. ☑ **D.** Writing is the laser printing stage in which the laser beam places an image on the photosensitive drum.
   ☒ **A**, cleaning, is incorrect because it is not the stage in which an image is placed on the drum, but the stage in which the drum is cleaned. **B**, developing, is incorrect because it is not the stage in which an image is placed on the drum, but the stage in which toner is attracted to the image on the drum. **C**, charging, is incorrect because it is not the stage in which an image is placed on the drum by the laser beam, but the stage in which a charge is applied to the drum.

4. ☑ **B.** Fusing is the stage in the laser printing process in which the image permanently fuses to the paper.
   ☒ **A**, cleaning, **C**, transferring, and **D**, writing, are incorrect because none of these is the stage that creates a permanent non-smearing image.

5. ☑ **D.** Inkjet is the type of printer that applies wet ink to paper.
   ☒ **A**, laser, is incorrect because this type of printer does not apply wet ink to paper, but rather dry toner that is fused to the paper. **B**, dot matrix, is incorrect because this type of printer does not apply wet ink to paper but uses an ink ribbon. **C**, thermal, is incorrect because this type of printer does not apply wet ink to paper.

6. ☑ **C.** Picoliter is the unit of measure used to describe the size of droplets created by the nozzles in an inkjet printer.
   ☒ **A**, millimeter, and **B**, meter, are both incorrect because neither one is the unit of measure used for the size of droplets from the nozzles in an inkjet printer. Both millimeter and meter are units of measure for distance, while we are looking for a measurement of the volume of ink, a liquid. **D**, liter, is incorrect because this is not the unit of measure used to describe the size of droplets created by the nozzles in an inkjet printer. While liter is the measure for liquid volume, it is far too large for such small drops.

7. ☑ **C.** Dye sublimation and thermal wax are two examples of solid ink technology.
   ☒ **A,** inkjet and bubblejet, is incorrect because these are printers that use liquid ink. **B,** laser jet and dot matrix, is incorrect because the one uses dry toner, and the other uses an ink ribbon. **D,** direct thermal and thermal wax transfer, is incorrect because, while thermal wax transfer uses solid ink technology, direct thermal does not but actually burns an image into paper.

8. ☑ **B.** OCR, or optical character recognition, is the software used to convert a scanned page of text from graphic format to editable text format.
   ☒ **A,** copy, is incorrect because this is not software that converts a scanned page of text from graphic format to editable text format. **C,** scanning, is incorrect because scanning is not the software that converts a scanned page of text from graphic format to editable text format. **D,** graphics editing, is incorrect because this software does not convert a scanned page of text from graphic format to editable text format.

Installing and Configuring Printers and Scanners

9. ☑ **A.** The Add Printer Wizard is the Windows GUI tool for installing a non-Plug-and-Play printer.
   ☒ **B,** Device Manager, **C,** My Computer, and **D,** Add or Remove Programs, are incorrect because none of these is the GUI tool for installing a non-Plug-and-Play printer.

10. ☑ **B.** Transportation lock is correct because engaging this will protect internal components when a scanner must move.
    ☒ **A,** OCR, is incorrect because this is not used to protect internal components during a move but is software used to convert scanned text from a graphics image into editable text. **C,** lid, is incorrect because while a flatbed scanner has a lid, engaging this does not protect internal components. **D,** scanning software, is incorrect because this is for the normal scanning operation of the printer, not to protect internal components while a printer is being moved.

Upgrading and Optimizing Printers and Scanners

11. ☑ **D.** New device driver is the most common software upgrade for a scanner or printer.
    ☒ **A,** graphics software, is incorrect because this is not the most common software upgrade for a scanner or printer. **B,** word processing software, is incorrect because this is not the most common software upgrade for a scanner or printer. **C,** firmware upgrade, is incorrect because it is not the most common software upgrade for a scanner or printer.

12. ☑ **B.** Display is another device (in addition to printers and scanners) that can benefit from color calibration.
    ☒ **A,** memory, is incorrect because memory will not benefit from color calibration. **C,** hard drive, is incorrect because a hard drive does not benefit at all from color calibration. **D,** paper tray, is incorrect because a paper tray cannot benefit from color calibration.

Troubleshooting Printers and Scanners

13. ☑ **A.** Dust can contribute to static build-up in a printer.
    ☒ **B**, ink, is incorrect because, while ink residue may build up in a printer, it does not appreciably contribute to static buildup. **C**, overloaded paper tray, is incorrect because this is not a cause of static build-up in a printer. **D**, paper jams, is incorrect because, while static build-up in a printer may occasionally cause a paper jam, it is not a primary cause.

14. ☑ **A.** Nozzles in an inkjet printer can become clogged with ink.
    ☒ **B**, hammers, **C**, friction-feed rollers, and **D**, tractor feeder, are incorrect because these components do not become clogged with ink.

15. ☑ **B.** The transfer corona wire is a possible source of a problem causing blank pages to print out on a laser printer.
    ☒ **A**, paper path, **C**, power supply, and **D**, paper tray, are incorrect because they are not considered possible sources for blank pages printing out on a laser printer.

16. ☑ **B.** The drum could be the source of a repeated patter of speckles printing out from a laser printer.
    ☒ **A**, fusion roller, **C**, toner, and **D**, primary corona wire, are incorrect because none of these is a probable source of repeated pattern of speckles printing out from a laser printer.

17. ☑ **B.** The drum is the probable source of a ghosted image printing on subsequent pages from a laser printer.
    ☒ **A**, fusion roller, **C**, toner, and **D**, primary corona wire, are incorrect because none of these is a probable source of a ghosted image.

18. ☑ **C.** The display color depth being set too low can cause scanned images to look distorted on a computer display.
    ☒ **A**, display resolution set too low, **B**, scanner resolution set too low, and **D**, scanner color depth set too low, are all incorrect because they are not likely to cause the distorted appearance caused by a low color density on a display when viewing an image scanned at a higher density.

Preventive Maintenance for Printers and Scanners

19. ☑ **B.** Reset the page count of a laser printer after installing a maintenance kit.
    ☒ **A**, reset the maintenance count, is incorrect because this will set the number at which the printer should receive maintenance to zero pages. **C**, reset the printer, is incorrect because this will not turn the page count to zero, and the printer will display a maintenance warning. **D**, call the manufacturer, is incorrect because this is unnecessary when all you need to do is reset the page count.

20. ☑ **D.** Cleaning is the simple maintenance task for both printers and scanners that helps maintain high-quality results.

☒ **A**, memory upgrade, is incorrect because this is not a simple maintenance task, and it will not help maintain high-quality results. **B**, installing a maintenance kit, is incorrect because this is not a simple maintenance task. **C**, calibration, is incorrect because this is not a simple task.

LAB ANSWER

Answers will vary. The answer provided here is correct at the time of this writing, and different printers will be available to the student.

Because we want a color printer that can print over 24 pages per minute, we decided to look for a color laser printer. And because it is to be shared on a network, we looked for a printer with an integrated network card. Manuals should be in permanent ink, another reason why a laser printer is the best choice. Manuals also do not generally require photo-quality printing, so a modestly priced laser printer will be adequate.

The printer we selected is a Dell 3100cn, a color laser printer with an integrated network card. The estimated cost of this printer is $400, with another $300 for a duplexer for two-sided printing. The duty cycle, of 45,000 pages per month, is more than adequate, as is the speed at 18 pages per minute. A set of cartridges is $313, with an expected life of 4000 pages, bringing the estimated cost of toner to eight cents a page.

Part V

Networks

12

Network Basics

Computer networks provide users with the ability to share files, printers, resources, and e-mail as though they resided locally on the user's computer. Computer networks have become so important in some settings that they provide the basis for nearly all business transactions. Networks make it possible to share documents and images with people all around the world, literally at the click of a mouse.

Obviously, a discussion of the full spectrum of network details and specifications is too broad in scope to be contained in this chapter and the two that follow. However, as a computer technician, you should be aware of basic networking concepts so that you can troubleshoot minor problems on already-established networks. This chapter focuses on basic concepts of physical networks; Chapter 13 guides you through simple network client-installation procedures, and Chapter 14 provides the basis for troubleshooting common network installation and connectivity problems.

CERTIFICATION OBJECTIVES

■ **601: 5.1   602: 5.1**   *Identify the fundamental principles of networks*

Computer networking is a very broad topic. There are many geographic types of networks, from simple personal area networks to wide area networks connecting huge networks, such as the Internet—a worldwide interconnection of networks. Each type of network can employ a different combination of network devices, computers, operating system, cabling, protocols, and security measures. These combinations are the network's architecture. In fact, while CompTIA's Network+ certification is based entirely on networking concepts and network architectures, networking is only one domain of the A+ exams. In addition, the CompTIA Server+ certification requires in-depth knowledge of network servers, and the Internet+ exam requires knowledge of the great array of Internet technologies. Therefore, the knowledge required for the A+ exams is that of an introductory overview, which we present here.

Network Overview

For a computer professional working with PCs, the networked computer is the norm, not the exception. A computer not connected to a network is a stand-alone computer, and this has become a nearly extinct species, as more and more PCs are networked—even in homes.

Geographic Network Classifications

To understand networks, you must first be familiar with the basic network classifications, which describe networks by scale, beginning with the smallest networks up to a globe-spanning network. Any of these network types will allow you to access and use resources, since that is the reason for having a network of any type.

While the range of a network—the distance over which signals are viable—is one important defining aspect of a network, bandwidth is another. Bandwidth is the amount of data that can travel over a network at a given time. It may be expressed in kilobits per second (Kbps), kilobytes per second (KBps), megabits per second (Mbps), and even gigabits per second (Gbps).

Personal Area Network (PAN)

You may have your own personal area network (PAN), if you have devices, such as phones and personal digital assistants (PDAs), that communicate with each other and/or your desktop computer. These devices frequently have a distance limit of one meter, or a theoretical limit of about ten meters.

Local Area Network (LAN)

A local area network (LAN) is a network that covers a relatively small area, such as a building, home, office, or campus. The typical distances are measured in hundreds of meters. A LAN may share resources such as printers, files, or other resources. LANs operate very fast—with speeds measured in megabits or gigabits per second—and have become extremely cost effective. An office or a home can share a single high-speed laser printer using a LAN, and each user can have equal access to the printer.

Metropolitan Area Network (MAN)

A metropolitan area network (MAN) is a network that covers a metropolitan area, connecting various networks together using a shared, community network, and often providing WAN connections to the Internet.

Wide Area Network (WAN)

A wide area network (WAN) can cover the largest geographic area. It is defined as two or more networks connected over long distances. A WAN connection is the connection between the networks. The generic term for such connected networks is an internetwork or intranet. The most famous, and largest, of these is the Internet. Your Internet connection from home is a WAN connection, even when the network at home consists of a single computer connected to a phone line.

Geographic Network Technologies

There are specific technologies designed for each of the geographic network types. Manufacturers select these technologies for their capabilities that match the distance and sometimes the security needs of the network type.

PAN Networks

A PAN network may use a wired connection, such as the old PC serial interface, or USB or FireWire, or it may communicate wirelessly using one of the standards developed for short-range communications, such as IrDA (an implementation of infrared wireless) or Bluetooth. We described these interfaces in Chapter 2.

> **exam**
> **ⓦatch** *While the term PAN is not included in the objectives for the CompTIA A+ exams, the wireless technologies used in a PAN are included, so be sure to be familiar with them and their distance limit, which is one meter for IrDA and ten meters for Bluetooth (see Chapter 5).*

LAN Networks

While there are many LAN technologies, the two most widely used are Ethernet and several standards that fall under the Wi-Fi heading.

Ethernet   Most wired LANs use hardware based on the IEEE-developed Ethernet standard that defines, among other things, how computer data is broken down into small chunks, prepared, and packaged before the Ethernet network interface card (NIC) places it on the Ethernet network. This chunk of data is an Ethernet frame.

Also known as IEEE 802.3, an Ethernet network uses the carrier sense multiple access/collision detection network access method. In this access method, when a computer wants to send a data packet, it first "listens" to the network to determine if another transmission is already in progress. If there is another transmission, the computer waits, and then listens again. When there is no other network activity, the computer sends its data packet. However, if another computer sends a packet at the same time, a collision occurs.

When a collision is detected, both computers stop transmitting, wait a random amount of time, and then begin the listening/transmitting process again. This procedure continues until the data transmits properly. These collisions are limited to a single network segment, the portion of a network between bridges. (Bridges are defined later in this chapter.)

On networks with many computers, the number of collisions can be quite high, so it can take a number of tries until a computer can send its packet. The collision problem can be dealt with by breaking a network into more segments (by adding more bridges) with fewer nodes per segment.

When a network medium allows for communications in both directions, it is bidirectional. Ethernet is half-duplex, meaning that while data can travel in either direction, it can only travel in one direction at a time.

Depending on the exact implementation, Ethernet supports a variety of transmission speeds and media. Here is a summary of different levels of Ethernet, and their speeds:

- **Ethernet** For many years the most widely used implementation, simply called Ethernet or 10Base-T, it transfers data at 10 Mbps over unshielded twisted pair (UTP) copper cabling.

- **Fast Ethernet** Using the same cabling as Ethernet, Fast Ethernet, or 100Base-T, operates at 100 Mbps and uses different network interface cards, many of which are also capable of the lower speeds of Ethernet, auto-detecting the speed of the network and working at whichever speed is in use.

- **Gigabit Ethernet** Supporting data transfer rates of 1 Gbps over UTP, Gigabit Ethernet is also called 1000Base-T. This standard supports speeds up to 10 Gbps but is normally implemented at 1 Gbps. Faster standards have also evolved using fiber optics. One that supports 5 Gbps is often used between specialized network equipment, rather than for connecting computers to the network.

Wireless LAN (WLAN) Local area networking using radio waves, wireless LAN (WLAN) communication, has become very popular. The most common wireless LAN implementations are based on the IEEE 802.11 group of standards, also called Wireless Fidelity (Wi-Fi). There are several 802.11 standards, and more are proposed. Most of these wireless standards use either 2.4 GHz or 5 GHz frequencies to communicate between systems. The range on these systems is relatively short, but they offer the advantage of not requiring cable for network connections.

In many homes, Wi-Fi networks give users access to the Internet. In these instances, the wireless communications network uses a wireless router connected to a broadband connection, such as a cable modem or DSL modem, as shown in Figure 12-1. In this figure, one computer connects via Wi-Fi, while another computer connects directly to the router via an Ethernet cable.

Laptops now come standard with Wi-Fi, and many public places, restaurants, and other businesses offer free or for-pay access to Wi-Fi networks connected to

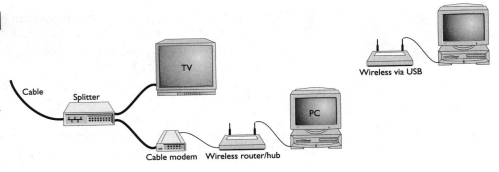

FIGURE 12-1

Internet access using a wireless network to connect to a broadband router

broadband Internet service. In large corporations, users with wireless-enabled laptops and handheld computers can move around the campus and continue to connect to the corporate network.

Wi-Fi now comes in several speeds, complying with various 802.11 standards. Here is a brief description of several of these standards:

- **802.11a** This standard was developed by the IEEE at the same time as the slower 802.11b standard, but the "a" standard was more expensive to implement. Therefore, manufacturers tended to make 802.11b devices. 802.11a uses the 5 GHz band, which makes 802.11a devices incompatible with 802.11b and the subsequent 802.11g devices. 802.11a devices are seldom used because they do not provide downward compatibility with existing equipment using the 802.11b or newer 802.11g standards because of this bandwidth issue. An 802.11a network has speeds up to 54 Mbps.

- **802.11b** This was the first widely (even "wildly") popular version of Wi-Fi, with a speed of 10 Mbps, and a range of up about 90 feet. Operating in the 2.4 GHz band, also used by other non-computer devices such as cordless phones and household appliances, these devices are vulnerable to interference if positioned near another device using the same portion of the radio spectrum.

- **802.11g** 802.11g replaced 802.11b as the most commonly implemented wireless standard. With a speed of up to 54 Mbps, it also uses the 2.4 GHz radio band, and 802.11g devices are normally downward compatible with 802.11b devices, although the reverse is not true.

SCENARIO & SOLUTION

Given the choice, why would I choose a Bluetooth-enabled mouse over a mouse that uses IrDA to communicate with my PC?	Bluetooth uses radio waves, but IrDA uses the infrared band, requiring a direct line of sight between the IrDA ports on each device.
What is the most common wired LAN technology?	Ethernet in all of its versions is the most common wired LAN technology.
Why can I find wireless network cards and access points that are compatible with both 802.11b and 802.11g, but not 802.11a?	While 802.11b and 802.11g both use the same bandwidth, 2.4 GHz, 802.11a uses a different, and therefore incompatible, bandwidth—5 GHz.

- ■ **802.11n** Currently under development, this standard promises speeds of up to 108, 240, and 350+ Mbps. Some manufacturers of wireless NICs, signal boosters, and access points manufactured before the release of the full specification (but including the promised improvements of this standard) use terms such as "802.11pre-n" to describe their equipment.

When considering using a wireless network, speed and range can be nebulous at best. In spite of the stated speeds just listed, many factors affect both speed and range. First, there is the limit of the standard, and then there is the distance between the wireless-enabled computers and the wireless access point (WAP), a network connection device at the core of a wireless network. Finally, there is the issue of interference, which can result from other wireless device signals operating in the same band, or from physical barriers to the signals. In Chapter 13 you will learn about installing a WLAN to avoid interference and devices that will extend the range of the signals.

exam
watch

Be sure that you understand that Wi-Fi alone does not give you a connection to the Internet, because it is a LAN technology. The reason people are able to connect to the Internet through a Wi-Fi connection is that the Wi-Fi network is connected through a device, usually a combination wireless access point (WAP)–router, to a broadband connection to the Internet.

MAN Networks

A MAN usually uses high-speed fiber-optic cable (operating in the gigabits-per-second range). Although people tend to be less aware of MANs, they nonetheless exist. In fact, a MAN may well be somewhere between you and the Internet. A MAN allows a community of LANs to connect to each other and to the Internet.

WAN Networks

WANs, which traditionally used phone lines or satellite communications, now also use cellular telecommunications and cable networks.

WAN speeds range from thousands of bits per second up into the low millions of bits per second. At the low end today are 56 Kbps modems (56,000 bits per second). At the high end of WAN speeds are parts of the Internet backbone, the connecting infrastructure of the Internet, which runs in the hundreds of millions of bits per second and faster.

o n t h e
ⓞo b *The speed of your communications on any network is a function of the speed of the slowest pathway between you and the servers you are accessing. The weakest link determines your speed.*

Dial-Up WAN Connections A dial-up network connection uses an analog modem (described in Chapter 2) rather than a network card and uses regular phone cables instead of network cables. In a dial-up connection, the client computer is configured to dial the host computer, and the host computer must be configured to permit dial-up access. Once a dial-up connection is established, the client can communicate with the host computer as though it were on the same LAN as that computer. If the host computer is already part of a LAN, and if the host configuration allows it, the client computer can access the network to which the host is connected. Many home PCs use a modem connection for dial-up Internet access. In this case, the host computer is just a gateway to the Internet. This is the slowest, but cheapest, form of Internet access, and in some areas, it may be all that is available.

Broadband WAN WAN connections that exceed the speed of a typical dial-up connection come under the heading of broadband connections. Broadband speeds are available over cellular, ISDN, DSL, cable, and satellite. WAN connections can connect private networks to the Internet, and to each other. Often, these connections are "always on," meaning that you do not have to initiate the connection every time you wish to access resources on the connected network, as you do with dial-up. If you wish to browse the Web, you simply open your Web browser.

■ **Cellular** Cellular Internet data connections, also referred to as wireless WAN (WWAN), vary in speed from less than dial-up speeds of 28.8 Kbps, to a range of broadband speeds. Because the trend in cellular is to provide faster-than-dial-up speeds, it is included under broadband WAN. This trend to higher speeds is supported by the move away from the original analog cellular networks to all-digital cellular networks in the United States. Several years ago, we were thrilled to have a cellular wireless network PC Card advertised as operating at 56 Kbps, but it functioned at 48 Kbps. New standards are in development to deliver broadband speeds over cellular networks. At this writing, these are available only in a few metropolitan areas. Laptops are available with built-in cellular devices, and if you need to share a cellular Internet connect, another new product is a box the size of a video cassette called a cell transceiver that converts and routes the cell signal through an integrated LAN hub, which can be either a wired Ethernet hub or a Wi-Fi access point. Currently the cellular device is "married" to a specific cellular provider, so you are locked in to that provider's offerings as long as you want to use that device. Depending on the cellular provider and the technology used, expect speeds between 170 Kbps and 384 Kbps. Speeds as high as 10 Mbps, or even higher, will soon be offered at reasonable prices.

on the
job *Cellular providers must continue to operate analog networks until February 18, 2008, to prevent a sudden abandonment of analog users, especially in rural areas where the digital cellular network was slow to develop.*

■ **ISDN** The Integrated Service Digital Network (ISDN) was an early international standard for sending voice and data over digital telephone wires. These days newer technologies, such as DSL and cable, largely replace it. ISDN uses existing telephone circuits or higher-speed conditioned lines to get speeds of either 64 Kbps or 128 Kbps. ISDN lines also have the ability to carry voice and data simultaneously over the circuit. In fact, the most common ISDN service, called Basic Rate Interface (BRI), includes three channels—two 64 Kbps channels, called B-channels, that carry the voice or data communications, and one 16 Kbps D-channel that carries control and signaling information. ISDN connections use an ISDN modem on both ends of the circuit. Figure 12-2 shows

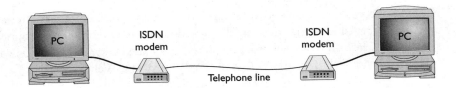

a typical ISDN connection between two networks. This connection uses a conditioned phone line provided by the phone company.

■ **DSL** Digital subscriber line (DSL) uses existing copper telephone wire for the communications circuit. A DSL modem splits the existing phone line into two bands to accomplish this; voice transmission uses the frequency below 4000 Hz, while data transmission uses everything else. Figure 12-3 shows the total bandwidth being separated into two channels; one is used for voice, the other for data. Voice communications operate normally, and the data connection is always on and available. DSL service is available through phone companies, which offer a variety of DSL services usually identified by a letter preceding "DSL," as in ADSL, CDSL, HDSL, SDSL, SHDSL, and many more. Therefore, when talking about DSL in general, the term *x*DSL is often used. Some of these services, such as ADSL (asymmetrical digital subscriber line), offer asymmetric service, in that the download speed is higher than the upload speed. The top speeds can range from 1.5 Mbps to 6 Mbps for download and between 16 Kbps and 640 Kbps for upload. However, CDSL (consumer DSL) service aims at the casual home user and offers lower speeds than this range. CDSL service is limited to download speeds of up to 1 Mbps, and upload speeds of up to 160 Kbps. The words "up to" indicate that the actual speeds can be lower. Other, more expensive, services aimed at business offer much higher rates. Symmetric DSL, high–data rate DSL, and symmetric HDSL all offer matching upload and download speeds. Table 12-1 shows some DSL services and their maximum data transfer speeds.

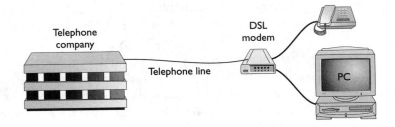

TABLE 12-1	DLS Services with Maximum Download and Upload Speeds		
Service	Range of Maximum Speeds Down	Range of Maximum Speeds Up	Comments
Asymmetric DSL (ADSL)	1.5–8.192 Mbps	16–640 Kbps	Different upload and download speeds
Rate-adaptive DSL (RADSL)	64 Kbps–8.192 Mbps	16–768 Kbps	Different upload and download speeds
Consumer DSL (CDSL)	1 Mbps	16–160 Kbps	Different upload and download speeds. Also called DSL-lite (G.lite)
High–data rate DSL (HDSL)	1.544 Mbps in North America 2.048 Mbps elsewhere	1.544 Mbps in North America 2.048 Mbps elsewhere	Same upload and download speeds
ISDN DSL (IDSL)	144 Kbps as Basic Rate Interface (BRI)	144 Kbps as BRI	Same upload and download speeds
Symmetric DSL (SDSL)	1.544 Mbps in North America 2.048 Mbps elsewhere	1.544 Mbps in North America 2.048 Mbps elsewhere	Same upload and download speeds
Very high data rate DSL (VDSL)	13–52 ±Mbps	1.5–6.0 Mbps	Different upload and download speeds
Symmetric high-speed DSL (SHDSL)	192 Kbps–2.360 Mbps or 384 Kbps–4.720 Mbps	192 Kbps–2.360 Mbps or 384 Kbps–4.720 Mbps	Same upload and download speeds

■ **Cable** Cable television service has been around for four decades. Most cable providers have added Internet connection services with promised higher speeds of up to 30 Mbps, which is three times the practical maximum for the typical DSL service. These speeds appear to be more promise than fact. Whereas DSL service is point-to-point from the client to the ISP, a cable client shares the network with their neighboring cable clients. It is like sharing a LAN that in turn has an Internet connection. For this reason, speed degrades as more people share the local cable network. You still get impressive speeds with cable, depending on the level of service you buy. Cable networks use coaxial cable to connect a special cable modem to the network. The PC normally connects to this cable modem with twisted pair cable that, in turn, is connected to the PC's Ethernet network adapter. Figure 12-4 shows a cable modem installation for a home that also has cable TV service.

FIGURE 12-4

A cable modem configuration

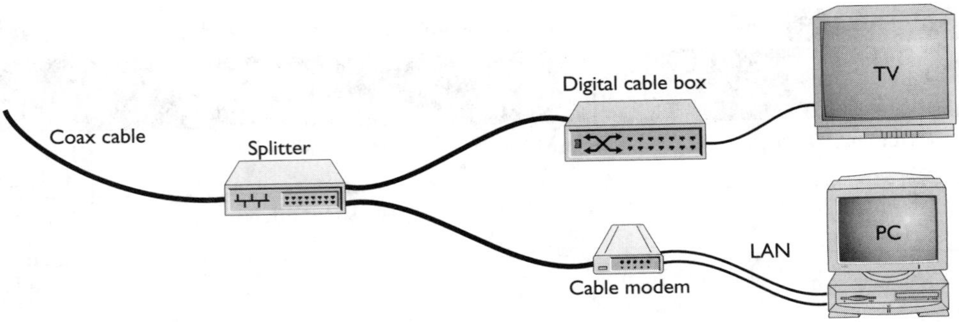

- **T-carrier** Developed by Bell Labs in the 1960s, the T-carrier system multiplexes voice and data signals onto digital transmission lines. Where previously one cable pair carried each telephone conversation, the multiplexing of the T-carrier system allows for a single pair to carry multiple conversations. Over the years, the T-carrier system has evolved, and telephone companies have offered various levels of service over the T-carrier system. For instance, a T1 circuit provides full-duplex transmissions at 1.544 Mbps, carrying digital voice, data, or video signals. A complete T1 circuit provides point-to-point connections, with a channel service unit (CSU) at both ends. On the customer side a T1 multiplexer or a special LAN bridge, referred to as the customer premises equipment (CPE), connects to the CSU. The CSU receives data from the CPE and encodes it for transmission on the T1 circuit. T1 is just one of several levels of T-carrier services offered by telephone companies over the telephone network.

- **Satellite** Satellite communications systems have come a long way over the last several years. Satellite communication systems initially allowed extensive communications with remote locations and for military purposes. These systems usually use microwave radio frequencies and require a dish antenna, a receiver, and a transmitter. Early satellite communications systems were very expensive to maintain and operate. Today a number of companies offer relatively high bandwidth at affordable prices for Internet connection and other applications. The bandwidth capabilities of these systems rival those of cable or DSL networks and offer speeds for downloading of up to 2 Mbps (uploading speeds typically range from 40 to 90 Kbps). Satellite connections are now available for both fixed and mobile applications. Satellite providers offer different levels of service.

The highest speeds require a larger dish antenna. The authors currently use a 0.74-meter dish (larger than modern TV dish antennas) with a special digital receiver/transmitter referred to as a modem. This dish and modem combination gives a certain range of speeds, and larger and more expensive dishes provide greater speeds. As with TV satellite service, you must have a place to mount the dish antenna with a clear view of the southern sky. Using a plan designed for homes and small business, the download speed is 700 Kbps and upload speed is 128 Kbps. The next level of service offers speeds of 1000 Kbps down and 200 Kbps up.

EXERCISE 12-1

Testing Broadband Speeds

Regardless of the broadband service you use, they all vary in the actual speeds they provide from moment to moment. Connect to one of the many broadband speed-testing sites on the Internet and test yours now.

1. Open your favorite search engine and enter a search string. We used "network speed test."

2. From the results list in the search engine select a site.

3. Follow the instructions for testing your connection. Some sites test as soon as you connect.

4. View the results (see Figure 12-5). Are the results congruent with the service you expect from your broadband connection?

5. Time permitting, try this at another time—even another day.

Network Hardware

Network hardware is a very broad topic including many network connection devices that are part of the infrastructure of a large network, and of the largest network—the Internet. The hardware described in this section is limited to the network adapters used in PCs, and the medium that connects these adapters to the network.

FIGURE 12-5 The speed of a broadband Internet connection can vary.

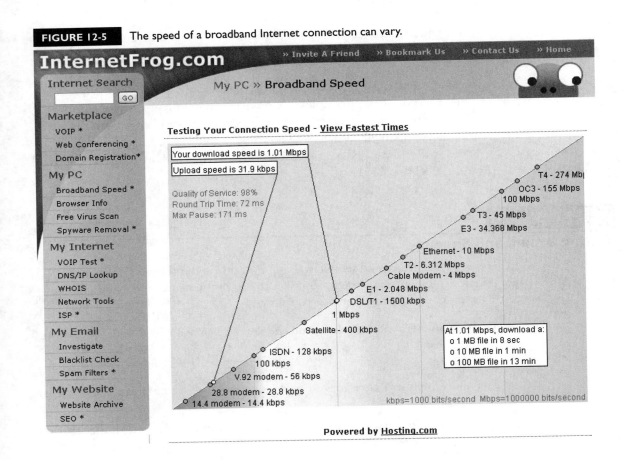

Network Adapters

Each computer on a network must have a connection to the network provided by a network interface card (NIC), also called a network adapter, and some form of network medium that makes the connection between the NIC and the network. NICs are identified by the network technology (Ethernet or Wi-Fi) used, and the type of interface used between the card and the PC, such as the PCI and PCIe interfaces introduced in Chapter 1, the USB or FireWire interfaces defined in Chapter 2, or for a laptop, the PC Card interfaces explored in Chapter 5.

Most NICs come with status indicators, as lights on the card itself, and/or as software that displays the status on the notification area of the taskbar.

Transmission Medium

The transmission medium for a network carries the signals. These signals may be electrical signals carried over copper wire cabling, light signals carried over fiber-optic cabling, or infrared or radio waves transmitted through the atmosphere. In these examples, the copper wire, fiber-optic cable, and atmosphere are the media.

Plenum vs. PVC

Many commonly used network cables use a PVC outer sheath to protect the cable. PVC is not fire resistant and, by code, cannot be used in overhead or plenum areas in offices—those spaces in a building through which air conditioning and heating ducts run. Plenum cable uses a special fire-resistant outer sheath that will not burn as quickly as PVC. Plenum cable frequently costs more but is required in most areas. Most of the standard cables discussed in this chapter are available with plenum-grade ratings.

Twisted Pair

Twisted-pair cable is the most popular cable type for internal networks. The term "twisted pair" indicates that it contains pairs of wires twisted around each other. These twists help "boost" each wire's signals and make them less susceptible to electromagnetic interference (EMI). The most common type of twisted-pair wiring is unshielded twisted pair (UTP), which, while it has a plastic sheathing, does not have actual metal shielding.

Twisted-pair cable is also available as shielded twisted pair (STP), with an extra insulating layer that helps prevent data loss and blocks EMI. However, due to the expense of STP, UTP is more commonly used.

There are several standards for twisted-pair cables, each with a different number of wires, certified speed, and implementation. These standards are often referred to as CAT*—for example, CAT3, CAT5 (CAT is short for category). CAT5, a type of UTP, is the most common twisted-pair cable. Table 12-2 presents a summary of twisted-pair cable standards. CAT 5e is an enhanced version of CAT5 that is more stringently tested and offers better transmission characteristics than CAT5. CAT6 offers higher bandwidth and improved signal handling characteristics.

You can identify a twisted-pair cable by its use of RJ45 connectors, which look like regular RJ11 phone connectors but are slightly larger, as they contain eight wires, while RJ11 connectors contain four wires.

on the
iob

The oldest cabling you should normally encounter in a business is CAT5, although it is certainly possible to find very old installations of CAT3 cabling, which is not adequate for modern networks running 100 Mbps or faster.

TABLE 12-2	Type	Speed	Common Use
	CAT1	1 Mbps	Phone lines
Cable Categories	CAT2	4 Mbps	Token Ring networks
	CAT3	16 Mbps	Ethernet networks
	CAT4	20 Mbps	Token Ring networks
	CAT5	100 Mbps	Ethernet networks
	CAT5e	100 Mbps	Ethernet networks
	CAT6	200 Mbps	Ethernet networks

Fiber-Optic Cable

Until recently, local area networks (LANs) seldom used fiber-optic cable (fiber for short), but fiber is often used to join separate networks over long distances. Increasingly, however, some new homes, apartments, and businesses have both fiber and copper wiring installed when being built. Also, some phone companies are using fiber to connect to homes and businesses.

Fiber transmits light rather than electrical signals, so it is not susceptible to electromagnetic interference (EMI). It is capable of faster transmission than other types of cable, but it is also the most expensive cable.

A single light wave passing down a cable is a mode. Two variants of fiber-optic cables are single-mode and multimode. A single-mode cable allows only a single wave to pass down the cable. Multimode fiber allows for multiple modes or waves to pass simultaneously. Multimodes usually use a larger diameter fiber, and each wave uses a certain portion of the fiber cable for transmission.

Fiber-optic data transmission requires two cables—one to send and another to receive. Over the years, the various standards for connectors have continued to evolve, moving toward smaller connectors. Connectors enable fiber-optic cable to connect to transmitters, receivers, or other devices. Here are brief descriptions of four types of connectors used with fiber cable:

- **Straight tip (ST)** This connector is a straight, round connector used to connect fiber to a network device. It has a twist-type coupling.
- **Subscriber connector (SC)** This connector is a square snap coupling, about 2.5 mm, used for cable-to-cable connections or to connect cable to network devices. It latches with a push-pull action similar to audio and video jacks.

FIGURE 12-6

The ST and SC connectors used with fiber-optic cable

- **Lucent connector (LC)**   This type (also called local connector), has a snap coupling and, at 1.25 mm, is half the size of the SC connector.
- **Mechanical Transfer Registered Jack (MT-RJ)**   This connector type resembles an RJ45 network connector and is less expensive and easier to work with than ST or SC.

Figure 12-6 shows the ST and SC connectors.

The CompTIA A+ exam objectives only require knowledge of network adapters and the medium they connect to, because these are the network hardware components PC technicians encounter most often.

Connecting LANs

Most LANs now connect to other LANs, or through WAN connections to internetworks, such as the Internet. A variety of network connection devices connect networks. Each serves a special purpose, and two or more of these functions may be contained in a single box.

Repeater

A *repeater* is a device used to extend the range of a network by taking the signals it receives from one port and regenerating (repeating) those signals to another port. Repeaters are available for various networks. For instance, on an Ethernet network you would use an Ethernet repeater, and in a Wi-Fi network you would use a wireless repeater (often called a signal booster) to boost the signal between wireless networks. In both cases, the repeater must be at the appropriate level and speed for the network (Ethernet, Fast Ethernet, Gigabit Ethernet, 802.11b, 802.11g, etc.).

Bridge

A *bridge* is a device used to connect two networks and pass traffic between them using the physical address of the destination device. Bridges are specific to the hardware technology in use. For instance, an Ethernet bridge looks at physical Ethernet addresses and forwards Ethernet frames with destination addresses that are not on the local network.

Hub/Switch

A *hub* is a device that is the central connecting point of a LAN. It is little more than a multiport repeater because it takes a signal received on one port and repeats it on all other ports. The most basic hub is a passive device that does not have power to it. The next level up is a powered active hub, which amplifies and cleans up the signal before sending it to other ports. More intelligent devices called *switches* or switching hubs, which take an incoming signal and only send it to the destination port, have replaced both types of hubs. This type of switch is both a bridge and a hub. At one time switches were very expensive, but now small eight-port switches are inexpensive and commonly used—even in very small LANs.

Each computer or other device in a network attaches to a hub of the type appropriate for the type of LAN. For instance, computers using Ethernet cards must connect to an Ethernet hub or switch. Wireless devices attach wirelessly to a wireless hub—more often called a wireless access point (WAP). Devices may combine these functions, as in the case of a WAP that includes an Ethernet switch (look for one or more RJ45 connectors on a WAP).

Router

Connections between networks usually require some form of routing capability. In the case of a connection to the Internet, each computer or device connected to the network requires a TCP/IP address.

In order to reach a computer on another network, the originating computer must have a means of sending information to the other computer. To accomplish this, routes are established and a router—a device that sits at the connection between networks—is used to store information about destinations.

A router is specific to one protocol. The type of router used to connect TCP/IP networks is an IP router. An IP router knows the IP addresses of the networks to which it connects, and the addresses of other routers on those networks. At the least, a router knows the next destination to which it can transfer information.

Many routers include bridging circuitry, a hub, and the necessary hardware to connect multiple network technologies together, such as a LAN and a T1 network, or a LAN to any of the other broadband networks. The Internet has thousands of routers managing the connections between the millions of computers and networks connected to it. Figure 12-7 shows a router between a LAN and a WAN.

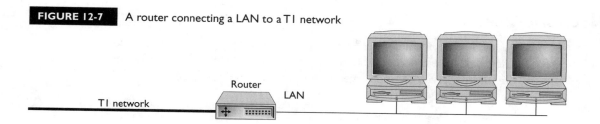

FIGURE 12-7 A router connecting a LAN to a T1 network

EXERCISE 12-2

Identifying Network Hardware

See what network hardware you can identify in your home, office, or school.

1. If you have a PC in your home, and it has a connection to the Internet, locate and identify the network components.

2. If you use a dial-up connection, look for the modem, the telephone cable between the modem and the phone jack on the wall, and the RJ11 connectors at either end of the telephone cable.

3. If you have a DSL connection, look for the Ethernet cable that runs between your computer and the hub/switch, or modem. Examine the RJ45 connectors on either end of the cable. The cable may connect to a single box that performs all of these functions.

4. If you have cable Internet service, look for an Ethernet cable between your computer and the cable modem, and then look for a coaxial cable between the modem and the wall connector.

5. At school or work, all you may find is an Ethernet cable connecting your computer to a wall jack, where the cable in the walls connects to the network. Ask the network administrator to describe how you connect to the Internet through the network.

Network Software

The software on a network gives us the network that we know and use. This is the logical network—although it certainly could not exist without the network hardware. In this section, explore the network roles, protocol suites, and network addressing of the logical network.

Network Roles

You can describe a network by the types of roles played by the computers on the network. The two general computer roles in a network are clients, computers requesting services, and servers, computers providing services.

Peer-to-Peer Networks

In a peer-to-peer network all computer systems in the network may play both roles—client and server. They have equal capabilities and responsibilities; each computer user is responsible for controlling access, sharing resources, and storing data on their computer. All of the computers essentially operate as both servers (providing access to shared resources) and clients (accessing those shared resources). In Figure 12-8 each of the computers can be sharing their files, and the computer connected to the printer can share the printer. A typical peer-to-peer network is very small, with users working at each computer. Peer-to-peer works best in a very small LAN environment with fewer than a dozen computers and users. A small business office may have a peer-to-peer network. Microsoft's term for a peer-to-peer network is a workgroup. Each Microsoft workgroup must have a unique name, as must each computer. More on naming later.

Client/Server-Based Networks

A client/server-based network uses dedicated computers called *servers* to store data, provide print services and other capabilities. Servers are generally more powerful computer systems with more capacity than a typical workstation. Client/server-based models also allow for centralized administration and security. These types of networks are also considerably more scalable in that they can grow very large without adding additional administrative complexity to the network. A large private internetwork for a globe-spanning corporation is an example of a client/server-based network. The network administrator can establish a single model for security, access,

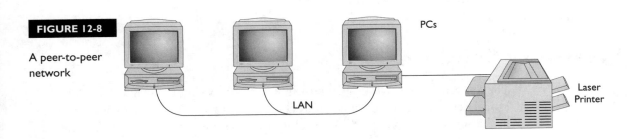

FIGURE 12-8

A peer-to-peer network

PCs

LAN

Laser Printer

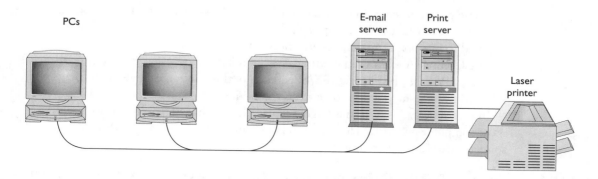

FIGURE 12-9 A client/server environment where dedicated or special-purpose servers perform assigned functions

and file sharing when configuring the network. This configuration may remain unchanged as the network grows, but if changes are needed, they can be done from a central point by the administrator. who does not need to go to each computer on the network to make administrative changes. The term for a Microsoft client/server network is a domain. The domain must have a unique name, and each client or server computer must have a unique name.

Client/server environments are used extensively in situations where a centralized system of administration is needed. Servers can be multipurpose, performing a number of functions, or dedicated, as in the case of a Web or mail server. Figure 12-9 shows a network with servers used for e-mail and printing. Notice in this situation that each of the servers is dedicated to the task that it is assigned.

Protocol Suites

Every computer network consists of physical and logical components controlled by software. Standards, also often called protocols, describe the rules for how hardware and software work and interact. Ethernet, detailed earlier in this chapter, is a standard for the physical components, such as cabling and network adapters, as well as for the software that controls the hardware, such as the ROM BIOS in the network adapters and device drivers, which allow the network adapters to be controlled from the operating system.

However, in most discussions about networks and related documentation, the term *protocol* describes certain software components that work on top of such underlying protocols as Ethernet. These protocols control communications at a higher level, including the addressing and naming of computers on the network, among other tasks.

These protocols combine into suites that include a group of protocols built around the same set of rules, with each protocol describing a small portion of the tasks required to prepare, send, and receive network data.

The CompTIA exams require that A+ candidates understand three protocols suites: TCP/IP, NetBEUI, and IPX/SPX. Each of these involves several protocols and other software components, and each is sometimes called a "protocol stack."

In recent years, TCP/IP has largely replaced the other two protocols for use on most computer networks. However, you may encounter NetBEUI or IPX/SPX in some organizations that continue to use these protocols.

on the
job

Although TCP/IP, IPX/SPX, and NetBEUI are protocol suites, it is very common for techs to refer to each suite as "a protocol." This is also how the published CompTIA A+ exam objectives refer to them. On the job, take your cue from the experienced techs, and use the terms they use for easy communication. Hey, that sounds like a protocol!

TCP/IP

Transmission Control Protocol/Internet Protocol (TCP/IP) is by far the most common protocol suite on both internal LANs and public networks. It is the protocol suite of the Internet. TCP/IP requires more configuration than the other two protocol suites mentioned here, but it is the most robust, is usable on very large networks, and is routable. The term routable refers to the ability to send data to other networks. At the junction of each network is a router that uses special router protocols to send each packet on its way toward its destination.

There are several protocols in the TCP/IP suite; the two main protocols are the Transmission Control Protocol (TCP) and the Internet Protocol (IP). There are many sub-protocols, such as UDP, ARP, ICMP, and IGMP.

TCP/IP allows for cross-platform communication. That means that computers using different OSs (such as Windows and Unix) can send data back and forth, as long as they are both using TCP/IP. The following briefly describes the two cornerstone protocols of the TCP/IP suite.

exam
watch *The A+ exams only expect you to understand the very basics about the TCP/IP protocol suite.*

Internet Protocol (IP)   Messages sent over a network are broken up into smaller chunks of data, called *packets*. Each packet has information attached to the beginning of the packet, called a *header*. This packet header contains the IP address of the sending computer and that of the destination computer. The Internet Protocol (IP) manages this logical addressing of the packet so that routing protocols can route it over the network to its destination. We will describe addressing later in this chapter.

Transmission Control Protocol (TCP)   When preparing to send data over a network, the Transmission Control Protocol (TCP) breaks the data into chunks, called datagrams. Each datagram contains information to use on the receiving end to reassemble the chunks of data into the original message. This information—both a byte-count value and a datagram sequence—is placed into the datagram header before being given to the IP protocol, which encapsulates the datagrams into packets with addressing information.

When receiving data from a network, the Transmission Control Protocol (TCP) uses the information in this header to reassemble the data. If TCP is able to reassemble the message, it sends an acknowledgment (ACK) message to the sending address. The sender can then discard datagrams that it is saving while waiting for an acknowledgment. If pieces are missing, TCP sends a non-acknowledgment (NAK) message back to the sending address, whereupon TCP will resend the missing pieces.

An excellent movie describing how TCP/IP works in an amusing and interesting fashion is available free at www.warriorsofthe.net. It is a 73 MB download. It is well worth watching.

IPX/SPX

IPX/SPX stands for Internet Packet Exchange/Sequenced Exchange. It is the protocol suite of early Novell networks and contains these two core protocols along with several supporting ones. Novell designed IPX/SPX specifically for the Novell NetWare network operating system. It is routable and otherwise similar to TCP/IP, except that it has limited cross-platform support and cannot be used on the Internet. Beginning with NetWare version 5.0, Novell moved to TCP/IP, although they continue to support the old protocol stack for networks with mixed NetWare versions.

The Microsoft implementation of IPX/SPX is NWLink, used mainly to communicate with the older NetWare servers in a Microsoft network.

NetBEUI

NetBEUI (the name stands for NetBIOS Extended User Interface) is usable only in small networks. It requires no address configuration and provides faster data transfer than TCP/IP, but it cannot be routed—the main reason it is limited to small networks.

An early Microsoft LAN protocol, NetBEUI only requires a computer name and a workgroup name for each computer on the network. There is no notion of a computer or network address. We will explore addressing later in this chapter.

At one time NetBEUI installed by default on a Windows computer. This is no longer true, and if you have a reason for using NetBEUI, you can install it from the Windows distribution CD or download it from the Microsoft Web site.

People often confuse NetBEUI with NetBIOS, but NetBIOS is not a network protocol suite. It is a single protocol for managing names on a network. In a Windows network, you can use NetBIOS names and the protocol with any of the protocol suites. However, NetBIOS naming has limited value in modern networks, and the Internet-style names of the DNS protocol (which requires TCP/IP) have replaced it. Learn more about DNS later in this chapter.

SCENARIO & SOLUTION

My computer is part of a large corporate network. What role is my desktop computer most likely to be playing in this network?	A large corporate network is a client/server network. A desktop PC in this network has the role of a client.
What is the protocol suite of the Internet?	The protocol suite of the Internet is TCP/IP.
I understand that NetBEUI is very easy to install and use. Why does our corporate internetwork not use it?	A corporate internetwork consists, by definition, of interconnected networks requiring a protocol suite routable between networks. NetBEUI, as a non-routable protocol, would therefore not be used.

Network Addressing

It is very important to identify each computer or device directly connected to a network. This is done at two levels—the hardware level, in which the network adapter in each computer or network device has an address, and the logical level, in which a logical address is assigned to each network adapter.

Hardware Addressing

Every NIC and every device connected to a network has a unique address, placed in ROM by the manufacturer. This address, usually permanent, is called by many names, including Media Access Control (MAC) address, physical address, Ethernet address (on Ethernet devices), and NIC address. For the sake of simplicity, we will use the term physical address in this book.

FIGURE 12-10

The physical address of a NIC, labeled "MAC," is shown on a label.

A physical address is 48 bits long and usually expressed in hexadecimal. You can view the physical address of a NIC several ways. It is usually, but not always, written on a label attached to the NIC. Figure 12-10 shows the label on a wireless USB NIC. The word "MAC" precedes the physical address. The actual address on this NIC is six two-digit hexadecimal numbers, but on this label, there are no separating characters. It is easier to read these numbers if separated by a dash, period, or space, like this: 00-11-50-A4-C7-20.

It is not always so easy to locate this address. You can also discover the address of a NIC in Windows. Simply open a command prompt and type the **ipconfig /all** command. The physical address is in the middle of the listing. Notice that it shows six two-digit hexadecimal numbers, each separated by a dash.

This physical address identifies a computer located in a segment of a network. However, we use logical addresses to locate a computer that is beyond the local network segment.

Logical Addressing

In addition to the hardware address, a computer in a TCP/IP network must have a logical address that identifies both the computer and the network. This comes under the purview of the IP protocol.

The Internet Protocol addressing scheme described here offers almost 4.3 billion possible IP addresses, but the way in which they have been allocated throughout the world has reduced that number. Someday we will use a different addressing scheme that will provide many more addresses, but this new addressing scheme depends on a new version of the IP protocol. The current version is Internet Protocol version 4 (IPv4), so we will stick to the present addressing scheme in this explanation.

An IP address identifies both the computer, a "host" in Internet terms, and the logical network on which the computer resides. This allows messages to move from one network to another on the Internet. At the connecting point between networks, a special network device called a router uses its routing protocols to determine the route to the destination address, sending each packet along to the next router closer to the destination network. Each computer and network device that directly attaches to the Internet must have a globally unique IP address.

An IP address is 32 bits long and is usually shown as four decimal numbers, 1–255 (in some octets they can be between 1 and 255), each separated by a period. An example of an IP address is 192.168.1.41. Called dotted decimal notation, this is the format that is shown in the user interface. However, the IP protocol works with addresses in binary form, in which the preceding address looks like this: 11000000.1 0101000.00000001.00101001.

on the Job

In case you are curious, the next version is IPv6, and parts of it have already been implemented and added to IPv4. Some very high-end network equipment already supports the next version. In fact, some high-speed internetworks already use IPv6. IPv6 has 128-bit addressing, which theoretically supports a huge number of unique addresses—340,282,366,920,938,463,463,374,607,431, 768,211,456, to be exact.

IP addresses are routable because an IP address contains within it both the address of the host, called the host ID, and the address of the network on which that host resides, called the network ID. A mask of ones and zeros separates the two parts. The ones "cover up" the first part, or network ID, and the zeros "cover up" the remaining part, or host ID. The portion of the address that falls under the ones is your network address, and the portion of the address that falls under the zeros is your host address. In the preceding example, with a mask of 11111111.11111111.11111111.00000000, or 255.255.255.0, the network ID is 11000000.10101000.00000001.00000000 and the host ID is 00101001 (see Figure 12-11). In dotted decimal form, the network ID is 192.168.1.0, and the host ID is 41. Often called a subnet mask, this mask is an important component in a proper IP configuration. After all, the IP address of a host does not make any sense until masked into its two IDs.

FIGURE 12-11

The subnet mask defines the network ID and host ID portions of an IP address.

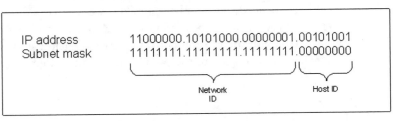

| IP address | 11000000.10101000.00000001.00101001 |
| Subnet mask | 11111111.11111111.11111111.00000000 |

Network ID   Host ID

When you view the IP configuration for the NIC on your PC, you may be surprised to see other IP addresses besides that of the NIC. These include addresses labeled Default Gateway, DHCP Server, DNS Server, and Primary WINS Server.

Default Gateway   When your IP protocol has a packet ready to send, it examines the destination IP address and determines if it is on the same IP network (in the earlier example, this is 192.168.1.0) as your computer. If it is, then it can send the packet directly to that computer (host ID 41 in the example). If the destination IP address is on another IP network, then your computer sends it to the IP address identified as the Default Gateway. This address is on your network (same IP network ID), and it belongs to a router that will send the packet on to the next router in its journey to the destination. Without a Default Gateway, your computer does not know what to do with packets that have a destination address beyond your IP network.

DNS Server   For name resolution, a DNS client uses the DNS Server IP address. The Domain Name Service (DNS) manages access to the Internet domain names, like mcgraw-hill.com. The server-side service maintains a database of domain names and responds to queries from DNS clients (called resolvers) that request resolution of Internet names to IP addresses. A client will do this before sending data over the Internet, when all it knows is the domain name. For instance, if you wish to connect to a McGraw-Hill Web server, you might enter "www.mcgraw-hill.com" in the address bar of your browser. Then, your computer's DNS client (the resolver) sends a request to a DNS server, asking it to resolve the name to an IP address. Once the server has the answer (which it most likely had to request from another DNS server), it sends a response to your computer. The IP protocol on your computer now attaches the address to the packets your computer sends requesting a Web page.

Primary WINS Server   Windows Internet Naming Service (WINS) has a function similar to that of DNS, but it resolves NetBIOS names rather than DNS host names. WINS works in Microsoft networks, but the need to use it has diminished over the years. Newer versions of Windows and its client/server environment, Active Directory, can locate computers strictly by DNS names. Sometimes the WINS service is required on a network because of old operating systems or applications that only know how to work with NetBIOS names and depend on querying the WINS service.

DHCP Server   There are two ways to assign an IP address to a network host: manually and automatically.

When you assign an address manually in Windows, you must open the Properties dialog box for the NIC and enter the exact IP address (obtained from your network administrator), subnet mask, and other configuration information, which includes the addresses for the Default Gateway, DNS Server, and (if necessary) WINS Server. An IP address configured in this manner is a static address. This address is not permanent, although that term may be used by some documentation, because an administrator can easily change it.

exam
ⓦatch
Be sure you understand how the subnet mask divides the host ID and network ID of an IP address, and that you understand the purpose of the following addresses: Default Gateway, DNS Server, WINS Server, and DHCP Server.

In order to receive an IP address automatically, you must configure a computer to do so. This is the default setting for Windows desktop operating systems. A computer configured to receive an address automatically will send a special request out on the network when it starts up.

Now, you would think that a client computer without an IP address would not be able to communicate on the network, but it can in a very limited way. Using a special protocol (BOOTP), the computer sends a very small message that a Dynamic Host Configuration Protocol (DHCP) server can read. It cannot communicate with most other types of servers until it has an IP address. A properly configured DHCP server will respond by sending the computer (now called a DHCP client) an IP address and subnet mask. This is the minimum configuration it will assign to the client computer. In most cases, the server will provide the other IP configuration addresses, including Default Gateway, DNS Server, and Primary WINS Server. Only Windows networks that require this last address get it.

A DHCP server does not permanently assign an IP address to a client. It leases it. Lease is the term used, even though no money changes hands in this transaction between a DHCP client and a DHCP server. A client will release the IP address, giving up the lease, every time it reboots. When one-half of the leased time for an IP address (and its associated configuration) has expired, the client tries to contact the DHCP server in order to renew the lease. It can do this because it remembers the DHCP server's IP address. As long as the DHCP server has an adequate number of unassigned IP addresses, it will continue to reassign the same address to the same client each session.

Exercise 12-3 will walk you through using a command that will display the physical address, as well as the IP address for your network card. This is a very handy command to use because, while you can see the manually configured IP addresses in the properties of a dialog box, you cannot see the automatically configured IP information in this box for a DHCP client.

EXERCISE 12-3

Viewing the Physical and IP Addresses of a NIC

To view the physical and IP addresses of a NIC, follow these steps:

1. Open a command prompt.
2. In the command prompt enter the command **ipconfig /all** and press ENTER.
3. The result should look something like Figure 12-12, only with different addresses.
4. The address of the NIC is in the middle, labeled Physical Address. Notice that it is six pairs of hexadecimal numbers separated by hyphens.
5. Three lines below that is the IP Address of the NIC.
6. Locate the other addresses discussed in the preceding text, including Default Gateway, DNS Server, DHCP Server (if present), and WINS Server (if present).

FIGURE 12-12   Use the ipconfig/all command to view the physical address and the IP address of a NIC, and the other addresses that are part of the IP configuration.

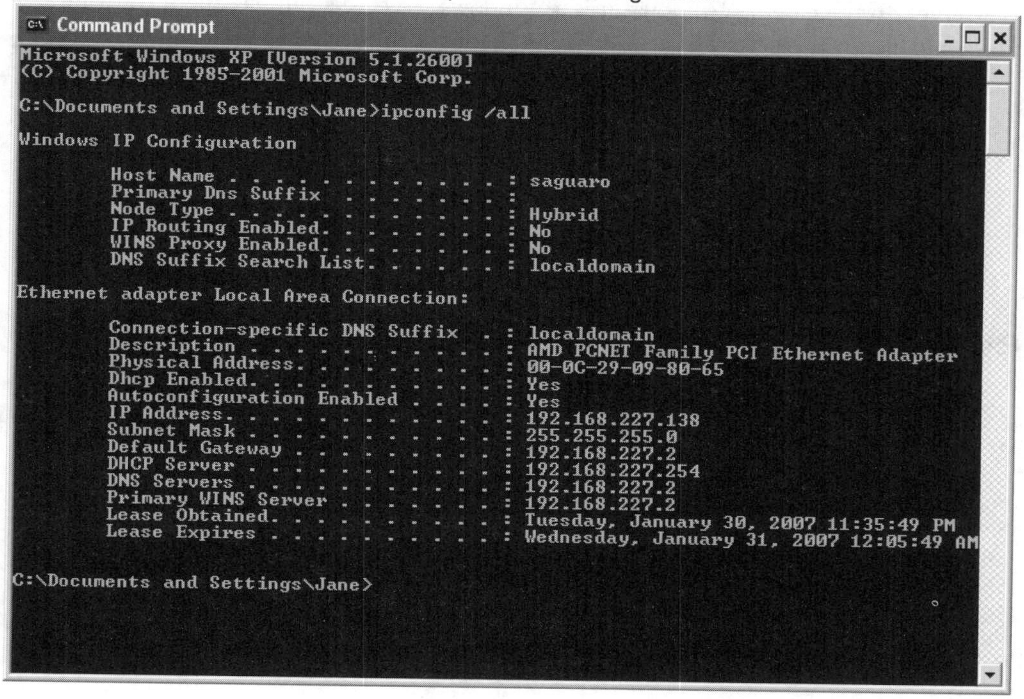

```
Command Prompt                                                            _ □ ×
Microsoft Windows XP [Version 5.1.2600]
(C) Copyright 1985-2001 Microsoft Corp.

C:\Documents and Settings\Jane>ipconfig /all

Windows IP Configuration

        Host Name . . . . . . . . . . . . : saguaro
        Primary Dns Suffix  . . . . . . . :
        Node Type . . . . . . . . . . . . : Hybrid
        IP Routing Enabled. . . . . . . . : No
        WINS Proxy Enabled. . . . . . . . : No
        DNS Suffix Search List. . . . . . : localdomain

Ethernet adapter Local Area Connection:

        Connection-specific DNS Suffix  . : localdomain
        Description . . . . . . . . . . . : AMD PCNET Family PCI Ethernet Adapter
        Physical Address. . . . . . . . . : 00-0C-29-09-80-65
        Dhcp Enabled. . . . . . . . . . . : Yes
        Autoconfiguration Enabled . . . . : Yes
        IP Address. . . . . . . . . . . . : 192.168.227.138
        Subnet Mask . . . . . . . . . . . : 255.255.255.0
        Default Gateway . . . . . . . . . : 192.168.227.2
        DHCP Server . . . . . . . . . . . : 192.168.227.254
        DNS Servers . . . . . . . . . . . : 192.168.227.2
        Primary WINS Server . . . . . . . : 192.168.227.2
        Lease Obtained. . . . . . . . . . : Tuesday, January 30, 2007 11:35:49 PM
        Lease Expires . . . . . . . . . . : Wednesday, January 31, 2007 12:05:49 AM

C:\Documents and Settings\Jane>
```

Network Operating System (NOS)

A network operating system (NOS) is an operating system that runs on a network server and provides file sharing and access to other resources, account management, authentication, and authorization services. Microsoft Windows Server operating systems, Novell Server operating system, and Linux are examples of network operating systems. The distinction is clouded somewhat by the ability of desktop operating systems such as Windows XP and Windows 2000 Professional to allow file sharing, but these operating systems do not provide the robust services that, coupled with high-performance servers and fast network connections, add up to reliable server operating systems.

Network Client

A network client is software that runs on the computers in a network and that receives services from servers. Windows, Mac OS, and Linux, when installed on desktop computers that have a network connection, automatically install a basic network client that can connect to servers and request file and print services. In each case, the automatically installed clients can only connect to a certain type of server. In the case of Windows, it is a Windows server. Novell has client software available for their Novell servers. Their client software comes in versions that install on various operating systems.

Beyond a basic file and print client, Windows and other OSs usually come with an e-mail client, a browser (Web server client), and other clients, depending on the options selected during installation. You can add other clients. For instance, if you install an office suite such as Microsoft Office 2007, you will have a more advanced e-mail client than the one that comes with the OS.

Internet Concepts

The largest internetwork in the world is the Internet. All computers that provide a service for, or that access, the Internet are part of the Internet itself. Each server is responsible for one or more services, such as supplying Web pages, transferring e-mail, or relaying messages to other servers. Many other network devices on the Internet are not, strictly speaking, servers. The most important of these are routers, network devices that direct the flow of packets from one network to another. Without routers, the Internet could not exist in its present state.

Many concepts, services, and procedures are associated with the Internet that are not associated with simple private LANs. While many small networks use the TCP/IP protocol suite, they do not require an ISP (described in the next section) to access their private network. On the other hand, many private internetworks use many of the services described next. Of course, they also do not need an ISP to access the private network. These Internet-style private networks are intranets. In this section, we will review some of the most common terms associated with the Internet, from ISP to the variety of services that run on TCP/IP.

Internet Service Provider (ISP)

An Internet service provider (ISP) is a company in the business of providing Internet access to users. ISPs have traditionally been phone companies, but now ISPs include cable companies and organizations that lease phone or cable network usage. When you connect to the Internet from home or office, you connect through your ISP. While you are on the Internet, your ISP relays all data transfers to and from locations on the Internet.

The ISP you select will depend on the type of connection available to you. For instance, a cellular provider will be your ISP if you chose to connect to the Internet via the cellular network, and a cable company will be your ISP if you connect over the cable network. As for DSL, at first this service was offered mainly through local phone companies, but many other companies now offer DSL using the telephone network. Some ISPs specialize in satellite Internet access.

There are also levels of ISPs, with the highest-level ISPs only serving very large corporations and providing Internet access to the ISPs at the next level. These connections are called network access points (NAPs). The largest ISPs include AT&T WorldNet, IBM Global Network, MCI, Netcom, UUNet, and PSINet. The ISP you use from home may be at the bottom of several layers of ISPs.

In addition to Internet connection services, ISPs now provide a huge number of other services. Some of these services, such as e-mail, are free, but others, such as hosting Web servers, come at a cost based on the complexity of the Web services provided. An e-commerce site in which you sell products and maintain customer lists is an example of a service that would come at additional cost.

Internet Services and Protocols

There are a large number of Internet services. You may use many every day if you frequent the Internet. In this section, we will describe a few of these services.

Simple Mail Transfer Protocol (SMTP)

Simple Mail Transfer Protocol (SMTP) transfers e-mail messages between mail servers. Clients also use this protocol to send e-mail to mail servers. When configuring a computer to access Internet e-mail, you will need the address or name of an SMTP server to which your mail client software will send mail.

Post Office Protocol (POP)

Post Office Protocol (POP) is the protocol used to allow client computers to pick up e-mail from mail servers. The current version is POP3.

Internet Message Access Protocol (IMAP)

Internet Message Access Protocol (IMAP) is a protocol used by e-mail clients for communicating with e-mail servers. This protocol is replacing the POP protocol. IMAP allows users to connect to e-mail servers and not only retrieve e-mail, which removes the messages from the server, as they can do with the POP protocol, but also manage their stored messages without removing them from the server.

Hypertext Markup Language (HTML)

Hypertext Markup Language (HTML) is the language of Web pages. Web designers use the HTML language to create Web page code, which your Web browser converts into the pages you view on your screen.

Hypertext Transfer Protocol (HTTP)

The Hypertext Transfer Protocol (HTTP) is the information transfer protocol of the World Wide Web (WWW). Included in HTTP are the commands Web browsers use to request Web pages from Web servers and then display them on the screen of the local computer.

Secure Sockets Layer (SSL)

The Secure Sockets Layer (SSL) is a protocol for securing data for transmission by encrypting it. Encryption is a term for converting data into a special format that cannot be read by anyone unless they have a software key to convert it back to its usable form. When you buy merchandise online, you go to a special page where you enter your personal and credit card information. These Web merchants almost universally use some form of SSL encryption to protect the sensitive data you enter on this page. When you send your personal information over the Internet, it is encrypted, and only the merchant site has the key to decrypt it. As with most computing technologies, SSL has been improved upon, and a newer encryption technology, Transport Layer Security (TLS), is used for secure transmission over the Internet.

Hypertext Transfer Protocol Secure (HTTPS)

Hypertext Transfer Protocol over Secure Sockets Layer (HTTPS) is a protocol that encrypts and decrypts each user page request, as well as the pages downloaded to the user's computer. The next time you are shopping on a Web site, notice the address box of your browser. You will see the URL preceded by "HTTP" until you go to pay for your purchases. Then the prefix changes to "HTTPS" because the HTTPS protocol is in use while you are at the page where you will enter your personal information and credit card number.

Telnet

At one time, all access to mainframes or minicomputers was through specialized network equipment called *terminals*. At first, a terminal was not much more than a display, a keyboard, and the minimal circuitry for connecting to the mainframe. People called it a dumb terminal. With the growing popularity of PCs in the 1980s, it wasn't unusual to see both a terminal and a PC on a user's desktop taking up a great deal of space. Eventually, by adding both software and hardware to a PC, the PC could emulate a terminal, and the user would switch it between terminal mode and PC mode.

The Telnet utility provides remote terminal emulation for connecting to computers and network devices running server software that can respond. This is done without concern for the actual operating system running on either system.

The original Telnet client was character-based, and it was a popular tool for network administrators who needed to access and manage certain network equipment, such as the routers used to connect networks.

File Transfer Protocol (FTP)

File Transfer Protocol (FTP) is a protocol for computer-to-computer (called host-to-host) transfer of files over a TCP/IP network. The two computers do not need to be running the same operating system; they only need to be running the FTP service on the server computer and the FTP utility on the client computer. FTP supports the use of user names and passwords for access by the FTP client to the server. FTP is widely used on the Internet for making files available for download to clients.

Voice over IP (VoIP)

Voice over IP (VoIP) is a set of technologies that allows voice transmission over an IP network—specifically used for placing phone calls over the Internet—rather than the public switched telephone network (PSTN), the worldwide network that carries traditional voice traffic.

CERTIFICATION SUMMARY

IT professionals preparing for the CompTIA A+ exams must understand only the basic concepts of computer networks. More in-depth knowledge is required for other exams, such as the CompTIA Network+, Server+, and Internet+ exams. Basic concepts include the geographic classifications of networks into LANs, MANs, and WANs. Understand LAN technologies, such as Ethernet and Wi-Fi, and the various WAN connection methods, including dial-up and broadband WAN connections, such as ISDN, cable, DSL, satellite, and cellular. Be able to identify the most common cabling types for networks and common network adapters used in PCs.

Be able to identify the roles desktop computers play in a peer-to-peer network as opposed to a client/server network. Have knowledge of the common protocol suites, and understand that TCP/IP is a protocol suite designed for the Internet and now used on most interconnected networks. IPX/SPX and NetBEUI are now rarely used network protocol suites.

Understand network-addressing concepts, including physical addresses assigned to network adapters, and logical addresses assigned and used through the network protocols. The most important logical network addressing to understand is that of the IP protocol, in which a 32-bit address displays in dotted decimal format. An example of an IP address is 192.168.1.41.

Understand the various addresses that are part of an IP configuration and their roles. These include the IP address and subnet mask of the network adapter, Default Gateway, DNS Server, DHCP Server, and WINS Server addresses.

Identify and describe basic Internet concepts, including the role of ISPs and the basic functions of Internet services and protocols such as SMTP, POP, IMAP, HTML, HTTP, HTTPS, SSL, FTP, and VoIP.

TWO-MINUTE DRILL

Here are some of the key points covered in Chapter 12.

Network Overview

❑ Networks fall into several network classifications, including PAN, LAN, MAN, and WAN.

❑ PAN technologies include the use of standards for wireless transmissions over very short distances. These include IrDA, limited to about one meter, and Bluetooth, which has a range of up to ten meters.

❑ Common LAN technologies include Ethernet in wired LANs and Wi-Fi in wireless LANs.

❑ There are several implementations of Ethernet with increasing speeds, from Ethernet (10Base-T) at 10 Mbps, to Fast Ethernet (100Base-T) at 100 Mbps, and Gigabit Ethernet (1000Base-T) at 1 Gbps over UTP (speeds up to 10 Gbps are supported). In addition, fast speeds are supported over fiber-optic cable, and 5 Gbps Gigabit Ethernet is often used between specialized network equipment.

❑ The Wi-Fi standard 802.11a supports speeds up to 54 Gbps using the 5 GHz frequency. Other Wi-Fi standards are more popular. These include 802.11g, which also supports speeds of up to 54 Gbps but uses the same frequency (2.4 GHz) as its predecessor, 802.11b. Because 802.11g equipment usually is downward compatible with the slower and older 802.11b equipment, the equally fast 802.11a standard has not really taken off.

❑ The 802.11n Wi-Fi standard, promising speeds of up to 108, 240, and 350 Mbps, is currently in development.

❑ Dial-up WAN connections are the slowest and require initiation of the connection every time a user wishes to connect to a remote resource.

❑ Broadband WAN connections, all offering speeds greater than dial-up, include cellular, ISDN, DSL, cable, T-carrier, and satellite.

Network Hardware

❑ Network adapters are available for the various networking technologies. Common network adapters include Ethernet and Wi-Fi.

❑ A network adapter provides the connection to the network medium.

❑ Physical transmission media include twisted-pair and fiber-optic cable.

❑ Networking requires various network connection devices. A repeater is a device used to extend the range of a network by taking the signals it receives from one port and regenerating (repeating) those signals to another port.

❑ A bridge is a device used to connect two networks and pass traffic between them based on the physical address of the destination device.

❑ A hub is a device that is the central connecting point of a LAN, with all network devices on a LAN connecting to one or more hubs. A passive hub is little more than a multiport repeater. An active hub is powered and amplified, and cleans up the signal before sending it to other ports.

❑ Both active and passive hubs are now replaced by more intelligent devices called switches or switching hubs. These take an incoming signal and send it only to the destination port.

❑ An IP router sits between networks and routes packets according to their IP addresses.

❑ Many routers combine routing and bridging, and connect multiple network technologies, such as a LAN and a T1 network.

Network Software

❑ The roles played by the computer on the network describe the network. The two most general roles are those of clients and servers.

❑ A network in which any computer can be both a client and a server is a peer-to-peer network.

❑ A client/server network is one in which most desktop computer are clients, and dedicated computers act as servers.

❑ Protocol suites are groups of related protocols that work together to support the functioning of a network.

❑ Three network protocol suites are NetBEUI, IPX/SPX, and TCP/IP. Only the last one is widely used today, and it is the protocol suite of the Internet.

❑ TCP/IP supports small to large networks, and interconnected networks called internetworks. The Internet is the largest internetwork.

❑ Network addressing occurs at both the physical level and the logical level. Every network adapter from every manufacturer in the world has a unique physical address, also called a MAC address. A physical address is 48 bits long and is usually in hexadecimal.

❏ Internet Protocol is concerned with logical addresses. An IP address is 32 bits long and usually in dotted decimal notation, as in 192.168.1.41.

❏ An IP address configuration will include a subnet mask, which determines the host ID and network ID portions of an IP address. In addition, the IP configuration may include addresses for a Default Gateway, DNS Server, Primary WINS Server, and DHCP Server.

❏ A network operating system (NOS) is an operating system that runs on a network server and provides file sharing and access to other resources, account management, authentication, and authorization services.

❏ Examples of NOSs are Microsoft Windows Server operating systems, Novell Server operating systems, and Linux.

❏ A network client is software that requests services from compatible servers. Windows, Mac OS, and Linux, when installed on desktop computers that have a network connection, automatically install a basic network client.

❏ Novell has client software that will run on various operating systems.

Internet Concepts

❏ An ISP is a company in the business of providing access to the Internet.

❏ There are a large number of Internet protocols and services.

❏ SMTP transfers e-mail messages between mail servers. Clients also use this protocol to send mail to mail servers.

❏ POP is the protocol used to allow client computers to pick up e-mail from mail servers. The current version is POP3.

❏ IMAP is a protocol used by e-mail clients for communicating with e-mail servers. It is replacing the POP protocol. It allows users to connect to e-mail servers and not only retrieve e-mail, which removes the messages from the servers, but also manage their stored messages without removing them from the server.

❏ HTML is the language of Web pages that your browser converts into the pages you view on your screen.

❏ HTTP is the transfer protocol used to transmit browser-requested Web pages over the Internet to your computer.

❏ SSL is a protocol for securing data for transmission by encrypting it. When you pay for merchandise over the Internet, you connect to a page that uses SSL to encrypt your personal and financial data before sending it to the Web site where it is decrypted.

❑ HTTPS is a protocol that uses SSL to encrypt data and then transports it to the Web site for decryption.

❑ Telnet is a utility that provides remote terminal emulation for connecting to computers and network devices that are running the Telnet server software.

❑ FTP is a file transfer protocol for computer-to-computer transfer of files over a TCP/IP network.

❑ VoIP is a set of technologies that allows voice transmission over an IP network. You use it to place phone calls over the Internet rather than using the public switched telephone network.

SELF TEST

The following questions will help you measure your understanding of the material presented in this chapter. Read all of the choices carefully because there might be more than one correct answer. Choose all correct answers for each question.

Network Overview

1. Which of the following statements is true about a LAN versus a WAN?
   A. A LAN spans a larger distance than a WAN.
   B. A WAN spans a larger distance than a LAN.
   C. A LAN is generally slower than a WAN.
   D. A WAN is used within a home or within a small business.

2. Which of the following is a PAN technology?
   A. Ethernet
   B. Satellite
   C. Bluetooth
   D. 802.11a

3. What is the type of network that connects many private networks in one metropolitan community?
   A. PAN
   B. MAN
   C. WAN
   D. LAN

4. Of the following technologies, which is downward compatible with 802.11b?
   A. 802.11a
   B. 802.11g
   C. Bluetooth
   D. IrDA

5. Which of the following is usually the slowest WAN connection?
   A. Dial-up
   B. DSL
   C. Cable
   D. Satellite

6. Which of the following WAN technologies uses a network originally created for television transmissions?
   A. DSL
   B. Cellular
   C. Cable
   D. Dial-up

7. MCI is an example of what type of Internet organization?
   A. File server
   B. Dial-up
   C. Phone company
   D. ISP

Network Hardware

8. Which of the following attaches to a PC with a bus connector, USB, or other interface, and gives it a connecting point to a network?
   A. WAP
   B. NIC
   C. LAN
   D. PAN

9. Which of the following is not a network medium?
   A. Plenum
   B. Twisted-pair cable
   C. Fiber-optic cable
   D. Atmosphere

10. Which type of cable uses ST, SC, LC, or MT-RJ connectors?
    A. STP
    B. UTP
    C. Fiber-optic
    D. Coaxial

11. Thousands of these devices exist on the Internet between networks, direct the traffic of the Internet using the destination IP address of each packet, and pass them to their destinations along the interconnected networks of the Internet.
    A. Router
    B. Modem

    C. NIC

    D. Hub

Network Software

12. A large corporate internetwork is likely to be this type of network, based on the roles of the connected computers.

    A. Peer-to-peer

    B. Client-to-client

    C. Client/server

    D. Server-to-server

13. What is the protocol suite of the Internet?

    A. TCP/IP

    B. NetBEUI

    C. IPX/SPX

    D. TCP

14. What protocol used on the Internet is concerned with the logical addressing of hosts?

    A. TCP

    B. IP

    C. UDP

    D. ARP

15. What was the old Novell network protocol suite?

    A. NetBEUI

    B. NetBIOS

    C. SPX

    D. IPX/SPX

16. What divides an IP address into its host ID and network ID components?

    A. Default gateway

    B. DNS server

    C. DHCP server

    D. Subnet mask

17. A NIC has this type of a permanent address assigned to it by the manufacturer.

    A. IP address

    B. Physical address

    C. Host ID

    D. Automatic address

18. A packet with a destination address not on the local network will be sent to the address identified by which label in the IP configuration?

    A. Default gateway

    B. DNS server

    C. DHCP server

    D. Subnet mask

Internet Concepts

19. What type of organization provides Internet access to its customers?

    A. Server

    B. Client

    C. ISP

    D. DHCP

20. What Internet service allows users to connect to a mail server and manage their messages, giving them the choice to leave the messages they have read on the server?

    A. SMTP

    B. POP

    C. FTP

    D. IMAP

LAB QUESTION

The two main wired broadband services are cable and DSL. Cable providers and telephone carriers are in a battle to capture the broadband market with their services. But since these both require considerable infrastructure, the services they provide vary, especially in the case of cable, which is not available in many rural areas. Use the Internet or other sources to discover what service is available to you at your home address. Is there only one option, or are several available? Find out the exact service provided, including speeds (both up and down) and pricing. Then write a paragraph or two on your findings.

SELF TEST ANSWERS

Network Overview

1. ☑ **B.** A WAN spans a larger distance than a LAN.

    ☒ **A,** that a LAN spans a larger distance than a WAN, is not true. **C,** that a LAN is generally slower than a WAN, is not true. **D,** that a WAN is used within a home or a small business, is not true.

2. ☑ **C.** Bluetooth is a personal area network (PAN) technology used to connect devices and computers over very short distances.

    ☒ **A,** Ethernet, **B,** satellite, and **D,** 802.11a, are all incorrect because none of these is a PAN technology. Ethernet is a wired LAN technology, satellite is a WAN technology, and 802.11a is a WLAN technology.

3. ☑ **B.** MAN is the type of network that connects many private networks in one community.

    ☒ **A,** PAN, is incorrect because this is a very small personal area network that only connects devices in a very small (usually a few meters) area. **C,** WAN, is incorrect because this connects over long distances. **D,** LAN, is incorrect because this is limited to a distance of hundreds of meters that would not span an entire metropolitan community.

4. ☑ **B.** 802.11g is downward compatible with the slower 802.11b standard, because they both use the 2.4 GHz bandwidth.

    ☒ **A,** 802.11a, is incorrect because this Wi-Fi standard operates in the 5 MHz band, which makes it totally incompatible with 802.11b. **C,** Bluetooth, is incorrect because it is a standard for very short distances and is not downward compatible with 802.11b. **D,** IrDA, is incorrect because this is a standard for very short-range infrared communications, which is totally incompatible with 802.11b.

5. ☑ **A.** Dial-up is usually the slowest WAN connection at an advertised rate of 56 Kbps, but top actual rate of about 48 Kbps.

    ☒ **B,** DSL, **C,** cable, and **D,** satellite, are all incorrect because each of these is a broadband service with maximum speeds that go up to several times that of dial-up.

6. ☑ **C.** Cable is the WAN technology that uses a network originally created for television transmissions.

    ☒ **A,** DSL, is incorrect because it uses the telephone network, not a network created for television transmissions. **B,** cellular, is incorrect because it uses the cellular network, which was originally created for voice transmissions but has been upgraded to digital and can be used for broadband data transmissions. **D,** dial-up, is incorrect because it uses the telephone network, not a network created for television transmissions.

7. ☑ **D.** MCI is an ISP type of Internet organization.
☒ **A**, file server, is incorrect because this is a type of network server computer, not an Internet organization. **B**, dial-up, is incorrect because this is a type of WAN connection, not a type of Internet service organization. **C**, phone company, is incorrect because, while MCI is a telephone company, that does not really explain the type of Internet organization it is.

Network Hardware

8. ☑ **B.** NIC is a device that attaches to a PC with a bus connector, USB, or other interface and gives it a connecting point to a network.
☒ **A**, WAP, is incorrect because this is a network connecting device. A PC would require a wireless NIC to connect to a WAP. **C**, LAN, is incorrect because this is a type of network that a PC would connect to, not a device that would connect the PC to the network. **D**, PAN, is incorrect because this is a type of network of devices connecting to each other and to a computer over very short distances.

9. ☑ **A.** Plenum is not a network medium, but rather a characteristic of certain network media (cables) indicating that the cable sheath is fire resistant and appropriate to run in plenum space.
☒ **B**, twisted-pair cable, **C**, fiber-optic cable, and **D**, atmosphere, are all network media.

10. ☑ **C.** Fiber-optic cable uses ST, SC, LC, or MT-RJ connectors.
☒ **A,** STP, **B**, UTP, and **D**, coaxial cabling do not use ST, SC, LC, or MT-RJ connectors.

11. ☑ **A.** Devices that exist on the Internet and pass IP packets from many sources to their destinations along the Internet are called routers.
☒ **B**, modem, is incorrect because it does not pass packets along the Internet, although it is a beginning point for a single computer to send packets. **C**, NIC, is incorrect because this is simply a device for connecting a single computer to a network. **D**, hub, is incorrect because this is a device at the heart of a LAN but not an Internet device.

Network Software

12. ☑ **C.** Client/server is the type of network found in a large corporate internetwork.
☒ **A**, peer-to-peer, is incorrect because this type of network, where each computer can serve as both client and server, is only used in very small networks of less than a dozen computers. **B**, client-to-client, is incorrect because this is not really a network type. **D**, server-to-server, is incorrect because this is not a network type.

13. ☑ **A.** TCP/IP is the protocol suite of the Internet.
☒ **B**, NetBEUI, and **C**, IPX/SPX, are not the protocol suites of the Internet, although both are protocol suites. **D**, TCP, is incorrect because this is just one of the many protocols in the TCP/IP protocol suite.

14.   ☑   **B.** IP is the protocol used on the Internet that is concerned with the logical addressing of hosts.

    ☒   **A**, TCP, is incorrect because this protocol is not concerned with the logical addressing of hosts. **C**, UDP, is incorrect because this protocol, which we only mentioned and did not describe, is not concerned with the logical addressing of hosts. **D**, ARP, is incorrect because this protocol is not concerned with the logical addressing of hosts.

15.   ☑   **D.** IPX/SPX is the old Novell network protocol suite.

    ☒   **A**, NetBEUI, is incorrect because this is the old Microsoft network protocol suite and was not used by Novell. **B**, NetBIOS, is incorrect because not only is it not a protocol suite at all, but it is a naming system for network computers that has been largely replaced by DNS. **C**, SPX, is incorrect because this is only one protocol of the IPX/SPX suite.

16.   ☑   **D.** A subnet mask divides an IP address into its host ID and network ID components.

    ☒   **A**, default gateway, is incorrect because this is the name of the router address to which a computer directs packets with destinations beyond the local network. **B**, DNS server, is incorrect because this is where a network client sends queries to resolve DNS names into IP addresses. **C**, DHCP server, is incorrect because this is what automatically assigns IP addresses to DHCP client computers.

17.   ☑   **B.** The physical address is the type of permanent address assigned to a network card by the manufacturer.

    ☒   **A**, IP address, is incorrect because this is not a permanent address but a logical address not permanently assigned to a NIC. **C**, Host ID, is incorrect because this portion of an IP address identifies the host. **D**, automatic address, is incorrect because this usually refers to an IP address assigned to a PC by a DHCP server.

18.   ☑   **A.** The default gateway is the address to which the router sends packets that have addresses not on the local network.

    ☒   **B**, DNS server, is incorrect because this server resolves DNS names. **C**, DHCP server, is incorrect because this server assigns IP addresses automatically. **D**, subnet mask, is incorrect because this is not an address but a mask used to divide an IP address into its host ID and network ID components.

Internet Concepts

19.   ☑   **C.** An ISP is an organization that provides Internet access to its customers.

    ☒   **A**, server, is incorrect because it is a term that describes a single computer role, not an organization. **B**, client, is incorrect because it is a term that describes a single computer role, not an organization. **D**, DHCP, is incorrect because this term describes a service for assigning IP addresses, not an organization that provides Internet access to customers.

20. ☑ **D.** IMAP is an Internet service that allows users to connect to a mail server and manage their messages, giving them the choice to leave messages they have read on the server.

☒ **A,** SMTP, is incorrect because this is a service used to send e-mail, not to pick it up or manage it. **B,** POP, is incorrect because IMAP is replacing this service. POP allows users to connect to a mail server and pick up mail, which is then deleted from the server. **C,** FTP, is incorrect because this service has nothing to do with e-mail but is used for transferring files over the Internet.

LAB ANSWER

Answers will vary according to location and offerings available at the time this question is completed. For example, our home area has no cable service, and the only DSL provider is a very small telephone company that serves several scattered rural communities. They offer two levels of DSL service, both of which are in addition to the charge for basic voice services. The $25/month package provides 128 Kbps down and 56 Kbps up, while the $40/month service offers 512 Kbps down and 256 Kbps up. We doubt that they are able to provide the upload speeds that they quote.

13

Installing Networks

N

etworks allow individual computers to share network resources, which include anything that you can share over a network. It is the ability for a user at one computer to access a resource on another computer that makes today's computing so powerful. A resource is not simply, or only, data. Resources include objects (data files and folders) and physical entities, such as modems, printers, CD and DVD player/recorders, and backup devices. Resources also include services, such as e-mail and fax. You can even sit in front of one PC, and take over and control the functions of another PC on the network.

In this chapter, you will learn the tasks required to install and configure client computer access to a LAN or WLAN. Then you will explore how to create file and printer shares in Windows desktop and server computers. On the client side of things, you will learn the installation and use of file and printer clients from Microsoft and Novell.

Finally, you will learn about the two most popular Web browsers—Microsoft Internet Explorer and Mozilla Firefox. You need to be familiar with these Web browsers and know how to install, configure, and upgrade them.

CERTIFICATION OBJECTIVES

■ **601: 5.2   602: 5.2   603: 5.2**   *Install, configure, and upgrade networks*

An A+ certification candidate must know how to connect desktop and laptop computers to a LAN or WAN. This requires understanding how to install and configure common network hardware, and how to configure the OS to recognize and work with the hardware. As with all other hardware, vendors occasionally upgrade network hardware drivers, and the technician must understand how to update the network drivers and protocols.

Learn how to create file and printer shares and how to assign permissions to shares. Be prepared to explain the difference between a Microsoft workgroup and a domain, and know how to configure a computer to join a workgroup or domain. Understand how to configure the Client for Microsoft Networks and where to find the clients for connecting Windows computers to Novell networks.

Installing and Configuring Networks

A connection to a LAN requires a network interface card (NIC) for each computer. Therefore, the first step in connecting a computer to a network is to install a NIC. If you need to connect to an Ethernet network, which is the most common type of wired LAN, you may not need to add a NIC to new computers, since most of them come standard with an Ethernet NIC, which may be part of the circuitry of the motherboard, or it may be a bus adapter.

If you work with older PCs, or if the installed NIC in a newer computer fails, you will need to know how to install and configure a replacement NIC. If the network you are connecting to is not a wired Ethernet network, then you will need to install an appropriate NIC, such as a Wi-Fi NIC.

Physical Installation

When installing any NIC into a PC or laptop, there are two connections to consider—the connection to the computer and the connection to the network. You must first decide how the NIC will interface with the computer based on the choices available to you in the computer. NICs are available for all of the expansion bus types for desktop PCs described in Chapter 1. If you need a NIC for a laptop, you will also find NICs for the various laptop expansion slots described in Chapter 5. There is also a selection of NICs with USB interfaces to either the PC or laptop.

Installing a Bus NIC

Because of the array of expansion slots in PCs and laptops, you must first determine what expansion bus type or types are available in the computer before choosing a NIC to install. In the case of a bus NIC for a desktop computer, before removing the new NIC from its packaging, review the instructions for handling computer circuitry, which were included in the first three steps of Exercise 3-2 of Chapter 3. When installing the NIC, follow the steps for installing an adapter card given in Exercise 3-12 in Chapter 3. Then, in the case of an Ethernet NIC, connect the network cable, and then start up the computer.

In most cases, you will first physically install a bus NIC and then install the driver and other software, but check the documentation to make sure before installing it.

If you are unsure of the standard that a PCMCIA slot in a laptop supports, follow the instructions in Exercise 5-1 in Chapter 5 to use Device Manager to view the

CardBus Controller. When installing a NIC in a PC Card, CardBus, or ExpressCard slot, follow the manufacturer's instructions for inserting the card into the slot, which is accessible without opening the case.

Installing a USB or FireWire NIC

Before installing a USB or FireWire NIC, check the manufacturer's instructions because in most cases you will need to install the software before connecting the NIC. Then connect the NIC as you would any other USB or FireWire device. These are the overall steps for installing a USB or FireWire NIC:

1. Insert the Installation CD and run the Setup Wizard.
2. Connect the NIC to the USB or FireWire port.
3. Connect the NIC to the network.

Connecting a Wired NIC to the Network

An Ethernet NIC will need to connect to the LAN using UTP CAT5 or better cabling that has an RJ45 connector. Before connecting the cable, turn off power to the PC and the hub/switch, if applicable. This step may seem a bit extreme and is generally not required, but we have found that some Ethernet switches include this instruction, which ensures that the switch will properly detect the new connection. Connect one end to the NIC and the other to a wall jack, or directly to a hub or switch. In a large organization, a network administrator or technician will instruct you where to connect to the LAN, which will probably be to a wall jack with an RJ45 connector. At home or in a small office, you will normally connect directly to a small hub or switch.

Figure 13-1 shows a device that acts as an Ethernet switch, as well as a router to a cable or DSL WAN connection. The cable on the left connects to a cable modem, while the center cable connects to the PC. The cord on the right provides power to the device. The manufacturer calls this device a router, although it is a multifunction device, as described in Chapter 12.

FIGURE 13-1

FIGURE 13-1

A device that performs the functions of an Ethernet switch, and an IP router between WAN and LAN networks.

EXERCISE 13-1

Connecting an Ethernet Cable

You can easily connect an Ethernet cable to an RJ45 outlet on a PC, switch, or hub.

1. Align the RJ45 cable connector with the RJ45 outlet on the computer so that the clip on the cable connector lines up with the notch in the center of one side of the outlet.

2. Push the connector into the outlet until you hear the clip click into place. This secures the cable so that it makes a good connection and cannot accidentally fall out of the outlet.

3. Use the same technique to connect the cable to an outlet on an Ethernet switch or wall-mounted plate. (See Figure 13-2, in which the cable connector is shown in front of the outlet on the router.)

4. If this is the first time you have connected an Ethernet cable, practice unplugging it by grasping the connector, pressing on the clip, and gently pulling the connector out. Never force it, or you will break off the clip, and then your cable will be not be securely connected. Now plug it back in.

The next step is to configure the TCP/IP properties of the connection in Windows. Since this configuration is common to both wired Ethernet connections and Wi-Fi connections, we will explore the IP configuration after we examine how to create a Wi-Fi network.

Creating a Wi-Fi Network

Before you install a wireless network, you must consider some special issues for selecting and positioning wireless hardware. These include obstacles between the computers and the WLAN, the distances involved, any possible interference, the standards supported by the devices on the Wi-Fi network, and the wireless mode for your WLAN.

Obstacles and Interference   Certain devices emit radio signals that can interfere with Wi-Fi networks. These include microwave ovens and cordless telephones that use the 2.4 GHz radio band. WAPs normally support channel selection. Therefore, if you

FIGURE 13-2

The clip on the RJ45 connector must align properly with the RJ45 outlet.

have a 2.4 GHz cordless phone that supports channel selection, configure the phone to use one channel (channel 1, for instance) and the WAP and each wireless NIC to use another channel, like channel 11. In addition, metal furniture and appliances, metal-based UV tint on windows, and metal construction materials within walls can all block or reduce Wi-Fi signals.

on the Job *When a computer or other physical device is connected to a network, it is called a node.*

If there are other WLANs within range of yours, use the site survey feature of your wireless NIC to see what channel each of them is using. Then configure all the wireless nodes and the WAP in your WLAN to use a different channel. The site survey feature may simply be called Available Network, as in Figure 13-3, in which a list of wireless networks is shown. Clicking a network in the list reveals the channel in use and other important information.

Distances and Speeds   A huge issue with wireless networks is the signal range of the communicating devices. All of the Wi-Fi standards commonly used, as well as the new 802.11n (not yet ratified) standard, give maximum signal ranges of 75 to 125 meters, but that is for a signal that is not interrupted by potential barriers, such as walls that may contain signal-stopping materials like metal lath in stucco walls. Position a WAP in a central location within easy range of all devices, NICs, and access points.

The farther a wireless NIC is from a WAP, the more the signal degrades and the greater the chance of slowing down the connection speed. Actual ranges for these

FIGURE 13-3

The box titled Available Network shows the networks detected within range of a wireless adapter.

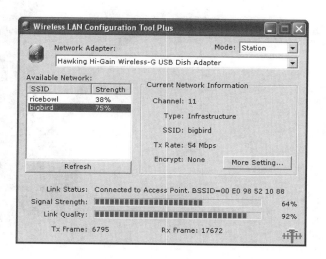

TABLE 13-1	Summary of Common Wi-Fi Standards				
IEEE Standard	**Operating Frequency**	**Typical Data Rate**	**Maximum Data Rate**	**Indoor Range**	**Outdoor Range**
802.11b	2.4 GHz	6.5 Mbps	11 Mbps	~35 meters	~100 meters
802.11g	2.4 GHz	25 Mbps	54 Mbps	~25 meters	~75 meters
802.11n	2.4 GHz or 5 GHz	200 Mbps	540 Mbps	~50 meters	~125 meters

devices in place vary greatly. For instance, the documentation for our 802.11g WAP shows that the outdoor range of this device is 40 meters at 54 Mbps and 300 meters at 6 Mbps or lower. Indoor range is 15 meters at 54 Mbps and 120 meters at 6 Mbps. Compare that with the ranges for the standards shown in Table 13-1.

We prefer to use USB NICs attached to a USB cable (Figure 13-4) rather than bus or PC Card NICs that are rigidly fixed to the computer. The cable gives you more flexibility in positioning the wireless antenna for best signal reception. We find this is important, even when the WAP is located within just dozens of feet of most of our computers.

FIGURE 13-4

A USB wireless NIC you can position for better signal strength

When a wireless network spans buildings, there are special problems. For instance, the material in the walls of the building may interfere with the signal. This is where you need to get creative. For instance, consider a wireless NIC with a directional dish antenna (see Figure 13-5) that you can position in a window and point directly toward the WAP. Another option is a wireless range extender—a device that resembles a WAP but is designed to boost the signals from a WAP and extend its coverage distance.

Another issue is the standard supported by each device. If possible, for each wireless network installation, select NICs and wireless access points (WAPs) that comply with the exact same Wi-Fi standard. Even though 802.11g, which is faster than 802.11b, is downward compatible with the slower standard, even a single

FIGURE 13-5   A wireless NIC with a directional dish antenna

802.11b device on the wireless network will slow down the entire WLAN. Similarly, an 802.11n device that complies with the proposed standard will be downward compatible with 802.11a, 802.11b, and 802.11g devices. However, a single, slower non-802.11n device may slow down the entire WLAN.

Additionally, we prefer to use devices from the same manufacturer, when possible. This is because some manufacturers build in special proprietary features—support for higher speeds or greater range—that are only available to their devices. However, this is a difficult rule to enforce in practice, especially when you add a laptop with a built-in wireless NIC to your network.

Basically, a Service Set ID (SSID) is a network name used to identify a wireless network. Consisting of up to 32 characters, the SSID travels with the messages on the wireless network. All of the wireless devices on a WLAN must use the same SSID in order to communicate. Therefore, assigning a SSID is part of a wireless network setup. WAPs come with a preconfigured SSID name used in all WAPs by that manufacturer. You must change this name, as well as the default administrator user name and password, in the WAP. Otherwise, anyone who can access the wireless network can log on to the WAP and change its configuration.

The steps required to set up a wireless network depend on the wireless mode you select—ad hoc mode or infrastructure mode.

Wireless Modes   There are two basic wireless modes: ad hoc and infrastructure. If your goal is to have just two or three PCs communicate with each other wirelessly, and they do not need connections to other LANs or the Internet, you can consider having these computers communicate directly—without the use of a WAP—in ad hoc mode. In this case, each computer will require a wireless NIC, which you must position within range of the others. Then you will configure the wireless cards in each computer to work in ad hoc mode. The wireless nodes communicating together in this mode make up an Independent Basic Service Set (IBSS). This small group of computers is similar to the peer-to-peer model of Microsoft workgroup administrative models.

However, ad hoc is a minimal configuration. Even in a small home network, when you wish to use a Wi-Fi connection to gain access to an Internet connection, you will rarely use this model. In most cases, the reason for a wireless network is to have access to a wired network, or to connect to a broadband connection to the Internet. For this, you will use infrastructure mode, which requires a wireless access point (WAP), which is a hub for a wireless network.

Many wireless nodes can connect to a single WAP. In fact, the WAP itself may be a multifunction device, acting as a WAP, an Ethernet switch, and an IP router.

It, in turn, can connect to a wired Ethernet network, a cable, or a DSL modem. Figure 13-6 shows a WAP. Many manufacturers refer to these as wireless routers. The one pictured is a WAP for both 802.11b and 802.11g that you can use to share a broadband connection; it includes a four-port Ethernet switch with four Ethernet ports (10BaseT/100BaseT).

The wireless nodes (including the WAP) communicating together in infrastructure mode make up a Basic Service Set (BSS).

Ad Hoc Setup   If you are setting up two or more computers to communicate wirelessly in ad hoc mode, follow the manufacturer's instructions for the proper order of things. For instance, for a USB NIC you will install the software from the NIC's installation CD-ROM first, and then connect the NIC. Once the NIC is connected, the Found New Hardware Wizard will run and install the software for your NIC. If prompted for configuration information, select ad hoc mode. It will now communicate peer-to-peer with other ad hoc wireless NICs within range.

FIGURE 13-6

A wireless access point

Infrastructure Setup: WAP   Position a WAP in the center of all the computers that will participate in the wireless network. If there are barriers to the wireless signals, you will need to determine if you can overcome them with the use of an enhanced antenna on the WAP, as shown in Figure 13-7, or a wireless signal booster to reach computers that are beyond the range of the WAP. A wireless signal booster physically resembles a WAP.

A wireless access point with an enhanced antenna attached

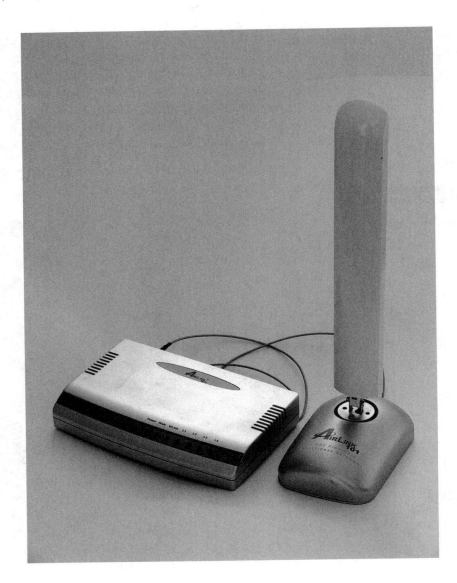

In order to configure a new WAP, you normally connect to it using an Ethernet cable between a computer with an Ethernet NIC and the WAP. Check the documentation that comes with the WAP in case you need to use a special cable. Direct connection via the Ethernet port is only required for the initial setup of the WAP. Once it is up and running, you can connect from any computer on the network and modify the configuration.

It only takes a few minutes to physically set up a WAP and then configure it to create your wireless LAN. You will need a WAP and its User Manual, a computer with an Ethernet NIC, two Ethernet cables (one may have come with the WAP), and the IP address of the WAP, obtained from the User Manual. If you are setting this up as a broadband router, you will need the DSL or cable modem. With all the materials assembled, follow these general instructions for connecting and configuring a WAP that is a DSL/cable router. The actual steps required to configure a WAP may vary from these steps.

These instructions work for most WAPs we have used:

1. Before connecting the WAP, turn off the computer and the DSL or cable modem.

2. Connect one end of an Ethernet cable to the WAN port of the WAP, and connect the other end of the cable to the DSL or cable modem.

3. Take another network cable and connect one end of the cable to your computer's Ethernet NIC, and the other end to one of the Ethernet ports on the WAP.

4. Turn power to the modem on, and wait for the lights on the modem to settle down.

5. Turn the WAP's power on by connecting the power cable that came with the WAP, to the WAP first, and then to an electrical outlet. If the WAP has a power switch, turn it on now.

6. Turn the computer's power on.

7. Now look at the WAP and verify that the indicator lights for the WAN and WLAN ports light up. Ensure that the indicator light for the LAN port to which the computer connects is lit.

Once you have completed these steps, you can test the connection to the WAP, and if all works well you can configure the WAP settings. Exercise 13-2 will walk you through testing the connection to the WAP, and then using your Web browser to connect and configure the WAP settings.

EXERCISE 13-2

Configuring a WAP

You will need to obtain the IP address for the WAP, and then use the PING command to test the connection between the computer and the WAP. Once you determine that the connection works, you can connect and configure the WAP.

1. Open a command prompt in Windows. Select Start | Run, type **cmd**, and click OK. The command prompt will display in a window.

2. Test the connection using the ping command. Type **ping *ip_address_of_WAP***. A successful test will show results similar to Figure 13-8.

3. Now you can configure the WAP through your Web browser (Internet Explorer or Firefox). Open the browser and enter the address you successfully tested in Step 2.

4. If prompted for a user name and password, use the one provided in the User Manual for the WAP. Change this user name as well as the password so that no one else familiar with the default settings for your WAP can connect and change the settings.

5. The next screen should be a setup utility for the WAP. Follow the instructions and provide the type of Internet Access (using information from your ISP). Perform other steps appropriate to your type of Internet access, and provide the user name and password required for Internet access so that the router can connect to the Internet.

6. Most WAPs, by default, act as DHCP servers, running the DHCP service and giving out IP addresses to computers on the internal WLAN and LAN (if appropriate). If there is no other DHCP server on your network, leave this default. If there is a DHCP server for your LAN, disable DHCP for the LAN (all Ethernet connections), but leave it enabled for the WLAN (all wireless connections), unless an administrator for your LAN advises otherwise.

7. A screen will display in which you can configure other settings for the wireless router. Look for the SSID setting, and change it from the default name to a unique name.

8. Figure 13-9 shows a configuration screen for a WAP with a changed SSID.

9. If all the nodes on the wireless LAN will be using the same 802.11 standard, select that standard for the WAP; otherwise, select a standard that will allow NICs using an older standard to connect. After completing the configuration, save your settings and then log out of the setup program.

FIGURE 13-8

A successful test
of the Ethernet
connection to
the WAP

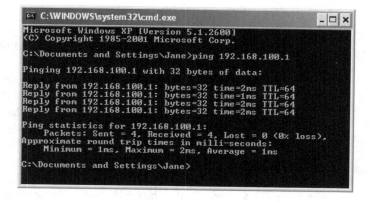

Your wireless access point/router is set up and configured, but not quite ready for
use, because you should not use any wireless network without turning on security.
In Chapter 16 you will learn how to configure security settings for a WAP. For now,
move on to installation and configuration of the wireless NICs for this WLAN.

FIGURE 13-9   Change the SSID and other settings, as needed.

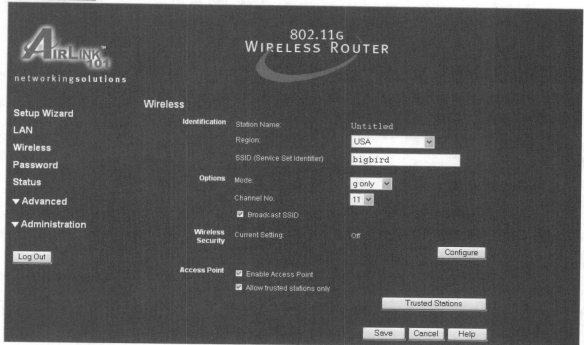

Infrastructure Setup: Wireless NIC   Follow the manufacturer's instructions for installing, connecting, and configuring your wireless NIC. For instance, for a USB wireless NIC, first install the software from the installation CD-ROM onto the PC. Then connect the wireless NIC.

After the NIC is connected, Windows will detect the new hardware, and the Windows Found New Hardware Installation Wizard will display. Select the option "Install the software automatically" and click Next. Follow the instructions to install the NIC, including providing the SSID of your wireless network. Once the installation is complete, an icon for the wireless NIC will appear on the notification area of the toolbar.

on the
ⓙob

Windows XP Service Pack 2 has a Wireless Network Setup Wizard that you may launch from an applet in the Control Panel. However, we recommend using the instructions in this chapter for setting up your first wireless network so that you are familiar with the manual procedure.

Once you have installed the software, you can change the configuration by double-clicking the icon for your wireless NIC. This program will let you search for available wireless networks, change the mode in which your wireless NIC is operating, set security settings for encryption of the data transmitted, change channels, and much more.

Status messages will appear over your notification area when a wireless connection is established (shown in Figure 13-10) and when a wireless connection fails. These messages only display briefly, so most NICs also change the appearance of the icon, showing perhaps a blue or green icon when the NIC is connected and a red icon, or an icon with an *x* over it, when the NIC is disconnected.

FIGURE 13-10

A status notification displays above the toolbar.

IP Configuration

By default, Windows assumes that each network connection will receive an IP address automatically via a DHCP server on your network. This is true of connections made via an Ethernet NIC as well as through a wireless NIC.

Beginning with Windows 98, Microsoft added a new twist to the DHCP client—Automatic Private IP Addressing (APIPA), whereby a DHCP client computer that fails to receive an address from a DHCP server will automatically give itself an address from a special range that has 169.254 in the first two octets of the IP address. If a

TABLE 13-2	IP address	192.168.227.138
	Subnet mask	255.255.255.0
Sample IP	Default Gateway	192.168.227.2
Configuration	DNS Server	192.168.227.3
Settings	WINS Server	192.168.227.4

computer uses this range of addresses, it will not be able to communicate with other devices on the network, unless they also have addresses using the same network ID and subnet mask.

You may need to set up a computer on a LAN in which all the computers are assigned IP addresses manually. In that case, you will obtain the configuration information from a LAN administrator and then manually enter an IP configuration into Windows. This information should include the IP configuration addresses described in Chapter 12. The list will resemble Table 13-2, although the actual addresses will be unique to your network. Add the address for a WINS server only if the computer is part of a large network that requires WINS.

If you need to manually configure IP settings, make a list similar to that in Table 13-2 showing the required settings that you received from your network administrator. Then open the IP configuration for your network adapter, as described in Exercise 13-3.

EXERCISE 13-3

Manually Configuring IP Settings

The following steps will guide you through entering IP configuration settings into Windows XP. The steps are very similar in Windows 2000.

1. Open Control Panel, select Network Connections, and right-click the icon for the network connection you wish to configure. Select Properties from the context menu.

2. In the Properties dialog box, scroll through the list of items used by the connection and click to select Internet Protocol (TCP/IP). Then click the Properties dialog box.

3. In the Internet Protocol (TCP/IP) Properties dialog box, click the radio button labeled Use The Following IP Address.

4. Enter the IP address, subnet mask, and Default Gateway settings.

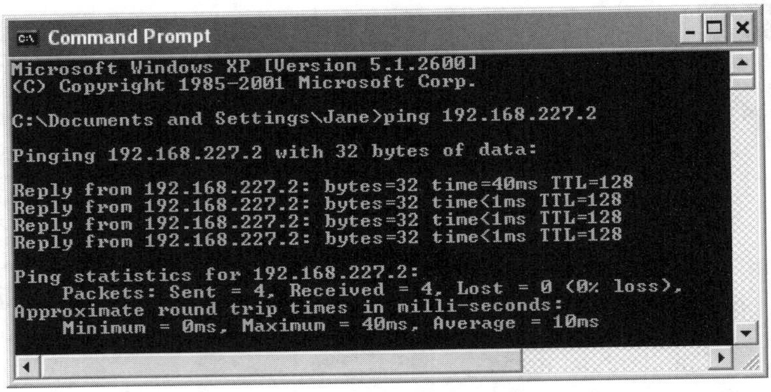

FIGURE 13-11

Test the configuration by pinging the gateway.

```
Command Prompt                                            _ □ ✕

Microsoft Windows XP [Version 5.1.2600]
(C) Copyright 1985-2001 Microsoft Corp.

C:\Documents and Settings\Jane>ping 192.168.227.2

Pinging 192.168.227.2 with 32 bytes of data:

Reply from 192.168.227.2: bytes=32 time=40ms TTL=128
Reply from 192.168.227.2: bytes=32 time<1ms TTL=128
Reply from 192.168.227.2: bytes=32 time<1ms TTL=128
Reply from 192.168.227.2: bytes=32 time<1ms TTL=128

Ping statistics for 192.168.227.2:
    Packets: Sent = 4, Received = 4, Lost = 0 (0% loss),
Approximate round trip times in milli-seconds:
    Minimum = 0ms, Maximum = 40ms, Average = 10ms
```

5. If you have a DNS server address to use, click the radio button labeled Use The Following DNS Server Addresses and enter the Preferred DNS Server. If you have an address for the Alternate Server, enter that address too.

6. Check the numbers you entered, click OK to accept these settings, and then click the Close button in the Properties dialog box.

7. To test your settings, open a command prompt and ping the gateway address to ensure that your computer can communicate on the LAN. If your configuration is correct, and if the gateway router is functioning, you should see four replies. Figure 13-11 shows the results of pinging a gateway address of 192.168.227.2.

NWLink IPX/SPX

In Windows, it is possible to have more than one protocol stack installed, although you normally will not have more than one protocol stack. The reason is that it can slow down your network access, as one protocol stack will be preferred, and the system will tend to use it before using the other(s). Things will slow down until it uses the correct protocols for the access requested.

If you plan to connect to Novell NetWare servers in addition to Microsoft servers, you may need to install Microsoft's version of the IPX/SPX protocol stack, called NWLink IPX/SPX, in addition to TCP/IP. While Novell server networks now use the TCP/IP protocol suite, occasionally you may need to install Microsoft's version of Novell's old protocol stack, which is only required if you wish to connect to an older Novell NetWare server and you use the Microsoft Client Service for NetWare

SCENARIO & SOLUTION

I have installed bus NICs many times, and I need to install a USB NIC for the first time. What is the biggest difference I will find in the methods of installing NICs for these two types of interfaces?	Normally, when you install a bus NIC, you install the card, and then install the drivers. When you install a USB NIC, you normally first install the software, and then connect the NIC to the USB port, at which time Windows detects the NIC and completes the installation.
At home, we have two computers and a broadband Internet connection. We have decided that we want our two computers to connect to the WAN connection via WLAN. Can we use ad hoc mode and save the cost of a wireless router?	No, an ad hoc WLAN cannot connect to another network. Use a wireless router and infrastructure mode to connect these computers to the Internet.
Someone told me that if I want to use the NWLink IPX/SPX protocol stack to connect to an older Novell server, I must uninstall TCP/IP. Is this true?	It is not true. You can have more than one protocol stack installed in Windows. While we do not normally recommend this, it is possible, and sometimes necessary.

(described later in this chapter). If you install this client, NWLink IPX/SPX will install automatically.

on the
() o b   *If you install a client for a Novell network that requires IPX/SPX, it will install the Novell protocol stack, and it does not use the Microsoft NWLink protocol stack at all. It may even uninstall NWLink if it is present.*

You can also install this protocol manually. To do this, open the Properties dialog box for the network connection, click Install, select Protocol, and click Add. In Select Network Protocol, select NWLink IPX/SPX/NetBIOS Compatible Transport Protocol. Click OK and supply the Windows distribution CD if prompted.

Sharing Network Resources

On a Microsoft Windows network, when you make a file or print resource available, you are creating a *share*—the point at which a user, using client software, can access your file system or printers. While you can share other resources, on a Windows desktop computer, the other resource that a PC technician should know how to share is an Internet connection. In this section, first learn about creating file and printer shares. Then explore the steps for sharing an Internet connection.

Sharing Files and Printers

Before you can share files or printers over a network, the File and Printer Services must be functioning on your computer. Then you can create a file share pointing to a folder on your hard drive, or a printer share pointing to a local printer. Finally, you set permissions on the share, and on the underlying file system.

Enabling File and Printer Services

The default configuration for a Windows computer is to have the two most important requirements for file and printer sharing installed and enabled. These are the Server service and the file and printer sharing component. View the status of the Server service in the Computer Management console, which you open by right-clicking My Computer and selecting Manage from the context menu. Now open the Services and Applications node and expand Services. Scroll down until you see Server. Its status should be Started and its Startup Type should be Automatic. If it is not started, right-click and select Start. Close the console.

Now check on file and printer sharing by opening the Properties of the NIC connected to the network over which you wish to share files or printers. On the General tab look for File And Printer Sharing For Microsoft Networks and ensure that there is a check in the box, indicating that it is enabled. If not, click to place a check in the box. Now you are ready to create shares.

on the
Job
If you are preparing to share files on a newly installed Windows computer, with a standard installation, you will not need to check the Server service or file and printer sharing status because they are on by default.

Simple File Sharing vs. Classic File Sharing

Windows 2000 has just one user interface (UI) for sharing, the classic file sharing interface. Windows XP has two UIs for this purpose. In both cases, the UI is found on the Sharing tab of the properties for a folder. The simpler of the two, Simple File Sharing, is always on in Windows XP Home Edition computers but turns on automatically in Windows XP Professional only when the computer is a member of a workgroup. In that case, you have the option to turn it off, and you can then use what is termed the classic file sharing interface. The classic file sharing interface is the only file sharing UI for a Windows XP Professional computer that is a member of a domain.

Simple File Sharing sets very restrictive permissions on a share and does not allow other permissions to apply to a share. Therefore, the Security tab is removed from the properties dialog box on files and folders on an NTFS volume. In fact, it disregards user names and passwords because with Simple File Sharing turned on, anyone connecting to the computer is connected as the Guest account, even if they have user accounts that are valid on the local computer. The Guest account is assigned only the Read permission to any share so they can only read a file, not change it. And, if the Guest account is disabled, no one can connect to a share.

In a Windows XP Professional computer you have more options when assigning permissions to users if you turn off Simple File Sharing, which you can do using the steps in Exercise 13-4. With Simple File Sharing turned off, the Security tab is enabled in the properties dialog box for a file or folder on an NTFS volume and an administrator can assign any level of permissions to user and group accounts. Only then can you allow network users to have various levels of control, including full control, of files in the share.

EXERCISE 13-4

Turning Off Simple File Sharing

Turn off Simple File Sharing in order to have more control over permissions.

1. Click My Computer to open the My Computer folder.
2. On the Tools menu, select Folder Options.
3. Click the View tab and then scroll down the list under Advanced Settings until you can see the choice labeled Use Simple File Sharing (Recommended). Clear this check box, which is at the bottom of the list in Figure 13-12.
4. Click OK to close the Folder Options dialog box.

Creating a Share and Setting Share-Level Permissions

Enabling file and printer sharing on a Windows computer does not make every file or every printer available to network users. In fact, you would not want to share every file on your computer, and any attached printer, over the network. For that reason, you must take an additional step to make files and printers available on the network. In Windows, a share is a special folder that represents a file folder or a printer. The share is available to network users and is visible over the network.

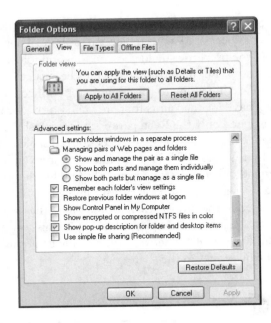

Files and folders within a shared folder are available to network users. Similarly, a shared printer is available to network users.

Creating a Printer Share   When you install a printer using the Add Printer Wizard, you have an opportunity to share the printer by creating a printer share. If you decide to share a printer after installing it, simply open the Properties for the printer, select the Sharing tab, and select Share This Printer. You can accept the Share name or give the printer's share a new name. If the network's client computers are running the same version of Windows that this computer is, you are done and can click OK. If there are other versions of Windows on the network, click Additional Drivers and select the other versions of Windows. If prompted to provide a printer driver, insert the driver disc that came with the printer and continue.

Creating a File Share   Although called file sharing, a share must point to a file folder, not to a single file. To create a file share, use My Computer or Windows Explorer to browse to a folder you wish to share, right-click that folder, and select Properties. Click the Sharing tab in the folder's Properties dialog box. Select Share This Folder and complete the rest of the settings. The share name will show the name of the file folder, but you can choose to give it another name to represent it on

FIGURE 13-13

A share name can be different from the file folder name.

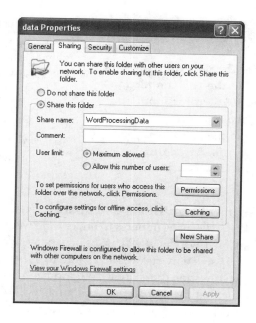

the network. In Figure 13-13, the folder named "data" was assigned the share name "WordProcessingData."

When you log on locally to a computer with a file share, and you view the shared file folder in My Computer, the folder icon will include a hand that appears to be holding the folder. This is the sharing icon. The displayed name is the name for this folder in your file system, not the share name. You can view the share name on the Share page of the Properties dialog box for this folder.

A user connecting to your computer over the network will see this folder with its share name only.

e x a m

ⓦatch   *Understand the difference between a file share and the file folder that it points to. A folder icon represents both, and each can have a unique name, or they can both have the same name. This also applies to a share for a printer.*

Under User Limit in the Sharing tab, selecting Maximum Allowed will automatically allow the number of users that Windows will permit to connect at one time. Windows 2000 Professional and Windows XP Professional have a limit of ten simultaneous user connections. Additional connections will fail until a connection has been released.

Windows Server operating systems do not have such connection limits—only legal limits.

The connections to Microsoft Windows server operating systems are managed using purchased client licenses. A certain number may come with a server, and you can purchase additional licenses.

If you do not use the Permissions button on the Sharing dialog page but click OK without assigning permissions, the created share will have the default permissions, which we will explore next.

Assigning Permissions to a Share   Once created, you can set share permissions. But first, take a few minutes to understand what happens when a user connects to a share on a Windows XP Professional or Windows 2000 Professional computer. When a user connects over a network to a shared folder, the security system of the computer hosting the share will perform authorization, authenticating the user, and verifying that the user account has some level of access to the folder.

You can set one set of permissions on the share and another set of permissions on an NTFS file system. If the underlying file system is not NTFS but FAT16 or FAT32, there can be no file or folder-level permissions under the share. The only protection is the authentication and the share-level permissions.

When a network user is accessing a share that exists on an NTFS volume, the share permissions and NTFS permissions combine, with the most restrictive permissions applying. For instance, if the share-level permissions grant a user Full Control, but the folder or file-level permissions only grant the Read permission, the user will only have Read permission.

When the underlying file system is NTFS, and the share permission is more restrictive than the file system permission, the users will not be able to access the underlying files, or will not be able to perform actions on the files that they could do if logged on locally. Share-level permissions do not affect local users who are accessing the file system directly.

Further, on an NTFS file system, folders have a slightly different set of permissions than those that can be set on individual files, although they share several common permissions. For instance, you can open a folder and view a list of the files and folders it contains, which is different from opening a file in an application. Therefore, folders need the List Folder Contents permission.

In both cases, there are standard permissions, each of which is composed of several special permissions. For example, the standard file permission called Read permission consists of the following special permissions: Read Data, Read Attributes, Read Extended Attributes, Read Permissions (the permissions on the file), and Synchronize. Most of the time, standard permissions are all you need to use. Therefore, we only list the standard permissions here.

The standard folder permissions are:

- Full Control
- Modify
- Read and Execute
- List Folder Contents
- Read
- Write

The standard file permissions are:

- Full Control
- Modify
- Read and Execute
- Read
- Write

When folder permissions and the permissions on the files within the folder combine, the least restrictive permissions apply. However, when a user connects to files through a share, first the file and folder permissions are combined with the resulting least-restrictive permission applying, and then the resulting file system permission is combined with the share-level permission and the most-restrictive permission is applied.

The best practice is to first set the NTFS permissions, and then set the share-level permissions. On a FAT32 volume, it is important to change the permissions on a share as soon as you create it because the default permissions on a share in Windows 2000 Professional, and some of the server versions, give the group Everyone full control, which allows all users full access to files, including the right to change or delete them. Windows XP and Windows Server 2003, on the other hand, only grant the Read permission to the Everyone group by default, which means that without any other permissions assigned in addition to the Read permission, users can open and read the files under the share, but not change or delete them.

You can change the permissions on a share that you create. First, you can add and remove users to whom you will grant permissions. We recommend that you add other users or groups. As soon as you have added at least one user or group, remove the group Everyone, unless you really want anyone who can access your network to also access the share. Normally, you would not want to grant permissions so globally. The Authenticated Users group is all users who have been authenticated. When we want to assign permissions to "everybody," we add the group Authenticated Users and remove the group Everyone.

If we want even a single user connecting over the network to be able to change files in the share, we give the Authenticated Users the Full Control permission. This may sound too permissive, but we make things more restrictive at the file system level if the share is on an NTFS volume. If it is not, but is on a FAT or FAT32 volume, the share permissions should be set to exactly what you desire for users because the FAT file systems have no way to apply permissions. However, there is only one common reason for having a FAT or FAT32 volume on a Windows 2000, Windows XP, or newer version of Windows. That reason would be if you are dual-booting the computer between one of these OSs and one that does not support NTFS. An example would be a computer dual-booting between Windows 9x and Windows XP. This should be a very rare configuration.

In addition to the share permission, the file permissions on files and folders in an NTFS volume that fall within a share are the last defense against unauthorized users coming over the network. Set permissions at the most restrictive level that will allow the right users to accomplish their work.

Internet Connection Sharing

Sharing an Internet connection to a single Windows computer is much like sharing an Internet connection to a LAN. One situation in which you may wish to share the Internet connection through a single computer is if you have one computer that has a dial-up or broadband connection to the Internet. In this case, the PC sharing the connection is acting as a router to the Internet as well as a PC for an end user. The computer with the WAN connection will have one NIC or modem for the WAN connection, and another NIC (Ethernet or Wi-Fi) over which other computers may connect to share the connection.

There are drawbacks to this model. One is that the computer with the WAN connection must remain powered on in order for the other computers to connect. Another is that the shared computer may not be able to communicate with any other computer on the shared interface.

Before turning on Internet Connection Sharing, be sure that you have a firewall turned on for the interface that is sharing its connection. Learn more about firewalls in Chapter 15. To enable the firewall that comes with Windows XP Service Pack 2, open the Windows Firewall applet in Control Panel and select the radio button labeled On and click OK. This will turn it on for all network adapters in your computer.

To turn on Internet Connection Sharing, open the properties of the network connection to the Internet. Open the Advanced page in the Properties of that connection. On the Advanced page click to place a check in the box labeled "Allow other network users to connect through this computer's Internet connection." A warning will appear stating that once ICS is turned on, the adapter with the Internet connection will be configured with an IP address of 192.168.0.1, and the computer may not be able to communicate with other computers on that network.

If you connect to the Internet over an Ethernet LAN connection and are providing ICS to computers connected via a WLAN interface, this means that you will not be able to communicate with every computer on the LAN unless they have addresses on the same IP network. In short, ICS is for home use and perhaps a very small office. Only consider it if you need to share a dial-up connection. There are plenty of inexpensive routers available for sharing a broadband connection.

on the
job *We strongly recommend that, even in a home environment, when you wish to share a broadband connection between as few as two computers, you purchase a broadband router, which does a better job of sharing the connection.*

In Figure 13-14, the computer connects to the Internet through its wireless connection, and users on the Local Area Connection share the connection. We do not recommend the option labeled "Allow other network users to control or disable the shared Internet connection."

Once Internet Connection Sharing (ICS) is turned on for a connection, its status in the Network Connections folder should show as "Connected, Shared, Firewalled."

FIGURE 13-14

Turn on Internet
Connection
Sharing.

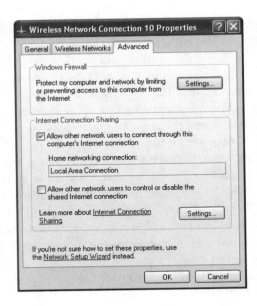

To enable the use of this connection on other computers on the LAN, simply make sure that the IP configuration on each computer (excluding the one with the shared connection) is set to Obtain An IP Address Automatically. ICS will act as a DHCP server on the LAN and give out IP addresses and configuration information to the other computers. The Gateway address for those computers will be that of the LAN connection of the ICS computer.

e x a m

ⓦ a t c h   *The preferred method for sharing an Internet connection is through a broadband router that also contains an Ethernet switch. Then, as long as the router and the broadband modem are powered, network users can access the Internet without depending on a computer that is acting as the router.*

Accessing Network Resources

Think of all the reasons for using a computer network, and you will find that there is a server role for each reason and a service for each role. The most basic network server role is a file and printer server. The server service, installed by default on every Windows computer, allows that computer to share its files and printers with client computers on the network.

SCENARIO & SOLUTION

I would like to create a share on my computer for files that two other users in my workgroup must be able to modify. Can I do this with Simple File Sharing?	No, because all users who connect under Simple File Sharing are members of the Guests group, and only have the Read permission. You need to turn off Simple File Sharing and assign the Full Control permission to the accounts for these two people.
I need to create a share that points to the folder named "daily" on my local hard drive. I would like to name the share "reports" when users view it over the network. Do I need to change the file folder name?	No, you do not need to change the name of the file folder. Just name the share "reports" and it will be seen over the network as "reports."
I have a dial-up connection on my home PC. I would like to share this connection with my spouse's computer. Both computers have wireless NICs, and they communicate with each other in ad hoc mode.	While sharing a dial-up connection is rather slow, you can share it by turning on Internet sharing for the modem connection and selecting the wireless LAN as the Home Networking Connection.

A client computer must have the appropriate client software to access a server. A single computer can play both client and server roles simply by having both the server and client components installed and enabled, which is the default for file and printer sharing in Windows desktop computers. You will find the file and printer service in the most basic administrative network model, a workgroup, as well as in the client/server administrative model.

Microsoft Workgroups

In a small, basic network, there are no dedicated servers, only peer computers that share their files and printers with other users on the network. This model, which Microsoft calls a workgroup, has no centralized administration but has a distributed administration model. That means that someone must do the work of creating shares and assigning permissions to those shares on each computer that shares its files and/ or printers. This does not scale well as the number of participating computers grows, because the administrative work becomes more and more time consuming.

Microsoft Domains

A second model has centralized administration of one or more servers, which contain a shared database of user accounts used to authenticate users before they can access any resources on the network. The Microsoft version of this administrative model is a *domain*, an administrative organization with a centralized security accounts database, maintained on one or more special servers called *domain controllers*.

Domain Accounts

This centralized database contains security accounts for users, groups, and computers participating in the domain, and you can use it to authenticate a user for access to any resource of the domain. A security account is one to which you can assign permissions and rights. A user account represents a single user. Group accounts exist in a security accounts database to simplify administration. Rather than assign rights and permissions to individual users, an administrator can place many users (and some groups) into a single group and assign one set of permissions to all.

This model allows one administrator, or relatively few administrators, to perform the administrative tasks for a great number of computers—both client and server computers—from one or more centralized locations. This includes creating accounts and shares, and assigning permissions to shares and other resources.

An organization can have more than one Microsoft domain, in which case they may establish a special relationship between the domains called a *trust*. This relationship allows the accounts from one domain to use the resources of another domain.

> **exam**
> **⊙atch** *For the exam, you need to know the overall administrative differences between a workgroup and a Windows domain. You will not need to understand the trust that can exist between domains. We define the term trust here because it is mentioned in the description of domain group accounts.*

Local Accounts Beginning with Windows NT and continuing in all the Windows desktop operating systems that directly evolved from the Windows NT operating system, each installation of Windows maintains a local security accounts database. These operating systems include Windows 2000 Professional, Windows XP Professional, and Windows Vista.

Each installation contains local user accounts and local group accounts. A user account used for authentication is a record in the security accounts database that normally represents a single person. Authentication is validation of a user account and password that occurs before the security components of Windows will give the user access to the computer. At this point, you might envision the user account as standing on the threshold of the network or the remote computer to which it has connected, but it is the authorization process that allows the user in after assessing the permissions assigned to the user to each requested resource (like a file share).

A local group account can contain one or more local user accounts, and when the computer is a member of a Windows domain, a local group may also contain domain users or domain group accounts in order to give domain users and groups access to resources on the local computer.

During installation, the local security accounts database for Windows 2000 Professional and Windows XP Professional is created, with two user accounts: Administrator and Guest, but only the Administrator account is enabled by default. Administrator cannot be renamed or disabled.

Both versions of Windows also have several built-in groups, including (but not limited to) Administrators, Backup Operators, Guests, Power Users, and Users. Some special groups are created automatically when certain services and applications are installed.

By default, Administrator is the only member of the Administrators group, and Guest is the only member of the Guests group. The other built-in groups are empty until an administrator creates additional local user accounts. At that point, all local user accounts are automatically members of the Users group. The administrator may make users members of any group, including new groups the administrator creates.

Creating Local Accounts   During installation of Windows, you provide a password for the Administrator, and that is the user account you must log on with immediately after installing. Whatever you do, do not log on as the Administrator account for ordinary tasks. Create a user account that is not a member of the Administrators group and use this account when you are simply doing common office tasks on your computer.

On both Windows 2000 Professional and Windows XP Professional computers, an administrator can choose between a simple and a more complex tool for managing users and groups. In Windows 2000 Professional, the simple tool is a Control Panel applet called Users and Passwords, while Windows XP has the User Accounts applet. These simple applets are the preferred tools to use if your computer is a member of a workgroup and only one or two users log on to each computer or need to connect to shares on the computer over the network.

In both versions of Windows more experienced administrators use the more complex tool—the Local Users and Groups node of the Computer Management console. Even in a domain, the need for this tool may be limited, since another tool manages domain accounts, which can access any computer in the domain.

Both the Windows XP User Accounts applet and the Windows 2000 Professional Users and Passwords applet hide the complete list of user groups, using a simple reference to account types defined by an account's group membership. In Windows 2000, when you make a user a Standard User, the account becomes a member of the Power Users Group. An account that is a Restricted User is a member of the Users Group, and the third type of user account is a member of the Administrators group. In Windows XP, the types of accounts an administrator can create in User Accounts is Limited (a member of the Users group) and Computer Administrator (a member of the local Administrators group). Figure 13-15 shows the User Accounts applet with three accounts visible: Jane, Dingo, and Guest. The individual Administrator account is only visible in the User Accounts applet when the logged-on user is Administrator.

Domain Users and Group Membership   In a Windows domain, there are three types of security accounts: users, groups, and computers. A domain has a domain administrator who can create new user and group accounts.

Once accounts are created, the administrator can assign permissions and user rights to them. A permission is a level of access to a single object, such as a file or folder. A user right is the privilege to perform a system-wide function, such as

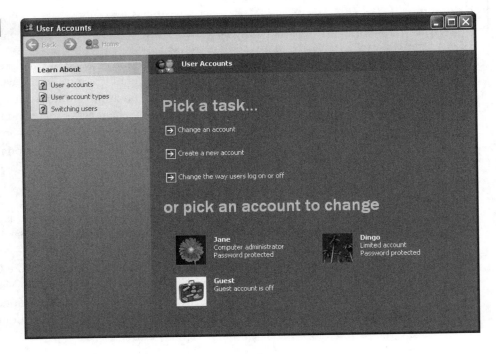

FIGURE 13-15

The Windows XP User Accounts applet

access the computer from the network, log on locally, log on to a computer from the network, back up files, change the system time, or load and unload device drivers. In this chapter, we are only concerned with permissions, not user rights.

Domain User Accounts   Each user who logs on to a Windows computer that is a member of a domain must have a domain user account. *Domain user* accounts contain identifying information about each user. At minimum, each user must have a user name and password to use in order to log on. This name can be up to 20 characters, and most organizations establish a standard for creating the user name. Optionally, a user account can contain a great deal of data, including a user's full name, job function, location, and much more.

Windows NT Domain Groups   An NT domain (one in which all the domain controllers are Windows NT Server systems) has two types of groups: local and global. A *local* group is used to assign permissions to resources on the same domain controller and can contain user and group accounts from that domain and trusted domains. A *global* group assigns permissions and user rights to resources on other computers in the domain, and to resources in a domain that trusts the domain in which the global group resides. A global group can contain only users and groups from the local domain.

Active Directory Domain Groups   Active Directory domains are those with Windows 2000 or newer domain controllers. Active Directory is a directory service, a network service that can manage all types of network resources, based on certain international standards. The Active Directory group account story is much more complicated than that of Windows NT domains, and we will tell only part of it here, because the finer details are necessary only if you are preparing to become an Active Directory administrator.

An Active Directory domain also has local and global security groups, but the local groups are called *domain* local groups. Domain local groups can contain user accounts from the same domain, global groups from the same domain or trusted domains, and other domain local groups. This last is a practice called nesting, and administrators use it with caution, because it adds a level of real complexity to the administrator's job.

Special Groups   *Special* groups are groups no user can create or modify. The membership of a special group is predefined, and it is available to you only when you assign permissions or rights. Some Microsoft documentation for Windows XP calls special groups "built-in security principals." A few important special groups are Creator Owner (membership consists of the user who created a file or folder), System (the operating system), and the Everyone group, which includes all users on a network, even those who have not been authenticated.

Joining a Computer to a Workgroup or Domain

Windows computers participate in a network through membership in one of two types of administrative models: a workgroup or a domain. A Microsoft workgroup must have a unique name on the network with up to 15 characters, but the only user accounts available in a workgroup exist independently on member computers that are capable of maintaining a local accounts database. All Windows computers can join a workgroup.

While Windows 9x and Windows Me cannot maintain local accounts databases, the newest versions of Windows do. This ability is in Windows NT, Windows 2000, Windows XP, and beyond.

In a workgroup, you can only use locally maintained user accounts to authenticate users to the local computer, and to give users rights and permissions to the resources on the local computer. All it takes to be a member of a workgroup is to specify the workgroup name, either in the identification page of the Windows setup program, or in the Computer Name page of the System Properties dialog box. Any Windows computer, new or old, can join a workgroup. In fact, a workgroup is created when the first computer on a network provides a unique workgroup name and joins that workgroup.

The centralized database of a Microsoft Windows domain contains security accounts for users, groups, and computers participating in the domain. For a user to log on to a domain, the Windows 2000 or Windows XP computer from which they are logging on must have an account in the same domain as the user, or in a domain that trusts the user's domain.

A domain administrator must first create an account for the computer in the domain, and then the computer must join the domain.

Some Windows computers cannot join a domain. In particular, computers running Windows 9x or Windows XP Home cannot join a domain or have a security account in the domain. What they can do is enjoy some of the benefits of membership. The first one is that a user can log on to a domain from a Windows 9x computer (but not a Windows XP Home computer) if it is configured for a user domain logon. Then, once logged on to the domain, a user can assign permissions to access local shares to users and groups in the domain.

With Windows NT, Windows 2000, Windows XP Professional, and Windows Server 2003 computers, each computer must have an account in a domain and be logged on to a domain before a user sitting at that computer can log on to a domain. When a computer is a member of a domain, it performs a computer logon automatically.

Joining a computer to a domain is important even if you never intend to share a folder or printer on that computer, because there are other benefits of membership. These include centralized management of the desktop computer by administrators in the domain, and your ability to log on to that computer using a domain user account. These things are possible because when the computer joins the domain, certain group accounts in the domain become members of local groups. This gives the domain administrators administrative rights on the local computer and allows domain users to log on to the local computer.

These are important benefits in most organizations, because centralized administration reduces the costs of keeping computers secure and up-to-date, as well as supporting the users in their daily use of computers. Exercise 13-5 describes the steps for adding a Windows XP computer to a domain. The steps are similar in Windows 2000.

EXERCISE 13-5

Adding a Computer to a Domain

To complete this exercise, you will need a computer with Windows 2000 or Windows XP Professional (or a newer Windows OS) that is a member of a workgroup. This, of course, excludes the Home versions of Windows XP and Vista, which cannot participate in a domain. You will need a user name and password of an account with local administrator rights, a user name and password of a user account in the domain, and the name of a Windows domain on your network (an administrator account for a Windows NT domain, but an ordinary user account for an Active Directory domain).

1. Log on to the local machine with an account that is a member of the local Administrators group. Right-click My Computer, and then select Properties. In the System Properties dialog box, select Computer Name.

2. Click Network ID to run the Network Identification Wizard. Click Next on the Welcome page, select the radio button titled "This computer is part of a business network…," and click Next (see Figure 13-16). Continue, providing the information you gathered for joining the domain.

3. When you reach the Access Level page, select Standard User unless advised otherwise by your network administrator.

FIGURE 13-16

Use the Network Identification Wizard to join a computer to the domain.

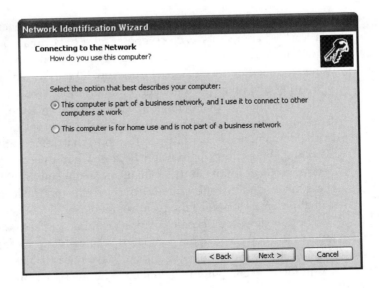

4. Then, unless an administrator has already created a computer account in the domain, provide a user name and password for a domain account that can join a computer to a domain. A member of the Domain Administrators group works in both types of Microsoft domains. Click OK twice and then click Yes to reboot.

5. After the reboot, log on to the domain using a domain user account. Be sure to select the domain by clicking Options to make the Log On To box visible.

Viewing Workgroups, Domains, and Computers

To see other workgroups and domains, open Network Places, click Find, and click the link labeled "Microsoft Windows Network" in the task pane under Other Places. Figure 13-17 shows three workgroups or domains: Htc, Osborne, and Workgroup. My Network Places refers to all groupings of computers as workgroups, even though in Figure 13-17, Htc is a domain and the others are workgroups. Just seeing other workgroups and domains on the network is confirmation that a network connection is working, because you must be connected and communicating on a network to be aware of the other workgroups, domains, and computers.

FIGURE 13-17

Microsoft
Windows
Network showing
three workgroups
or domains

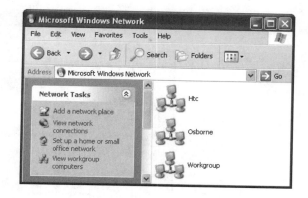

To see other computers, open a workgroup or domain. The computers listed are either actual server computers or Windows desktop computers with file and printer sharing turned on. Other computers will not be visible on the network.

If you have a Novell client installed in Windows, you will also see Novell servers.

Configuring File and Printer Clients

In order to see and connect to shares on servers, you must have a file and printer client installed. A file and printer client includes both the user interface and the underlying file sharing protocols to access a file sharing service on a network server.

Examples of file sharing protocols are Microsoft's Server Message Block (SMB) protocol, Novell's NetWare Core Protocol (NCP), and the newer Common Internet File System (CIFS), a standard used by Microsoft, Novell, and many others. In addition, Linux and some UNIX versions use the network file system (NFS), and some Internet file sharing systems use the P2P protocol. Most of these file sharing protocols include support for sharing a printer attached to the local server, and they are also contained in dedicated network devices for sharing a printer.

Because many corporate networks may have more than one type of file sharing server, Windows allows you to have more than one client installed, so your connection properties may look like Figure 13-18. When you install a new service or client, it is, by default, installed for all available network connections. For instance, if you have a modem, that is considered a network connection, and each file sharing service and client you install will be configured for that connection, as well as Ethernet and Wi-Fi connections (if present).

If you have both the Microsoft and Novell clients installed, you will be able to view and connect to both types of servers on the network. The client software and

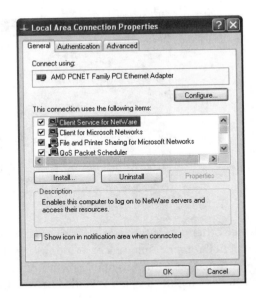

security components that are installed in Windows allow users to log on to Microsoft or Novell networks. Learn more about the Microsoft and Novell file and printer clients in the following sections.

Client for Microsoft Networks

The Client for Microsoft Networks is automatically installed and enabled when a Windows operating system is installed. With the client installed you are able to use the Windows GUI to see those Microsoft computers on the network that have file and printer sharing turned on, whether they are using the older SMB file sharing protocol or the newer CIFS protocol standards.

You can see both dedicated Windows network servers and Windows desktops that have file and printer sharing turned on. You will be able to see these servers on your network in My Computer | My Network Places, but your ability to connect to any shares on those computers depends on the permissions applied to each share.

You will also have mixed results viewing the properties of these objects in My Network Places. You may even be surprised at what you find. Figure 13-19 shows the properties of a print server, a dedicated device packaged in a small case that uses the Microsoft SMB protocol to allow users to print to one or more printers attached to it.

FIGURE 13-19

Print server
properties

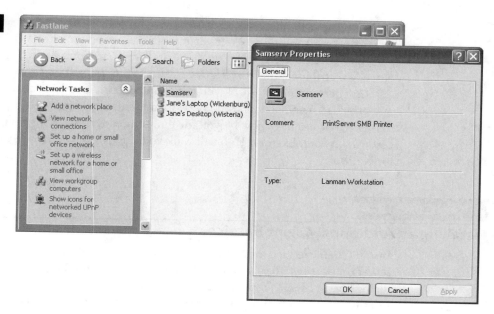

Novell Clients

A computer requiring access to file and printer services on a Novell server needs
a Novell client. Both Microsoft and Novell offer Windows clients for Novell
networks. Novell offers clients for almost any operating system, including several
versions of UNIX and Linux, Macintosh, mainframes, and several versions of
Windows.

Microsoft Client Service for NetWare   While Microsoft's Novell client for
Windows does not install automatically on a Windows computer, one comes with
each version of Windows and can be installed after the fact through the properties of
a network connection. You will have to restart the computer after installation.

on the job

*Before Windows XP, the Client Service for NetWare was known as Novell
Client by Microsoft for Windows. You will see this term used in certain articles
and documentation.*

After the restart, complete the Select NetWare Logon dialog box, in which
you select either a NetWare server or a NetWare Directory Services (NDS) tree
and context. If you select a server, you will need the name of a Novell NetWare

server on the network that either is running an older version (before version 4) of NetWare, or is running a newer version but emulating the older version for logon purposes. Alternatively, selecting a tree and context allows you to log on to NDS, Novell's distributed directory service introduced in Novell NetWare 4.0.

The Microsoft client for Novell is generally considered less capable than the one provided by Novell, and the network administrators may select this client for a network that has just a few Novell file and printer servers, or for compatibility with certain software. Exercise 13-6 will walk you through installing the Client Service for NetWare.

EXERCISE 13-6

Installing an Additional Client Service

Install Client Service for NetWare as a second client. If you do not have a Novell server on your network, you may still complete this exercise, but cancel out of the dialog box in Step 3. You will need the installation CD for the version of Windows installed on the computer. If a NetWare server is on your network, you will need a user account on a NetWare server, or one that is valid in an NDS tree and context. You will also need the name of the tree and context.

1. Open Control Panel | Network Connections. Right-click a network connection, and select Properties.

2. In the Connection Properties dialog box, click Install. The choices will normally be Client, Service, or Protocol. Select Client and click Add.

3. In the Select Network Client dialog box, select Client Service for NetWare, and click OK (see Figure 13-20). If requested, provide the Windows CD. When prompted, select Yes to restart the computer.

Novell Client by Novell for Windows   Novell also offers a client to allow a Microsoft computer to connect to Novell services. If your network is primarily a Novell network, in which all or most of the servers are Novell servers, this is the preferred client for your Windows computers, because it has better software tools for use by the Novell server administrators who will normally administer the server or servers from a desktop computer. There are separate Novell clients for the various Windows versions, and for other operating systems. The clients themselves are also issued in numbered versions.

You can download Novell clients free from the Novell site (www.novell.com).

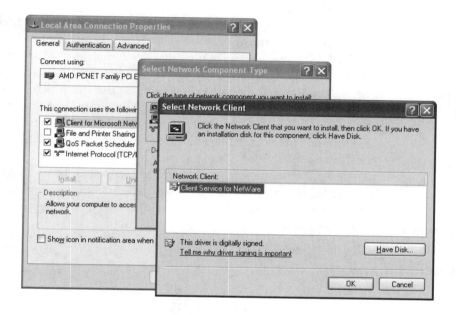

FIGURE 13-20

Select Network
Client

Installing and Configuring Web Browsers

While the World Wide Web (the Web) is just one of the many services that exist
on the Internet, it alone is responsible for most of the huge growth in Internet use
that began after the Web's introduction in the 1990s. Web technologies changed the

SCENARIO & SOLUTION

What is the difference between administering user accounts and shared resources in a workgroup versus those in a domain?	In a workgroup administration is distributed, meaning that someone must go to each computer to administer accounts and shares. In a domain administration is centralized and can be performed from one location.
I have heard about the Everyone group and I would like to make changes to restrict the membership of this group, but I can't find a way to do that.	The Everyone group cannot be altered. It is created by default and includes all users on the network—even those who have not been authenticated. The only way to control this is when you are assigning permissions. Add other users or groups and then remove the Everyone group from the list.

look of the Internet content from all text to rich and colorful graphics, and made it simple to navigate the Web by using a special type of client called a Web browser.

The Web browser's ease of use hides the complexity of the Internet, because protocols are used to transfer the content of a Web page to the user's computer, where the Web browser translates the plain-text language into a rich, colorful document that may contain links to other pages—often at disparate locations on the Internet. The two most common Web browsers used by Windows computers are Internet Explorer and Mozilla Firefox, described in the next sections. We will describe security settings for these two Web browsers in Chapter 16.

A related service is a proxy server, also described in the next sections. If this service is available on your network, you may need to configure your computer as a proxy client. Learn more about the relationship between proxy servers and Web browsers and other services.

Internet Explorer

In August 1995, Microsoft introduced the Internet Explorer (IE) Web browser along with the launch of the Windows 95 operating system. IE was included (or bundled) free with the operating system and has been included in each subsequent Windows OS. Free updates to newer versions of IE for Windows and Mac OSs are available at the Microsoft Web site.

Installing and Upgrading Internet Explorer

Internet Explorer is, by default, installed with Windows and is well integrated into the OS. You should not need to install IE, but expect to upgrade it as Microsoft releases a new version every few years. If you have Automatic Update turned on, it will download and install updates to IE automatically. You can also use Windows Update from the Start menu or go directly to the Microsoft download site at www .microsoft.com/downloads.

If you install a second Web browser, do not uninstall IE. Not only is it not advisable to uninstall IE, some Web pages do not display correctly in other browsers, but look fine in IE. This has to do with content on the Web page that is running small programs in ActiveX, which run best in IE. ActiveX is a technology developed by Microsoft for making Web pages more interactive by downloading small programs from Web sites and running them in an ActiveX-enabled browser—mainly Internet Explorer. These programs include sound, Java applets, and animation.

Conversely, some Web pages may not display properly in IE but work fine in other Web browsers, including Mozilla's Firefox. In this scenario, the problem may be one or more Java scripts that are not compatible with IE. We have run into more problems with Web pages not working in Firefox than with pages not working in IE. For instance, browsing pages at Microsoft or MSN, we need to use IE because objects are missing on some pages when we use Firefox. This is especially true when using Hotmail, and we found that we could not send mail from Hotmail from within Firefox. These problems could go away in the future as these browsers are updated.

Configuring Internet Explorer

Configure Internet Explorer through its Tools menu. From here, in IE 7, you can turn on and configure the Pop-up Blocker, turn on and configure a Phishing Filter (learn about phishing in Chapter 15), run Windows Update, diagnose connection problems, and open the Internet Options dialog box, which has pages of settings to further control the behavior of IE. You can also manage add-ons, which are small programs installed into Internet Explorer. Called browser extensions, they include such programs as Adobe PDF Reader Link Helper, Diagnose Connection Problems, Sun Java Console, and Windows Messenger.

Firefox

Firefox, by Mozilla, is an increasingly popular free Web browser. People consider it to be a safer Web browser than Internet Explorer, because it is not targeted by malicious attacks as much as the Microsoft browser is. You still need to have security in place when you use Firefox.

Installing and Upgrading Firefox

To download Firefox, point your browser to www.mozilla.com and follow the instructions for downloading and installing Firefox. The installation process will copy your Favorites from Internet Explorer. You will have an opportunity to select Firefox as your default browser during installation. The default browser is the browser Windows opens when the user clicks on a URL. If you do not select it at that time, and you want to do so later, select Tools | Options. On the General tab click the Check Now button under Default Browser. When it detects that Firefox is not your default browser, it will offer to change the setting.

Once it is installed, open the Options dialog box from the Tool menu and select Advanced, and then select the Update page. If you have an Internet connection, make sure that Firefox is set to automatically check for updates for Firefox, installed extensions and themes, and search engines. Then decide what action you want taken when updates are discovered.

Configuring Firefox

Use the Options dialog box to configure Firefox further. In addition to the Default Browser setting, the General page allows you to configure the home page—the page that appears when you first open the browser—and the connection settings. Configure the setting for Privacy, Content, Tabs, and Downloads. Find additional settings on the Advanced page.

Configure Proxy Settings

In many instances an Internet connection includes a proxy server—a network service that handles the requests for Internet services, such as Web pages, files on an FTP server, and mail for a proxy client without exposing that client's IP address to the Internet. There is specific proxy server and client software for each type of service. Most proxy servers combine these services and accept requests for HTTP, FTP, POP3, SMTP, and other types of services. The proxy server will often cache a copy of the requested resource in memory, making it available for subsequent requests from clients without having to go to the Internet again.

If there is a proxy server on your network, you can configure your browser to send requests to the proxy server, which will forward and handle all requests. To configure Windows XP to use a proxy server, open the Control Panel's Internet Options applet and click the Connections tab. There are two places for configuring a proxy server on this tab, depending on how you connect to the Internet.

If you have a dial-up connection, click the Settings button under Dial-up and Virtual Private Network settings. Follow the instructions for configuring the proxy server, which will include the IP address of the server.

If your computer connects to the Internet through a LAN, go to the bottom of the Connection page and click the LAN Settings button. This will open the Local Area Network (LAN) Settings box. Under Proxy Server click to put a check in the box labeled Use A Proxy Server for your LAN. (These setting will not apply to dial-up or VPN connections.) Then enter the IP address in the Address box, and the Port number (obtained from your network administrator or the documentation for the proxy server) in the Port box. Click Advanced if you need to add more ports. The OS uses ports as a way to identify a service at a specific address. They have numbers, like 3128, and you must supply a port for each service the proxy service supports. For instance, when you send an e-mail to your SMTP server, the packets that your TCP/IP stack sends have the IP address of the server, and the port number (usually 25). This identifies both the IP address of the computer and the service your packet is targeting.

SCENARIO & SOLUTION

I plan to use Mozilla Firefox as my Web browser. Should I uninstall Internet Explorer?	No. Do not uninstall Internet Explorer. You can make Firefox your default browser.
When I browse to MSN using Firefox, the pages do not appear correct, and I cannot access all the features.	Firefox does not work well with pages that use ActiveX programs. IE has problems with some pages that use Java applets. Therefore, when a page does not look right, change to the other Web browser.
I connect to the Internet via the company LAN, and my LAN administrator has e-mailed me proxy server addresses. Where in Windows do I enter these?	Open Control Panel | Internet Options. On the Connections page click the LAN Settings button at the bottom. On the Local Area Network Settings place a check in the check box under Proxy Server and enter the settings provided by your administrator.

However, Windows only provides options for four types of proxy servers: HTTP, Secure (HTTPS), FTP, and SOCKS. You should be familiar with all but the last of these terms. SOCKS is a protocol used by proxy servers. If you have a proxy server for other services, not supported by Windows, you will need to install a proxy client provided by the vendor of the server software.

CERTIFICATION SUMMARY

An A+ certification candidate must understand the tasks required to install, configure, and upgrade networks for client computers on a network. Installation and upgrade tasks include the physical installation of both wired and wireless NICs, setting up a wireless LAN, configuring IP settings, and adding additional clients or protocols.

The most basic form of sharing network resources is file and printer sharing, and you need to understand how to enable this and create shares on a Windows computer. Be prepared to create file and printer shares and to assign permissions to the shares. A share folder can have two separate names: a share name visible to network users, and a file folder name visible to those users logged on locally to the computer. Understand the difference between using Simple File Sharing and classic file sharing, and how to disable Simple File Sharing if an administrator needs to have more control over setting permissions on shares.

A Windows computer can belong to one of two types of Microsoft administrative organizations: a workgroup or a domain. A PC technician must know how to join a computer to a workgroup or domain, and must understand the difference between the distributed administration of a workgroup versus the centralized administration of a domain. This includes a basic knowledge of the user and group accounts that exist in the local security accounts database of a Windows computer versus those that exist in the centralized accounts database of a Windows Active Directory domain.

The two most popular Web browsers are Microsoft Internet Explorer and Mozilla Firefox. A PC technician should be familiar with both, knowing how to install, configure, and update them.

Finally, a technician must know how to configure settings for a proxy server for HTTP, FTP, POP3, SMTP, and other types of services using the Connection tab of the Internet Options applet.

✓ TWO-MINUTE DRILL

Here are some of the key points covered in Chapter 13.

Installing and Configuring Networks

❑ Each computer on a network requires a NIC for its physical installation.

❑ Decide how a NIC should interface with your computer (bus, USB, or other interface) and select a NIC for the type of network you require—LAN or WLAN.

❑ For a bus NIC installation, first install the NIC, then, if it is an Ethernet NIC, connect the cable, and lastly start up the computer and install the drivers.

❑ The order of things differs for a USB or FireWire NIC. First, install the software, and then connect the NIC to the computer. Finally, connect the NIC to the network.

❑ When connecting to a wired Ethernet network, use CAT5 or better UTP cabling with an RJ45 connector. Connect one end to the NIC and the other to the wall jack, or directly to a hub or switch.

❑ Once a NIC connects to the network and the drivers are installed, configure the TCP/IP properties. If your network has a DHCP server, you can leave these settings at their default, and your computer will acquire an IP address automatically from the DHCP server.

❑ When creating a Wi-Fi network, check for possible obstacles and interference sources that can block the signal. Signals degrade over distance causing slower data speeds, so verify that the distances between the wireless devices are well within the published signal range of the devices.

❑ A service set ID (SSID) is a network name used to identify a wireless network. All of the wireless devices on a WLAN must use the same SSID in order to communicate

❑ Ad hoc wireless mode is useful for only a very few computers and cannot connect directly to another network.

❑ To connect a wireless network directly to another network you need to use a wireless access point (WAP) and infrastructure mode for all nodes on the network.

❑ You normally do the initial setup of a WAP with a directly wired Ethernet connection between a PC and the WAP. Then you use a Web browser to access the configuration program on the WAP. You can make subsequent changes over the wireless network.

❑ Most WAPs run the DHCP service to give out IP addresses on the WLAN. Most can also do the same over their Ethernet port or ports. If your wired network already has a DHCP server, you will want to disable this service on the WAP for the LAN ports.

❑ Change the default SSID of a WAP to a unique name, change the default user name and password to ones that will not be easily guessed, and set other options, as appropriate for your WLAN.

❑ When Windows installs, it assumes that the TCP/IP configuration should be set to obtain an IP address automatically. If there is a DHCP server on the network, this will be adequate. If not, you must configure IP settings manually, including IP address, subnet mask, Default Gateway, and DNS Server.

❑ The important IP configuration settings are: IP address of the network card; subnet mask, Default Gateway, DNS Server, and WINS Server (if required).

❑ You can install more than one protocol stack in Windows, but we do not recommend it unless it is absolutely necessary because it can slow down network access.

❑ NWLink IPX/SPX is Microsoft's implementation of Novell's IPX/SPX. It only works with the Microsoft Client Service for NetWare.

Sharing Network Resources

❑ A share is the point at which a user, using client software, can access your file system or printers.

❑ Sharing a file or printer requires the Server service and the File and Printer component, which are installed and turned on by default.

❑ Internet Connection Sharing (ICS) turns a Windows computer connected to the Internet into a router to the Internet for other computers that connect to the ICS computer over a second network interface. It is intended only for very small networks and has drawbacks, including the need to keep the ICS computer turned on when the others need to connect, and the fact that it manually reconfigures the IP configuration of the shared connection.

❑ The preferred method for sharing a broadband network connection is through a broadband router.

❑ Simple File Sharing sets very restrictive permissions of Read (only) on all shares and disregards user accounts, assigning all network users to the Guest group, so that you cannot apply less restrictive permissions to the share for individual users and groups.

❑ Simple File Sharing is the only way to share in Windows XP Home Edition. In Windows XP Professional, you can have more control over the permissions on shares if you disable Simple File Sharing.

❑ Turn on sharing for a printer in the Add Printer Wizard during the installation process or from the Properties of the printer.

❑ Turn on sharing for files on the Sharing tab of the Properties of a folder. First, browse to the folder and open the Properties dialog box.

❑ A share name can be different from a file folder name.

❑ A file share and the file folder that it points to each can have a unique name. Users connecting over the network see the share name, but only local users see a folder name in the file system.

❑ Windows 2000 Professional and Windows XP Professional have a limit of ten simultaneous user connections. Additional connections will fail until a connection is released.

❑ Standard NTFS folder permissions are Full Control, Modify, Read and Execute, List Folder Contents, Read, and Write.

❑ Standard NTFS file permissions are Full Control, Modify, Read and Execute, Read, and Write.

❑ A user connecting to a share on an NTFS volume is affected by both the share permissions and the NTFS permissions on the folder and the files.

❑ Sharing an Internet connection to a single Windows computer is much like sharing an Internet connection to a LAN, except that it requires a computer to act as a router to its Internet connection, such as a dial-up connection. We don't recommend this for sharing a broadband connection, which is better shared among computers via a separate device called a broadband router.

Accessing Network Resources

❑ A Microsoft workgroup has a distributed administration model, meaning that someone must do the work of creating shares and assigning permission to those shares on each computer that shares its files and/or printers. This does not scale well as the number of participating computers grows.

❑ The domain model uses a centralized administration model, allowing one administrator, or just a relatively few administrators, to perform the administrative tasks for a great number of computers, both client and server computers, from one or more centralized locations.

❑ Local accounts exist in the local security accounts database in each Windows computer that directly evolved from the Windows NT operating system. These include Windows 2000, Windows XP, and Windows Vista.

❑ Local user accounts are used for authentication, and normally represent a single person. Authentication is validation of a user account that must occur before the security components of Windows give the user access to the computer.

❑ A local group can contain one or more local user accounts, and when the computer is a member of a Windows domain, a local group may contain domain users and groups from the same domain and trusted domains.

❑ The local security accounts database for Windows 2000 and Windows XP is created with two default user accounts: Administrator and Guest.

❑ What the user can do on that computer is determined by the authorization process, which assesses the permissions assigned to the user to each requested resource (like a file share).

❑ Windows 2000 Professional and Windows XP Professional each have two administrative tools—one simple and one more complex. In Windows 2000 Professional, the simple tool is Users and Passwords, while Windows XP has the User Accounts applet.

❑ Users and Passwords and User Accounts are the preferred tools to use if your computer is a member of a workgroup and only a few users log on to each computer or access shares on the computer over the network.

❑ In both versions of Windows, more experienced administrators use the more complex tool—the Local Users and Groups node of the Computer Management console.

❑ Both the Windows XP User Accounts applet and the Windows 2000 Professional Users and Passwords applet hide the complete list of user groups, using a simple reference to account types defined by an account's group membership.

❑ If a Windows computer is a member of a domain, each user must log on with a domain user account.

❑ A Windows NT domain has two types of groups: local and global. An Active Directory domain has domain local and global groups.

❑ Special groups have predefined members and are only available when you assign permissions or rights. In Windows 2000, these are called special groups, but some of the documentation for Windows XP refers to these groups as built-in security principals.

❑ The Creator Owner special group's membership consists of the user who created a file or folder. The System special group contains just the operating system, and the Everyone special group includes all users on a network, even those who have not been authenticated.

❑ All Windows computers can join a workgroup simply by specifying the workgroup name (up to 15 alphanumeric characters) in the user interface for joining a workgroup.

❑ Only computers running versions of Windows that maintain local security accounts databases can join a domain. For a user to log on to a domain from one of these computers, that computer must first be a member of the domain within which the user has an account, or a member of a domain that trusts the user's domain.

❑ Computers running Windows 9x or Windows XP Home cannot join a domain. However, a Windows 9x computer can be configured to allow a user to log on to a domain, but this is not true of a Windows XP Home computer.

❑ View workgroups, domains, and computers in Network Places. The only computers that are visible are either true servers or Windows desktop computers with file and printer sharing turned on. Other computers on the network will not be visible.

❑ The Client for Microsoft Networks is the client component that allows a Windows computer to view and connect to Windows servers on the network. It automatically installs in Windows.

❑ You can optionally add one of the Novell clients (from Microsoft or Novell) to your Windows computer, and view and log on to Novell servers.

Installing and Configuring Web Browsers

❑ A Web browser is software that transfers the contents of a Web page to a computer, and translates the plain-text language into a rich, colorful document.

❑ The two most common Web browsers for Windows computers are Microsoft Internet Explorer (IE) and Mozilla Firefox.

❑ IE is installed in Windows by default, and, while you can and should upgrade it as updates and new versions are available, do not uninstall it from Windows—even if you install a second browser.

❑ Web pages that use ActiveX programs may not appear correctly in Firefox, and some that use Java scripts may not appear correctly in IE. When this occurs, use the other browser to open the problem Web page.

❑ Configure IE 7 through its Tools menu where you can turn on and configure the Pop-up Blocker, turn on and configure a Phishing Filter, manage add-ons, run Windows Update, diagnose connection problems, and open the Internet Options dialog box, which has pages of settings to further configure IE.

❑ Mozilla Firefox is an increasingly popular free Web browser that is not as big a target of malicious attacks as is the more prevalent IE. Download Firefox from www.mozilla.com.

❑ Configure Firefox from Tools | Options. Be sure to configure it to update automatically.

❑ A proxy server handles requests for Internet resources, such as Web pages, files on an FTP server, and mail for a proxy client. It does this without directly exposing the proxy client's IP address to the Internet. Proxy servers combine services and accept requests for HTTP, FTP, POP3, SMTP, and other types of services.

❑ To configure Windows XP to use a proxy server, open Control Panel | Internet Options and click the Connections tab. You can configure a proxy server for a dial-up connection or for a LAN connection in the Internet Options Control Panel applet.

SELF TEST

The following questions will help you measure your understanding of the material presented in this chapter. Read all of the choices carefully because there might be more than one correct answer. Choose all correct answers for each question.

Installing and Configuring Networks

1. What is the first step in connecting a client computer to a LAN?
- A. Finding an ISP
- B. Installing a proxy server
- C. Configuring TCP/IP
- D. Installing a NIC

2. What are the two connections required for every PC NIC?
- A. Computer and network
- B. USB and FireWire
- C. Bus and PC Card
- D. Wi-Fi and Ethernet

3. What is the normal order for installing a USB NIC and driver in Windows?
- A. First install the NIC, and then install the driver.
- B. First install TCP/IP, and then install the driver.
- C. First install the driver, and then connect the NIC.
- D. Insert the NIC in the PC Card slot, and then install the driver.

4. What is the normal order for installing a bus NIC and driver in Windows?
- A. First install the NIC, and then install the driver.
- B. First connect the Ethernet cable, and then install the NIC.
- C. First install the driver, and then connect the NIC.
- D. Insert the NIC in the PC Card slot, and then install the driver.

5. What is one way to determine the standard used in a PCMCIA slot in a laptop?
- A. Purchase and test a card in the slot.
- B. Use Task Manager to view the properties of the controller.
- C. Read the label on the bottom of the laptop case.
- D. Use Device Manager to view the CardBus Controller.

6. What secures an RJ45 connector to an outlet on a PC or switch?

   A. A torx screw

   B. A clip on the connector

   C. A latch on the outlet

   D. A slot cover

7. What term describes a name that identifies a wireless network?

   A. BSS

   B. IBSS

   C. SSID

   D. WAP

8. What radio band do three Wi-Fi wireless standards use?

   A. 2.4 GHz

   B. 4.2 GHz

   C. 5 GHz

   D. 7 GHz

9. What happens as you move a wireless NIC and host computer further away from a WAP?

   A. Signal increases.

   B. Connection speed is increased.

   C. No change.

   D. Connection speed is reduced.

Sharing Network Resources

10. Which server role is included by default in all Windows desktop and server computers?

   A. Proxy server

   B. Database server

   C. File and Printer server

   D. Backup server

11. When a share on a Windows XP computer points to a folder on a FAT32 volume, what permissions apply to network users?

   A. Share-level, file, and folder permissions

   B. Share-level and folder permissions

   C. Only share-level permissions

   D. Only file and folder permissions

12. When a share on a Windows XP computer points to a folder on a FAT32 volume, what permissions apply to local users?

    A. Share-level, file, and folder permissions

    B. No permissions

    C. Only share-level permissions

    D. Only file and folder permissions

13. When a network user accesses a share that exists on an NTFS volume, what is the effect of combining the share-level and NTFS permissions?

    A. Least restrictive permissions apply.

    B. Most restrictive permissions apply.

    C. Full Control permission is granted.

    D. Only the Read permission is granted.

Accessing Network Resources

14. To what type of administrative organization does a Windows computer that is solely part of a peer-to-peer network belong?

    A. Domain

    B. Workgroup

    C. Group

    D. Security Account

15. How can a single computer be both a client and a server?

    A. By having both client and a server services installed and enabled

    B. By having the Client Service for NetWare installed

    C. By having the Client for Microsoft Networks installed

    D. By having a Web browser installed

16. In a Windows Active Directory domain which of the following *cannot* be members of a domain local group?

    A. User accounts from the same domain

    B. Shared folders

    C. Global groups from the same domain

    D. Global groups from a trusted domain

17. Where in Windows XP can I view Windows servers on the network?
- **A.** Client Service for NetWare
- **B.** My Network Places
- **C.** Outlook Express
- **D.** Network Connections

18. What is the preferred client for connecting to Novell servers from a Windows computer?
- **A.** Microsoft Client Service for NetWare
- **B.** Novell Client by Novell for Windows
- **C.** My Network Places
- **D.** Network Connections

Installing and Configuring Web Browsers

19. What is the recommend action to take when you install Firefox?
- **A.** Uninstall Internet Explorer
- **B.** Disable Internet Explorer
- **C.** Leave Internet Explorer installed
- **D.** Make Internet Explorer the default browser

20. What service handles requests for Internet services for a client without exposing the client's IP address to the Internet?
- **A.** File and Printer
- **B.** Server Message Block
- **C.** Proxy
- **D.** Common Internet File System

LAB QUESTION

Rather than answer a question, build a network. Maybe you can do this at school through some special arrangement, or at home. Or maybe you work in a company that supports your effort to prepare for the A+ exams. Building even the simplest of networks is a good hands-on learning experience.

Use as few as two computers, each with a NIC, and each with Windows 2000 Professional or newer. Connect the computers. If you are connecting only two computers, assuming that the NICs are Ethernet, you could use a simple Ethernet cross-over cable to connect them directly. Otherwise, if you have an Ethernet hub or switch, you can connect each computer to that device using a standard Ethernet cable from each computer to the hub or switch.

SELF TEST ANSWERS

Installing and Configuring Networks

1. ☑ **D.** Installing a NIC is the first step to connecting a client computer to a LAN.
    ☒ **A**, finding an ISP, is incorrect because it is not necessary to have an ISP in order to connect to a LAN. **B**, installing a proxy server, is incorrect because you would not normally install a proxy server on a client computer, and it is definitely not the first step in connecting a computer to a LAN. **C**, configuring TCP/IP, while an important step, is not the first step in connecting a computer to a LAN.

2. ☑ **A.** Computer and network are the two connections required for every PC NIC.
    ☒ **B**, USB and FireWire, is incorrect because both of these are computer connections, and with each a connection to a network (wired or wireless) is required. **C**, bus and PC Card, is incorrect because both of these are computer connections, and with each a connection to a network (wired or wireless) is also required. **D**, Wi-Fi and Ethernet, is incorrect because both of these are network connections, and with each a connection to a computer is also required.

3. ☑ **C.** To first install the driver and then connect the NIC is the correct order for installing a USB NIC.
    ☒ **A**, first install the NIC, and then install the driver, is incorrect because this is not the normal order for installing a USB NIC. **B**, first install TCP/IP, is incorrect because this has nothing to do with the installation of a USB NIC, and a protocol stack can be installed before or after the installation of a NIC. It is installed in Windows by default. **D**, insert the NIC in the PC Card slot, and then install the driver, is incorrect because a PC Card slot has nothing to do with the normal installation of a USB NIC.

4. ☑ **A.** To first install the NIC and then install the driver is the normal order for installing a bus NIC in Windows.
    ☒ **B**, first connect the Ethernet cable, and then install the NIC, is incorrect because this is not a correct order described in the book, and it does not mention installing the driver. **C**, first install the driver, and then connect the NIC, is incorrect because this is the order for installing a USB NIC. **D**, insert the NIC in the PC Card slot, and then install the driver, is incorrect because a PC Card slot has nothing to do with the normal installation of a bus NIC.

5. ☑ **D.** To use Device Manager to view the CardBus Controller is correct.
    ☒ **A**, purchase and test a card in the slot, is incorrect because you should determine the type of slot and therefore the type of card before purchasing one. **B**, use Task Manager to view the properties of the controller, is incorrect because Task Manager does not display the properties of a controller. **C**, read the label on the bottom of the laptop, is incorrect because laptop manufacturers do not usually put this information in a label on the case.

6. ☑ **B.** A clip on the connector is what secures an RJ45 connector to an outlet on a PC or switch.
☒ **A**, a torx screw, is incorrect because this is not used to secure an RJ45 connector to an outlet on a PC or switch. **C**, a latch on the outlet, is incorrect because, while the outlet has a notch into which the connector clip fits, this is not a latch. **D**, a slot cover, is incorrect because this covers an empty slot in the back of a PC and does not secure an RJ45 connector to an outlet on a PC or switch.

7. ☑ **C.** SSID, or Service Set ID, is the term that describes a name that identifies a wireless network.
☒ **A**, BSS, or Basic Service Set, is incorrect because this term describes the wireless nodes (including the WAP) communicating together in infrastructure mode. **B**, IBSS, or Independent Basic Service Set, is incorrect because this term describes the wireless nodes communicating together in ad hoc mode. **D**, WAP, or Wireless Access Point, is incorrect because this is a hub for a wireless network.

8. ☑ **A.** 2.4 GHz is the band used by three Wi-Fi wireless standards: 802.11b, 802.11g, and 802.11n (just one of two bands used by this last standard).
☒ **B**, 4.2 GHz, is incorrect because none of the Wi-Fi wireless standards use it. **C**, 5 GHz, is incorrect because only two of the Wi-Fi wireless standards use it: 802.11a and 802.11n (just one of two bands used by 802.11n). **D**, 7 GHz, is incorrect because none of the Wi-Fi wireless standards use it.

9. ☑ **D.** Connection speed is reduced as you move a wireless NIC and host computer further away from a WAP.
☒ **A**, signal increases, is incorrect because the opposite happens as you move a wireless NIC and host computer further away from a WAP. **B**, connection speed is increased, is incorrect because the opposite happens as you move a wireless NIC and host computer further away from a WAP. **C**, no change, is incorrect because there definitely is a decrease in connection speed because the signal degrades as distance increases.

Sharing Network Resources

10. ☑ **C.** File and Printer server is the role included by default in Windows desktop and server computers.
☒ **A**, proxy server, is incorrect because this server role is not included in all Windows desktop and server computers. A proxy client is included for a few services and must be configured in order to work. **B**, database server, is incorrect because this server role is not included in all Windows desktop and server computers. **D**, backup server, is incorrect because this server role is not included in all Windows desktop and server computers.

11. ☑ **C.** Only share-level permissions are applied to network users connecting to a share on a Windows XP computer that points to a folder on a FAT32 volume. It is not possible to apply file and folder permissions in this file system.

☒ **A**, share-level, file, and folder permissions, is incorrect because it is not possible to apply file and folder permissions in the FAT32 file system. **B**, share-level and folder permissions, is incorrect because it is not possible to apply file and folder permissions in the FAT32 file system. **D**, only file and folder permissions, is incorrect because it is not possible to apply file and folder permissions in the FAT32 file system.

12. ☑ **B.** No permissions are applied to local users when a share points to a folder on a FAT32 volume because they access the file system directly, not through the share.

☒ **A**, share-level, file, and folder permissions, is incorrect for two reasons. First, local users do not need to connect through a share where share-level permissions apply, and second, it is not possible to apply file and folder permissions in the FAT32 file system. **C**, only share-level permissions, is incorrect because the local users do not need to connect through a share where share-level permissions apply. **D**, only file and folder permissions, is incorrect because it is not possible to apply file and folder permissions in the FAT32 file system.

13. ☑ **B.** Most restrictive permissions apply when a network user accesses a share that exists on an NTFS volume and the share-level and NTFS permissions are combined.

☒ **A**, least restrictive permissions apply, is incorrect because least restrictive only applies when you combine folder and file NTFS permissions. **C**, Full Control permission, is only granted when you combine share-level and NTFS permissions if both have Full Control permission. **D**, only the Read permission is granted, applies only if the Read permission is on either the share or NTFS permissions, and if this is the most restrictive permission of the two levels.

Accessing Network Resources

14. ☑ **B.** Workgroup is the type of administrative organization to which a Windows computer belongs if it is solely part of a peer-to-peer network.

☒ **A**, domain, is incorrect because this is not the type of administrative organization used in a peer-to-peer network. **C**, group, is incorrect because this is not a type of administrative organization but a type of account in a security accounts database. **D**, Security Account, is incorrect because this is not a type of administrative organization.

15. ☑ **A.** A single computer can be both a client and a server by having both client and server services installed and enabled.

☒ **B**, by having the Client Service for NetWare installed, is incorrect because this only makes a computer a client in a NetWare network, not a server. **C**, by having the Client for Microsoft Networks installed, is incorrect because this is only the client side; the file and printer service is the other half that would make this both a client and server for Microsoft's server service. **D**, by having a Web browser installed, is incorrect because this is only the client for a Web server, so it would require that the Web server service be installed for the computer to be both client and server for this service.

16. ☑ **B.** Shared folders cannot be members of a domain local group.

    ☒ **A**, user accounts from the same domain, **C**, global groups from the same domain, and **D**, global groups from a trusted domain, are all incorrect because these *can* all be members of a domain local group.

17. ☑ **B.** My Network Places is where you can view Windows servers on the network.

    ☒ **A**, Client Service for NetWare, **C**, Outlook Express, and **D**, Network Connections, are incorrect because these are not places you can view Windows servers on the network.

18. ☑ **B.** Novell Client by Novell for Windows is correct.

    ☒ **A**, Microsoft Client Service for NetWare, is incorrect because this is not the preferred client for connecting to Novell servers from a Windows computer in most cases, although there may be situations in which this one is the preferred client. **C**, My Network Places, is incorrect because My Network Places is not a client but a user interface for viewing workgroups, domains, and servers on a network. **D**, Network Connections, is incorrect because this is not a client but a tool for viewing network connection status and modifying network connection properties.

Installing and Configuring Web Browsers

19. ☑ **C.** To leave Internet Explorer installed is the recommended action to take when you install Firefox because some Web pages appear better in Internet Explorer than in Firefox. The opposite is also true.

    ☒ **A**, uninstall Internet Explorer, is incorrect because some Web pages appear better in Internet Explorer than in Firefox. **B**, disable Internet Explorer, is incorrect because some Web pages appear better in Internet Explorer than in Firefox. **D**, make Internet Explorer the default browser, is incorrect because you can set either of these browsers as the default, which only affects which browser opens automatically when the user clicks on a URL.

20. ☑ **C.** The Proxy service handles requests for Internet services for a client without exposing the client to the Internet.

    ☒ **A**, File and Printer, is incorrect because this is the component for sharing files and printers, not the service that handles requests for Internet services for a client without exposing the client's IP address to the Internet. **B**, Server Message Block, and **D**, Common Internet File System, are incorrect because they are both file sharing protocols, not the service that handles requests for Internet services for a client without exposing the client's IP address to the Internet.

LAB ANSWER

There is no single correct answer to this lab because it is completely hands-on and depends on the availability of equipment and software for your use.

14
Troubleshooting Networks

To troubleshoot networks, a PC professional must call on all the skills required for hardware and software support, plus apply a structured approach to determining the problem, applying solutions, and testing. However, keep in mind that if you make all connections properly, and all the hardware is working properly, the most common problems will involve the TCP/IP configuration of NICs.

While there are many network problems only a trained network specialist can resolve, there are also many common and simple network problems that you will be able to resolve without extensive training and experience. There are also certain tests you can run that will give you important information to pass on to more highly trained network specialists, such as those in a large corporation or at your local ISP.

In this chapter you will explore the tools and techniques for troubleshooting common network problems. You will also learn about preventive maintenance tasks for networks.

CERTIFICATION OBJECTIVES

- **601: 5.3   603: 4.3**   *Identify tools, diagnostic procedures, and troubleshooting techniques for networks*

- **602: 5.3**   *Use tools and diagnostic procedures to troubleshoot network problems*

  CompTIA expects the A+ certification candidates for the 601, 602, and 603 exams to be prepared to troubleshoot common network problems. However, in-depth knowledge of networks is not required for these exams, because there is a separate CompTIA certification for network technicians: Network+. Be prepared to identify hardware and software tools for basic network troubleshooting and understand how they are used. You should practice and review troubleshooting techniques for networks.

Tools for Network Troubleshooting

There are many tools for network troubleshooting. In this section learn about basic network troubleshooting tools the A+ certification candidate should know how to use. These include status indicators, command-line utilities, cable testers, Remote Desktop, and Remote Assistance.

Status Indicators

Status indicators for network hardware include LED lights on the physical device itself, and/or software installed along with the driver. With a quick glance at the lights on a device, or icons and messages on your computer screen, you will know that the device is powered up, that it is receiving and transmitting data, and (in the case of wireless devices) the strength of the signal.

Most NICs—both Ethernet and Wi-Fi—install with a configuration utility that can be opened from an icon in the system tray of the taskbar. A balloon message may appear over the system tray when the status of one of these devices changes. The icon may also change to indicate the current status, and pausing your mouse over one of these icons will cause it to display the status of the devices. Figure 14-1 shows a status message that appeared when we passed a mouse over the status icon for the Local Area Connection. The icon for this connection also had a red "X" over it, so we knew there was a problem.

Command-Line Tools

If you are unable to access another computer on the network, several command-line utilities will help in pinpointing the source of a problem and arriving at a solution. When the TCP/IP protocol suite installs into Windows, it also installs a variety of command-line tools, such as IPCONFIG, PING, TRACERT, NETSTAT, and NSLOOKUP. These are the handiest and cheapest tools you can use for network troubleshooting.

Later in this chapter we describe common problems and how to use command-line tools for each of them. Each utility provides different information and is most valuable when used appropriately. For instance, you should first view the IP configuration using the IPCONFIG utility and verify that it is correct for the network to which you are connected. If you discover any obvious problems when you view the IP configuration, correct them before proceeding. Then, select the tool that will help you diagnose and—in some instances—resolve the problem.

One more important note about command-line tools: most of them have many optional parameters you can enter at the command line to change the behavior of

FIGURE 14-1   A status message that appeared when the mouse was paused over the icon for the Local Area Connection

```
Local Area Connection
A network cable is unplugged.
```

the command. In this book, we provide the simplest and/or most often used syntax. If you would like to learn more about each command, simply open a command prompt in Windows and enter the command name followed by a space, a slash, and a question mark followed by the ENTER key. For the IPCONFIG command enter the following: **ipconfig /?**.

on the
Job

When entering commands at the command prompt, separate the command name, such as "ipconfig," from any parameters with a space. In the case of "ipconfig /?" the slash and question mark together comprise a parameter and are separated from the command name with a space. Do not insert a space between the slash and what follows, such as "?" or "all." If additional parameters must be used, separate each parameter with a space.

Cable Testers

As we stated in the beginning of this chapter, no one expects an A+ candidate to have the knowledge and skills of a network professional, but you should be able to diagnose and correct common network problems. An inexpensive cable testing device, such as the one shown in Figure 14-2, should be included in your hardware toolkit. Notice that there are two separate components: a master unit, and a smaller remote terminator. This makes it possible to connect to each end of a cable when those ends are in separate rooms or even on separate floors. To test an Ethernet cable, plug one end into the master unit and the other end into the remote unit.

FIGURE 14-2

A cable testing
tool

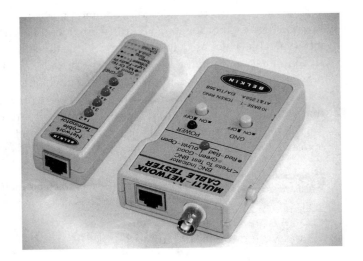

Turn on the master unit and watch the lights on the remote unit. The LEDs on the remote terminator will light up in turn as the master unit sends signals down each pair of wires. If the cable wiring is intact, the LEDs corresponding to each pair will show green. If there is damage to the cable wiring, the LEDs will not light up at all, or may first show green and then turn red. This is true for each pair of wires tested.

Some cable testers will test more than one type of cabling, but in most LANs, being able to test Ethernet cable is very useful and may be all you need.

on the
job

If you use your favorite search engine to query "cable tester" you will find a large selection of cable testers. You are sure to find one that fits your budget and needs. Some vendors, such as Lanshack (www.lanshack.com), publish free tutorials on working with various types of cables.

Remote Desktop

Remote Desktop is a network service available in Windows XP Professional, Windows XP Media Center, and Windows Vista. Although it is not strictly a troubleshooting tool, we include it here as both a productivity tool and a means for troubleshooting Windows problems over a network. Remote Desktop allows a remote user to connect to a Windows computer and have total access to the desktop and local resources, including files, printers, and other attached devices. The remote user can see the remote desktop in a window or as a full-screen view. The entire experience is nearly identical to working physically at the computer.

This is ideal for the user who must work from home but wants access to all the files and programs on his or her office PC. There are other scenarios in which this is a great productivity tool. Perhaps you are on vacation or at work and need to access files and programs on your home computer. Set up Remote Desktop and you are good to go.

exam
watch

In the CompTIA 602 exam objectives, Remote Desktop falls under the Operating Systems domain as a system management tool. While we covered the other related subobjectives in Chapter 7, we include Remote Desktop in this chapter under troubleshooting tools. For the exam, remember its primary function is as a productivity tool, allowing someone to work on his or her own Windows PC from a remote location.

Remote Desktop can also be a tool for a PC professional requiring access to files and programs on a user's computer for troubleshooting and maintenance. Spend a few minutes learning how to set up and use Remote Desktop. Then, in the following section learn about Remote Assistance, a Windows service designed to allow a user to invite someone to help troubleshoot a problem.

Required Windows Versions

Before you can even begin to set up Remote Desktop, you must ensure that you have the correct Windows versions on both computers. While the server side, which is the computer you wish to connect to remotely, must be running Windows XP Professional, Windows XP Media Center, or Windows Vista, the client computer at the remote site can be running Windows 95 or newer. In the following discussion, we assume a scenario in which you need to connect from home to your desktop PC at work.

Preparing the Server Side of Remote Desktop

On the server side (the desktop PC at your workplace), open Control Panel and double-click the System icon. In the System Properties dialog box, shown in Figure 14-3, open the Remote tab. Select "Allow users to connect remotely to this computer" and click OK. When you make this change, Windows also modifies Windows Firewall to allow Remote Desktop messages to pass through the firewall.

Turn on Remote Desktop.

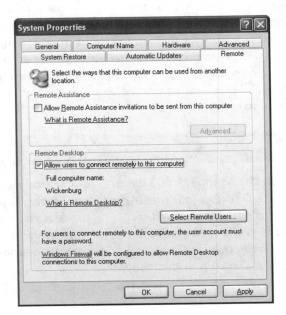

If you have disabled Windows Firewall and are using a third-party firewall, you will need to check the manufacturer's instructions. In this case, you need to make an exception so that the firewall will allow the Remote Desktop messages through. To do this, you need to find how to configure the firewall to allow traffic that is using TCP port 3389.

Now, while you are working on the office PC, you also need to make a note of the computer name or domain name and the IP address. Even if you are sure you know the computer name or domain name, double-check it now by opening the System applet in Control Panel and selecting the Computer Name tab. If your computer is a member of a workgroup, you will need the computer name. If it is a member of a domain, you will need the domain name.

In the middle of the Computer Name page you will see either Domain or Workgroup followed by a name. If a domain name shows, write down that name. If a workgroup name shows, write down the name shown after Full Computer Name. You will need this name when you are configuring the client (remote) side of Remote Desktop. The reason for this is that you will need to configure the remote client to log on just as you do at work. That is, if your computer is a member of a domain, you will log on to the domain with your user name and password. If the computer is a member of a workgroup, you will log on to the computer itself. When you have collected this information, close the System Properties dialog box.

Now find the IP address of the work PC using the IPCONFIG command. If you need help with the command, flip back to Exercise 12-3 in Chapter 12. Write down the IP address. You will need the IP address and computer name or domain when you configure the Remote Desktop client.

Preparing the Client Side of Remote Desktop

In this scenario the client computer is the computer you will use from a remote location to connect to your office PC. If the Remote Desktop Connection client software is not yet installed on the remote computer, you will need to download it from the Microsoft Web site (www.microsoft.com). Connect to this site and search on "download remote desktop connection." Follow the instructions provided with the download to install Remote Desktop Connection for the client computer.

Once the Remote Desktop Connection software is installed, start the program from Start | All Programs | Accessories | Communications | Remote Desktop Connection. Enter the IP address of your office PC in the box labeled Computer. Click Options, and on the General tab page type the user name and password for your office computer. If your office computer is in a domain, enter the domain name in the domain box. If the computer is a member of a workgroup, enter the computer name.

Click Connect, and a window will open on your desktop containing the desktop of your office computer. You will have access to all programs and files, just as if you were sitting at that computer.

There are several third-party programs that you could use for the same purpose. Just a few are GoToMyPC, LapLink Everywhere, and Anyplace Control.

Remote Assistance

Remote Assistance is another service that is available for connecting computers running Windows XP (including Home Edition) or Windows Vista. The major difference between this and Remote Desktop is that Remote Assistance requires Windows Messenger to run, and the user needing assistance must send an invitation. A remote assistant cannot connect without this invitation.

There are three requirements for using Remote Assistance:

- Both computers must be running Windows XP Professional or Windows XP Home Edition.
- Both computers must be connected via a network.
- Both computers must have Windows Messenger installed.

In addition, the computer seeking assistance must have a Remote Assistance setting turned on. Do this by opening the System applet in Control Panel, selecting the Remote tab, and placing a check in the box labeled "Allow Remote Assistance invitations to be sent from this computer" (see Figure 14-4). Click OK to close the System Properties dialog box.

If a user has a problem with a computer and still has network access, the user can send a remote assistance request to someone who can help solve the problem. This request allows another person to remotely access the computer over any network. The person providing this assistance can be anyone the user knows and trusts who has the skills to help. In the discussions that follow we refer to this person as a remote assistant.

Requesting Remote Assistance

As a computer professional, you may find yourself on either side of this service and should understand how to initiate it. There are three ways to request assistance and to initiate the session that allows the remote assistant to remotely access a computer: via Windows Messenger, via e-mail, and by sending a file. In all the methods described, you will need to set a password for the Remote Assistance session. It is up to you to communicate this password separately to the person you are asking to help you.

FIGURE 14-4

The computer
requesting
help must have
the Remote
Assistance setting
enabled.

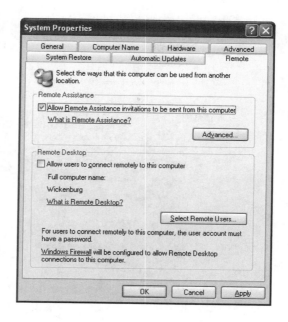

Consider doing this via phone or in a separate e-mail message. We wrote the following descriptions as if you are the person requesting remote assistance, but be sure that you understand both roles in the Remote Assistance transaction.

Before requesting remote assistance, check your firewall settings. If you are using Windows Firewall in Windows XP, open the Windows Firewall applet from Control Panel. On the General page remove the check (if one exists) from the check box labeled Don't Allow Exceptions. Click the Exceptions tab, and on the Exceptions page scroll through the list of Programs and Services and place a check in the box labeled Remote Assistance. Click OK to close the Windows Firewall dialog box. If you are using the Windows Vista Firewall, the steps are similar for allowing incoming Remote Assistance traffic.

If you have disabled Windows Firewall and are using another firewall, you will need to check the manufacturer's instructions.

With all three methods of sending an invitation you can begin the process by opening Windows Help and Support, available from the Start menu. Under Ask For Assistance click "Invite a friend to connect to your computer with Remote Assistance"; on the next page select "Invite someone to help you." This will open the Remote Assistance page shown in Figure 14-5. Notice the choices for contacting your assistant. Select one of these, and it will guide you through the process of sending the invitation.

FIGURE 14-5

Select the method for contacting your assistant.

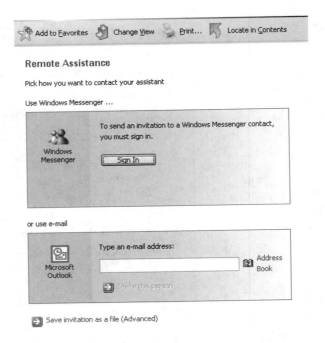

Requesting Assistance via Windows Messenger   You can send a request for remote assistance via Windows Messenger. This requires that you have Windows Messenger enabled on your computer and that the person you wish to ask for help is in your list of contacts. If the remote assistant is not in your contacts list, you will need to add this person's information, including e-mail address. You can begin this method either from Help and Support, as just described, or directly from Windows Messenger. The instructions that follow are for Windows Messenger.

Open Windows Messenger and enter your user name and password. Open the Tools menu and select "Ask For Remote Assistance." Select the remote assistant who can help you from your list of contacts. Alternatively, if you are already in a Windows Messenger session, simply click Invite and select "To Start Remote Assistance," and click the e-mail address of the remote assistant.

At this point, the remote assistant will receive an instant message in Windows Messenger and must first click Accept, which will result in the display of a password dialog box.

Once the assistant enters the password and clicks Yes, the Remote Assistance session window opens on his desktop. He must click Take Control.

The assistant's computer sends a request to your computer and a dialog box opens requesting your permission. Click Yes to continue. Your Windows desktop appears in the largest pane of the Remote Assistance window on his computer. The remote assistant should click the Show Chat button in the top-left corner of the Remote Assistance window so that you can continue chatting as you work together to solve your problem.

During the session both you and the remote assistant can control the mouse and keyboard while trying to solve a problem.

Requesting Assistance via E-Mail

Use Windows Help and Support Center to initiate a Remote Assistance request via an e-mail message. On the main page locate Ask For Assistance and select "Invite a friend to connect to your computer with Remote Assistance." On the Remote Assistance page select "Invite someone to help you." On the next page enter the e-mail address of a remote assistant, and then click the green arrow labeled Invite This Person.

On the E-Mail An Invitation page enter your name, and then type a message describing the problem. You will need to set an expiration time for the session and create a password. Remember to communicate the password separately to the remote assistant.

The remote assistant must open the e-mail message and its attachment, enter the password in the dialog box, and click Yes. The Remote Assistance screen will open, and the remote assistant must click Take Control, which will result in a message appearing on your computer requesting your permission. Click Yes to give your permission and continue. Now the remote assistant can proceed with the session.

Remote Assistance via a File

You can create a Remote Assistance invitation in a file that you can then send to the remote assistant via any mode you wish. You can post it to an FTP site, send it as an attachment to an e-mail, give it to the remote assistant on a flash drive, or use any other mode of transferring the file.

First create the file and then send it to the remote assistant. To get to the page that will create the file, open the Help and Support Center and select "Invite a friend to connect to your computer with Remote Assistance," and then select "Invite someone to help you." Finally, select "Save invitation as a file (Advanced)."

On the Remote Assistance—Save Invitation page (shown in Figure 14-6), enter your name and then set the time after which the invitation will expire. Click Continue.

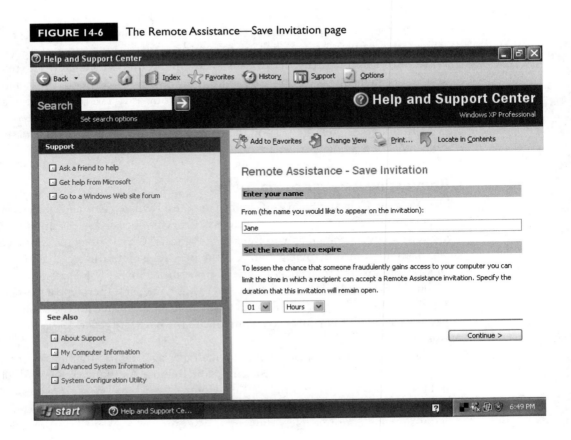

FIGURE 14-6   The Remote Assistance—Save Invitation page

On the next page, enter the password the user must enter to access your computer. You will need to send this password separately to the remote assistant. Click Save Invitation to save the file. A Save As dialog box will open, and you can select the location for saving the file.

Inform the remote assistant of the password, and that when he double-clicks the file, it will open the Remote Assistance Invitation, which will show your name (or the name you provided), the time the invitation expires, and a password box. When the remote assistant enters a password and clicks Yes, a message box will display "Attempting to start remote assistance session." Meanwhile, you will receive a message on your computer requesting your permission. Click Yes to give your permission and continue. Now the remote assistant can proceed with the session.

SCENARIO & SOLUTION

My wireless NIC contains no status lights. How can I tell if it is working?	Look in the system tray for an icon for the NIC. Double-click the icon to open a configuration utility, which will show the status.
I have heard experienced technicians talk about network utilities like "ipconfig" and "ping," but I cannot find these programs listed anywhere on the Start menu. Where are they?	You will not find these programs on the Start menu because they are command-line tools that you must enter from the command prompt. Enter the name of one of these followed by a /? to learn more about it.
I am having trouble understanding the difference between Remote Desktop and Remote Assistance. Which one should I use to help a new user with a Windows problem?	Remote Desktop mainly exists as a means for someone to access their own PC from a remote location, while Remote Assistance is a way for a user to invite someone to act as a remote assistant and help solve a problem. This is the one you should use to help the new user.

Troubleshooting Common Network Problems

When troubleshooting network problems, keep in mind the troubleshooting theory and techniques you learned in Chapter 4 and assess the problem systematically. In the case of bandwidth problems, you often must rely on the user's perception of network slowness. Learn techniques for reducing the unnecessary use of bandwidth, and then learn ways to increase the bandwidth. Connectivity problems are more obvious because the user simply fails to connect to a computer and usually receives an error message. For the PC technician supporting connectivity problems involving the Internet, there are literally worlds of possible locations for the problems. Learn how to pinpoint a connection problem from the local computer to Internet routers. Finally, when you see error messages associated with a NIC that is no longer present on the computer, learn a technique for removing the driver to eliminate these messages.

Resolving Insufficient Bandwidth

Chapter 12 described bandwidth as the amount of data that can travel over a network at a given time. If a user perceives a network to be slow, increasing the bandwidth can improve its speed. The more data you can send at once, the faster data will move from beginning to end, and the faster the network will run overall.

There are two ways to increase bandwidth. One is the low-cost method of reducing the sources of broadcasts, and the second, more costly, method is hardware upgrade.

Reducing Sources of Network Broadcasts

Most protocols suites have at least a few subprotocols that rely on network broadcasts. While these broadcasts do not cross routers, they still persist within the network segments between routers, thus taking up valuable bandwidth. Reduce these sources by first searching for the unnecessary protocol suites, and then look within the suites that are necessary and reduce the amount of broadcasting within those suites.

The following section describes how to remove entire suites from a network by checking computers and network devices for installed suites that are not truly necessary to connect to any network resources. The section following describes what to do if you discover that certain client computers have the NWLink protocol stack installed. If this is truly required to connect to servers, and you must leave this protocol on these clients, learn how to configure NWLink to reduce broadcasts from the clients.

Removing Unnecessary Protocol Suites
Before spending money to increase the bandwidth of a network, first look for inefficient use of bandwidth. You do not have to be a network technician to do this. One inefficient use of network bandwidth is when unnecessary network protocol suites exist on a network. Why is this a problem? Because all protocol suites do some broadcasting on the local network, even when no other host is using the same protocol. A broadcast is a transmission of packets addressed to all nodes on a network. With some protocols, especially NetBEUI, there is a great deal of broadcast traffic. Broadcast traffic is, to some extent, unavoidable within a network segment, but too much of it takes up bandwidth needed for other traffic.

The very nature of NetBEUI is to broadcast. Each node sends out broadcasts saying that it is on the network. (Hey there, I'm up and running.) This is true even if there are no other NetBEUI nodes on the network. This is a waste of bandwidth.

Why do unnecessary protocols exist on a network? As you know, you can install more than one protocol suite on a Windows computer. Some technicians still believe that they should always install NetBEUI on a computer, even when all the hosts on a network are using TCP/IP. This stems from a very old technician's trick of installing NetBEUI as a very easy protocol suite to work with for downloading software images to a computer. If you find NetBEUI installed on a computer, and there is no reason to have it, remove it. The same goes for Novell's IPX/SPX or Microsoft's NWLink.

When it comes to the use of excess protocol suites, the most common offenders are not usually computers, but print servers, which may come with several protocol suites enabled. Whether a print server is a separate box or integrated into a network printer, find out how to access the print server configuration. In the case of a separate print server box, you will normally enter the print server's IP address into a Web browser's address box and access it remotely. You will need the administrative user name and password to access it. For a print server integrated into a printer, it all depends on its design. Access its configuration through a Web browser, or through a control panel on the printer. In both instances, look for protocols and remove protocol suites that are not required on your network.

Reducing IPX/SPX (NWLink) Broadcasts

NWLink, the Microsoft implementation of IPX/SPX, is a self-configuring protocol. It does not need configuring, but if many clients on a network use this protocol, consider manually configuring it. This will reduce network traffic. When a system using NWLink starts up, the system monitors network traffic and uses the IPX/SPX parameters it detects to configure NWLink. The main configuration element is the frame type, which defines the structure of the IPX frames that carry the message on an IPX/SPX network. Computers can only communicate via IPX/SPX if each one is using the same frame type.

The process of automatically detecting the IPX/SPX frame type generates additional traffic on the transmission media. When a Windows system configured to auto-detect IPX/SPX parameters starts up, it broadcasts packets to determine the frame type used for IPX/SPX. These broadcast packets reach each device on an Ethernet network.

To reduce the amount of traffic, you can specify the Ethernet frame type used by the NetWare systems. Configure this in the properties of the NWLink IPX/SPX, as shown in Figure 14-7. The drop-down box displays the list of frame types. Select the one used by the NetWare servers on the network.

Upgrading Network Hardware

Once you have eliminated unnecessary protocol suites and unnecessary broadcasting, if there is still a bandwidth problem, increase the bandwidth by upgrading the network's components. If the network has any Ethernet hubs, replace them with switches. Recall that a hub takes a signal received on one port and repeats it on all other ports. This consumes bandwidth. A switch, on the other hand, is a more intelligent device, which takes an incoming signal and only sends it to the destination port. This saves bandwidth.

Manually
configure the
frame type to
reduce NWLink
broadcasts.

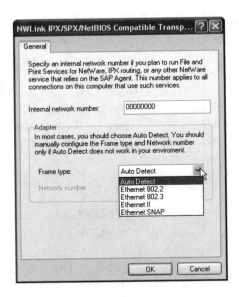

If the network already has switches, then consider upgrading to faster equipment. For example, a LAN with Ethernet (10 Mbps) equipment can be upgraded to Fast Ethernet (100 Mbps), and a network that currently has Fast Ethernet equipment can be upgraded to Gigabit Ethernet (1 to 10 Gbps).

Be sure that when you upgrade to increase bandwidth, the upgrade is thorough. That is, all the NICs, switches, and routers must support the new, higher speed. While the faster equipment is downward compatible with the slower equipment, the network will only be as fast as its slowest hardware component. Also, on an Ethernet network, do not forget to upgrade the cabling to the grade required for the network speed you want to achieve.

Similarly, to upgrade a wireless network, replace slower equipment with newer, faster equipment. Increase signal strength with proper placement of the wireless antenna, and install signal boosters, if necessary.

Troubleshooting Network Connectivity Problems

When you suspect that a computer does not have network connectivity, gather information from error messages and status lights or software status indicators. If no obvious source of the problem is apparent, check the NIC and its connection to the network, and check other connecting hardware, such as hubs, switches, WAPs, and routers. Once you have eliminated hardware as a problem, move on to verifying the IP configuration, and performing tests of the connection using command-line tools.

Checking the Network Hardware

Check the NIC, cables (for a wired network), hub, switch, WAP, and router. Check the NIC by looking at status indicator lights on the NIC itself, if available. Most NICs with status indicator lights have, at minimum, a power light and a link light. The power light only indicates that the NIC is receiving power, but since most NICs receive power from the PC, this is a good indication that the NIC's connection to the PC is working (at least the power lines are). The link light indicates that the connection to the network is live, and it will usually blink when transmitting or receiving. There may be other lights indicating that data is actively transmitting. In addition, some wireless NICs have five LEDs that indicate signal strength, much like the bars on a cell phone. One lit light indicates a poor connection, and five lit lights indicate an excellent connection.

With many Ethernet and wireless NICs now built into computers, you often do not have physical status lights but must rely on status information provided in Windows. Check the system tray on the taskbar for an icon for the NIC.

If you have determined that a NIC has power, but there is no evidence of a connection, take steps to correct this. In the case of a wired Ethernet NIC, check for a loose or damaged cable and examine the RJ-45 connectors for damage. Follow the cable to the hub or switch.

If the cable appears okay, check that the hub, switch, WAP, and router are functioning. Check for power to each device. These devices also have status lights similar to those of NICs. If all the lights are off, check the power supply. In the case of an Ethernet hub or switch, if it has power, look at the status light for each Ethernet connection on the device. If the light is out for the port to which the computer connects, swap the cable with a known good cable, and recheck the status. Also check the cable standard that is in use. You may still find very old CAT3 cabling in use on a Fast Ethernet network. Upgrade the cabling to, at minimum, CAT5e.

Check for any source of electrical interference affecting the cabling. UTP cabling does not have shielding from interference, relying instead on the twists in the cable pairs to resist electromagnetic interference (EMI). Many things can cause EMI. Heavy power cables running parallel to network cabling can cause interference, especially if there are intermittent loads on the power cable such as when a large electric motor starts and stops. Radio frequency interference (RFI) can also affect networks if an RFI generator, such as a poorly shielded electronic device, is located near network cabling.

If you cannot find any physical problems with the NIC, cabling, hub, switch, or WAP, check the IP configuration of the NIC in Network Connections. To do this, open the properties dialog box of the connection and click the Configure button to the right of the Connect Using box that displays the name of the NIC. This opens the Properties dialog box of the NIC.

FIGURE 14-8

Check the device
status in the
Properties
of the NIC.

Figure 14-8 shows the Properties dialog box of a Fast Ethernet NIC with no problems indicated in Device Status. This does not necessarily mean that there is absolutely no problem with the NIC, but when you are first troubleshooting a network problem, accept this opinion at least temporarily, and perform other tests before doing anything drastic, like replacing the NIC.

The following section describes how to use IPCONFIG to view the TCP/IP configuration of a NIC. If this test indicates that nothing could bind to the NIC, then swap out the NIC with an identical NIC, reboot the computer, and test the replacement. This may solve the problem.

Testing IP Configuration and Connectivity

When a computer has the TCP/IP suite installed, it includes many protocols and many handy little programs that computer professionals quickly learn to use. IPCONFIG and PING are two that you should learn right away, if you have not used them before.

Verifying IP Configuration with IPCONFIG   When you are troubleshooting network connectivity problems on an IP network, after eliminating an obviously disconnected or failed NIC use the IPCONFIG command to verify the IP configuration. If you completed Exercise 12-3 in Chapter 12 you already saw what this command can do.

The IPCONFIG command will display the IP configuration of all network interfaces on the local computer, even those that receive their addresses and configuration through DHCP. In fact, if your NIC is a DHCP client, IPCONFIG is the best way to see the resulting IP configuration, since the TCP/IP Properties dialog will only show that it is configured to receive an IP address automatically, and it will not show its IP configuration.

Figure 14-9 shows an example of running the IPCONFIG command on a computer with a single network adapter.

When the output from the IPCONFIG command shows an IP address other than 0.0.0.0, you know that the IP settings have been successfully bound to your network adapter. Bound means that there is a linking relationship, called a binding, between the network protocol and the adapter. A binding establishes the order in which each network component handles network communications.

In addition, when viewing the IP configuration information, verify that each item is correct for the IP network segment on which the NIC is connected. There are three rules to keep in mind when evaluating an IP configuration:

1. The network ID and the subnet mask of each host on an IP segment must match.

2. The Gateway address must be the IP address of a router on the same subnet.

3. Each host on an IP segment must have a unique host ID.

Therefore, if there are other hosts on the same subnet, run IPCONFIG on each of them to determine if all the hosts comply with these rules. If not, correct the problem.

Finally, if the computer in question has an IP address that begins with 169.254, this is an Automatic Private IP Address (APIPA)—an address that a DHCP client

FIGURE 14-9

The result of running the IPCONFIG /ALL command

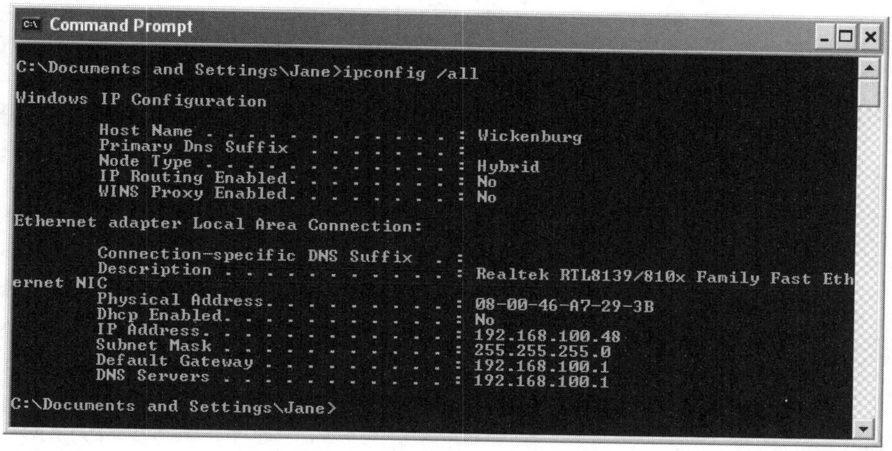

```
Command Prompt                                                           _ □ X

C:\Documents and Settings\Jane>ipconfig /all

Windows IP Configuration

        Host Name . . . . . . . . . . . . : Wickenburg
        Primary Dns Suffix  . . . . . . . :
        Node Type . . . . . . . . . . . . : Hybrid
        IP Routing Enabled. . . . . . . . : No
        WINS Proxy Enabled. . . . . . . . : No

Ethernet adapter Local Area Connection:

        Connection-specific DNS Suffix  . :
        Description . . . . . . . . . . . : Realtek RTL8139/810x Family Fast Eth
ernet NIC
        Physical Address. . . . . . . . . : 08-00-46-A7-29-3B
        Dhcp Enabled. . . . . . . . . . . : No
        IP Address. . . . . . . . . . . . : 192.168.100.48
        Subnet Mask . . . . . . . . . . . : 255.255.255.0
        Default Gateway . . . . . . . . . : 192.168.100.1
        DNS Servers . . . . . . . . . . . : 192.168.100.1

C:\Documents and Settings\Jane>
```

can assign to itself when it cannot reach a DHCP server. If this is a very small network of just a few computers in which all of the computers use APIPA, this may be okay, but in most cases, consider this address a sign of a failure. If possible, check to see if the DHCP server is available. In a large network you will need to contact a network administrator.

In a small or home network, the DHCP server may be part of a broadband router. In that case, reset the router. If you wait long enough, the DHCP server should assign an address to the DHCP client computer. If you wish to take control of the process, open a command prompt on the PC and enter the following command: **ipconfig /renew**. This allows you to force the DHCP client to request an IP address. It may take several seconds before you see a response, but it should receive a new address if it is able to reach the DHCP server. The output from the IPCONFIG command will make it clear whether the computer receives an address.

Troubleshooting Connection Errors with the PING Command   The PING command is useful for testing communications between two hosts. The name of this command is an acronym for *Packet Internet Groper*. We prefer to think (as many do) that it was named after the action of underwater sonar. Instead of bouncing sound waves off surfaces, the PING command uses data packets, sending them to specific IP addresses and requesting a response (hence the idea of pinging). Then, PING "listens" for a reply.

If you completed Exercise 13-2 or 13-3 in Chapter 13, you know the syntax of the PING command, which is **ping *target-IP-address***. Use the PING command to test a new network connection, and for troubleshooting a connection failure. The first address you should ping is the local NIC using a special name for the local computer, *localhost*, which does not require using or knowing the IP address.

1. PING the local NIC using the following command: **ping localhost**. If the ping results in four responses, move on to the next step. If this fails, troubleshoot the NIC as you would any hardware component. If you have another identical NIC known to work, swap it with the current NIC. If the replacement NIC works, replace the original NIC.

2. PING the IP address of the Gateway. If this does not work, verify that the Gateway address is correct. If there are other computers on the network, compare the IP configuration settings. If the local settings match those of other hosts on the network, ping the Gateway address from another computer.

3. PING the IP address or DNS name of a computer beyond the Gateway.

This order confirms, first, that the NIC is working. It also confirms that the address works within your LAN, because the Gateway address is on the LAN and has the same network ID as the local NIC. Finally, pinging an address beyond the Gateway confirms at least two things: the router works, and the NIC of the target host is functioning and can respond to PING requests. If you cannot ping any computer beyond the router, the problem may be in the router itself.

Now you need some technical information about PING and related commands. The PING command uses a subprotocol of IP called the Internet Control Message Protocol (ICMP). This little protocol has a big job in a TCP/IP internetwork. It detects problems that can cause errors. Such problems include congestion and downed routers. When ICMP detects these problems, it notifies other protocols and services in the TCP/IP suite, resulting in routing of packets around the problem area.

PING sends ICMP Echo packets to the target node. An Echo packet contains a request to respond. Once the target node receives the packets, it sends out one response packet for each one that it received.

on the **Ü** o b *Practice working with these command-line tools before there is a problem with your network. Then you will be more comfortable with the tools and their screen output.*

e x a m
w a t c h
Be sure that you understand the type of results you get from each of the command-line commands.

Using TRACERT to Troubleshoot Slow Communications   You may have situations in which you can connect to a Web site or other remote resource, but the connection is very slow. If this connection is critical to business, you will want to gather information so that a network administrator or ISP can troubleshoot the source of the bottleneck. You can use the TRACERT command to gather this information. TRACERT is a command-line utility that traces the route taken by packets to a destination.

When you use TRACERT with the name or IP address of the target host, it will ping each of the intervening routers, from the nearest to the farthest. You see the delay at each router, and you will be able to determine the location of the bottleneck. You can then provide this information to the people who will troubleshoot it for you.

It is also important to understand time to live (TTL). Each IP packet header has a TTL field that shows how many routers the packet can cross before being discarded. Like PING, TRACERT creates ICMP Echo packets. The packet sent to the first host or router has a TTL of one (1). The TTL of each subsequent packet is increased by one (1). Each router, in turn, decreases the TTL value by one. The computer that sends the TRACERT waits a predetermined amount of time before it increments the TTL value by one for each additional packet. This repeats until the destination is reached. This has the effect of pinging each router along the way, without needing to know the actual IP address of each router.

Consider a scenario in which your connection to the Google Web site (www. google.com) is extremely slow. You are working from a small office that has a cable modem connection to the Internet and you are accustomed to very fast responses when you browse the Web. You have connected in the last few minutes to other Web sites without significant delay, so you believe there is a bottleneck between you and Google.

Use TRACERT as described in Exercise 14-1 and report the results to your ISP. Normally, the first and last numbered lines in the output represent the source IP address and the target IP address. Every line in between is a router located between your computer and the target. You can verify that the last line is the target by matching the IP address to the one you entered at the command line. If you entered a DNS name at the command line, the IP address will display below the command line.

EXERCISE 14-1

Using TRACERT

Use TRACERT to discover the address of the router that is the bottleneck between you and a target host. In this exercise, we use Google as the target, but you can substitute another domain name or IP address.

1. Open a command prompt.

2. Type **tracert www.google.com**.

3. In Figure 14-10, none of the routers shows a value that is much greater than the others, so no single router is a bottleneck relative to the others. If your test shows a router with a much greater value, report this to your ISP or to a network professional in your company, if appropriate.

On the Internet, which is besieged with all types of attacks, the TRACERT command may not give you valuable information if one or more of the routers in the path to the target is configured to block and not respond to PING requests.

FIGURE 14-10

Using TRACERT
to trace the
route to
www.google.com

```
C:\WINDOWS\system32\cmd.exe                                          _ □ ×

C:\>tracert www.google.com

Tracing route to www.google.akadns.net [216.239.41.99]
over a maximum of 30 hops:

  1    <1 ms    <1 ms    <1 ms  192.168.100.1
  2   858 ms   810 ms   812 ms  hh1095067.direcpc.com [205.177.62.67]
  3   875 ms   819 ms   807 ms  dpc6682016181.direcpc.com [66.82.16.181]
  4   803 ms   746 ms   872 ms  dpc6682016073.direcpc.com [66.82.16.73]
  5   749 ms   820 ms   747 ms  so-5-1.hsa1.Washington1.Level3.net [63.215.128.129]
  6   806 ms   867 ms   879 ms  ge-9-2.ipcolo2.Washington1.Level3.net [4.68.121.172]

  7   815 ms   806 ms   760 ms  unknown.Level3.net [166.90.148.174]
  8   749 ms   812 ms   811 ms  216.239.47.69
  9   821 ms   805 ms   812 ms  216.239.47.154
 10   871 ms   747 ms   811 ms  216.239.48.77
 11   755 ms   867 ms   880 ms  216.239.41.99

Trace complete.

C:\>_
```

Using the NETSTAT Command to Troubleshoot Connection Errors   The NETSTAT command will give you statistical information about the TCP/IP protocols and network connections involving your computer, depending on the switches you use when you enter the command. While it has many options, there are a few to remember. For instance running **netstat** without any parameters, as shown in Figure 14-11, will show the current connections. This can show you a connection that is not working—perhaps because an application has failed. Running **netstat -s** displays statistics on outgoing and incoming traffic on your computer. If this shows there is no traffic in one direction, you may have a bad cable.

Troubleshooting DNS Problems

DNS problems show themselves as messages such as "Server not found." These messages can occur in your Web browser, your e-mail client, or any software that attempts to connect to a server. How do you know it is a DNS problem? You do

FIGURE 14-11

The NETSTAT
command
shows current
connections.

```
C:\>netstat

Active Connections

  Proto  Local Address          Foreign Address             State
  TCP    Wickenburg:1422        localhost:1423              ESTABLISHED
  TCP    Wickenburg:1423        localhost:1422              ESTABLISHED
  TCP    Wickenburg:1427        localhost:1428              ESTABLISHED
  TCP    Wickenburg:1428        localhost:1427              ESTABLISHED
  TCP    Wickenburg:1456        he-in-f91.google.com:http   TIME_WAIT
  TCP    Wickenburg:1490        80.67.74.223:http           TIME_WAIT
  TCP    Wickenburg:1495        80.67.74.224:http           ESTABLISHED
  TCP    Wickenburg:1499        wwwbaytest1.microsoft.com:http  ESTABLISHED
  TCP    Wickenburg:1500        80.67.74.224:http           ESTABLISHED
  TCP    Wickenburg:1503        65.55.194.61:https          TIME_WAIT
  TCP    Wickenburg:1504        microsoft.iad.webtrends.com:http  ESTABLISHED
  TCP    Wickenburg:1506        wwwbaytest1.microsoft.com:http  TIME_WAIT
```

not know this until you eliminate other problems, such as a failed NIC, a broken connection, a typo, or an incorrect IP configuration. But once you have eliminated these problems, use the following tests to troubleshoot DNS problems.

Using PING to Troubleshoot DNS Problems   Notice that in the steps provided for using both the PING and TRACERT commands in the previous sections, you can use either the IP address or the DNS name. When you use the DNS name with either of these commands, it is also a test of DNS. For instance, if you open a command prompt and enter the following command: **ping www.mcgraw-hill .com**, before the PING command can send packets to the target, www.mcgraw-hill .com, the DNS client must resolve the DNS name to an IP address. This is exactly what happens when you enter a URL in the address box of a Web browser. The DNS client resolves the name to an IP address before the browser can send a request to view the page.

When pinging a DNS name is successful, you know several things: your DNS client is working, your DNS server is responding and working, and the target DNS name has been found on the Internet. Now, notice that the name we used has three parts to it. Read from right to left, "com" is the top-level domain (TLD) name, and mcgraw-hill is the second-level domain (SLD) name within the com TLD. We usually refer to both of these together as a domain name. So what is "www"? The owner of the second-level domain name defines anything to the left of the second-level domain name.

For instance, www.mcgraw-hill.com is listed in DNS servers that are probably under the control of McGraw-Hill or its ISP. The entry points to a server, named "www," where Web pages can be found. So, to the left of the second-level domain name are the names of servers or child domains of McGraw-Hill.com. This allows them to organize their portion of the DNS name space and help client computers locate resources on these servers.

And what about all those letters, numbers, slashes, and other characters to the right of the TLD? They point to specific documents on the servers. Simple? To the casual observer, yes, because DNS hides the complexity of the organization and the locations of servers and documents. Understanding this much will help you to work with DNS and do basic troubleshooting.

So, the next time you cannot connect to a Web site from your browser, first double-check your spelling. If you entered the URL correctly, then open up a command prompt and ping on the portion of the URL that contains the TLD and SLD. If the PING is not successful, you should immediately PING another domain name, and/or try connecting to another URL through your browser. If you are successful on all but the first, suspect that the problem between your computer and the target is a DNS problem only if you have proof that the name cannot be resolved. If it is not a DNS problem, use TRACERT, described earlier, to pinpoint the problem router.

Using NSLOOKUP to Troubleshoot DNS Problems   To further troubleshoot DNS problems, use the NSLOOKUP command, which lets you troubleshoot DNS problems by allowing you to query DNS name servers and see the result of the queries. In using NSLOOKUP you are looking for problems such as a DNS server not responding to clients, DNS servers not resolving names correctly, or other general name resolution problems.

NSLOOKUP has two modes: *interactive* and *non-interactive*.

- **Interactive mode**   In interactive mode NSLOOKUP has its own command prompt, a greater than sign (>) within the system command prompt. You enter this mode by typing **nslookup** without any parameters, or **nslookup** followed by a space, a hyphen, and the name of a name server. In the first instance, it will use your default name server, as shown in Figure 14-12, and in the second instance, it will use the name server you specify. While in interactive mode enter commands at the NSLOOKUP prompt, and type **exit** to end interactive mode and return to the system command prompt.

- **Non-interactive mode**   In non-interactive mode, you enter the NSLOOKUP command plus a command-line parameter for using one or more NSLOOKUP subcommands. The response is sent to the screen, and you are returned to the command prompt. Exercise 14-2 uses the non-interactive mode.

FIGURE 14-12

NSLOOKUP in interactive mode

EXERCISE 14-2

Using NSLOOKUP to Troubleshoot DNS

Use NSLOOKUP to resolve any Internet domain name to an IP address.

1. Open a command prompt and enter the following command: **nslookup mcgraw-hill.com**. If the name server is working, the result will resemble Figure 14-13.

2. The Server and Address in the first and second lines of the output are the name and IP address of the DNS server that responded to your request. They will be the name server used by your ISP or your company.

3. The second group of lines shows the result of the query. It is called a non-authoritative answer because the name server queried had to query other name servers to find the name.

4. The results in Figure 14-13 show that DNS name resolution is working. Therefore, if we are unable to connect to a server in this domain it may be because the server is offline, or a critical link or router between it and the Internet has failed. If you were troubleshooting a connection problem to this domain, you would pass this information on to a network administrator or ISP.

Troubleshooting WINS Problems

The Windows Internet Naming Service (WINS) is like DNS, only it resolves NetBIOS names to IP addresses, while DNS resolves DNS names to IP addresses. WINS is nearly extinct because it was mostly a Microsoft naming system, and Microsoft networks now use DNS. Windows 2000 and Windows XP do not require NetBIOS, as earlier versions of Windows did, but they both use it. However, if you have a network that is using TCP/IP and has older versions of Windows, you will still need WINS.

FIGURE 14-13

The NSLOOKUP command queries the default name server.

The most likely scenario you will find for problems with WINS will be a computer running Windows 9*x* that cannot see a Windows server in Network Neighborhood and cannot connect to it. Windows 2000 and newer computers can see that server on the network and, depending on permissions, can connect to it. If you have eliminated TCP/IP configuration problems and hardware problems, then suspect a WINS problem.

If the remote host is located on the same IP network, then the Windows 9*x* computer will use NetBIOS broadcasts rather than contacting a WINS server to resolve the name. In this case, check that the remote computer is online and functioning, and that the user on the Windows 9*x* computer is using the correct NetBIOS name. Verify that the problem is not due to two computers with the same NetBIOS names.

If the host the Windows 9*x* computer cannot locate is a network segment beyond the local router, verify that the Windows 9*x* TCP/IP configuration is correct. It may not be a WINS problem, but a configuration problem, if either the Gateway address or the WINS address is incorrect. If you have eliminated configuration as the problem, this is the point at which you consult a network administrator who must ensure that the WINS server is online and that it has the target host name and address in its database.

Removing a Driver for a Non-Present NIC

In Chapter 10 you learned that Device Manager is a tool that allows you to view and change device properties, update device drivers, and disable or enable devices. You learned that you can use Device Manager in Windows after a normal startup, and that you can also use it in Safe Mode. One scenario given in the Chapter 10 section "Safe Mode with Networking" described how to use Device Manager to disable a network adapter driver that was causing startup problems. Exercise 10-5 introduced you to many features of Device Manager.

There is another scenario in which Device Manager is a valuable tool. We have experienced situations in which we had error messages for a network adapter that was no longer physically present. In one instance, the formerly installed NIC was manually configured with an IP address. When we removed the NIC, and we tried to manually assign the same IP address to the replacement NIC, we received an error message. We opened Device Manager but found we could not remove the device driver because it was not visible. The network administrator told us that we had to use that IP address for that computer, so assigning a different IP address was out of the question.

Once a non-present device is visible, you can remove the driver, and that eliminates the error messages for this device. After some research, we learned the two-step process for making non-present devices visible in Device Manager. You must turn on the Show Hidden Devices setting and create a special environment variable. An environment variable consists of a name and a value and is stored in a special location in the Windows registry. Windows and a number of applications look for specific environment variables and modify their behavior according to the value. In the case of the Show Hidden Devices setting, when the variable name devmgr_show_nonpresent_devices has a value of one (1), non-present devices are visible when Show Hidden Devices is turned on. If there is no setting in the environment for devmgr_show_nonpresent_devices, or if the value is zero (0), then non-present devices will not show when Show Hidden Devices is turned on.

Exercise 14-3 will walk you through the steps required to make non-present devices visible in Device Manager. Be sure to take the time to notice the changes in Device Manager first when you turn on Show Hidden Devices, and then after you add the non-present devices setting to the Windows environment. Remember that both of these settings are necessary to view non-present devices.

EXERCISE 14-3

Making Non-Present Devices Visible in Device Manager

These steps will allow you to make a non-present device visible in Device Manager so that you can delete it to remove the device driver. This is a very handy technique, but you will not see any noticeable change in Device Manager if you do not have a non-present device problem.

1. Open Device Manager from the Hardware page of the System applet and verify that the *Show Hidden Devices* setting on the View menu is not selected. Look at the contents in Device Manager, noticing the displayed nodes.

2. Turn on the Show Hidden Devices setting, and then notice the differences in the devices displayed in Device Manager. Close Device Manager.

3. Open Control Panel and double-click the System applet to open the System Properties dialog box.

4. Select the Advanced tab and then click the Environment Variables button at the bottom of the page.

5. In the Environment Variables dialog box locate the System Variables list and click the New button below this list.

6. In the New System Variable box carefully type the following in the Variable name box: **devmgr_show_nonpresent_devices**.

7. Also in the New System Variable box carefully type a number one (1) in the Variable value box. Click OK to close the New System Variable box.

8. Verify that the new variable appears in the System Variables list (see Figure 14-14) and click OK in the Environment Variables box and again in the System Properties dialog box.

9. Open Device Manager and notice the difference in the visible devices.

10. Now that the non-present devices are visible in Device Manager, you can select and delete any that have caused problems. However, do not delete all non-present devices, because some of these may be devices that are only temporarily absent, and the next time one of these devices is connected, the device's driver must be available.

FIGURE 14-14

The Environment Variables setting for non-present devices

SCENARIO & SOLUTION

My network has a DHCP server. I need to see if the NIC received an IP address, but when I look at the properties of the Local Area Connection the IP address is empty. What can I do?	Open a command prompt and enter the following command: **ipconfig /all**. This will display the IP configuration.
I have connected to a certain Web site many times, but today the connection to just this one Web site is very slow. I would like to talk to my ISP about this, but I need more information. How can I tell where the problem is?	Since other Web sites do not seem as slow, use the TRACERT command to trace the route to the Web site and determine where a bottleneck may be.

CERTIFICATION OBJECTIVE

■ **602: 5.4** *Perform preventive maintenance of networks including securing and protecting network cabling*

CompTIA A+ Exam 602 is the only one of the A+ exams to list an objective involving preventive maintenance for networks. All that is required for this exam is knowledge of the tasks for securing and protecting network cabling.

Preventive Maintenance for Networks

It is always better to prevent problems than to spend your time solving them. In this section learn the basic maintenance tasks specific to networks, which include maintaining all the equipment directly attached to the network and the media over which the signals travel. However, the value and usability of a network also depend on proper functioning of the attached computers (clients and servers), as well as other shared devices, such as printers. In previous chapters you learned preventive maintenance for computers and printers. Preventive maintenance for network devices, such as NICs, hubs, switches, WAPs, and routers, is identical to that for computers and printers.

A network also depends on the maintenance of an appropriate and secure environment for both the equipment and data. Chapters 15 and 16 explore security issues for computers and networks, and Chapter 17 presents safety and environmental issues.

Therefore, although this chapter presents some network-specific maintenance tasks, keep in mind that a computer professional must look beyond the components and software that are specific to a network and approach network maintenance holistically.

Maintaining Equipment

Network equipment, from the NICs in the computers to the bridging and routing devices that connect networks together, all have similar requirements. For instance, they all require sufficient ventilation and cooling systems to maintain the appropriate operating environment.

Reliable Power

All computer and network components must have electrical power. Providing reliable power begins with the power company supplying the power, but your responsibility begins at the meter. Do not assume that the power will always be reliable. Most of us have experienced power outages and can understand how disrupting they are. However, bad power, in the form of surges, spikes, and voltage sags, can do a great deal of damage. Prevent damage and disruption from these events by using uninterruptible power supply (UPS) devices or other protective devices discussed in Chapter 4. Versions of these power protection devices come in a form factor for mounting in equipment racks. Equipment racks are discussed in the following section.

Be aware of the number and location of circuits in the building, and the total power requirements of the equipment you have on each circuit. If you have network equipment unprotected by a UPS, be sure that this equipment is not sharing a circuit with a device that has high demands, such as a laser printer or photocopier.

Consider using a dedicated circuit for the most critical equipment. A dedicated circuit has only one, or very few, outlets.

Housing Servers and Network Devices

Servers and network devices such as switches and routers should be in a physically secure room or closet with proper climate controls. The humidity should at or near 40 percent, and the temperature should be no higher than 70 degrees. Provide adequate spacing around the equipment for proper ventilation. When dealing with more than a few servers plus network equipment, use rack-mounted servers that fit into the specially designed equipment racks for holding servers and other devices, such as UPSs, routers, and switches. These take up less space and, unlike tables and desks, allow more air to flow around the equipment.

Dedicate the room or closet to the equipment. Do not make this a multipurpose room for storage or office space because that is inviting disaster, especially if the space is readily accessible by people who have no professional reason to be in contact with the servers or network equipment. The unintended consequences of such an arrangement can be damage to the equipment.

As a new technician you may find yourself in a new and growing company. Take a professional approach to organizing and protecting the networking equipment from the beginning. This will make the changes required to accommodate a larger network easier.

Securing and Protecting Network Cabling

Regardless of the size of the network, keep network cabling neat and labeled. In the equipment room or closet use patch panels. A patch panel is a rack-mounted panel containing multiple network ports. Cables running from various locations in the building connect to ports on the back of the patch panel. Then shorter cables, called patch cables, connect each port to switches and routers in the closet or equipment room. This keeps cables organized and even allows for labeling the ports. This will help prevent damaged cables and confusion when troubleshooting a cable run.

e x a m

w a t c h *Knowledge of how to secure and protect network cabling is required for CompTIA A+ Exam 602.*

Horizontal runs of cabling often must run through suspended ceilings. Resist the urge to simply lay the cabling on the top of the ceiling tiles. This may be okay for a very small number of cables, but it only takes a few cables to make a tangle. Further, running additional cables into this space can be very difficult. Therefore, bundle cables together and run them through channels where possible. If the budget allows, it is well worth the investment in specialized cable management systems. Use cable trays for running cables in the ceiling. A cable tray is a lightweight bridge-like structure for containing the cables in a building.

CERTIFICATION SUMMARY

This chapter explored the tools for troubleshooting networks, techniques for troubleshooting network problems, and preventive maintenance for networks.

The tools included physical and software status indicators, command-line tools, cable testers, Windows Remote Desktop, and Windows Remote Assistance. We introduced you to two of these commands, IPCONFIG and PING, in Chapters 12 and 13 respectively. In this chapter, you learned strategies for using these commands to analyze network problems. You also learned how to use TRACERT, NETSTAT, and NSLOOKUP for specific network problems.

A problem that may appear to be caused by insufficient bandwidth may actually be caused by inefficient use of bandwidth. Remove unnecessary protocol suites from computers and network devices, such as print servers, because every active protocol generates a certain amount of broadcast traffic, even when there is no other device using the same protocol. If the NWLink protocol suite is required on the network, reduce the broadcast traffic from all the hosts using NWLink by manually configuring the frame type.

Analyze network connectivity problems based on error messages or other symptoms. If you see no obvious source of the problem, check the hardware, beginning with the NIC, cables, hubs, switches, WAPs, and routers. Check for any source of EMI. If you detect no physical source of the problem, check the IP configuration of the NIC in Network Connections.

At this point it is time to use command-line tools that you must enter from a Windows command prompt. Use these tools to reveal the IP configuration, test connectivity, locate a bottleneck on the Internet, reveal statistics about the TCP/IP protocols and network connections involving the local computer, and detect DNS and WINS problems.

Back in the Windows GUI, you used a two-step process for revealing non-present devices in Device Manager.

Most preventive maintenance for network devices is identical to that for computers. There are some special considerations for the servers, network devices, and the cabling, for which preventive maintenance begins with providing a proper and secure environment and carefully organizing the cabling and the cable runs through ceilings and walls. Restrict access to network-specific devices to protect them from people with no professional reason to be in contact with the servers or network equipment.

TWO-MINUTE DRILL

Here are some of the key points covered in Chapter 14.

Tools for Network Troubleshooting

❑ Status indicators for network hardware include LED lights on physical devices and/or status information from software installed along with the driver.

❑ A quick glance at indicator lights on a device, or icons and messages on the computer screen, reveals valuable information.

❑ The typical NIC installs with a configuration utility that you can open from an icon in the system tray of the taskbar. A change in status, or pausing your mouse over this icon, will cause a message to appear over the system tray.

❑ A group of command-line commands installs with the TCP/IP protocol suite. These include IPCONFIG, PING, TRACERT, NETSTAT, and NSLOOKUP.

❑ Use the /? switch with any command-line command to learn about the variety of parameters that alter the behavior of the command.

❑ A cable tester connects to the ends of a cable and sends a signal down the cable in order to detect breaks in the cable.

❑ Remote Desktop allows someone running a Windows computer to connect to a Windows XP Professional, Windows XP Media Center, or Windows Vista computer and have total access to the desktop and local resources, including files, printers, and other attached devices.

❑ Although it is not designed to be a network troubleshooting tool, support professionals use Remote Desktop to access files and programs on a user's computer for troubleshooting and maintenance.

❑ Remote Assistance allows someone working at a computer running Windows XP (including Home Edition) or Windows Vista to invite someone to connect over a network to the desktop for the purpose of troubleshooting. This is not strictly a network troubleshooting tool, since the network must be working before you can use Remote Assistance.

Troubleshooting Common Network Problems

❑ One way to increase network bandwidth is to remove unnecessary protocol suites from the network. Check computers for unneeded protocol suites and other network devices, such as print servers, which may come with several protocols enabled.

❑ A more costly method of increasing network bandwidth is by upgrading hardware. Begin by replacing hubs with switches, and consider changing all the network hardware (NICs, switches, cabling, etc.) to hardware capable of higher speeds than the existing equipment.

❑ When troubleshooting network connectivity problems, physically check the local network hardware. Next, check the status of the NIC driver in the Properties of the NIC.

❑ Use the IPCONFIG command to check the IP configuration.

❑ Use the PING command to test for connectivity to another host.

❑ Find a network bottleneck on a routed network (like the Internet) using the TRACERT command.

❑ Use the NETSTAT command to view statistics about connections to the local computer.

❑ Troubleshoot DNS problems with PING and NSLOOKUP.

❑ WINS problems involve NetBIOS names within Microsoft networks. Check for duplication of NetBIOS names or problems with the WINS server.

❑ When an error involves a NIC (or other device) that has been physically removed, remove the driver for the missing device. To do this from Device Manager, you must first make the non-present device visible in Device Manager, and then the driver can be removed.

Preventive Maintenance for Networks

❑ Preventive maintenance for network devices, such as NICs, hubs, switches, WAPs, and routers, is identical to what we described in previous chapters for computers and printers.

❑ Do not overload circuits, and provide reliable power using power protection devices, as described in Chapter 4. Consider using a dedicated circuit for the most critical equipment.

❑ Locate servers and network devices in a dedicated space, such as a room or closet. Make sure that the environment in this space is appropriate, and restrict access to the equipment.

❑ Secure, protect, and organize network cabling using patch panels in the closet or room housing the network devices, and by using cable management systems, such as cable trays for horizontal runs through ceilings.

SELF TEST

The following questions will help you measure your understanding of the material presented in this chapter. Read all of the choices carefully because there might be more than one correct answer. Choose all correct answers for each question.

Tools for Network Troubleshooting

1. Which of the following items can be either one or more lights on a physical device or a message in software?
   - A. Wi-Fi NIC
   - B. Ethernet NIC
   - C. Command-line utility
   - D. Status indicator

2. In what form will you find the handiest and cheapest network troubleshooting tools?
   - A. Status indicators
   - B. Command-line utilities
   - C. Ethernet NIC
   - D. Cable tester

3. Which of the following would you use to view the IP configuration of a local NIC?
   - A. NETSTAT
   - B. PING
   - C. IPCONFIG
   - D. NSLOOKUP

4. What tool would you use if you suspected that a cable was bad?
   - A. Cable ping
   - B. Cable tester
   - C. Status indicator
   - D. LED

5. Which of the following allows a user to connect to a Windows PC from another location over the Internet and work with the Windows desktop, programs, files, and other resources, as if sitting at the PC?
   - A. Remote Desktop
   - B. Remote Assistance

    C. Remote Control

    D. Network Connections

6. What version of Windows is required on the computer of the person providing the assistance with Remote Assistance? Select all that apply.

    A. Windows 9x

    B. Windows Me

    C. Windows XP Professional

    D. Windows XP Home

Troubleshooting Common Network Problems

7. What should you look for on a network that seems to have a bandwidth problem?

    A. Unnecessary protocol suites

    B. Unnecessary servers

    C. Unnecessary network printers

    D. Unnecessary print servers

8. How can you reduce the network traffic produced by the NWLink protocol stack?

    A. Switch to NetBEUI.

    B. Replace it with TCP/IP.

    C. Set Frame Type to Auto Detect.

    D. Manually configure the frame type.

9. Which of the following devices reduces network traffic within an Ethernet LAN?

    A. Hub

    B. Switch

    C. Router

    D. WAP

10. How would you check the signal strength received by a wireless NIC? Select all that apply.

    A. Check indicator lights on the wireless NIC.

    B. Check indicator lights on the WAP.

    C. Open the NIC's program from the system tray.

    D. Run IPCONFIG.

11. What is the result of mixing 802.11b and 802.11g equipment on the same wireless LAN?

    A. Network speed will be at the 802.11g level.

    B. Network speed will be mixed.

    C. Nothing. The two do not work together.

    D. Network speed will be at the 802.11b level.

12. What is the result of mixing Ethernet and Fast Ethernet hardware?

    A. Transmissions at 100 Mbps

    B. Transmissions at 10 Mbps

    C. Transmissions at 1 Gbps

    D. Transmissions at 10 Gbps

13. The distance between a WAP and one group of wireless hosts causes the signal to degrade so badly that the transmissions are too slow and users are complaining. What can you do?

    A. Install a signal booster.

    B. Upgrade all the wireless devices to a faster speed.

    C. Install an Ethernet network.

    D. Install a router.

14. Which type of server automatically assigns IP addresses to hosts?

    A. DHCP

    B. WINS

    C. DNS

    D. APIPA

15. What command can you use to force a DHCP client to request an IP address assignment?

    A. ping localhost

    B. ipconfig /renew

    C. ipconfig /all

    D. tracert www.mcgraw-hill.com

16. A user complains that an Internet connection to a Web site she needs to access for her work is extremely slow. Which of the following commands will you use first to analyze the problem?

    A. NETSTAT

    B. IPCONFIG

    C. TRACERT

    D. NSLOOKUP

17. Which two programs can you use when troubleshooting a possible DNS problem?

    A. NETSTAT

    B. PING

    C. TRACERT

    D. NSLOOKUP

18. After replacing a failed NIC, and assigning to the new NIC the IP address previously assigned to the old NIC, an error message appears that there is an IP address conflict with another NIC (the one that was removed). The network administrator will not allow you to use another IP address. What can you do?

    A. Delete the old NIC in My Computer.

    B. Use IPCONFIG to configure the new NIC.

    C. Delete the old NIC using Device Manager.

    D. Move the new NIC to another connector or port.

Preventive Maintenance for Networks

19. Which of the following is the preferred environment for network equipment and servers in a law office?

    A. A broom closet

    B. A reception desk

    C. A dedicated, climate-controlled room

    D. A conference room

20. You need to run a group of wires through a suspended ceiling. What should you use to keep the wires organized within the ceiling area?

    A. An equipment rack

    B. A UPS

    C. Cable wraps

    D. Cable trays

LAB QUESTION

Visit a server room, or wiring closet. Ask the network administrator at your place of work or school for a tour of the facility. Ask what type of network equipment they have, how they have organized their cable runs, and how they restrict access to the network equipment. Write a few paragraphs on what you learned.

SELF TEST ANSWERS

Tools for Network Troubleshooting

1. ☑ **D.** A status indicator can be either one or more lights on a physical device or a message in software.
   ☒ **A**, Wi-Fi NIC, and **B**, Ethernet NIC, are both incorrect because, while both can have status indicators, neither is itself a status indicator. **C**, command-line utility, is incorrect because a command-line utility is not one or more lights on a physical device or a message in software, but a program.

2. ☑ **B.** Command-line utilities are the handiest and cheapest network troubleshooting tools.
   ☒ **A**, status indicators, is incorrect because this is not the form of the handiest and cheapest network troubleshooting tools. **C**, Ethernet NIC, is incorrect because this is a network device, not a troubleshooting tool. **D**, cable tester, is incorrect because while this is a good troubleshooting tool, it is not the handiest or cheapest compared to command-line utilities.

3. ☑ **C.** Use IPCONFIG to view the IP configuration of a local NIC.
   ☒ **A**, NETSTAT, is incorrect because this displays network statistics but does not display the IP configuration. **B**, PING, is incorrect because this tests a connection between two hosts but does not display the IP configuration of a local NIC. **D**, NSLOOKUP, is incorrect because this tests for DNS problems and does not display the IP configuration.

4. ☑ **B.** You would use a cable tester if you suspected that a cable was bad.
   ☒ **A**, cable ping, is incorrect because such a tool was not even mentioned and may not exist. **C**, status indicator, and **D**, LED, are incorrect because neither is a tool you would use if you suspected that a cable was bad.

5. ☑ **A.** Remote Desktop allows a user to connect to a Windows PC from another location over the Internet and work with the Windows desktop, programs, files, and other resources, as if sitting at the PC.
   ☒ **B**, Remote Assistance, is incorrect because this only allows a user to invite someone to connect over a network and help the user. **C**, Remote Control, is incorrect because this term was not used in this chapter. **D**, Network Connections, is incorrect because this is a Control Panel applet that allows you to configure NICs and protocols.

6. ☑ **C and D.** Windows XP Professional and Windows XP Home are both versions of Windows that the person providing the assistance with Remote Assistance can use.
   ☒ **A**, Windows 9x, and **B**, Windows Me, are both incorrect because neither can be used for Remote Assistance.

Troubleshooting Common Network Problems

7. ☑ **A.** Unnecessary protocol suites are what you should look for on a network that seems to have a bandwidth problem.

☒ **B,** unnecessary servers, **C,** unnecessary network printers, and **D,** unnecessary print servers, are all incorrect because none of these contribute to bandwidth as much as unnecessary protocol suites.

8. ☑ **D.** Manually configure the frame type of the NWLink protocol stack to reduce the broadcast traffic generated if the frame type is set to Auto.

☒ **A,** switch to NetBEUI, and **B,** replace it with TCP/IP, are both incorrect because neither of these would solve the problem, and computers that need NWLink cannot use NetBEUI or TCP/IP to communicate to servers that are using NWLink. **C,** set Frame Type to Auto Detect, is incorrect because the broadcasts generated for the auto detection are the source of network traffic.

9. ☑ **B.** A switch is the device that reduces network broadcasts in an Ethernet network.

☒ **A,** hub, is incorrect because a hub sends a packet to every port, which increases traffic, while a switch only sends packets to the destination port. **C,** router, is incorrect because a router connects LANs, while a switch is within a LAN. It is true that a router will keep broadcast traffic from traveling between LANs. **D,** WAP, is incorrect because this device is a wireless version of a hub.

10. ☑ **A and C.** The indicator lights on the wireless NIC and the NIC's program available from the system tray are both correct as places where you look for the signal strength received by a wireless NIC.

☒ **B,** To check indicator lights on the WAP, is incorrect because, since the WAP is the source of the signals, these do not indicate the strength of the signal received by a wireless NIC. **D,** to run IPCONFIG, is incorrect because it is not where you would look for the signal strength received by a wireless NIC.

11. ☑ **D.** Network speed will be at the 802.11b level.

☒ **A,** network speed will be at the 802.11g level, and **B,** network speed will be mixed, are both incorrect because the presence of 802.11b devices will make the wireless LAN operate at the lower level. **C,** nothing—the two do not work together, is incorrect because they do work together, just at the speed of the slower devices.

12. ☑ **B.** The result of mixing Ethernet (10 Mbps) and Fast Ethernet (100 Mbps) is transmissions at 10 Mbps.

☒ **A,** transmissions at 100 Mbps, is incorrect because the presence of the slower Ethernet devices will cause communications between the slower and faster devices to run at the slower rate. **C,** transmissions at 1 Gbps, and **D,** transmissions at 10 Gbps, are both incorrect because neither Ethernet nor Fast Ethernet runs at these speeds.

13. ☑ **A.** The solution to the degraded signal due to distance is to install a signal booster.
☒ **B,** upgrade all the wireless devices to a faster speed, is incorrect because the question does not mention the standard of the device in use, and it may be at the highest level available. **C,** install an Ethernet network, is incorrect because a wireless network is often installed where it is not possible or practical to install a wired network. **D,** install a router, is incorrect because this would not solve the problem of the weak signal within the wireless LAN.

14. ☑ **A.** DHCP is the type of server that automatically assigns IP addresses to hosts.
☒ **B,** WINS, is incorrect because a WINS server resolves NetBIOS names to IP addresses. **C,** DNS, is incorrect because the DNS server resolves Internet domain names to IP addresses. **D,** APIPA, is incorrect because this does not describe a server, but an IP address (beginning with 169.254) that a DHCP client can assign to itself if it does not get a response from a DHCP server.

15. ☑ **B.** You use the ipconfig /renew command to force a DHCP client to request an IP address assignment.
☒ **A,** ping localhost, is incorrect because this command is used to ping the local NIC. **C,** ipconfig /all, is incorrect because this command is used to look at the TCP/IP configuration, not to analyze a TCP/IP configuration. **D,** tracert www.mcgraw-hill.com, is incorrect because this command displays a trace of the route taken by packets to the destination.

16. ☑ **C.** TRACERT is the command to use to analyze the problem of a slow connection to a Web site.
☒ **A,** NETSTAT, **B,** IPCONFIG, and **D,** NSLOOKUP, are all incorrect because none of these is the correct command to analyze the problem described.

17. ☑ **B** and **D.** PING and NSLOOKUP are the two programs you can use when troubleshooting a possible DNS problem.
☒ **A,** NETSTAT, and **C,** TRACERT, are not programs used to troubleshoot a DNS problem.

18. ☑ **C.** Delete the old NIC using Device Manager. You may also have to take steps to make the old NIC visible in Device Manager.
☒ **A,** delete the old NIC in My Computer, is incorrect because you cannot delete the old NIC in My Computer. **B,** use IPCONFIG to configure the new NIC, is incorrect because this is not where you would configure the new NIC, and it would not solve the problem. **D,** move the new NIC to another connector or port, is incorrect because this would not solve the problem with the old NIC.

Preventive Maintenance for Networks

19. ☑   **C.** A dedicated, climate-controlled room is the preferred environment for network equipment and servers in any organization.

☒   **A,** a broom closet, **B,** a reception desk, and **D,** a conference room, are all unsuitable locations because they do not restrict access to the equipment and do not provide the correct climate-controlled environment.

20. ☑   **D.** You should use cable trays to keep the wires organized within the ceiling area.

☒   **A,** an equipment rack, is incorrect because an equipment rack is not used within ceiling areas. **B,** a UPS, is incorrect because this is a power protection device, not something for organizing cables. **C,** cable wraps, is incorrect because while you could use these to organize cables, they are not mentioned in the chapter and are not the best solution for organizing cables within the ceiling area.

LAB ANSWER

Answers will vary based on the individual's experience.

Part VI

Security

15

Computer Security
Fundamentals

All the latest operating systems—Linux, Mac OS, and Windows—have a long list of security features. Further, each operating system is updated as new vulnerabilities are discovered. The savvy computer user knows to apply security patches to any operating system. An entire industry has grown up to provide security products for home and business computers. Computer security is a multi-billion-dollar business worldwide. It is a dangerous world out there, and today "out there" is everywhere.

No form of computing is safe from threats as long as the computer connects to any network, and those few that do not connect to networks can still be infected by malicious code on flash drives, floppy disks, and even optical disks.

In this chapter, learn what the threats are to your data, to your identity, and even to your hardware. Then explore the fundamentals for protecting yourself and your computer against threats. In the following chapter learn how to implement computer security.

CERTIFICATION OBJECTIVES

■ **601: 6.1   602: 6.1   603: 5.1**   *Identify the fundamental principles of security*

■ **604: 4.1**   *Identify the names, purposes, and characteristics of physical security devices and processes*

All four of the CompTIA A+ certification exams covered in this book require knowledge of security fundamentals and principles, although, as with other objectives, each exam has a slightly different focus. The greatest difference in the four exams is in exam 604, which emphasizes knowledge of physical security devices over the variety of security objectives in the other three exams.

Threats

There was a time when threats to users and computers were very few in number and limited in scope, and when networks were isolated without connections to other networks. Then, networks became more connected and were joined into intranetworks of private networks, often under the umbrella of a single organization, but with a large geographic footprint—many spanning the globe. The more networks we connected together and the larger the number of people with access, the greater the opportunity for evil, mischief, or carelessness to cause damage and loss of data. The problem was compounded beginning in the mid-1990s; with the advent of the World Wide Web more of these networks became connected to the Internet. As the number of networks and individual computers connected to the Internet really exploded, the threats also grew.

What are the threats? In this chapter we will look at some of the ways threats affect individuals and entire organizations, including hardware theft, identity theft, and a long list of other threats. This is not a complete list, since new threats appear every day. Are you paranoid yet? Read on.

e x a m

ⓦ a t c h *The CompTIA A+ exams require that you be able to identify the various types of threats to computers and networks.*

Computer Hardware Theft

Security begins with the simple, time-honored act of locking doors, keeping hardware locked away, and protecting all hardware devices from physical damage or theft. People steal an astounding number of computers, especially laptops, each year from businesses and homes. The result is loss of an important tool and valuable data files, and perhaps even a loss of identity. A large percentage of computer equipment thieves simply want to sell the hardware quickly for cash—at a fraction of the value of your computer and data to you or your business.

Identity Theft

An increasing number of thieves are technically sophisticated and will go through your hard drive looking for bank account, credit card, and other financial data so that they can steal your identity. Identity theft occurs when someone collects personal information belonging to another person and uses that information to fraudulently make purchases, open new credit accounts, and even obtain new driver's licenses and other forms of identification in the victim's name. They may not even be interested in actual financial information; simply obtaining your social security number and other key personal information may be enough to steal your identity.

Thieves can steal your identity in many ways that are not directly involved with your use of computers. Several Web sites maintained by the U.S. government offer valuable information for consumers who wish to protect themselves from identify theft.

Fraud

Fraud is the use of deceit and trickery to persuade someone to hand over money or valuables. Fraud is often associated with identity theft, because the perpetrator will falsely pose as the victim when using the victim's credit cards and other personal and financial information.

Accidents, Mistakes, and Natural and Unnatural Disasters

Accidents and mistakes happen. It seems as if everyone has at one time or another accidentally erased an important file, pressed the wrong button at the wrong instant, or created a file and immediately forgotten its name and location. To the person who made the error, these are disasters.

Disasters happen in many forms. Just to name a few, there are fires, earthquakes, and weather-induced disasters resulting from tornados, lightning strikes, and floods. Predicting such events is imperfect at best. The principal protection against accidents, mistakes, and disasters is to make frequent, comprehensive backups.

You can make backups of an entire hard drive using programs that make an image of the drive, or use programs that back up your critical data files on a periodic basis. Organizations should make multiple backups, saving one set on-site and another set off-site. Then, in case of a disaster that destroys not only the on-site backups but the computers and facilities, they can still recover.

Malicious Software Attacks

Malicious software attacks are, sadly, now common on both private networks and public networks like the Internet. The perpetrators of these malicious attacks, commonly called hackers, are people who make an avocation or vocation out of creating ways to invade computers and networks. At one time this term described a clever programmer, or anyone who enjoyed exploring the software innards of computers. The term hacker has less favorable connotations today.

You probably have heard of many of the types of software threats against computers, such as viruses, worms, Trojan horses, or spam. But have you ever heard of pop-up downloads, drive-by downloads, war driving, Bluesnarfing, adware, spyware, back doors, spim, phishing, or hoaxes? Read on to learn about these various forms of deliberate attacks.

Viruses

A *virus* is a program installed and activated on a computer without the knowledge or permission of the user. At the least, the intent is mischief, but most often the intent is to cause damage. Like a living virus that infects humans, a computer virus can result in a wide range of symptoms and outcomes. Loss of data, damage to or complete failure of an operating system, or theft of personal and financial information are just a few of the potential results of viruses infecting an individual computer. If you extend the range of a virus to a corporate or government network or portions of the Internet, the results are devastating and costly in lost productivity, lost data, lost revenues, and more.

Password Crackers

A huge number of programs and techniques are available to people who want to discover passwords. One commonly used technique is to invade an unsecured Web site to access information unwitting users provide to the site, such as user names and passwords. Another technique is to use a *password cracker,* a program used to discover a password. Some password crackers fall into the category of brute-force password crackers, which simply means the program tries a huge number of permutations of possible passwords. Because most people tend to use simple passwords such as their initials, birthdates, addresses, and so on, the brute-force method works. Other password crackers use more sophisticated statistical or mathematical methods to discover passwords.

Worms

A *worm* is a virus that is self-replicating. Worms travel between machines in many different ways. Several worms in recent years have moved from one computer to another as compressed (Zipped) attachments to e-mail, but they can also be executables. The file has an innocent-sounding or enticing name to tempt the user to open and execute the program. Some of these worms, upon execution, scan the local address book and replicate themselves to the addresses. Variants of such worms as Netsky and MyDoom slowed down networks just by the amount of network traffic they generated.

Trojan Horses

The purpose of the modern-day *Trojan horse* type of virus is to gain access to computers, much like the ancient Greek warriors who, in Homer's famous tale, *The Iliad,* gained access to the city of Troy by hiding in a large wooden horse, presented as a gift to the city. A Trojan horse virus masquerades as a harmless program that a user innocently installs on a computer. The host program may actually work and provide some benefit. These programs are additionally attractive to users because they are often free. After installation the virus activates itself and infects the computer.

Keystroke Loggers

A *keystroke logger* is either a hardware device or a program that monitors and records a user's every keystroke, usually without the user's knowledge. In the case of a hardware logger, the person desiring the keystroke log must physically install it before recording and then remove it afterward in order to collect the stored log of keystrokes. A software keystroke logger program may not require physical access to the target computer, but simply needs a method for downloading and installing it on the computer. Any one of several methods—for instance, a pop-up downloader or drive-by downloader (see the following sections)—can be used to install a keystroke logger. A keystroke logger can send the collected information over a network to the person desiring the log.

Some parents install keystroke loggers to monitor children's Internet activity, but such programs have the potential for abuse by people with less benign motives, including stalking, identity theft, and more.

Pop-Up Downloads

A *pop-up download* is a virus that downloads to a user's computer through a pop-up window that appears in a Web browser. It requires an action on the part of a user, such as clicking on a button that implies acceptance of something like free information, although what that something may actually be is not really clear. The downloaded program may be a virus or worm.

Drive-By Downloads

A *drive-by download* is a program downloaded to a computer without the user's consent. Any drive-by download can install a virus, a worm, adware, or spyware. The user unwittingly initiates the download by some simple act, such as browsing to a Web site or opening an e-mail message written in HTML. Or a user may initiate a drive-by download by installing an application—one of several file sharing programs that allow the sharing of music, data, or photo files over the Internet. Some drive-by downloads may alter your browser home page and/or redirect all your browser searches to one site. This last action is called Web browser hijacking.

Grayware

The term *grayware* describes threats that are not truly malicious code, but these programs have indirect negative effects, such as decreasing performance or using up bandwidth. They are still undesirable, and computers should have protection against grayware, which includes spyware, adware, spam, and spim.

Spyware

Spyware is a category of software that runs surreptitiously on a user's computer in order to gather information without permission from the user, and then sends that information to the people who requested it. Internet-based spyware, sometimes called tracking software or a spybot, may be installed on a computer by one of many means of secretly installing software. Companies use spyware to trace users' surfing patterns in order to improve the company's marketing efforts. Some individuals use it for industrial espionage. With appropriate legal permissions, law enforcement officers use it to find sexual predators and other criminals. Governments use forms of spyware to investigate terrorism.

Adware

Adware, which also installs on a computer without permission, collects information about a user in order to display targeted advertisements, either in the form of inline banners or pop-ups. Inline banners are advertisements that run within the context of the current page, just taking up screen real estate. Pop-ups are a greater annoyance, because they are ads that run in separate browser windows that you must close before you can continue with your present task. Clicking to accept an offer presented on an inline banner or pop-up may trigger a pop-up download that can install a virus or worm.

Spam

Spam is unsolicited e-mail. This includes e-mail from a legitimate source selling a real service or product, as well as from sources with intent to do more harm than to sell you something. If you did not give the sender permission to send such information to you, it is spam. Spam can be the vehicle for bringing a variety of threats to you and your computer. Too often spam involves some form of scam—a bogus offer to sell a service or product that does not exist—or tries to include you in a questionable money-making deal. The latter often turns out to be outright fraud. If it sounds too good to be true, it is! We call the perpetrators of spam "spammers," and laws now make some spam illegal.

Spam accounts for a huge amount of traffic on both the Internet and private networks, and a great loss in productivity as administrators work to protect their users from spam, and as individuals sort through and eliminate spam. Some corporate network administrators report that as much as 60 percent of the incoming e-mail traffic to their individual organizations is spam. One compilation derived from reputable sources estimates that 40 percent of e-mail in 2006 was spam. That makes a total of 12.4 billion spam e-mails, or an average of 2200 per person.

The costs to the spammers are very low, and they will continue to spam as long as people reward them for their efforts. One estimate holds that 8 percent of users who received spam made a purchase as a direct result of the spam.

Spim

Spim is an acronym for Spam over Instant Messaging, and the perpetrators are known as "spimmers." Instant messaging screen names are often collected by small programs, called bots (short for robot, a program that runs automatically), that are sent out over the Internet to collect information. The spimbot then sends unsolicited instant messages to the screen names. A typical spim message may contain a link to a Web site, where, as with spam, the recipient will find products or services for sale—legitimate or otherwise.

Dialers

A *dialer* is a program that causes a modem to surreptitiously dial phone numbers. These are often pay-per-call or international numbers that are charged to the user's phone bill.

Prank Programs

Prank programs, also called joke programs, produce strange behavior, such as screen distortions, erratic cursor behavior, or strange icons on the screen. Even though these programs do not normally directly harm data, they are costly in lost productivity and time to rid the computer of the problem.

Methods for Gaining Access and Obtaining Information

Malicious software and grayware gain access to computers and networks through a large variety of techniques. The following are just a few of these methods.

Back Door

In computing, a *back door* is program code that provides a way in which someone can gain access to a computer while bypassing security. Only a person who knows how the back door works can use it, but once in, that individual has the same access as the host program to all the internal operating system code.

Sometimes a developer installs a back door into a single program for easy access later for administering the program and/or for troubleshooting the program after it is installed on a client's computer. Or, an attacker may create a back door in an operating system or other program by taking advantage of a discovered weakness in the program's security.

In one well-known situation, hackers used the Code Red worm, which took advantage of a vulnerability in Microsoft's Internet Information Server (its Web server software), to install a back door into Windows. Then, they infected PCs with the Nimda worm, which used that back door to invade each computer.

War Driving

War driving is the name given to the act of moving through a neighborhood in a vehicle or on foot, using either a laptop equipped with Wi-Fi wireless network capability, or a simple Wi-Fi sensor available for a few dollars from many sources. War drivers are searching for open hotspots, areas where a Wi-Fi network connects to the Internet without using security to keep out intruders. Using a practice called war chalking, a war driver will often make a mark on a building wherever a hotspot exists. People "in the know" look for these marks to identify hotspots for their use.

People who use these hotspots without permission are trespassing, and, in addition to gaining Internet access, they can prey on other users of the wireless network who are vulnerable if not protected from intrusions to their computers. With this access to the network, the intruder can capture keystrokes, passwords, and user names. Further, if the wireless network connects to an organization's internal wired network, the intruder may gain access to the resources on that network.

Intentionally created hotspots are increasing in number as more and more are made available for free or for a small charge by various businesses, such as coffee shops, bookstores, restaurants, hotels, and even campgrounds.

Bluesnarfing

Similar to war driving, *Bluesnarfing* is the act of covertly obtaining information broadcast from wireless devices using the Bluetooth standard. Using a cell phone, a Bluesnarfer can eavesdrop to acquire information, or even use the synchronizing feature of the device to pick up the user's information without detection by the victim.

Exposure to Inappropriate or Distasteful Content

The Internet, and especially the World Wide Web, is a treasure trove of information. It is hard to imagine a subject that cannot be found somewhere on the Internet. However, some of this content is inappropriate or distasteful.

What is inappropriate or distasteful content? To some extent, only an individual can judge. However, there are circumstances in which one should filter content to avoid exposing a certain group or individual to inappropriate or distasteful content. In that case, use content filtering, a feature in popular Web browsers. For instance, a company may choose to enable content filtering to avoid having employees or customers offended by certain content becoming visible on a computer. Parents can use content filters to protect children from exposure to content the parents believe would be harmful.

Invasion of Privacy

Many of the threats we have described are also clearly invasions of privacy. Protecting against privacy invasion includes protecting your personal information at your bank, credit union, retail stores and Web sites, health clinics, and any organization in which you are a customer, member, patient, or employee.

Every step you take to make your computer more secure contributes to the protection of your privacy.

Cookies—the Good and the Bad

Cookies are good. Mostly. Under some circumstances people can use them for the wrong purposes, but for the most part their benefits far outweigh the negatives. There is a great deal of misinformation about cookies, the small files a Web browser saves on the local hard drive at the request of a Web site. The next time you connect to that same site, it will request the cookie saved on previous visits. Cookies are text files, so they cannot contain viruses, which are executable code, but they may contain the following information:

- User preferences when visiting a specific site
- Information a user entered into a form at the Web site, including personal information
- Browsing activity
- Shopping selections on a Web site

The use of cookies is a convenience to users. Thanks to cookies you do not have to reenter preferences and pertinent information on every visit to a favorite Web site.

The cookies act as electronic notes about your preferences and activities within a Web site, remembering selections you have made on each page so that when you return to the page you do not have to reselect them. Just one example of this is when you are at a retail site and make selections that you add to your "shopping cart." In all likelihood, these selections are saved in one or more cookies, and when you finally decide to check out, the checkout page reads the cookie files to calculate your order.

Although users are not overtly aware when the Web site saves or retrieves cookies on the local hard disk, most good Web sites clearly detail whether they use cookies and what they are used for. Look for this information in the privacy statement or policy of the site.

Normally, only the Web site that created the cookies can access them. However, some advertisers on Web sites have the browser create cookies, and then other sites that include this advertiser can use them. These are "third-party cookies." Learn about browser settings for cookies in Chapter 16.

Your browser cookies are stored in a hidden folder named Cookies in your personal folders. If you cannot see this folder in My Computer or Windows Explorer, modify the View settings found in Tools | Folder Options to Show Hidden Files And Folders.

In Firefox select Tools | Options | Privacy. On the Privacy page click Show Cookies to open a window in which you can search for and view cookies listed in alphabetical order (see Figure 15-1).

FIGURE 15-1

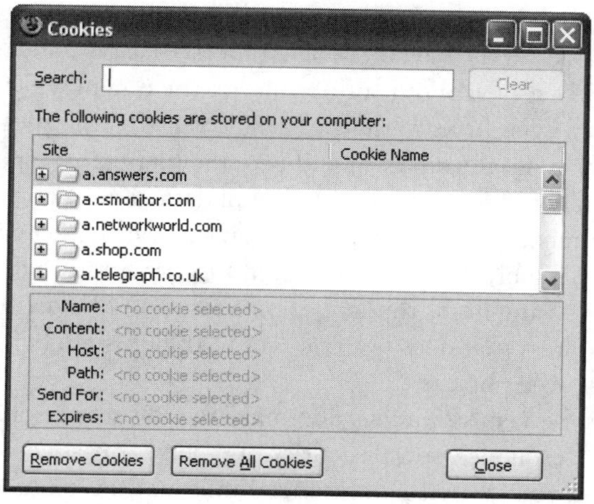

Search for and view cookies in Firefox.

Social Engineering

Social engineering encompasses a variety of persuasion techniques that are used for many purposes—good and bad. People with malicious intent use social engineering to persuade someone to reveal confidential information or give something else of value to the perpetrator. The information sought may be in the form of confidential corporate data, personal identifying or financial information, user names and passwords, or anything you can imagine that could be of value to another person.

While social engineering is as old as Homo sapiens, and there are countless techniques employed, there are a few types of social engineering techniques that everyone should learn to recognize. They all count on the natural trusting behavior of the targeted people. Once you understand the forms of social engineering threats, you are less likely to become a victim. In this section we will explore social engineering threats and appropriate responses. On the Internet the most common vehicle for social engineering communications is e-mail.

The best response to any form of social engineering is to not respond and to not reveal any information. And you should never send money in response to a communication from a stranger, no matter how enticing the offer may be.

Phishing

Phishing is a fraudulent method of obtaining personal and financial information through the use of pop-ups or e-mail messages that purport to be from a legitimate organization, such as a bank, credit card company, retailer, and so on. They often (falsely) appear to be from well-known organizations and Web sites, such as various banks, eBay, PayPal, MSN, Yahoo, Best Buy, and America Online.

In a typical phishing scenario, the e-mail will contain authentic-looking logos, and even links to the actual site, but the link specified for supplying personal financial information will take recipients to a "spoofed" Web page where they are supposed to enter their personal data. The Web page may look exactly like the company's real Web page, but it's not at the legitimate site. A common practice is for a phisher to use the credit information to make purchases over the Internet, choosing items that are easy to resell and having them delivered to a destination address that does not connect to the phisher, but to which he has access, such as a vacant house.

Be very suspicious of e-mails requesting personal financial information, such as access codes, social security numbers, or passwords. Legitimate businesses will never ask you for personal financial information in an e-mail.

To learn more about phishing, and to see the latest examples of phishing, point your Web browser to www.antiphishing.org, the Web site of the Anti-Phishing Working Group. See a list of reported phishing scams, and you can also report phishing attacks at this site.

Would you recognize a phishing e-mail? There are Web sites that try to educate people to recognize a phishing scam when they receive it in e-mail or other communications. Exercise 15-1 describes how to use just one of these sites.

EXERCISE 15-1

What Is Your Phishing IQ?

You can test your Phishing IQ and learn to identify phishing scams.

1. Use your Web browser to connect to the Phishing IQ test at www.sonicwall.com/phishing.

2. You will see ten e-mails. You must decide whether each is legitimate or phish.

3. When you finish, you can review the correct answers, along with a detailed explanation as to why each is either legitimate or phish.

If you completed Exercise 15-1, you will have noticed that phishing e-mails look very official, but in some cases, careful scrutiny reveals problems. While the signs identified in these messages are not the full extent of the problems you can find in a phishing e-mail, this type of test helps to educate us so that we do not become victims of phishing.

While not all phishing e-mails have the same characteristics, the following lists just a few problems detected in phishing e-mails:

- The "To:" field is not addressed to you, even though it appeared in your inbox.
- There is no greeting, or one that omits your name.
- The message text shows bad grammar or punctuation.
- When you click a link, the URL you are directed to does not match what appears in the e-mail.
- A link does not use HTTPS.
- The title bar reveals that a foreign character set (e.g., Cyrillic) is used.
- What appears to be a protected account number (revealing only the last four digits) is not your number at all.

- What appears to be an account expiration date is not the correct expiration date for your account.
- A URL has a slightly misspelled domain name that resembles the legitimate domain name.
- No additional contact information is given, such as a toll-free phone number and a name and title of a contact person.

Now, to make things more confusing, some legitimate e-mails may show some of these problems or practices, and not all phishing e-mails have all of these negative characteristics.

A safer way to include a URL in a legitimate e-mail is to not make it a link, but to include it in the e-mail as unformatted text, with instructions to cut and paste it into a Web browser. This way, malware cannot redirect the recipient to a bogus Web site. The user must still be diligent and examine the URL before using it.

Phone Phishing

Phone phishing is another form of phishing. In order to gain the intended victim's confidence, a phishing e-mail will urge the reader to call a phone number to verify information, at which point the person on the phone will ask the victim to reveal the valuable information.

What makes this so compelling to the user is that phone phishing often involves a very authentic-sounding professional Interactive Voice Response (IVR) menu system, just like a legitimate financial institute would have. It may ask the user to enter their password or personal identifying number (PIN). To ensure that the system captures the correct password or PIN, the system may even ask the victim to repeat it. Some systems then have the victim talk to a "representative" who gathers more information.

on the job

Keep yourself up-to-date on the latest threats. Microsoft and other software vendors, particularly those who specialize in security products, offer a wealth of information on their Web sites. You can also subscribe to newsletters from these same organizations.

Hoaxes

A *hoax* may take many forms. One is an e-mail message claiming to be from Microsoft notifying the receiver of the availability of an update, and providing a link to a Web site for downloading the fix. When recipients click the link, rather than receive the latest security update, they may be downloading a virus or other invasive program. Microsoft never sends out updates through e-mail.

Enticements to Open Attachments

Social engineering is also involved in the enticements, called "gimmes" in e-mails—either in the subject line or the body of the e-mail—to open the attachments. Opening the attachment then executes and infects the local computer with some form of malware. There are a huge number of methods used. Sadly, enticements often appeal to basic characteristics in people, such as greed (an offer too good to be true), vanity (physical enhancements), or simple curiosity. Some bogus enticements appeal to people's sympathy and compassion by way of a non-existent charity. Or the author of the e-mail will pose as a legitimate charity—anything to get you to open the attachment.

Defense Against Threats

Protection from threats begins with realistic security policies, which this section defines and describes. Most of the other topics in this section are included under the umbrella of security policies. These include access control, firewalls, equipment disposal, and recovery. In addition, users must also learn to identify social engineering ploys.

SCENARIO & SOLUTION

What type of threat uses deceit and trickery to gain money or valuables?	Fraud is the use of deceit and trickery to persuade a person to give up money or valuables. Fraud is a crime.
What is the term used to describe a software attack that captures keystrokes, usually without the user's knowledge?	Keystroke logger
Phishing, phone phishing, hoaxes, and enticement to open attachments are all examples of techniques used to persuade someone to reveal confidential information or give something else of value to the perpetrator. What is the term used for this?	Social engineering

Security Policies

A security policy is a set of rules and practices describing how an organization protects and manages sensitive information. A security policy applies to all employees. Most medium- to large-sized organizations have an explicit, written security policy. Small organizations may have a written policy but often only have an implicit policy—one that is not formally defined, in writing, and available to all employees or members. All organizations should have a security policy. If you belong to an organization that does not, and you are not in a position to change that situation, at the very least protect yourself by behaving as if there were an explicit security policy in place. Many of the basic concepts of a security policy are universal, and any computer professional with integrity should observe them.

Background

Security policy has become critical for more organizations since the 1996 enactment of the Health Insurance Portability and Accountability Act (HIPAA) by the U.S. Congress. All health care companies are required to comply with the HIPAA requirements for storing patient information, and they must follow certain guidelines for risk analysis, awareness training, audit trails, disaster recovery plans, and information access control and encryption. HIPAA is one of the most compelling reasons you are required to study security for the A+ exams.

Security Policy Defined

A security policy is a set of rules or requirements that all employees or members must meet. A policy covers a single area. Security policies define appropriate behavior and the expected consequences of inappropriate behavior. In fact, you should pay close attention to policies because a violation could cost you your job or worse, since in some cases, an employer can bring legal action against an employee who violates security policy.

Security policy defines who has access to what resources. This requires good judgment in determining how much access you can entrust to anyone. If you completely trust everyone, you can be vulnerable to a betrayal of the trust. In fact, the officers and managers of an organization may be in violation of HIPAA or some other regulation if they are too trusting. However, security policy must involve some level of trust, or compliance will get in the way of accomplishing work.

A security policy must allow the needed amount of trust, and the most trusted people become administrators. They must put practices in place to restrict access and to allow administrators to adjust access.

Security policies are all-inclusive. They apply to all employees or members. The typical employee will be affected by the need to provide credentials (e.g., user name and password) to authenticate and receive authorization for access to resources. Administrators and other PC support personnel have the task of administering and managing systems. The company must absorb the cost of implementing and managing security policy.

Creating Security Policies

A committee normally creates security policies. The makeup of this committee varies from company to company, but the membership should ideally include the following:

- One or more senior-level administrators
- A manager with authority to enforce the policy
- A lawyer or other member of the legal staff
- One or more employees representing the user community
- A competent and experienced writer

Implementing Security Policy

A security policy will fail if it is not enforceable or understood by all involved. An organization should formally present security policies to all employees, and the security policies should be included in new employee orientations. Once an employee has had an opportunity to review security policy, you must obtain some form of confirmation that the employee understands and agrees to comply with the policy. Give annual review seminars on policy, if possible.

IT Security Policies

IT security policies can include a variety of policies. The following outlines the major policy areas that should be included in IT security policies.

Acceptable Use Policy   An acceptable use policy covers the responsibility of the user when using equipment, programs, and data. Some organizations will not issue a user account until an employee reviews and signs an acceptable use policy.

Remote Access Policy   A remote access policy covers how users remotely access the company network. This will detail the authorized methods and security procedures required of the user.

Data Protection Policy A data (or information) protection policy details the appropriate use, storage, transmission, and even the printing of corporate data, especially data identified as sensitive data critical to the organization, or personal data, such as medical or financial records. Only employees whose jobs require it should have access to sensitive data.

Physical Security Policy A physical security policy, also called a perimeter security policy, describes the methods for allowing employees access to the physical site. It may include security at all entrances and/or security to server rooms, equipment closets, and printers. It should also define who (often by job title) may have access to an area, and who has knowledge of the details of physical security access.

Malicious Software Protection Policy A malicious software protection policy defines the requirements for protection against the various malicious software threats. This will include specific protection software, such as antivirus, antispyware, and antispam software. This policy should also define rules for downloading files and programs to company computers, and for scanning e-mail and e-mail attachments.

Password Policy A password policy details how to create passwords for maximum protection, including length and complexity. This policy must also describe requirements for protecting passwords, and may require changing certain passwords at a specified interval.

Incident Reporting The security policies of an organization should define incident reporting. The type of incidents reported depends on the security policy of your organization. For instance, the security policy might state that you should report any action that violates or attempts to violate the company's security policy.

It is very important to report incidents, and to report them to the correct people. When an incident involves a third party, such as a fraudulently represented bank in a phishing e-mail, reporting the incident to the bank will enable them to take action, for instance, reporting the incident to the police and perhaps taking legal action against the perpetrators if they can be identified. They may have grounds for a civil suit against the wrongdoer. Organizations track incident reports in order to evaluate the effectiveness of security measures, and to determine if additional action is required to protect systems.

The process for incident reporting will depend on the organization. Many organizations publish a Web page that defines a reportable incident and contains instructions on the incident reporting procedure. An incident normally includes

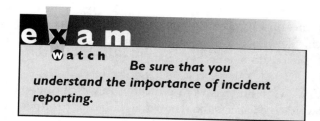

any attempt to access the physical site, computer systems, and network, as well as the introduction of malicious code to computers or the network. Depending on the nature of the incident, and the level of security required by the organization, the organization will evaluate a reported incident for impact, investigate for the source of the incident, and take steps to correct any security flaws the investigation reveals.

Controlling Access to Restricted Spaces

The best defense against common threats is well-managed access control. Access control is management of access to resources. Properly implemented, access control allows the good guys in and keeps the bad guys out. For hardware resources, access control involves managing who can physically access equipment within physical sites, and involves restricting physical access only to authorized personnel.

Sometimes, in our quest to protect computers from attacks, we forget the most basic source of threat from someone with malicious intent who can physically access computers or other equipment. Restricted spaces are those rooms, closets, offices, or desks that only authorized persons should have physical access to. Ironically, gaining physical access to restricted spaces is often very easy. Even in facilities with state-of-the-art security, intruders can gain access using stolen credentials or by taking advantage of lax enforcement of security policies.

Access Control to Computers and Networks

Access control of resources on a local computer or over a network involves the processes of authentication (verifying a user's identity) and authorization (determining the level of access someone has to a resource). In the following sections, explore types of access control.

Password-Based vs. User-Based Access Control

Control of access to computer resources can be very simple password-based access control, or more elaborate and secure user-based access control.

Password-based access control requires only that a resource has a password assigned to it. It does not require identification of the user in any way. Operating systems that do not have access to an accounts database perform password-based access control. This is the type that you could place on shares on a Windows 9x computer participating in a workgroup. It cannot be used on the file system in Windows 9x because the file system does not support access control. Therefore, local users have complete access to the local files and folders.

You could create a share in Windows 9x and password-protect it. In which case, anyone who has the correct password could access the share. Your choice is to either leave a share without any security, or to assign a password to it and to every other share you wish to protect. We like to think that pure password-based access control is a thing of the past.

User-based access control requires authentication and authorization. Each user must have an account. In a Windows network the account can be a local account or a domain account. Of course, whenever possible use centralized accounts so that each user only needs to log on to the centralized database for authentication, and, as the user attempts to access each resource, the system performs authorization to verify the user's level of access to the resource. The user can use one user account to gain access to any network resources to which the user is granted access in the form of permissions.

Authentication and Authorization

One of the first defenses against threats is authentication and authorization by security systems built into the operating systems on your local computer and network servers. Recall from Chapter 13 that authentication is the verification of who you are, and authorization determines your level of access to a computer or a resource. The most recent Windows desktop OSs support both of these.

Authentication Factors

Authentication verification uses up to three factors, which include something you know, something you have, and something you are. An example of something you know is a user name and password, or a personal identification number (PIN). Something you have may be a smart card, and something you are may be a measurement of a body part, such as a fingerprint or retina scan. Authentication involves one or more of these factors and can therefore be one-factor, two-factor, or three-factor authentication. We describe individual factors and their uses in the following sections.

Passwords

We have used the term password many times in the previous chapters of this book, but until now we have not stopped to define it. Most of us have had to use passwords, but it does not hurt to stop and define this term. A *password* is a string of characters that a user enters, along with an identifier, such as a user name, in order for authentication to take place.

A password is an important security tool for anyone who uses a computer, especially one connected to any network, including the Internet. Do not take your passwords for granted! You may have habits or practices that make you vulnerable to identity theft and other threats. Consider the following questions:

- Do you have too many passwords to remember?
- When you have an opportunity to create a new password, do you use your favorite password?
- At school or work, do you have your password written on sticky notes or your desk calendar?
- Have you used the same password for more than a few months?

If you answered "yes" to any of these questions, you are at risk, and you need to change your behavior.

Best Practices with User Names and Passwords

Here are some best practices to keep in mind when working with user names and passwords.

Don't Give Away Your User Name and Password If you use the same user name and password at your bank as you do at an unrelated Web site where you innocently provided personal information, you may have put your bank account and your other financial assets at risk. Perhaps the Web site was created just for the purpose of gathering personal information, or it may be harmless except that it has weak security. Either way, the outcome may be the same—someone has information that could enable them to access your bank account.

Someone can piece together information gathered from several Web sites and other sources to figure out where you bank, and to use the user name and password you provided elsewhere to access your account. Even if your bank uses the best security practices (which most do), if someone else provides your user name and password, that person will have full access to your account.

Create Strong Passwords A strong password is one that meets certain criteria in order to be difficult to crack. The criteria change over time as people with malicious intent (hackers) create more and more techniques and tools for discovering passwords. One definition of a strong password is one that contains at least eight characters, includes a combination of letters, numbers, and other symbols (_, -, $, and so on), and is easy for you to remember but difficult for others to guess.

Never Reuse Passwords   Every account should have a unique user name (if possible) and a unique password (always). Many Web sites require your e-mail address as the user name, so these will not be unique.

Avoid Creating Unnecessary Online Accounts   Many Web sites ask that you create an account and "join," but what are the benefits of joining? Why do they need information about you?

Don't Provide More Information Than Necessary   Avoid creating accounts with Web sites that request your social security number and other personal and financial information. Avoid having your credit card numbers and bank account information stored on a Web site. Although it is not easy to do online, when a merchant asks you for your social security number, ask these four questions:

1. Why do you need it?
2. How will you protect it?
3. How will you use it?
4. What happens if I don't give it to you?

You may have to make a decision as to whether to do business with that merchant if they do not give you satisfactory answers.

Always Use Strong Passwords for Certain Types of Accounts   Use strong passwords for the following account types:

- Banks, investments, credit cards, and online payment providers
- E-mail
- Work-related
- Online auction sites and retailers
- Sites where you have provided personal information

Authentication Technologies

Authentication comes after a user presents credentials. In the vast majority of cases, you gain access to computers and networks with a standard interactive logon using a keyboard—most often the ubiquitous computer keyboard. Organizations requiring more stringent authentication practices will use specialized technologies, such as smart cards, key fobs, and even biometric scanners. All of these technologies provide more secure authentication at an additional cost, but the costs are coming down, and they are becoming more widespread. Learn more about just a few of them now.

Standard Interactive Logon   The type of authentication most commonly used on Windows PCs is a standard interactive logon in which the user enters a user name and password into a security dialog box. This does not require any special hardware, as the user name and password can be entered using the keyboard or, in the case of someone with special needs, an adaptive input device.

Depending on the configuration of your Windows computer, the logon dialog box will not display automatically. In this case, when a user is not logged on, as occurs immediately after Windows starts up, the Welcome to Windows dialog box (see Figure 15-2) displays with special instructions. A user must use a secure attention sequence (SAS), the CTRL-ALT-DELETE key combination, before the Log On To Windows dialog box will appear. This is for security purposes, clearing memory of certain types of viruses that may be lurking. If not disabled by this action, malicious code could wait to capture the keystrokes you enter for your user name and password. In some instances, you may be able to disable this requirement, but you will lose the security it offers.

A standard installation of Windows XP in a workgroup will not require CTRL-ALT-DELETE, but an administrator who desires a higher level of security should enable it. Exercise 15-2 describes the steps to enable or disable this setting in Local Security Policy.

FIGURE 15-2   Press CTRL-ALT-DELETE.

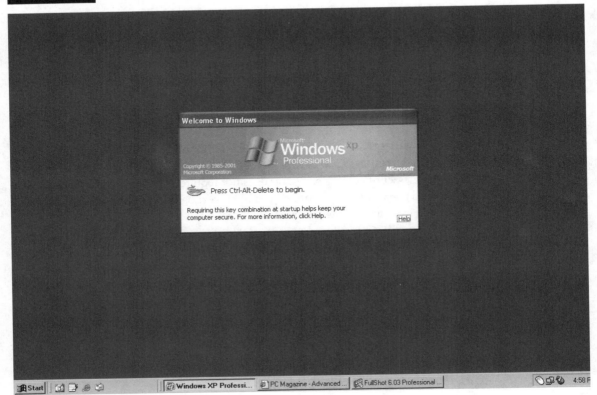

EXERCISE 15-2

Enabling or Disabling the CTRL-ALT-DELETE Requirement

An administrator can enable or disable the CTRL-ALT-DELETE requirement for an interactive logon by making a change in Local Security Settings. You must log on as the Administrator account or as a member of the Administrators group.

1. Select Start | Control Panel. In Control Panel double-click Administrative Tools.

2. In Administrative Tools double-click Local Security Policy.

3. In the Local Security Settings console expand Security Settings | Local Policies | Security Options.

4. In the details pane double-click Interactive Logon: Do Not Require CTRL+ALT+DEL. In the Setting dialog box click the radio button for the setting you want to use, Enabled or Disabled, as shown here.

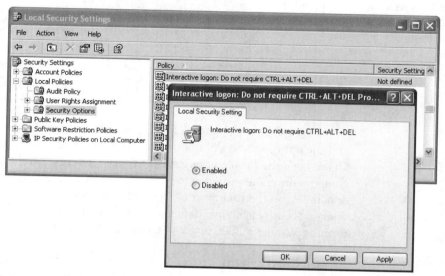

5. Click OK to close the dialog box, and verify that the Security Setting for this policy reflects the setting you chose. Then close the Local Security Settings dialog box. If you chose to enable this policy, the next time you log off or restart your computer you will be required to first use this key combination before you can log on.

The contents of the Log On To Windows dialog box depend on whether the computer is a member of a workgroup or a domain. If it is a member of a workgroup, then the only possible logon is a local logon to the computer and the Log On To Windows dialog box will reflect this limit (see Figure 15-3). During a local logon, the local computer's logon security components authenticate the user, who must use a user name and password from the local security accounts database.

If you click Options in the Log On To Windows dialog box, it will expand the dialog box so that you will see the Log On To box. In the case of a computer that is a member of a workgroup, this box is a simple text box that only contains the name of the local computer. If the computer is a member of a Windows domain, the user may log on to the local computer or to the domain, and the dialog box will allow for these choices with a drop-down box. Figure 15-4 shows the Log On To drop-down box, in which the user can select the local computer or a domain logon. The parenthetical phrase automatically shows to inform the user.

FIGURE 15-3

This dialog box
only allows a
logon to the local
computer.

If a computer is a member of a domain, the preferred logon is to the domain, and the options view will not display unless a user clicks Options. During a domain logon, both the local computer security components and the domain security components come into play to make the logon as secure as possible. During a domain logon the user must use a user name and password of an account in the domain security accounts database. In a domain in which the domain controllers are running Windows 2000 or greater, this accounts database is called Active Directory.

Smart Card Logon A *smart card* is a plastic card, often the size of a credit card, which contains a microchip. The microchip can store information and perform functions, depending on the type of smart card. Some smart cards only store data, while others may have a variety of functions, including security cards for logging on to facilities or computers. If configuration of the Windows domain controllers and local Windows computers allows acceptance of smart card logons, users may use this method of presenting credentials and logging on. The domain controllers require certain software security components, while the local computer must have a special piece of hardware called a smart card reader or card terminal. When the user inserts the card into the reader, the reader sends commands to the card in order to complete

FIGURE 15-4

This dialog box
allows the user
to log on to the
local computer or
to a domain.

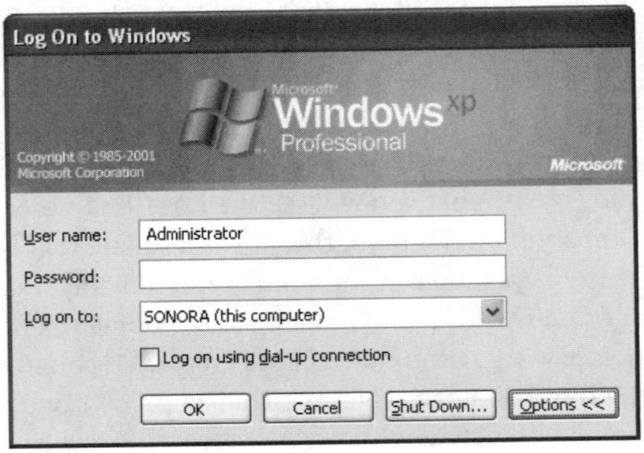

the authentication process. As is true of a bank cash card, the user may also need to enter a PIN (Personal Identification Number) into the keyboard in conjunction with the smart card. The two together comprise two-factor authentication.

Key Fob Logon   Much like a smart card, a *key fob* is a small device containing a microchip, and you can use it for logging on to a computer or a network. Also called a security token, it has a form factor that suggests something you might attach to a key chain, as its name implies. A common procedure for using a key fob is to insert the key fob and enter the PIN, which identifies the user as the owner of the key fob. Then, the key fob displays a string of characters. Either it transmits the characters to the computer, or the user manually enters the string to gain access. This string is a one-time password (OTP). The key fob generates a different password at each use, and this guarantees that the user has a unique, strong password protected from the vulnerabilities of ordinary user-generated passwords, which may be too easy to guess, or which the user may write down somewhere to avoid having to memorize.

Biometric Logon   Users can easily forget passwords or PINs, and lose smart cards. But each person can be uniquely identified by measurements of body parts— a biometric. A logon based on one of these measurements is a *biometric logon*. Commonly used biometrics include fingerprints, handprints, and retinal scans. It uses a hardware device that can perform the scan, and through an interface with a local computer, the scanned information goes to the security components for processing. As with smart card logon, this requires specialized hardware attached to the local computer and specialized software on the domain controllers (in the case of a domain logon). The domain accounts database must contain the biometric information for each user account for which this type of logon is enabled.

Access Control to File Systems

File system security comes in the form of access control to the file systems. It begins with an authentication and authorization system for restricting access to the computer itself. Next, the file system must support the application of permissions to restrict the level of access for each user or group in an accounts database. For sensitive files, consider adding encryption to the mix. File and folder permissions and encryption are only available on NTFS volumes; none of the FAT file systems used in Windows supports these. NTFS is your preferred file system.

In Chapter 13 you learned the basics of file and folder permissions, including the two sets of standard permissions for files and folders. If you need a refresher, flip back to Chapter 13 and review those permissions. Next we will discuss some of the more technical aspects of permissions, including ACLs, ACEs, and inheritance.

ACLs and ACEs

Each file and folder on an NTFS volume has an associated access control list (ACL), which is a table of users and/or groups and their permissions to the file or folder. Each ACL has at least one access control entry (ACE), which is like a record in this tiny ACL database that contains just one user or group account name and the permissions assigned to that account.

An administrator, or someone with the permissions to create ACEs for the file or folder, creates ACEs. To view the ACEs in an ACL for a file or folder, open its Properties dialog box and select the Security tab. Figure 15-5 shows the Security page for a folder named Spreadsheets. Notice the list of permissions for the user jholcombe. This is an ACE.

NTFS Permission Inheritance

Arrangement of the folders and files on a disk volume is in a hierarchy, with the drive itself at the top, followed by the root folder and subfolders. When you create a new folder or file, it inherits the permission settings of the parent folder, unless you choose to block this inheritance through an option in the Security page of the file or folder.

When you view permissions on a file or folder, the permissions inherited from the parent will be grayed out, and you will not be able to modify those permissions at the child (inherited) level.

You can assign new permissions, but inherited permissions cannot be altered. However, you can modify them in the folder in which they originated. You can choose to block inheritance on a folder or file to which you wish to assign different (usually more restrictive) permissions. To do this, you must log on with a user account that can modify the ACL for the child folder. Click on Advanced on the

FIGURE 15-5

The list of
permissions for
a folder

Security page of the folder. Then, in the Advanced Security Settings page clear the check box with a description that begins with the word "Inherit." When you do this, a prompt will display with the option to copy the permissions of the parent folder. Once you have copied the permissions to the ACL for this folder, you can alter them, which is something you cannot do to inherited permissions.

Permissions Assigned to Personal Folders

When a user logs on to Windows for the first time, the operating system creates personal folders on the local hard drive for that use. If that local drive is an NTFS partition, Windows will assign a default set of permissions to those folders designed to keep other users out. The user has full control over their personal folders, as does the Administrators group and the System. No other user has permissions to these folders or can even view their contents.

The default location for these folders is in a folder that Windows assigns the user's logon name and places in C:\Documents and Settings. See Figure 15-6, which shows the Documents and Settings folder with personal folders for several users. We expanded the ssmith folder to show the contents.

If you have a computer running Windows, and with an NTFS drive C:, use the steps in Exercise 15-3 to view permissions on your personal folders.

FIGURE 15-6

Personal folders in Windows XP

EXERCISE 15-3

Viewing Folder Permissions

View the permissions on your personal folders. In order to complete this exercise, you need to use the Security tab on the properties of a folder on an NTFS volume. If this tab is not available on an NTFS volume, Simple File Sharing must be turned off. Exercise 13-4 in Chapter 13 describes how to do this.

1. Open My Computer and browse to C:\Documents and Settings. Notice the folders. There should be one for each user who has logged on, plus one titled All Users.

2. Open the folder with the user name that you used when you logged on. View the contents of this folder. These folders make up the user profile for your user account on this computer. Close the folder.

3. Right-click the folder with the user name that you used to log on. Select Properties, and then select the Security tab. Click Permissions to see the list of users and groups that have permissions to the folder.

4. As shown here, the only accounts given permissions to personal folders are the user's account (Sue Smith), the Administrators group, and the SYSTEM (the Windows operating system). No other user has permission to access these folders. Close the window when you are finished.

Encryption

Encryption is the transformation of data into a code that one can only decrypt through the use of a secret key or password. A secret key is a special code used to decrypt encrypted data. You can use encryption on data files that are stored on a local computer or on a network server. In addition, data being sent over a network can be encrypted. Encryption protects sensitive or valuable data, and only someone who knows the password or holds the secret key can decrypt the data back to its original state. The secret key may be held in a digital certificate, which is a special file stored on a computer. Encryption is very useful for data stored on a laptop or in a professional setting where data theft is a real concern. The NTFS file system on Windows 2000 or newer computers includes the ability to encrypt files and folders. Learn how to implement encryption in Chapter 16.

Firewalls

Firewalls protect you against the dangers presented by having an unprotected connection to an untrusted network, such as the Internet. A firewall sits between a private network and the untrusted network and examines all traffic in and out of the network it is protecting. It will block any traffic it recognizes as a potential threat, using a variety of techniques.

Firewall Technologies

A firewall may perform a large number of related tasks, but the most common and traditional tasks include IP packet filtering, proxy service, network address translation (NAT), encrypted authentication, and support for virtual private networks (VPNs).

IP Packet Filtering An IP packet filter inspects (or filters) each packet that enters or leaves the network, applying a set of security rules defined by a network administrator. Packets that fail inspection are not allowed to pass between the connected networks.

Proxy Server A proxy server, described in Chapter 13, is often an important part of a firewall. The proxy server intercepts outbound connection requests from internal clients to external servers and directs the resulting incoming traffic to the correct internal computer. While doing this, the proxy server hides the internal address of the client computer, acting as a stand-in (proxy) for the internal computers.

Network Address Translation   Another method for hiding internal IP addresses is network address translation (NAT). A TCP/IP protocol developed as a solution to the dwindling number of IP addresses on the Internet, NAT is available on most broadband routers, although you will rarely see the term NAT used and rarely need to configure NAT. The NAT component is often referred to as a NAT router.

To understand NAT, you need to first understand public and private IP addresses. Public IP addresses are those that are used on the Internet and are globally unique. The current IP protocol, IPv4, with its 32-bit address (usually shown in dotted decimal format) is running out of these public addresses. This was predicted many years ago, and many measures have been taken to extend the life of IPv4 and its 32-bit addresses. One such action was to designate blocks of IP addresses as private addresses. These addresses are reserved for private networks and never assigned to a device that is directly on the Internet. Perhaps millions of computers worldwide use these private addresses on their internal networks.

The addresses are in the following ranges: 10.0.0.1 to 10.255.255.254, 172.16.0.1 to 172.31.255.254, and 192.168.0.0 to 192.168.255.254. Most NAT-enabled devices use this last group of addresses for the private network.

With a public address on the external NIC and a private address on the internal NIC, a typical NAT device translates the source address of each outgoing packet from hosts on the private network (NAT clients) into the NAT router's public address (sometimes using more than one public address). Along with changing the source IP address to the public address, the NAT device also identifies all traffic from each host with a special identifier called a port number. Port numbers play a much larger role in networking than the numbers assigned by a NAT router. When a packet is sent to an IP address, a port number in the packet identifies what service the packet is accessing. There are many well-known port numbers used to identify standard services like SMTP and FTP. What NAT does during translation of outgoing packets is to renumber source ports and maintain a port mapping table that it uses to redirect the resulting incoming traffic to the correct host.

NAT routing works faster than a proxy service, but it has some significant limits. It basically is only practical for a small private network in which there is only a single private IP network and no servers that must be accessed from the Internet. It does not examine the contents of packets, which a proxy server will do.

Encrypted Authentication   Encrypted authentication is a security service that is not limited to firewalls. When a firewall receives connection requests originating from outside the private, protected network, some firewalls require the external users to provide a user name and password before giving access. Since authentication information passes over the untrusted network, these firewalls often support and require encrypted authentication using one of several encryption protocols to encrypt the authentication credentials (user name and password) during transmission.

Virtual Private Network   Not truly a firewall technology, a virtual private network (VPN) is a virtual tunnel created between two endpoints over an untrusted network. This is done by encapsulating the packets within special packets for the tunnel. Other security methods are also usually applied to a VPN, such as encryption of the data before encapsulating it, and encrypted authentication. When set up in combination with a properly configured firewall, a VPN is the safest way to connect two private networks over the Internet.

Hardware Firewalls

Your ISP and most corporations employ hardware firewalls, expensive and specialized devices manufactured by companies such as Cisco, NETGEAR, and others. These sophisticated firewalls require highly trained people to configure and manage them. At work or at school such a firewall normally protects the internal network.

on the
job

Cisco offers certification in their router technologies. These certifications require experience and hands-on practice and are highly respected and valued by employers.

Based on its configuration, a firewall makes decisions about allowing traffic into a private network. The administrator determines the actual configuration to allow necessary traffic in and out of the private network. The type of computer on the private network, in turn, determines the necessary traffic.

If all the computers on a private network are desktop computers connecting to the Internet to browse Web pages and access FTP sites, the firewall protecting the network has a simple job. It blocks all inbound traffic that is not the result of a request from a computer on the internal network; matching incoming traffic with previous outgoing traffic that made requests that would result in incoming traffic. For instance, when you connect to a Web site, there is outgoing traffic from your computer to the Web site requesting to see a page. That page comes to you in the form of incoming traffic. A firewall will allow it through because of your initial request.

If the private network includes servers that offer services on the Internet, then it must allow initiating traffic to come through the firewall, but it does not allow all incoming traffic through. In this case, the firewall configuration allows incoming traffic of the type that can communicate with the internally based servers. The various types of traffic include e-mail, HTTP (Web), FTP, and others. Each type of traffic has a certain port number recognized by the firewall. Figure 15-7 shows a firewall protecting a network containing both servers and desktop computers (shown as clients).

A network professional would look at the simplified firewall example in Figure 15-7 and immediately recommend setting up a DMZ, a network between the internal network and the Internet with a firewall on both sides. The DMZ, named for a wartime demilitarized zone, would contain any servers an organization wishes to use to offer services to the Internet. The firewall between the DMZ and the private network would isolate the private network from the incoming traffic destined for the servers.

Software Firewalls

A software firewall is one that you can install on any computer, as opposed to the software built into a hardware firewall. The most common software firewalls are called personal firewalls because they are designed to be installed on individual desktop computers.

FIGURE 15-7

A private network protected by a firewall

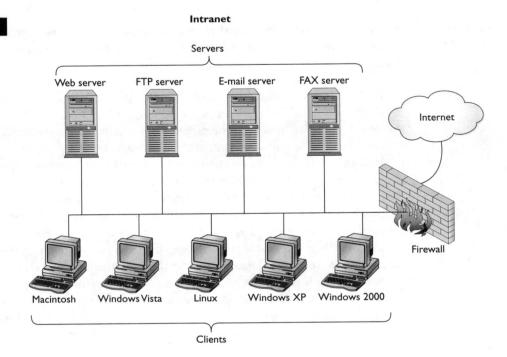

Both Windows XP and Windows Vista come with a firewall, and there are many third-party firewalls to choose from, including Symantec's Norton Personal Firewall, Sunbelt/Kerio Personal Firewall, CheckPoint's ZoneAlarm Pro Personal Firewall, and many more. Before installing a third-party firewall in Windows, be sure to turn off the Windows Firewall, which you will find as an applet in the Control Panel.

Equipment Disposal

How does your organization dispose of old computer equipment? This is a topic that will be pursued in Chapter 17 in regard to keeping computer waste out of the waste stream, recycling components, and disposing of hazardous waste contained in computers and related equipment. Whatever the policy on equipment disposal, it should include the thorough removal of all data from hard drives and destruction of optical media containing data. The best practice is to destroy all the data on the hard drives before sending them to a recycler. Ordinary deletion of the files in Windows will not permanently delete these files, even if you reformat the hard drives. Therefore, use a program that will truly erase all the data from the hard drives so that it cannot be recovered, even with very sophisticated tools.

Recovery

The ability to recover from an attack depends on the preparation work. For instance, have good backup procedures in place so that you can restore destroyed data. Have all the protections in place for possible threats, including access control, antivirus,

SCENARIO & SOLUTION

I want to set a more restrictive level of permissions on a folder, but the user permissions are grayed out. What can I do?	If your account has permissions to modify the ACLs on the folder, turn off inheritance on the folder in the Advanced Security Settings page of the folder's Properties dialog box.
I plan to travel with a laptop running Windows XP Professional that contains very sensitive data. How can I protect the data in the event of theft of the laptop?	If you save the data to an NTFS volume, you can use file and folder encryption to protect it.
Our company disposes of old computer equipment through a service that recycles many of the components. How can we protect the sensitive data on the hard drives?	Take measures to permanently delete the data before sending the computers to the recycler.

antispam, firewalls, and other procedures available for protecting systems and data. If these are in place, recovery will take a minimum of time.

Auditing

Security auditing is a way to monitor security-related events. Windows does not record security events by default, but an administrator can configure Event Viewer to audit selected categories of events. Once configured, you have an audit trail of these events. This will not protect against unauthorized access, but it will give you proof of activity. For instance, auditing the successful logon events in a Windows domain will tell you who logged on and when. Auditing logon failures may tell you when logons failed. These failures may not be intruders—just users who forgot their passwords, but they may be someone trying to guess a password. If you view the Security log frequently, you may see evidence of an intruder attempting to guess passwords. For instance, look for logon activity success or failure after work hours. You can limit logon hours to work hours, but with so many people working late, or from their homes after hours or while on business trips, this may not be practical.

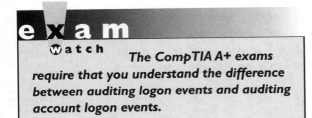

The CompTIA A+ exams require that you understand the difference between auditing logon events and auditing account logon events.

Auditing is turned on or off through the Local Security Settings console that is launched from the Local Security Policy selection in the Administrative Tools menu. In the Local Security Settings console navigate to Security Settings | Local Policies | Audit Policy, where the Audit policies are listed, as shown in Figure 15-8.

FIGURE 15-8

Audit Policy

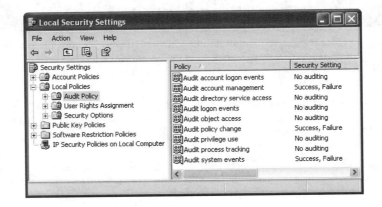

Use discretion when setting up auditing. Do not audit every type of event on every user, file, or folder that you choose, because too much auditing can slow down a computer. Auditing many events also creates large log files very quickly, giving the administrator a great deal of data to sift through.

Auditing Logon Events vs. Auditing Account Logon Events

When working in an Active Directory domain, is it important to understand the difference between auditing logon events and auditing account logon events. Auditing logon events is computer specific. That is, it only audits logon events for the computer on which the logon event occurs. Auditing account logon events tracks all logon accounts. This is especially valuable for auditing domain account logon events, because it will audit any logon no matter what computer is used for the logon. You must log on as the Administrator or a member of the Administrators group to make changes to local Security Policy on a Windows computer. You must be a Domain Administrator to administer Domain Audit Policy. Exercise 15-4 describes the steps for turning on the auditing of account logons for Windows XP.

EXERCISE 15-4

Auditing Logons

In this exercise you will turn on auditing for logon events and for account logon events for a Windows XP computer.

1. Select Start | Control Panel. In Control Panel double-click Administrative Tools.
2. In Administrative Tools double-click Local Security Policy.
3. In the Local Security Settings console expand Security Settings | Local Policies | Audit Policy.
4. In the details pane double-click Audit Account Logon Events. In the Audit Account Logon Events Properties place a check mark in the box next to Success and place another one in the box labeled Failure, as shown here, and then click OK. You do not have to choose both of these, and can audit just success or just failure.

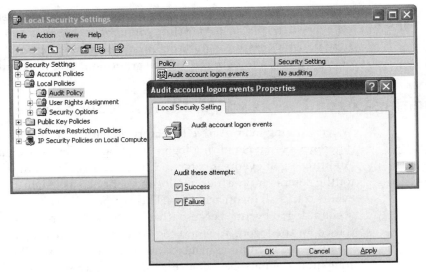

5. Click OK to close the dialog box, and then close the Local Security Settings console.

6. Your Windows XP computer will now log account logon events.

7. Check back in a day or two to see the results. At that time open Event Viewer from Administrative Tools and expand the Security node. Look for logon activity from other computers on your network. This should not be occurring if you are not actively sharing resources on your computer.

We once realized that there was a virus on one of our computers because the Security log on another computer showed that the logged-on user account on the infected computer was attempting to log on over the network. Each failed attempt to log on with the user name was followed by an attempt to log on using the Guest account. The user sitting at these computers was totally unaware of this activity until we informed him. It took an upgrade of his security software to find and remove the virus from the one machine that was attempting to replicate to the other machine.

Auditing Files and Folders

Windows allows you to audit files and folders for security-related events performed by specified users or groups. You can audit events initiated by any user or group, even for special groups such as Everyone and Authenticated Users. The actions can include a variety of tasks performed on files and folders, such as creating folders and assigning permissions.

Exercise 15-5 will guide you through the process of turning on auditing of file and folder access.

EXERCISE 15-5

Auditing File and Folders Access

In this exercise you will turn on auditing for file and folder access for a Windows XP computer. This is a two-step procedure. First you enable the auditing of object access, and then you select the files or folders to audit.

1. Select Start | Control Panel. In Control Panel double-click Administrative Tools.

2. In Administrative Tools double-click Local Security Policy.

3. In the Local Security Settings console expand Security Settings | Local Policies | Audit Policy.

4. In the details pane, double-click Audit Object Access, and in the Audit Object Access Properties dialog box, place a check mark in the box next to Success and place another one in the box labeled Failure, as shown here. You can choose to audit just success or failure.

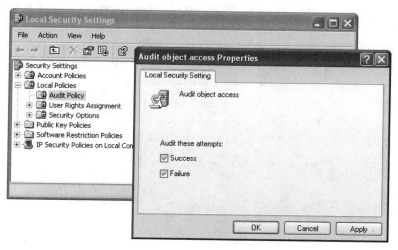

5. Click OK to close this dialog box, and then close the Local Security Settings folder.

6. Now open My Computer and browse to the file or folder you wish to audit, right-click, and select Properties.

7. In the Properties dialog box select the Security tab and click Advanced.

8. In the Advanced Security Settings dialog box select the Auditing tab.

9. On the Auditing page click Add to open the Select User Or Group box. Enter the users or groups whose access you wish to audit. If you know the name, you can type it into the box and click Check Names. If the name is in the accounts database, it will be underlined in the list. Click OK.

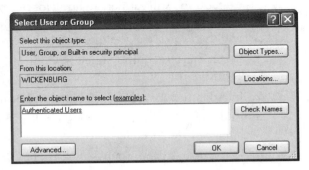

10. The Auditing Entry dialog box will open. Select the type of access you would like audited and select Successful and/or Failed for each one, and then click OK.

11. Repeat Steps 9 and 10 for each user or group you wish to add. When you have finished, click OK three times to close all the dialog boxes.

12. You have now turned auditing on for the users or groups you selected and for the level of access to the file or folder you selected.

As with all auditing, auditing of files and folders can slow the system down as it uses the CPU, memory, and disk. Therefore, only turn on auditing for the most important data in your organization.

CERTIFICATION SUMMARY

A computer professional must understand the threats to people, computers, and networks. To that end, this chapter begins with an overview of the various threats, including computer hardware theft, identity fraud, disasters, malicious software attacks, grayware, various methods for gaining access and obtaining information, inappropriate or distasteful content, invasions of privacy, and social engineering. Computer professionals must also understand the nature of cookies, including the benefits of cookies and how cookies are exploited.

Defense against threats begins with security policies that define the parameters of computer security. Following the guidelines, managers and technical staff implement access control to equipment as well as to computer, network, and file systems. Firewalls further protect networks and individual computers by examining and filtering traffic between a private network and an untrusted network like the Internet.

Also, according to good security policy, hardware is disposed of in a way that is both environmentally sound (more on this in Chapter 17), and that removes sensitive data previously stored on discarded hard drives. Further, security policy determines how recovery will occur, by defining a backup policy.

Both computer professionals and ordinary users should identify and report social engineering ploys.

Auditing of selected security events, such as account logons and access to sensitive files, gives an administrator a way to discover usage trends that may indicate a threat. It also creates a trail of evidence an organization can use in bringing charges against offenders.

TWO-MINUTE DRILL

Here are some of the key points covered in Chapter 15.

Threats

❑ Threats to users, computers, and networks include a large variety of attacks, including hardware theft, identify theft, fraud, disasters, malicious software, grayware, and a variety of methods for gaining access and obtaining information. In addition, users can be exposed to inappropriate or distasteful content, and endure an invasion of privacy.

❑ Security begins with protection of hardware from theft. While many thieves only want to sell the hardware quickly, this is also an opportunity to steal data.

❑ Identify theft occurs when someone collects personal information belonging to another person, and uses that information to fraudulently make purchases, open new credit accounts, and even obtain new driver's licenses and other forms of identification in the victim's name.

❑ Fraud is the use of deceit and trickery to persuade someone to hand over money or valuables.

❑ Disasters that affect computers, networks, and data come in many forms, including accidents, mistakes, and natural and unnatural disasters.

❑ Malicious software attacks are common on both private and public networks. Some forms include viruses, password crackers, worms, Trojan horses, keystroke loggers, pop-up downloads, and drive-by downloads.

❑ Grayware is a term for threats that are not truly malicious code but can have indirect negative effects, such as decreasing performance or using up bandwidth. Grayware includes spyware, adware, spam, spim, dialers, and prank programs.

❑ Perpetrators use a variety of methods for gaining access and obtaining information. Some common methods include back doors, war driving, and Bluesnarfing.

❑ The wealth of information on the Internet also includes information that is inappropriate for some individuals, such as children, or generally distasteful.

❑ Many of the threats described in this chapter are clearly invasions of privacy. Any steps you take to make your computer more secure contribute to protection of your privacy.

❑ Cookies are small files a Web browser saves on the local hard drive at the request of a Web site. For the most part cookies are harmless because they are not program code but small text files, and they can normally only be read by the Web site that created them. Such a cookie is called a first-party cookie.

❑ Some advertisers on Web sites create cookies that the program code from the same advertiser can read from other Web sites. These are third-party cookies, and you can configure a Web browser to disable third-party cookie reading.

❑ Social engineering involves a variety of techniques used to persuade someone to reveal confidential information or give something else of value to the perpetrator. Phishing, phone phishing, hoaxes, and enticements to open attachments all employ persuasive social engineering tactics.

Defense Against Threats

❑ A security policy is a set of rules and practices describing how an organization protects and manages sensitive information. Applied to all employees, most medium to large organizations have an explicit, written security policy.

❑ HIPAA and other government regulations have made security policies mandatory for many organizations in the health care or finance industries.

❑ A committee that includes one or more senior-level administrators, a manager with authority to enforce the policy, a lawyer or member of the legal staff, one or more employees representing the general user community, and a competent and experienced writer, should create an organization's security policy.

❑ Control access to restricted spaces, equipment, files, folders, and other resources of the organization.

❑ Access control to computers and networks includes authentication. Access to resources then requires authorization and evaluation of the level of access granted to the user.

❑ Follow best practices for passwords, which include protecting the confidentiality of passwords, creating strong passwords, never reusing passwords, avoiding creating unnecessary online accounts, avoiding providing more information than necessary, and always using strong passwords for certain accounts.

❑ There are a variety of authentication technologies. Just a few include ordinary logons using the standard keyboard, smart card logons, key fob logons, and biometric logons.

❑ The NTFS file system in Windows supports file and folder permissions through use of an access control list (ACL) on each file and folder. This table contains at least one access control entry (ACE), which is a record containing just one user or group account name and the permissions assigned to that account.

❑ Administrators, or someone using an account with the permissions to create ACEs for the file or folder, can create ACEs. Manage permissions using the Security page in the properties dialog box of a file or folder.

❑ A newly created folder or file inherits the permission settings of the parent folder, unless you choose to block this inheritance through an option in the Security page of the file or folder. Inherited permissions appear grayed out, and you cannot modify inherited permissions at the child level.

❑ Block inheritance on a folder or file to which you wish to assign different (usually more restrictive) permissions.

❑ When Windows creates personal folders for a user, it assigns a default set of permissions to the folders and their contents. The user, Administrators, and System all have full control, but no other user has any level of permissions to these folders.

❑ Encryption is the transformation of data into a code that can be decrypted only through use of a secret key or password. Windows NTFS5 (in Windows 2000 and newer) supports encryption.

❑ A firewall sits between a private network and an untrusted network and examines all traffic in and out of the network it is protecting. Firewalls use a variety of software technologies, including IP packet filtering, proxy servers, encrypted authentication, and virtual private networks.

❑ ISPs and most corporations use hardware firewalls, expensive and specialized devices manufactured by companies such as Cisco, NETGEAR, and others. They often require highly trained people to configure and manage them.

❑ A software firewall is one installable on almost any computer (allowing for minimum hardware and operating system requirements). The most common software firewalls are personal firewalls installed on desktop computers.

❑ Microsoft includes a firewall with Windows XP and Vista, and there are many third-party software firewalls.

❑ When disposing of old computer equipment, be sure to remove all data from hard drives and destroy optical media containing confidential data.

❑ Recovery from an attack depends on the preparation work of good backups, and protections against the threats outlined in this chapter.

Auditing

❑ Security auditing gives you an audit trail of security activity that may include evidence that an intruder is attempting to log on after hours.

SELF TEST

The following questions will help you measure your understanding of the material presented in this chapter. Read all of the choices carefully, because there might be more than one correct answer. Choose all correct answers for each question.

Threats

1. What is the term for activity that results in someone using your personal information to obtain new credit or credentials?
   A. Virus
   B. Identity theft
   C. Trojan horse
   D. Social engineering

2. Netsky and MyDoom were this type of virus, which replicates itself, moving from computer to computer.
   A. Trojan horse
   B. Password cracker
   C. Worm
   D. Keystroke logger

3. What is the term used to describe the delivery of malicious code to a user's computer through the use of a pop-up window in a Web browser?
   A. Worm
   B. Grayware
   C. Trojan horse
   D. Pop-up download

4. Which of the following is a category of software that runs surreptitiously on a user's computer for the purpose of gathering personal and financial information without permission from the user, and then sends that information to the people who requested it?
   A. Spam
   B. Spyware
   C. Adware
   D. Spim

5. Which of the following is a term for unsolicited e-mail?
- A. Spyware
- B. Spam
- C. Back door
- D. Worm

6. What type of program attempts to guess passwords on a computer?
- A. Keystroke logger
- B. Password cracker
- C. Virus
- D. Fraud

7. This program code gets its name from the way that it allows someone who knows how to use it to bypass security and have the privileges of the host program.
- A. Back door
- B. Bluesnarfing
- C. Cookies
- D. Phishing

8. Web browsers save these small text files at the direction of programs on a Web site.
- A. Back door
- B. Spam
- C. Cookies
- D. Prank programs

Defense Against Threats

9. What term describes a set of rules and practices designed for an organization that applies to all employees, and describes how an organization protects and manages sensitive information?
- A. Audit policy
- B. Security policy
- C. HIPAA
- D. Remote access policy

10. This procedure informs security and technical personnel of actual violations of an organization's security policy.
- A. Security policy
- B. Phishing

    C. Phone phishing

    D. Incident reporting

11. What type of access control only requires that a resource have a password assigned to it? It does not require authentication to a user accounts database.

    A. User-based

    B. Password-based

    C. Three-factor

    D. Two-factor

12. What term describes a password meeting certain criteria in its construction that make it very difficult to crack?

    A. User-based

    B. Healthy

    C. Strong

    D. Two-factor

13. What is the term that describes the CTRL-ALT-DELETE key combination that must be entered before the Log On To Windows dialog box will appear on many Windows computers?

    A. Secure attention sequence

    B. Interactive logon

    C. Secure computing sequence

    D. Authentication factor

14. This device uses a PIN and generates a new password every time a PIN is entered.

    A. Smart card

    B. Key fob

    C. Biometric logon

    D. Keyboard

15. What is the term for the table of users and/or groups and their permissions that is associated with a file or folder on an NTFS volume in Windows?

    A. Access control list (ACL)

    B. Security page

    C. Properties dialog

    D. Access control entry (ACE)

16. When a user logs on to Windows for the first time, what is the name of the set of folders Windows creates for that user on the local hard drive?
    A. My Documents
    B. My Computer
    C. Personal folders
    D. Logon folders

17. What term is used for the transformation of data into a code that can only be decrypted through the use of a secret key or password?
    A. Compression
    B. Encryption
    C. Deletion
    D. Programming

18. When a firewall inspects each incoming or outgoing packet and does not allow some to pass, it is performing this function.
    A. Proxy service
    B. VPN
    C. Encrypted authentication
    D. IP packet filtering

Auditing

19. If you want to audit the logon of a domain account no matter what computer it uses to log on, use this domain Audit Policy setting.
    A. Audit logon events
    B. Audit account management
    C. Audit account logon events
    D. Audit object access

20. To audit the success or failure of access to a file or folder, use this Audit Policy setting and then enable auditing on the Audit tab of the Advanced Security Settings in the Properties of the file or folder you wish to audit.
    A. Audit object access
    B. Audit privilege use
    C. Audit process tracking
    D. Audit system events

LAB QUESTION

What would you do if you thought your identity was stolen? The U.S. Government has a great resource for reporting identify theft, and for taking steps to recover from identify theft. The URL for this site is currently www.ftc.gov/bcp/edu/microsites/idtheft/. If you cannot find it with this URL, use a search engine to find it with the search string: identity theft gov. Go to this site and learn the steps you should take. Then write a paragraph or two on the action you should take if you suspect you have been a victim of identify theft.

SELF TEST ANSWERS

Threats

1. ☑ **B.** Identity theft is the term for activity that results in someone using your personal information to obtain new credit or credentials.

   ☒ **A** and **C** are incorrect because they are both malicious code, not an activity. **D**, social engineering, is incorrect because it is a collection of persuasion techniques used for many purposes. Social engineering may be involved with identity theft, but the two terms do not identify the exact same behavior.

2. ☑ **C.** A worm is a type of virus that replicates itself, moving from computer to computer.

   ☒ **A**, Trojan horse, is incorrect because this is a type of virus that is hidden within an apparently harmless program. A worm, like any other virus, can transfer to a computer as a Trojan horse. **B**, password cracker, is incorrect because this is a program that attempts to discover passwords. **D**, keystroke logger, is incorrect because this is a program that logs the user's keystrokes.

3. ☑ **D.** Pop-up download describes the delivery of malicious code to a user's computer through the use of a pop-up window in a Web browser.

   ☒ **A** and **C** are both incorrect because they are both types of viruses, not the method for delivering a virus. **B**, grayware, is incorrect because this describes threats that are not truly malicious code but that still have indirect negative effects.

4. ☑ **B.** Spyware is a category of software that runs surreptitiously on a user's computer for the purpose of gathering personal and financial information without permission from the user.

   ☒ **A** and **D** are both incorrect because they represent unwanted messages—spam being unwanted e-mail, and spim being unwanted instant messaging messages. **C**, adware, is incorrect because although it also installs on a computer without permission and collects information, it has a different purpose. Adware collects information in order to display targeted advertisements.

5. ☑ **B.** Spam is a term for unsolicited e-mail.

   ☒ **A**, **C**, and **D** are all incorrect because they are examples of malicious program code and grayware, not e-mail. The e-mail could contain malicious code, but that is not part of the definition.

6. ☑ **B.** Password crackers attempt to guess passwords on a computer.

   ☒ **A** and **C** are both incorrect because while both a keystroke logger and a virus are malicious code, they do not match the definition of a program that attempts to guess passwords on a computer. **D**, fraud, is incorrect because this includes the use of deceit and trickery to persuade someone to hand over money or valuables. It does not match the narrow definition of a password cracker.

7. ☑ **A.** Back door is the name for code that allows someone to bypass security and access the operating system with the same privileges as the host program.
☒ **B,** Bluesnarfing, is incorrect because this is the act of covertly obtaining information broadcast from wireless devices using the Bluetooth standard. **C,** cookies, is incorrect because cookies are not program code, and they do not allow access to an operating system. **D,** phishing, is incorrect because phishing is a fraudulent method of obtaining personal and financial information through the use of pop-ups or e-mail messages that purport to be from a legitimate organization.

8. ☑ **C.** Cookies are small text files saved by a Web browser at the direction of programs on a Web site.
☒ **A,** back door, is incorrect because this is program code and is used for an entirely different purpose. **B,** spam, is incorrect because spam is unsolicited e-mail. **D,** prank programs, is incorrect because these are programs and do not serve the same purpose as cookies.

Defense Against Threats

9. ☑ **B.** Security policy is a set of rules and practices designed for an organization that applies to all employees and describes how an organization protects and manages sensitive information.
☒ **A,** audit policy, is incorrect because it is just a small part of a security policy. **C,** HIPAA, the Health Insurance Portability and Accountability Act, is incorrect because this is an act of the U.S. Congress, not a set of rules and practices for an organization. HIPAA or other laws often influence security policy. **D,** remote access policy, is incorrect because this is just one small part of a security policy.

10. ☑ **D.** Incident reporting informs security and technical personnel of actual violations of an organization's security policy.
☒ **A,** security policy, is incorrect because, while security policy may define incident reporting procedures, incident reporting is just one part of the actions taken within an organization in compliance with security policy. **B** and **C,** phishing and phone phishing, are both incorrect because neither is a procedure that informs security and technical personnel of actual violations of security policy. Both are violations of security policy.

11. ☑ **B.** Password-based access control only requires that a resource have a password assigned to it.
☒ **A,** user-based access control, is incorrect because this requires authentication and authorization. **C** and **D,** three-factor access control and two-factor access control, are both incorrect because they require more than just a password and require actual authentication and authorization.

12. ☑ **C.** A strong password is one that meets certain criteria in its construction that make it very difficult to crack.
☒ **A, B,** and **D,** user-based, healthy, and two-factor, are all incorrect because they do not describe a password that meets certain criteria that makes it difficult to crack.

13. ☑ **A.** Secure attention sequence, or SAS, describes the CTRL-ALT-DELETE key combination because it clears memory of certain types of viruses that may be lurking.

☒ **B**, interactive logon, is incorrect because this describes the logon process that occurs when a user logs on in Windows. The CTRL-ALT-DELETE key combination precedes an interactive logon on many Windows computers. **C** and **D**, secure computing sequence and authentication factor, are both incorrect because they are not terms used in this chapter.

14. ☑ **B.** A key fob is a device that uses a PIN and generates a new password every time a PIN is entered.

☒ **A**, smart card, is incorrect because, while it may be similar to a key fob, it is not usually used in the manner described in the question. **C**, biometric logon, is incorrect because it is a logon that uses a body measurement for authentication. **D**, keyboard, is incorrect because you cannot use a keyboard in the manner described in the question.

15. ☑ **A.** Access control list (ACL) is the term for the table of users and/or groups and their permissions that is associated with a file or folder on an NTFS volume in Windows.

☒ **B** and **C** are both incorrect because both a Security page and the Properties dialog are part of the user interface that allows you to administer the ACL to a file or folder object in Windows, not the ACL itself. **D**, access control entry (ACE), is incorrect because this is just a single entry in an ACL, not the entire table.

16. ☑ **C.** Windows creates personal folders the first time a user logs on to Windows.

☒ **A** and **B** are incorrect because both My Documents and My Computer are folders a user can access, but neither entirely constitutes the personal folders of that user. **D**, logon folders, is incorrect because this is not a term used to describe the user's folders in Windows.

17. ☑ **B.** Encryption is the transformation of data into a code that only the use of a secret key or password can decrypt.

☒ **A**, compression, is incorrect because it is not the transformation of data into a code that only the use of a secret key or password can decrypt. Compression is a method for reducing the size of a file. **C**, deletion, is incorrect because this is the action of removing something, as in the deletion of a file from a hard drive. **D**, programming, is incorrect because this is not the transformation of data into a code that only the use of a secret key or password can decrypt. Programming is the creating of executable code.

18. ☑ **D.** IP packet filtering is a firewall function in which it inspects each incoming or outgoing packet and does not allow some to pass.

☒ **A**, proxy service, is incorrect because this is a different function that intercepts outbound connection requests from internal clients to external servers and directs the resulting incoming traffic to the correct internal computer. **B**, VPN, is incorrect because this is a virtual tunnel created between two endpoints over an untrusted network. **C**, encrypted authentication, is incorrect because this is encryption of authentication credentials.

Auditing

19. ☑ **C.** Audit account logon events is the setting that should be used to audit the logon of a domain account no matter what computer it uses to log on.

    ☒ **A**, audit logon events, is incorrect because this will only audit logon events on the computer on which the policy is used. **B**, audit account management, is incorrect because this only audits any changes made to accounts. A logon is not a change to an account. **D**, audit object access, is incorrect because this audits access to objects, such as files and folders.

20. ☑ **A.** Audit object access is the Audit Policy setting for auditing the success or failure of access to a file or folder.

    ☒ **B, C,** and **D** are all incorrect because, while they are all individual Audit Policies, they do not track the success or failure of access to a file or folder.

LAB ANSWER

Answers may vary as the site updates. At this writing, the steps this site recommends that you should take when you suspect that you have been a victim of identify theft are outlined here:

1. Contact the fraud department of one of three consumer reporting companies and place a fraud alert on your credit report. Creditors who see the fraud alert will contact you directly and take other steps before allowing anyone to open a new account in your name.

2. Close all accounts that appear to have been tampered with or were opened without your knowledge. You will need to file an ID Theft Affidavit form with creditors to dispute these new accounts. This form is available at this site.

3. File a complaint with the Federal Trade Commission. You can file the FTC claim through this site or by mail using the FTC ID Theft complaint form available at this site. Print it out to use in the next step.

4. File a report with law enforcement in your community or the community in which the identity theft occurred. Give them a copy of your completed FTC ID Theft complaint form. Be sure to get a copy of the police report or the report number.

16

Implementing and Troubleshooting Security

Possibly the most important set of tasks on a network is applying and managing the necessary security to network resources, and to the network in general. Placing resources on networks has led to the need for centralized management of those resources, including security. Implementing security in this environment involves many different tasks, such as making a resource (a file folder or printer, for example) available on the network with adequate permissions and taking all necessary steps to prevent the invasion of malicious software and to discover if malicious software is already on a system.

CERTIFICATION OBJECTIVES

■ **601: 6.2   602: 6.2   603: 5.2**   *Install, configure, upgrade, and optimize security*

■ **604: 4.2**   *Install hardware security*

The security objectives for the CompTIA A+ exams, like all the objective domains, reflect the target skills for each exam. Exams 601, 602, and 603 include security subobjectives that involve both software and hardware security skills, while the security subobjectives for exam 604 are light on operating systems security, with more emphasis on hardware security. The most important thing to understand about computer security is that there are no easy answers to security, and you must continue to keep up-to-date on the latest security techniques and know how to implement several security tasks to fully protect PCs.

Implementing Authentication

Authentication to a PC is most often performed by Windows—by authenticating a user using a local account or a domain account. However, depending on the options in CMOS setup, a PC can also have a password that is required before it will start up an operating system—BIOS passwords. In Chapter 15 you learned about authentication technologies that go beyond basic interactive logon, such as smart card readers, key fobs, and biometric logon. Learn more about the implementation of these types of authentication in the following text. Also learn how to use the Lock Computer option in Windows to protect your computer while preserving your present workspace when you need to leave your computer unattended for brief periods of time. Security auditing is also important for monitoring computers for unauthorized logons.

BIOS Password

In Chapter 3 you learned about the settings stored in a PC's CMOS chips. These are often called BIOS settings because the programs that use these settings are stored in each PC's ROM-BIOS. Many BIOS manufacturers include CMOS settings for one or more passwords. Recall that some BIOS settings allow for setting one password to restrict the booting of the system and another password to restrict access to the CMOS settings program itself. A password set in this manner is separate from a password required by Windows to log on to your computer or network. This is merely password-based access control, not the user-based access control performed against a user's accounts database.

When a computer is started up, if a password is set on the system startup, a password dialog box will display even before Windows (or any other operating system) loads. The Windows startup will not begin until the user enters a password. A password that is set to restrict access to the CMOS settings program will only be required if the user attempts to access that program, and will not be seen at bootup. Again, in both cases, this is merely password-based access control, not the user-based access control performed against a user's accounts database.

We do not normally recommend setting BIOS passwords, but we have been in environments in which it is prudent to set at least one of these passwords. For instance, computers in a classroom lab should have a password set for entering the CMOS settings program. This will keep all but the most determined from accessing and changing the CMOS settings on the lab computers. This works well if unauthorized persons are also restricted from physically opening up the computer cases, because the fix for removing the BIOS password, if you do not know (or have forgotten) the password, usually requires opening up the case.

Smart Card Readers

Before smart cards can be used a special device called a *smart card reader* must be connected to the computer where the smart card will be used. This will require the device itself and the drivers and other software for the device. Further, a special service, called Certificate Services, must be installed on the domain controllers for the Windows domain.

Once the reader is installed and the domain controllers are configured to support Certificate Services, users can log on to the computer. Inserting the card into the reader has the same effect as pressing the CTRL-ALT-DELETE key combination. Both actions are considered a secure attention sequence (SAS), defined in Chapter 15. Smart cards are considered a very secure and tamper-resistant method of authentication.

There are three instances in which smart card authentication is not appropriate:

- When a user is required to join his or her computer to a domain. A computer must be part of a domain before a user can authenticate using the smart card.
- When a user needs to promote the logon computer to a domain controller.
- When a user is configuring a network connection for remote access.

Key Fobs

As described in Chapter 15, a key fob only requires that a user remember a PIN number, which identifies that person as the owner of the key fob. The key fob generates a unique password used for authenticating the user. Installing support for a key fob involves installing an agent that runs on the local computer and a service on the active directory domain controllers. The agent acts as a front end to the authentication process at the computer at which the logon is occurring, passing encrypted authentication information to the domain controller that responded to

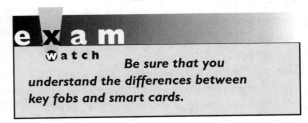

Be sure that you understand the differences between key fobs and smart cards.

the authentication request. On the domain controller the service decrypts the password and provides the password and the user name to the Active Directory security components for authentication. If the password and user name match a domain user account, the user is allowed access to resources to which permissions and rights have been granted.

Biometrics

While theoretically many types of biometrics can be used for computer login, the most popular and least expensive are fingerprint scanners (also called fingertip scanners). In fact, some Tablet PCs have a fingerprint scanner built in or packaged with the PC. These built-in devices are the size of a USB port, with a slender scanning slot.

External fingerprint scanners are available as PC Card devices, in which the scanner protrudes from the PC Card slot. USB devices, available from several vendors, are approximately the size of a CompactFlash card and have a small, flat sensor pad to which you touch your finger. Both the built-in and external devices require drivers and software to integrate with the computer's security system, including Windows domain controllers, if your computer is a member of a Windows domain.

Follow the manufacturer's instructions for installing the software and hardware. Do not forget that most USB devices require that you install the software before connecting the device. After installing the software, run the software to configure it to recognize your fingerprint and associate it with your user account. To do this, you will need to provide a user name and password. If your computer is a member of a workgroup, you will need to provide either the computer name or the workgroup name. If your computer is a member of a domain, provide the domain name and your user name and password in the domain. You will be prompted when the configuration utility is ready to scan your fingertip and associate it with your user account. To do this, swipe your finger across the scanner's sensor. You can scan one or more fingers, and any one of the scanned fingers can then be used for login. In most cases, the scanner's associated software will also save passwords for applications and Web sites and associate them with your profile.

Lock Computer

Lock Computer is an option in Windows that is preferred to logging off when you want to leave all your programs running exactly where you left off. It is very simple to do if you signed in to Windows through the Windows Security dialog box. Before leaving your computer unattended, simply press CTRL-ALT-DELETE to open the Windows Security dialog box and click Lock Computer. That's it. Your desktop will disappear, and the Computer Locked dialog box will appear on the screen. Then when you return, simply press CTRL-ALT-DELETE to open the Unlock Computer dialog box, shown next. Enter the password for your account, and you will be back to the desktop exactly as you left it.

If you did not sign in to Windows through the Windows Security dialog box, pressing CTRL-ALT-DELETE brings up the Task Manager. Then, from the Task Manager menu bar, select Shut Down | Lock Computer. Finally, there is a keyboard shortcut that works no matter how you logged on. If your keyboard has the WinKey (also called the Windows Key), a key with a Windows logo, located between the CTRL and

ALT key, press and hold this key while pressing the "l" key (that is the "L" key, but it only works in lowercase).

Auditing

In Chapter 15 you learned how to turn on auditing of Logon Events and of Account Logon Events. Once these are enabled, be sure that you use Event Viewer to monitor these events. If you need to turn off auditing, follow the instructions in Chapter 15

SCENARIO & SOLUTION	
I am preparing a new computer for a computer lab. How can I configure the computer so that students will not be able to access the system setup and change the BIOS settings, making the computer unusable?	Check out the manufacturer's documentation on the computer's system settings and look for the password settings. Set the password on the access to the system menu only. Do not set the password on the system startup unless the security policy for the computer lab requires this.
We are getting ready to order ten laptops for traveling auditors who will have sensitive data on the hard drives. We are looking for a secure authentication method beyond a simple user name and password for basic interactive logon to a Windows domain. What do you recommend?	Since you are in the process of purchasing the laptops, check out biometric devices, such as fingerprint scanners. These are more secure than the basic interactive logon and work with a Windows domain.
Our employees' computers are in a public area where customers and others can easily wander in and out. Employees must frequently leave their computers unattended during the workday for brief periods. How can they keep their desktops secure without shutting down their applications and Windows?	We suggest that you show the employees how to use Windows' Lock Computer option.

for turning auditing on, and turn it off for the specific policy. For instance, if you wanted to turn off auditing of account logon events, open Local Security Policy from the Administrative Tools. Expand Security Settings | Local Policies | Audit Policy. In the right pane double-click Audit Account Logon Events. In the Properties dialog box, shown here, clear both check boxes to turn off Auditing for both success and failure events for this action. If you only wish to turn on one, clear that check box. Then click OK to close the Properties dialog box, and then close the Local Security Setting folder when you are finished.

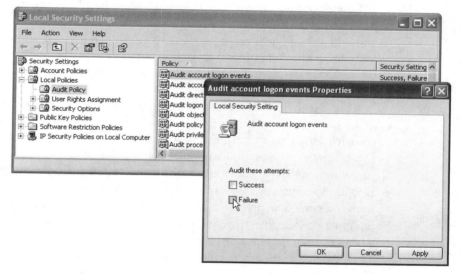

Implementing Data Security

In Chapter 15 you learned about the support built into NTFS for permissions and encryption, both used for data security. In this chapter learn how to apply NTFS permissions and encryption, strategies for backing up data, data migration in Windows XP, and permanent data removal from hard drives.

Applying NTFS and Share Permissions

In previous chapters you learned about NTFS standard permissions, share permissions, and how the two permissions interact. In this chapter learn how to plan for and apply NTFS and share permissions.

The last line of defense for securing data on a Windows computer is NTFS file and folder permissions. Properly set, these permissions protect data against unauthorized users coming over the network, and they also apply to local users. Set NTFS permissions at the most restrictive level that will allow the right users to accomplish their work. Therefore, an administrator should plan carefully before setting NTFS permissions—perhaps coordinating with managers to discover just what level of access to what files and folders is required for various users. The outcome of these meetings should include planning worksheets.

One worksheet will include the groups the administrator determines are needed and the user accounts that will be made members of these groups. The administrator will assign the same level of permissions to all members of a single group. Therefore, each group often identifies a single job function or related job function. This saves time when it comes to assigning permissions to these groups, giving them access to resources.

Consider the creation of a group planning worksheet for the managers and clerks in a school registration office. The school has a Microsoft Windows Active Directory domain, which we will call SchoolReg. The plan includes the use of two Active Directory group types: domain local and global. Domain local groups can be used to assign permissions to resources on any computer with an account in the domain. Domain local groups can contain user accounts from the same domain, global groups from the same domain or a trusted domain, and other domain local groups. This last is a practice called nesting, and it should be used with caution, because it does add a level of real complexity to your administration.

One practice when working with these group types is to create domain local groups to which permissions are assigned to resources. Then create global groups into which domain users with common security needs are grouped. Then, global groups will be made members of the local groups. The local groups will then be assigned permissions to resources. Let's apply this practice to a scenario. Simplified, you place users into global groups; place global groups into domain local groups; and assign permissions to local groups.

The SchoolReg domain has several shared folders and printers that should be accessed only by the managers and clerks in the school registration office. The group membership plan recognizes that the managers and clerks will have different access needs to various resources. Therefore, they will be placed into two separate global groups, named RegMgrs and RegClerks. A third global group, RegNight, is needed for the night clerks in the registration office. Now let's look at the local groups to which permissions will be assigned.

The registration printers should be available to all registration employees, but not to other employees; therefore, a local group, RegPrint, will be created for assigning permissions to registration printers. The night clerks produce reports on a special printer for which a separate domain local group is created, RegPrint2. They also must print to the same printers as the RegPrint domain local group. Therefore, these groups are nested.

on the
Ⓘob

Case is not significant in user and group names. RegMgrs and regmgrs are considered the same group. A mixture of uppercase and lowercase is used only for ease of reading.

There are certain data files that only managers need to access, so another local group, RegData1, is created for giving access to these folders. Another set of data files must be available to all of the users in the Registration department; therefore, another local group is created, RegData2.

Table 16-1 shows a planning worksheet based on this scenario. The Group Membership column includes group names and user names. The user names show each user's full name and that person's user name, in parentheses, which will be used to log on.

Use your desktop computer to practice working with user groups. Follow Exercise 16-1 to create local user accounts with the same names as the domain user accounts in

TABLE 16-1

Group Membership Planning Worksheet

Group Name	Group Type	Group Membership
RegPrint	Domain local	RegMgrs RegClerks RegPrint2
RegData1	Domain local	RegMgrs
RegData2	Domain local	RegClerks
RegPrint2	Domain local	RegNight
RegMgrs	Global	Mai Ling (mling) Juan Martinez (jmartinez)
RegClerk	Global	Sarah Webster (swebster) Allison Romain (aromain) Tom Harrah (tharrah) Walter Brown (wbrown)
RegNight	Global	Marisa Tortelli (mtortelli) Glen Olson (golson)

Table 16-1. Then create local groups with the same names as the groups in Table 16-1. Follow the worksheet to place users in the appropriate group. You must be logged on using the local Administrator account or an account that is a member of the local Administrators group.

This is practice for creating user and group accounts. You will create all the groups named, but you will not be able to create them as Domain Local or Global groups and then place Global groups inside Domain Local groups as you can in a domain. The local accounts database does not have a group type similar to Global. The Local groups on a Windows desktop computer only exist on that computer and cannot be used to assign permissions to any other computer.

If you are lucky enough to have access to a school lab or other practice lab with an Active Directory domain created just for such experimentation, request that you be given an account that will allow you to create the users and groups listed in the planning worksheet in Table 16-1. In this case, you will use the Domain Users and Groups user interface to create these accounts.

EXERCISE 16-1

Creating Users and Groups

Practice creating user and group accounts on your Windows XP Professional computer. The steps are similar for Windows 2000 and Vista.

1. Right-click My Computer and select Manage.

2. Expand Local Users and Groups, and then Groups.

3. Right-click on an empty area in the right window pane, and then select New Group.

4. In the New Group dialog box (shown next), enter a Group Name from the list. A Description is optional. Do not add members at this time. Click Create to create the group. The group will be created and the box will remain open and ready for the next group. Create a group account for each item in the Group Name column, and then click Close to close the New Group dialog box. Remain in the Computer Management console for the next step.

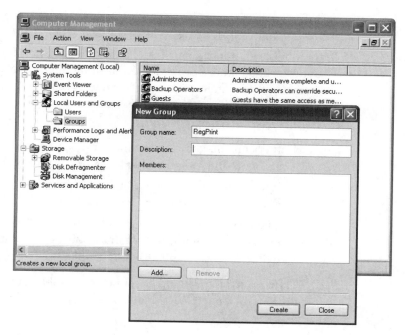

5. Now click the Users folder to expand it.

6. Right-click on an empty area in the right window pane, and then select New User.

7. Beginning with Mai Ling, enter the User Name (shown in parentheses in Table 16-1) and the Full Name for each user. If you do not provide a password and leave the box checked (User Must Change Password At Next Logon), the user will be able to log on without using a password and then will be prompted to immediately create a password before getting access to the desktop. For simplicity, leave this default and click Create to create each account.

8. When you have created all the user accounts in the list, click Close.

9. Verify that all the users in the planning form appear under Users, and that all the groups that you created appear under Groups. If any are missing, create them before moving on. When you are finished, close the Computer Management console.

Next, the administrator and the managers identify the file and printer resources that require permissions and determine the level of permissions to assign to each group.

The result of this process is another worksheet. Table 16-2 shows a sample worksheet for assigning permissions to NTFS folders according to the SchoolReg scenario. In the worksheet, notice that a folder named Registration contains two other folders, Database and Forms. Case is not significant in file and folder names in Windows; therefore, the capitalization in these names is only for ease of reading.

For a very small organization, this amount of detailed preparation seems unnecessary, but this serves several purposes.

- It documents the memberships of the groups for use when creating group accounts and assigning user account membership in the groups.
- It documents the memberships of the groups for future use by this administrator, or others in the same job.
- The administrator can have the managers sign off on the document. This protects the administrator from making errors due to misunderstanding the manager's intent and assigning inappropriate permissions to accounts.

NTFS permissions should be set before you share a folder because the default permissions on a new folder share are very open. Further, when a folder is shared,

TABLE 16-2	Folder	Users/Groups	Permissions
NTFS Permissions Worksheet	Registration	RegData1	Everything but Full Control and Special Permissions
		RegData2	Read & Execute, List Folder Contents, and Read
		Administrators (local computer) SYSTEM CREATOR OWNER	Full Control
	Registration \ Database	RegData1	Everything but Full Control and Special Permissions
		RegData2	Read, Write, and Execute
		Administrators (local computer) SYSTEM CREATOR OWNER	Full Control
	Registration \ Forms	RegData1	Everything but Full Control and Special Permissions
		RegData2	Read, Write, and Execute
		Administrators (local computer) SYSTEM CREATOR OWNER	Full Control

you will need to plan the permissions to apply at the share level. Beginning with Windows XP Service Pack 1, the default permission on a new share is only Read for the group Everyone. Previous to that, the Everyone group was granted full control on a new share. Keep in mind that share permissions must be open enough to allow for the most privileged access, but you will normally want to assign specific users or groups to a share and remove the group Everyone from the share.

In the example we are using here, the Registration folder is shared and the RegData1 group should be given Full Control permission, while the RegData2 group should be given Read access, and the group Everyone should be removed from the share. Share permissions can also be included in a planning worksheet, especially when several shares are involved.

As with user group accounts, you can practice creating folders and assigning NTFS permissions on your desktop computer. Then create a share and set the appropriate share permissions. Follow the steps in Exercise 16-2 to do these tasks on a computer running Windows 2000 Professional or Windows XP Professional.

EXERCISE 16-2

Assigning Permissions to Folders in NTFS

Create folders and assign NTFS permissions to those folders. Then create a share and set permissions on the share. You must be logged on using the local Administrator account or an account that is a member of the local Administrators group. You will also need the groups created in Exercise 16-1 to complete this exercise.

1. Open Windows Explorer or My Computer. Expand drive C: and create the folders shown on the NTFS Permissions Worksheet in Table 16-2 detailed in the following steps.

2. Right-click on an empty area in the right pane of the window, being careful not to click any file or folder. In the context menu select New, and then from the resulting pop-up menu select Folder, as shown here.

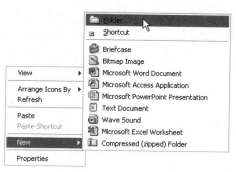

3. Name the new folder **Registration** and press ENTER.

4. Open the new Registration folder, right-click in the right pane, and create a new folder within this folder. Name this folder **Database**. Create another new folder inside the Registration folder and name it **Forms**.

5. Block inheritance on the Registration folder so that it will not inherit the permissions of the parent folder (the root of drive C:). To begin blocking inheritance, right-click the Registration folder and then select Properties | Security. On the Security page, click Advanced,

6. In the Advanced Security Settings dialog box, clear the check box labeled Inherit From Parent The Permission Entries That Apply To Child Objects.

7. This will result in the Security box, shown here. Click Copy.

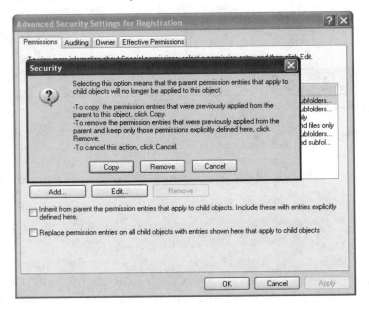

8. The Permissions page will display with the list of users granted permissions. These were copied from the parent. Click each user who is not listed on the NTFS Permissions Worksheet in Table 16-2 for this folder and remove the user from the list using the Remove button.

9. Add the permissions for the RegDat1 and RegDat2 groups to the Registration folder. If you need help in assigning permissions, check out Help and Support. The resulting Security page should resemble the one shown here. Click OK when you have finished, to close the Registration Properties dialog box.

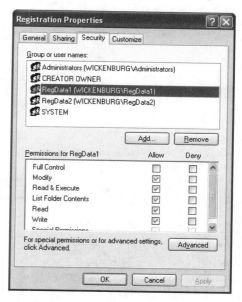

10. Now that NTFS permissions have been assigned, create a share pointing to the Registration folder. Right-click the Registration folder, select Sharing And Security. This opens the sharing tab of the Properties dialog box. Select Share This Folder. Leave the share name as Registration.

11. Click Permissions to open the Permissions For Registration dialog box. Click Add to open the Select Users Or Groups dialog box. Type the name **RegData1**.

12. Set the share permissions for RegData1 to Full Control, which will turn on Change and Read. Add **RegData2** and set the permissions for RegData2 to Read.

13. Now select the Group Everyone and click Remove. The resulting Permissions for Registration should resemble the ones shown next. Click OK to close the Permissions dialog box. You have now set the share permissions.

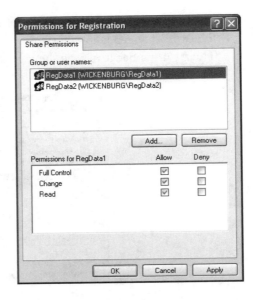

When you click the Advanced button on the General page of the Properties dialog box for a file or folder, the Advanced Security Settings dialog box will display. It has four tabs. Select the Owner tab and it will list the user who is the owner of the file or folder. The list in the Change Owner To box shows the list of users to whom you can change ownership of the file or folder. Normally you can change ownership to only individual user accounts or to the Administrators group.

Select the Effective Permissions tab and select a user or group name for the Group Or User Name box. The result will be a list of the Effective permissions for that user or group to the file or folder. Effective permissions include all permissions that are granted to the user or group. These are based on the permissions assigned directly to the selected user or group, as well as those assigned to groups to which the user or group has members.

Applying NTFS File and Folder Encryption

Beginning in Windows 2000, NTFS supports file and folder encryption. When you encrypt a folder the folder itself is not actually encrypted, but all files in the folder are encrypted, and any new files saved into the folder are automatically encrypted. NTFS encryption only applies to files while they are saved in the encrypted folder, and when they are moved or copied into unencrypted folders on NTFS volumes that support encryption. This is true, even if the folder to which the files are moved does not have encryption turned on. The files are not encrypted if they are copied to non-NTFS volumes or if they are e-mailed to someone.

Conversely, moving a non-encrypted file into an encrypted folder by using drag-and-drop will not result in the file being encrypted. Therefore, be sure to only use cutting and pasting (or saving from within an application) to move files into an encrypted folder.

It is simple to encrypt a folder. Simply open the properties dialog box of the folder and click Advanced. In the Advanced Attributes dialog box click Encrypt Contents To Secure Data (see Figure 16-1), and then click OK.

It is important to know that you can only decrypt a file when you are logged on with the account used to encrypt it. Then, decryption is transparent; simply open the file using the usual application for that file type. Both normal permissions and a special authorization to decrypt are applied. Even when logged on with another account with full control permissions to the file, you will not be able to decrypt the file, and therefore, you will not be able to use it in any way.

The Encrypting File System (EFS) in Windows XP Professional has the following features not available in Windows 2000:

FIGURE 16-1

Turn on the Encrypt attribute.

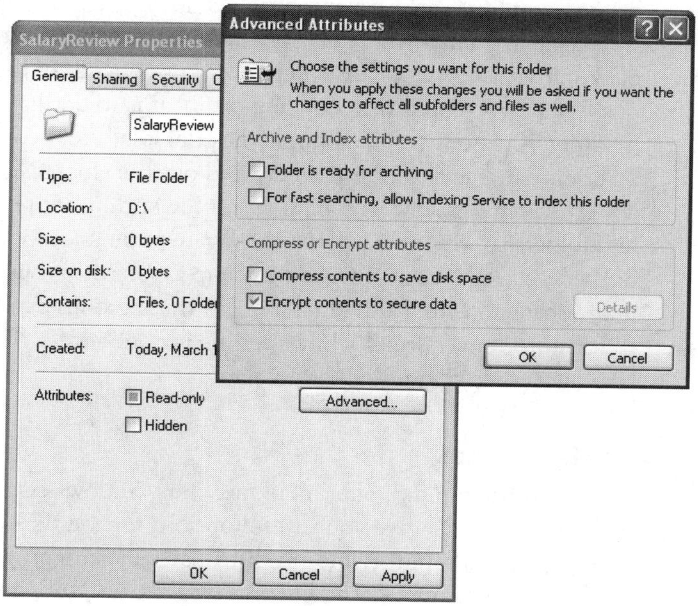

■ A user can share encrypted files with other users.

■ A user may encrypt offline files, which are files that are stored on a network server but cached in local memory when the local computer is disconnected from the server.

The only person who can decrypt a file or folder is the person who encrypted it or a member of a special group called Recovery Agents. By default, only the local administrator is a member of this group. Recovery is not the same as being able to directly access the data; it is a very advanced task, described in Windows 2000 Help and in Windows XP Professional Help and Support.

on the **Job** *While the CompTIA A+ exam objectives require that you understand NTFS encryption, there are shortcomings to this encryption, which you will learn about later in this chapter in the section "Troubleshooting Security."*

Implementing Data Backup Procedures

An important part of data security is a backup policy that includes frequent backups of data to removable media. Storage of the media should also be part of the policy. While backup media should be handy for quick restores, a full backup set should also be stored off-site in case something occurs to the building in which the computer is housed, as well as to the computer. The frequency of the backups, and of the full backup that is stored off-site, depends on the needs of the organization. It is not possible to overemphasize how important it is to do this. Backup was discussed in Chapter 10. We will talk about additional issues related to backup here.

Users can back up files they created on their local NTFS volume, including the My Documents folder in their own profile and its contents. Users can restore files and folders to which they have the Write permission on an NTFS volume. Members of the local Administrators and Backup Operators groups have the right to back up and restore all files. Individual users in these groups can back up and restore files that they do not normally have permissions to access. This does not give them any other access to these files and folders.

Backup Types

Any good backup program, including the Windows Backup program, also called NTBACKUP, will give you several options for the type of backup. While they may have slightly different names in third-party backup programs, in Windows Backup the backup types are Normal, Copy, Differential, Incremental, and Daily. Which of these types you select when you back up depends on several things, including the frequency of the scheduled backups, how much time you are willing to spend restoring data, and how much space you can afford to devote to backups. Figure 16-2 shows the Options dialog box, which you open in Windows Backup by selecting Tools | Options. The list box for Default Backup Type is open, showing all the backup type choices.

In Chapter 9 you learned about the archive file attribute and its relationship to backup programs. This attribute is normally turned on when a file is first created or modified. Any copied file also has this attribute turned on. Backup programs can therefore use the attribute to identify files that have not been backed up, which would be true of a file after it has been created, modified, or copied. Conversely, a backup program can turn off, or "clear," the archive attribute on a file to indicate that it has been backed up. All of the backup types, with the exception of copy, use the archive attribute in some way. What follows is a description of each backup type, the files it backs up, and whether or not it clears the archive attribute.

Normal When Windows Backup does a normal backup, it backs up all selected folders and files regardless of the status of the archive attribute on each file. However, during the backup Windows Backup turns off, or clears, the archive attribute on each file that it backs up.

Copy When Windows Backup does a copy backup type, it backs up all selected folders and files regardless of the status of the archive attribute on each file, and it

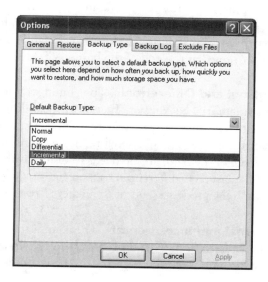

FIGURE 16-2

Select the default backup type from the Options dialog box.

does not clear the archive attribute on the backed-up files. This type of backup is done between other backup types, such as normal and incremental, in order to get a backup set without disturbing the backup strategy.

Differential   During a differential backup, Windows Backup backs up all selected folders and files on which the archive attribute is turned on. This indicates that they were created or modified since the last backup. The archive attributes are not cleared during a differential backup.

Incremental   During an incremental backup, Windows Backup backs up all selected folders and files on which the archive attribute is turned on. This indicates that they were created or modified since the last backup. The archive attributes are cleared during an incremental backup.

Daily   A daily backup backs up all selected files that have changed during the day. It does not clear archive attributes during the backup.

Backup Strategies

Regardless of the backup software used, an effective administrator plans a backup strategy that fits the needs and budget of the organization. And whether it is a sophisticated tape backup system with an automated tape changer, or a simple system in which the backup medium is changed by an individual, the most popular backup strategies normally combine two or three of the backup types described in the preceding section. What follows are descriptions of three backup strategies and how they are used during a Monday through Friday workweek. In all cases, backups are performed at the end of the business day.

Normal and Differential   The administrator runs a normal backup on Monday and differential backups on Tuesday through Friday. Because differential backups do not clear the archive attribute, each day's differential backup contains all the changes since Monday. Therefore, if the administrator discovers a problem requiring a restore of the data, all she needs to restore is the normal backup set from Monday and the last day's differential backup. This strategy takes longer to back up each day as the week progresses, but it is quicker to restore.

Normal and Incremental   The administrator runs a normal backup on Monday and incremental backups on Tuesday through Friday. Because incremental backups do clear the archive attribute, each day's incremental backup contains only the files that changed since the previous day's backup. If the administrator needs to restore the data, he needs to restore Monday's normal backup set followed by each day's incremental backup set up to the last incremental backup before the problem occurred. This strategy takes less time each day to back up, but more time to restore.

Be sure that you can differentiate among the three backup strategies, and show that you understand the backup types used with each strategy.

Normal, Differential, and Copy This strategy is the same as the normal and differential strategy with the exception of a copy backup on Wednesday. Since copy backup does not clear the archive attribute, this does not interfere with the overall backup strategy of normal and differential. The purpose of a copy backup is to create a snapshot of a point in time. Copy backups are handy to do at any point in the week when you want to create a backup set to send off-site for storage.

Data Migration

There are two general types of computer data migration. One involves translating data from one data format to another, while the second type involves moving data from one storage device to another. An organization may need to do both types of migration at the same time.

The translation of data from one data format to another is necessary when changing from one type of system and application for managing the data to another. This type of migration normally involves large databases. For instance, Microsoft provides software tools for migrating customer relationship management (CRM) data from other formats to that of Microsoft Business Solutions CRM.

The second type, in which data is moved from one storage device to another, is more common. Data migration can be as local and personal as migrating data from a Windows 2000 computer to a Windows XP computer. Or it can be as big as migrating terabytes of data for a large enterprise from one storage system to another. Both involve careful planning, which results in a strategy for safely and securely migrating the data without an interruption of business. The resulting plan will determine the migration media: network or backup media, or a combination of both. The plan will define the hardware and software used for the migration. This will determine the transfer rate and hence the duration of the migration, and the method for monitoring data for quality and maintaining security of the data during the entire process.

The migration of data from one PC to another, as required when you purchase a new computer and need to move the data from the old computer to the new computer, is made easier by migration programs from Microsoft and other vendors. Microsoft provides the Files and Settings Transfer Wizard in Windows XP. This wizard brings over your data and places it in the correct locations on your hard drive, fulfilling the basic task of data migration. It goes further by also migrating settings for Windows and certain Windows applications. This includes the desktop preferences, and preferences for Internet Explorer and all Microsoft applications installed on both the old and the new computers. It does not include installing any applications on the new PC, so you will need to install your applications on the new PC before migrating the data and settings from the old PC.

The Files and Settings Transfer Wizard must be run on both the old and new computer. It can be started from Start | All Programs | Accessories | System Tools on a Windows XP computer, or from the main menu of the Windows XP CD on an old computer running Windows 95, Windows 98, Windows 98SE, Windows ME, Windows NT 4.0, Windows 2000, or Windows XP. Choose the local computer's role in the transfer, as shown in Figure 16-3. When the wizard runs on any version of Windows other than Windows XP, the only role available is that of Old Computer.

When you select Old Computer, the wizard collects files and settings and places them in the location you define. This can be any local hard drive or flash drive or

FIGURE 16-3

The Files and Settings Transfer Wizard

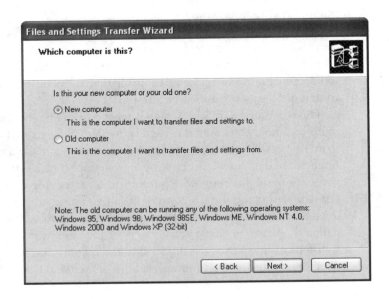

a network share. You can specify a floppy disk, but the data is normally too large for a single floppy disk, and many newer PCs do not come with a floppy drive. Another option is a direct cable attached to serial ports. This option is rarely used for a similar reason—serial ports are disappearing from new PCs.

Once the data is collected, run the wizard on the new computer and point to the location of the data and the wizard will complete the transfer. This replacement process greatly simplifies the time it once took to move your data and configure a new PC with your preferences.

on the
O o b
When you upgrade a computer with Windows Setup, the new installation will acquire the settings of the old installation, and the data files will be preserved and usable in the new installation. This is achieved by installing the new version of Windows into the same disk folder as the old installation. This is not a migration.

Data Removal

In many organizations the permanent removal of data is recognized as an important security function, but in too many organizations data removal is overlooked. There are several scenarios in which permanent data removal is necessary. One scenario involves moving computers from user to user in an organization. Another scenario is when a computer is removed from service in an organization. At this point the computer may be donated to a charity or disposed of. In the later case, the recommended path is to a recycling and disposal company contracted to recycle all suitable components and safely and legally dispose of other components. In this scenario, the data should be permanently removed, or the hard drives destroyed.

Further, the ordinary user deletes data every day that is not really deleted, but saved in the Recycle Bin. Suppose that you delete confidential files and then walk away from your computer without logging off. Someone with malicious intent could sit at your computer in your absence, open the Recycle Bin, and restore the deleted files.

In a scenario in which computers are removed from service, it is important to thoroughly remove the data from the hard drives. It turns out that Windows' delete, format, and even partition programs do not truly destroy the data saved on hard drives. Therefore, a determined person can recover the data, or even remnants of data files. The length to which people are willing to go depends on the perceived value of the data in question. So, whether it is your personal financial data, or your employer's super-secret research and development information, start being smarter about removing data from hard drives before they fall into the wrong hands. In the extreme, you could remove a hard drive from a user computer and physically destroy it. Most of us do not need extreme measures but can use one of the many inexpensive software tools for permanently removing data from hard drives.

To begin with, be smarter about deleting files from your hard drive in Windows. A simple delete from any menu in Windows will only move the file from its present folder into the special Recycle Bin folder. There are conditions under which normally deleted files are not sent to the Recycle Bin. These include files stored on removable disks, files stored on network drives, and files deleted from compressed folders. These are said to be "permanently" deleted, but even these files can be recovered, but not quite as easily as from the Recycle Bin. It takes special software to undelete these files.

A file can easily be recovered from the Recycle Bin. This is great for those times when you change your mind after deleting a file, or accidentally delete the wrong file. It is also a security hole. So, when you are absolutely sure that you want to permanently delete a file, you can avoid sending it to the Recycle Bin by selecting the file and holding down the SHIFT key while pressing the DELETE key.

This only protects you from the user who gains access to your computer and uses the Recycle Bin to recover deleted files. It does not protect you from someone who gains access to your computer or hard drive and uses specialized software (and hardware) to recover deleted files or files from a partition that has been reformatted or repartitioned.

on the job

Use the staying power of data on a hard drive to your advantage. If a hard drive with valuable data fails or is somehow damaged so that you cannot access the data on the drive, you can send the drive to a company that will recover your data—at a price. If recovering the data is well worth thousands of dollars, then this is an option to explore. You will find these services by searching on "hard drive data recovery" in a search engine. Remember that the bad guys can do this, too.

To protect your data from malicious attempts to recover it, use programs that remove the data from the hard drive. The most recent name for this class of program is "shredder."

A shredder overwrites deleted files using random data. It overwrites the same space multiple times, and you can choose to shred an entire disk or any one or more documents. Most of these programs will protect your data from all but the most aggressive attempts to recover data using very high-end software and equipment. There are several shredders available for free, and several commercial products. Use a shredder program to wipe out a hard drive before moving a computer to another user or donating it or sending it to a recycler.

Consider using a shredder program on a regular basis to ensure that deleted files are truly deleted. Microsoft Windows XP comes with a command-line utility for encrypting files and folders. However, one option of this command can be used to permanently remove all deleted files from a folder or an entire volume. When you enter the command

```
cipher /w:drive:\folder
```

all the empty space in the folder specified will be overwritten. If you enter the command with this syntax and only specify a drive, all the "empty" space on the drive will be overwritten. Figure 16-4 shows the CIPHER command with the correct syntax to overwrite the deleted files in D:\SalaryReview. The line of dots act as a progress bar, with more dots showing as the program works until it is completed. CIPHER makes three passes: in the first pass it write all zeros onto the empty space, on the second pass it writes the hexadecimal value FF over the same space, and on the final pass it writes random numbers. This is the same technique used by shredder programs.

Neither the CIPHER command nor third-party shredder programs should be used without taking the precaution of first backing up any data on the same drive, because the way these programs manipulate data on the drives has the potential of damaging good files if anything goes wrong during the shredding process.

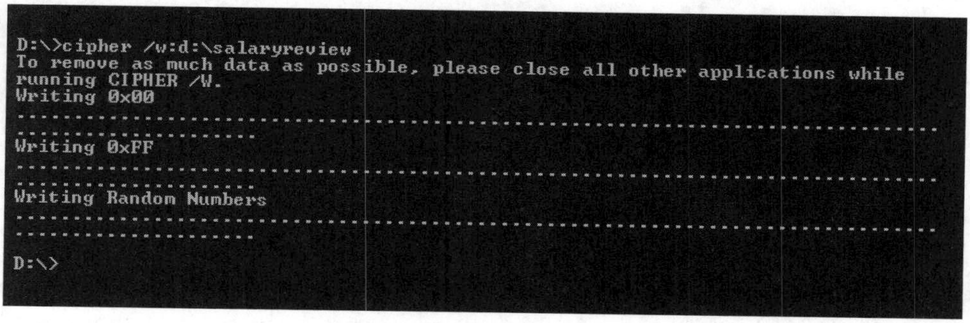

FIGURE 16-4

The CIPHER command used to permanently remove all deleted files in a single folder

Implementing a Defense Against Malicious Software

There are many small building blocks to an effective defense against malicious software. It begins with a foundation of secure authentication and data protection techniques, and continues with the protection of a firewall and related technologies at the junction between a private network and the Internet. Then, each computer in the private network must use a group of technologies to protect them from attacks. These include software firewalls, antivirus programs, phishing filters, and management of the mostly beneficial Internet cookies, other temporary Internet files, and browser add-ons.

Software Firewalls

As you learned in Chapter 15, the first line of defense for a network is a firewall placed at the point the network connects to another network, such as the Internet. This keeps unwanted traffic from entering the network. In a large organization this firewall is in the form of a very expensive hardware device that is best managed by highly trained personnel. This device is often a multifunction device combining routing, firewall, and other functions. It is also placed at the point at which the company connects to the Internet using a high-end connection like one of the T-carrier services.

At home and in a small business, the firewall is also normally a multifunction hardware device, usually a broadband router for use with a WAN connection, such as cable, DSL, or satellite. The differences between what the big guys use and what the rest of us use are price and capability. You get what you pay for.

If your computer is behind a well-configured hardware firewall, that is all the firewall protection you should require for attacks coming from outside the private network. However, many attacks come from within a private network. Therefore, whether your computer is behind an expensive well-managed hardware firewall or a firewall that is part of one of the inexpensive broadband routers found in homes and small businesses, you still need to install and configure a software firewall on every Windows computer.

Of course, you always need antivirus software and all the other protections against malicious code and threats.

Windows Firewalls

Until Windows XP Service Pack 2, the Windows firewall was called Internet Connection Firewall (ICF) and was intended to be enabled on a Windows computer that was sharing its Internet connection with other computers on a LAN. When Windows XP was installed, this firewall was not turned on. If you have a computer that has not been upgraded to Service Pack 2, you can still see this option on the Advanced page of the network connection dialog box, as shown in Figure 16-5.

FIGURE 16-5

The Internet
Connection
Firewall settings
in pre–Service
Pack 2 Windows
XP

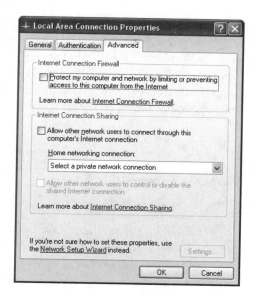

When Windows XP Service Pack 2 installs, it includes the Windows Firewall, which is more configurable than ICF. Windows Firewall is turned on by default. Figure 16-6 shows the Windows Firewall dialog box with three tabbed pages.

FIGURE 16-6

Windows Firewall
dialog box

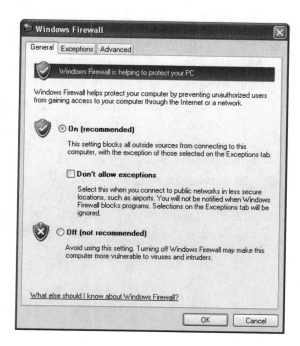

Exercise 16-3 will help you learn more about the Windows Firewall. You must be logged on as the local Administrator or a member of the local Administrators group to work with the Windows Firewall, and to complete this exercise. If you install a third-party firewall, you should turn off Windows Firewall because multiple firewalls on the same computer do not cooperate. Therefore, when you do Exercise 16-3, if you find that it is turned off, do not turn it on unless you are sure that no other firewall is installed.

EXERCISE 16-3

Configuring the Windows Firewall

Explore the Windows Firewall options.

1. Select Start | Control Panel | Windows Firewall. Notice the current setting on the General page, and then click the Exceptions tab to see a list of the types of traffic allowed through your firewall as exceptions. All other traffic that was not requested by your computer will be blocked.

2. Only place a check in boxes next to services you need to use. For instance, turn on File and Printer Sharing only if you have enabled this on your computer and have created one or more shared folders.

3. The Add Program button will allow you to add a program or service to the list. We do not recommend adding a program unless you have very reliable information that this is required and will not cause harm.

4. Similarly, the Add Port button should only be used if you have expert advice on adding a port, or port ID, the identifying information for an IP packet.

5. When you have finished with the Exceptions page, click the Advanced tab.

6. The Network Connection Settings section of the Advanced page will allow you to enable or disable the firewall for network connections to this computer. If you only have a single network connection, you will see only one connection listed, as shown next.

7. The Security Logging section allows you to turn on logging of certain firewall activity. You can choose to log all packets refused by the firewall. These are called dropped packets. You can also log all successful connections and select the location and name for the log file as well as a size limit.

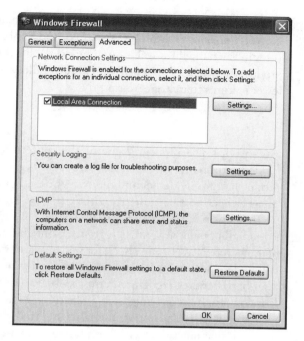

8. The ICMP settings allow you to configure the types of Internet-based requests for ICMP error and status information to which the computer will respond.

9. Finally, the Restore Defaults button at the bottom of this page allows you to restore Windows Firewall to the default settings.

10. When you are finished, close the Windows Firewall dialog box by clicking OK (to accept changes) or Cancel to quit without making changes.

One shortcoming of Windows Firewall is that it does not stop traffic generated from your computer, including connections to the Internet that are originated by locally installed malware. Once malware gets installed, it can initiate a connection to the Internet, and traffic coming from this connection is allowed by the firewall because it is in response to requests from your computer.

Third-Party Software Firewalls

There are many inexpensive third-party software firewalls—some commercial and some free. What third-party software firewalls offer is additional features and greater support than Windows Firewall does.

Examples of personal firewalls are ZoneAlarm and ZoneAlarm Pro by CheckPoint, Norton Personal Firewall by Symantec, and Sunbelt Personal Firewall from Sunbelt (previously named Kerio Personal Firewall). Each of these is available as a separate product or as part of a security software bundle. ZoneAlarm is a free program with fewer features than ZoneAlarm Pro.

Antivirus

An antivirus program can examine the contents of a disk and RAM looking for hidden viruses and files that may act as hosts for virus code. Effective antivirus products not only detect and remove viruses, but they also help you recover data that has been lost because of a virus.

To keep an antivirus program up-to-date, always enable the update option you will find in all popular antivirus programs. Configure it to automatically connect to the manufacturer's Web site, check for updates, and install them. An antivirus program will update at least two components: the antivirus engine (the main program) and a set of patterns of recognized viruses, usually contained in files called definition files. It is common practice among manufacturers of antivirus software to charge an annual fee for updates to the antivirus engine and to the definitions. Common commercial antivirus manufacturers with both home and business solutions include Symantec, TrendMicro, CA, McAfee, Kaspersky, and Grisoft. There are excellent free services for home users. One example is AVG Anti-Virus from Grisoft. Even the commercial vendors who do not offer a completely free product often allow you to try their product for free for a period of time, usually 30 days.

Phishing Filter

In Chapter 15 you learned of the dangers of phishing, a practice in which authentic-looking communications attempt to fool you into providing personal financial information. Phishing is often very difficult to detect for what it truly is. Along with educating yourself on what to look for, be sure to install or enable a phishing filter for your Web browser. You may already have one that is not enabled. Keep in mind that, even with a phishing filter, you must still be alert to possible phishing attacks. A phishing filter will check for suspicious behavior on the Web sites you visit. It will also usually maintain a list of reported phishing sites. For instance, Internet Explorer 7 has Phishing Filter, a feature that detects phishing Web sites. Here is how it works:

- Microsoft maintains a list of legitimate Web sites, which are downloaded to your computer on a regular basis. As you browse the Web, the Phishing Filter compares each site you visit with the list.

■ Phishing Filter looks at the information posted on Web sites and compares it to traits typical of phishing Web sites on each site you visit. If it detects these traits it will warn you that the Web site is flagged as suspicious. This means that it is not on the list of legitimate sites, nor is it on the list of reported phishing sites. If you receive a message that a site is suspicious do not submit any personal information to the site.

■ Depending on how you configure Phishing Filter, it will automatically send addresses of Web sites you visit to Microsoft where they are compared to a list of reported phishing Web sites. Alternatively, you can manually request this check. When the information is sent, it includes your IP address, which is encrypted using SSL, and only the domain and path of the Web site. No other information identifying your activities at the Web site is sent.

To configure Phishing Filter, open Internet Options. Internet Options is a Control Panel applet. You can open Internet Options from Control Panel, or from within IE by selecting Tools | Phishing Filter | Phishing Filter Settings. In Internet Options select the Advanced tab and scroll down to Phishing Filter in the Settings list (see Figure 16-7).

FIGURE 16-7

The Phishing Filter settings in Internet Options

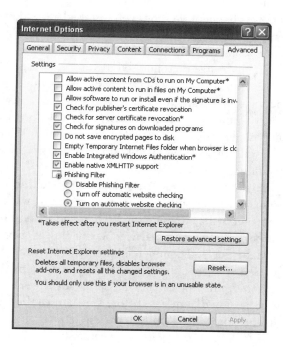

While browsing the Web, selecting the Tools | Phishing Filter option on the Tools menu in IE will allow you to check the current Web site, turn off (or on) Automatic Website checking, report a site, or open the Internet Options menu to change Phishing Filter settings.

Keep one thing in mind. A phishing filter is only an aid. You must educate yourself and the people whose computers you support about the tactics used by phishers. Never provide your social security number or other financial information in response to an unsolicited message—no matter how official the message or the method of transmitting it appears to be. Phishing attacks can come to you via any means—through the mail or over a computer network.

Antispyware/Antiadware/Pop-Up Blocker

As you learned in Chapter 15, spyware and adware are types of programs that install on your computer, and perform functions on behalf of others. The intent of spyware can be very malicious, including identity theft, while the intent of adware is generally less malicious, even if the people responsible for the adware hope to profit from you by advertising their products to you.

How spyware and adware are installed on your computer is yet another issue. It is hard for users to believe that their actions invite malicious programs in, but that is how it happens. Perhaps you installed a wonderful free program. You may be very happy with the program itself, but you may have also installed spyware, adware, or worse along with the program.

The most insidious method used to install spyware and adware on your computer comes in the form of a pop-up window resembling a Windows alert. These bogus messages may warn you that spyware has been installed on your computer, and that you must take some action, such as clicking OK in the pop-up window. This supposedly starts a download of software from Microsoft or another credible source to install software to rid you of the threat. In reality, it is only a disguised method for installing spyware or adware.

Do not fall for these tricks. Fighting these threats begins with being very careful about how you respond to messages in pop-up windows, and what you install onto your computer while browsing the Web. If you are unsure of a message, do not click any buttons or links within the window, but close it using the close button at the upper right.

Many free and commercial programs are available that effectively block various forms of spyware and adware, especially pop-ups. These are the easiest to block, and the most annoying because a pop-up advertisement appears in its own window and must be closed or moved before you can see the content you were seeking. Such a blocking program is called a pop-up blocker. Configure a pop-up blocker so that it will block pop-ups quietly. You can also opt to configure it to make a sound and/or display a message allowing you to make a decision on each pop-up.

We have found a few Web sites where blocking all pop-ups has blocked much of the content we were seeking. If you find that to be the case, configure the pop-up blocker to allow pop-ups for that session, or configure it to display a message. You can also configure it to always allow pop-ups from specified sites.

Pop-up blockers are now the norm in Web browsers, and third-party pop-up blockers are also available. If your Web browser does not have a pop-up blocker option, you may simply need to update it. Exercise 16-4 shows how to enable it in Internet Explorer 7.

EXERCISE 16-4

Configuring a Pop-Up Blocker

You can easily configure the Internet Explorer 7 Pop-up Blocker using the following steps.

1. Open Internet Explorer and Select Tools | Pop-up Blocker. If there is a choice for turning off Pop-up Blocker, then it is already on and you should not select this option. If there is a choice to turn it on, select it so that you will be protected from pop-ups.

2. Now configure Pop-up Blocker. Once again from the Tools menu select Pop-up Blocker and then select Pop-up Blocker Settings, shown here.

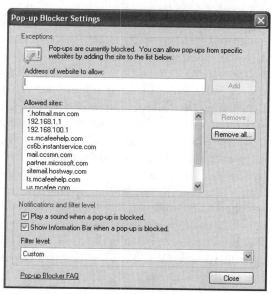

3. Make any changes you desire, including adding sites in which you want to always allow pop-ups, and determining how you want to be notified of a blocked pop-up:

with a sound and/or via the Information Bar, a bar that appears at the top of the IE window below all the other bars. You can also select the Filter Level.

4. When you have finished, click Close.

Antispyware software is now often part of an Internet security package that includes a software firewall, antivirus, antispam, as well as antispyware. Many vendors offer these packages, including Symantec, Trend, AVG, and others. You can also find free or inexpensive individual antispyware programs.

Managing Browser Cookies

Another Web browser issue is third-party cookies, which can be opened by software running on a Web page other than the Web page that saved the cookie. In Chapter 15 you learned about first-party and third-party cookies. Now learn how to manage those cookies.

First-party cookies are, for the most part, harmless and actually have benefits in allowing a Web site to save information about you between visits. Since this information is normally saved in cookies on your local hard drive, they are generally thought to be harmless. However, as you learned, third-party cookies can be used for malicious intent. It is important to disable the use of third-party cookies.

Cookies are not the only files saved on your local hard drive when you are browsing the Web. Popular Web browsers Internet Explorer and Firefox also save entire Web pages and other components of Web pages, such as images and media files. These files are called stored pages in Internet Explorer. The reason for doing this is that on subsequent visits to the same Web site the page will download to your computer faster because in most cases it will not need to download as much from the Web page. By default, after Internet Explorer does a check to see if any of the files have changed on the Web site, it then downloads only those files from your local hard drive that have not changed since your last visit. This practice is sometimes called Web page caching and the location used to store them locally is called a Web cache, but IE does not use these terms.

All the various files that IE saves are lumped together under the heading Temporary Internet Files. The Temporary Internet Files and History Settings page in Internet Properties will allow you to configure several options for handling these files, including how often IE checks for new versions of the locally stored pages, how much disk space is used for all of the files, and the location of the files (see Figure 16-8). You can also view the files from this page.

FIGURE 16-8

Temporary
Internet Files and
History Settings

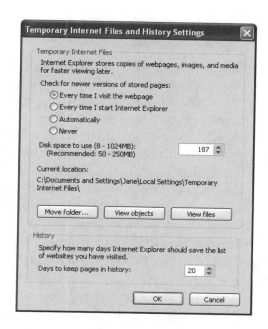

Use the Internet Options applet in Control Panel to manage cookies for Internet Explorer. This also allows you to manage files other temporary Internet files. Follow the steps in Exercise 16-5 to begin managing temporary Internet files in IE.

EXERCISE 16-5

Managing Temporary Internet Files in IE

You can manage temporary Internet files, including cookies, using the Internet Options applet.

1. Open Control Panel and launch the Internet Options applet (also available from the Tools menu in IE). On the General tab locate Browsing History and select the Settings button.

2. Most of the settings are under Temporary Internet Files. Four radio buttons allow you to choose when IE checks for newer versions of stored pages. You can turn this Web page caching off altogether by selecting the Never button.

3. The next setting, Disk Space To Use, controls the space used by Temporary Internet Files. You can enlarge it by clicking the up arrow in the spin box to

make the value larger. Conversely, click the down arrow to use less disk space for Temporary Internet Files.

4. You can change the location of Temporary Internet Files by clicking the Move Folder button. The default location is within the Personal folders for the currently logged-on user. Each user has a location that is separate from other users for these files. If you have a computer in which drive C: (the default drive for these files) is getting low on space, you can change the location to another internal hard drive.

5. Click the View Objects button to reveal downloaded program files. These were downloaded by all users of this computer using IE. Some of them were subsequently installed as add-ons to IE; others may or may not have been installed into Windows in general. Close the folder and return to Temporary Internet Files and History Settings.

6. Click the View Files button to reveal the Temporary Internet Files for the currently logged-on user. Once you have viewed these files, close this folder and return to the Temporary Internet Files and History Settings dialog box.

7. The next setting is History, which determines how many days IE will save the list of visited Web sites. Use the spin box to increase or decrease the number of days.

8. Click OK to close the Temporary Internet Files and History Settings page.

9. Back on the General page click the Delete button. This opens a dialog box from which you can select the type of file to delete including Temporary Internet files, Cookies, the list of Web sites visited, form data, and passwords.

You can also clean up the files that you viewed in the last exercise, as well as others by using the Disk Cleanup utility. To do this, select Start | All Programs | Accessories | System Tools | Disk Cleanup. A small dialog box displays with the message shown here.

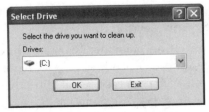

Once you have selected the drive, click OK and Disk Cleanup will calculate how much space it can free up on the drive, and, after a slight delay, it will display

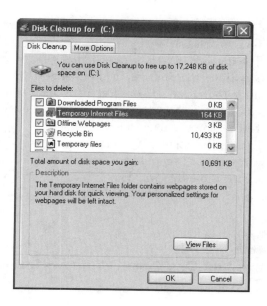

a dialog box showing how much space you will gain and allow you to select or deselect groups of files to delete (Figure 16-9). Before you make a decision, click the More Options tab and look at other ways that you can clean up the drive. These choices include removing optional Windows components, removing installed programs that you do not use, and removing all but the most recent restore point. Do not make any hasty decision here; only use this page if you cannot free up enough space using the first page. Return to the Disk Cleanup page. Once you have selected the files you wish to delete, click OK.

Managing Add-Ons in Web Browsers

Add-ons are small programs that only run in a Web browser. Many add-ons are written in Microsoft's ActiveX language. These programs are often called ActiveX controls. Others are written in Java, which is a programming language developed by Sun Microsystems and designed for use on the Internet. Additionally, some add-ons are written in yet another language, JavaScript, developed by Netscape. Less powerful than Java, JavaScript was designed for creating very small programs that run on Web servers or browsers.

While not truly malicious code, add-ons still require management. Some add-ons are installed when you install a program like Adobe Acrobat; others, such as Windows Messenger, are installed as part of Windows. Certain add-ons are installed without requiring your permission. These are pre-approved add-ons that Microsoft has checked and digitally signed, although Microsoft is not the only source of the add-ons in this list.

The number of Web browser add-ons to choose from is large, and you encounter opportunities to install new add-ons almost any time you browse the Web. In addition to the two add-ons just mentioned, you will find browser toolbars from Google and other search engines, animated mouse pointers, stock tickers, and pop-up blockers, just to name a few.

Each of the popular Web browsers gives you a tool for managing add-ons. It is worth using this tool just to find out what add-ons you have, and disabling or removing those that you do not want or trust. Exercise 16-6 describes the steps for using the Manage Add-ons tool in Windows Internet Explorer 7.

EXERCISE 16-6

Using the Manage Add-Ons Tool in Windows Internet Explorer

Internet Explorer has a simple-to-use Manage Add-ons tool.

1. Open Internet Explorer 7 and select Tools | Manage Add-ons | Enable Or Disable Add-ons. This will open the Manage Add-ons dialog box shown here.

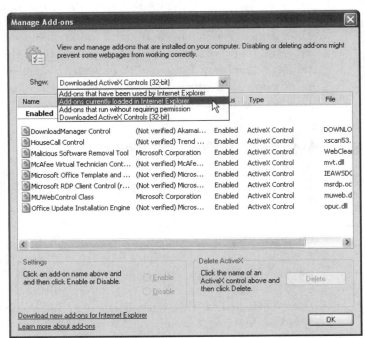

2. View the add-ons using the Show drop-down list to select from four different views.

3. Select an add-on and Enable or Disable it by selecting one of the radio buttons under Settings.

4. You can also delete an add-on by selecting it in the list and clicking the Delete button. Disabling or deleting an add-on may affect the function of certain Web pages. Disable a suspect add-on, and then browse to important Web pages to see if this change has a negative effect.

5. When you are done, click OK to close the Manage Add-ons page.

You can search for add-ons to install by selecting Tools | Manage Add-ons | Find More Add-ons. This will take you to the Add-Ons for Internet Explorer page of the Windows Marketplace site. Here you will find add-ons that you can download to your computer. Many are free; others are usually priced under $20. They are rated by people who tried them and posted their ratings. Be sure to read all the information on any add-on before you download. Some are not compatible with the latest version of IE, or with other installed programs.

SCENARIO & SOLUTION

I support computers in a large organization that uses CISCO routers and firewalls at all connections to the Internet. Why should we use personal firewalls on all our Windows computers?	A properly configured hardware firewall will protect against invasions to the network, but it will not protect each computer from invasion from within the private network.
Now that I have a phishing filter enabled in Windows, do I need to be on the watch for phishing?	Yes, you still must be watchful of phishing attempts. Educate yourself on the techniques used by phishers to obtain your personal financial information.
I heard that cookies are bad, so should I simply block all cookies on my home computer? I browse the Internet frequently, and often go to the same sites for shopping or research.	Blocking all cookies might make your browsing less enjoyable, because without cookies, the sites have no way of remembering your preferences or interests. If you are concerned about cookies, block them for all but your favorite Web sites. Internet Explorer and Firefox have settings that will allow you to do this.

Securing a Wireless Network

In Chapter 13 you learned about creating a Wi-Fi network. The major focus of the installation in that chapter was positioning the hardware components for maximum signal strength, avoiding obstacles and interference, and selecting the correct mode. The radio signals Wi-Fi uses make your Wi-Fi network vulnerable. Anyone with a computer with a Wi-Fi adapter can pick up these radio waves and access your network and your computers, unless you take steps to secure your wireless network.

Access Point Configuration

The heart and soul of a wireless network is the wireless access point, and this is where security is implemented. The important security tasks involve DHCP, the SSID, MAC filtering, the administrator password, keeping the WAP updated, encryption of transmitted signals, and firewall settings. You should implement as many of these changes as is practical, and be sure to document all the settings on your WAP and your wireless client computers. This will help you to restore the WLAN to the same level of protection if something should happen to the WAP, such as a complete failure or an invasion by someone who manages to lock you out of the WAP. More on this last a bit later in the following discussion.

DHCP

One task that will make your wireless network less vulnerable is to disable DHCP on the wireless access point. Unwelcome wireless clients must have an IP address to access your wireless network, and if you lack other security, and the DHCP server gives out addresses indiscriminately, it makes it easy for intruders.

To set up a wireless network without a DHCP server requires some knowledge of IP addressing because once you disable the DHCP server on the WAP you will need to go to each wireless client on the network and give it a unique IP address. You must make sure that the IP address for each wireless client is on the same logical network as the access point. To do this, look at the IP address of the access point. This is normally the only address that is static because the access point includes the DHCP server, which gives out addresses.

A very common IP address for a WAP is 192.168.0.1, but you should check the manufacturer's documentation for the correct address. We often change this default address, but it is not necessary. Consider a WAP with an address of 192.168.100.1 and a Network Mask of 255.255.255.0. You would connect to this access point using your Web browser, because WAPs, like many other network devices, have a Web server built in.

Simply enter the IP address in the address box of the browser. The Web page of the WAP will open in the browser, and from here you can navigate to the settings you need to change. Leave the IP address as it is and locate the setting for the DHCP server. Turn off the DHCP server. See the instructions for manually configuring a client with an IP configuration later in this chapter under Wireless Client Configuration.

If you do not wish to disable DHCP, then limit the number of IP addresses the DHCP server can give out to the number of wireless clients on your network. This will at least avoid unused wireless connections.

Change SSID and Disable Broadcast

Always change the default SSID to a unique name and disable the SSID broadcast. This makes it difficult for the casual user to see your wireless network, since the wireless configuration software that comes with most wireless NICs only displays wireless networks they detect from the access point's broadcast of the SSID name. Disabling this also reduces the volume of wireless traffic incrementally. As with the IP address, you will need to search for the SSID broadcast setting using the access point's Web site.

Once the SSID broadcast is disabled, you will need to manually configure each wireless client with the SSID. Remember that you changed it from the default.

MAC Filtering

All wireless adapters that we have worked with have also allowed you to limit users of the wireless network based on the MAC address of each wireless NIC. Recall that all NICs have a universally unique physical address, called the MAC address. This will require that you visit each wireless computer and obtain the MAC address for each one. There are several ways to do this, but we like using the IPCONFIG command on each computer. Write down the MAC address and connect to the WAP using the browser. Search for the page where you can configure MAC filtering and enter the MAC address for each wireless NIC. If you cannot find a setting on the WAP that uses the term "MAC filtering," look for other terms that may be used, such as Trusted Wireless Stations, as shown in Figure 16-10.

Change Default Administrator Password

Most WAPs come with a default administrator account with a blank password. It may not be possible to change the administrator name, but you can try. At the very least,

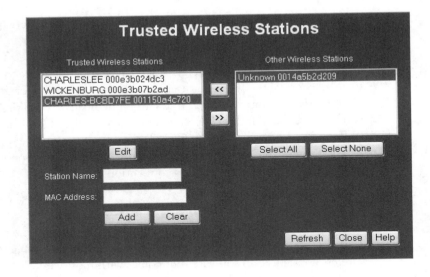

MAC filtering settings are found under Trusted Wireless Stations on this WAP.

change the password to a complex password that will not be easy to crack. You will not be happy if someone accesses your WAP, changes settings, and then changes the password so that you cannot get in and change the settings back.

Update Firmware

Manufacturers of all types of equipment provide updates to the firmware in their devices. In the case of a wireless access point, check the manufacturer's Web site on a regular basis, especially after you learn of new features for WAPs. You do not always need to buy a new WAP in order to have these new features. If the manufacturer makes an update available, follow the instruction for downloading it from the Web site and installing it to the WAP.

Encryption

The most important setting you will find involves encryption of the wireless transmissions. On the wireless router's Web site this setting may simply be labeled "Security" or "Encryption." Once you locate it, look for the latest Wi-Fi encryption. At this time it is Wi-Fi Protected Access (WPA), which uses an encryption standard that is approved by the U.S. government—Advanced Encryption Standard (AES). WPA is based on the IEEE 802.11i security standard for wireless networks. WPA is considered transitional because it supports most older NICs. Wi-Fi Protected Access 2 (WPA2) more fully supports the 802.11i standard, and, as such, does not support older network cards.

If you do not see a setting for WPA or WPA2, it may be labeled WPA-PSK, for WPA pre-shared key. Enter a passphrase of from 8 to 63 characters. Make sure that you combine letters, numbers, and symbols so that this passphrase cannot be cracked. The more complicated and the longer the passphrase, the more secure it will be. Also, be sure that you remember this passphrase, because you will need to enter it in the wireless configuration utility at each computer on the WLAN. Once you have done this, go to each client computer and configure encryption.

One big problem you could encounter is a mixture of old and new equipment. If your WAP supports WPA2, but your NICs do not, you need to make a choice. Use one of the weaker encryption standards that all the wireless devices support, or spend the time and money upgrading to newer NICs that support the same encryption standard as the WAP.

A wireless device manufactured before 2003 may only support an older encryption standard, Wired Equivalent Privacy (WEP). WEP uses 64-bit encryption. In some cases, manufacturers modified WEP to use 128-bit encryption. Even at this higher level, the WEP key can be easily cracked. Further, WEP does not provide true end-to-end data encryption with authentication, as does WPA. If wireless security is important to you, ensure that all of your wireless devices support WPA2. This may require upgrading the BIOS in the device, or replacing it.

Firewall

Enable the firewall in your WAP. This setting may be buried under several menu layers, but locate it and ensure that it is turned on. Then enable the options appropriate for your network. A wireless firewall may be minimal, because it assumes that you do not have servers on the wireless LAN. If available enable the Denial of Service protection, which may be labeled "DoS Firewall."

Wireless Client Configuration

Wireless client configuration follows the access point configuration and must be compatible with the settings on the access point.

DHCP Client Configuration

By default, when a new network interface card is installed on a computer that has the TCP/IP stack, Windows configures the card as a DHCP client. Therefore, you should not have to touch this if a DHCP server is enabled on the network.

Manual IP Configuration

However, if you have chosen to disable the DHCP server on the wireless access point and do not have another one on the network, you must manually configure the wireless NIC on each client computer with an appropriate IP configuration.

To do this, go to each PC that has a wireless NIC and open the Network Connections applet from Control Panel. Right-click the connection for the wireless NIC, and select Properties. On the General page, scroll down and select Internet Protocol (TCP/IP) and click Properties. In the Internet Protocol (TCP/IP) Properties dialog box enter a unique IP address that is on the same network as the WAP, enter the same subnet mask as that of the WAP, enter the WAP's IP address in the Default Gateway box, and enter the DNS service addresses provided by your ISP or network administrator. Figure 16-11 shows an example of a static IP address setting. Do not use the settings shown in this figure.

Manually Configure the SSID

If you have disabled the SSID broadcast on the WAP, then you will need to manually configure each wireless client with the SSID name, since the name cannot be easily discovered otherwise when SSID broadcast is turned off.

FIGURE 16-11

Manually enter the IP settings for each wireless NIC.

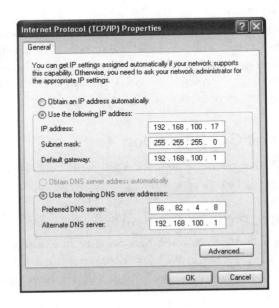

MAC Filtering

If you have configured the WAP to allow only specified MAC addresses, then every time you add a new client to the WLAN, you need to discover the MAC address of the wireless NIC on the new client and add it to the list on the WAP. The MAC address can usually be found on the wireless device itself or on the packaging, or else you can find it after installing the wireless NIC by running the IPCONFIG command using the following syntax: **ipconfig /all**.

Update Firmware

Just as it is important to update the firmware on a wireless access point, you need to check for available firmware upgrades for each wireless NIC. Do this even with a brand-new NIC, since updates may have been released since the NIC was manufactured. Then, follow the manufacturer's instructions for updating the NIC.

Encryption

Each wireless client will need to be configured to match the encryption setting of the WAP. In most cases, this will involve entering the appropriate passphrase—the one you configured on the WAP. If the client is not up to the same level of encryption as the WAP, determine if an upgrade is available from the manufacturer. If not, consider purchasing a new wireless NIC.

Firewall

You normally will not need to make any configuration changes on the wireless client for working with the WAP's built-in firewall. However, always install and configure a personal firewall. Use the Windows Firewall, or disable it and install a third-party personal firewall.

CERTIFICATION OBJECTIVES

■ **601: 6.3   602: 6.3   603: 5.3** *Identify tools, diagnostic procedures, and troubleshooting techniques for security*

■ **601: 6.4** *Perform preventive maintenance for computer security*

■ **602: 6.4   603: 5.4** *Perform preventive maintenance for security*

Recall that the 604 exam is testing the knowledge and skills required for such job functions as depot technician, bench technician, and similar vocations. Notice the similarities between objective 601: 6.4 and the objectives shared by 602: 6.4 and 603: 5.4. There is an important distinction. While the only subobjective for 601: 6.4 is computer-specific, the only subobjective defined under both 602: 6.4 and 603: 5.4 is not strictly computer-related. Specifically, the subobjective under 601: 6.4 states, "Implement software security preventive maintenance techniques such as installing service packs and patches and training users about malicious software prevention technologies." This has been covered, in part, in Chapter 10, which describes how to update the Windows operating system. Good security practices include regular updates. The subobjectives under 602: 6.4 and 603: 5.4 both state: "Recognize social engineering and address social engineering situations." This was described in Chapter 15.

Troubleshooting Security

Troubleshooting security follows the same lines as all computer troubleshooting. Gather information, perform an analysis, arrive at possible solutions, apply the solution, and test the solution. Once you are successful, document the process so that you or your coworkers will not have to "solve" the same problem twice. There are certain problems that are specific to security on a PC, and you will explore some of these in the following sections.

BIOS Password Problems

Earlier in this chapter we explored the issue of setting passwords in BIOS. Like all passwords, it is easy to forget a BIOS password. How this will affect the user depends on the type of BIOS password that was set.

If a BIOS password is set on the system startup, no one will be able to get beyond the BIOS password prompt and boot up the computer until the password is provided. Forget the password, and you are locked out of using the computer.

If a BIOS password is set on the system settings menu, and only on this menu, the computer will boot up normally without requiring a BIOS system startup password. Forget the password and you can start up the computer just fine, but you will not be able to go into the system settings menu and make changes. As we mentioned earlier, this password is necessary in situations in which people have physical access to computers, as in a computer lab.

In both cases, documentation of the password or passwords is very important and should be maintained and kept in a safe place, available to all authorized personnel. The password should not be something only the head techie knows and does not share with anyone else. There are better ways to gain job security.

Before we go on, you must understand that the procedure for removing a BIOS password will also normally erase all the settings, since both are saved in CMOS. Therefore, you will need to reconfigure the CMOS settings after you remove the password. Recall Exercise 3-6 in Chapter 3, in which you learned how to back up CMOS settings. If you have access to a copy of the CMOS settings for the computer, the configuration process will be far easier than trying to guess what the settings were.

Unless a computer case is physically locked, anyone who knows how can remove a BIOS password. Locate the PC or BIOS manufacturer's documentation for the computer or the version of BIOS. This should be in a user manual that came with the computer, but if you cannot locate this, check the manufacturer's Web site. What must be done after that depends on the system, and can range from temporarily removing the battery that supports CMOS to changing a jumper setting and restarting the computer. As you can see, if the computer cases are physically locked, or if access to the lab is only allowed when the computers are supervised, this activity is restricted.

Biometrics

Sometimes users cannot log on to a Windows XP computer using biometrics as the computer resumes from standby or hibernation. This problem was solved in a hotfix from Microsoft. A hotfix is program code that fixes a specific problem. A hotfix is normally only available from Microsoft Product Support Services to persons who identify the problem. In these cases, Microsoft usually waives the normal charges for Microsoft Product Support Services. When we last checked, this was the only manner in which this fix was available. However, it is worth running Windows Update to see if this hotfix has been added to the updates that are available free through this service. If you support one or more Windows computers that are using biometric authentication, check to see if they have been updated and update them before this becomes a problem.

When this problem occurs the computer will still accept a basic interactive logon from the keyboard. Therefore, enter a user name and password from the keyboard. Then take steps to update the computer.

Forgotten Windows Password

If you have forgotten your password, there is help. For one thing, if you are part of a Windows domain, tell the network administrator about your problem. Lost passwords are at the top of the list of things administrators must fix, especially in an environment where people log on with a standard interactive logon—entering user names and passwords at their keyboard. The administrator can log on with the Domain Administrator account (or any account with appropriate rights), access your domain user account, and reset the password. The administrator can assign a password and configure your account so that you will sign on with the assigned password but must change your password during that logon.

Now, if you are not part of a Windows domain, there is still some hope if you can log on with the Administrator account. This can be done the easy way or the hard way. The best way to do this is if you know the local Administrator password or an account that is a member of the local administrator's group. Then simply log on using this user name and password. Then select Start | Run. In the dialog box type **control userpasswords2**. Then click OK. This opens the User Accounts dialog box (the version previously found in Windows 2000). Select the user name of the account with the lost password and click the Reset Password button. In the Reset Password dialog box enter the new password twice and click OK.

If you do not know the Administrator password, it is possible that your installation of Windows has a hidden Administrator account. To access this account, simply restart your computer in Safe Mode. Basic Safe Mode will do. If you need help with Safe Mode, flip back to Chapter 10 and read about Safe Mode. Log on in Safe Mode with the Administrator account. Unless it has been changed, you can leave the password blank when you log on. After logging on as the Administrator, run the User Accounts dialog box, as described previously, and reset the password or your user account.

Missing Security Tab

It has happened to many of us. We want to share a folder on a Windows XP computer. The folder is on an NTFS volume, but the Properties dialog box for the folder does not have a Security tab. What happened to the Security tab and how can we set permissions on this NTFS folder?

It sounds like Simple File Sharing is turned on. In Chapter 13 you learned about Simple File Sharing. When Simple File Sharing is turned on, the Security dialog box is removed from the Properties of NTFS folders and files. You must turn off Simple File Sharing if you want to be able to set specific permissions. Exercise 13-4 in Chapter 13 describes the steps for turning off Simple File Sharing.

No Permissions on FAT32

You would like to set permissions on a folder that you plan to share. You first notice that there is no Security tab in the Properties dialog box for the folder. Perhaps Simple File Sharing is turned on. Then you notice that the volume is not NTFS but FAT32. FAT32 does not support file- and folder-level permissions. The only permissions in this case will be at the share level, and you want to set NTFS permissions so that you can give permissions to each subfolder under the shared folder. What can you do?

If there is no compelling reason for using FAT32 on the volume, convert it to NTFS. Before doing this, back up the entire drive that you plan to convert, just in case something goes wrong with the process. Once the backup is completed, convert the volume using the Disk Management node of the Computer Management console, or by opening a command prompt and running the CONVERT program. The syntax for running the convert program is

```
convert d: /fs:ntfs
```

where *d:* is the drive you wish to convert. Whether you use Disk Management or the CONVERT program, if the drive you are converting is not in use by the OS or any other program, the conversion will occur immediately. If the drive is in use, as is always the case with the system drive (normally drive C:), you will see a message that the conversion will occur the next time Windows is restarted.

This is a one-way conversion. You cannot convert back from NTFS to FAT32 unless you reformat the drive, and then you lose all the data on the hard drive.

Once the file system is converted from FAT32 to NTFS, you can assign permissions to files and folders and use other features of NTFS not available in FAT32.

Be sure that you understand how to convert a volume from FAT32 to NTFS. Understand that there is no reversing this without losing the data on the drive.

Encryption Issues

If you, or users you support, encrypt files using NTFS encryption, you risk having the encryption defeated or being locked out of your own encrypted files. Sometimes we leave the worst news for last. After learning about NTFS encryption in Chapter 15, we will now explain the shortcomings and why we do not use NTFS encryption.

NTFS Encryption Can Be Broken

One way in which NTFS encryption can be broken is by guessing your password. Once someone does that, that person can log on with your user name, which is often displayed in the logon dialog box as the last logged-on user. Once logged on, the invader has access to everything on your computer, including your encrypted files.

The key is to not allow any unauthorized person physical access to your computer. With physical access someone can use a variety of tools to access your encrypted files. There are inexpensive software tools, classified as password recovery software, that can crack passwords on Windows accounts—both local and domain. ElcomSoft (www.elcomsoft.com) has a suite of password recovery products. If you need such a tool, use an Internet search engine to search on this category of software.

Encrypted Files Can Become Inaccessible

You have been careful to encrypt sensitive data files, and to back up your computer. Then, one day your computer crashes. After trying many recovery options, you reformatted the hard drive, reinstalled Windows, and restored your data from the most recent backup set. Your new installation of Windows has an account with the same user name as your old one. You believe you did everything you were supposed to do, but you cannot access the encrypted files that were restored to your computer. What can you do?

First we will explain what went wrong in spite of your diligence. Your user account in the original installation of Windows had a unique security identifier (SID). The NTFS encryption associated this key with the encrypted file, and the only person who can open and use the encrypted files is someone who logs on with the account using this SID. Unfortunately, when Windows failed, it took your account and this identifier with it. After you reinstalled Windows and created a new account, even though you used the old name, the new account received an entirely different SID. Therefore, when logged on with this account, you cannot use the encrypted files.

Products such as ElcomSoft's Advanced EFS Recovery program may be able to decrypt NTFS files.

Software Firewall Issues

A firewall may pop up a message that a program running on your computer is trying to access the Internet, and the firewall then requires that you make a decision to allow this action or not. When this happens, use a search engine to discover if the program is harmful. There is a wealth of information on the Web about problem programs.

If your firewall has blocked a program, you can be sure that others' firewalls have also. Your search will normally result in many hits, and some of the Web sites it discovers may not be well-monitored, or the advice may not be from experienced and qualified people. Do not make a decision based on just one Web site. Check out several. If you know and trust the company posting the information, such as one of the top security software companies, you may accept their answers as authoritative.

Some personal firewalls provide additional information on blocked files with a recommended action you may choose to take. It still often comes down to your having to make a decision without being absolutely sure of the safety of the program, even when it appears to be one that you are familiar with. Windows does have safeguards to protect certain operating system files in the form of digital signatures. If Windows indicates that a program has been digitally signed, you can usually trust the program.

Wireless Access Point Problems

You are the administrator of a wireless LAN and find that although you could once access the wireless access point's Web page, you no longer can do this from any computer on the WLAN. You also fear that someone has gotten into the WAP and made changes in the security settings. What can you do? You will need to reset the WAP using the manufacturer's instructions. Then, because resetting the WAP erases all your settings, you will need to reconfigure it. Be sure to set a complex password on the administrative account to keep intruders out, and set all the security settings on the WLAN.

Preventive Maintenance for Security

As all steps you take to implement security are preventive steps, we do not need a long description of preventive maintenance for security. There are certain tasks that should be added to those described so far in this chapter.

Installing Service Packs and Patches

Although this point has been made previously in this book, it is important to the security of your computer and your confidential data that you keep your computer updated with the latest service packs and patches. If you have Internet access, turn on Automatic Updates in Windows. Further, any security software you install will normally have an automatic update feature. Be sure to turn this on.

Training Users

Knowledge of the danger of threats and how to prevent malicious software from invading computers is important to both the computer professional and to each PC user. Do your part to keep yourself current on security technologies. Depending on your role in an organization, take all opportunities to educate users. Make them aware of the company's security policy, and the role they need to play in preventing attacks.

While every security measure you take is preventive against threats, the CompTIA A+ exams stress the importance of keeping your operating system and security software up-to-date with service packs and patches and training of users. User training should include the software prevention technologies in use on their systems and the social engineering situations they may encounter. This last point was addressed in Chapter 15.

Recognize Social Engineering

In Chapter 15 you learned about social engineering and how to recognize social engineering when you encounter it in e-mails and other messages. Do your part to inform other users about social engineering by sharing what you have learned and directing them to look at a site that educates people about these threats. We gave one example in Exercise 15-1.

CERTIFICATION SUMMARY

There are no easy answers or quick fixes when it comes to computer security. In Chapter 15 you learned that security threats go beyond simple computer invasions to inflict damage, to threats against your very identity. Therefore, computer security must be multifaceted to protect computers, data, and users.

This multifaceted approach includes implementing a variety of security programs and features, including authentication, permissions at both the file system level and the share level, backing up of data, performing data migration when necessary, and removing data from computers that are moved from one place to another or taken out of service with your organization. Audit certain security events and be sure to monitor the resulting events in Event Viewer.

Additionally, train users to protect their computers when they must temporarily walk away. One effective and simple solution is to use Windows' Lock Computer, which preserves the desktop and open files, while protecting them from intruders until the user enters a password to unlock the computer.

Take steps to secure wireless networks, beginning with the access point configuration and extending to the wireless clients, which must be compatible with that of the WAP. You will need to make decisions about the configuration based on what is supported in all the wireless devices in the WLAN. Areas of concern are DHCP, SSID name and broadcasting, MAC filtering, administrative password, firmware updates, encryption, and firewall settings.

Approach security troubleshooting as you would any PC troubleshooting. Some special security issues are BIOS passwords, biometric devices, lost Windows passwords, missing Security tab in the properties dialog box of an NTFS file or folder, lack of permissions on FAT32 volumes, problems with NTFS encryption, software firewall messages, and preventive maintenance for security.

✓ # TWO-MINUTE DRILL

Here are some of the key points covered in Chapter 16.

Implementing Authentication

❑ Two types of BIOS passwords can be set—one that must be entered at startup before an operating system is loaded, and another that is required for access to the BIOS system settings (also known as CMOS settings).

❑ A smart card reader is a device for authenticating with a smart card. It requires software and drivers on the local computer and Certificate Services installed on the domain controllers for the Windows domain.

❑ A smart card cannot be used in three scenarios:

  ❑ When a user is required to join his or her computer to a domain

  ❑ When a user needs to promote the logon computer to a domain controller

  ❑ When a user is configuring a network connection for remote access

❑ Installing support for a key fob involves installing an agent that runs on the local computer, and a service on the active directory domain controllers.

❑ The most popular biometric devices are fingerprint scanners. Some are built into computers, such as Tablet PCs, and others can be added as external devices.

❑ Both the built-in and external biometric devices require drivers and software to integrate with the computer's security system.

❑ When a user needs to walk away from a PC for short periods of time, the Lock Computer option will hide the desktop until the user returns and enters his or her account password.

❑ Enable auditing for Logon Events and Account Logon Events. Then be sure to use Event Viewer to monitor these events to see if there is unusual activity indicating that an intruder is trying to log on to your computer.

Implementing Data Security

❑ In addition to authentication, take steps to directly protect data through the use of NTFS and share permissions.

❑ Use NTFS encryption on the most sensitive of data files, although NTFS encryption has shortcomings, which are detailed under "Troubleshooting Security" in this chapter.

❑ Data backup procedures involve using the data backup types in a combination that provides the best strategy for you. These backup types in Windows Backup are normal, copy, differential, incremental, and daily.

❑ The two major types of data migration are the translation of data from one data format to another, and the moving of data from one storage device to another.

❑ The translation of data from one data format to another is necessary when changing from one type of system and the application for managing the data to another.

❑ One example of the moving of data from one storage device to another is when you purchase a computer with a new version of Windows.

❑ Windows has the Files and Settings Transfer Wizard for moving not just data, but settings for Windows and applications.

❑ Permanent data removal is an important security task, required when a computer is moved from one user to another in an organization, or when it is removed from service within the organization.

❑ Data deleted by users is not truly deleted, but saved in the Recycle Bin and easily recovered. Even when data has been removed from the Recycle Bin and "permanently" deleted, it can be recovered.

❑ A class of programs, called "shredders," removes data from hard drives. Run a shredder on your files as you delete them.

Implementing a Defense Against Malicious Software

❑ A properly configured hardware firewall will protect a network from certain types of invasions from the Internet or other untrusted network, but personal firewalls on each computer will protect from attacks that originate on the private network.

❑ Previous to Windows XP Service Pack 2, the Internet Connection Firewall (ICF) was available, but not turned on.

❑ The Windows Firewall that comes with Windows XP Service Pack 2 is an improvement on ICF but does not stop traffic generated from your computer, including connections to the Internet that originate from locally installed malware.

❑ Antivirus programs examine the contents of a disk and RAM looking for hidden viruses and files that may act as hosts for virus code.

❑ Always enable the update option in an antivirus program and configure it to automatically connect to the manufacturer's Web site, check for updates, and install them. These updates will include changes to the antivirus engine and definition files.

❑ Install or enable a phishing filter for your Web browser. This will check for suspicious behavior on the Web sites you visit. You will still need to be watchful of possible phishing attacks.

❑ Your response to an innocent-looking pop-up can result in installing spyware or adware on your computer. A pop-up blocker can prevent unwanted windows from opening in your browser.

❑ Pop-up blockers are available in Web browsers or as add-ons to Web browsers. Because pop-ups are often necessary on some legitimate Web sites, configure your pop-up blocker to allow certain sites, or just temporarily allow pop-ups for a single session at a site.

❑ For the most part first-party cookies—those that can only be used by the originating site—are harmless. Third-party cookies are usually those created by an advertiser on one site, but configured to be read by software from the same advertiser at other sites.

❑ Configure your browser to disable the use of third-party cookies.

❑ There are many other temporary Internet files saved on your local hard drive. The most common are the entire contents of Web pages, which are saved to increase performance when you revisit the same Web sites.

❑ Internet Options in Control Panel (and from the Tools menu of IE) will allow you to manage temporary Internet files, including cookies.

❑ Use the Disk Cleanup utility to remove temporary Internet files and other files when disk space is running low.

❑ Common Web browsers allow you to manage browser add-ons. In IE 7 this option is found by selecting Tools | Manage Add-ons | Enable Or Disable Add-ons.

Securing a Wireless Network

❑ First configure the wireless access point (WAP), including DHCP (enable or disable). Then change the SSID name, disable SSID broadcast, enable MAC filtering, change the default administrator password, update firmware, enable the strongest encryption available on the WAP, and enable the firewall.

❑ Configure each wireless client with settings compatible with the WAP.

Troubleshooting Security

❑ A forgotten BIOS password, depending on its function, will keep users from starting up the OS, or just keep everyone out of the systems settings menu.

❑ To remove a BIOS password, follow the manufacturer's instructions, which may require opening the computer and setting jumpers to erase the contents of CMOS, which is where the BIOS password is saved.

❑ If you remove the BIOS password by erasing the contents of CMOS, you will need to run the system setup program and enter the correct settings for the system.

❑ If users cannot log on to a Windows XP computer using biometrics as the computer resumes from standby or hibernation, check to see if the computer is up-to-date on updates. When this happens, the short-term fix is to log on with a basic interactive logon from the keyboard.

❑ The preceding problem was solved in a Windows hotfix that was not generally available, but it may be by the time you read this. If not, contact Microsoft for the hotfix.

❑ If you forget your password, there are several options, depending on the situation. If your logon account is in a Windows domain, ask the domain administrator to reset the password.

❑ If the forgotten password is for a local user account, there are also several options. Log on as the local Administrator if you know that password. Then reset the password for the user account.

❑ Or perhaps your installation of Windows has a hidden Administrator account. Access this account by restarting in Safe Mode and logging on with the Administrator account. Unless it has been changed, you can leave the password blank. Then reset the password for the user account.

❑ If the Security tab is missing from the properties of a file or folder on an NTFS volume, it is probably because Simple File Sharing is turned on. Turn this off, and the Security tab will become available.

❑ FAT32 does not support file and folder permissions. Therefore, unless there is a special reason for having a FAT32 volume, convert FAT32 volumes to NTFS using the following syntax:

```
convert d: /fs:ntfs
```

where *d:* is the drive you wish to convert.

❑ Two major problems with NTFS file encryption are that it can be broken and that encrypted files can become inaccessible. Third-party programs may be able to recover the encrypted files.

❑ A firewall may pop up a message that a program running on your computer is trying to access the Internet, and the firewall then requires that you make a decision to allow this action or not. You should research the filename displayed in the message to determine the action you should take. Use a search engine, and/or information available from the firewall.

❑ If you cannot access a WAP's Web page, and you previously could, reset the WAP using the manufacturer's instruction. This will erase the WAP's settings, and you will need to reconfigure it. Be sure to set a complex password on the administrative account to keep intruders out, and set all the security settings on the WLAN.

❑ Preventive maintenance for security includes installing service packs and patches, training users, recognizing social engineering, and performing all the security implementation steps described in this chapter.

SELF TEST

The following questions will help you measure your understanding of the material presented in this chapter. Read all of the choices carefully because there might be more than one correct answer. Choose all correct answers for each question.

Implementing Authentication

1. What is the term for a password that must be entered before a PC will start up the operating system? This term also applies to a password required before you can access the system settings menu.
    A. Biometric password
    B. BIOS password
    C. Windows password
    D. Share-level password

2. What service must be installed on domain controllers before users can log on to a client computer using a smart card?
    A. Smart Services
    B. Secure attention sequence (SAS)
    C. Remote access
    D. Certificate Services

Implementing Data Security

3. What strategy should you use when setting NTFS permissions?
    A. Set the least restrictive level for all users.
    B. Set the most restrictive level that still allows users to accomplish their work.
    C. Keep user groups small.
    D. Assign permissions to users, not to groups.

4. Which of the following procedures is recommended when planning permissions assignments to users in the domain on a computer that is a member of a domain?
    A. Make domain users members of global groups, make global groups members of local groups, and assign permissions to local groups.
    B. Make domain users members of local groups, make local groups members of global groups, and assign permissions to global groups.

   C. Assign permissions directly to individual domain users.

   D. Only assign permissions directly to local users.

5. Create one of these when you work with managers to document which users require the same level of permissions to resources and will therefore be organized into groups.

   A. Permissions planning worksheet

   B. User membership planning worksheet

   C. Group membership planning worksheet

   D. User auditing worksheet

6. What is the recommended order of tasks for creating shares and applying permissions?

   A. Create the share, apply NTFS permissions, and apply share-level permissions.

   B. Give Everyone Read access, apply NTFS permissions, apply share-level permissions, and create the share.

   C. Apply NTFS permissions, create the share, and apply share-level permissions.

   D. Apply NTFS permissions, apply share-level permissions, and create the share.

7. What setting do you turn off on a child folder when you do not want it to inherit the permissions of the parent folder?

   A. Inherit from parent the permission entries that apply to child objects

   B. Block inheritance

   C. Inherit permissions

   D. Effective permissions

8. If an encrypted file is moved or copied into an unencrypted folder on an NTFS volume, which of the following will occur?

   A. It will be decrypted.

   B. It will remain encrypted.

   C. It will be Read-Only.

   D. Encrypted files cannot be moved or copied.

9. Which daily backup strategy takes longer to back up each day as the week progresses, but is quicker to restore?

   A. Normal

   B. Normal and incidental

   C. Normal and incremental

   D. Normal and differential

10. What wizard will move files and settings from one Windows computer to another?
    A. Files and Settings Transfer
    B. CIPHER
    C. Windows Setup
    D. Windows Backup

Implementing a Defense Against Malicious Software

11. What hardware device or software program uses several technologies to prevent unwanted traffic from entering a network?
    A. Proxy server
    B. Firewall
    C. Router
    D. Switch

12. What two antivirus components are frequently updated?
    A. Antispyware
    B. Engine and definitions file
    C. Engine and spam filter
    D. Definition files and phishing filter

13. What type of security software looks at Web site contents for certain traits of social engineering, and will warn you if it detects one of these traits while you are browsing?
    A. Antispyware
    B. Spam filter
    C. Phishing filter
    D. Antivirus

14. What service do popular Web browsers, such as IE and Firefox, offer to prevent unwelcome browser windows from opening on your desktop?
    A. Phishing filter
    B. Spam filter
    C. Pop-up blocker
    D. Personal firewall

15. What security software examines the contents of a disk and RAM looking for hidden viruses and files that may act as hosts for virus code?
    A. Phishing filter
    B. Antivirus

    C. Personal firewall

    D. Pop-up blocker

16. What Control Panel applet allows you to manage temporary Internet files?

    A. Internet Options

    B. Computer Management

    C. Event Viewer

    D. Administrative Tools

Securing a Wireless Network

17. Where do you begin when configuring security for a wireless network?

    A. Wireless clients

    B. Windows

    C. Access point

    D. Ethernet router

18. When possible, which wireless encryption should you use to secure your wireless network?

    A. WEP

    B. WPA2

    C. WPA1

    D. NTFS

Troubleshooting Security

19. What are the direct consequences of forgetting the password on the systems settings menu?

    A. Inability to start up Windows

    B. All systems settings will be reset

    C. The Windows password will be reset

    D. Inability to access the system settings menu

20. What administrative program for user accounts will open in Windows XP when you enter "control userpasswords2" from Start | Run?

    A. Local Users and Groups

    B. User Accounts (Windows XP version)

    C. User Accounts (Windows 2000 version)

    D. Reset Password

LAB QUESTION

Is your computer secure? Whether it is your home computer, or the PC you use at school or work, do your own security audit. Use the list in the following table and look for each of these security items. Feel free to add questions to this list. When you have completed the audit and filled in the Secure Setting column, write a paragraph or two describing the improvements, if any, you would recommend for your computer or network.

Security Setting	Yes or No?
Is authentication required to access the computer?	
If authentication is required, is the password complex?	
If authentication is required, is an authentication method used other than a basic interactive logon at a keyboard?	
Do you use the Lock Computer option when you need to leave your computer while you are logged on?	
Are NTFS permissions applied to locally stored data?	
Is a backup procedure in place for making regular backups of your data, either on the local computer or on a server?	
Is a software firewall in place on your computer?	
Does your computer have antivirus, antispyware, a phishing filter, and a pop-up blocker configured?	

SELF TEST ANSWERS

Implementing Authentication

1. ☑ **B.** BIOS password is the term for a password that must be entered before a PC will start up the operating system.

   ☒ **A**, biometric password, is incorrect. **C**, Windows password, is incorrect because this password is required after the operating system is started, but before the user is granted access to the desktop. **D**, share-level password, is incorrect because this would also be required after the operating system is started. A share-level password is a password you might use when trying to access a share on a Windows 9x computer.

2. ☑ **D.** Certificate Services must be installed on domain controllers before users can log on to a client computer using a smart card.

   ☒ **A**, Smart Services, is incorrect. **B**, secure attention sequence (SAS), is incorrect because this is a special key sequence used to access the logon dialog box in Windows. **C**, remote access, is incorrect because this service has nothing to do with using smart cards to log on to a domain.

Implementing Data Security

3. ☑ **B.** Set the most restrictive level that still allows users to accomplish their work.

   ☒ **A**, set the least restrictive level for all users, is incorrect because this would expose data to unauthorized users. **C**, keep user groups small, is incorrect because this is not part of the strategy described in this chapter for setting NTFS permissions. **D**, assign permission to users, not to groups, is incorrect because this is the opposite of the strategy described in the chapter.

4. ☑ **A.** Make domain users members of global groups, make global groups members of local groups, and assign permissions to local groups.

   ☒ **B**, make domain users members of local groups, make local groups members of global groups, and assign permissions to global groups, is incorrect because this is not the procedure described in the chapter, and you cannot make local groups members of global groups. **C**, assign permissions directly to individual domain users, is incorrect because this is not the procedure described in the chapter, and this would also create more work for the administrator. **D**, only assign permissions directly to local users, is incorrect because this would not allow you to assign permissions to domain accounts.

5. ☑ **C.** A group membership planning worksheet is an aid to help document which users require the same level of permissions to resources.

   ☒ **A**, permissions planning worksheet, is incorrect because this is not used to document which users require the same level of permissions to resources and will therefore be organized into groups.

B, user membership planning worksheet, is incorrect because this does not mention "groups." **D**, user auditing worksheet, is incorrect because this would not describe something that documents groups.

6. ☑ **C.** Apply NTFS permissions, create the share, and apply share-level permissions.
   ☒ **A**, create the share, apply NTFS permissions, and apply share-level permissions, is incorrect because if you create the share before applying NTFS permissions, the share-level default permissions will leave the shared files and folder too vulnerable. **B**, give Everyone Read access, apply NTFS permissions, apply share-level permissions, and create the share, is incorrect for two reasons: Everyone Read is too open for most situations, and you cannot apply share-level permissions before you create a share. **D**, apply NTFS permissions, apply share-level permissions, and create the share, is also incorrect because you cannot apply share-level permissions before you create the share.

7. ☑ **A.** "Inherit from parent the permission entries that apply to child objects" is the setting to turn off on a child folder when you do not want it to inherit the permissions of the parent folder.
   ☒ **B**, block inheritance, is incorrect because, while this is the effect you want, the setting does not use this term. **C**, inherit permissions, is incorrect because this describes the opposite result than is described in the question. **D**, effective permissions, is incorrect because this is not a setting for a child folder, but just one page on the Advanced dialog box available from the Advanced button on the Security page of the properties dialog box for a file or folder.

8. ☑ **B.** It will remain encrypted if moved or copied into an unencrypted folder on an NTFS volume.
   ☒ **A**, it will be decrypted, is incorrect because as long as the move or copy is not performed as a drag-and-drop operation, an encrypted file will remain encrypted. **C**, it will be Read-Only, is incorrect because this is not the result of moving or copying an encrypted file into an unencrypted folder on an NTFS volume. **D**, encrypted files cannot be moved or copied, is incorrect because encrypted files can be moved or copied.

9. ☑ **D.** A normal and differential weekly backup strategy takes longer to back up each day as the week progresses, but is quicker to restore.
   ☒ **A**, normal, is incorrect because it will not result in a strategy that takes longer to back up each day as the week progresses, but is quicker to restore. The relative length of time for each backup will depend on the amount of changed data in the selected files, and it will take longer to restore because each day's backup will have to be restored. **B**, normal and incidental, is incorrect because this is not specified as a backup strategy and there is no "incidental" backup type. **C**, normal and incremental, is incorrect because this backup strategy takes longer to restore, because each day's backup must be restored.

10. ☑ **A.** The Files and Settings Transfer Wizard will move files and settings from one Windows computer to another.
☒ **B,** CIPHER, is incorrect because this is a command-line utility for encrypting files on an NTFS volume. **C,** Windows Setup, is incorrect because, although this can be used to upgrade an installation of Windows, it is not used to transfer files and settings from one Windows computer to another. **D,** Windows Backup, is incorrect because, although it can be run as a wizard, this is not the tool for moving files and settings.

Implementing a Defense Against Malicious Software

11. ☑ **B.** A firewall is the hardware device or software program that uses several technologies to prevent unwanted traffic from entering a network.
☒ **A,** proxy server, is incorrect because although this is one of the technologies used by a firewall, it does not fully describe a firewall. **C,** router, is incorrect because this is a separate device (or software), although it may use one or more of the technologies associated with a firewall. **D,** switch, is incorrect because this is not a device or software that prevents unwanted traffic from entering a network. A switch is a cable-connecting device used within a network.

12. ☑ **B.** The engine and definitions file are the two antivirus components that are frequently updated.
☒ **A,** antispyware, is incorrect because this is not a component of antivirus, although antispyware and antivirus may both be part of a security bundle. **C,** engine and spam filter, is incorrect because, although the antivirus engine is one of the components that is updated, the spam filter is not part of antivirus, even though it may be bundled with antivirus software in a security package. **D,** definition files and phishing filter, is incorrect because, although definition file is part of the correct answer, phishing filter is not part of an antivirus program, but an add-on or feature of a Web browser.

13. ☑ **C.** Phishing filter is the type of security software that looks at Web site contents for certain traits, and will warn you if it detects one of these traits while you are browsing.
☒ **A,** antispyware, is incorrect because antispyware looks for spyware on your computer, not traits of social engineering. **B,** spam filter, is incorrect because this does not look for traits of social engineering but for spam in your e-mail. **D,** antivirus, is incorrect because this does not look for traits of social engineering, but for viruses on disk or in memory.

14. ☑ **C.** Pop-up blocker is the service Web browsers offer to prevent browser windows from opening up on the desktop.
☒ **A,** phishing filter, is incorrect because, while this works within a browser, it scans Web sites for certain traits of social engineering. **B,** spam filter, is incorrect because this scans incoming e-mails for suspected spam messages. **D,** personal firewall, is incorrect because it does not work

within a Web browser but blocks certain types of incoming messages based on information in the packet header.

15. ☑ **B.** Antivirus is security software that examines the contents of a disk and RAM looking for hidden viruses and files that may act as hosts for virus code.

☒ **A,** phishing filter, is incorrect because this works within a browser and scans Web sites for certain traits of social engineering. **C,** personal firewall, is incorrect because it blocks certain types of incoming messages based on information in the packet header but does not look at the contents to determine if it is virus code. **D,** pop-up blocker, is incorrect because it only works within a browser to prevent unwanted browser windows from opening.

16. ☑ **A.** Internet Options is where you can manage temporary Internet files.

☒ **B,** Computer Management, **C,** Event Viewer, and **D,** Administrative Tools, are all incorrect because none of these administrative tools allows you to manage temporary Internet files.

Securing a Wireless Network

17. ☑ **C.** An access point is the place to begin when configuring security for a wireless network.

☒ **A,** wireless clients, is incorrect because the access point must be configured before the wireless clients can be configured to connect. **B,** Windows, is incorrect because this is also on the client side of things and should not be configured until after configuring the access point. **D,** Ethernet router, is incorrect because, while a wireless network may be connected through the access point to an Ethernet router, this has no other connection to the configuration of the wireless network.

18. ☑ **B.** WPA2 is the latest encryption method, and the preferred one to use as of the writing of this book.

☒ **A,** WEP, is incorrect because this was replaced by WPA in 2003 and is no longer considered secure. **C,** WPA1, is incorrect because WPA2 is more secure. **D,** NTFS, is incorrect because NTFS encryption has nothing to do with wireless networks.

Troubleshooting Security

19. ☑ **D.** Inability to access the system settings menu is the direct consequences of forgetting the password on the systems settings menu.

☒ **A,** inability to start up Windows, is incorrect because forgetting the password on the systems settings menu will have no effect on starting up Windows. **B,** all systems settings will be reset, is incorrect because this will not happen just because you forget the systems settings menu password. **C,** the Windows password will be reset, is incorrect because the password on the systems settings menu will not affect the Windows password for any user account.

20. ☑ **C.** User Accounts (Windows 2000 version) is the program for user accounts that opens in Windows XP when you enter "control userpasswords2" from Start | Run.

☒ **A**, Local Users and Groups, **B**, User Accounts (Windows XP version), and **D**, Reset Password, are all incorrect because none of these will open when you enter "control userpasswords2" from Start | Run. In fact, Reset Password does not exist as a separate program.

LAB ANSWER

Answers will vary, but if the table shows any "No's" in the "Secure Setting?" column, then you should recommend changing the security configuration so that the computer or network is more secure.

Part VII

Safety and Environmental Issues

17

Safety and Environmental Issues

The 2006 601, 602, and 604 A+ exams, like the former 2003 A+ Core Hardware exam, include safety and environmental issues, but it is clear that this topic is more important in the newer exams and you should expect more questions in this area than previously. In the old A+ Core Hardware exam objectives, safety and environmental issues were only a subobjective comprising about half of the listed objectives under the Preventive Maintenance domain, and this domain was only 5 percent of the entire exam. In the three new exams listed here, Safety and Environmental Issues is a separate domain that carries of weight of 10 percent of the 601 and 604 exams and 5 percent of the 602 exam. Exam 603 does not include safety and environmental objectives.

CERTIFICATION OBJECTIVES

- **601: 7.1** *Describe the aspects and importance of safety and environmental issues*

- **601: 7.2** *Identify potential hazards and implement proper safety procedures, including ESD precautions and procedures, safe work environment, and equipment handling*

- **602: 7.1   604: 5.1** *Identify potential hazards and proper safety procedures, including power supply, display devices, and environment*

The A+ candidate must prove that he or she understands that everyone must take responsibility for a safe work environment and safe equipment handling to protect both the equipment and people. Further, in spite of all efforts to make the workplace safe, accidents will happen, and it is expected that technicians and all other workers will prepare to respond by acquiring first aid skills and, in case of an accident, contacting emergency personnel immediately.

Maintaining a Safe Work Environment

While your company may have specific people assigned direct responsibility for safety compliance and implementation, safety truly is everyone's job, regardless of job description. Everyone in an organization must play an active role in maintaining a safe work environment. This includes developing an awareness of common safety hazards, such as spilled liquids, floor clutter, electrical dangers, and atmospheric hazards. From this awareness come precautions against all anticipated hazards. Be proactive to avoid disasters that can harm people and equipment.

Liquids

Liquids can pose a risk to both equipment and to personnel. Understand the risks posed by liquids in the workplace, and how to avoid damage and injury.

Computer Damage from Liquids

Liquids—even the most benign, such as water—are very dangerous to computers and peripherals. Liquids can quickly short out a computer or peripheral if spilled onto the circuitry, causing permanent damage. With a computer on nearly every office desktop in the world, liquids may be the most common threat to computer keyboards. It is hard to enforce a policy of no beverages around computers, so at least educate users on the dangers. Encourage them to place beverages on a separate surface, perhaps a small table that is lower than the computer keyboard, and nowhere near the computer system itself.

If clean water spills into a computer or peripheral, such as a keyboard, the extent of damage will depend on whether power was on at the time. If power is off, do not turn it on until the computer or peripheral is completely dry. Open it to inspect it before turning it back on.

If power is on, the computer or peripheral will probably short out and cause permanent damage. The only possible recoverable clean water spill when power is on is to a keyboard—and then only if the keyboard has a film membrane that may (in the best of circumstances) protect the keyboard's circuitry from the spill. If you spill clean water on a keyboard connected to a powered-up computer, turn the keyboard over immediately, and disconnect it from the computer (to turn off the power). Do not reconnect it until it is completely dry. You can hasten this process by carefully removing the keys and using a clean lint-free cloth to gently blot up water. You can also use a blow dryer, but only on a low setting. There are two risks in using a blow dryer: the risk of creating a low-humidity environment in the keyboard, which may generate static, and the risk of melting the keyboard and deforming its plastic body. We know about this last from personal experience.

It is bad enough when clean water spills into a computer or keyboard. When dirty water or, even worse, sugary soft drinks, spill they leave behind a residue that may also permanently damage the computer, even if the computer or peripheral does not have power turned on at the time. In this case, even if you allow the liquid to dry before turning on the power, the residue can cause malfunctions with the keys or short-circuit the circuitry in the keyboard.

If workers must, as part of their jobs, have their hands wet or dirty while using a computer, consider purchasing an inexpensive see-through membrane keyboard cover that protects the keyboard but still allows the user to use the keyboard.

on the !Job *Check out availability of keyboard covers by using the keywords "keyboard protection" in your favorite Web search engine.*

Injury Accidents Caused by Liquids

Liquids are also dangerous in any work environment, because liquids spilled on floors and stairways create opportunities for slipping and falling. Another potential danger from a liquid spill is electrical shock if the spill creates a pathway between a power source and a person.

How many times have you been in a grocery store or your favorite big box store and heard a request for a cleanup, identifying the location of the spill. No one wants their customers or employees injured for any reason, and spills are a big contributor to injuries from falls.

Tripping

Another problem in all types of work environments is injury from tripping over unexpected obstacles. Keep all aisles, walkways, hallways, and other traffic areas clear of clutter that can cause employees or customers to trip and fall. Be especially careful with electrical cords.

Worn or damaged flooring can become a hazard to people. Pay special attention to stairways and entrances, where stair pads or floor mats can become loose. You should remove or repair such hazards as soon as possible. If it is not possible to remove the hazard immediately, post a sign and/or block off the area from traffic until the situation is corrected. However, do not block building exits while doing this.

Electrical Dangers

Leave servicing high-voltage peripherals such as monitors, laser printers, and power supplies to technicians trained in that area. Even when left unplugged for an extended period, such devices can store enough voltage to cause severe injury or even death from electrical shock. Do not use an antistatic wristband or other antistatic equipment when working with high-voltage devices.

While we think of high voltage as being the most dangerous, which it is, low voltage, under certain circumstances, can also cause serious injury or death. People have died from electrical injuries involving as little as 50 volts. Many variables determine the amount of damage to a victim of electric shock. These include (but are not limited to) the body's resistance to the current (or lack of resistance due to wetness), the path of the current through the body, and how long the body is in contact with the electrical current.

In cases in which the skin offered little resistance (for instance, wet skin), the skin may appear undamaged, but perhaps internal organs were damaged. In cases in which the skin, due to dryness or thickness, or a combination of characteristics, offered greater resistance, there may be bad burns on the skin but no damage to internal organs.

Atmospheric Hazards

Atmospheric hazards include all possible weather phenomena, such as cold, flood, rain, heat, snow, hurricanes, ice storms, lightning, tornados, and wind. In addition, very fine particulates in the air can also cause lung damage. These particulates can come from many sources, including general pollution, manufacturing, and even ordinary equipment.

For instance, laser printer toner is a very fine particulate, and while the chemical makeup of toner may not be dangerous, its very fine form means that it can be inhaled and cause lung damage. This should not happen in ordinary handling of laser toner cartridges, but even an "empty" toner cartridge still has toner in the reservoir where it stores the excess toner cleaned from the drum during the printing process. Mishandling of a toner cartridge, such as by opening up the toner reservoir or accidentally breaking open the cartridge, can release the ultra-fine toner particles into the air. If this happens, immediately leave the area and only return when you have breathing protection from the particulates and are able to clean up the toner.

SCENARIO & SOLUTION

Our organization has workers whose hands are constantly dirty and greasy from servicing manufacturing equipment, but they must frequently use a computer to access the online repair manuals. How can we protect the keyboards so that we do not have to frequently replace them because of malfunctions caused by the dirt and grease?	Purchase keyboard protection covers, which are available from many sources. Use a Web search engine to research the available covers.
I noticed that some of the stair treads in a frequently used stairway are loose and may pose a hazard. What should I do?	Report the problem to the appropriate person, remove or correct the hazard if you can, or block off the hazard if you cannot correct it immediately.

Excess toner also accumulates inside a laser printer. Using a vacuum for cleaning toner is not recommended because the microscopic particles will pass through most filters, and you risk inhaling the toner. Seek advice from the cartridge manufacturer on a safe method of cleanup.

Safe Equipment Handling

Safe equipment handling begins with using the appropriate tools, taking care when moving equipment, protecting yourself and equipment from electrostatic discharge, avoiding damage to transmissions and data from electromagnetic interference, and taking appropriate precautions when working with power supplies, displays, and printers.

Using Appropriate Repair Tools

The typical computer technician's repair toolkit is not extensive. Recall the tools listed under "The Hardware Toolkit" in Chapter 4: various types and sizes of screwdrivers, a parts grabber, a flashlight, a small container for holding extra screws and jumpers, a multimeter, and antistatic equipment, such as a wrist strap and antistatic mat.

Use each tool only for its intended purposes. Attempting to use a flat-bladed screwdriver on a Phillips head screw can damage the screw. It also does not work very well. Worse yet, using the wrong tool that does not fit properly may cause your hand to slip and damage a component, such as the motherboard, or even injure yourself.

 on the **Job**

Do not carry loose objects like screwdrivers in shirt pockets, because these can fall into computers and other equipment when you lean over.

Moving Equipment

Power down all equipment and disconnect it from power outlets before moving it—even when moving it from one side of a desk to another. This includes laptops. Yes, they are portable devices, but moving a laptop around while it is actively running can harm the hard drive. Moving any computer while powered up could damage the hard drives.

Do not just flip the power switch. For instance, in Windows XP you have three appropriate choices before you move the laptop or other computer: Turn Off, Stand By, or Hibernate (depending on the configuration). All of these will shut down the hard drive until you turn the computer back on or it is Resumed. After the computer turns off or goes into one of these other states, do not forget to unplug the power cord.

You may question the advice to always unplug a device before moving—even from one side of a desk to another. However, we have seen too many instances in which the connected power cord caused damage or injury. You simply are not in complete control of a device when it is still tethered to the wall.

Be very careful when moving displays—whether they are CRTs or flat panel displays. Both types are fragile, and you must take care not to drop a display or put any pressure on the front of the display.

Other devices require special handling when moved. If you are unsure of the proper way to move a computer or peripheral, check out the documentation. For instance, some scanners have a transportation lock that you must engage before moving them, in order to protect fragile components.

Of course, consider your own safety when moving equipment. Protect your back when you lift equipment: wear a safety belt, keep the back straight, and use your knees. Do not try to carry heavy computer components farther than a few feet without the aid of a utility cart.

Whenever handling computer components, be very careful of the sharp edges on sheet metal in computer cases and in some peripherals. It is very easy to cut yourself on these. Similarly, the backs of many circuit boards contain very sharp wire ends that can cause puncture wounds. Work gloves offer protection, but most of us feel too awkward wearing gloves while handling delicate computer equipment. If you cannot wear gloves, be very cautious.

Electrostatic Discharge (ESD)

One of the most prevalent threats to a computer component is electrostatic discharge (ESD), also known as static electricity, or simply static. Static is all around us, especially when both the humidity and the temperature are low. When you put on a jacket that makes the hair on your arm stand up, or when you run a balloon on your hair to make it stick to the wall, you are encountering static electricity. When you slide your feet across a carpet and then touch someone else, or a door knob or light switch, and receive a jolt, you are experiencing a static discharge.

The Dangers of ESD

ESD happens when two objects of uneven electrical charge come in contact with one another. Electricity has the property of traveling from an area of higher charge to an area of lower charge, and the static shock that you feel is the result of electrons jumping from your skin to the other object. The same process can occur within a computer. If your body has a high electric potential, electrons will transfer to the first computer component that you touch.

Electrostatic discharge, or static electricity, can cause irreparable damage to your computer components and peripherals. Typical ESD discharges range from 600 to 25,000 volts, although at minute amperages. Most computer components can safely receive voltages of ±12 volts. Therefore, damage to computer components can occur with as little as 30 volts—a charge you will not even detect because your body can withstand 25,000 volts under the right conditions.

on the job

Do not count on the body's ability to withstand 25,000 volts. This is under the right circumstances. Learn more about this in the section titled "Protection from ESD Damage and Injury."

People call these very low-voltage static charges "hidden ESD," and they can come from dust buildup inside the computer. Dust and other foreign particles can hold an electric charge that slowly bleeds into nearby components. Hidden ESD can cause serious problems because you will have no hint of trouble until damage has occurred to the component and it malfunctions. This is very difficult to pinpoint.

ESD can cause the immediate, catastrophic malfunction of a device, or it can cause a gradually worsening problem in a device—a process called degradation. As unlikely as it might seem, degradation damage can be more costly in lost work time and in time spent to troubleshoot and repair than catastrophic damage. When a device suffers catastrophic damage, the result is immediate and typically quite obvious, so you will know to replace the device right away. Degradation, on the other hand, can cause a component to malfunction sporadically, sometimes working and sometimes not. This makes it harder to pinpoint the cause, and the problem will persist for a longer period of time and be more disruptive to the user and to the support professional.

Additionally, a total failure of one component will typically not affect the usability of other components. However, degradation can cause a component to fail in ways that also result in the failure of other components.

exam
watch

Most static discharges are well above 600 volts, but it takes a charge of only about 30 volts to destroy a computer component.

Protection from ESD Damage and Injury

There are many ways to prevent ESD from damaging computer equipment. First, low humidity contributes to ESD. Therefore, when possible, keep computer equipment in a room in which the humidity is between 50 and 80 percent. Do not allow it to go above 80 percent, or condensation could form on the equipment and cause it to short out.

To prevent damage to the system, you must equalize the electrical charge between your body and the components inside your computer. Touching a grounded portion of your computer's chassis will work to some extent, but for complete safety, use an antistatic wristband with a ground wire attached to the computer frame.

Antistatic devices, such as an antistatic wrist or ankle strap, drain static charge from your body to ground. If a static charge has built up in the computer equipment, it will also bleed from the computer through your body to ground. This is also true of any electrical flow. Therefore, you must never use an antistatic strap attached to your body when working around high-voltage devices. Nor should you use other antistatic devices in a manner that puts your body between a power source and ground.

Many computer assembly and repair shops use an antistatic floor mat that discharges static when you stand on it. Similarly, an antistatic mat on the bench table is often used. An antistatic mat looks like a vinyl placemat, but it has a wire lead and (usually) an alligator clip to connect it to ground. An antistatic mat is a safe place to put expansion cards or other internal components that you have removed from the computer.

Before you pick up a loose computer component, if you are not wearing or touching an antistatic device, discharge any static electricity on your body by touching something metal, such as a table leg or chair. Equipment placed on the mat will discharge static through the mat. All of these antistatic devices usually have cables that you must attach to a grounded metal object. Some have a single prong that you insert into the ground socket in a regular wall outlet. In the United States and Canada, the ground socket is the single round socket offset from the two slender blade sockets. Other cables on antistatic wrist or ankle straps or on antistatic mats may use alligator clips for making this attachment.

Another name for antistatic devices is ESD devices. You will find a wide array of these devices under either name. Searching on "ESD," we found the expected ESD floor mats and wrist straps, plus gloves, finger cots, labels, bags, cleaners, bins, and meters.

Use antistatic spray to remove static from clothing and carpet. Never spray it directly on computer equipment or components. Exercise 17-1 will lead you through the process of protecting your workspace and computer from ESD damage.

EXERCISE 17-1

ESD-Proofing Your Workspace

Whether your workspace is a cubicle or desk at which you do minor repairs, or a computer workbench where you do more extensive service on computers and peripherals, follow these simple steps to ESD-proof your workspace.

1. Maintain the room's humidity between 50 percent and 80 percent.

2. Spray your clothing and the work area with antistatic spray. Never directly spray the computer, its components, printers, or scanners.

3. Place an ESD mat on the workspace and attach its alligator clip to something stationary and metal, such as the leg of a table.

4. Remove all jewelry, including rings.

5. Put an ESD strap around your wrist or ankle, and attach the other end to a stationary metal object (if it has an alligator clip) or plug it into a wall outlet's ground socket (only if the strap has an outlet prong).

Electromagnetic Interference (EMI)

Another problem related to electricity is electromagnetic interference (EMI), which we described in Chapter 4. Be aware of nearby electrical devices. A high-voltage transformer, electrical panels, fluorescent lights, and electric motors produce EMI, which can temporarily interfere with the functioning of computer equipment, such as monitors. For instance, a monitor experiencing EMI will have a jittery or distorted picture, but when you remove the source of the interference or move the monitor, the picture will return to normal. The biggest problem with EMI is that it disturbs the transmission of data over copper wires, such as Ethernet cables.

e x a m

w a t c h *Do not be confused by the similarity in the names: ESD can damage or destroy hardware, while EMI usually causes temporary problems and is more dangerous to data than to hardware. ESD damage usually requires replacing a component, while EMI may damage data but not hardware. Remove the source of EMI, or move the computer away from the source, and the problem with transmissions goes away. If EMI is strong enough, it can damage data stored magnetically. Restore the data and you are in business again.*

Proper Component Storage

When they are in use, keep all computers and components in a working environment that is most conducive to prolonged operation. Whenever you remove a component from a computer, it becomes susceptible to damage from external sources. Therefore, you must ensure that you properly protect it when you store it. Always store computer components in a cool, dry place (but not dry enough to generate static electricity). Heat can damage a component's circuits and cause magnetically stored data to be lost. Furthermore, damp environments can cause condensation to form, leading to corrosion, or they can cause the component to short-circuit when it is reinstalled in a computer.

You should also make sure that components, especially those that use magnetic storage, are kept safely away from high-voltage devices, as well as electromagnetic interference (EMI)–causing devices and other sources of magnetism. You should always place internal components such as chips and circuit boards in antistatic bags before storing or transporting them.

Antistatic bags dissipate static charges away from the contents by moving a static charge from the inside of the bag to the outside. Components normally come packaged in these bags, and you should save the bags and always store unused components in these bags. One precaution: do not set any components down on top of one of these bags, because the bag's exterior can pass a static charge onto the component. Simply do not consider the exterior of the bag as safe for your component, but immediately place the component inside the bag. When preparing to install a component that is stored in one of these bags, leave the component inside the bag until you are ready to install it.

on the
Job

Many technicians place components on top of the antistatic bags they arrived in. This can cause damage, and you should not do this unless specifically instructed to do so by the manufacturer. If the bag in question is one that moves the static charges from inside the bag to the outside, placing a component on one of these bags can expose the component to harmful static.

Power Supplies

The power found in a computer's high-voltage power supply is enough to cause injury or death. Always unplug the power supply from the wall outlet when you are working inside a computer or printer. Simply turning off the power switch is not enough. Even when turned off, the power supply in a computer can conduct electricity, and most motherboards continue to have power applied—a practice called soft power that we described in Chapter 2. To be safe, unplug the power supply. Some technicians prefer to leave the power supply plugged in while they work on the computer to allow static to bleed away from the computer into the wall outlet's ground wire. However, we do not recommend this, because there are safer methods for removing static, such as placing the computer on an antistatic mat.

Power supplies store electrical charges for long periods of time, even when unplugged. Never open the power supply's case, and never wear an antistatic wrist strap when replacing or handling a power supply. The high voltage from the power supply is sufficient to cause grave injury or death.

Display Devices

Like power supplies, CRT monitors are high-voltage equipment and can store a harmful electrical charge, even when unplugged. Never open a CRT case, and never wear a wrist strap when handling a CRT. You do not want to provide a path to ground through your body for this charge.

Printers

Printers have lots of moving parts, so there are several safety procedures you should follow whenever you work with or around a printer. Do not let long hair, clothing, jewelry, or other objects near the moving parts of a printer, including (but not limited to) feed or exit rollers. There are two different hazards involved in wearing a tie. First, the tie itself may build up a static charge, and if it touches a component, it will pass the charge to the component. The second hazard, which is very dangerous to the wearer, is the danger of loose clothing being entangled in the moving parts of a device like a printer. When wearing a tie or scarf, make sure that you either tuck it into your shirt or use some kind of clip or tie tack. Figure 17-1 shows an open printer and the cartridge assembly, which rapidly moves back and forth when it is operating.

on the
Job   *Some employers require technicians to dress like office professionals, which may include having men wear neckties.*

FIGURE 17-1   Keep loose clothing and jewelry away from open printers.

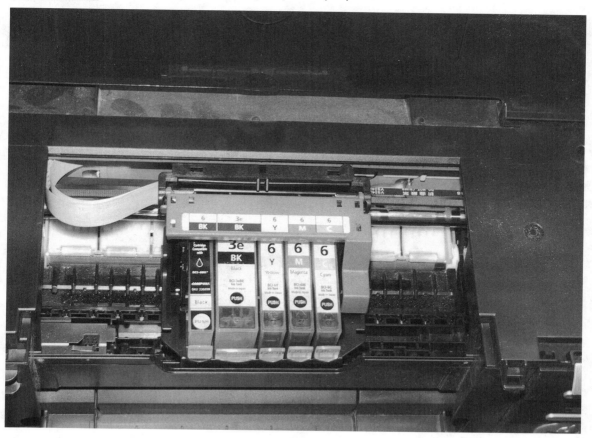

Furthermore, do not try to operate a printer with the cover off. The cartridge in an inkjet printer and the print head in a dot matrix printer move back and forth quickly across the page, and it is possible to get your hands or other objects in the way. This can harm you and the printer's components. You must be especially careful when working around laser printers because the laser beam can cause eye damage. Fortunately, most printers do not work when their covers are open.

The two biggest dangers associated with working with a laser printer are the fusion assembly and the power supply. Avoid touching the fusing roller in a laser printer because it can be hot enough to burn. Power down a laser printer and allow it to cool off before opening it. Laser printers also use high-voltage and low-voltage/high-current power supplies. Make sure the laser printer is powered off and unplugged before opening it. See Figure 17-2.

Compressed Air

In Chapter 4 you learned about the use of canned compressed air to blow dust out of computers and peripherals. Recall that you should take care to keep the can upright while spraying; avoid tilting or turning the can upside down, because the liquid gas that forces the air out may spill and cause freeze burns on your skin and/or damage components.

FIGURE 17-2

A laser printer with the toner cartridge removed, showing the fusion area deep in the back

SCENARIO & SOLUTION

I need to remove a Phillips head screw from a computer case, but I do not have a Phillips head screwdriver that will fit. I would like to try a flat-bladed screwdriver. What should I do?	Do not use a flat-bladed screwdriver in a Phillips head screw unless it is an emergency. To avoid damaging the screw or the computer, wait until you can obtain the correct tool.
Since a laptop is portable, is there any reason why I should not move it from desk to desk while it is turned on and operating?	A laptop's portability does not apply to when it is up and running, with the hard drive spinning. Do one of these actions from within Windows before moving a PC, even a laptop: Turn Off, Stand By, or Hibernate.
We have excellent climate control in our computer server room and equipment closet, but the manager prefers to keep the setting very cool and with a humidity level below 50 percent. Is this OK?	This is a formula for ESD. At the very least, the manager should adjust the climate controls so that the humidity is above 50 percent and raise the temperature to a comfortable level for employees.

Additionally, when you are using compressed air to clean anything, you should wear eye protection and even a simple mask to keep dust and particles from getting in the eye or being inhaled.

Responding to Accidents

In spite of the most stringent precautions, accidents will happen, hazardous material will spill into the environment, and people will be injured. What's important is how you handle the accident in both the immediate response and in creating a truthful incident report so that the organization can learn from the incident and prevent similar accidents from occurring.

First Aid Training

The best response to an accident is quick response by trained personnel. The sooner injuries receive appropriate aid, the better the outcomes will be for the victims. Employees should be prepared for accidents and other disasters, and know how to give aid and summon help as fast as possible. All organizations should evaluate their accident risks, determine the types of accidents that are probable in their organization, and provide opportunities for first aid training to all personnel. This training may be conducted by qualified employees, it may be brought in-house from outside experts, or employees may be given paid time in which to take training available in their communities from the Red Cross or other organizations.

Giving First Aid

In the following sections, explore how to handle electrical, chemical, and physical accidents. These descriptions are rough guidelines, and you should not consider them to be official first aid instructions. They do not replace appropriate first aid training. Further, first aid is only for giving aid until professional medical care is available. In all cases, if the injured person has collapsed or stopped breathing, call 911 or your local emergency responders at once, and request emergency personnel to your site. If the injury is minor, consult by phone with qualified medical persons and take the victim to a clinic or hospital for further treatment, if necessary.

on the **job**

Make sure you know the number to call for emergency services. While the 911 emergency response number works in many communities, there are some, especially rural, communities in which it does not work at all or not as you would expect. In our rural community, 911 is answered in the county seat, 50 miles away, and is not well coordinated with our local emergency response facility. For prompt emergency care, we need to call a more conventional phone number that is not easy to remember. Then there is the issue of calling 911 from a cell phone. Some 911 centers cannot pinpoint the location of such a call.

If the victim is conscious, gather all information about the accident and the symptoms and pass this on to emergency personnel. There is only one area in which you should not necessarily trust the victim. Many victims will protest that they do not need attention. This can be due to embarrassment, or even to impaired perception from the accident. You may follow the victim's instructions after an extremely minor injury, but in the case of most accidents, especially those involving falls, fire, or electrical shock, let a qualified person decide on the needed care. Overreaction is better than paying too little attention to a serious injury that is not apparent at the time of the accident.

exam
watch

Always call emergency personnel when you believe someone has a possibly serious injury. Do not pay attention to the victim's insistence that he or she does not need treatment when you detect symptoms that tell you otherwise.

Electrical Accidents

If someone appears to have suffered an electric shock, first make sure there is no longer any danger of shock to yourself and others. Turn off the power, if necessary. If you cannot easily or quickly turn off the power, and the power appears to be flowing through the victim, attempt to remove the victim from the power. To do this, first stand on a non-conducting surface. You may have to fashion this surface by putting folded newspaper or layers of cardboard on the floor and standing on it. Then use a non-conducting object, like a wooden broom handle, to push the victim away from the current.

Then immediately assist the injured person and summon emergency personnel. An inexperienced person cannot accurately assess the actual damage to an electrical shock victim. Electrical shock can affect the brain and nervous system, as well as the kidney, muscles, heart, and lungs, so the stakes are high when someone suffers this type of injury.

Chemical Accidents

These guidelines for chemical accidents are very general and the actual first aid treatment will vary, depending on the exact nature of the chemical and the location of the injury. Also, refer to the chemical's material safety data sheet (MSDS). This document should be available for any chemical used on the job. Learn more about MSDSs later in this chapter, in the section titled "Disposing of Computing Waste."

on the
()o b

Time is precious. If you have any concerns about the chemical involved, and you are in the U.S.A., call the poison control center hotline at 800-222-1222. This number, provided by the American Association of Poison Control Centers (AAPCC), will connect you to the nearest poison control center.

Chemical Splash in the Eye   A common chemical accident, regardless of the chemical, is when a chemical splashes in the eye. The recommended first aid for this is to flush the eye with clean, lukewarm tap water for at least twenty minutes. However, be aware that while this is generally the best action for most chemicals, some chemicals cause greater damage if you add water to them, and you must use other treatment. The best precaution is to be aware of the types of chemicals you must handle and learn about the proper treatment before an accident occurs.

An organization with a high risk of this type of accident will have instructions posted and emergency showers or eye-wash stations located near areas where people handle chemicals. In this case, the victim must get into the shower and point a gentle stream of water at the forehead and allow it to flow over the injured eye. If both eyes are affected, direct the water at the bridge of the nose and let it flow into both eyes equally.

After thoroughly bathing the eyes, wash the victim's hands to ensure that the chemical is not on their hands. If the victim was wearing contact lenses when the accident occurred, and if the lenses did not wash out, he or she should remove them after the hand washing. If possible, put sunglasses on the victim, because the injury and the treatment will make the eyes sensitive to light. Next, bathe any other body parts and remove clothing contaminated with the chemical.

Inhaled Chemical Immediately move away from the chemical source into fresh air and call 911. Be very specific about the chemical involved. Then, unless the 911 operator provides information on what to do until emergency help arrives, call poison control and ask what you should do until help arrives.

Chemical Burns Remove all clothing and jewelry that the chemical has touched. If a powdered chemical burns the skin, brush it off the skin, and then if it is not a chemical that becomes more harmful with water, flush it with cool tap water for at least fifteen minutes. Loosely wrap a clean wound with a dry, sterile dressing. If no sterile dressing is available, use a clean cloth. A very mild injury will not require further treatment, but check with emergency personnel and provide them with the name of the chemical or chemicals so that they can advise you about further treatment.

Immediately seek emergency medical help in the following instances:

- **Shock**   When a victim shows signs of shock. Symptoms of shock include fainting, an unusually pale complexion, or shallow breathing.
- **Skin damage**   If the chemical caused a second-degree burn (or worse) and covers an area more than two to three inches in diameter. A second-degree burn is one that penetrates the first layer of skin, evidenced by blisters, skin damage, and intense pain, relative to a first-degree burn. A first-degree burn causes red skin without blistering and very mild pain.
- **Injury location**   If the chemical burn affects any of these areas: eye, hands, feet, face, groin, buttocks, or a major joint, or if the chemical was inhaled.

Other Injury Accidents

The list of possible accidents and injuries that can occur in the workplace is interminable. First aid education is not the immediate aim of the A+ certification.

SCENARIO & SOLUTION

Our organization goes to great lengths to prevent accidents. Therefore, I do not see any need to get first aid training, although we are encouraged to do so. What do you advise?	Even with extreme care to prevent accidents, they will happen, and everyone should have first aid skills.
My coworker appears dazed, and I believe he was injured, but he does not want to be treated. What should I do?	Call for emergency treatment immediately. The injury, or embarrassment, may be keeping the coworker from making a good decision.
It appears that a coworker has received an electrical shock. He seems stunned, but I do not see any burn marks. What should I do?	Call 911 or your local emergency number immediately. A person can sustain a very severe injury from electric shock without an obvious burn on the body.
What should I do if I see someone who appears to be injured and unconscious from an electric shock, but I believe he is still in contact with the power source?	Immediately turn off the power source if you can do so without harming yourself. Or, quickly position yourself on a non-conductive surface, even if you have to improvise by throwing non-conductive material on the floor to stand on. Then use a non-conductive object to move the victim off the power source.

Rather, this objective requires that you have an awareness of, and understand, the types of accidents that are most likely in your organization, and that you prepare for accidents by acquiring first aid skills through your company or a qualified third party, such as the Red Cross.

Incident Reporting

Report all accidents involving physical injury. Many organizations have a formal incident reporting procedure. For a variety of reasons people are often reluctant to report accidents. These can include fear of someone holding them accountable for the accident, or pressure from peers or managers to not report an accident. However, the organization cannot correct the condition or circumstances that caused the accident unless people are open about it. Therefore, a formal reporting process has the advantage of obliging employees to report accidents. Then, a well-managed organization will analyze the cause and search for ways to prevent future accidents.

■ **601: 7.3** *Identify proper disposal procedures for batteries, display devices, and chemical solvents and cans*

Computing waste is becoming a major problem throughout the world. For years much of it ended up in landfills, taking up rapidly depleting landfill space, releasing toxic ingredients into the environment, and wasting reusable materials (both toxic and non-toxic). Governments and organizations throughout the world are taking actions to stop these wasteful land polluting practices, making this knowledge important for the A+ certification candidate.

Disposing of Computing Waste

Lead, mercury, cadmium, chromium, brominated flame retardants, and polychlorinated biphenyls (PCBs)—what do they all have in common? They are toxic to the environment and to humans if mishandled, and they are widely used in electronics, including computers, printers, and monitors. These items must be recycled or disposed of in the proper manner. You should never discard them directly into the trash, where they will end up in landfills and potentially pollute the ground water.

In addition, electronics also contain plastic, steel, aluminum, and precious metals—all of which should be recovered and recycled. Provide containers in which to collect these components for proper sorting and disposal.

Manufacturers' Recycling Programs

Computer companies, such as Dell and Hewlett-Packard (HP), and other electronics companies such as Nokia, are using more environmentally friendly components and working to recycle components from discarded computers. In fact there is a relationship between these two activities. The more a manufacturer is involved in recycling the wastes from its products, the more changes that company makes to use more eco-friendly material. If we don't use environmentally hazardous materials in electronic components in the first place, then the danger to the environment is less. We are a long way from eliminating hazardous materials from electronics, and we will continue to have a recycling need for both hazardous materials and non-renewable materials, such as gold, copper, and aluminum.

Dell is widely considered to be the leader in electronics recycling. Not only do they offer free recycling for all their products, but they are phasing out some toxic chemicals in the production of their products.

In September of 2006 Dell introduced a recycling program in the U.S. that offered free recycling—even free shipping to recycling centers—of Dell products without requiring that customer purchase a new product. A customer who purchases a new Dell system gets free recycling of an old PC and monitor, even if it is not a Dell product.

HP's recycling efforts began over two decades ago. At HP's recycling plant near Sacramento, workers first remove motherboards, batteries, and other possible hazardous components, and then feed the remains into a machine that shreds and separates the material into aluminum, plastic, and precious metals. After that, the plastic and metals are recycled.

In spite of such efforts, estimates are that only 10 to 15 percent of electronics are recycled.

Material Safety Data Sheets (MSDS)

If you are unsure of the proper handling or disposal procedures for a chemical, look for its material safety data sheet (MSDS). An MSDS is a standardized document that contains general information, ingredients, and fire and explosion warnings as well as health, disposal, and safe transportation information about a particular product. Any manufacturer that sells a potentially hazardous product is required to issue an MSDS for it.

If an MSDS did not come with a particular chemical, contact the manufacturer or search for it on the Internet. A number of Web sites contain large lists of MSDSs. There have been some major changes in these Web sites. Therefore, if you wish to find an MSDS on a particular product or type of product, use a search engine with appropriate keywords, including "MSDS" and terms associated with the product.

Make a practice of asking a retailer or vendor of computer products to include any applicable MSDS with the product at purchase.

Batteries

Many batteries contain environmentally hazardous materials, such as lithium, mercury, or nickel-cadmium. Therefore you cannot place them in the trash where they will end up in a landfill. Many communities have special recycling depots that accept batteries to be recharged, reused, or properly processed so that they do not introduce harmful elements into the environment. Many communities periodically conduct hazardous material pickups to homes or businesses, in which you can hand over all toxic materials, such as batteries and paint, for proper disposal.

Never store computer batteries for extended periods of time. Never leave batteries in equipment that is being stored for extended periods of time. Battery casings are notorious for corroding, allowing the chemicals inside to leak or explode out. This can cause a large mess, destroy nearby components, and cause skin burns if you touch it.

Toner Cartridges

Printer toner cartridges also provide a potential environmental hazard, simply due to their large numbers and the space they can take up in a landfill. For this reason you should not simply throw them away. Fortunately, most toner cartridges have reusable components. That is, many companies will buy back used toner cartridges, refill and recondition them (if necessary), and then resell them. Figure 17-3 shows a laser toner cartridge removed from a printer.

Display Devices

Cathode ray tube (CRT) displays contain lead, which is toxic to the environment and is a useful metal that can be recycled. Therefore, never throw CRTs in trash destined for a landfill. Always search for ways to recycle a CRT. Call your local waste disposal organization and arrange to have CRTs picked up or dropped off at its site. Many communities advertise locations and hours for these recycling services.

FIGURE 17-3

A laser printer toner cartridge, showing the drum

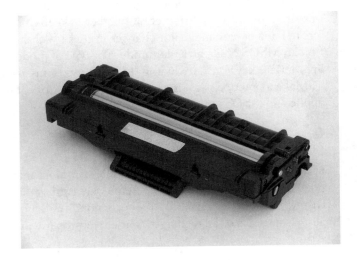

Chemical Solvents and Cans

Chemical solvents designed for the computer are just as hazardous to the environment as non-computer-related chemical solvents. They must be disposed of in a similar manner. Many communities collect chemical solvents and paints, and make them available for recycling. Residents can go to the recycling center and obtain the paints for free or at a very reduced cost. Those solvents and paints deemed unsafe for recycling are disposed of properly. Look for a hazardous material pickup or depot in your area.

Similarly, the empty cans, including aerosol cans, should be disposed of in an appropriate manner. Contact your local waste disposal company for the proper handling and disposal of empty cans that once held solvents and other toxic materials. They may be as dangerous as the contents they once held.

EXERCISE 17-2

Researching Recycling Centers

Research the recycling options in your community.

1. First, use the local phone book and look under the local government listings for recycling. List the nearest center to your home here:

   _____

2. Call the center and determine if they accept the following items: CRTs, chemicals, empty paint and solvent cans, circuit boards, old computers, batteries.

3. Find out the days and times when the center accepts these items for recycling and list them here:

   _____

4. Ask if the center has a pick-up service for recycling for private homes, and how you can arrange this.

5. Ask if the center has a pick-up service for recycling for businesses, and how you can arrange this.

CERTIFICATION SUMMARY

This chapter explores ways to maintain a safe work environment. It covers the safe handling of computer equipment, proper response to accidents, and disposal of computing waste.

Safety in an organization is everyone's responsibility. Always be aware of potential safety hazards such as liquid spills, clutter in walkways and stairways, and exposure to high- and low-voltage devices.

Practice safe equipment handling to protect both yourself and equipment. Use appropriate repair tools as they were meant to be used. Take precautions when moving computer equipment to protect both the equipment and yourself.

Protect yourself and computer equipment from electrostatic discharge (ESD) using appropriate antistatic devices. ESD can cause the immediate malfunction of a device or it can cause a gradual degradation, leading to total failure. Maintain humidity between 50 and 80 percent to avoid ESD.

Electromagnetic interference (EMI) will not damage equipment, but it will disrupt usage and damage data. Removal of the source of EMI (or moving equipment away from it) will eliminate the problem.

Improper handling of power supplies can cause injury or death. Always unplug the power supply from the wall outlet when you are working inside a computer or printer. A power supply stores electrical charges for long periods of time. Never open a power supply's case, and never wear an antistatic wrist strap when replacing or handling a power supply. Similarly, CRT monitors are high-voltage equipment and can store a harmful electrical charge, even when unplugged. Never open a CRT case, and never wear an antistatic wrist strap when handling a CRT.

Avoid the moving parts in printers. Keep long hair, clothing, jewelry, and other objects away from the moving parts in a printer.

Be prepared to give first aid to accident victims and call emergency personnel when needed. Learn the best methods for aiding victims of electrical shock, chemical spills, and other types of accidents.

Always dispose of computer components properly. You can check the component's MSDS for proper disposal instructions. You should also be wary of components that use high voltage or lasers, such as the monitor, power supply, and optical drives. Handle components carefully when you store them. Keep them out of hot or damp places, and keep magnetic storage devices away from EMI-emitting devices.

TWO-MINUTE DRILL

Here are some of the key points covered in Chapter 17.

Maintaining a Safe Work Environment

❏ Safety is everyone's job. Be aware of common safety hazards and be proactive to avoid disasters.

❏ Liquids are dangerous to computers and peripherals because they can cause electrical shorts. Purchase keyboard covers for those employees who must use a PC with wet or dirty hands.

❏ Liquids spilled on floors and stairways can cause falls and injuries.

❏ Avoid injury from tripping by keeping floors, stairways, and doorways clear of obstacles and clutter, including loose flooring and electrical wires.

❏ Do not try to service high-voltage peripherals, such as monitors, laser printers, and power supplies, because there is a high danger of electrical shock.

❏ Do not use an antistatic wristband when working with high-voltage devices.

❏ Low-voltage devices can also cause serious injury or death under certain circumstances. As little as 50 volts can cause death, depending on many variables, including, but not limited to, the body's resistance to the current, the path of the current through the body, and how long the body is in contact with the electrical current.

Safe Equipment Handling

❏ Use appropriate repair tools, and use each tool only for its intended purposes.

❏ Power down all equipment before moving it, even laptops. Moving any computer while powered up could damage the hard drive(s).

❏ Displays are very fragile, and you should move them with great care.

❏ Some devices require special handling when moved. For instance, you should power down computers (even laptops) or put them into Standby or Hibernate mode. Some scanners have a locking mechanism. Also disconnect power and equipment cords before moving computer equipment.

❏ Take care to protect your back when lifting equipment, and use a utility cart to move equipment more than a few feet.

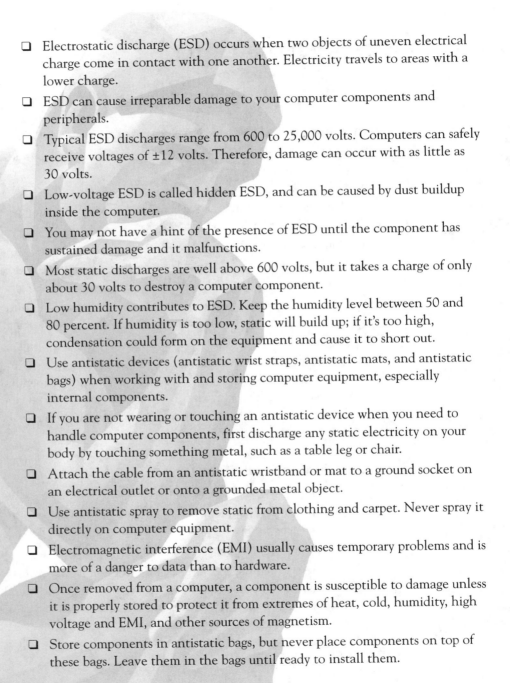

❑ Electrostatic discharge (ESD) occurs when two objects of uneven electrical charge come in contact with one another. Electricity travels to areas with a lower charge.

❑ ESD can cause irreparable damage to your computer components and peripherals.

❑ Typical ESD discharges range from 600 to 25,000 volts. Computers can safely receive voltages of ±12 volts. Therefore, damage can occur with as little as 30 volts.

❑ Low-voltage ESD is called hidden ESD, and can be caused by dust buildup inside the computer.

❑ You may not have a hint of the presence of ESD until the component has sustained damage and it malfunctions.

❑ Most static discharges are well above 600 volts, but it takes a charge of only about 30 volts to destroy a computer component.

❑ Low humidity contributes to ESD. Keep the humidity level between 50 and 80 percent. If humidity is too low, static will build up; if it's too high, condensation could form on the equipment and cause it to short out.

❑ Use antistatic devices (antistatic wrist straps, antistatic mats, and antistatic bags) when working with and storing computer equipment, especially internal components.

❑ If you are not wearing or touching an antistatic device when you need to handle computer components, first discharge any static electricity on your body by touching something metal, such as a table leg or chair.

❑ Attach the cable from an antistatic wristband or mat to a ground socket on an electrical outlet or onto a grounded metal object.

❑ Use antistatic spray to remove static from clothing and carpet. Never spray it directly on computer equipment.

❑ Electromagnetic interference (EMI) usually causes temporary problems and is more of a danger to data than to hardware.

❑ Once removed from a computer, a component is susceptible to damage unless it is properly stored to protect it from extremes of heat, cold, humidity, high voltage and EMI, and other sources of magnetism.

❑ Store components in antistatic bags, but never place components on top of these bags. Leave them in the bags until ready to install them.

❑ Never open power supplies for service. Even when powered off, a computer power supply continues to store electricity, supplying the motherboard with a small amount of current.

❑ Do not leave a power supply plugged in while servicing a PC.

❑ CRT monitors are high-voltage equipment and can store a harmful electrical charge, even when unplugged. Never open a CRT.

❑ Never wear a wrist strap when handling a power supply or a CRT.

❑ Take extra precautions when working with a printer, because long hair, loose clothing, and jewelry can catch in the moving parts. In addition, any of these objects can pass ESD to the printer.

❑ Do not try to operate a printer with the cover off. Some printers will not operate in this state, but some, like inkjets, must be open when you change the print cartridges, and the cartridge assembly moves to allow access.

❑ Avoid touching the fusing roller in a laser printer, because it can be hot enough to burn. Power down a laser printer and allow it to cool off before opening it.

Responding to Accidents

❑ Accidents will occur, no matter what precautions you take.

❑ The best response to an accident is quick action by trained personnel. Employees should be prepared for accidents and disasters, and know how to give first aid and to summon help as fast as possible.

❑ If you suspect someone has suffered an electric shock, first make sure there is no longer danger of shock to yourself and others.

❑ If necessary, stand on non-conducting material and use another non-conducting object, like a wooden broom handle, to move the victim away from the current.

❑ Immediately assist the victim and summon emergency personnel. An inexperienced person cannot accurately assess the actual damage to a shock victim.

❑ Electrical shock can affect all major organs, especially the brain and nervous system, as well as the kidney, muscles, heart, and lungs.

❑ Injuries from chemicals must be treated appropriately for the type of chemical, and as quickly as possible.

- ❑ If you are concerned about how to treat a chemical accident, call the poison control center hotline at 800-222-1222.
- ❑ Treat a chemical splashed in the eye by flushing the eye or eyes with clean, lukewarm water for at least twenty minutes. Then wash the victim's hands and remove contact lenses if the water did not wash them out.
- ❑ Bathe any other body parts and remove clothing contaminated by the chemical.
- ❑ If someone has inhaled a chemical, move the victim away from the chemical source into fresh air and seek emergency help.
- ❑ If someone suffers chemical burns, remove all clothing and jewelry that the chemical has touched. If a powdered chemical burns the skin, brush it off the skin, and then flush it with cool tap water for at least fifteen minutes.
- ❑ Seek immediate emergency medical help if a victim shows signs of shock, if skin damage involves second-degree burns over two to three inches in diameter, and if the burn is located in or around the eyes, hands, feet, face, groin, buttocks, or a major joint.
- ❑ Report all accidents involving physical injury.

Disposing of Computing Waste

- ❑ Toxic metals and chemicals used in computers and peripherals include mercury, cadmium, chromium, brominated flame retardants, and polychlorinated biphenyls (PCBs).
- ❑ When a computer or component reaches the end of its useful life, dispose of it appropriately, taking time to send all equipment that cannot be donated to a charity to a recycling center so that the toxic and reusable components can be replaced.

SELF TEST

The following questions will help you measure your understanding of the material presented in this chapter. Read all of the choices carefully because there might be more than one correct answer. Choose all correct answers for each question.

Maintaining a Safe Work Environment

1. Who is responsible for maintaining a safe work environment? Select the single best answer.

   A. Managers

   B. All employees

   C. Safety experts

   D. IT personnel

2. What immediate danger do liquid spills pose to computers?

   A. Electrical shock

   B. Rust

   C. Electrical short

   D. EMI

3. My CRT display is only a few years old and was quite expensive. It is now malfunctioning, and none of the external buttons on the monitor help, nor can I fix it using the Properties settings in Windows. What should I do?

   A. Open the CRT case and look for a loose connection.

   B. Take it to a qualified repair center.

   C. Immediately discard it.

   D. Recycle it.

4. I have a used laser printer toner cartridge and I plan to open it to satisfy my curiosity about its inner workings. What do you advise?

   A. Use a flat-bladed screwdriver to pry it open.

   B. Be sure to touch a metal object to ground yourself.

   C. Never open a toner cartridge, because the toner is dangerous to breathe.

   D. Throw the toner cartridge in the trash.

Safe Equipment Handling

5. What should you do before moving any computer equipment?
   A. Power down and disconnect the power cord.
   B. Select Stand By.
   C. Select Hibernate.
   D. Remove the power supply.

6. What is the ideal environment for ESD to occur?
   A. Hot and humid
   B. Cold and humid
   C. Hot and dry
   D. Cold and dry

7. You are getting ready to install a new component, a memory stick that came in its own antistatic bag. What is the correct way to handle this component and the bag?
   A. Remove the component from the bag and place on top of the bag until ready to install.
   B. Remove the component from the bag and immediately discard the bag.
   C. Leave the component in the bag until you are ready to install it.
   D. Remove the component from the bag and turn the bag inside out before placing the component on the bag.

8. Which statement is a true general comparison of the effects of EMI versus ESD?
   A. ESD can damage hardware; EMI harms data.
   B. EMI can harm hardware; ESD harms data.
   C. ESD only destroys data; EMI destroys hardware.
   D. EMI can cause injury or death; ESD is less harmful to people.

9. My computer display is jittery; should I replace the display?
   A. Yes, this is a fatal defect.
   B. No, look for a source of EMI and increase the distance between that source and the display.
   C. Yes, and buy a display that resists ESD.
   D. No, look for a source of ESD and move it away from the display.

10. I plan to replace the power supply in a computer. What is the most important safety measure I should take?
    A. Wear an antistatic wristband.
    B. Do *not* ground yourself.

    C. Bend your knees when you lift it.

    D. Buy a name brand power supply.

11. What can I use to protect my PC from power sags?

    A. Surge protector

    B. SPS

    C. UPS

    D. APS

12. I understand there is an adjustment I can make to a CRT display if I open the case. How do I do open it?

    A. Read the CRT's user manual.

    B. Never open a CRT case.

    C. Log on as Administrator.

    D. Look for four Phillips screws in the CRT case.

13. What are the two most dangerous areas of a laser printer?

    A. Toner cartridge and paper feed

    B. Paper feed and drum

    C. Output and input trays

    D. Fusion assembly and power supply

Responding to Accidents

14. A coworker tripped and fell in the stairwell while carrying a computer. He cannot put his weight on his left leg and appears to have a bump on his head. He has asked that I leave him alone and not summon help. What should I do?

    A. Administer first aid and be quiet.

    B. Administer first aid and summon help.

    C. Call your boss.

    D. Walk away.

15. A coworker seems to have received an electrical shock. She is slightly disoriented but does not have any burn marks on her body. My boss wants us to just watch her before calling 911. What should we do?

    A. Do as your boss says.

    B. Send her home to rest.

    C. Call 911 and administer first aid.

    D. Administer first aid and send her back to work.

16. A coworker was using window cleaner on the exterior of a PC case and splashed it in his eyes. What is the best immediate treatment until he can be seen by emergency personnel?

    A. Put two eye drops in each eye.

    B. Bathe both eyes at once with lukewarm tap water for at least 20 minutes.

    C. Bathe each eye in turn with lukewarm tap water for at least 20 minutes.

    D. Remove his contacts and then bathe both eyes in tap water for at least 20 minutes.

17. A technician was using a solvent to clean electrical contacts and accidentally inhaled the solvent. What should be done?

    A. Move him into fresh air and watch him for a few hours.

    B. Give him a glass of water.

    C. Have him sit down immediately.

    D. Move him into fresh air immediately and call 911 and poison control.

Disposing of Computing Waste

18. When a computer system is no longer functioning and is not repairable, how should you dispose of it?

    A. Put it in the trash.

    B. Donate it to a charity.

    C. Send it to a recycling center.

    D. Send it to a landfill.

19. We do not know the proper handling of an old solvent previously used in our company, but now we need to discard it. How can I find out more about it?

    A. Contact the manufacturer and ask for an MSDS.

    B. Send it to a recycling center.

    C. Transfer it to a glass jar for safe storage.

    D. Call 911.

20. What should we do with the large number of used batteries we accumulate in our office?

    A. Dispose of them in the trash.

    B. Find a recycling center that will accept them.

    C. Send them back to the manufacturers.

    D. Let them accumulate and dispose of them about once a year.

LAB QUESTION

First aid training is valuable to everyone at home, at school, or at work. Research the first aid training available to you. At work, ask your manager and/or the Human Resources department what, if any, first aid training the company offers. If you are a student, ask about first aid training through the school. Look in your community for sources for free or inexpensive first aid training. Write a few sentences on your findings.

SELF TEST ANSWERS

Maintaining a Safe Work Environment

1. ☑ **B.** All employees are responsible for maintaining a safe work environment.
   ☒ **A, C,** and **D** are each incorrect as the single best answer. This is only because these people and all others are responsible for maintaining a safe work environment.

2. ☑ **C.** An electrical short is the immediate danger posed to computers by liquid spills.
   ☒ **A,** electrical shock, is incorrect because this is a danger to people who come in contact with both liquids and an electrical circuit. **B,** rust, is incorrect because although a wet component may rust over time, this is not an immediate danger. **D,** EMI, is incorrect because this would not be an effect of a liquid spill.

3. ☑ **B.** Take it to a qualified repair center. Never open a CRT.
   ☒ **A,** open the CRT case and look for a loose connection, is incorrect because only highly trained technicians should open a CRT case. **C,** immediately discard it, is incorrect because this is an extreme reaction until you know more about the nature of the problem and whether the CRT can be repaired. If it cannot, then recycle it, rather than "discard" it. **D,** recycle it, is also incorrect until you have more information about the problem and whether the CRT can be repaired. If you cannot get it repaired, then you will need to recycle it.

4. ☑ **C.** Never open a toner cartridge, because the toner is dangerous to breathe. This is not because the toner is necessarily toxic, but because the powder is so fine it poses a threat to the lungs.
   ☒ **A,** Use a flat-bladed screw driver to pry it open, is incorrect. See the explanation for the correct answer. **B,** be sure to touch a metal object to ground yourself, is incorrect and irrelevant when working with an old toner cartridge. **D,** throw the toner cartridge in the trash, is incorrect. Toner cartridges should always be recycled.

Safe Equipment Handling

5. ☑ **A.** Power down and disconnect the power cord before moving any computer component.
   ☒ **B** and **C,** select Stand By and Hibernate, are both incorrect because they do not apply to all computer equipment. They only apply to Windows PCs, and they do not include the need to disconnect the power cord. **D,** remove the power supply, is incorrect because this is a very extreme and unnecessary action to take before moving computer equipment.

6. ☑ **D.** Cold and dry is the ideal environment for ESD to occur.
   ☒ **A, B,** and **C** are all incorrect because none of these is an ideal environment for ESD.

7. ☑ **C.** Leave the component in the bag until you are ready to install it.

☒ **A**, remove the component and place on top of the bag until ready to install, is incorrect because the outside of the bag may hold a static charge. **B**, remove the component from the bag and immediately discard the bag, is incorrect because you may want to reuse the bag if you need to store this or another component at some time. **D**, remove the component from the bag and turn the bag inside out before placing the component on the bag, is incorrect because this procedure is not recommended and could expose the component to ESD.

8. ☑ **A.** ESD can damage hardware; EMI harms data. This is a true general comparison of the effects of EMI versus ESD.

☒ **B** and **C** are both incorrect because they basically say the same thing, and the opposite is true. **D**, EMI can cause injury or death; ESD is less harmful to people, is incorrect because ESD is potentially more harmful.

9. ☑ **B.** To look for a source of EMI and increase the distance between that source and the display is correct because you should not replace the display until you know more about the problem, and it sounds like an EMI problem.

☒ **A**, yes, this is a fatal defect, is incorrect because you do not know that it is a defect at all, and it sounds like a possible EMI problem. **C**, yes, and buy a display that resists ESD, is incorrect because you do not yet know that the display should be replaced, and there is no reason to believe that the problem has anything to do with ESD. **D**, no, look for a source of ESD and move it away from the display, is incorrect because the symptom is more likely to be caused by EMI.

10. ☑ **B.** To *not* ground yourself is the most important safety measure. You do *not* want to make your body a path to ground. Wearing an antistatic wristband, standing on a grounding mat, or touching something already grounded would do this and put you in danger.

☒ **A**, wear an antistatic wristband, is incorrect because this would expose you to possible electrical shock. **C**, bend your knees when you lift it, is incorrect because replacing a power supply should not require heavy lifting. **D**, buy a name brand power supply, is incorrect because this is not a safety measure.

11. ☑ **C.** A UPS will protect a PC from power sags because it provides conditioned power, free from the surges, spikes, and sags coming from the power company.

☒ **A**, a surge protector, is incorrect because this only protects from power surges, not from power sags. **B**, an SPS, is incorrect because this device kicks in and provides battery power to a PC when the power from the power company fails. It does not protect from sags. **D**, an APS, is incorrect because this is not a standard acronym for a power protection device.

12. ☑ **B.** Never open a CRT case, because this is dangerous and only a trained technician should do it.

     ☒ **A**, read the CRT's user manual, is incorrect because you should never open a CRT case if you are not qualified. The manufacturer's instruction will probably include that warning. **C**, log on as Administrator, is incorrect because this has nothing to do with opening a CRT. **D**, look for Phillips screws in the CRT case, is incorrect because you should not even think of opening a CRT.

13. ☑ **D.** The fusion assembly and power supply are the two most dangerous areas of a laser printer.

     ☒ **A, B**, and **C** are all incorrect because none of these components are the two most dangerous areas of a laser printer.

Responding to Accidents

14. ☑ **B.** To administer first aid and summon help is correct. Disregard the victim's protests because an injured person may be too disoriented to make a good judgment about the need for treatment.

     ☒ **A, C**, and **D** are all incorrect and the resulting delay in getting treatment caused by all of these could endanger your coworker.

15. ☑ **C.** To call 911 and administer first aid is correct.

     ☒ **A, B**, and **D** are all incorrect. As with the wrong answers in question 14, these would all delay treatment for what could be a very serious injury.

16. ☑ **B.** Bathe both eyes at once with lukewarm tap water for at least 20 minutes.

     ☒ **A**, put two eye drops in each eye, is incorrect because this is inadequate to wash out the chemical and would allow it to do greater damage. **C**, bathe each eye in turn with lukewarm water for at least 20 minutes, is incorrect because the treatment could be too late for the second eye. **D**, remove his contacts and then bathe both eyes, is incorrect because this is the reverse order. Bathe the eyes first. If the victim wears contacts and they have not been washed out, remove the contacts after the water bath.

17. ☑ **D.** Move him into fresh air immediately and call 911 and poison control.

     ☒ **A**, move him into fresh air and watch him for a few hours, is incorrect because he may need further treatment and this delay could endanger him. **B**, give him a glass of water, is incorrect because this will have no direct effect in treating the problem. **C**, have him sit down immediately, is incorrect because you need to move him away from the solvent and into fresh air.

Disposing of Computing Waste

18.   ☑   **C.** To send it to a recycling center is correct. Even a non-functioning computer has material in it that can and should be recycled.

☒   **A** and **B** are both incorrect for the same reason. Something put into the trash will end up in a landfill. **D**, send it to a landfill, is incorrect because computers contain components that can contaminate the environment and they also contain components that should be recycled.

19.   ☑   **A.** To contact the manufacturer and ask for an MSDS is correct because this document will contain instructions on safe handling and safe disposal of the chemical.

☒   **B**, send it to a recycling center, is incorrect although this is what you may ultimately do. You first need to know how to safely handle the chemical. **C**, transfer it to a glass jar for safe storage, is incorrect because there is no information to lead us to believe that the original container is not adequate. **D**, call 911, is incorrect because there is no emergency.

20.   ☑   **B.** To find a recycling center that will accept them is correct.

☒   **A**, dispose of them in the trash, is incorrect because batteries should never be thrown in the trash. They contain environmentally dangerous components and chemicals. **C**, send them back to the manufacturer, is incorrect in general. Some manufacturers may have a program for used batteries, but it is better to first locate a recycling center. **D**, let them accumulate and dispose of them about once a year, is incorrect because batteries stored for long periods can leak toxic chemicals.

LAB ANSWER

Answers will vary. Companies in which hazardous materials are handled on a routine basis will normally have appropriate training available on site, on a regular schedule. Similarly, companies in which there are physical risks, such as moving machinery, will also have first aid training offered to employees. Small businesses and companies that offer services over the Internet are among those that may have very little or no first aid training. Schools may offer first aid training through extension services. There are many sources of first aid training in the community, including the local fire and rescue, the American Red Cross, and other service organizations.

Part VIII

Communication and Professionalism

18

Communication and Professionalism

Communication and professionalism together make up a single domain in three of the four 2006 CompTIA A+ exam objectives. This domain involves aspects of human behavior not covered in the previous A+ exams. It carries a weight of 5 percent in the 601 exam, 15 percent of the 602 exam, and 20 percent of 603. We believe that all job functions require good communication skills and professionalism—whether you are interacting with coworkers, customers, or your boss.

In this chapter learn the principles of effective communication and how to integrate professionalism into all your interactions with customers and colleagues. You will consider both non-verbal and verbal skills, as well as behaviors, mindset, and attitude. First explore some of the universals of personal interactions, including predictable responses and body language. Learn how to recognize predictable responses in yourself and others and to steer conversations toward positive and productive results. Learn that not only must you say the right words, but your body language must also convey the same message as your words. Professionalism includes your behavior in all interactions, as well as how you treat property belonging to your employer and customers. Use what you learn here to improve all your relationships.

CERTIFICATION OBJECTIVES

■ **601: 8.1   602: 8.1   603: 6.1**   *Use good communication skills, including listening and tact/discretion, when communicating with customers and colleagues*

CompTIA requires that an A+ candidate demonstrates knowledge of good interpersonal communication skills. Communication is the total of all verbal and non-verbal behavior that results in the exchange of thoughts, messages, or information. The skills required include showing tact and discretion in all dealings with customers and colleagues, and an understanding of how to engage them in positive and productive communications.

Basics of Human Interactions

Human interactions are unavoidable—on the job, at school, and at home. How you interact with other people affects much more than your personal life, it affects your career. Learn about predictable human behavior and responses in this section. Learn that if your words are positive, but your body language is negative, people will believe the latter.

Predictable Human Behavior and Responses

In this section, learn about two common and predictable reactions that can interfere with effective communication: the egocentric state and psychological reciprocity. Learn how either of these can trap you into communication failure. However, you will also learn that you can use one of these, psychological reciprocity, to create good results to improve a situation that starts out bad.

Both of these are reactions to perceived or actual words or actions of others. Learning about these behaviors will not make you totally immune to them, but it will increase your ability to recognize when you are experiencing one of them.

Learn that once you understand what is happening, with practice you can pull yourself out of an egocentric state. Understanding how people tend to echo the behavior they receive can help you to change your own behavior, and possibly cause a positive change in their behavior.

And, while it is very important to recognize reactions in yourself and counteract the impulse to act on them, you must also learn to recognize when someone else has entered one of these states. Learn how to bring someone out of an egocentric state and how to use psychological reciprocity to help resolve a situation.

Egocentric State

What is an egocentric state? The word "ego" means "self," and the word "centric" means "centered"; thus "egocentric" means "self-centered." So an *egocentric state* is the name for what happens when you focus internally and fail to pay attention to what is going on around you, or to the person with whom you are talking. Think of it as a self-centered sticking place.

An egocentric state can occur to you if you are startled, shocked, surprised, feeling attacked, puzzled, or feeling any other emotion that causes you to retreat inside your head to try to figure out what is going on and what to do about it. It can last from a split second to many minutes, or more. Don't confuse this with introspection, which is simply thinking about what you might want to do next. Introspection is not what happens when you are stuck in an egocentric state.

What happens is that when you focus internally trying to figure out what is going on, or what to do next, it is physiologically almost impossible to be aware of what is going on outside of you. In effect, for the moments when you are stuck in an egocentric state, you are unaware of what is going on in front of you—you stop hearing what people are saying and you stop seeing what they are doing. Furthermore, this most often occurs when you are in a situation in which you must not shut down incoming information. Instead you need to be gathering information, to stay in the moment, in order to achieve an appropriate outcome.

For instance, imagine that you are working at your desk when you receive a call from a customer who has a serious computer problem. You answer with a pleasant greeting; the customer responds and explains the problem with a note of desperation in his voice. If he cannot get a quick fix, he will miss an important deadline. But before you can respond, you overhear your boss remind a coworker in the next cubicle that registration for a very important technical training class will close in only 15 minutes. Upon hearing that, your thoughts turn inward as you realize that this training class is a requirement for your next promotion, and the class will not be offered for another six months. You really do not want to miss registering for this class.

You are now busy mentally solving your own problem of how to both register for the class and take care of the caller's problem. By the time you recover, you have missed some important information the customer was telling you, and you will probably have to ask him to repeat it. This does not help the customer calm down, and it delays your arriving at a possible solution. The answer is for you to learn to recognize when this happens to you, resist withdrawing into yourself, and stay focused on the customer.

When the situation is reversed, and it occurs to someone else, you will see a difference in their expression as their eyes become unfocused and he or she becomes very quiet, not responding to you. Use the technique demonstrated in the following scenario for helping another person out of an egocentric state.

In this scenario a PC support specialist (the Tech) is helping a customer with a problem. Both are in front of, and looking at, the customer's display. The Tech notices a note taped to the front of the monitor with what appears to be the user's password. They both work in an organization that is very strict about security and forbids doing this. The boss, however, has given the Tech some discretion in handling problems like this. Rather than immediately report someone, the Tech can work with the customer to help develop methods for creating and memorizing unique passwords that are difficult for password hackers to break.

> *Tech:* "Is that your password on this note on your display?"
>
> *Customer:* "Sure, it's easier than memorizing a password every month!"
>
> *Tech:* "Did you know it's against company policy to have your password written down where others can find it?" [Unbeknownst to the Tech, the Customer got in trouble for another, unrelated violation of company policy recently, and management told him that another such violation would mean dismissal from work. Customer looks away and is very quiet while he envisions his firing and the impact it will have on his family.]
>
> *Tech:* [Recognizing that the customer is in an egocentric state, pauses long enough to allow him to come out of that state, and regains eye contact

with him.] "Hey, it's no big deal! If you want I'll teach you how to create easy-to-memorize passwords from your favorite phrases or books or album titles so you won't have to write the password down."

Customer: "What? Oh, that would be great! I was afraid I would get into more trouble over this."

The Tech in this scenario is paying attention to the customer, and realizes that he has retreated into an egocentric state. Guessing that it has to do with the company's strict security policy, the Tech offers a solution and gets the customer back into the dialogue by reducing his tension. Even if you have no idea what caused the egocentric state, you can use this technique of being quiet until you have the person's attention again, and then proceed with the problem solving process. If it recurs, you may need to take time to ask about the customer's concern. You may say something like, "It seems as though you are having trouble concentrating; is there anything I can do?" This will get the customer talking, and may reveal more information about the problem. At the minimum, it will help you establish rapport with the person.

Psychological Reciprocity

Another interesting fact of human behavior is that everybody, usually without being aware of it, automatically responds in kind to whatever another person says or does to them. For example, if a clerk in a store greets you with warmth and apparent sincere interest in what you need, you automatically tend to respond with warmth and politeness. But if the clerk is abrupt, focused on what he is doing, and apparently uninterested in you or what you need, you will tend to respond abruptly too. In other words we humans tend to automatically reciprocate what we receive. We give back what we get. We call this *psychological reciprocity*, but you can call it "payback" if you don't like the more scientific term.

The important thing is to be aware that this behavior is a human universal. Everybody does it. And, usually, people are completely unaware they are doing it.

When you initiate a conversation, remember that you set the tone, and you can start it out at a cheerful, helpful, professional level.

When the other person starts the conversation with a negative tone, discipline yourself to not reciprocate with similar (or worse) behavior. This will not accomplish anything. In fact, if you stay calm, you may cause the other person to calm down so that you can have a productive conversation.

Consider a situation in which an angry customer comes into your workplace with a complaint, and his voice and demeanor seem attacking. You must not allow yourself to reciprocate the customer's angry behavior, and you must behave toward him in such a way as to cause him to calm down and be willing to listen to you.

Here is an example of how you might defuse an angry customer simply by not reflecting the angry behavior and staying calm and professional. In this scenario the Tech is sitting, and the Customer is standing.

> *Customer:* [Appearing red-faced at the Tech's desk and looming over him] "You and your whole department are a waste of money for this company!"
>
> *Tech:* [Slowly turning to face the Customer, rising from the chair and remaining calm]: "Hello, what can I do to help you?"
>
> *Customer:* [Backing away slightly, and calming down a notch and holding up a laptop case] "It's this worthless laptop you gave me last month. It was okay for a while, but now it is so slow it is worthless, especially when I work at home. Why would a computer work differently at home than here at work? Did you put some kind of spy software in it to see what I'm doing at home?"
>
> *Tech:* [Ignoring the last two questions and reaching out toward the laptop case] "Here, let's take it over to the table and see what's going on. I'll power it up and take a look."
>
> *Customer:* "Okay, but I didn't do anything to it. It just suddenly slowed down."
>
> *Tech:* [Looking at the Start menu] "Well, it looks like someone installed Space Nerd Invaders. That's a pretty complex game—something people usually install on a really powerful computer. Do you run that often?"
>
> *Customer:* "Sure, my son installed it for me. I have it on whenever I work at home. We like to play against each other over our home network."
>
> *Tech:* "Well, I think we have found the problem that is slowing your machine down, but to be sure, I will run a few tests on the computer to be sure there is nothing else causing this problem. Then I'll make sure all your security software is up to date, and return it to you this afternoon."

Notice how the Tech first ignored the customer's angry behavior, defusing the situation and staying focused on solving the customer's problem. Then, the Tech also ignored the customer's denial that he did anything that would cause the problem, and was matter-of-fact about his discovery of the software that may have caused the problem, subsequently offering to do a more thorough check of the computer and return it to him. If company policy forbids installing game software on company computers—which is highly likely—the Tech will need to inform the customer of that and remove the software.

e x a m
⊛ a t c h

The A+ exams do not require that you understand the terms egocentric state or psychological reciprocity. We include this information because knowing it will help you in your interpersonal communications and support your understanding of the exam objectives.

Body Language

Good, effective communication between people involves much more than just talking and listening. It involves body language, the silent message you send with movements and gestures, as well as facial expressions. What you do with your body, whether you are leaning forward showing interest or leaning back showing disinterest, how you move your arms and hands, and so forth, speak as clearly as your words. Folding your arms across your chest or clasping your hands behind your back are both body language that tells the person that you are not open to what they say. It is better to have your hands in front of you in a resting position, if you are not holding anything. Shaking your head from side to side shows disapproval of, or disagreement with, the other person. Nodding your head shows acknowledgment, agreement, and understanding of what you are hearing.

Do not just say the right things; back up your words with appropriate body language. Have you ever approached a checkout counter and had the clerk say all the right words of a professional greeting (obviously from a memorized script), but her body language is broadcasting an entirely different message? Sure you have. It may have unfolded something like this:

As you walk up to the checkout stand, the clerk, who is surreptitiously text messaging on her cell phone, avoids looking at you, but you can tell she senses your approach, because she moves closer to the register. You set your selection of expensive merchandise down on the counter. The clerk, still avoiding eye contact, slips the phone into her pocket, drags the first item over the scanner while saying (in a very fast, mumbled monotone) "Hello. It's a pleasure to serve you. Did you find everything you were looking for?"

The clerk's body language and her verbal language are not sending the same message. She did greet you, but do you believe for one second that she is interested in your answer or even cares whether you found everything you wanted? She probably does not, and even something as small as this may keep you from returning to this store.

on the
! o b

Regardless of your role—customer or service person—you do not have to ignore all bad behavior. There are times when someone crosses the line with extremely inappropriate behavior that is either threatening or insulting. If this should happen, you should remain calm, and state that you will not tolerate the behavior. Resist reciprocating their behavior at any level. What you do next depends on many things, including whether safety is an issue. You may need to walk away from the person and notify your boss, or the other person's, depending on your role.

EXERCISE 18-1

Reacting to Body Language

Find someone who will partner with you while you practice using body language to change the meaning of your words.

1. Stand about three feet apart facing each other.

2. Participant A: Fold your arms across your chest and take one step backward. Then, while staring at the floor and avoiding eye contact, say "Hello, it's a pleasure to serve you, what can I do to help you?"

3. Participant B: While trying to make eye contact say: "Thank you. I am looking for a flangermatic axiomatic plunger."

4. Participant A: Still staring at the floor, say, "I will have to research that. Here, write your name down on this pad of paper." Extend your hand to Participant B as if handing him a pad and pencil, but still not making eye contact.

5. Now Participant B should talk about how that exchange felt. Did Participant B feel like Participant A was sincere in his greeting?

6. Reverse roles, and repeat the dialog. Talk again about how it felt.

7. Now have a more engaged conversation, with Participant A reprising her role, rather than stepping back, lean forward with arms unfolded and smile and look at Participant B while repeating the greeting in Step 2.

8. Now talk with each other about how the body language affects the interaction.

Communicating with Customers and Colleagues

Communicating with customers and colleagues involves many important communication skills that are part of active communication. In other words, it isn't just what you say, it's the way you say it, and what you do while you are saying it.

In this section, go beyond the basics of human interactions described previously and consider communication goals and keys to effective communications. Then learn how to use active communication and tact and discretion in your communications.

Communication Goals

On the job there are several reasons or goals for communicating effectively. First, it lets you establish some rapport with the other person, which leads to building trust between you. It helps to avoid misunderstandings between you, and communicating respectfully makes everything easier for everybody.

Establish Rapport and Build Trust

Any interaction with another person is easier if you can establish some level of rapport with them because it tends to increase the trust level between people. And yes, even in a brief telephone conversation, you can establish some rapport and build some trust.

Establishing Rapport   What is rapport? It is when two people recognize that they share a commonality of perspective, of being in "sync," of sharing a bond, or having an affinity. Whenever people must interact, there is a natural tendency to identify similarities between them. Focusing some energy on this will improve communications between you. One effective strategy is to mirror the other person to some degree to invoke a positive psychological reciprocity. Most people do this unconsciously. Mirroring the other person's speech cadence (whether they speak rapidly or slowly), for example, is a simple thing to do and makes the other person more comfortable with you.

During a phone conversation, you can only mirror the audible components, such as modulating your voice tone and tempo to match the caller. But be sure to exclude negative aspects of the caller's behavior. If the caller raises his voice, use a calm voice, but adopt the same tempo. If the caller has a different accent than you, don't do an outright imitation, but simply match the cadence, or use some of the caller's expressions. For example, if the caller says a long, leisurely "Well," with a gentle rising inflection, you may want to use this word in the same way as you introduce a solution to their problem.

In a face-to-face conversation, mirror the other person's body posture and movements, but be careful to not make the person feel like you are mocking a behavior. When you mirror effectively the other person feels more comfortable, and therefore more likely to be open to what you are saying or doing.

Build Trust   Trust is confidence and faith in a person—a belief that the person will always deliver on promises and be reliable. You must earn trust. While it is difficult to build trust in a single conversation, you can do it to a significant degree, and you should also treat each encounter with a customer or coworker as part of an ongoing relationship. Consider the following methods for building trust.

- **Be consistent**   Always behave in a consistent manner when dealing with other people. For instance, if you walked a caller through installing a new device in Windows, and he calls again for the same help with another device, do not give him an excuse to not help him. Even if, since the last incident, another person had been assigned this duty, do your best to walk him through the steps briefly, and then tell him that from now on the other person will help with this problem. However, if your boss is very strict, and you cannot do this, then be very professional in explaining the new situation, putting it into a positive light. Then make sure your replacement in this duty is available to help the user.

- **Demonstrate congruence**   Congruence is a harmonious relationship between parts. In the context of communicating with customers and colleagues, think of the parts of your behavior during a conversation or the parts of your entire relationship with another person. For instance, when you earlier learned that your body language should match your words, you were actually working toward congruency. Don't just say that you want to help someone, have a helpful tone in your voice, a smile on your face, and a posture that shows you really do want to help them.

- **Honor commitments**   If you make any commitment to another person, be sure to follow through. For instance, if you tell a customer that you will help them solve a problem, work toward resolution of that problem. If you find that you must turn the customer over to another person, then follow up and make sure that the person now responsible for helping the customer does indeed resolve the problem.

- **Model trustworthy behavior**   As you practice the behaviors you have learned here, and continue to do your work with integrity, you are showing that you are trustworthy. Your very behavior becomes a model for others to follow—whether they are customers or coworkers.

- **Avoid misunderstandings**   A misunderstanding is a mix-up in communication between two or more people that leaves at least one person with a false impression of facts. Misunderstandings are very damaging to any type of relationship. When a misunderstanding occurs, communication can completely break down. It is difficult to recover from misunderstandings, and therefore, you need to work to avoid them. Here are some ways to avoid misunderstandings:

  - Be constantly aware of how you are communicating with the other party. Imagine how you sound and appear to the other person.

  - As you explain something (especially technical things) to a customer, make sure he or she heard what you said by "checking in." This means you intersperse the explanation with phrases, like, "Does that make sense to you? Do you understand? What do you think of this approach?"

  - Make sure you heard and understand what they said by paraphrasing it or repeating it back for their confirmation.

  - Focus your intentions in order to influence the way you approach others, the manner in which you communicate, and the outcomes of your interactions.

  - Use the keys to effective communications, described later in this chapter.

- **Communicate respectfully**   A little respect goes a long way, and using it in all your interactions will bring you rewards in better relationships with others and more efficient interactions that produce good results. Use the following techniques to show respect to customers and coworkers.

  - Do not allow anything to undermine the meaning of what you say. Be as clear as possible and immediately correct any misunderstandings before they become a problem.

  - Treat others the way you like to be treated (psychological reciprocity). This old adage is as true today as it was thousands of years ago. Unfortunately, in the crush of deadlines, changing priorities, and the need to be more efficient and more productive, we often neglect to do this and need a reminder.

■ Avoid disregarding what someone else tells you. This is called "minimizing," and it is very disrespectful.

■ Use the Keys to Effective Communications.

Keys to Effective Communications

The Keys to Effective Communications will help you to improve the results of your interactions with others. They include providing context, using active communication, gathering information, noticing, and empathizing.

Providing Context

When you say something to another person, you understand exactly how you mean it, but the odds are high that they won't understand it exactly the same way because their life experience, education, and attitudes are different from your own. Similarly, when you do something, they will interpret your action in ways that make sense to them, but that are not necessarily how you mean it. Context provides the framework that surrounds what you are saying or doing, and can throw light on its meaning. When you give context for your words or actions, it helps others to understand your intentions, which helps avoid a misunderstanding.

For instance, if you are at a customer site, and you find you need to take a printer in for service, don't just unplug the printer and carry it out. Tell the customer what you are about to do, and why. They deserve to know why you need to do this because it will be an inconvenience to them.

When you are gathering information about a computer problem, you will often need to ask questions that may seem unnecessary to the customer. Your experience will have taught you to gather information that goes beyond what the user believes you need to know to solve the problems. For example, non-technical users may not see the connection between a failure to connect to the Internet and a power failure that occurred overnight, so you might not learn that when he arrived at work, his computer, which he had left on the night before, was off. To get this kind of information, provide him with context for why you want to ask him questions by telling him that many things can affect an Internet connection and you need to ask some questions that may seem odd. For instance, asking him whether he had noticed if anything unusual happened.

Using Active Communication

Active communication involves a set of behaviors that lets the other party know that you are engaged in the conversation and that enhances your effectiveness. Active communication is described later in this chapter.

Gathering Information

A common requirement of the job descriptions for people who take the 601, 602, and 603 exams is interaction with users to solve computer problems. This requires gathering information from the user.

Let the Customer Demonstrate   Users are often uncomfortable with the technology involved, and they may not have the vocabulary to describe the problem in terms that will allow you to resolve the problem quickly. So you need to couch the questions you must ask in language the user is comfortable with. Try to use words the user understands, and relate your questions to the user's job function and how she uses the computer and peripherals. Use questions like "When you tried to print the Daily Report, did you notice any messages on your screen?" Or ask the user to show you the exact steps that led up to the problem. Remember, users often do many tasks without having the vocabulary to describe what they are doing. Therefore, asking the user to demonstrate what she did in the few minutes before the problem occurred keeps her in her comfort zone of common activities and does not require her to find the words to describe her actions.

Relieve the Customer of Guilt   The customer may be worried about being held accountable for the problem and may withhold information that would help you solve the problem, but (in his mind, at least) reveal that he was responsible. You will need to deal with this type of situation more often than you may believe, and it may help to assure the customer that the more you know, the quicker you can solve the problem.

Noticing

Noticing means understanding what you are seeing, and it requires you to pay close attention to what is going on so that you can make accurate and astute observations about the interactions you are having, and decisions about your actions. Good noticing skills come into play with all professional interactions, whether with customers or coworkers.

Noticing can provide you with valuable information and insights into the person with whom you are interacting. When you notice the other person's body language, tone of voice, eye movements, words, tone, pacing, and style, you learn about that person's feelings and concerns so that you can respond appropriately. When you can tell that someone is upset and stressed out, it is worth asking a few questions to put her behavior in context. Perhaps she is under a great deal of pressure to produce a report that now seems to be lost in her computer. This may put her into an egocentric state in which all she can think about are the consequences of not having that report on time.

Do not rely strictly on the customer for information. Be willing to calmly assess the entire situation and notice things beyond what the user believes are associated with the problem.

Noticing the surroundings and details of the situation can help you solve problems. For instance, even though the customer insists that the monitor worked when she came into the office, and failed when she opened her word processor, you may notice that the monitor is actually unplugged.

Empathizing

When you empathize with another person, you identify with and understand that person's situation, feelings, and/or motives. We often describe empathy as putting yourself in another person's shoes. But in reality, before you can put yourself in another person's shoes, you must remove your own. In other words, you must consciously step out of your own mindset and, for a moment or two, mentally take on the identity and perspective of that person. Imagine that you share the same experiences, have the same problems, and have the same needs. You must be sincere, and what is most important, the other party must know that you empathize.

Mirror the other person's movements and behavior patterns and exercise good listening skills so that you can truly understand him or her. Verbally acknowledge significant points that the other person makes in the conversation. Relate relevant points from your own experiences and volunteer your assistance.

Active Communication

Remember that communication is a two-way street and involves much more than simply talking and hearing. The best communication is active communication, which involves a set of behaviors we call active listening and active speaking that shows that you are fully engaged in the conversation and encourages the other person to also communicate in a positive manner. Active listening includes using a set of skills, behaviors, and attitudes while you are listening to the other person, while active speaking covers the appropriate responses that you make during a conversation.

Active Listening

One of the most important tasks technical personnel perform involves working directly with computer users—often gathering information in order to help them solve problems or to teach them how to use their computers. Active listening is critical to these tasks.

Active listening requires that you give the speaker your complete attention. This must be apparent to the speaker, even during a phone conversation. Do not interrupt; allow the speaker to complete statements. Do not jump to conclusions. If necessary, clarify customer statements by asking pertinent questions. This shows that you are listening and helps you to avoid making incorrect assumptions. Following are several components of active listening.

Benefits of Active Listening   When you listen attentively, you gather valuable information that you need, with the added benefit of showing the other person how to be an active listener. As with all the good behavior you do, this serves as a model, and the other person will often respond by actively listening to you, also.

Skills for Active Listening   There are several active listening skills that are very easy to acquire simply by practicing them. After a while, you will find that these skills become second nature in your interactions.

- Make good eye contact.
- Physically respond to what the other person is saying with a nod, or by shifting your weight to lean toward them. This last also shows interest in what they are saying.
- Repeat the key points you heard to show that you are listening.
- Mentally check that you understand what they mean, not simply "hear" what the other person is saying.

on the Job   *Resist the bad habits of communication that tell the other person that you are not interested in what he has to say. Do not interrupt to finish his sentences. Do not let your gaze turn into the stare of a daydreamer.*

Be Engaged   In a face-to-face conversation, engagement involves using eye contact and body language that tells the customer that she is important to you. Nod your head and maintain a pleasant expression appropriate to the conversation.

A big smile is not always the correct expression. Show concern with a serious and sympathetic expression if the customer is frustrated or angry. You can empathize with the customer by saying something like "I don't blame you for being upset. If I were going through what you have gone through I'd be upset too."

In a phone conversation, when the customer pauses or takes a breath, use phrases such as "I understand" and "Please tell me more." Even a short "Yes" or "Okay" lets the customer know that you are listening and engaged in the conversation.

Allow the Customer to Fully Explain   The most important act a computer professional does is to allow the customer to fully explain the reason for the conversation: the problem as the customer perceives it. Listen without interruption; do not be distracted by the customer's misuse of or total lack of technical language. Work toward gathering information without correcting the customer. Make a note if you notice that the customer could use appropriate training to make their use of the computer more effective, but do not let the conversation get sidetracked from solving the problem.

Active Speaking

Active speaking involves speaking clearly, avoiding direct "you" statements, avoiding jargon, and confirming that the customer understands what you are saying.

Speak Clearly   Speak in clear, concise, and direct statements. Use language appropriate to the user without being condescending.

Do Not Start with "You"   Avoid beginning sentences with the word "you." This practice is sometimes called a direct "you" statement, and when you start off this way, it tends to put the other party in a defensive position. It is also easy to fall into the trap of saying things like "You didn't … ?" or "You should have … ." Once this happens, communication can break down.

Do not completely eliminate the word "you," because it is a great word in sentences such as "What can I do to help you?" or "What did you notice just before this occurred?" The first phrase lets the customer tell you what they want from you, while the second one shows them that their input will be important in solving the problem. Repeat these two sentences out loud, and then do the same with the following sentences and notice the difference in the emphasis on the word "you." "You must have changed something!" "You need to be careful when using … ."

Avoid Jargon   Jargon is not necessarily bad. Jargon is simply the use of words, often technical and uncommon, that both parties understand in the same way. The problems come when you use technical words that are familiar to you but that are completely unknown to the other person.

Avoid using technical jargon, abbreviations, and acronyms with non-technical customers and coworkers. This is confusing to the listener because they don't know what you are talking about, and it can work against you by breaking down communications. It clearly shows a lack of respect for the other person and for what you are trying to achieve and communicate. Sometimes people use jargon almost deliberately as a way to "one up" themselves over the other person—to subtly show their superiority. The problem is that psychological reciprocity will come into play and you will have started a contest for control of the situation. Not what you want!

In avoiding jargon, do not speak down to the other person. Here is an opportunity to be creative in describing things to the customer. If you have been a good listener, you will find ways to express yourself without giving the customer too much technical detail.

exam

watch *Be sure that you understand the concept and practice of active communication, employing both active listening and active speaking.*

Get Acknowledgment Frequently confirm that the customer understands what you are saying by asking questions like "Does that make sense?" "Does that sound okay to you?" "Would you like to go through those steps while I am here?" Think of the conversation as a train, with you as the engineer. The customer is a passenger waiting on the platform, if you do not stop or slow down, the customer cannot get on the train, and you will find yourself at the destination, but the customer will still be back at the station. Slow down and confirm that he is on board before you race ahead with a technical explanation that would please your coworkers but bewilder the customer.

on the **job** *There is not a single profession in the world that does not have its own jargon. Since professions tend to be separate cultures, the use of jargon, abbreviations, and acronyms strictly among peers is generally acceptable, but do not let this spill over to your communications with people who are not part of your technical culture.*

Tact and Discretion

Tact and discretion are very important characteristics of effective communicators. Tact involves showing consideration for others, which is also part of discretion. Tactful communication is more about what you do not say than what you do say.

Take care to not offend no matter what you may think of the other person, or what your own situation is. Being discreet includes not revealing information about someone that would be harmful to them or embarrass them.

People often see discretion and tact as synonyms. While discretion does relate closely to tact, there is a subtle difference between them. For instance, a person who is tactful or discreet avoids embarrassing or distressing another. But discretion assumes a measure of good judgment based on the situation. It doesn't matter whether your encounters with customers are face-to-face, by phone, or purely via electronic messages (e-mail, newsgroups, or messaging)—you can still use tact and discretion.

Using Tact

We have seen it many times. A customer who does not seem to understand the connection between the power switch and the computer manages to figure out how to customize the Windows desktop with family photos on the background, customized pointers, and a desktop cluttered with dozens of files, folders, and shortcuts. Unless you were summoned there for the purpose of helping the customer clean up the desktop, stick to the reason for the visit, and do not offer your opinion of the desktop. This is using tact.

You can further demonstrate your command of tact after you have solved the problem. At that point, you might inquire if she has had any end-user training on using the Windows desktop. If the answer is "Yes," then you may want to drop the subject, unless you find that her own desktop actually bewilders the customer, and she would like help cleaning it up and organizing her files. This is an opportunity to spend a few minutes demonstrating the use of the My Documents folder and subfolders, if time permits.

Using Discretion

Use discretion by simply not revealing unnecessary information to customers or coworkers. This may be information about other people, unannounced company policies, and information about the company's research and development, just to name very few things. If the information would hurt or offend a third party, even someone of whom you have a low opinion, keep it to yourself. If the information could harm your company, also keep it to yourself.

If you do not follow this advice, and you divulge information you have no authority to share, you will find it difficult to build trust with other people. Even when someone seems to enjoy the information, this behavior tells them that you are not trustworthy.

SCENARIO & SOLUTION

I get very bored with talking to customers at the front counter, and I find that I can pick up my e-mail while listening to a customer's description of a problem. My boss has told me not to do this? Why is that?	There are many reasons this behavior is inappropriate. Just one reason is that you are not showing the customer respect by letting him or her know that you are listening. You actually may miss important information if you do not use active listening techniques.
They tell me not to begin sentences with "you" when speaking to customers. Why is this?	Starting a sentence with "you" tends to make the other party feel defensive.
I enjoy sharing information about office politics and unannounced changes in company policy. My boss has reprimanded me for this, but people seem to enjoy hearing this news. Why is doing this a problem?	Once again, there are many reasons this is inappropriate behavior. At the very least, revealing this information shows a lack of tact and discretion, and does not engender trust in you, even though people seem to enjoy hearing this information.

Do Not Speak Your Mind

Do not speak your mind if it means that you are moving the interaction away from the purpose of solving the customer's problem. Sometimes technicians go too far in showing empathy for the customer's plight, and speak negatively about the customer's working conditions or the very equipment or software that the technician is paid to support. The customer does not need to know that you think the printer the company bought for him is substandard, or that you hate driving out to his office because of the terrible traffic conditions.

CERTIFICATION OBJECTIVES

■ **601: 8.2   602: 8.2   603: 6.2**   *Use job-related professional behavior, including notation of privacy, confidentiality, and respect for the customer and customer's property*

Professionalism

Professionalism involves using a set of behaviors that each of us should do whether we are being observed or not, because behavior you do only when being observed is not behavior that you believe in. You cannot fake professional behavior. People who do try to fake it will eventually fall into a trap of their own making, and they may well lose their job as a result. Many professions have a formal code of ethics that defines professionalism framed in the context of that profession. In this section we will explore a general definition of professionalism as it applies to behavior in dealing with others, and in the treatment of property.

Respectful Behavior Toward Others

Professional behavior is respectful. This includes being pleasant, reasonable, and positive in the face of the variety of events that occur in the work environment.

Maintaining a Positive Attitude

Always maintain a positive attitude and tone of voice. This takes practice and discipline because everyone has personal problems and challenges in their lives, along with all the issues that revolve around a job, such as politics, personalities, work goals, and more. You literally need to compartmentalize your life. Hold an image in your mind that, when you are at work, the other parts of your life are behind doors. Visualize the labels on those doors. They will be different for everyone, but they may look like this: Family, School, Personal, and Office. There may be more doors behind each of these, too. Try to keep the doors to these other parts of your life closed most of the time you are at work, and only open each one at an appropriate time. Open the Family door when you call home during a break or lunch hour. Open the School door when you take out a book to study during lunch hour or while commuting by train to work. When you become successful at this, you will find that you are more effective in all the areas of your life, because you can give each the full attention it deserves at the appropriate time.

Avoid Confrontations

Avoid arguing with customers or coworkers. If you discover something that makes you angry, pause to calm yourself down before engaging in a conversation about the problem. When others approach you in an angry fashion, stay calm and avoid becoming defensive. Resist falling into the trap of psychological reciprocity. These measured responses can defuse a potentially volatile situation.

Do Not Minimize Other's Concerns

Never minimize another person's problems and concerns. We minimize when we interrupt an explanation, and show through body language, such as a dismissive wave of the hand, that their concern is not important to us. Do not tell the customer about someone else who has a worse predicament. That is irrelevant. Imagine how you would feel if you could not get some work completed on time due to a computer problem and while trying to explain your plight to a technician she minimized or dismissed your concern as being of no importance.

However, there is a balance between not minimizing and assuring the customer that you have an easy fix for the problem. An easy fix just means that you can solve the problem soon; it does not mean that the customer has no reason to mourn the lost time, lost deadline, or loss of productivity.

Avoid Judgmental Behavior

Avoid being judgmental and/or insulting to anyone. Never resort to name-calling. This behavior is damaging to any relationship and is completely uncalled for in a professional environment. For instance, if the workings of computer hardware and software fascinate you, it may be difficult for you to be patient with people who cannot seem to understand or even care how they work, and frequently need help with hardware and software. You believe that anyone can understand computers if they just take the time to learn more. If you feel this way, you are judging another's decision to not study computers the way you have. It is just a small baby step from here to behaving judgmentally toward the customer.

Be Attentive

Avoid distractions and/or interruptions when talking with customers or coworkers. You may have two sets of standards for customers versus coworkers. Customers must have your complete attention, and only an emergency should distract you when talking with the customer. Even when you are talking on the phone with a customer, resist the urge to read e-mail and browse the Internet. You may relax these rules a bit with coworkers, depending on your working relationship, but be very careful not to be disrespectful of anyone.

Confidentiality and Respect for Privacy

In all human interactions we learn things about one another, and some of what we learn is personal and we should not share it with others. Part of professionalism is knowing when to keep what you know confidential. This includes both knowledge about company matters and knowledge involving someone's personal life. This shows respect for the privacy of others. When you keep such information to yourself, you will gain the trust of your coworkers and customers. Of course, when you respect someone's privacy, you do not try to gain personal information, but sometimes you learn it inadvertently. However you learn such information, keep it to yourself. If you are unsure if the information you have can be shared with others, then do not divulge it to anyone.

The practice of respecting the privacy of others extends to Web sites where you will find a privacy policy that describes how they use information about visitors to their Web site. This information may be limited to your name and e-mail address, but it is still personal information, and it is important to know what the privacy policy is before divulging even this minimal information. What you want to see is a statement that they will not in any way provide your information to anyone else without your permission.

Where can you find a privacy statement on a Web site? Sometimes you will find a link to a company's privacy statement on the home page, or on a page that contains a form for you to fill in with information about yourself. Other times you will need to search for it. When you click the link, it will take you to a page with the company's Privacy Statement. Figure 18-1 shows a portion of Microsoft's privacy page.

The CompTIA exam objectives for 601: 8.2, 602: 8.2, and 602: 6.2 use the term "notation of privacy" rather than privacy policy.

You should also have a privacy policy, even if your organization does not formally provide one. This is your personal privacy policy that should be part of your personal standards of behavior.

FIGURE 18-1

The Microsoft Online Privacy Statement

Microsoft Online Privacy Notice Highlights
(last updated January 2006)

Scope

This notice provides highlights of the full Microsoft Online Privacy Statement. This notice and the full privacy statement apply to those Microsoft websites and services that display or link to this notice.

Personal Information — Additional Details

- When you register for certain Microsoft services, we will ask you to provide personal information.
- The information we collect may be combined with information obtained from other Microsoft services and other companies.
- We use cookies and other technologies to keep track of your interactions with our sites and services to offer a personalized experience.

Your Choices — Additional Details

- You can stop the delivery of promotional e-mail from a Microsoft site or service by following the instructions in the e-mail you receive.
- To make proactive choices about how we communicate with you, follow the instructions listed in the Communication Preferences of the full privacy statement.
- To view and edit your personal information, go to the access section of the full privacy statement.

Uses of Information — Additional Details

- We use the information we collect to provide the services you request. Our services may include the display of personalized content and advertising.
- We use your information to inform you of other products or services offered by Microsoft and its affiliates, and to send you relevant survey invitations related to Microsoft services.
- We do not sell, rent, or lease our customer lists to third parties. In order to help provide our services, we occasionally provide information to other companies that work on our behalf.

Important Information

- The full Microsoft Online Privacy Statement contains links to supplementary information about specific Microsoft sites or services.
- The sign in credentials (e-mail address and password) used to sign in to most Microsoft sites and services are part of the Microsoft Passport Network.
- For more information on how to help protect your personal computer, your personal information and your family online, visit our online safety resources.

Respect for Property

Respect for property includes both the physical treatment of property and equipment belonging to others, and the exact manner in which you use the property or equipment. This includes the building, parking lot, and office space, as well as all the furniture and equipment within. Oddly enough, company policy manuals often define respect for property better than they do the interpersonal aspects of professional behavior. So consult policy manuals for details of how to treat company property. If you did not know before, you learned in this book what the proper physical treatment is for laptop and desktop computers, printers, displays, and other equipment. But do not forget the telephone—whether it is a wired telephone on your desktop, a wireless one for use in the office, or a company-provided cell phone. Use of company property is both a privilege and great responsibility. Whatever the equipment, treat it with respect, because it is a tool of your trade.

You show respect for property in other ways than proper physical handling. Never forget that you should treat any equipment that belongs to the organization as its property. Do not let family members use it, unless you have specific permission to do so. Follow company guidelines for personal use of company equipment. Even if they allow it, be sure that you are not abusing this privilege. This type of misuse includes using the company computer to shop online or to play Internet games—this is doubly unprofessional when you do it on company time.

This respect for property extends beyond company property to that property belonging to all persons with whom you have contact, including your customers and coworkers.

SCENARIO & SOLUTION

How can I avoid a confrontation when someone else shows anger toward me?	Try to stay calm, avoid becoming defensive, and do not reciprocate the anger.
I try to put customers' concerns into perspective for them by telling them about others who are worse off. Is this a good practice?	No, this is not a good practice because the customers will believe (rightly so) that you are minimizing their concerns.
If the company gives me a laptop to take home, do I have the right to use it for personal purposes?	No. Unless you have an unusual arrangement, you are to use the laptop given to you by the company for business purposes only. It is unprofessional to use it for personal purposes.

CERTIFICATION SUMMARY

A+ candidates taking the 601, 602, or 603 exam must understand the communication skills required for success on the job. This includes listening skills and communicating clearly while employing tact and discretion with all interpersonal contacts. It is helpful to understand predictable human behavior and responses so that you can keep interactions positive, avoid falling into certain traps, and recognize when the other party in a conversation has fallen into an egocentric state. You can also use the human tendency toward psychological reciprocity to avoid mirroring bad behavior and to be a model for the behavior you wish the other person to do. Be conscious of your body language to ensure that your words and actions are not sending conflicting messages.

Good communication skills include what you say, the way you say it, and what you do while you are saying it. Communication goals include establishing rapport and building trust. Keys to effective communication includes providing context, using active communication, gathering information, noticing, and empathizing.

Active communication is a set of behaviors that come under the headings of active listening and active speaking. These behaviors show that you are fully engaged in the conversation and encourage the other person to also communicate in a positive manner.

Tact and discretion are very important characteristics of effective communicators. Tact involves showing consideration for others, which is also part of discretion. Tact is more about what you do not say, while discretion includes not revealing information that would be harmful or embarrassing to someone.

Professionalism includes a set of behaviors that each of us should do whether we are being observed or not. Many professions have a formal code of ethics that defines professionalism framed in the context of that profession. Respectful behavior includes respect for others and respect for privacy and property.

✓ TWO-MINUTE DRILL

Here are some of the key points covered in Chapter 18.

Basics of Human Interactions

❑ Two predictable reactions that can interfere with communications are the egocentric state and psychological reciprocity.

❑ An egocentric state is a reaction in which the person focuses internally and fails to pay attention to what is going on around him or her.

❑ An egocentric state can result when someone is startled, shocked, surprised, feeling attacked, puzzled, or any other emotional reaction that causes him to retreat inside his head.

❑ Learn to recognize when something has triggered an egocentric state in yourself and resist the urge to go inside yourself so that you can remain attentive to the other person.

❑ Learn to recognize the signs that another person has entered an egocentric state and try to draw him or her out of it.

❑ Psychological reciprocity occurs when one person automatically responds in kind to whatever another person says or does to him or her.

❑ The negative side of psychological reciprocity is when someone responds with negative behavior to actual or perceived bad behavior from another.

❑ Learn to avoid responding in kind when the other person is negative, and you can turn the tone of a conversation to something more positive and productive.

❑ When you initiate a conversation, you set the tone. Start out a conversation on a positive note to avoid psychological reciprocity from the other person because, even if you feel a strong emotion, things will go downhill fast, and you will not accomplish anything if you both engage in negative behavior.

❑ Knowing the right things to say is just part of the story; you also must back up what you say with appropriate body language.

Communicating with Customers and Colleagues

❑ Communication goals include establishing rapport and trust.

❑ Keys to effective communication include providing context, using active communication, gathering information, noticing, and empathizing.

❑ Active communication involves behavior that shows you are fully engaged and that encourages the other person to also communicate in a positive manner.

❑ An active listener makes good eye contact, uses body language to confirm that she is listening and interested, and mentally checks her understanding.

❑ Always allow the other person (especially a customer) to fully explain.

❑ An active speaker speaks clearly, does not start sentences with "you," avoids jargon, and confirms that the other person understands.

❑ Always practice tact and discretion in interactions with other people.

Professionalism

❑ Professionalism is a set of behaviors that everyone should do whether or not we are being observed.

❑ Professional behavior is respectful and includes a positive attitude, avoiding confrontation and a judgmental attitude, and never minimizing others' concerns.

❑ When you are respectful, you are attentive and respect confidentiality and privacy.

❑ Respect for property includes both the physical treatment of property and equipment belonging to others, and the exact manner in which you use the property or equipment.

❑ Most companies have a formal policy for the use of company property, and you should always be mindful of your use of company property, even when allowed to bring it into your own home.

❑ Be especially careful of equipment belonging to a customer. Showing respect and care in the way you handle their often expensive property goes a long way toward establishing rapport and trust.

SELF TEST

The following questions will help you measure your understanding of the material presented in this chapter. Read all of the choices carefully because there might be more than one correct answer. Choose all correct answers for each question.

Basics of Human Interactions

1. Which of these is a predictable response that causes you to focus internally and fail to pay attention to what is going on around you?
    A. Psychological reciprocity
    B. Active communication
    C. Egocentric state
    D. Direct "you" statement

2. When approached by an angry person, which type of intentional response can you utilize to change the customer's behavior?
    A. Active communication
    B. Psychological reciprocity
    C. Egocentric state
    D. Direct "you" statement

3. When put to good use, which predictable response takes advantage of the tendency to mirror behavior?
    A. Active "you" statement
    B. Egocentric state
    C. Psychological reciprocity
    D. Active communication

4. When this predictable response occurs to someone else, you will see signs, such as a different expression as the eyes become unfocused, and he or she becomes unresponsive to your questions.
    A. Direct "you" statement
    B. Active communication
    C. Egocentric state
    D. Psychological reciprocity

5. When someone else is in an egocentric state, which of the following is the best tactic for dealing with it?
   A. Remain quiet until he or she comes out of that state.
   B. Clap your hands loudly.
   C. Shout "Fire!"
   D. Keep talking until you have his or her attention.

6. Which is an example of good, positive body language for someone who is listening to a customer?
   A. Folding your arms across your chest
   B. Shaking your head from side to side
   C. Leaning toward the customer
   D. Clasping your hands behind your back

7. What predictable human reaction is a self-centered state?
   A. Surprise
   B. Egocentric state
   C. Psychological reciprocity
   D. Anger

Communicating with Customers and Colleagues

8. What word listed below describes the bond that people tend to create between one another based on their similarities?
   A. Trust
   B. Body language
   C. Misunderstanding
   D. Rapport

9. Which of these actions builds trust? Select all that apply.
   A. Being consistent
   B. Demonstrating knowledge of office politics
   C. Honoring commitments
   D. Avoiding misunderstandings

10. Your boss and coworkers have criticized you for being too abrupt with customers, even as you take all the correct actions to fix their computers. What are you failing to do in your contacts with customers that would make them more comfortable with your actions?
    A. Showing them the owners manual for the computer
    B. Providing context for what you are saying or doing

    C. Demonstrating how quickly you can un-cable their equipment and take it out of their office for repair

    D. Showing the customer the list of your technical certifications

11. What practices show that you are an active communicator? Select all that apply.

    A. Making good eye contact

    B. Interrupting the customer because you know the answer to their problem

    C. Allowing the customer to completely explain the problem

    D. Repeating points the customer made to confirm that you understand

12. Which of the following are good ways to gather information when you are at the customer's desk? Select all that apply.

    A. Letting the customer demonstrate what he or she was doing when the problem occurred

    B. Asking the customer to leave the room so that you can work on the computer

    C. Noticing the surroundings

    D. Noticing the customer's body language and tone of voice

13. Which technique tends to put the other party into a defensive position?

    A. Empathizing

    B. Using direct "you" statements

    C. Allowing the other person to explain fully

    D. Being engaged

14. When you are explaining something technical to a customer, which of the following is the best technique to use to confirm understanding of your explanation?

    A. Intersperse phrases to "check in" with the customer.

    B. After the explanation, give the customer a quiz.

    C. Give the customer a printed explanation to read as you speak.

    D. Maintain eye contact.

15. When someone has explained something to you, how can you make sure that you heard and understand what they say?

    A. Focus.

    B. Repeat it back in your own words.

    C. Imagine how you sound and appear to the other person.

    D. Nod your head frequently.

16. Which of the following is a technique used to show respect? Select all that apply.

    A. Be as clear as possible and correct any misunderstandings.

    B. Show the customer your privacy policy.

    C. Avoid disregarding what someone else tells you.

    D. Treat others the way you like to be treated.

17. Which phrase describes active listening in a face-to-face context?

    A. Words and actions that tell the speaker that you are paying attention

    B. Closing your eyes to concentrate on what is said

    C. Taking notes

    D. Helping the speaker by finishing sentences

18. When a customer is explaining a problem, what is the most important thing an active listener must do?

    A. Nodding your head to show understanding

    B. Empathizing

    C. Allowing the customer to explain the problem without interruption

    D. Show respect

Professionalism

19. What behavior shows a positive and professional attitude? Select all that apply.

    A. Avoiding confrontation

    B. Avoiding judgmental behavior

    C. Showing respect

    D. Minimizing another's concerns

20. Which statement below is true in regard to respect for property?

    A. It only includes the company building.

    B. It includes the office space and furniture only.

    C. It includes both the physical treatment of property and the manner in which it is used.

    D. You can use a company laptop as you please in your own home.

LAB QUESTION

Your boss manages fifty people, and she has determined that the best way to ensure that everyone practices good communications skills and professionalism is through appropriate customer service training. Among the staff people there are several job titles, including Technical Support Technician, Field Service Technician, and Call Center Operator. She has asked you to find appropriate training for each of these three job descriptions. Then, because e-mail is the primary communication method among her group, she also wants training that would teach all employees how to write professional and concise e-mail messages. She would prefer using one source and has the following requirements for the training:

- The training must be available online to accommodate the various schedules of the participants.
- The training must provide relevant usable skills for each job title.
- The training must include a test by which the students demonstrate that they have learned the content of the training program.
- The training must lead to an industry-recognized accreditation.

Use a Web search engine to find a company that can provide training products that meet the manager's requirements. Consider using the following keywords: "customer service training technical." Once you have found a company with appropriate products, write a paragraph or two listing the company and the products it offers that meet these needs.

SELF TEST ANSWERS

Basics of Human Interactions

1. ☑ **C.** An egocentric state is a predictable response that causes you to focus internally and fail to pay attention to what is going on around you.

   ☒ **A**, psychological reciprocity, is incorrect because this is the name used for the behavior in which a person responds in kind to another's words or actions. **B**, active communication, is incorrect because this is a set of skills for effective communication. **D**, a direct "you" statement, is incorrect because you should avoid using this in your communications.

2. ☑ **B.** Psychological reciprocity is the type of intentional response you can use to change a customer's behavior by not responding to the anger, but by being professional and calm.

   ☒ **A**, active communication, is incorrect because this will not change a customer's behavior as directly as using psychological reciprocity. **C**, an egocentric state, is incorrect because this is a state that you want to avoid, and it will not positively influence another's behavior. **D**, a direct "you" statement, is incorrect because beginning a sentence with "you" will tend to have a negative influence on the customer.

3. ☑ **C.** Psychological reciprocity is a predictable response that takes advantage of the tendency to mirror behavior.

   ☒ **A**, an active "you" statement, is incorrect because this is not a predictable response. **B**, an egocentric state, is incorrect because this predictable response does not involve mirroring behavior and is not a desirable behavior in itself. **D**, active communication, is incorrect because, while this is a set of good habits, it is not a predictable response that takes advantage of the tendency to mirror behavior.

4. ☑ **C.** An egocentric state is a predictable response in which the person shows signs such as the eyes becoming unfocused, and he or she becomes unresponsive to your questions.

   ☒ **A**, a direct "you" statement, is incorrect because this is a statement beginning with the word "you." **B**, active communication, is incorrect because this is communication using a variety of verbal and non-verbal skills. **D**, psychological reciprocity, is incorrect because this is a predictable response in which someone returns the behavior of another with like behavior.

5. ☑ **A.** Remain quiet until he or she comes out of that state.

   ☒ **B**, **C**, and **D** are all incorrect because they are all disrespectful of the person and will not help the situation.

6. ☑ **C.** Leaning toward the customer is good body language while listening to a customer.

   ☒ **A**, folding your arms across your chest, is not good body language because it tells the other person that you are not open to what they are saying. **B**, shaking your head from side to side, is incorrect because this shows disapproval or disagreement with the customer. **D**, clasping your hands behind your back, is incorrect because it shows the other person you are not open to what they are saying.

7. ☑ **B.** An egocentric state is a self-centered state.
   ☒ **A**, surprise, and **D**, anger, are both incorrect because each of them is an emotion, not a self-centered predictable human reaction. **C**, psychological reciprocity, is incorrect because this is the predictable response in which you treat the other person in the manner that they treated you, or that you perceive that they did.

Communicating with Customers and Colleagues

8. ☑ **D.** Rapport describes the bond that people tend to create between one another based on their similarities.
   ☒ **A**, trust, is incorrect because trust is confidence and faith in a person. **B**, body language, is incorrect because this is the silent messages you send with movements and gestures, as well as with facial expressions. **C**, misunderstanding, is incorrect because this is a mix-up in communications.

9. ☑ **A, C,** and **D.** These are all correct because they all work to build trust.
   ☒ **B**, demonstrating knowledge of office politics, is incorrect because this would not build trust and is behavior that is detrimental and non-professional.

10. ☑ **B.** Providing context for what you are saying or doing would make customers more comfortable with your actions.
    ☒ **A**, showing them the owner's manual for the computer, would not make a customer more comfortable with your actions. **C**, demonstrating how quickly you can un-cable their equipment and take it out of their office for repair, would not make the customer more comfortable with your actions. **D**, showing the customer the list of your technical certifications, would not make them more comfortable with your actions.

11. ☑ **A, C,** and **D.** These are all correct because these are all practices of an active communicator.
    ☒ **B**, interrupting the customer because you know the answer to their problem, is incorrect because this is not a practice of an active communicator and is disrespectful.

12. ☑ **A, C,** and **D.** These are all correct because they are all good ways to gather information when you are at the customer's desk.
    ☒ **B**, asking the customer to leave the room so that you can work on the computer, is incorrect because this is not a way to gather information. It may be necessary to do this after you discover the problem, but this behavior would not gain the customer's trust, nor is it a way to gather information.

13. ☑ **B.** Using direct "you" statements tends to put the other party into a defensive position.
     ☒ **A, C,** and **D** are all incorrect because they are all good behaviors that are part of active communication and would not put the other party into a defensive position.

14. ☑ **A.** Intersperse phrases to "check in" with the customer.
     ☒ **B,** after the explanation, to give the customer a quiz, is incorrect because, while it would confirm understanding, it is certainly not the best technique and would probably make the customer angry. **C,** to give the customer a printed explanation to read as you speak, is incorrect because this is not the best way to treat a customer. **D,** maintain eye contact, is incorrect because while this should always be part of face-to-face interactions, it is not the best technique to use to confirm understanding.

15. ☑ **B.** Repeat it back in your own words. This confirms that you heard and understand.
     ☒ **A,** focus, is incorrect although focusing on the customer and the problem is an important thing to do. **C,** imagine how you sound and appear to the other person, is incorrect, although this is a good habit when you are the one doing the speaking. **D,** nod your head frequently, is incorrect because while this tells the speaker that you are listening it does not confirm that you heard and understand what they said.

16. ☑ **A, C,** and **D.** These are all correct techniques for showing respect.
     ☒ **B,** show the customer your privacy policy, is incorrect because, while this is an important policy for an organization, and you should practice respect for privacy, this does not directly show respect at the personal level.

17. ☑ **A.** Words and actions that tell the speaker that you are paying attention describe active listening.
     ☒ **B,** closing your eyes to concentrate on what is said, is incorrect because this does not give the other person any clue that you are an active listener who is engaged in the conversation. However, this may be effective in a phone conversation. **C,** taking notes, is incorrect because, while you may want to do this, it is not part of active listening. **D,** helping the speaker by finishing sentences, is incorrect because this is not active listening, and it is certainly not respectful.

18. ☑ **C.** Allowing the customer to explain the problem without interruption is the most important thing an active listener must do when a customer is explaining a problem.
     ☒ **A, B,** and **D** are all incorrect because, while all of these should be used in your interaction with the customer, the most important thing to do in this case is to allow the customer to explain without interruption.

Professionalism

19. ☑ **A, B,** and **C.** These are all correct behaviors that show a positive and professional attitude.
☒ **D,** minimizing another's concerns, is incorrect because this is negative and unprofessional behavior.

20. ☑ **C.** That it includes both the physical treatment of property and the manner in which it is used is a true statement about respect for property.
☒ **A** and **B** are both incorrect because respect for property includes more than just the company building and office space and furniture. **D** is incorrect because a company policy for how a laptop is used normally covers the laptop no matter where it is used.

LAB ANSWER

Answers will vary based on the students' research. For example, we found several products that meet the requirements at Impact Learning Systems International (www.impactlearning.com). The four training programs include Getting to the Heart of Technical Support™, Getting to the Heart of Field Service™, Making it Happen™ (call center training), and Getting to the Heart of E-mail Communications™. While not directly requested by the boss, another course may be of interest, Getting to the Heart of Diagnostic Troubleshooting™.

After each course, the student takes an online test, and the manager can control the pass/fail grade level requirement for this group. The products selected prepare students for CompTIA's Customer Service Skills certification and the Service Support Professional Association (SSPA) certification in Professional Support.

Appendix

About the CD

The CD-ROM included with this book comes complete with MasterExam practice exam software, MasterSim task simulations, CertCam movie clips, the electronic version of the book, and Session #1 of LearnKey's online training. The software is easy to install on any Windows 98/NT/2000/XP/Vista computer and must be installed to access the MasterExam and MasterSim features. You may, however, browse the electronic book and CertCams directly from the CD without installation. To register for LearnKey's online training and additional bonus MasterExams, simply click the Online Training link on the Main page and follow the directions to the free online registration.

System Requirements

The software requires Windows 98 or higher, Internet Explorer 5.0 or above, and 20MB of hard disk space for full installation. The Electronic book requires Adobe Acrobat Reader. To access the Online Training from LearnKey, you must have RealPlayer Basic 8 or the Real1 Plugin, which will be automatically installed when you launch the online training.

LearnKey Online Training

The **LearnKey Online Training** link will allow you to access online training from Osborne.Onlineexpert.com. The first session of this course is provided at no charge. Additional sessions for this course and other courses may be purchased directly from www.LearnKey.com or by calling (800) 865-0165.

The first time that you run the Training, you will be required to register with the online product. Follow the instructions for a first-time user. Please make sure to use a valid e-mail address.

Prior to running the Online Training you will need to add the Real Plugin and the RealCBT Plugin to your system. This will automatically be adapted to your system when you run the training the first time.

Installing and Running MasterExam and MasterSim

If your computer CD-ROM drive is configured to autorun, the CD-ROM will automatically start up when you insert the disk. From the opening screen you may install MasterExam or MasterSim by pressing the MasterExam or MasterSim button.

This will begin the installation process and create a program group named "LearnKey." To run MasterExam or MasterSim, use Start | Programs | Learnkey. If the autorun feature did not launch your CD, browse to the CD and click the LaunchTraining.exe icon.

MasterExam

MasterExam provides you with a simulation of the actual exam. The number of questions, the type of questions, and the time allowed are intended to be an accurate representation of the exam environment. You have the option to take an open-book exam; including hints, references, and answers; a closed-book exam; or the timed MasterExam simulation.

When you launch MasterExam, a digital clock display will appear in the upper left-hand corner of your screen. The clock will continue to count down to zero unless you choose to end the exam before the time expires.

To access any additional bonus MasterExams, simply click the Online Training link on the Main page and follow the directions to the free online registration.

MasterSim

The MasterSim is a set of interactive labs that will provide you with a wide variety of tasks to help you experience the software environment even if the software is not installed. Once you have installed the MasterSim, you may access it quickly through this CD launch page, or you may also access it through Start | Programs | Learnkey.

Electronic Book

The entire contents of the Study Guide are provided in PDF form. In addition, there is a Glossary, which is available only on the CD. Adobe's Acrobat Reader has been included on the CD, as well.

CertCam

CertCam .AVI clips walk you through the steps of a selection of the exercises in the book. These videos show exactly what occurs on the screen in Windows, while a voice-over provides helpful commentary. You can access the clips directly from the CertCam table of contents by pressing the CertCam button on the Main page.

The CertCam .AVI clips are recorded and produced using TechSmith's Camtasia Producer. Since .AVI clips can be very large, ExamSim uses TechSmith's special AVI codec to compress the clips. The file named tsccvid.dll is copied to your Windows\ System folder during the first autorun. If the .AVI clip runs with audio but no video, you may need to re-install the file from the CD-ROM. Browse to the Programs | Certcams folder and run TSCC.

Help

A help file is provided through the help button on the main page in the lower left-hand corner. Individual help features are also available through MasterExam, MasterSim, and LearnKey's Online Training.

Removing Installation(s)

MasterExam and MasterSim are installed to your hard drive. For *best* results for removal of programs use the Start | Programs | Learnkey | Uninstall option to remove MasterExam or MasterSim.

If you desire to remove the Real Player, use the Add/Remove Programs applet from your Control Panel. You may also remove the LearnKey training program from this location.

Technical Support

For questions regarding the technical content of the electronic book, MasterExam, or CertCams, please visit www.osborne.com or e-mail customer.service@mcgraw-hill. com. For customers outside the 50 United States, e-mail: international_cs@mcgraw-hill.com.

LearnKey Technical Support

For technical problems with the software (installation, operation, removal of installations), and for questions regarding LearnKey Online Training and MasterSim content, please visit www.learnkey.com or e-mail techsupport@learnkey.com.

INDEX

U